# AMERICAN SOCIOLOGY SERIES

## KIMBALL YOUNG, GENERAL EDITOR

## American Sociology Series

# Rural Sociology

*by* *LOWRY NELSON*

PROFESSOR OF SOCIOLOGY, UNIVERSITY OF MINNESOTA

SECOND
EDITION

*AMERICAN BOOK COMPANY* NEW YORK

HT
421
.N4

## PREFACE TO THE SECOND EDITION

Since the first edition of this book was published in 1948, the world has seen the results of World War II and of its aftermath, the Cold War, made manifest in human affairs. These events have had a serious impact upon rural life in the United States. In the main, the result has been to accelerate the rate of social change. All aspects of life, material and non-material, seem to have been affected. The advances in agricultural technology have never been equaled in a comparable period in American history. For example, electricity has been brought to nearly all the farms of the nation for the first time; as late as 1935, only one in ten farms was served from a central electric generator. Farm production has steadily mounted, while the number of farms has steadily declined. The farm population has become "thinner." Tractors have largely replaced horses; and the ingenious machines associated with the tractor have so reduced the need for human labor that migration from farms to cities, towns, and villages has become a spectacle rivaling the enclosures in Britain in the early stages of the Industrial Revolution.

These changes have affected the social relations of rural people. The institutions of education, religion, government, and family have had important adjustments to make. Even so, the full effects of this New Industrial Revolution in agriculture have not been fully experienced and understood. More changes are yet to come.

In this revision, the author has introduced facts to indicate the remarkable changes that have taken place during the past decade and a half. Since the changes are still in process, it is impossible to do more than indicate the trends and suggest directions.

Just as changes have taken place in society, so have great advances been made in the science of society. Much new light has been shed on the nature of rural society by the studies which have been made in the last decade and a half. It has been the author's purpose to include the results of new research wherever possible. Throughout the book, data from the Federal Census of 1950 and the results of sample census surveys since that time have been incorporated. The student will note that for the first time in the preparation of textbooks it is possible to incorporate data more recent than that of the decennial census, thanks to the excellent sample surveys made annually by the Bureau of the Census. Refer-

v

ences to late literature bearing on each chapter have been included in this revision.

Grateful acknowledgement is given to my colleagues Dr. Charles E. Ramsey and Dr. Marvin J. Taves for assistance in the preparation of Chapters 11 and 15, respectively.

LOWRY  NELSON

Minneapolis, Minnesota

# CONTENTS

# LIST OF FIGURES

# LIST OF TABLES

# LIST OF PICTURES

# PART I

# *INTRODUCTION*

## INTRODUCTION

THE OBJECT of Part I is to review some of the basic concepts of sociology, to which the student may have been introduced in previous courses, and to present some of the main characteristics that distinguish rural from urban life. The material in Chapter 1 is devoted to the first purpose, that of introducing or reviewing, as the case may be, some of the fundamental concepts. In addition, in this first chapter the field of rural sociology is defined and distinguished from other social science fields, and there is a brief discussion of the nature of the scientific method as applied to social data. Chapter 2 points out the special characteristics of rural life as distinguished from urban life. It must not be inferred, however, that rural society exists as a self-contained society. Quite to the contrary, the organic relations between urban and rural societies are stressed. Nevertheless, the justification for rural sociology as a field of study lies in the distinctive features of the rural environment as set forth in this chapter.

*CHAPTER 1*

# CONCEPTS AND METHOD

As a science, sociology is concerned with the development of knowledge about the behavior of human groups. The subject matter of rural sociology is the description and analysis of groups of various kinds as they exist in the rural environment. By the same token, the subject matter of urban sociology is human groups and institutions in the urban environment. Just as a physical scientist applies the scientific method to the study of physical phenomena, so the social scientist applies the same method to the study of the phenomena we call "social," that is, those arising from the interaction of human beings. The difference is not in method but in the phenomena under study.

It is not to be inferred that the rural sociologist lacks interest in the betterment of rural life. Quite the contrary. But *as a scientist* he is interested only in understanding. As a scientist he seeks the facts concerning rural society and tries to relate them in a meaningful way. He aims to describe as accurately as possible the behavior of people living in a rural environment and the factors which govern or condition that behavior.

As a member of society, the sociologist is interested in human betterment and therefore in the application of the results of his scientific research to the welfare of the community. It is largely a matter of training the mind to pursue rigidly the canons of the scientific method when engaged in research, howsoever one may exercise his influence as a citizen at times when he is not acting as a scientist.

**Relation to other social sciences.** There are other social sciences, as every student knows. There is *economics*, which deals with the relations of men arising from their activities in creating useful goods and services and in exchanging or distributing them in terms of money. There is *political science*, which deals with the forms and functions of government. There

3

is *anthropology*, which has given primary attention to the description of prehistoric and contemporary primitive societies. There is *history*, which aims at describing the social situations, problems, and events of the human past. All of these subjects represent the effort of the human mind to understand social relations. All of them overlap more or less in their content; often the points of view differ. Each one develops its own body of theory, methods of study, and terminology.

Yet in spite of the division and subdivision of social science, there is a fundamental unity of purpose and a growing unity in method and point of view. No special guild of scholars, whether economists, political scientists, psychologists, historians, or sociologists can find within the scope of its own knowledge all of the explanations of social phenomena. On the other hand, interchange of ideas will bring more adequate explanations of the nature of man. Rural sociology, as the scientific study of rural society, should certainly avail itself of the approaches, methods, and techniques of all other sciences, insofar as they may be useful in understanding and describing that society.

**Science and scientific method.** Science may be considered in two aspects: as a body of verified knowledge, and as a method of study. Method is the crucial quality of science because it determines the validity of the results. Certainty is attained only if the processes of defining a problem, the collection and analysis of facts, and the drawing of inferences or conclusions are all carried through with intelligence and meticulous care. Such procedures depend upon the scientist's possession of certain attitudes. He must be patient and have the "capacity for taking infinite pains." He must rid himself of any sort of bias and be willing to "face the facts," especially when they go counter to his wishes. He must be cautious in interpretations and not "go beyond the facts." There are other virtues of the scientist which could be added; those listed are indispensable.

In rural sociology it cannot be said that there is as yet a general system of verified laws or principles in the sense familiar to physical scientists. There has not yet been a sufficient refinement of techniques of observing and measuring phenomena to warrant sweeping generalizations. But it is evident to everyone that there are certain general uniformities in human conduct, which can in time be accurately described. Such confidence in the orderliness of nature underlies the efforts of all scientists.

**Accurate observation essential in science.** In the development of any science, accurate observation is indispensable. The process of observation rests in part upon the sense-perception of the human organism. But unaided sensory-perceptive processes enable us to perceive only certain qualitative characteristics of phenomena. We can say that an object is hot or cold, a sound, loud or faint, but only roughly do we perceive quantitative attributes. We know only that the object is *very* hot or *very* cold. The senses therefore need to be supplemented by devices for measurement. We can say that a table is long, but with the aid of the yardstick we are able to say that it is so many inches long. Standards of weights and measures are basic to the development of scientific observation. While the social sciences have as yet developed few such standards of measurement for general use, noteworthy progress has been made. The Intelligence Quotient is an example from the field of psychology. The development and use of aptitude tests are further illustrations. The general use of statistical techniques in the social sciences has done much to increase precision in observing and describing social phenomena. Chapin's scale for the measurement of socio-economic status of urban families and a similar scale developed by Sewell for use in rural areas are only two of many measuring devices which have proved useful in sociological research. By means of such scales, families in a community, for example, can be appraised in terms of a numerical score, and thus may be conveniently compared one with another or arranged significantly into groups or classes.

**Verbal description as a scientific tool.** But while there has been marked development in techniques of quantitative measurement of social life, it seems apparent that there will remain for a long time to come, if not always, a large number of social phenomena which cannot be subjected to precise quantitative measurement. How can one, for example, reduce to numerical terms the behavior of a lynching mob, the intensity of religious fervor at a camp meeting, the relationship of members of a family or members of a neighborhood of rural people? Some aspects of these problems may be reduced to quantitative terms, but when everything possible in this respect has been accomplished, the results are bound to be inadequate. Verbal description which aims at portraying the qualitative aspects of social phenomena must continue to be a necessary, though inexact, tool of the social sciences.

The case-study method is often used in the analysis of situations which do not lend themselves to quantitative treatment. By careful observation a competent investigator may record the behavior of, say, a rural community in wartime; or the life history of an individual may be reconstructed from his memory, from existing documents, and the like. Similarly, an institution may be studied from its beginning through the various phases of its development, by using historical documents, interviews with informed persons, and other sources. It is a matter of relying largely on verbal description rather than on the measuring devices mentioned previously; however, both may be used in combination.

**Concepts as tools for analysis.** Social concepts refer to social phenomena. Certain forms of social behavior are found to be common enough so that words can be used to indicate and roughly to describe them. For example, in sociology we use concepts such as primary group, secondary group, institution, social process, conflict, accommodation, assimilation, isolation, folkways, ethnocentrism, and many more. Concepts once established and in common use can be used for purposes of classification and analysis. For example, if one sets out to study a group of people he may, on the basis of his observations, be able to indicate whether or not it is a primary or secondary group; whether conflict exists and if so, of what nature or intensity; and what the relations of the group are to other groups in terms of such processes as accommodation or assimilation.

These concepts become a language, or "universe of discourse" among students, and facilitate the communication of ideas. For example, after the concept of the primary group is once established and in current use, it no longer becomes necessary for each investigator to describe in detail the type of behavior to which the concept alludes. He may take it for granted that his fellow students understand the meaning of the concept. It must be borne in mind, however, that in a new branch of science such as sociology there are many concepts which are not fully and satisfactorily defined—or refined—and many investigators may use the same word with varying shades of meaning.[1] Moreover, many of the words used by sociologists to designate strictly defined concepts are often the same as those used loosely in popular speech. The word "culture" is a case in point. The sociologist uses it in a sense quite different from that understood by the man in the street.

**Some general concepts.** In these beginning paragraphs there have occurred such words as *society, culture, science, rural, urban;* it is well, at the outset, to have in mind the meaning that is commonly attached to them. While the concepts are used in so many different ways by different scholars as to cause some dismay, we are able to see increasing general agreement upon their use. The student of social science soon comes to expect a large measure of disagreement among scholars concerning the precise meaning of concepts. The lack of standard nomenclature is simply evidence of the comparative immaturity of social science and represents an experience common to the history of older sciences such as physics, astronomy, and biology.

**What is society?** As used by the scientist, the term signifies simply a group of interacting human beings. Without social interaction, there is no society. It is used broadly when we refer to *human* society; or specifically when we refer to *rural* society, *Malay* society, and so on. The essential point is that in using the term we make clear whether we are using it in a broad or in a specific sense.

**Meaning of culture.** This term is frequently used by social scientists as synonymous with the word society. As a concept it has been developed by the anthropologists, and as used by them it includes material as well as nonmaterial things. Wallis defines culture as "the artificial objects, institutions, and modes of life or of thought which are not peculiarly individual, but which characterize a group." [2] Like the term society, culture

---

[1] Thus the American Sociological Society at one time appointed a committee on Conceptual Integration, the purpose of which was to try and bring about consensus among sociologists on the precise meaning of certain concepts.

[2] Wilson D. Wallis, *Culture and Progress*, p. 9. New York: McGraw-Hill Book Co., 1930.

is often used in a general and a specific sense. However, the tendency is more in the direction of a specific point of reference. It is, therefore, common to speak of Winnebago culture, Osage culture, Trobriand culture, etc. In recent years the term has been widely accepted by sociologists, and it will frequently be used in this book. When used in a critical sense, the words "culture" and "society" have distinctly different meanings. Culture refers to the nature and patterning of the folkways, institutions, beliefs, and customs, while society refers to the interacting groups or persons.[3]

Culture is made up of units called *culture traits*. Examples of culture traits in contemporary rural society are the steel plow, the mechanical corn picker, isolated farm residence as contrasted with village residence, and various food items. Culture traits are interrelated and interdependent; moreover, they occur in clusters: the corn picker, for example, is related to the whole process of corn production, which itself could be called a *culture trait-complex* or *culture pattern*. Corn production also illustrates another concept, namely the *culture area*, since it is highly concentrated in what we refer to as the "Corn Belt." A culture area is a geographic space which is characterized by a predominance of certain culture traits or patterns which distinguish it from other areas.

**The meaning of rural and urban.** While precise definitions of "rural" and "urban" are not possible, nor necessary for our purposes, it is important that the two fields be roughly defined. Because everyone has a general idea of the meaning of these terms, the student may be surprised to learn that a precise definition cannot be given. It may be well, therefore, briefly to elaborate. The problems involved are these: (1) What occupational groups, besides farmers, should be included under the heading of "rural"? One may be inclined to say that no other occupational groups than farmers should be called rural. But what about the operator of a crossroads store, an open-country tavern, or a filling station? They could hardly be classed as city folks. Nor is it even safe to include all farmers as rural.

[3] For a fuller discussion of the differences in meaning of these terms, consult Kimball Young, *Sociology: A Study of Society and Culture*, Second Edition, pp. 17–20. New York: American Book Co., 1949.

There were 283,000 people in 1950 classified by the census as "urban farm"; [4] that is, they lived on farms which were located, at least in part, within the corporate limits of a city. For example, there were 1,101 "farmers and farm managers" reported within the city of New York. They no doubt operate very intensive farms such as those producing truck crops and poultry.

This brings up the next problem: (2) How big should a community be in order to be classified as urban, or how small to be considered rural? The answer to this question should bring us close to the crux of the problem of defining rurality. For there can be no doubt that social life is different in a small community from what it is in a large one, whatever the dominant occupation. The primary difference between life in a large and in a small community is *the relative extent of one's personal acquaintance with other members of the community.* Many other differences between rural and urban life are derived from this factor.[5] In a small place of not more than 1,000 population, the writer knows from personal experience that it is possible for everyone to know nearly everyone else. It cannot be demonstrated from existing information how much larger a community would have to be in order to reduce to, say, 50 per cent the number of the inhabitants with whom one could be personally acquainted. But it is highly probable that in a place of no more than 2,500 population one could be personally acquainted with at least 50 per cent of the people. In the large city, of course, the individual leads a rather "anonymous" existence—a definite characteristic of urban life.

Yet despite the attempt to consider range of acquaintanceship as the criterion, there is no sharp dividing line between urban and rural, and the best one can do is to recognize that the extremes of rural and urban societies are identifiable and to admit that there is a transition zone between the extremes in which the social life partakes of the nature of both urban and rural communities. But for practical purposes, one must set a rather arbitrary boundary. This has been done, as far as the United States is concerned, by the Bureau of the Census, which

[4] *United States Census of Population: 1950,* "U.S. Summary, General Characteristics," Table 90.

[5] To be treated in Chapter 2.

defines the rural population as those people residing in all unincorporated territory and in incorporated places of less than
2,500 population.[6] Such an arbitrary definition has the disadvantage that it is based entirely upon one criterion—size
of the community—and leaves out of consideration any qualitative characteristics.[7] Moreover, it takes no account of the fact
that there can be very little difference in the nature of community life in a place of 2,400—which would be classed as
rural—and one of 2,500, which would be considered urban. In
short, the weakness of the definition is that it is arbitrary.

The advantage in using the Census definition is that our most
important body of data for the United States—the Census
itself—is reported on the basis of this definition. Indeed, it
becomes almost inevitable that we follow the lead of the
Bureau of the Census in this respect so far as the United States
is concerned. Moreover, there is some justification for doing so
because of the primary importance of the criterion of size of
community, for many of the other possible social characteristics
are derived from this fact.

Landis states his own procedure—and the one commonly
followed by rural sociologists—as follows:

For statistical purposes, rural consists of places with less than 2,500
people, unless otherwise noted. For purposes of social-psychological
analysis, rural consists of those areas in which a high degree of intimacy
and informality characterizes relationships, the urban beginning at that
ill-defined point where people assume impersonal attitudes toward each
other. For purposes of economic-occupational analysis, farming is the
central point of interest.[8]

While the Census definition will include as rural a considerable
number of people in small communities who may be wholly
engaged in mining, forestry, fishing, or manufacturing, the
emphasis in this text will be upon the agricultural workers

---

[6] Some exceptions occur in the New England and a few other states, where it is
not the practice to incorporate places of less than 10,000 population. For full explanation see *Sixteenth Census of the United States, Population:* Vol. I, p. 10.

[7] See Chapter 2 for a discussion of some of the qualitative characteristics, and
consult Louis Wirth, "Urbanism As a Way of Life," *American Journal of Sociology,*
1938, 44:1–24.

[8] Reprinted by permission from *Rural Life in Process,* by Paul H. Landis, Copyrighted, 1940, by the McGraw-Hill Book Co., Inc. p. 18.

and those in the small towns engaged in operating service agencies primarily for farm people.

**The importance of the study of rural society.** Up to comparatively recent times the story of man is largely the story of *rural* man. Human beings have, no doubt, lived most of their history in small groups; not primarily as craftsmen and sedentary workers, but as hunters of food animals, and collectors of native fruits, or, since the invention of agriculture, as tillers of the soil. Cities are of comparatively recent times; indeed, cities as we know them today are largely a development of the past two centuries. While it is true that relatively large cities existed in very early historic times, those which arose before the Industrial Revolution were largely what Werner Sombart, the German economist, calls "consuming cities," or cities "which do not pay for [their] maintenance . . . with [their] own products because they do not need to do so, since they receive their maintenance by virtue of a legal title [taxes, rent, or the like] without being obliged to return an equivalent." [9] Therefore, if we would understand the historical roots of our contemporary rural-urban society, we should know something of the underlying rural experience of mankind.

Moreover, the contemporary citizen, whether he be urban or rural, cannot consider himself fully educated until he knows how the "other half" lives. The urbanite, as well as the ruralite, should know something about both rural and urban societies, their interrelations, common and differing characteristics. In other words, rural sociology is not exclusively for the student who comes from rural areas. In training for the professions, medicine, law, the ministry, social work, and teaching, many individuals with urban background find that their careers are spent at least partly in rural communities.

**Our culture a unity.** Contemporary society, with all its many diversities, is after all a functioning unit. No group exists in isolation from the rest of the world. Before the development of rapid means of communication, it was possible for groups of people to live with little or no contact with other groups.

[9] Werner Sombart, *Der moderne Kapitalismus:* quoted in translation in P. A. Sorokin, C. C. Zimmerman, and C. J. Galpin, A *Systematic Source Book in Rural Sociology,* Vol. I, p. 175. Minneapolis: University of Minnesota Press, 1930.

That time is now gone, and the social world is steadily and rapidly contracting. What with our heritage of group differences, the present situation creates many problems of adjustment among groups. World Wars I and II were undoubtedly the result of the failure of national groups to develop peaceful modes of accommodating one to the other. Our new means of communication have made the world a *technological* unit, but societies have not yet developed adequate social techniques to create a world *social* unit. The working hypothesis of intelligent humans the world over is that such a cultural world unit can be achieved. Also within the national groups themselves there are many problems of social adjustment to be worked out. The United States, for example, has problems of adjustment among rural and urban groups, among the numerous political or governmental units (township, county, state, and nation), and among purely geographic regions. Our point of view is that our civilization is one and the various segments are but parts of an organic whole; that rural society is to be studied as a part of the "Great Society." While we narrow our attention on the rural scene, let us not lose sight of its relation to the total cultural landscape.

## QUESTIONS FOR DISCUSSION

1. What is, or should be, the relationship between general and rural sociology?
2. Is it possible for a person to be both a social scientist and a social reformer?
3. Is it possible or feasible to divide the several social sciences into "watertight" compartments?
4. What elements do the social sciences have in common?
5. In what two senses is the word *science* used? Which of the two ways of using the term should be given the most importance?
6. In what way have the social sciences lagged behind the physical or exact sciences?
7. Discuss the need and methods for achieving more refined observation of social phenomena.
8. What are the principal methods of scientific study?
9. What are some language difficulties encountered by the social scientists?
10. What is the relationship between a *concept* and an *hypothesis?*

11. How are such concepts as *society, culture, rural,* and *urban* customarily used by social scientists?
12. Mention some difficulties involved in the use of the terms *urban* and *rural.*
13. Why should some knowledge of rural culture be a part of every person's education?
14. In what sense can contemporary American culture be regarded as a unity? In what way or ways does our culture lack integration?

## SELECTED REFERENCES

Kluckhohn, Clyde, and Kelly, William H. "The Concept of Culture," in *The Science of Man in the World Crisis,* pp. 78–106. Ralph Linton, ed. New York: Columbia University Press, 1945.

Pearson, Karl. *The Grammar of Science,* Chapter 1. London: J. M. Dent and Sons, Ltd. (Everyman's Library), 1937.

Young, Kimball. *Sociology: The Study of Society and Culture,* Second Edition, Chapter 1, "What Sociology Is and What It Tries to Do," New York: American Book Co., 1949.

CHAPTER 2

# CHARACTERISTICS OF RURAL LIFE

The distinctive characteristics of rural life are most easily discerned by comparing them with those of city life. Some differences are apparent to everyone. The culture of cities is one thing, the culture of the country is quite another. Cities are by comparison large, impersonal, and complex in social structure; country communities are small, intimate, and simple in organization. Rural-urban differences have found expression in the common tendency for urban and rural groups to coin words or phrases (stereotypes) to designate one another. Thus, "peasant," "hayseed," "clod-hopper" become designations for the ruralite, while the urbanite becomes a "city slicker."

But the emphasis on differences between the two segments of culture should not deny recognition of the underlying similarities. While the differences may seem to be many and socially important, they cannot equal the likenesses either in number or in qualitative significance.

Thinking in terms of the United States, what are some of the elements common to both rural and urban cultures? Perhaps the factor of first importance in binding the parts together as a single society is a common language and the literature, science, philosophy, and religion which are recorded in that language. Second, of course, are the common institutions of education, religion, family life, and business and political organization. There are rural as well as urban Methodists, Presbyterians, Catholics, Democrats, Republicans, PTA members, Masons, Odd Fellows, alumni of the universities. Practically all of the numerous ethnic groups occur in both rural and urban areas. In other words, we are fruit of the same tree, howsoever we may differ in size, shape, and color. There are within the United States innumerable occupations, groupings, societies, organi-

14

zations, all partaking of the general character of the fundamental culture.

What is it, then, that gives to rural society a character different in certain particulars from that of urban life? The answer will not be found in any one factor, but in several factors. For one thing, the historical development of the two ways of life has followed somewhat divergent paths. In the beginning all human beings were rural; cities are a later development. In the United States the national life was predominantly agricultural until about 1900. City life may be looked upon, therefore, as a stream diverted from the river of rural culture.

Since the possibilities for cultural differentiation are almost infinite, the separation of the two ways—rural and urban—was bound to set the stage for divergent patterns of change. The occupational and geographic environment of the city is very different from that of the country. The impacts of invention affect the city and country variously. The Industrial Revolution in England, which stemmed from such inventions as the steam engine (1769) and the power loom (1787), wrought drastic though different changes both to the city and to the country. For the city it meant expansion because of the proliferation of new occupations; for the country it meant depopulation and decay of institutions. The development of the internal combustion engine has had a similar effect. The cities have continued to grow, the country to decline. On the other hand, the benefits and conveniences which both ways of life have inherited from the Industrial Revolution should not be disparaged.

These differing historical developments have not taken place in a vacuum. Changes in culture usually result from the response of human beings to stimuli arising from their environment. We need therefore to examine two other major factors which have influenced the development of rural society: occupation, and population density.

## THE OCCUPATION OF AGRICULTURE

While rural people are engaged in a considerable variety of occupations, it is agriculture that gives to rural life many of its peculiar characteristics. Farming involves the raising of

plants and animals for human consumption—as food, and as
fiber for the manufacture of clothing and other utilities. Of
the approximately 20 million persons 14 years of age or over
living on farms in the United States in 1940, more than 9
million were listed as belonging to the experienced labor force
in agriculture. Here is accounted for about 18 per cent of the
total labor force of the nation. The number of workers in
agriculture exceeds that in any other specific industry except
manufacturing.

**The farmer's work-environment.** In contrast with the situation in most other occupations, the farmer does his work in
the open air, in close association with the soil and living things.
While farming involves hard physical labor, the agricultural
worker is exposed to an abundance of fresh air and sunshine,
so important in maintaining health. The work routine on the
farm is determined by the seasons and the fluctuations of the
weather. In the springtime, the animals need special attention,
since, as a rule, it is the season when they give birth to their
young. If losses are to be prevented, special care must be taken.
Many sheep growers, for example, suffer heavy losses during
the lambing season unless adequate precautions are taken
against inclement weather and other contingencies. In the
spring, also, other essential jobs to be done are plowing, preparation of the seedbed, and planting the crops. Once the crops
are up, they must be cultivated to eliminate weeds and to
conserve moisture. Some crops, like sugar beets, require thinning
which must be done by hand. In growing some specialty crops
such as vegetables and fruits, farmers must be prepared against
untimely frosts by covering the tender shoots with paper; or,
as in the case of citrus crops, farmers must be equipped with
smudge pots, which are scattered through the orchard and
fired to provide warmth against freezing. Harvest of some crops,
mainly hay and fall-planted grain, commences in June and runs
into the autumn.

The fall is, of course, the season for harvesting most crops.
It is a critical period on the farm, demanding the maximum
effort of the farmer, his family, and his hired help. Failure to
get the crop gathered at the right time may result in heavy
losses and wipe out the year's profits.

After the harvest, the farmer's work routine shifts again, and his primary tasks become caring for his livestock and marketing his crops. In diversified farming areas, care of livestock, especially dairy cattle, occupies the chief attention of farm people. Barns must be cleaned daily and feed must be prepared and brought to the animals. Milking cows and processing the milk require much time. Throughout all the seasons of the year the daily chores must be done; they concern primarily the care of livestock.

**Farming requires a wide range of knowledge and skills.** One can readily see from the cursory enumeration of farm jobs given above that the successful farmer must be something of a jack-of-all-trades. First of all, he must understand the soil. Soils vary widely in texture and fertility. He must know when the soil is dry enough in the spring to plow. If the soil is of heavy texture so that it holds moisture longer, he cannot begin to work it as early in the spring as he might if it were of lighter texture. Moreover, there are usually considerable variations in soil types on his own farm. He must know also what fertilizers his varying soil requires and in what quantity.

Secondly, he must know about the soil and moisture requirements of various crops. Perhaps not all of the farm is suited to the production of corn, or of wheat, clover, cotton, and so on. He cannot grow the same crop on the same piece of land year after year without suffering a decline in yield. He must rotate his crops and work out the best system of rotation for his particular farm. He must be careful in the selection of seed to be planted. Some varieties will do well on his farm; others will not. He will come to learn about such matters through experience, or from his neighbors, or from the county agricultural agent.

In the third place, he must be skilled in the use and care of livestock. A good husbandman comes to know the individual characteristics of his animals and how to manage them to get the best possible results. A good teamster can often persuade a balky horse to pull, after he "gets acquainted" with him. On the other hand, an inexperienced horseman can "ruin" what had been a perfectly good work horse. During World War II dairymen objected to hiring inexperienced help, because of the

loss in production resulting from improper milking and feeding
of the cows. In short, the management and care of animals
requires a high degree of skill, usually attained only after long
experience.

Fourthly, the farmer must know a good deal about plant
and animal diseases and pests, and how to protect his growing
crops and animals from their attacks. The fruit grower must
spray his trees many times each season. The vegetable grower
must spray his crops against the numerous insects and diseases
that afflict them. For his animals he may be able to secure the
services of a trained veterinarian, but he must take care of his
crops by himself: he is his own crop "doctor."

Fifthly, the contemporary farmer must be something of a
mechanic. On the average diversified farm today there are many
machines, some of them rather complicated. Care and use of
tractors, combine harvesters, gasoline and electric motors,
milking machines, and many others, must be within the range
of skills of the successful farmer. Some of his repair work is
done by specialized mechanics, though it is not always possible
to get such service when it is needed, and in any case it may
be had only at considerable expense. Most farmers or their
sons come to know enough about the various machines, so
that they themselves can cope with most of the repairs needed.

Finally, the farmer must have managerial ability. Each of
the six million farmers of the United States is an entrepreneur.
The average value of their farms in 1952 was over $25,000.
In view of the complexity of the enterprise itself, successful
operation requires considerable ability. This is a fact often not
fully realized by those unfamilar with agriculture, and it accounts for many failures. The city man, who all his life has
dreamed of a little farm of his own, where he can live a life
close to nature and free from the bustle and cares of urban
life, may suffer a rude disillusionment when he attempts to
transform his dream into reality. Farming does have many
favorable characteristics as a way of life. But the inexperienced,
who are contemplating investing their life-savings in a farm
they expect to operate, should not underestimate the managerial
ability which success demands.

**Farming is a family enterprise.** Another important distinguishing characteristic of most farming is that it is a joint family undertaking. It is true that there is specialization and division of labor among the family members, but essentially the farmer and his wife, as well as the children, all take some part in most of the farm operations. Ordinarily, the mother and daughters are occupied with the home, the family garden, and usually the poultry, but at times they may help with other farm tasks as well. Nevertheless, division of labor, such as it is, does not weaken the generalization that the family as a unit operates the farm. This is true of practically no other occupation, and tends to give to the farm family its well-known solidarity.

**The farmer lives close to his work.** By virtue of the fact that most American farmers live on their farms, the home is near the daily work. Unlike the urban dweller, who often travels many miles daily to and from his work, the farmer nearly always lives in the midst of his occupation. The nearest urban equivalent would probably be the small shopkeeper whose dwelling place is in the back part of the structure that houses the store.

**The farmer's neighbors engage in the same occupation.** The farmer lives his life among neighbors who are also farmers. At very much the same hour of the day, all the farmers of a neighborhood will be doing very much the same sort of tasks. This sameness of activity is socially important because it gives to the neighborhood of farm people a homogeneity of interest in their occupation, which is characteristic of few other groups.

### NONAGRICULTURAL OCCUPATIONS IN RURAL AMERICA

By no means are all of the nearly 60 million people classified in the United States Census as "rural" engaged in agriculture. As a predominant pursuit, agriculture occupies only the 30 million farm dwellers. In the broad countryside of the nation and in the numerous villages and hamlets there is a great range of diverse occupations; they are mainly those which characterize urban centers. They derive, however, a distinctive rural quality from their very proximity to agriculture. As one drives out through the open country he will notice here and there an oil station, a crossroads store, a beer tavern, a roadside market, and of course, a schoolhouse, or an open-country church. For the most part, these agencies exist primarily to serve the needs of farmers. Indeed, many of the business establishments are operated by part-time farmers.

In the rural trade centers it is equally true that most of the merchants owe their livelihood primarily to the patronage of farmers in the surrounding territory. The villagers are for the most part engaged in performing services which farm families require. Essentially, villages constitute the avenues through which farm products find their way to the outside world, and through which the products of the urban world enter the farm homes. Village merchandising, transportation, banking, and much village manufacture are but a step removed from farming itself.

The close association of villager and farmer in the matter of occupation is suggested in our familiar reference to the "country" merchant, "country" doctor, banker, lawyer, preacher, editor, etc.[1] They differ from their counterparts in the larger city in the close personal relations they have with their customers, clients, and patients, and in the generalization rather than specialization of their services.

## POPULATION DENSITY

How much land there is to how many men is the fundamental consideration in the life of any society. The ratio between these two factors means the ratio of numbers to sustenance, or of mouths to food; for the fact that all food comes in the last analysis from the earth should not be let slip because it is obvious. This relation of numbers to sustenance affords a firm, unspeculative, unselected footing for a science of society. . . . [2]

Sumner and Keller, the authors of this statement, proceed to point out the relation between land and numbers of people in determining the struggle for existence, the formation of groups, and the development of ways of meeting life situations, especially the "maintenance-ways, by which an actual living

[1] Celebrated in such books as: Arthur E. Hertzler, *Horse and Buggy Doctor*, New York: Harper and Brothers, 1938; Bellamy Partridge, *Country Lawyer*, New York: McGraw-Hill Book Co., 1939; Henry B. Hough, *Country Editor*, New York: Doubleday-Doran and Co., 1940.

[2] William Graham Sumner and Albert G. Keller, *The Science of Society*, Vol. I, p. 4. New Haven: Yale University Press, 1927.

is acquired."[3] "Out of the blocks of customs thus evolved and controlled, issue all human institutions. Hence the type of society's institutions derives ultimately from the ratio of men to land. . . . "[4] It is safe to say that few contemporary students of society would go as far as these authors in ascribing to this factor such an all-inclusive role. Nevertheless, there can be no question of its being very important.

In terms of the number of people per square unit of area, the country has a low man-land ratio and the city has a high one. This means that the number of human beings with whom the farmer has daily contact is small, while for the city dweller it is large. The farm dweller, as a result, comes to know more intimately the people in the area in which he lives. Contacts are fewer but more intense, and knowledge about others in the area is much more complete. If a farmer goes on a trip, even to the village, the neighbors usually know about it. There is still much borrowing and lending among rural neighbors, exchange of labor during busy seasons, and mutual aid in time of illness or death. There is family visiting back and forth, and bonds of friendship are strong. In other words, the primary group characteristics defined by Cooley as "face-to-face relations" apply more exactly to rural areas than to urban.

**Social status and stratification.** Under rural conditions social status is likely to be determined more by the personal qualities of the individual rather than by the secondary criteria of income, occupation, and other general attributes. Class consciousness is not conspicuous in such a society, not only because of the personal knowledge which each has of the other, but also because of the fact that all are engaged in the same occupation, as we have already noted. Thus, the degree of social stratification in areas of low population density would be expected to be less than in an area where large numbers occupy a limited space.

While we usually think of the primary group as especially characteristic of the open-country dweller, it is common also to the rural trade center. In a village of no more than 2,500 people it is possible for everyone to know almost everyone else in the community and a large number of the dwellers in the adjacent countryside as well. The world of social interaction of the village

[3] *Ibid.*, p. 5.     [4] *Ibid.*, p. 5.

is not so large as to create highly impersonal relations, such as those which typify the urban environment.

**Size and nature of institutions.** The low population density in rural areas limits the growth of communities to relatively small size. This fact has significance for social institutions such as the school, the church, and the local government. Rural institutions in general are small in membership and their services are not highly specialized. The one-room school, for example, is a direct result of low population density. The teacher in such a school is perforce not specialized in any one subject or in the teaching of any one grade. He or she must be prepared to teach all ages of children all of the subjects in the curriculum. The rural church, similarly, has a small membership as a rule. It often does not maintain a Sunday school or a young people's organization, nor does it carry on many of the extra activities common in large urban churches. Other agencies, including the business enterprises in the villages are likewise affected, but the illustrations already given will serve to make clear the point that rural institutions are small in size and simple and undifferentiated in structure.

**Leadership.** The smallness of rural groups also tends to influence the character of local leadership. Since relations are so largely on a personal level, leaders are usually chosen with reference to personal qualities to a much greater degree than is possible in the city.

MacLeish and Young in their study of Landaff, New Hampshire, point out that in this community

> . . . the leader must be a person who will carry out the duties inherent in his role, but who will not go beyond them. The roles are set up in accordance with the ideas of personal independence, self-reliance, and individualism. In short, the leader must be a man who shows in himself the prime virtues of this culture: self-reliance, respect for others, and independence.[5]

In other words, leaders in a small community, because they are well known to the voters, can be chosen according to personal qualities which conform with the local system of values.

[5] Kenneth MacLeish and Kimball Young, "Culture of a Contemporary Rural Community, Landaff, New Hampshire," *Rural Life Studies: 3*, United States Department of Agriculture, April, 1942, p. 86.

**Social mobility.** Low density of population and homogeneity of occupation, results in less circulation of people from one occupational class or status-level to another. We shall see subsequently that this type of mobility is by no means absent from rural society, but it obviously is much less than in a more complex society, where the number of occupations and the range-of-status positions are much greater. There is also less moving about from place to place among rural people, as compared with urban.

**Social control.** In primary groups, social control—the establishment and maintenance of order—is achieved principally through the informal pressures of the folkways and mores, rather than by means of external or legal controls. It is true that legal enactments play an important role in rural society, but the relative strength of the folkways is much greater than in larger communities. The influence of folkways in rural society grows weaker as primary group gives way to secondary group organization.

**Standard of living.** Finally, the standard of living of rural people is directly proportional to the density of the population. This applies particularly to certain of the material factors in the living standard, such as household conveniences. In areas of high population density it is possible to obtain such things as running water in the home, electricity, sewage disposal, cooking gas, and the like. In areas of low population density it becomes a relatively costly undertaking to acquire them. Until the development of the Rural Electrification Administration in the United States, only one farm home in eight was able to have electricity. And even under the REA program, generous as it is, the per capita cost to the farm home is inevitably high when compared with that to the urban dweller. Water and sewage-disposal systems for the farmer are made possible by electricity, though each home has to have its own system with correspondingly large cost.

Discussion of the conditioning roles of occupation and low density of population could be extended. But enough has been said at this point to indicate the distinctive character of rural society. It will be readily seen that many social problems are traceable to the peculiarities enumerated. Moreover, the rural personality, insofar as it is a product of a particular social and physical environment, is sure to have traits which are peculiar to that environment. In Table 1, an attempt is made to indicate the rural-urban differences by use of qualitative adjectives. It is meant only as a guide and not as a precise characterization.

TABLE 1. *Approximate Qualitative Differences Among Farm, Village, and Urban Societies, With Reference Primarily to the United States*

|  | FARM | VILLAGE-TOWN | CITY |
|---|---|---|---|
| OCCUPATION | Agricultural, homogeneous | Nonagricultural, moderately diversified | Non-agricultural, highly diversified |
| Work Environment | Open air | Enclosed | Enclosed |
| Weather and Season | Highly important | Less important | Least important |
| Skills | General and diverse | More specialized | Highly specialized |
| Family Works as Unit | Common | Not usually | Very uncommon |
| Home and Work | Adjacent | Usually separate | Nearly always separate |
| POPULATION DENSITY | Low | Medium | High |
| Size of Community | Very small | Small to medium | Medium to large |
| Social Contacts | Few and personal | Moderate number, mostly personal | Numerous and mostly impersonal |
| Social Stratification | Little | Moderate | Much |
| Home Conveniences | Few (high cost) | Many (moderate cost) | Many (low cost) |
| Institutions | Small and simple | Medium in size and complex | Large and complex |
| Social Control | Folkways-Mores | Legislative-Mores | Legislative |
| Nature of Group | Primary | Primary-Secondary | Secondary |
| Mobility Rate | Low | Medium | High |
| Social Status | Stable—Rests upon personal acquaintance | Moderately stable | Unstable-Determined by secondary criteria, such as occupation and wealth |

## QUESTIONS FOR DISCUSSION

1. Compare the city dweller and the farmer with respect to their responses to, and dependence on, such things as precipitation, temperature, seasonal changes, and plant and animal life.

2. What are the social effects of living in a sparsely settled area? How are social contacts, attitudes, and organization likely to be influenced?
3. Does a low-density population have any specific advantages or disadvantages as compared with a high-density population? Discuss.
4. In what way is the size of a community related to the number and variety of social institutions? Racial and nationality differences? Number of social classes? Vertical and horizontal social mobility? Spatial mobility?
5. Why would you expect such institutions as the family, church, school, business, and government in rural areas to be more traditional in structure, function, and outlook?
6. What reason is there for believing that farming, as compared with most urban occupations, is more self-sufficient? Do you think the farmer has a greater choice in setting his own pace and choosing his day-by-day activities? Does he think and act within a narrower range of experience? Discuss.
7. Are urban and rural primary group relations likely to be different in quality or quantity? Give reasons for your answer.

### SELECTED REFERENCES

Heberle, Rudolph. "The Application of Fundamental Concepts in Rural Community Studies," *Rural Sociology*, 6:3, pp. 203–215, September, 1941.

Loomis, C. P., and Beegle, J. Allan. *Rural Social Systems*, Chapter 1. New York: Prentice-Hall, 1950.

Redfield, Robert. "Rural Sociology and the Folk Society," *Rural Sociology*, 8:1, pp. 68–71, March, 1943.

Sorokin, P. A., and Zimmerman, C. C. *Principles of Rural-Urban Sociology*, Chapter 2. New York: Henry Holt and Co., 1929.

Taylor, C. C., and others. *Rural Life in the United States*, Chapter 1. New York: Alfred A. Knopf, 1949.

# PART II

# THE PHYSICAL ENVIRONMENT AND SPATIAL
# PATTERNS OF RURAL LIFE

## INTRODUCTION

ALL LIFE subsists upon a superficial layer of the earth's crust, usually not more than a foot in thickness. This topsoil furnishes the nourishment that makes plant and animal life possible. Man, no less than the other animals and the plants, is dependent upon this thin coating of the planet. He not only must recognize this dependence and adapt himself to it, but his adaptation must also be to other physical conditions such as topography, temperature, and precipitation. This process of adaptation affects society and culture. Rural people especially have direct relations with the soil, the lay of the land, the wind, and the rain. They are not only acted upon by these forces, but they themselves act upon and influence them as well.

In man's adaptation to the physical environment there arise certain patterns of arrangement, which the geographer calls the cultural landscape. Regions with homogeneous characteristics can be delineated and constituent areas described.

In this section the reader is introduced in Chapter 3 to the regional patterns—both physical and cultural—as they have been described for the United States. In Chapter 4 the basic forms of settlement or of land occupancy are discussed. In Chapter 5 there is a description of the rural community as it has been delineated in the United States.

# REGIONAL PATTERNS IN THE
# UNITED STATES

Any discussion of regions involves consideration of the interplay of the physical environment and culture. Before presenting detailed information regarding regions themselves, it is pertinent to review briefly the more general question of the relation of man and his culture to geographic environment.

Every people, no matter how primitive and simple or advanced and complex, has to face the problem of adapting itself to the physical environment. From this environment are derived the necessities for maintaining life, especially food, clothing, and shelter. While the problem of adaptation is more apparent in the case of the simpler societies, it is no less real in the case of more complex societies. Anyone can readily recognize the close association between the physical environment and the Eskimo civilization, but one is not immediately aware of a similar relationship in some large metropolis like New York City. Nevertheless, the great metropolis exists ultimately because there is such a thing as agricultural land and because climatic factors are favorable to the growth of crops. New Yorkers may not be conscious of their dependence upon soil and rainfall, simply because in our system of division of labor it is not necessary for them to grow their own food. They take for granted the appearance of the milkman each morning to leave the family milk supply for the day, or the grocer's truck which delivers the fresh vegetables, fruit, and meat. They have no direct contact with the process of producing these commodities.

Yet when we think in terms of the aggregate population of the United States, or of the world, rather than a small specialized segment, we realize that there is a close connection between its welfare and the condition of the natural resources. During the decade from 1930 to 1940 there was much discussion among urban—as well as rural—groups regarding the conservation of natural resources in general and of the soil in particular. It is significant in that it represents a growing awareness of the final stake which city people have in the soil resources. They, no less than country people, depend for survival upon the maintenance of the fertility of the soil. One could go much further and say that city people may in large measure determine the kind of public policies adopted for protecting land resources.

**Does geography determine culture?** There are few subjects which have aroused so much speculation among scholars as the causal role of physical environment in shaping human civilization. Do climate, soil, location, topography, or other "aspects of nature" determine the kind of civilization that will arise in any given area? That society is influenced by such factors, few would deny, but there is great difference of opinion as to the extent and nature of the influence. The English historian, Henry Thomas Buckle, after speculating on the question, came to the conclusion that the geographical factors of soil, climate, food, and the general aspect of nature were the most important influences on mankind.[1]

The human geographers refined the theories of the effect of environment upon culture and particularly stressed the reciprocal relation of the two forces; that is, while the physical environment influences culture, it is also true that man modifies his physical environment. The anthropologists,[2] while dismissing the notion of a causal or determining relation between physical environment and culture, do not disregard the environmental influences. They recognize that the physical environ-

[1] "If we inquire," says Buckle, "what those physical agents are by which the human race is most powerfully influenced, we shall find that they may be classed under four heads: namely, Climate, Food, Soil and the General Aspect of Nature; by which last, I mean those appearances which, though presented chiefly to the sight, have, through the medium of that or other senses, directed the association of ideas, and hence in different countries have given rise to different habits of national thought." Henry Thomas Buckle, *History of Civilization in England*, Vol. I, p. 29. New York: D. Appleton and Co., 1901 (from the second London edition).

[2] For a good, brief review of the problem as seen by an anthropologist, see Alexander Goldenweiser, *Anthropology: An Introduction to Primitive Culture*, pp. 443–454. New York: F. S. Crofts and Co., 1937. On page 450 is found the pertinent sentence, "most important of all is to realize that in its relations to material culture, nature can set limits and furnish materials, but it cannot do more."

ment may condition culture and that it does set limits in a broad sense to the development of culture. That it is invalid to assign a causal influence to physical environment may be demonstrated by the differences in the use of American land by the Indians and by the Europeans. Before the coming of the Europeans, continental United States supported at most a few hundred thousand aborigines, whereas today it supports about 140 million people. The difference certainly cannot be attributed to the physical environment, but rather to the differences in the respective cultures.

This reciprocal relationship between society and its geographic environment has been well stated by a soil technologist as follows:

Man lives and must work to supply his needs in an environment that is both social and physical. All the land in the United States could be made to produce crops, and there is none that will produce without labor. What land will be used at any moment, with what techniques, and with what success, depends upon the social and economic frame of reference within which people work, as well as upon the physical environment. Every time the economic and social conditions change, a new physical problem is created, and each time a new technique is developed, a new economic question appears. New problems for both the physical scientist and the social scientist will arise as long as society changes. And when society ceases to change, the end will have come. Students of agriculture are coming to this realization. Soil studies in an economic vacuum and economic studies in a physical vacuum compete for uselessness as contributions to a solution of our land problems.[3]

We would do well to recognize that culture and physical environment react upon each other. Both are dynamic and changeful; culture must make adjustments to changes in the physical world and within itself, if it is to survive.

The agricultural land, climate, and topography constitute the main physical basis for rural society. Variations over the earth's surface of the character of these elements result in variations in the cultural response of the human inhabitants. There is, for example, one kind of social organization in a dry,

---

[3] Charles E. Kellogg, "Soil and Society," in *Soils and Men: Yearbook of Agriculture*, p. 886. Washington, D.C.: United States Department of Agriculture, 1938.

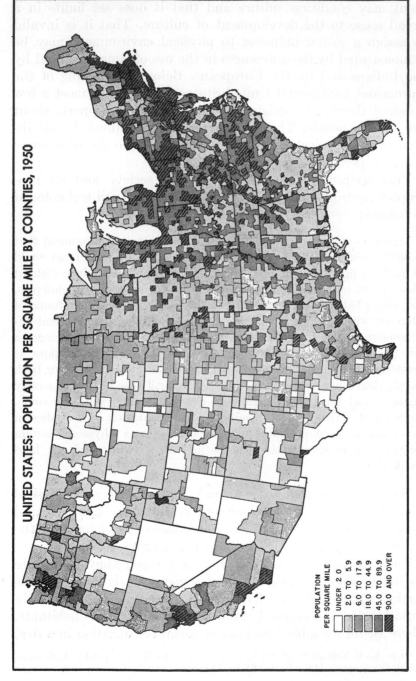

FIGURE 1. *Population Density of the United States by Counties, 1950*

temperate climate and quite another in one that is humid and tropical. Even in the same zone wide variations occur. Webb points out that a marked change occurs in the social structure as the 98th meridian is crossed in the United States. He says:

As one contrasts the civilization of the Great Plains with that of the eastern timberland, one sees what may be called an institutional *fault* (comparable to a geological *fault*) running from Middle Texas to Illinois or Dakota roughly following the ninety-eighth meridian. At this fault the ways of life and living changed. Practically every institution that was carried across it was either broken and remade or else greatly altered.[4]

Illustrating his point the author goes on to mention the differences in travel, weapons, methods of agriculture, plows, and other implements on the two sides of this borderline.

This "fault," in Webb's terminology, is illustrated by the sharp break in the density of the population at about the midpoint of the continent. (See Figure 1.) This difference, is of course, due to the differences in rainfall, since near the 100th meridian the humid area ends and the arid begins. Thus, in climate itself we have one factor contributing to the creation of the region.[5]

**Meaning of region.** The term "region" has become prominent in the literature of social science only in recent years, particularly since 1930. Earlier, the word "sectionalism" had gained wide currency among historians and political scientists, especially through the writings of Frederick J. Turner.[6]

From the early beginning of settlement in the United States divergent interests developed in the North and the South, based upon differences in types of farming and in farm organization. In the North there was the small farm agriculture

[4] W. P. Webb, *The Great Plains*, pp. 8, 9. Boston: Ginn and Company, 1931. (Quoted by permission of the author.)

[5] For an extensive discussion of the manner in which climate has influenced agricultural settlement in various climatic regions of the United States, how it affects health, the production of crops and livestock, etc., see *Climate and Man: Yearbook of Agriculture*. Washington, D.C.: United States Department of Agriculture, 1941. See also the novel by George R. Stewart, *Storm*. New York: Random House, 1941. It portrays dramatically the innumerable ways in which a storm affects the daily lives and fortunes of human beings.

[6] Frederick Jackson Turner, *The Significance of Sections in American History*. New York: Henry Holt and Co., 1932.

carried on by freemen, while in the South there was the large slave plantation which developed on the basis of cotton and tobacco culture. Subsequently, the West developed a new set of interests based upon the drive for free land and the homestead principle of settlement. The respective agrarian interests of North and South expressed themselves in political and finally in military conflict.

The concept of the region has its origin in physical geography. In this connection, the term is used to denote areas which have sufficiently homogeneous physical features to differentiate one from another. One finds such phrases as Coastal Region, the Appalachian Plateau, the Great Plains, and so on. Sometimes a river basin is considered as a region, although this is not a very satisfactory use of the term because of the wide variations which may occur within the same river valley. Woofter defines a region as "an area within which the combination of environmental and demographic factors have created a homogeneity of economic and social structure." [7]

The *cultural region* is an area in which society is characterized by a sufficient homogeneity in patterns of behavior—including ways of living, values, beliefs, and social organization—to differentiate it from other areas. This use of the term will be illustrated as we proceed. The adjustment of rural society in the United States can be better indicated by a brief examination of the various physical and cultural areas as they have thus far been delineated.

**Soil regions.** Basic to agriculture and the social organization of the rural community is the nature of the soil. Soil technologists have classified the soils of the United States into a number of major zones with numerous subclasses. The major soil groups tend to occur in specific areas or regions of the country. The regional variations are the result of a number of factors, including the rock materials from which the soils have been weathered by the elements, the variety and abundance of plant life which grew upon them before the introduction of agriculture,

---

[7] Quoted in *Regional Factors in National Planning*, p. 142. Washington, D.C.: National Resources Committee, 1935. This Report contains much valuable information on regionalism in the United States, approached from the standpoint of regional planning.

and the extent to which organic matter has been incorporated in the soil through the action of microorganisms. Plant life and its decomposition are largely a function of climatic factors, such as precipitation and temperature.

It will be noted by reference to the map (Figure 2) that approximately the eastern two-fifths of the United States is

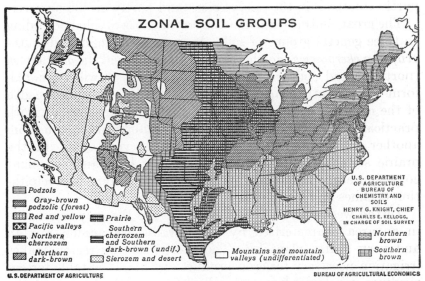

FIGURE 2. *Soil Zones of the United States*

divided into three main soil groups. Soils classified as *podzols* are found in the northern Great Lakes region, New York, northern New England, Pennsylvania, and West Virginia. These sandy-textured soils occupy areas where the rainfall is high and the mean annual temperature low, and remain damp a large part of the year. Conifers and other plants which flourish on an acid soil characterize the area; owing to the dampness and coolness of the soil, they are not readily decomposed. Peat bogs are therefore common.

Next, to the southward, are located the *gray-brown podzolic* soils. The rainfall is abundant, but temperatures are higher. There are few conifers; hardwoods and other deciduous trees predominate. The formation of humus—decomposed organic matter in the soil—has been more rapid than in the podzol region. In the Southeast, extending as far west as eastern Texas, are the *red and yellow* soils, the bright colors of which are familiar to anyone who has visited this section. Rainfall is high, topography is broken in most of the area, and temperatures are rather high. The open winters, the uneven topography, and the wide extent of cultivated row-crops, make this area particularly subject to heavy erosion. The original plant cover was partly conifers—in the sandy soils—and partly deciduous trees.

The great central section of the continent is divided according to three general groups of soils, the *prairie* (northern and southern), the *chernozems* (northern and southern), and the *dark brown* (northern and southern). These soils zones, it will be noted, form north-south strips running practically the full breadth of the country. All of them were originally grass-covered, with practically no trees. The factor that differentiates one from another is the abundance or sparsity of vegetation. In the prairie soil belt, rainfall is comparatively high and the plant cover more luxuriant. Moving westward, the annual precipitation declines and the vegetation becomes sparse.

To the west of the dark-brown zone are the *gray desert* soils in an area characterized by a generally low annual rainfall and very sparse plant life. The aridity of the region makes irrigation necessary for crop production. Lands suitable for agriculture are limited to the valley floors and plateaus of the Rocky Mountains.

The *Pacific valley* soils show great diversity, resulting from the wide range of climatic conditions, from extremely high rainfall on the northern coastal areas to very low in Southern California. There is also considerable variation in the rock formations from which the soils were originally derived.

These soils vary in fertility and in their suitability for various agricultural uses. As a result of differences in soil as well as those in rainfall and temperature, different types of agriculture have developed.

**The agricultural regions.** Agriculture, it should be borne in mind, is one aspect of *culture*. It represents one adaptation of society to natural resources. Man, through his experience and scientific experimentation, has discovered the crops and animals best suited to the particular conditions of soil and climate. It will be noted that there is a considerable correspondence between the map showing the soil groups and that showing the agricultural regions (Figures 2 and 3). A detailed description of these regions is not necessary here, since their general character is indicated by names on the map.

**Type-of-farming areas.** This phrase developed by students of farm management in the United States denotes relatively small areas within which there exist relatively homogeneous patterns of crop and livestock production. As defined by F. F. Elliott:

> The term is descriptive of the kind of farming followed on a group of farms having a high degree of uniformity in the kind, relative amount, and proportion of the crops and livestock handled, and in the methods and practices followed in production. . . . When a type of farming is fairly well concentrated in one area, so that it is the prevailing or dominant type in that area, usually associated with a set of reasonably homogeneous, natural, and economic conditions occurring throughout a definite geographic area, an area so characterized may be called a type-of-farming area.[8]

Thus, various areas are characterized as "corn-hog," "cash-grain," "small grain, potatoes, and livestock," and so on, depending on the particular combinations of crops and livestock which predominate.

In a given state, therefore, there are several of these type-of-farming areas. Elliott delineated over 500 areas, making an average of over 10 of these areas per state. These smaller areas may be called sub-areas within the larger "agricultural regions" discussed previously. They are never absolutely fixed, since the type of farming will change somewhat with changes in demand for farm products of different kinds, as well as from changes in agricultural technology. Public policies may also bring about changes. The Agricultural Adjustment Administration, for example, has in recent years had considerable influence in reducing the cotton acreage and increasing the acreage devoted to hay and pasture grasses in the southern states, thus altering to some extent the nature of farming.

**Cultural regions.** Up to this point, we have considered

---

[8] F. F. Elliott, "Types of Farming in the United States," p. 1. Washington, D.C.: Bureau of the Census, 1933. Practically every state experiment station has also mapped the type-of-farming areas within the respective states, using not only the census data on which Elliott based his delineations, but supplementary field studies as well. These areas will not always correspond with those mapped by Elliott.

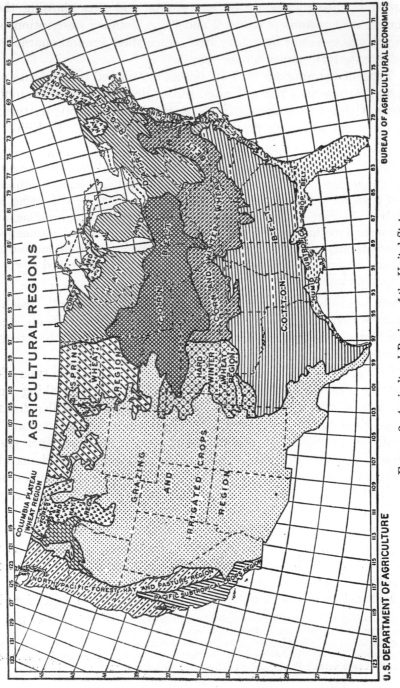

FIGURE 3. *Agricultural Regions of the United States*

"regions" and "areas" based primarily on physical factors and the resultant types of agriculture which have developed. While agriculture itself must be regarded as a cultural response to the physical environment, the question inevitably arises as to whether there may not be regional differences based upon other factors in culture, such as education, school attendance, level of living, population characteristics, and other social criteria. The concept of the "culture area" was developed by American ethnologists about a half century ago as a means of classifying museum materials and other ethnographic data. Clark Wissler elaborated the idea in 1917 and roughly mapped the cultural regions in the Americas so far as the aborigines were concerned.[9] A. L. Kroeber more recently has defined a culture area as "an area set off from others by relative internal homogeneity of culture and differentiation against the outside."[10]

The most definitive study of cultural regions in contemporary society in the United States has been made by Howard W. Odum and his associates of the University of North Carolina. Using upwards of 700 different measures of physical, economic, and social indices—including such factors as illiteracy, birth rates, death rates, school attendance, per capita wealth, and others— they grouped the 48 states into six major regions: the Northeast, the Middle States, the Southeast, Southwest, Northwest, and Far West.[11]

Among the rural sociologists, C. E. Lively, working in the state of Ohio in 1935, was the first to attempt to delineate regions based upon rural cultural characteristics. He used about 175 different statistical items for the counties in Ohio; by a process of statistical correlation and on the basis of the judgment of the investigator they were reduced to 60 and later to 25. A further computation of intercorrelations among these items indicated that some were closely related and "hang together,"

[9] Clark Wissler, The American Indian, Third Edition, pp. 220–248. New York: Oxford University Press, 1938.

[10] A. L. Kroeber, "Culture Area," in the Encyclopedia of the Social Sciences, Vol. 4, p. 646. New York: The Macmillan Company, 1937.

[11] Howard W. Odum, Southern Regions of the United States. Chapel Hill: University of North Carolina Press, 1936. See also H. W. Odum and H. E. Moore, American Regionalism. New York: Henry Holt and Co., 1938.

40

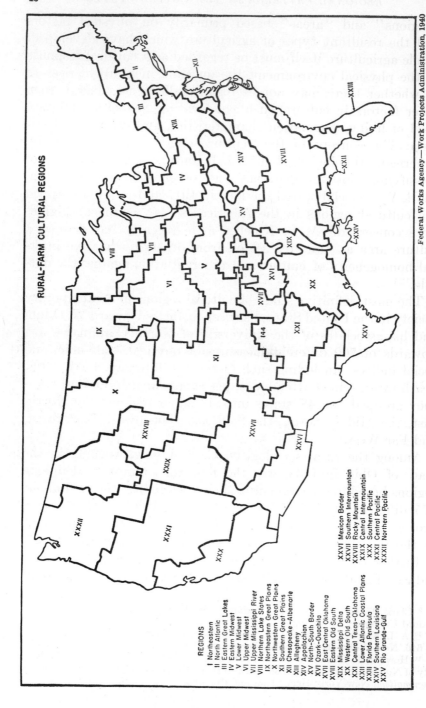

RURAL-FARM CULTURAL REGIONS

REGIONS
I Northeastern
II North Atlantic
III Eastern Great Lakes
IV Eastern Midwest
V Lower Midwest
VI Upper Midwest
VII Upper Mississippi River
VIII Northern Lake States
IX Northeastern Great Plains
X Northwestern Great Plains
XI Southern Great Plains
XII Chesapeake–Albemarle
XIII Alleghany
XIV Appalachian
XV North–South Border
XVI Ozark–Ouachita
XVII East Central Oklahoma
XVIII Eastern Old South
XIX Mississippi Delta
XX Western Old South
XXI Central Texas–Oklahoma
XXII Lower Atlantic Coastal Plains
XXIII Florida Peninsula
XXIV Southern Louisiana
XXV Rio Grande–Gulf

XXVI Mexican Border
XXVII Southern Intermountain
XXVIII Rocky Mountain
XXIX Central Intermountain
XXX Southern Pacific
XXXI Central Pacific
XXXII Northern Pacific

Federal Works Agency—Work Projects Administration, 1940

FIGURE 4. *Rural-Farm Cultural Regions*

making possible further elimination of items and combination of those remaining into an aggregate index, on which areas and subareas may be delineated.[12]

Using methods similar to those adopted by Odum and Lively, A. R. Mangus mapped rural cultural areas on the basis of data for farm population contained in the United States censuses of 1930 and 1935. He took as a point of departure the type-of-farming areas which had been delineated by Elliott, but he recognized type-of-farming as only one of many determinants of the type of rural culture. The indexes finally used as the criteria for mapping the cultural regions were (a) plane-of-living index, (b) the ratio of children under 5 years of age to 1,000 women 20–44 years of age (fertility ratio), (c) per cent of tenancy in 1935, (d) per cent of farms producing less than $1,000 in 1929, (e) per cent of agricultural products consumed on farms in 1929, (f) per capita land value, and (g) per cent of rural families residing on farms. In the South the per cent of Negroes in the population; in the Far West, the per cent of farm wage workers; and in the Southwest the per cent of "other races," were used as additional factors. As a result, Mangus was able to delineate 32 major accultural regions, and 218 subregions in the rural population.[13] (See Figure 4.)

Recently, Margaret J. Hagood has developed a rural level-of-living index for each county of the United States and for both the rural-farm and rural-nonfarm populations. The index was composed of such items as the per cent of occupied dwellings with fewer than 1.51 persons per room, the per cent with radios, farms with gross income under $600, the possession of automobiles, and the median grade of school completed by the adult population.[14]

The accompanying map based upon the rural-farm population

[12] C. E. Lively, "Social Planning and the Sociology of Sub-Regions," *Rural Sociology*, 1937, 2:288–298; C. E. Lively and R. B. Almack, "A Method of Determining Rural Social Sub-Areas with Application to Ohio," *Ohio AES, Department of Rural Economics Bulletin 106*, 1938.

[13] A. R. Mangus, *Rural Regions of the United States*, Chapter 4. Washington, D.C.: Work Projects Administration, 1940. Mangus also delineated regions for the rural nonfarm population and for the two rural groups combined.

[14] Margaret J. Hagood, "Rural Level of Living Indexes for Counties of the United States, 1940." Washington, D.C.: Bureau of Agricultural Economics, October, 1943.

42

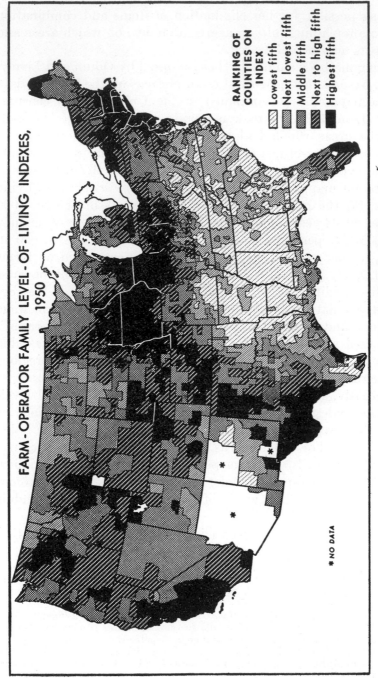

FIGURE 5. *Farm-Operator Family Level-of-Living Indexes, 1950*

index reveals in rather striking fashion the area differences in the United States, even though Hagood did not attempt to delineate specific regions (Figure 5). Comparison of this map with those given for soils and agricultural regions will reveal a certain degree of correspondence.

**Patterns of adjustment and maladjustment.** It has often been said that on a depleted soil will be found a depleted citizenry, while on a fertile soil will be found people enjoying considerable well-being. Although this generalization does not always hold good, there is evidence to show that people on good land compare to advantage on various social indexes. W. A. Anderson and others have found in New York state that people on the better soils show consistently higher rates of social participation than those on the poorer lands.[15] Investigators in Indiana found similar differences in a survey of 234 farm homes in Parke County. For example, on the poorest grade of land only 28 per cent of the families had one or more members participating in agricultural extension work, while on the best grade over 67 per cent were participating. In the proportions of homemakers contributing leadership in extension work, the range was from none on the two poorest grades of land to 14 per cent on the best grade. In regard to the number of household conveniences, the people on the poorer grades of land compared disadvantageously with those on the better grades.[16]

These data would seem to support the theory that the "A-grade farmers tend to get possession of the A-grade land"—meaning that in the competition for land the abler people will ultimately come to possess the better land. In other words, it is not the land that makes the people "better," but the fact that the better farmers select quality land on which they are able to make a better living. By virtue of their superior qualities they tend to be the leaders in, and supporters of, the social institutions.

That good soil in and of itself does not produce a superior

[15] W. A. Anderson and Hans Plambeck, "The Social Participation of Farm Families," *Cornell University AES, Rural Sociology Mimeograph Bulletin 8*, March, 1943. See also Bulletins 3, 4, and 7 in the same series.
[16] Starley M. Hunter, L. M. Busche, Gladys Gallup, and M. C. Wilson, "Home Situations on Different Classes of Land . . .," *Purdue University AES Extension Studies Circular 3*, May, 1941.

culture is demonstrated by the existence on some of the best soils of the nation of a culture which is characterized by the lowest level of living in the nation. In the Upper Mississippi Delta area of the South are some of the richest soils of the world. But reference to the level-of-living map (Figure 5) shows this area to be substandard. Along with the low index of family living will be found also inferior schools, churches, and other social institutions. "Rich land—poor people" is the way one government report characterizes a part of this general area.[17]

**Rural problem areas.** The severe depression of the early 1930's threw into prominence certain large areas of distress in the United States, areas which correspond roughly to soil zones and agricultural regions. In the 65 counties comprised in six problem areas of the country, were included approximately one half of the rural families receiving relief in the United States, although they contained but 36 per cent of the rural population of the country. The problem areas as delineated by P. G. Beck and M. C. Forster were as follows:

1) *The Appalachian-Ozark* area, characterized by small subsistence farms, very high birth rates, poor farming methods, and dependence on supplementary nonfarm employment.

2) *The Lake States Cutover* areas where farmers depend for part of their living on part-time employment in timber and mining; where farms are too small and often on poor soil unsuited to farming.

3-4) *The Short-Grass Wheat* areas of the Great Plains, characterized by climatic fluctuations which make farming hazardous. Periodic droughts greatly reduce the possibility of stable income. The *Spring Wheat* area includes the northern plains, while the *Winter Wheat* area includes the southern plains. In both, the problem of climate is crucial.

5) *The Eastern Cotton* area, characterized by dependence on the one crop of cotton, which has been subject to severe decline in prices and burdened with the sharecropper system, the biracial problem, and serious soil erosion.

6) *The Western Cotton* area, more subject to drought than the area to the East; has larger farms, and more mechanization, with growing displacement of human labor by machines. Drought was the main cause

[17] Max R. White, Douglas Ensminger, and Cecil L. Gregory, "Rich Land—Poor People," *Farm Security Administration Research Report I*, Indianapolis, 1938.

of the difficulty in the early 1930's, but the low price of cotton was associated with it.[18]

**Regionalism and rural planning.** The regional patterns of adjustment to the physical environment which have just been described have, as the saying goes, "just growed" up. There has been no deliberate planning to effect these adjustments. They have been influenced by such factors as the cultural tradition of the people, the introduction of technology, by public policies relating to tariffs, freight rates, and crop adjustments, by conditions of the market, and by climatic and other natural factors, including in the latter the introduction of plant diseases and insects. The crises of drought and depression of the 1930's have given rise to a great deal of thought as to whether and how more satisfactory adaptations to resources might be controlled and guided.

The process of attempting deliberately to influence adjustment to resources is called *planning*. In 1933 a number of programs were set in motion by the federal government to bring about desired changes in American rural life. One of these programs involved the "resettlement" of farm people from poor land—commonly designated as submarginal—to areas which were more suitable to agriculture. The submarginal lands were purchased from the owners by the government and the people thus displaced were assisted in getting relocated on better lands. Also, through the Agricultural Adjustment Administration and the Soil Conservation Service, attempts were made to prevent further destruction of the soil through erosion, to reduce the production of those crops of which we had a surplus, and to encourage more diversified crop production in the traditionally single-crop sections. Over all was the objective of increasing the flow of income into agriculture which since World War I had been in a more or less chronic state of depression.

One of the important steps taken during this period was the development of land-use planning committees in the various states, counties, and even townships. These planning commit-

[18] P. G. Beck and M. C. Forster, "Six Rural Problem Areas," *Federal Emergency Relief Administration Research Monograph I*, Washington, D.C., 1935.

tees composed of farmers, along with the technical employees of the government, mapped the areas of the county which were declared unsuitable for farming, and these areas were by county ordinance "zoned" against future settlement. Residents already in the areas were permitted to occupy their places as long as they desired, but after they left no other person might move in.

It should be clear from this presentation that, as the natural resources vary in regions of the earth's surface, different problems of adjustment are necessary on the part of man. Through these adaptations, regional differences in culture become apparent. Adaptation is never perfect and never completed. It is a continuous process for the reason that both natural resources and culture change. Mankind must always seek a desirable equilibrium between his social organization and the resources on which he depends. Wasteful use of soil, forests, metals, and other resources, goes on apace. It seems apparent that our civilization, by its disregard for the principles of conservative use of resources, is falling short of guaranteeing its future security.

### QUESTIONS FOR DISCUSSION

1. Cite examples of limitations on the development of culture which are imposed by (a) temperature; (b) rainfall; (c) soil.
2. Discuss the proposition that type-of-farming areas are expressions of the culture of people.
3. What factors are important in accounting for the differences in level of living among sections of the United States?
4. How would you explain the association of *poor people* on *rich land?*
5. Discuss the difference in meaning between *regionalism* and *sectionalism.*

### SELECTED REFERENCES

Beck, P. G., and Forster, M. C. "Six Rural Problem Areas." Washington, D.C. *Federal Emergency Relief Administration Research Monograph I.* 1935.

Lively, C. E. "Social Planning and the Sociology of Sub-Regions," *Rural Sociology,* Vol. 2, No. 3, pp. 288–298, September, 1937.

Odum, Howard W. *Southern Regions of the United States.* Chapel Hill: University of North Carolina Press, 1936.

Taylor, C. C., and others. *Rural Life in the United States,* Part IV. New York: Alfred A. Knopf, 1949.

# CHAPTER 4

# PATTERNS OF LAND SETTLEMENT

Another important aspect of the adaptation of people to land is the manner in which family dwellings are arranged and distributed over the area. Housing arrangements of farm families—unlike those of the city—are characterized by the practically universal "detached dwelling" and the almost total absence of "multiple unit" dwellings. Farm houses, however, are not arranged according to any single pattern, but may be in accordance with any one of several patterns. At the two extremes of dispersion and aggregation are, respectively, the *isolated farmstead* and the *farm village*. In between these extremes are several other patterns, the most significant of which are the *line village* and the *round village*. All these forms except the round village are represented in the United States, and are more or less common in all countries of the world. In the United States the isolated farmstead pattern is the dominant one.

## HISTORICAL BACKGROUND

The development of the forms of settlement in various colonies and throughout the Union is largely the result of convergence of social and geographic factors. The limited valley lands of New England did not permit the development of large estates. Moreover, it was a common practice of the trading company which held the land from the Crown to make grants to groups of persons rather than to individuals, a practice which in itself promoted the idea of small units of land for the several members of the group. Then, too, there was the ever present danger from the Indian, with whom the newcomers in the strange land did not for some years develop stable and peaceful social intercourse. Their sense of insecurity led quite naturally to compact communities which provided a more effective basis for defense.

Besides, there was the tradition of village or town residence into which they had been born. Finally, the Puritan group had reacted strongly against the feudal tenure of the Old World and sought greater equality in the distribution of land, leading naturally to the establishment of small freeholds.[1]

In contrast with the New England system of landholding, the South developed the plantation as the dominant unit of its agriculture from the beginning of colonization. At first the plantations of the South were primarily devoted to the production of tobacco, but cotton culture soon displaced tobacco in importance. Originally, the labor for the plantations was provided by free or indentured white workers. The introduction of Negro slave labor displaced the white workers, who were pushed into the less favorable agricultural areas. Their poverty and social isolation condemned them to become the "poor white trash"—the lowest stratum in the social hierarchy of the South.

Residence arrangements on the plantation, besides the owner's home, consisted of the nearby "slave quarters," essentially bunk houses; there were, therefore, few scattered dwellings during the slavery period. Following the War Between the States and the development of sharecropping and tenancy there appeared the "cabin in the cotton," which was essentially an isolated dwelling. Typically there is one of these cabins on each 20-acre tract which constitutes the allotment of the cropper family.

While smallholdings prevailed in New England and the large plantation in the South, a mixture of the two types developed in the Middle Colonies. The large estates of New York—particularly the Dutch manors in the Hudson River Valley—and those of New Jersey and Pennyslvania were interspersed among numerous smallholders settled in villages not unlike those in New England.

I. Elting, for example, quotes the following document providing for a "Towneshipp" on Staten Island:

---

[1] Amelia C. Ford, "Colonial Precedents of Our National Land System As It Existed in 1800," *University of Wisconsin History Series Bulletin 352*, p. 321 ff., Madison, 1910. See also Charles M. Andrews, *Colonial Folkways*, Chapter II, New Haven: Yale University Press, 1919.

A Towne, the which shall bee divided into lotts according to the number of Inhabitants proposed. . . . That each home lott shall have . . . acres of Ground to build a house upon and for gardens or other necessary accomodacons. . . . That there shall bee allotted of Ploughland or Arable ground . . . acres and of Meadow a convenient proporcon.[2]

The compact arrangements of dwellings on the large estates is indicated by the following description by Maud W. Goodwin:

How crude was the settlement which they established we may judge from the report made some years later by Father Jogues, a Jesuit missionary who visited Rensslaerswyck in 1643. He speaks of a miserable little fort built of logs and having four or five pieces of Breteuil cannon. He describes also the colony as composed of about a hundred persons, "who reside in some twenty-five or thirty houses built along the river as each found most convenient. . . ."

The fear of raids from the savages prompted the patron to advise that, with the exception of the brewers and tobacco planters who were obliged to live on their plantations, no other settlers should establish themselves at any distance from the church, which was the village center, for, says the prudent Van Rensselaer "every one residing where he thinks fit, separated far from others, would be unfortunately in danger of their lives in the same manner as sorrowful experience has taught around the Manhattans." [3]

It appears also that in the early settlement of Pennsylvania the practice was to establish villages rather than isolated farmsteads. About the settlement of Philadelphia, Holcomb says:

In laying out the lots they were to "let every house be placed in the middle of its platt as to the breadth of it, so that there may be ground on each side, for gardens or orchards, or fields, that it may be a green country Towne." [4]

The original intention was to lay out the city on a large scale; the agreement was that the adventurers were entitled to city lots in the proportion of ten acres to every five hundred bought in the country, if the place would allow it, but it would not.[5]

[2] Irving Elting, "Dutch Village Communities on the Hudson," *Johns Hopkins University Studies in Historical and Political Science*, Vol. IV, p. 28, Baltimore, 1886.

[3] From *Dutch and English on the Hudson*, by Maud Wilder Goodwin, Vol. 7, pp. 40, 41, "The Chronicles of America." Copyright, Yale University Press, 1919.

[4] William P. Holcomb, "Pennsylvania Boroughs," *Johns Hopkins University Studies in Historical and Political Science*, Vol. IV, p. 15, Baltimore, 1886.

[5] *Ibid.*, p. 15.

The town lots of ten acres proved to be too large and were finally reduced in size "but the owners were allowed to make up their proportion in the adjacent liberty lands." [6] It is clear, however, that the intention was to settle in communities rather than on dispersed farms. This is confirmed in a letter written by William Penn in February, 1764, which is quoted by Holcomb:

I suppose we may be five hundred farmers strong. I settle them in villages dividing five thousand acres among ten, fifteen or twenty families as their ability is to plant it. [7]

In spite of Penn's emphasis on "proportionate ownership in town and country," it was impossible with the rapid settlement of the country to maintain the village system, and in the course of time the dispersed farmsteads came to be dominant.

It is clear, therefore, that two major types of landholding —the large estate and the smallholding—have existed from the very beginning of land settlement in the United States. The large estates were based upon Negro slave labor and the production of cotton and tobacco, while the smallholdings represented the private property of freemen and were devoted essentially to diversified crop and animal production. The large estate was a characteristic of the South where climatic features favored specialization in crop production; the freehold was practically universal in New England and dominant in the Middle Colonies. The inhabitants of the slave plantation lived in compact bunk houses. After the emancipation the bunk houses gave way to the separate cabin of the sharecropper and tenant. The freeholders of New England were essentially village dwellers, while those of the Middle Colonies were both villagers and isolated farmsteaders. (See picture following page 56.)

These general characterizations tend to oversimplify the situation, however. As we have already indicated, the coming of Negro slavery to the South, resulted in the expulsion from the plantation areas of the white settlers, who established themselves upon small farms in the back country. At the same time, New England was not without its isolated farmsteads, even though the general rule was for the settlers to live in the village.

---

[6] William P. Holcomb, "Pennsylvania Boroughs," *Johns Hopkins University Studies in Historical and Political Science*, Vol. IV, p. 16, Baltimore, 1886.

[7] *Ibid.*, p. 17.

The two land systems were in conflict on the frontier, since it was obvious that the South could not extend its plantation area on the public domain and at the same time permit the settlement of small holders of the North in the same areas. This conflict of two agrarian systems, together with the moral controversy over slavery, culminated in the War Between the States and the emancipation of the slaves. Thus the expansion of the plantation system to new land areas was cut short. Besides, the outbreak of the war opened the way for the enactment of the Homestead Law in 1862, which southern representatives in Congress had opposed throughout the long debates over the national land policies. The passage of this act set the stage for the rapid settlement of the public domain in 160-acre tracts and the establishment of the family-farm as opposed to plantation agriculture.

### THE ISOLATED FARMSTEAD

The New England system of land tenure—small freeholds as contrasted with the large estate—became the basic land policy of the United States, but the New England village arrangement of farm dwellings was abandoned in favor of scattered homesteads. There we e several reasons, historically, why this happened. In the first place, it is important to note that village settlement is usually the result of the occupation of an area of land by a group that is essentially homogeneous, ethnically, religiously, or otherwise. The settlement of lands west of the Alleghanies for the most part was not begun by groups, but by individuals independently moving to the frontier and staking out land claims later to be validated by the government. Moreover, the population moving to the frontier was a heterogeneous one, being composed not only of persons from the many Atlantic seaboard communities, with a variety of social backgrounds, but also of immigrants from many foreign lands.

Another important factor contributing to the prevalence of the isolated pattern of settlement was the nature of the laws governing the alienation of land. Two aspects of these laws were especially important. The first was the adoption by Congress of the rectangular survey in 1785. This ordinance provided for the division of land into townships consisting of 36 sections of one square mile each. The sections, in turn, were divided into quarter sections of 160 acres. This system provided an excellent and almost infallible method of describing property; on the other hand, the gridiron pattern contributed to a wide dispersion of homes. The second important consideration was the requirement after 1841 that the settler had to establish a residence on the land as a prerequisite to securing a patent. While this provision was motivated by the commendable desire to avoid land speculation by getting the land into the hands of bona fide homeseekers, it had the practical result of imposing the isolated farmstead pattern upon the country.

Finally, the exigencies of pioneering in a new country made village settlement practically impossible. Settlement took place at such a rapid rate that it was impossible for the land survey to keep pace with it. The result was that there were great numbers of "unauthorized" settlers on the frontier. They were called "squatters"—individuals who had staked out a tract of land in advance of the survey. They cleared and developed these holdings in anticipation of being able to "bid it in" when the land "came on the market." However, it meant that their right to the land was no better than their ability to prevent someone else from jumping the claim. The protective vigilance required to make sure of their right when the time came could be exercised only by being on the land all the time. In other words, possession *was* nine points of the law. The rights of the squatter were recognized in the Preemption Act of 1841, which guaranteed him the prior right to purchase the land up to 160 acres in extent after it came on the market.

Living on the land rather than in a village was dictated, also, by the absence of roads. Once an individual decided upon his location he could ill afford the time and energy required to travel to and from a village center. It might have been possible to design village patterns that would have reduced such travel to a minimum, had it not been for the somewhat inflexible dictates of the rectangular survey. However, this system of survey was already established and, although attempts were made to change it, they were unavailing. It is debatable whether any other system would have served the country as well in the long run and especially under the conditions of rapid settlement which prevailed. The system had the advantage of being inexpensive, relatively rapid, and certainly definite. As contrasted with the alternative system of indiscriminate location, of describing boundaries by means of topographical features, it had the advantage of insuring a minimum of conflict and litigation over titles. (See pictures following page 56.)

**Advantages and disadvantages of the isolated farmstead.** The most obvious advantage of the system is that the farm family is close to its work. There is a minimum loss of time in getting from the home to work in the fields. There is also greater freedom in planning the farm enterprise. For example, the maintenance of a considerable herd of hogs, dairy cattle, or other livestock would scarcely be feasible if the barnyard were located on a village lot. Obviously, the amount of livestock that can be kept in a village is limited. Also, farming in the open country permits larger average units of land.

The disadvantages of the isolated farmstead are partly economic, but mainly social. In the first place, geographic isolation means social isolation. The farm family is removed by considerable distance from neighbors and from the village center, and this means that opportunity for social contacts is definitely limited. It was particularly true in the early days of settlement when roads were poor and often nonexistent. Now that most country roads have been improved and the automobile has become a common possession of farm families, the effects of distance and isolation have been greatly lessened. It is still a factor of significance, however, and there is the necessity of frequent trips to town for supplies and services which partly offsets in expense the higher cost which the village dweller has to pay in going to and from his fields.

Moreover, the isolated farmstead has long been denied the enjoyment of many modern living conveniences which have been readily available to the villager. Two thirds of farms in the United States in 1940 did not have electricity. In 1930, before the establishment of the Rural Electrification Administration, only 13 per cent of farms in the United States had electricity. Few had running water, and therefore could not very well have indoor toilets and well-equipped bathrooms.

Sanitary disposal of waste by a modern sewage system was an impossibility.

There are many other costs which accrue as a result of scattered homesteads. They are manifested in the tremendous mileage of public roads which have to be built and maintained in order to provide access for isolated farmers to the trade centers. They show up in the admitted inadequacies of local government and public institutions. The isolated farmer in the United States can scarcely be said to have a local municipality. As a rule he is not legally a part of the incorporated villages, and where the township system does prevail it is far short of an adequate governmental mechanism through which to achieve the extent or quality of services enjoyed by the village dweller. The one-room school and the open-country church are the direct result of the isolated farmstead pattern of settlement, and few will say that they represent even a near approach to the efficiency of comparable institutions in the compact settlement. They are makeshift adjustments to a sparsely populated area. In order to achieve a higher measure of adequacy in school or church, society has to stand a heavy burden of expense in operating transportation services for assembling a population from a widely scattered area.

There can be no doubt, however, that people who have been reared on isolated farms come to regard them as the only way of rural life, become inured to it, and are surprised at any suggestion that there are alternatives to it. Neither can there be any doubt that farm life in the United States will continue predominantly in the isolated pattern. The impetus or inertia of the original settlement is sufficient to guarantee its continuance. The automobile facilitates rapid and frequent contact with the trade center and neighbors and opens the way for replanning the educational system, while other technological developments may place within the reach of the isolated farmstead the conveniences of electricity, running water, and sewage disposal.

### THE FARM VILLAGE

This is probably the oldest form of land occupancy known to the human family. When our first nomadic forefathers, either from choice or necessity, decided to settle down permanently in one place, they pitched their dwellings close together. Often, if not usually, they farmed their lands communally rather than severally. The need for constant vigilance to protect themselves from enemy groups was often a sufficiently potent factor in itself to dictate village settlement. With the growth of population and the development of effective governments to protect the life and property of citizens, isolated farmsteads were possible and they developed throughout most of Europe and in parts of Asia alongside the villages.[8] The village remained, however, a common feature of the feudal economy in Europe and Asia.

As we have seen, the colonization of America saw the introduction of the village pattern as well as the isolated farmstead. There can be little doubt that at first the village predominated everywhere, although it was most conspicuous in New England. It has been briefly described by C. M. Andrews as follows:

The New Englander's house, with its barns, outbuildings, kitchen garden, and back lot, fronted the village street, while near at hand were the meetinghouse and schoolhouse, pillories, stocks, and signpost, all objects of constant interest and frequent concern. Beyond this clustered group of houses stretched the outlying arable land, meadows, pastures, and woodland, the scene of the villager's industry and the source of his livelihood. . . . While most of the New Englanders preferred to live in neighborly fashion near together, some built their houses on a convenient hillside or fertile upland away from the center. Here they set up "quarters" or "corners" which were often destined to become in time little villages by themselves, each the seat of a compound, a chapel, and a school. Sometimes these little centers developed into separate ecclesiastical societies and even into independent towns; but frequently they remained legally a part of the original church and township, and the residents often journeyed many miles to take part in town meetings or to join in the social and religious life of the older community.[9]

    [8] See A. Demangeon, "La Géographie de l'Habitat Rural," *Annales de Géographie*, Vol. 36, 1927. Reproduced in English in P. A. Sorokin, C. C. Zimmerman, and C. J. Galpin, *A Systematic Source Book in Rural Sociology*, Vol. I, pp. 266–304. Minneapolis: University of Minnesota Press, 1930.
    [9] Reprinted from *Colonial Folkways*, by C. M. Andrews, Vol. 9, pp. 25–26, "The Chronicles of America." Copyright, Yale University Press, 1919. See also: C. M. Andrews, "The River Towns of Connecticut," *Johns Hopkins University Studies in Historical and Political Science*, Vol. VII, pp. 331–457, Baltimore, 1889; Melville Egleston, "The Land System of the New England Colonies," Vol. IV, pp. 549–600, 1886.

There were strong protagonists in the post-Revolutionary days for making the village pattern the main form of settlement for rural America generally, but for reasons which were discussed in the previous section "town planting" gave way to isolated settlement.

**Advantages and disadvantages of the farm village.** Its advantages were indicated previously by comparison with those of the isolated farmstead. Chiefly they were social, although there were economic advantages which are frequently overlooked. It should be said that the village system does not appear to be practical in areas where large farms prevail. It is not possible to maintain in the village large numbers of livestock. Usually the village prevails only in areas where land holdings are relatively small, so that the average distance the villager has to travel to his farm is not too great. It is, moreover, usually found in places where settlement took place originally by homogeneous groups, rather than by heterogeneous individuals.

### MORMON VILLAGES

The most conspicuous occurrence of the farm village in the United States is found among the Mormons of the western United States, and among the Spanish-speaking population of the Southwest. The fact that the Mormons settled in the Great Salt Lake valley in 1847, at the time when settlement by the isolated farmstead pattern was rapidly progressing in other sections, raises an interesting question as to why they departed from the usual pattern. The answer lies in the religious ideology of the group. In common with a large proportion of the people of the United States in the early part of the nineteenth century, the Mormons had a strong conviction that the second coming of the Saviour was imminent. According to their prophet, Joseph Smith, they were the "chosen" group to prepare the way for the great event. Among other preparations the City of Zion was to be built as a headquarters for the Saviour during his reign on earth. It was the design for the City of Zion which constituted the basic plan for all the Mormon settlements. The original City of Zion was to be built in Jackson County, Missouri, on the site of what is now Independence. Before the

*Sharecropper family, with cabins in background, on cotton plantation in Mississippi County, Missouri. This is a type of dispersed farmstead. One family ordinarily has responsibility for about twenty acres. Sharecropping is also common in tobacco growing.*

*Above are dispersed farmsteads in a tobacco valley in Puerto Rico; below is a dispersed, highly intensive type of farming area in Yakima Valley, Washington.*

*View of Ephraim, Utah (above), shows farm homes located in villages. In El Cerrito, New Mexico (below), farm lands are along river bottoms, away from dwellings.*

*A line village in Quebec, Canada, is shown above. Pictured below is a Jewish agricultural settlement, Nahalal, in Palestine, designed on the circular plan.*

Mormons were able to execute their plans, they were driven out by the old settlers in the area who looked upon the newcomers as interlopers and as a threat to their own security.

The first settlement actually built by the Mormons in the Middle West was Nauvoo, Illinois. After being driven from Missouri in 1839, they moved to the present site of Nauvoo and there built a city which was the largest in the state at that time, containing at its peak upwards of 20,000 people. They were again driven from their homes in 1846, and decided to move west across the plains to the Rocky Mountains. The first group of them arrived in Salt Lake valley July 24, 1847, and there began the project in land settlement and community building which made them famous.

Salt Lake City was laid out after the plat of the City of Zion, with the following features: (a) 10-acre blocks, (b) 8-rod streets, (c) the blocks were square and the streets ran due north-south and east-west, intersecting at right angles. The original plat of the City of Zion also provided that each family should have a half-acre lot, on which not more than one house should be built. It further provided that all houses should be set back 25 feet from the street, to allow for parking and beautification. After all, this was to be the dwelling place of the Saviour. Another significant feature of the original plan was that barns and livestock should be kept outside the city, in communal facilities. The communal plan of living was never developed with success among the Mormons, although they still have in their scriptures a "revelation" describing the plan of the "United Order" and enjoining the members of the church to "live it." The "law of tithing" was subsequently "given" to the people as a "lesser law" until such time as they proved themselves worthy to live the "higher law" (the United Order). It is somewhat significant to find a communal system associated with the village pattern among the Mormons—even though it was never permanently established—because of the rather frequent association of these two factors among rural groups throughout the world.[10]

[10] See Lowry Nelson, "The Mormon Village: A Study in Social Origins," *Proceedings of the Utah Academy of Sciences*, Vol. VII, pp. 11-37, Provo, Utah, 1930. This is an abstract of the writer's Ph.D. thesis by the same title at the University of Wisconsin.

In the subsequent settlements established by the Mormons throughout the intermountain area from northern Mexico to southern Canada the village pattern of settlement has been retained, although modifications have been made in the original plat and a number of isolated farmstead settlements have arisen in some sections. The major change which was made in the original plat was the reduction in the size of blocks from 10 acres to 5, as a rule, and in the width of the streets. Eight rods were found to be an unnecessary width for the streets, and in nearly all places outside of Salt Lake City the streets are much narrower. Still, they are ordinarily wider than needed, and much good land is included in the excessively wide streets which might have better been put to other uses.

**Divided holdings.** One feature of the Mormon land system which is of considerable interest is the small size of the initial allotments. Impressed with the imminence of the millennium, the Mormons, for a time at least, had strong inclinations toward equality in the distribution of wealth. When they arrived in the Great Basin it was to be expected therefore that the land —and the irrigation water—should be equally distributed among the families. Equal distribution of property often meant the division of land into small parcels, in order that each family might have some. Not that land itself was scarce, but land *under the ditch* was. Without irrigation water the land itself was of no value. Getting water to the land was costly and slow. At the same time, population was increasing rapidly because of the high birth rate, and the immigration of many converts. It could almost be said that land was "scarce" from the beginning—that is, land with water to irrigate it.

The small allotments were suitable for an economy which at first was almost totally self-sufficing. However, as the commercial economy emerged, it was found that the small original allotments were insufficient to make an economic unit, and farmers began to try to enlarge their holdings. They found it possible to do so because not all of the men granted original allotments were interested in farming as a permanent occupation. Many of them were skilled tradesmen, and as soon as it was possible for them to specialize on their particular craft, they were ready to sell their land to someone who wished to buy.

In the process of enlarging units it was not possible in all cases to get adjacent tracts, with the result that a farmer may own many tracts around the village. In three villages in Utah where data were gathered, it was found that 40 per cent of the farmers had their farms in more than one tract. In the village of Ephraim 60 per cent of the farmers had more than one tract.[11] An extreme case was found in Ephraim where one farmer reported owning 12 different tracts, only two of which were contiguous, and even these two were separated by a railroad right-of-way. (See picture following page 56.) Incidentally, divided holdings will be more common in other sections also, as farmers continue to enlarge their farms.

**Distance between home and farm.** Since in the farm-village type, as it exists in Utah and other Mormon areas, the family has about $1\frac{1}{4}$ acres in the village, it is customary to build house and barns on the village lot. This means that the crops are hauled to the village for storage, and that the livestock is kept in the village through the winter months. During the growing season the farmer is therefore on the road between his home in the village and the farm during much of the day. It becomes a matter of interest therefore to know just how great this distance is. It will vary considerably among the villages, depending upon the density of settlement and the intensity of land utilization. The average distance of the farm from the home in the village is approximately two miles; more than three fourths of the farms of American Fork and Ephraim lie within three miles of the village. Some village dwellers stack their hay in the fields and either feed their livestock there during the winter by going out daily to the farm, or haul it to the village as needed in the winter season. It is coming to be common practice among the Mormons to keep dairy cows constantly in the pastures during the summer, rather than to drive them back and forth each day. They simply get in their automobiles and go to the pastures morning and evening to milk the cows. Where considerable numbers of livestock must be fed during the winter, it is almost a universal practice to build feed pens and sheds on the farms and drive out daily to do the feeding.

[11] Lowry Nelson, "The Utah Farm Village of Ephraim," *Brigham Young University Studies 2*, Provo, Utah, 1928.

### SPANISH–AMERICAN VILLAGES OF THE SOUTHWESTERN UNITED STATES

The other important contemporary rural group in the United States which lives in farm villages is the Spanish-American people of the Southwest. The story of one of their villages has been interestingly recorded by Olen Leonard and C. P. Loomis.[12] The settlements are of ancient origin, so far as pattern of life is concerned, although El Cerrito is relatively recent, "going back well over a century." [13] According to the authors:

The physical structure of these villages varies little. Houses are grouped closely together around a church, a school, and perhaps a store. None are farther separated than the distance across the plaza. Many are joined in long rows stretching along the sides of the plaza square. Away from the cluster no more houses appear until the next village is reached.[14] (See picture following page 56.)

The people who compose the village are native-born Americans, descended from Spanish and Indian forebears whose cultures came into contact during the conquests of the sixteenth century. The ethnic homogeneity is an important social bond in itself, and it is supported by that of religion, for the people are devout Roman Catholics.

The villages here, like those among the Mormons, are frequently—though not always—associated with areas of irrigation agriculture. There are also in New Mexico "scattered villages of the mountains, and dry-land farming villages." [15]

Along with the elements of homogeneity just mentioned, the compact grouping of dwellings also makes for close social relations. Say the authors:

The physical structure of the community is also a significant factor in the integration and stability of the village. The houses are compactly located to form the perimeter of a circle, with barns and corrals in the rear. Although such an arrangement interferes with efficient farming, it greatly facilitates living. The house is farther from fields and pastures but is closer to school, church, and neighbors. Such proximity of living

---

[12] Olen Leonard and C. P. Loomis, "Culture of a Contemporary Rural Community: El Cerrito, New Mexico," *Rural Life Studies I*, Bureau of Agricultural Economics, United States Department of Agriculture, Washington, D.C., November, 1941.
[13] *Ibid.*, p. 9.      [14] *Ibid.*, p. 2.      [15] *Ibid.*, p. 2.

has developed a sociability and an integration of group life that would be difficult, if not impossible, to duplicate in any other type of arrangement. Seldom does a day pass when a farmer does not converse with a number of his neighbors. Children are seen playing together, after the chores are done, both night and morning. Childhood associations are almost as close between playmates as between members of the same family. They grow up to know each other almost as well as if they had been reared under the same roof.

The sense of community is strong with these people. Individuals are identified as much by the community in which they live as by family name. To be born into a community is to inherit an identification with it that is never forgotten. The few families from El Cerrito who are living away always refer to the village as their home. The reputation of the home village fixes to a certain extent the general status of a resident.[16]

Here, as with the Mormons, the farms are small, often in less than one-acre plots. In general, village life is more likely to be found in association with small farms.

### OTHER VILLAGE SETTLEMENTS

Aside from the villages established in New England by the early colonists and those in the west by the Mormons, a great many communities were founded in various parts of the United States, chiefly in the middle decades of the nineteenth century. The "Fabulous Forties" [17] were especially marked by the rise of large numbers of "communities," resulting largely from the introduction and diffusion in this country of the socialist doctrines of Charles Fourier. The Fourier movement had been preceded by another which led to the establishment by Robert Owen of New Harmony, Indiana. Over a dozen other settlements following the communal pattern were established in Indiana, Ohio, New York, and Pennsylvania. Also a large number of pietistic and separatist religious groups founded village communities after a variety of religious principles, but all had in common the idea of communal ownership and operation of the land.

[16] *Ibid.*, p. 8.
[17] Meade Minnigerode, *The Fabulous Forties*. New York: G. P. Putnam's Sons, 1924.

Few of the hundreds of such communities that were organized lasted very long. Only one of the Owenite communities survived as many as four years; most of them were gone by the end of one or two years at most. The Fourier communities fared little better, although one (in Texas) continued for 21 years and another (in Kansas) for 14 years. Those founded by religious groups showed greater tenacity. The Shakers, originating in 1778, are now practically extinct, owing to their adherence to the practice of celibacy.[18] The Rappites survived a century, from 1805 to 1905. The Ephrata Cloister in Pennsylvania had an even greater longevity, from 1732 to 1905. Like the Shakers, many of this last group practiced celibacy and their numbers gradually declined.[19]

J. W. Eaton and S. M. Katz[20] have compiled a list of the known "cooperative group farming" settlements in the United States. The following tabulation is made from this list:

TABLE 2. *Cooperative Group Farming Settlements*

| Type of group | Number of communities | Number still going |
|---|---|---|
| Religious | 64 | 5 |
| Cooperative, socialist | 47 | 3* |
| Owenite | 13 | None |
| Fourier | 40 | None |
| Single tax | 10 | 10 |
| Miscellaneous | 26 | None |
| Total | 200 | 18 |

\* The authors are uncertain.

[18] For an account of a visit to a Shaker community in New York State, see Carl Carmer, *Listen for a Lonesome Drum*. New York: Farrar and Rinehart, 1936.

In the *Census of Religious Bodies*, Shakers are listed officially as the United Society of Believers. In 1936 only three churches were reported for the group, one each in Maine, New Hampshire, and New York. The total membership was 92, only 11 of whom were males. This represents a decline from 516 members reported in 1906. See the *Census of Religious Bodies*, Vol. II, p. 1262. United States Bureau of the Census, Washington, D.C., 1936.

[19] For brief historical accounts of a number of these communities, see Alice Felt Tyler, *Freedom's Ferment*. Minneapolis: University of Minnesota Press, 1944.

[20] Joseph W. Eaton and Saul M. Katz, *Research Guide on Cooperative Group Farming*. New York: H. W. Wilson Company, 1942. The authors state that their list is based on Julia Elizabeth Williams, "An Analytical Tabulation of the North American Communities by Type, Longevity and Location," University of South Dakota master's thesis, June, 1939; revised and brought up to date partly on the basis of an alphabetical list of communities found in Donald F. Blankertz, *Marketing Cooperatives*. New York: Ronald Press Company, 1940.

At the present time—except for the Mormons, the Spanish-Americans in El Cerrito, and the French-Canadians in Louisiana —there are few strictly farm-village settlements in the United States. The Amana Society in Iowa is one of these. It is a pietistic religious sect which had its origin in Germany in 1714, emigrated to the United States, and established its first settlement near Buffalo, New York, in 1843. In 1885, the group moved to Iowa where it secured some 26,000 acres of land 20 miles west of Iowa City. Here were established seven villages. It was a communistic group until 1932, when the form of organization was changed to a stock corporation.[21]

Another well-known contemporary group which lives in villages is the Hutterian Brethren, a sect of the Mennonite faith which had its origin in Austria in the sixteenth century. They came to the United States in 1874, settling in Bonhomme County, South Dakota. In 1936 there were five colonies in South Dakota, and there are a number located in the western provinces of Canada, where they moved during the first World War to escape conscription. The group practices communism, holding and operating its farm land in common. Each family has separate living quarters in a sort of dormitory where all meals are prepared in a common kitchen and eaten in a common dining room. They wear a distinctive style of dress which is uniform for the group. The total membership is not large. In the *Census of Religious Bodies* for 1936 they reported a membership of 501. It is not clear, however, whether this represents the total population or merely those who have been confirmed as members of the church.[22]

In Canada there have been a number of group settlement experiments in addition to the Hutterites who migrated from the United States. The French-Canadian farmers are by far

[21] A considerable amount of literature on this group has developed through the years. The most comprehensive treatment of the group will be found in Bertha M. Shambaugh, *Amana That Was and Amana That Is*. Iowa City: Iowa State Historical Society, 1932. In two parts; pt. 1, *Amana That Was*, published in 1908 under title *Amana, the Community of True Inspiration*. An excellent brief study of the group is Darrell H. Davis, "Amana: A Study of Occupance," *Economic Geography*, 1936, 12:217–230.

[22] The leading student in the United States of this group is Lee Emerson Deets. See his *The Hutterites: A Study of Social Cohesion*. Gettysburg, Pennsylvania: Times and News Publishing Company, 1939.

the most important in point of numbers as well as extent of landholdings. These farmers brought with them from France a form of land tenure which provides for the dwellings to be located along a common artery of transportation. This is usually referred to as a *line village* and will be discussed presently. In addition, Canada has the Doukhobors, a communistic sect who live in villages. Some other ethnic groups have shown tendencies toward the nucleated village pattern.[23]

### RECENT GROUP SETTLEMENT EXPERIMENTS

Since 1934 a number of land settlement projects have been initiated by the Federal Government. Beginning with the "rural-industrial" communities promoted by the Federal Emergency Relief Administration as a phase of its rural rehabilitation program which continued through the period of Resettlement Administration, 1935–1937, approximately 160 settlement projects were initiated. According to a summary, as of 1942, given by Eaton and Katz, twenty-seven of these were cooperative corporation farms.[24] They involved a total of 65,834 acres. Since under the cooperative plan of operation the land is not subdivided in order that it may be operated as a single unit, the residences of the settlers must be grouped in an area designated for the purpose.

Some of the cooperative-village settlements initiated under the Federal program have failed. One instance, known to the writer, was the Ethan Allen community in northern Minnesota. This project provided that each family would have a small plot of two acres on which to build its home, while the remainder of the tract would be operated as a single farm. It lasted about two years. The land was later subdivided and offered for sale to individual settlers.

What is undoubtedly the most extensive use of the village as a settlement design in modern times, is taking place in Palestine. Over a hundred such farm villages have come into

---

[23] For a discussion of these see Carl A. Dawson, *Group Settlement: Ethnic Communities in Western Canada*. Toronto: The Macmillan Co. of Canada, Ltd., 1936.

[24] Eaton and Katz, *op. cit.*, p. 56. See also Charles P. Loomis, "Social Relationships in Seven New Rural Communities," *Social Research Report 18*. Washington, D.C.. Farm Security Administration and Bureau of Agricultural Economics, January, 1940.

being within the last 50 years. In terms of the property in land, the communities are of two types: the Moshavah, in which the farms are rather large and require some hired labor; and the Kvutzah, the so-called "collective farms," in which the land is communally owned. Even in the villages of independent farms, according to Eaton, "the houses are built in a cluster, like most of the villages of Europe." [25] A third form of village, called the Moshae-Ovdim, is similar to the Moshavah except that the farms are small. While the farms in this type are individually owned, in many activities there is cooperation and mutual aid. Thus, they have cooperative buying and selling of farm products, group ownership of farm machinery, cooperative health insurance, and the like.

In Palestine the village is found in association with its ancient allies, geography, group homogeneity, religious motivation, necessity for protection, and communal property in land.

## THE LINE VILLAGE

This pattern of land occupancy is a modified form of village and is designed to provide the advantages of residence on the operated farm, while at the same time bringing the families as close and accessible to each other as possible. To accomplish these advantages the farms are laid out in such a way that they front on a single road or other artery of transportation. They are of oblong shape, with a relatively narrow width and much greater length. The pattern is characteristic of French land tenure, and is a conspicuous feature of French Canada and the French-Canadian settlements of Maine and Louisiana in the United States. Along the St. Lawrence River in Quebec the long fields can be observed extending back from the river on either side, with the homes of the farmers along the river front and the highways which transect the long strips of land into tiers at intervals across the valley. (See picture following page 56.)

During the eighteenth century the Acadians introduced this form of land division and settlement in French Louisiana along the bayous of the Mississippi Delta. Here the bayous were

[25] Joseph W. Eaton, "Jewish Agricultural Colonization in Palestine," *Rural Sociology*, 1940, 5:327–344, p. 328. See aso Walter C. Lowdermilk, *Palestine: Land of Promise*. New York: Harper and Brothers, 1943.

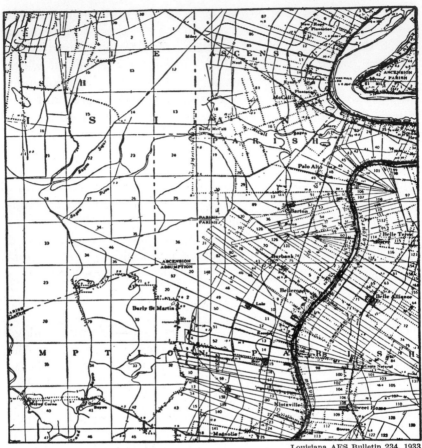

Louisiana AES Bulletin 234, 1933

FIGURE 6. *Map of Bayou La Fourche Showing Line Village Pattern*. This map of Bayou La Fourche in Louisiana shows the line village pattern in the area settled by the French-speaking population. The dwellings are along the bayou, which at the time of settlement was the artery of communication. The lands on the left side of the picture are swamplands; these have been surveyed by the usual checkerboard system.

the arteries of transportation and therefore became the base lines for dividing the land. Each farm had frontage on the bayou and extended back to the swamp land in the rear. The winding bayous did not permit the formation of regular rectangular-shaped fields so characteristic of the St. Lawrence Valley, but rather made for many triangular-shaped fields. Nevertheless, the principle of line village was maintained, and one can drive along the winding roads which today follow the course of the bayous and at frequent intervals pass homes which are separated from each other by only short distances of an eighth of a mile or less. Only one road needs to be maintained to insure the accessibility of all to the homes of the others and to the public services and institutions.[26] (See Figure 6.)

The line village exists in other than French settled areas. A considerable number of the Mormon villages in Utah have no more than a single street. Here it is not by special design, however, but is rather the consequence of location in valleys too narrow to permit more than a single village thoroughfare. Many of the villages of Germany and France are also of this type. It is interesting to note also that some of the Jewish communities in Palestine follow this pattern; the village street is in the form of a circle, rather than a more or less straight line, as in the cases which we have previously noted. (See picture following page 56.)

The *circular pattern* or *round village* has a very definite advantage in that it places the house and yard at the "apex" of a triangular plot, thus permitting the houses to be closer together, without creating correspondingly greater length in the farm tract. In Palestine irrigation is necessary and the amount of land which can be irrigated is limited. Thus the circular villages can be designed without reference to any necessity—such as would be faced in the humid areas of the United States—of having to fit them into a continuous pattern of settlement. In other words, in an area where the entire surface is arable—such as in Iowa, for example—a series of circular villages would leave interstitial areas to be accounted for. While this could be done short of great difficulty, a rectangular scheme of some sort is logically indicated.

Some advantages of the line village have already been indicated. Chiefly it is a compromise between the typical isolated farmstead and the farm village. In short, it permits the farmer to reside on his farm, without imposing the extreme of geographic isolation from his neighbor which is characteristic of

---

[26] For a description of the French-Canadian villages in Louisiana, see T. Lynn Smith, *The Sociology of Rural Life*, pp. 209–210. New York: Harper and Brothers, 1940. See also his "Farm Trade Centers in Louisiana," *Louisiana AES Bulletin 234*, January, 1933.

the scattered homesteads. This is a very marked advantage, to be sure. However, there is also a drawback to the line village, in that it compels exceptional elongation of the field. The long narrow strip cannot be effectively divided into fields for rotation of crops. There is also the expense of time getting to and from the far end of the field, with the necessity meanwhile of using a considerable portion of the land for a field road.

In speaking of the seigniorial tenure system of Canada, C. Gagné had this to say:

Our farms situated on the old seigniories are, as a rule, much longer and narrower than those in the townships. On the Island of Orleans and on the Beaupré Coast, there are farms which are more than two miles long and less than 300 feet wide. At Sante Anne de la Pocatière the farm lots of the old seigniory are $1\frac{1}{2}$ miles long and 384 feet wide. In the townships conditions in this regard, while not excellent, are better. There the lots are, as a rule, twice as wide as those of the seigniories and are seldom over one mile in length.[27]

Thus it is clear that a reasonable balance between the length and width of tracts needs to be maintained in the line-village pattern, if the disadvantage of extreme length is to be avoided. The problem of subdividing land among heirs is also raised by Gagné. Obviously, if dwellings are to be built along a single road, subdivision has to be lengthwise. The problem became so serious in Canada that the King of France in 1714 issued a decree prohibiting the construction of farm buildings where lots were less than 288 feet wide.

However, the apparent disadvantage should be carefully weighed against the many undeniable social and economic advantages derived from the more compact arrangement of the dwellings, the necessity of maintaining only one all-weather road to serve all the families, the better social institutions made possible by the larger number of participants per institution, etc.

T. Lynn Smith has proposed a plan whereby the rectangular survey might be adapted in such a way as to provide some of the advantages of the line village noted above. The essence of this plan is to divide the land into a series of oblongs in place

---

[27] C. Gagné, "Seigniorial Tenure in Canada," *Proceedings of the International Conference of Agricultural Economists*, p. 323. London: Oxford University Press, 1939.

of the present squares.[28] While the scheme would bring farm families closer together and reduce the amount of road mileage to be maintained, it will be criticized on the ground that the oblong shape for a farm does not admit of efficient organization and management. But again, defects must be weighed against the apparent advantages.

### QUESTIONS FOR DISCUSSION

1. Give several reasons why large estates were rare in the settlement of New England. What factors help to account for the many plantations that were established in the South?
2. In which colonies outside New England was the settlement of compact village communities encouraged? How do you account for the fact that nucleated farm villages became the exception rather than the rule in the colonies south and west of New England?
3. What two agrarian systems were in conflict during the decades preceding the War Between the States? List the main issues involved in this conflict. What bearing did the Homestead Law have on the outcome?
4. Describe the effect that such factors as population composition, the rectangular survey system, homestead regulations, and frontier life had upon the development and distribution of isolated farmsteads in this country.
5. In what ways is the rectangular survey system superior to the practice of using *meets and bounds* to mark land boundaries?
6. List the economic advantages and disadvantages of the dispersed farmstead type of settlement. Also, point out some social disadvantages of such an arrangement. Can you think of any social advantages it might have?
7. From what source did the Mormons get the idea of living in compact settlements? To what extent did communistic practices develop among them? Why did they find it necessary to divide up the land into small holdings? What happened to many of these small holdings later?
8. Describe the motivation and social organization which characterized the Fourier, Owenite, Shaker, Ephrata, and similar communities. Account for the fact that many of these settlements failed to persist, at least in their original form, while others, including the Amana colony, proved to be much more stable.

[28] T. Lynn Smith, *The Sociology of Rural Life*, p. 257. New York: Harper and Brothers, 1940.

9. What specific advantage does the line village have over either the dispersed farmstead or the New England types of settlement? Why did the French find it convenient to use this form of settlement in Louisiana? Where else have line villages or a close approximation been used?
10. What does T. Lynn Smith suggest as an appropriate type of rural settlement? Why?

### SELECTED REFERENCES

Nelson, Lowry. *The Mormon Village*, Chapter 1. Salt Lake City: The University of Utah Press, 1952.

Pederson, Harald A., and Raper, Arthur, "The Cotton Plantation in Transition," *Mississippi AES Bulletin 508*. 1954.

Sanderson, Dwight. *The Rural Community*, Chapter 6. Boston: Ginn and Company, 1932.

Smith, T. Lynn. *Brazil: People and Institutions*, Chapter 13. Baton Rouge: Louisiana State University Press, 1946.

——— *The Sociology of Rural Life*, Chapter 10. Third Edition. New York: Harper and Brothers, 1953.

Sorokin, P. A.; Zimmerman, C. C.; and Galpin, C. J. *A Systematic Source Book in Rural Sociology*, Vol. I. Article by A. Demangeon, "Geography of the Rural Habitat," pp. 266–304. Minneapolis: University of Minnesota Press, 1930.

Taylor, Carl C. *Rural Life in Argentina*. Baton Rouge: Louisiana State University Press, 1948.

Whetton, Nathan L. *Rural Mexico*, Chapter 4. Chicago: University of Chicago Press, 1948.

# CHAPTER 5

# THE RURAL COMMUNITY

Up to this point we have considered various arrangements of people on the land, including the broad regional adaptations and the various patterns of land occupancy. The final, and socially the most significant, aspect of man's spatial adaptation is the *community* itself. In this chapter we are concerned with the community primarily in terms of human ecology.[1] Subsequent chapters will consider in detail the social processes and institutions of the community.

**Definition of rural community.** In general, the term *community* refers to a group of people inhabiting a limited area, who have a sense of belonging together and who through their organized relationships share and carry on activities in pursuit of their common interests. It is a "locality group," whether the term is used to describe a neighborhood, a town, a city, or even a nation. In common usage the term is applied to the relatively small aggregates of population. The *rural community*, as it has come to be defined in the United States, is well characterized by Dwight Sanderson as "that form of association maintained between the people and their institutions in a local area in which they live on dispersed farmsteads and in a village which usually forms the center of their common activities." [2] In other words, the typical American rural community is made up of two population components, the people of the trade center, and the farm families in the area "tributary" to the center. Obviously, this definition applies only in those areas of the

---

[1] According to R. D. McKenzie, "human ecology deals with the spatial aspects of the symbiotic relations of human beings and human institutions. It aims to discover the principles and factors involved in the changing patterns of spatial arrangements of population and institutions resulting from the interplay of living beings in a continuously changing culture." *Encyclopedia of the Social Sciences*, Vol. 5, p. 314. New York: The Macmillan Company, 1931.

[2] Dwight Sanderson, *Rural Sociology and Rural Social Organization*, p. 278. New York: John Wiley and Sons, 1942.

71

country which were settled according to the "isolated farm-stead" pattern. It does not apply to any of the farm-village arrangements. However, because most of the United States was settled in the former way, Sanderson's definition has wide application.

This concept of the rural community in the United States is of recent origin and has an interesting history. One of the earliest sociologists to describe the rural community was Warren H. Wilson. As he observed the American countryside before the era of automobile transportation, he noted the farm families scattered on their separate holdings, and at the same time the small villages and towns to which these families went to market their produce and bring back their needed supplies. He concluded that "the country community is defined as the team haul. People in the country think of the community as that territory, with its people, which lies within the team haul of a given center." By "team haul," he meant the distance which for a farmer would be a "customary drive with a horse and wagon. . . . It is the radius within which men buy and sell. . . . It is the radius of social intercourse." [3]

Wilson's concept of the "trade area" community was the stimulus for C. J. Galpin to develop a technique for delineating and mapping what he came to designate the *rurban community*. About 1913 Galpin conceived the idea of going into a rural county in Wisconsin and actually mapping the trade areas of the communities in the county. The method was simple. He supplied himself with township maps which showed the location of farm families in the open country, and a questionnaire containing perhaps half a dozen questions, such as, where do you buy your hardware? Where do you send your children to high school? Where do you do your banking? Where do you buy your dry goods? With these devices he went out from the trade center along the country roads, locating by a mark on the map when he came to the last family on the road which traded at the center. When the survey was complete, he connected these marks on the maps so as to make a continuous line about the village for each of the services indicated on the schedule.

[3] Warren H. Wilson, *The Evolution of the Country Community*, pp. 91–92. Boston: The Pilgrim Press, 1912.

The lines for all services did not coincide entirely, but they did approximately. In this way he was able to indicate with some precision the community boundaries of each of these centers.

How service areas differ for various commodities is well illustrated by the results of a survey of Morrow County, Ohio, which was taken cooperatively in 1941 by the United States Census Bureau and Magazine Marketing Service. Reference to Figures 7 and 8 will show that the farm families tended to purchase groceries close to home; therefore there are numerous focal points on the map. On the other hand, there were remarkably fewer places at which they were purchasing the only slightly more specialized commodity, men's working clothes. The survey represents a very useful application of the technique developed by Galpin.

Galpin concluded that the trade zone was most important in determining community boundaries. Said he:

It is difficult, if not impossible, to avoid the conclusion that the trade zone about one of these complete agricultural civic centers forms the boundary of an actual, if not legal, community, within which the apparent entanglement of human life is resolved into a fairly unitary system of interrelatedness. The fundamental community is a composite of many expanding and contracting feature communities possessing the characteristic pulsating instability of all real life.[4]

The invention of a technique for more precise location of community boundaries has had a profound influence on subsequent rural studies in the United States. It has been applied by practically all rural sociologists working in the various states. Usually, though not always, their studies have verified Galpin's conclusion as to the determining role of trade in setting the boundaries. In Michigan, for example, it was found that the high-school attendance area most significantly determined community boundaries. The authors of the Michigan study concluded that "the high-school attendance area was a more satisfactory single factor in determining a community boundary than any other as it did not come and go as erratically

[4] C. J. Galpin, "The Social Anatomy of an Agricultural Community," *University of Wisconsin AES Research Bulletin 34*, 1915, p. 18. See also by the same author *Rural Life*, p. 86. New York: D. Appleton-Century Co., 1923.

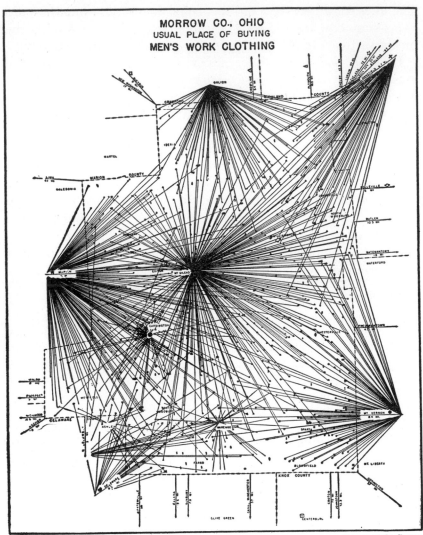

FIGURE 7. *Usual Place of Buying Men's Work Clothing by Farm Families in Morrow County, Ohio, 1941*

as other service areas, and tended to oscillate less." [5] This is due to the greatly increased high-school attendance rates of farm boys and girls. In his study Galpin found the high-school

[5] J. F. Thaden and Eben Mumford, "High School Communities in Michigan," *Michigan State College AES Special Bulletin 289*, 1938, p. 34.

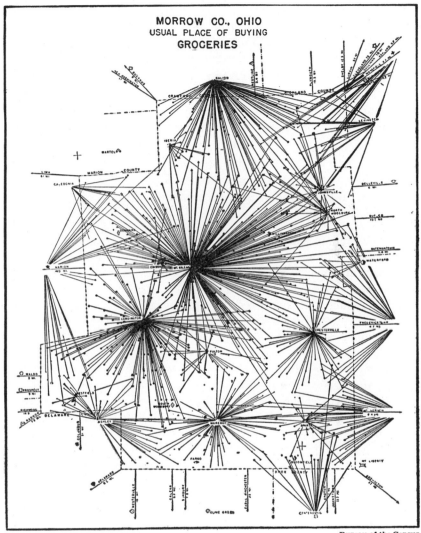

FIGURE 8. *Usual Place of Buying Groceries by Farm Families in Morrow County, Ohio, 1941*

zone to be much smaller than the other zones. Although **practically** every farm family in Walworth county was **within 5 miles** of a high school, the children from only 15 per cent of them attended. It is clear that in Galpin's time, the high-school attendance area could not be used as a criterion of the community. As attendance at high school becomes practically universal, however, it appears that it may become the most important item in designating community boundaries.

Irwin T. Sanders and Douglas Ensminger, in the process of mapping the community areas of Chilton County, Alabama, developed what may be an improvement in the Galpin technique. While accepting the basic principle that the trade and service area is the best measure of the natural rural community, they conceived the idea of grouping within the community boundaries not merely the individual families, as is customarily done, but rather the neighborhood units. The technique they refer to as the "neighborhood cluster method," for which they claim the following advantages:

1) The layman can more easily understand the community boundaries obtained by clustering the neighborhoods. He knows that a family is part of a neighborhood, and can see why a neighborhood should be part of a community.

2) The cluster method does not split neighborhoods as the trade-service area method often does with its emphasis upon secondary rather than primary association.

3) The community obtained by the service-area method has a structure, considered geographically, divided into village and farm people; the cluster method gives a better defined structure consisting of several neighborhoods as well as the center. The latter structure is better adapted to serve as basis of representation in planning programs.

4) The cluster method is much less laborious than the trade-service area method where questionnaires are circulated, each home located and its attachments shown for the several services.[6]

**The rural neighborhood.** Within the larger community areas as designated by Galpin and others there are numerous smaller groupings of farm families, the neighborhoods. These social entities developed on the frontier before the trade centers or villages emerged. Under pioneer conditions, with poor transportation, the neighbors on adjacent farms constituted the only immediate social contacts for the family. Thus they were bound together by the factor of distance or locality itself. In addition

---

[6] Irwin T. Sanders and Douglas Ensminger, "Alabama Rural Communities: A Study of Chilton County," *Alabama College Bulletin 136.* 1940, 33:1A, p. 80.

there were often other bonds, such as those of common nationality and language, kinship, or common religion. But of crucial importance was the common need for social contact in the interest of cooperating to meet needs and crises of the frontier and to establish and maintain schools and social control. Often the needs for social intercourse and mutual aid were combined in such activities as quilting bees, husking bees, barn- and house-raisings, and the like.

But neighborhoods were rather informal groupings, seldom if ever rising to the distinction of a name on the map, though they were nonetheless real to the inhabitants. The families which composed them had a sense of social cohesion, of belonging together. Usually, they had a name for the locality even though it might not appear on any map. In short, neighborhoods must be considered as groups with social significance. As Kenyon Butterfield has said, "It is something more than a mere aggregation of families." [7] It is a group of families who "neighbor" with each other.

**Delineation of neighborhoods.** Following the classic study by Galpin in mapping the "rurban" community, J. H. Kolb in Wisconsin, Dwight Sanderson and W. S. Thompson in New York, C. C. Taylor and C. C. Zimmerman in North Carolina, and E. L. Morgan and O. Howells in Missouri began studies of what might be called "sub-areas" within the larger community.[8] These were designated by the various investigators as "neighborhoods," "primary groups," "rural groups," and "social areas." The studies were all aiming at a common goal, namely to identify and describe the nature of these small groups of open-country farm families. Various techniques were used. Kolb asked the farm family to give the name of the neighborhood, and decided that name consciousness was a criterion of neighborhood cohesion. On the basis of questionnaires distributed through the schools, he mapped the boundaries of the neighborhoods of Dane

[7] In the introduction to E. L. Morgan, "Mobilizing the Rural Community," *Massachusetts Agricultural College Extension Bulletin 9*, 1918, p. 19.

[8] J. H. Kolb, "Rural Primary Groups," *University of Wisconsin AES Research Bulletin 51*, 1921; Dwight Sanderson and Warren S. Thompson, "The Social Areas of Otsego County," *Cornell University AES Bulletin 422*, 1923; E. L. Morgan and Owen Howells, "Rural Population Groups," *University of Missouri AES Research Bulletin 74*, 1925; C. C. Zimmerman and C. C. Taylor, "Rural Organization," *North Carolina AES Bulletin 245*, 1922.

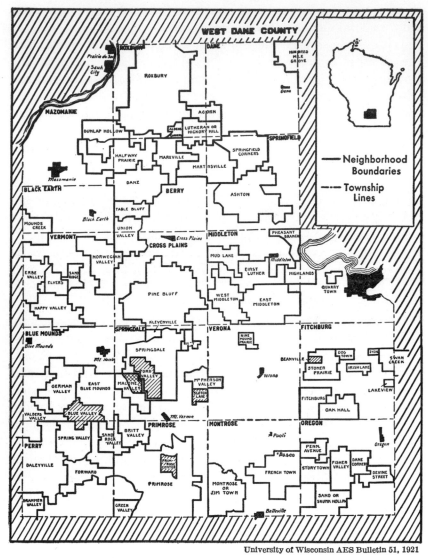

University of Wisconsin AES Bulletin 51, 1921

FIGURE 9. *Neighborhoods of West Dane County, Wisconsin*

County, Wisconsin. (See Figure 9.) The common use of a
"name" to identify the neighborhood did not prove adequate
as a criterion in some other states, however, and investigators
had to use other criteria, such as school districts and the various activities of the families. In North Carolina, Taylor and

Zimmerman found the "name area" quite lacking in reality as a means of designating a group which had social cohesion. In other words, the territorial grouping of families was not the sole bond which held them together, but there were other factors, such as a school, church, or some other institution, which modified the locality bond.

Sanderson and Thompson found 222 locality names in Otsego County, New York. "About 62 per cent of the farmhouses are located in areas having locality names, about 16 per cent are so near villages that they use the village name, and about 22 per cent have no local name or use a local name which is common to only three or four houses."[9] The average area of these neighborhoods was $2\frac{1}{4}$ square miles, and they contained about 12 homes each. The names of the neighborhoods were divided as follows: 71 from early settlers, 19 from geographic features, 2 from nationalities, 2 from churches, 5 from mills, and the rest from miscellaneous sources.

That areas of the country differ considerably in the neighborhood consciousness among farm families is indicated in a study in Minnesota, where farm people seemed to be more conscious of the township as a locality group than they were of the "name neighborhood."[10]

In his study of rural life in Brazil, T. Lynn Smith found territorial groupings of farm families similar to those in the United States:

In general in Brazil, as in the United States, the neighborhood is made up of a small number of families who live on adjacent farms, whose members frequently come into face-to-face contact with one another, and who have established a system of mutual aid amongst themselves. Brazilian neighborhoods owe their integration to a wide variety of causes: to the visiting and mutual aid among families who live near one another; to the pooling of efforts in order to secure and maintain a chapel or a school; to a mutual dependence upon a landed proprietor, a sugar mill, a cotton gin, a grist mill, a cooperative marketing association, a creamery or a cheese factory, a railroad station, or some other economic agency; to the grouping together in close proximity of farm

---

[9] Sanderson and Thompson, *op. cit.*, p. 10 ff.
[10] Vernon Davies, "Neighborhoods, Townships and Communities in Wright County, Minnesota," *Rural Sociology*, 1943, 8:51-61.

families who are intimately knit together by ties of kinship, national origins and language, and religion; or to the fact that a few families have been thrown into close and constant contact among themselves and isolated from the larger world, by establishing their residences in a small mountain valley or cove, a fertile and watered area in the midst of a barren region, on a small island, or even on a large fazenda or plantation.[11]

Similarly, C. C. Taylor found that rural people in Argentina grouped themselves into a territorial pattern not unlike that in the United States, in that there were: "(1) the neighborhood, which is identified by its lowest common denominator—family visiting; (2) a unit next above the neighborhood, often an open country pattern of association which falls some place between a visiting neighborhood and a trade-centered community; and (3) a trade-centered community."[12]

**Neighborhood bonds.** All of these early investigators found various social bonds which made the groups of families significant as social units. Sanderson and Thompson, for example, found the following interests or institutions in designated numbers of neighborhoods to be of greatest importance[13]:

TABLE 3. *Number of Neighborhoods in Otsego County, New York, Where Certain Institutions Existed at the Time of Study, and Number Where These Institutions Had Been Closed*

| INSTITUTIONS | No. NEIGHBORHOODS WHERE EXISTED | No. WHERE CLOSED |
|---|---|---|
| Churches | 15 | 8 |
| Schools | 95 | 15 |
| Granges | 7 | 1 |
| Blacksmith shops | 5 | 2 |
| Saw and grist mills | 12 | 5 |
| Cheese factories and creameries | 6 | 1 |

The social ties which supplement and give cohesion to these territorial groupings are classified by Kolb as "primary" and

---

[11] T. Lynn Smith, *Brazil: People and Institutions*, p. 588. Baton Rouge: Louisiana State University Press, 1945.

[12] C. C. Taylor, "Rural Locality Groups in Argentina," *American Sociological Review*, 1944, 9:162–170, p. 162.

[13] Sanderson and Thompson, *op. cit.*, p. 12.

"secondary." The relative importance of these activities in 94 Dane County, Wisconsin, neighborhoods are shown in Table 4 for the years 1921 and 1931.[14]

TABLE 4. *Relative Importance of Social Bonds in Dane County Rural Neighborhoods*

| FACTORS | PRIMARY | | SECONDARY | |
|---------|---------|------|-----------|------|
| | 1921 | 1931 | 1921 | 1931 |
| Religious | 32 | 27 | 5 | 10 |
| Educational | 29 | 31 | 9 | 15 |
| Economic | 14 | 18 | 6 | 7 |
| Social | 8 | 17 | 21 | 43 |
| Nationality | 5 | 0 | 10 | 0 |
| Topography | 5 | 0 | 10 | 0 |
| Kinship | 2 | 1 | 0 | 0 |

It is clear from these studies that religion, education, and economic activities are of primary importance in giving a neighborhood social cohesion. It is also important to note that over the ten-year period reported by Kolb important changes had taken place in the relative importance of these activities, notably the rise of "social" activities as a determining influence. These activities included clubs formed around various sociability interests.

**"Symbiotic" or accommodative neighborhoods.** In the biracial sections of the United States, characteristically the South, there are distinct neighborhoods for the Whites and for the Negroes in the same area. While the dwellings of the two groups may be interspersed and mingled and the two are "neighbors" in the geographic sense, each maintains its own "social area" or neighborhood. The two groups are in a relationship of mutual economic dependence in the broad social and economic sense, but they follow the "color line" in such activities as family visiting, borrowing and lending, school and church attendance, and the like. Thus L. S. Dodson and J. Woolley [15] have mapped the neighborhoods of the two color groups in Charles County, Maryland, as indicated on the accompanying maps (See Figures

[14] J. H. Kolb, "Trends of Country Neighborhoods," *University of Wisconsin AES Research Bulletin 120*, November, 1933, p. 15.

[15] Lindon S. Dodson and Jane Woolley, "Community Organization in Charles County, Maryland," *University of Maryland AES Bulletin A21*, 1943, pp. 275, 283.

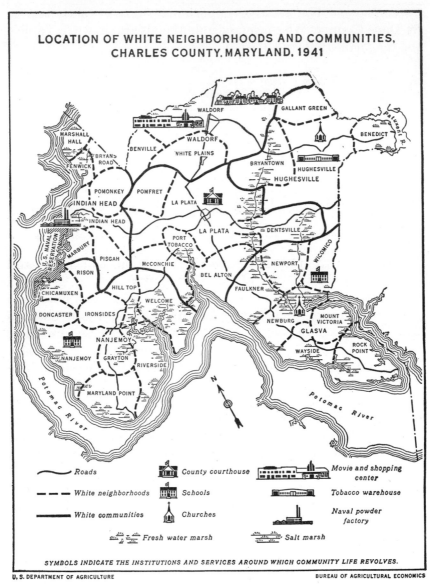

FIGURE 10. *Location of White Neighborhoods in Charles County, Maryland, 1941*

10 and 11). Zimmerman and Taylor found this symbiotic relationship among the two color groups in Wake County, North Carolina.[16]

[16] Zimmerman and Taylor, *op. cit.*

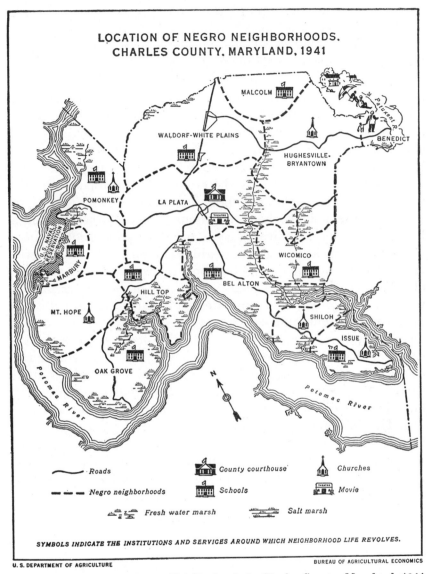

FIGURE 11. *Location of Negro Neighborhoods in Charles County, Maryland, 1941*

**Demographic changes and the neighborhood.** The decline of the farm population through the decreasing birth rate and migration, brings about changes in the total numbers of people in a given area and in the composition of the population as regards age and sex. Should the child population of a farm neighborhood decline, the one-room school, which is frequently a center of neighborhood consciousness, may be abandoned. Similarly, should the total population decline, the open-country church may close. The steady mechanization of agriculture also brings about a decline in the number of people per unit of area, both through the replacement of human labor by the machines and through the encouragement this replacement gives to the enlargement of the farm unit. Thus with the passage of time fewer people will live within the boundaries of the neighborhood. The neighborhood itself may therefore either disappear entirely as a natural social area or its boundaries may be enlarged.

**Changes in neighborhood functions.** Some of these changes have already been indicated as a result of population change and its consequent impact on neighborhood institutions. Migration into and out of a neighborhood tends to break down the old ties of face-to-face association which characterize the primary group. The newcomers cannot fit readily into the old patterns of neighborliness. There is, in other words, a growing anonymity here as in the city. With the decline of the significance of the neighborhood as a locality group in providing the social contacts of farm families, new groupings emerge around "interests." The focus of these interest groups is frequently outside the neighborhood, as such, and usually in the village.

J. H. Kolb and D. G. Marshall, in charting the changes in Dane County, Wisconsin, neighborhoods over a 20-year period, found a number of differences in the three surveys conducted in 1921, 1931, and 1941. While there was a difference of only one in the "active" [17] neighborhoods from 1921 to 1931, thirty-two of those which were active in 1921 were "inactive" by 1931, twenty-four were discovered for the first time in 1931, and seven which had been inactive in 1921 became active by 1931. In the 1930's, however, the number of active groups declined by 20 per cent. Only four inactive neighborhoods became active during the interval and no new ones were found. Further decreases in active neighborhoods are forecast for the period following 1941. Yet when the newly-discovered neighbor-

---

[17] A neighborhood was classified as "active" if it had "more than one function or activity."

hoods of 1931 were eliminated from the analysis, "it is surprising," say the authors, "how stable in form and regular in
activity the other active neighborhoods were throughout the
whole 20-year period." [18]

"The boundaries of the neighborhoods," they continue, "had
not changed significantly." There were some shifts, however,
as when a few neighborhoods merged. That the size of the
neighborhood has some relation to its tendency to persist or
remain active is observed, and the authors conclude that "the
main tendency . . . is for the larger ones to remain active, and
for the smaller ones and those too close to community centers
to become inactive."

The most important finding in this re-survey of neighborhoods was in the "shift in the relative strength of certain
functions." The comments of the authors deserve quotation:

The important finding in respect to functions or activities in neighborhoods is the shift in the relative strength of certain functions. While
the relative importance of certain functions within the combinations
changed, the major ones found in the various combinations did not change
significantly. This is further evidence of the degree of stability which many
active neighborhoods have acquired during the years. More specifically,
in 1941 in 100% of the cases there were educational activities, either
public or parochial, such as the elementary school, adult education
classes, 4-H clubs. In 83% there were social activities (sociability),
such as clubs or social organizations, parties, visiting. In 75% there were
economic activities, such as stores (half of the neighborhoods had them),
garages (one-third had them), filling stations, creameries and/or
cheese factories, cooperatives. Nearly 60% had religious activities, such
as church services, religious education, and societies. Thirty per cent
had taverns which classified both as economic and social. There were
other functions but they fell below the 15% level.

Functions or activities are found characteristically in certain combinations. The most frequent combination was three functions, occurring
in almost half of the cases. Educational, economic, and social was the
most frequent combination of three; religious, educational, and social
was second; and religious, educational, and economic, third. It was in
the combination of educational, religious, and/or economic and social,

---

[18] J. H. Kolb and Douglas G. Marshall, "Neighborhood-Community Relationships in Rural Society," *University of Wisconsin AES Research Bulletin 154*, 1944,
p. 3.

whether in the number of three or four, that the greatest stability seemed
to occur. When in the combination of four or five, made by adding
communication, 15 of the 27 cases were hamlets. The most significant
change from 1931 to 1941 was the relative decrease of the educational
and social combination, represented, for example, by school, mothers'
club, and/or 4-H club.

Not all functions have equal influence in a combination; some are
of major and some of minor importance. Therefore, a value of one was
assigned to a major and one-half to a minor emphasis. Thus a score
could be given each function in each neighborhood for each year studied,
and a rank order established. As can be observed from the ranking below,
the religious and the educational functions changed places with the
economic and the social from 1931 to 1941.[19]

TABLE 5. *Ranking of Functions for Active Neighborhoods*

| FUNCTIONS | 1941 | 1931 | 1921 |
|---|---|---|---|
| Religious | 1 | 3 | 1 |
| Educational | 2 | 1 | 2 |
| Economic | 3 | 4 | 4 |
| Social | 4 | 2 | 3 |

The persistence of these neighborhoods was most significantly
related to three factors: nationality, length of residence, and
tenancy. Interestingly enough, homogeneity on the basis of
nationality was not essential to active neighborhoods. As the
authors put it, " . . . neighborhoods in which at least 36 per
cent of the families have mixed or indefinite nationality background are more likely to be active than those with 64 per cent
or more of their families with similar recognized backgrounds." [20]
As might be expected, a high degree of farm ownership and
longer residence in the area are associated with "activeness."

It seems clear, therefore, that under the impact of the forces
of cultural change, neighborhood functions and to some extent
their areas are undergoing modification, though they tend to
persist as social groups.

[19] J. H Kolb and Douglas G. Marshall, "Neighborhood-Community Relationships in Rural Society," *University of Wisconsin AES Research Bulletin 154*, 1944,
p. 5
[20] *Ibid.*, p 7.

### AGRICULTURAL VILLAGES

As one travels through rural areas characterized by scattered farm settlement, one passes through many small clusters of homes and business establishments which constitute the nuclei of rural communities. These villages vary widely in size and in the number of business units which compose them. Many contain only a few dwellings and business structures, being practically little more than neighborhood centers. If the population of these small centers does not exceed 250 inhabitants, they are coming to be called *hamlets*. Those with populations from 250 to 1,000 are called *small villages*, while those from 1,000 to 2,500 are designated *large villages*. Places larger than 2,500 up to 5,000 inhabitants are referred to as *towns*, and those from 5,000 to 10,000 as *small cities*. Even the *towns* and *small cities* may be regarded from a functional standpoint as "rural" trade centers, even though the census designates them as "urban."

**Types of villages.** Several classifications of villages have been made according to the complexity and nature of the functions which they perform. In addition to those which are essentially service centers for the farm hinterlands, there are many primarily devoted to such activities as *mining, manufacturing,* or *timber products*. In the past quarter of a century, also, there have sprung up many *tourist* villages in recreational areas.

The more typical rural service centers have been classified by J. H. Kolb as follows:

1) *The single, simple service village* which is small in size, perhaps no larger than a hamlet, and contains usually no more than a general store, a small school, a gas station, and a tavern.

2) *The limited, simple service village,* usually providing at least two but less than six of the following services: economic, educational, religious, social, communication, and professional.

3) *The semi-complete intermediate type* may have some services in all six of the fields mentioned above, but not *complete* services. For instance, it may contain a bus service, but no railroad. Its other services may be relatively simple, and not adequate to meet fully the needs of the members of the community.

4) *The complete, partially specialized center* contains services

in all the six fields of activity, with a considerable degree of specialization in its stores and other services, and will range in size from 1,200 to 5,000 population. It approaches what might be termed self-sufficiency.

5) *The urban, highly specialized types* are the cities ranging in size from 5,000 population up to the great metropolitan centers. They are characterized by a high degree of specialization in services.[21]

Most of the services which farm families require are found in the first four types, and especially in the first three.

C. C. Zimmerman uses a slightly different terminology in the classification of trade centers, but one which is perhaps a little more precise. He groups the centers into *independent* and *dependent* or *elementary* categories. To be classified as independent a center had to have a post office, a telegraph office, an express office, a publisher, and a bank. Thus, the services of *communication* were the criteria used in this classification. The justification for this classification was, according to Zimmerman, the assumption that "the entire population depends, to some extent, upon the services furnished by these facilities, [and] any community that lacks one of them is to that extent dependent upon another for primary services." [22]

The independent centers were further classified by Zimmerman on the basis of the number of "business units" reported in *Bradstreet's Book of Commercial Ratings*. By this method he identified 68 trade centers in Minnesota with over 75 business units, 73 with from 50 to 75 units, and 211 with less than 50 units. In addition there were 1,211 elementary or dependent centers which lacked one or more of the communication services.

**Number and distribution of villages.** The United States Census provides a separate enumeration for incorporated villages and unincorporated places with 1,000 people or more. The number of incorporated places under 2,500 population in 1950 was 13,235; 3,408 of them contained from 1,000 to 2,500, and 9,827 had fewer than 1,000 people.

[21] J. H. Kolb, "Service Relations of Town and Country," *University of Wisconsin AES Research Bulletin 58*, 1923.

[22] C. C. Zimmerman, "Farm Trade Centers in Minnesota, 1905–29," *University of Minnesota AES Bulletin 269*, 1930, p. 10.

In addition to the places reported in the census there are several times as many small unreported centers, usually called *hamlets*, which do not appear on most maps but serve as farm trade centers. The number of these can be roughly determined from atlases and *Dun and Bradstreet Commercial Ratings*. The trend in these centers from 1920-1940 is shown in Table 6. During the period hamlets declined and villages remained about the same, while the total population remained constant. The 1950 census reported a small increase in the number and the population of places of 1,000 to 2,500, and, on the other hand, a decline both in number and population of places under 1,000.

TABLE 6. *Number and Population of Incorporated and Unincorporated Hamlets and Villages, 1920-1940.*

| YEAR | No. | TOTAL POPULATION (000) | No. | HAMLETS (UNDER 250) POPULATION (000) | No. | VILLAGES (250-2,500) POPULATION (000) |
|---|---|---|---|---|---|---|
| 1940 | 78,177 | 17,703 | 58,818 | 3,922 | 19,359 | 13,781 |
| 1930 | 74,502 | 17,889 | 55,135 | 3,580 | 19,367 | 14,310 |
| 1920 | 84,738 | 17,805 | 65,298 | 3,880 | 19,440 | 13,925 |

Adapted from D. G. Marshall, "Hamlets and Villages in the United States," *American Sociological Review*, Vol. 11, No. 2, April, 1946, pp. 159-165.

**Spacing of service centers.** The distribution of these different types of communities follows a rough spatial pattern in terms of distance from the farm family. Some services of a very simple kind, such as an oil and gas station or a general store, are located in the open country easily accessible to the farm family. Other services, calling for greater specialization, are located in slightly more distant and larger centers. This cumulative building up of specialized services continues from the simple neighborhood center to the great metropolis. Kolb decided the various types of centers in Wisconsin occurred at approximately four-mile intervals or multiples thereof. That is, a *single service* hamlet would be located under 4 miles of any farm home; a *limited* and *simple service* small village about 4 miles distant; a *semicomplete* or *intermediate* type about 8 miles away; the *complete* and *particularly specialized* town or small city, about 16 miles away; while the *urban* and *highly special-ized* city would be about 36 miles.[23]

In central New York, Sanderson[24] found a somewhat comparable distribution of villages according to size and distance from farm families. The local or nearest center patronized by the open-country farm family was about 2 or 3 miles away. From it they obtained groceries, automobile repairs, hardware, feed; there they went to attend church and the grange; and there they sent the children to school. The relationship of the farm family to the centers of various size and complexity is shown in Figure 12.

**Services villages perform.** As the "economic capitals of rural America" the agricultural villages are preeminently centers for implementing the trade relations of farmers with the Great Society. Through the village flow the goods and services used and consumed by farm families. Through it also, by way of exit, pass the crops and livestock which the farmer produces and sells to the "outside." The village is the nexus between the rural family and the rest of the world. As such it is dependent upon the farmer for the "raw material" of trade, for which it performs the middleman services. It is no less true that the farmer is dependent upon the village for performing these services.

In a social-cultural sense, also, the village is liaison between the farm family and the larger world. From it come ideas and values which have their origin in the urban world. The village "retails" these, as truly as it does the goods and services. Urban fashions in dress and in other ways of life spread to the farm hinterland through the village thoroughfares. Many of these ideas and values, it is true, are distributed directly to family homes via radio, the newspaper, magazines, and books. Nevertheless, the most effective contact is made in the village. It is truly the link between urban and rural (farm) societies. T. Lynn Smith has well summarized the functions of the village in our rural society under the following heads: (1) "trade as

[23] J. H. Kolb, "Service Relations of Town and Country," *University of Wisconsin AES Bulletin 58,* 1923.

[24] Dwight Sanderson, "Social and Economic Areas in Central New York," *Cornell University AES Bulletin 614,* 1934.

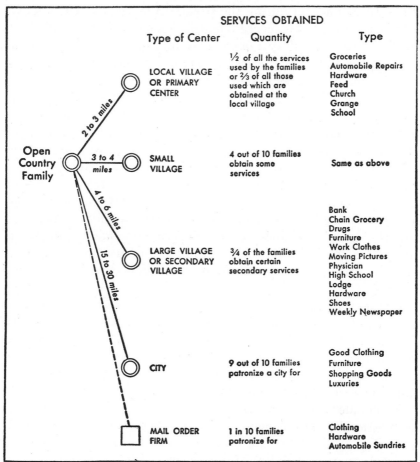

**SERVICES OBTAINED**

| Type of Center | Quantity | Type |
|---|---|---|
| LOCAL VILLAGE OR PRIMARY CENTER | ½ of all the services used by the families or ⅔ of all those used which are obtained at the local village | Groceries<br>Automobile Repairs<br>Hardware<br>Feed<br>Church<br>Grange<br>School |
| SMALL VILLAGE | 4 out of 10 families obtain some services | Same as above |
| LARGE VILLAGE OR SECONDARY VILLAGE | ¾ of the families obtain certain secondary services | Bank<br>Chain Grocery<br>Drugs<br>Furniture<br>Work Clothes<br>Moving Pictures<br>Physician<br>High School<br>Lodge<br>Hardware<br>Shoes<br>Weekly Newspaper |
| CITY | 9 out of 10 families patronize a city for | Good Clothing<br>Furniture<br>Shopping Goods<br>Luxuries |
| MAIL ORDER FIRM | 1 in 10 families patronize for | Clothing<br>Hardware<br>Automobile Sundries |

Open Country Family — 2 to 3 miles — 3 to 4 miles — 4 to 6 miles — 15 to 30 miles

Cornell University AES Bulletin 614, 1934

FIGURE 12. *Relationship of Farm Family to Various Service Centers*

the primary function of the village," (2) "the village as the nucleus of the emerging rural community," (3) "the village as America's 'old folks' home'," and (4) "the village as the arena of rural-urban conflict." [25]

**The disappearance of centers.** With changes in the field of transportation and communication, some of the small centers seem to disappear entirely. Thus, Landis found that the number of hamlets listed in 1900 had declined by over 30 per cent by

[25] T. Lynn Smith, "The Role of the Village in American Rural Society," *Rural Sociology*, 1942, 7:10–21, p. 16 f.

1930. In Minnesota during the period from 1905 to 1929, C. E. Lively found that 306 centers had disappeared from the listings in *Bradstreet's Book of Commercial Ratings*. The fundamental reasons for their disappearance were: (1) decline of tributary population or changes in its composition; (2) industrial changes, decline of or shifts in nonagricultural industry such as lumbering, and shifts in type of farming; (3) changes in communication and transportation facilities; (4) changes in marketing organization and buying habits; (5) social conflict; (6) competition with other trade centers. Some of the more immediate factors included loss of post office (as a result of the introduction of rural free delivery service), loss of county seat, destruction of a business establishment not subsequently rebuilt, death of a proprietor of a business establishment, breakdown of social unity due to the decline of a dominant institution such as a church, and poor merchandizing (too few goods and poor service).[26]

**Changes in village demography.** Villages either grow, remain static, decline, or disappear entirely. The question as to the future of villages in the matter of growth or decline according to whether they are large or small, has been the subject of considerable controversy. J. M. Gillette, on the basis of an analysis of changes in villages from 1890 to 1920, concluded that "the smaller the place, the greater is the liability of loss of population." [27] His conclusion carried the definite implication that the small centers were on the way to extinction, a state of affairs rather definitely foreshadowed by the trends during the period covered.

However, later trends (1930–1940) indicated a somewhat more hopeful outlook, at least for the places of more than 250 inhabitants. E. deS. Brunner and T. Lynn Smith, on the basis of an analysis of the incorporated places reported in the 1940 census, concluded that centers with 250 people or more showed

[26] C. E. Lively, "Growth and Decline of Farm Trade Centers in Minnesota, 1905–1930," *University of Minnesota AES Bulletin 287*, 1932. See also, as similar studies, T. Lynn Smith, "Farm Trade Centers in Louisiana, 1901–1931," *Louisiana State University AES Bulletin 234*, 1933; and Paul H. Landis, "The Growth and Decline of South Dakota Trade Centers, 1901–1933," *South Dakota State College AES Bulletin 279*, 1933.

[27] J. M. Gillette, *Rural Sociology*, p. 463. New York: The Macmillan Company, 1923.

a tendency for population either to grow or to remain static. "In every population group except the lowest (i.e. places with less than 250 population) well over two fifths of the villages showed only slight change in population; that is, lost or gained less than 10 per cent in the census period." [28] The great majority of the balance showed gains of 10 per cent or more, with a slight tendency toward higher percentages of growth in the larger places.

S. C. Ratcliffe, also using the census data for incorporated places, compared changes over the 50-year period from 1890 to 1940 and found that the rate of loss of population declined for all villages. He also noted that the rate of loss was less for the larger villages and higher for the smallest villages. [29]

As we have already noted for 1950, the places under 1,000 population lost somewhat, but, as Brunner has shown, much of this "loss" is due to the growth in the more than 1,000 category. He reports that 554 villages which had had less than 1,000 in 1940 "graduated" to the larger size. Of the places from 250 to 1,000, about one third gained 10 per cent or more, 18 per cent lost 10 per cent or more, while the remainder about held their own. Three fourths of the villages of 1,000 to 2,500 grew during the decade. [30]

There seems to be justification, therefore, for these conclusions: (*a*) the small hamlets show the most marked tendency toward population decline; (*b*) the rate of increase is roughly proportional to the size of the village; and (*c*) there is a recent tendency toward stability, or no marked increase or decrease. A word of caution, however, might be appropriate as to the interpretation of trends during the 1930's. The depression of that decade undoubtedly had an effect upon village growth. For one thing, the normal stream of migration to the cities was cut off. The demand for extra labor in industry was sharply reduced as a result of the depressed market and the steady increase in laborsaving devices. At the same time, work relief projects were organized throughout the country, in small as

[28] E. deS. Brunner and T. Lynn Smith, "Village Growth and Decline, 1930–1940," *Rural Sociology*, 1944, 9:103–115, p. 108.

[29] S. C. Ratcliffe, "Size As a Factor in Population Changes of Hamlets and Villages, 1930 to 1940," *Rural Sociology*, 1942, 7:318–328.

[30] Edmund deS. Brunner, "Village Growth 1940–50," *Rural Sociology*, 1951, 16:111–118.

well as large centers, and had the effect of stabilizing the population. During the 1940's however, the situation was reversed. The great surplus of farm people was drawn into the war industries and armed forces. At the same time prices of farm products rose to unprecedented levels, thus enhancing the buying power of farm families. Mechanization and electrification provided new business for the trade centers. The sale of tractors and farm machinery rose rapidly after 1940, as did that of electrical appliances. Farmers had more money to spend and more goods and services to spend it for.

To summarize, the typical rural community in the United States is composed of a village center and the farmers living in its trade hinterland. As sub-areas within the larger entity of the community are the neighborhoods which have been identified and delineated by several investigators in different states. The nature and social strength of these neighborhoods differ in various areas, but in general they show a tendency to persist. Changes, however, are taking place. Boundaries shift somewhat, for occasionally two neighborhoods coalesce to form one. Functions also change: where the church was important at a former period, a school or farm bureau unit may have taken its place. The village nuclei also show dynamic tendencies. Their populations grow or decline; the nature of the business units which compose them may undergo changes. The trade area itself may contract or expand. It is impressive, indeed, to contemplate the fluidity of community life, the flexibility manifest in man's adaptation to the earth's surface.

Surface arrangements, however, are not the totality of community life. The infinite complex of institutions, agencies, and other social interaction patterns will be described in other chapters to follow.

### QUESTIONS FOR DISCUSSION

1. What is meant by the *ecology* of a rural community?
2. What criteria have been found useful in defining the term *community?*
3. What is the origin and meaning of the phrase *team haul?*
4. Describe in detail how Galpin devised and carried out the idea of mapping what he chose to call the *rurban* community. Why has the

high-school attendance area become of increasing importance as a means of helping to map rural communities?

5. What kind of social grouping is a rural neighborhood? List several of the early neighborhood studies that have been made and describe the particular method of approach used in each study. In what way did the findings of the Taylor-Zimmerman study differ from the others? What institutions are most likely to be found in a neighborhood? State what is meant by a *symbiotic* neighborhood.

6. What are some recent trends as to the persistence of neighborhoods? Does the disappearance of a neighborhood, considered as a social unit, necessarily signify a condition of social disorganization? Discuss Kolb's use of the expression *inactive neighborhood?*

7. Classify hamlets, small villages, large villages, towns and small cities as to size of population.

8. If you happen to come from a rural community, what kind is it from the standpoint of Kolb's classification of agricultural villages?

9. How did Zimmerman use *communication* in his scheme of classifying rural communities?

10. In what way do Kolb's and Sanderson's findings differ as to the spacing of trade centers?

11. Give several reasons why the village plays a vital role in American society.

12. What factors are most closely associated with the disappearance of small trade centers?

### SELECTED REFERENCES

Alexander, Frank D., and Nelson, Lowry. "Rural Social Organization in Goodhue County, Minnesota," *Minnesota AES Bulletin 401.* 1949.

Anderson, A. H., and Hill, Randall C. "Rural Communities and Organizations: A Study of Group Life in Ellis County, Kansas," *Kansas AES Circular 143.* 1948.

Belcher, John C. "Service Relationships of Farmers in Lincoln County, Oklahoma," *Oklahoma AES Bulletin No. B–383.* 1952.

Grigsby, S. Earl, and Hoffsommer, Harold. "Rural Social Organization of Frederick County, Maryland," *Maryland AES Bulletin A51.* 1949.

Hay, Donald G., and others. "Rural Organizations in Three Maine Towns," *Maine Extension Bulletin 391.* 1949.

Hill, George W., and Smith, Ronald A. "Man in the Cut-Over," *Wisconsin AES Research Bulletin 139.* 1941.

Hill, George W., Slocum, Walter, and Hill, Ruth O. "Man-Land Adjustment: A Study of Family and Inter-Family Aspects of Land Settlement in the Central Wisconsin Land Purchase Area," *Wisconsin AES Bulletin 134*. 1938.

Jehlik, Paul J., and Wakeley, Ray E. "Rural Organization in Process," *Iowa AES Research Bulletin 365*. 1949.

Kolb, J. H., and Day, Leroy J. "Interdependence in Town and Country Relations in Rural Society," *Wisconsin AES Research Bulletin 172*. 1950.

Kolb, J. H., and Brunner, E. deS. *A Study of Rural Society*, Fourth Edition, Chapters 13 and 14. New York: Houghton Mifflin Co., 1952.

Kolb, J. H., and Marshall, Douglas. "Neighborhood-Community Relationships in Rural Society." *University of Wisconsin AES Bulletin 154*. Madison, 1944.

Loomis, Charles P. *Studies of Rural Social Organization in the United States, Latin America and Germany*. East Lansing: Michigan State College Press., 1946.

Mayo, Selz C., and Bobbitt, Robert McD. "Rural Organization: A Restudy of Locality Groups in Wake County, North Carolina," *North Carolina AES Technical Bulletin No. 95*. 1951.

Sanderson, Dwight. *Rural Sociology and Rural Social Organization*. New York: John Wiley and Sons, 1942.

———. "Locating the Rural Community." *Cornell Extension Bulletin 413*. 1939.

———, and Thompson, W. S. "The Social Areas of Otsego County, New York." *Cornell University AES Bulletin 422*. 1923.

Sorokin, P. A.; Zimmerman, C. C.; and Galpin, C. J. *A Systematic Source Book in Rural Sociology*, Vol. I, pp. 305–333. Minneapolis: University of Minnesota Press, 1930.

Stromberg, E. T. "The Influence of the Central Rural School on Community Organization." *Cornell University AES Bulletin 699*. 1938.

Zimmerman, C. C. *The Changing Community*. New York: Harper and Brothers, 1938.

# PART III

# THE BIOSOCIAL BASIS OF RURAL SOCIETY

## INTRODUCTION

BEFORE THERE can be a society there must be people. Men, women, and children, as biological organisms, constitute the raw material of society. It is important to the student of society that he have some understanding of the factors underlying population growth or decline, and the social consequences which result from these trends. It is also important to know the composition of the population, particularly with reference to age and sex, because these factors play an important role in social interaction and in determining the structure of society. Moreover, the movement of people from place to place is also an important dynamic force in social processes and organization and needs to be understood.

It may be well to reiterate here the explanation in the preface regarding the decision of the author to limit the material under the general heading of population. Conventionally, chapters on population in textbooks include discussions of composition in regard to marital status, ethnic elements, education, illiteracy, and the like. There frequently are separate chapters on mortality and fertility. It is the author's view, however, that the material on marital status might better be treated in connection with the institution of marriage and the family; that on ethnic composition, in connection with assimilation; that on education, under the discussion of the school; while mortality data might be more meaningful if treated in connection with the discussion of agencies of health. This arrangement will give additional meaning to the statistics.

# CHAPTER 6

# THE RURAL POPULATION

One of the most spectacular sociobiological facts of the period since 1800 is the tremendously rapid growth of the population of the world. During that 150 years the number of human beings on this planet has more than doubled. That is to say, as many people were added to the human family in that period as had been added in the whole previous period of human existence on the earth. This is a fact of vast social significance. It has meant that during that 150 years the population has spread over practically all of the remaining habitable areas of the globe. It has meant the development of new forms of social relations as a consequence of the increase in numbers.

The study of population has itself become a preoccupation of scholars chiefly during the past quarter of a century. Although John Graunt (1620–1674) had published his *Natural and Political Observations Upon the Bills of Mortality in 1662*, and some other English scholars had followed his lead in the latter half of the seventeenth and the forepart of the eighteenth century, it remained for Thomas Malthus really to establish the importance of population studies with the publication in 1798 of his famous *Essay on the Principle of Population as It Affects the Future Improvement of Society*. In this classic study, Malthus held that the increase in the population takes place more rapidly than the increase in the food supply.

While the study of population has been a continuing interest of scholars since the time of Malthus, it is fair to state that it has received the greatest attention during the period since World War I. The growth of interest in the subject immediately following World War I was due to a widespread conviction that the productivity of the planet in terms of food was fast approaching a maximum and that disaster might overtake the human family unless arbitrary reduction in the birth rate was invoked, or some new way could be found to increase the rate of food production.[1] The pessimistic outlook regarding the food supply changed rather suddenly during the postwar period, as food surpluses in the United States began to accumulate and the market deteriorated. Interest in population then became important not because of the imminence of starvation, but because of the changing composition of the population, the trend towards urbanization, and mounting unemployment.

### POPULATION CHANGES AND SOCIAL DYNAMICS

A numerical increase or decrease in the population can bring important changes throughout the social order. As numbers increase, the complexity of social organization, division of labor, and specialization all increase as well. Increase in numbers is usually accompanied by changes in property values, particularly in land. This is well illustrated by the experience of early American settlers on the frontier, who had only to wait a few years for the population to catch up with them in order to be able to sell their land for several times its original cost. Increase in numbers in a given area also gives rise to increase in social stratification. Declining populations are characterized by social changes involving the decline in the size of the family, changes in functions and number of social institutions, net out-migration, and the like.

The numerical trend of population growth in the United States is indicated by the accompanying graph (Figure 13). It will be noted immediately that since the first census was taken in 1790 the population has grown steadily from the approximately 4 million inhabitants at that time to 150,697,361 in 1950.

The extraordinary population growth during the 1940's was unexpected. In 1937 two able students of population changes, W. S. Thompson and P. K. Whelpton, predicted a population of 153 million by 1980, a figure actually surpassed in 1951.[2] The

---

[1] Among the books published during this wave of neo-Malthusian interest were E. M. East, *Mankind at the Crossroads*, New York: Charles Scribner's Sons, 1923; and E. A. Ross, *Standing Room Only*, New York: The Century Company, 1927.

[2] W. S. Thompson and P. K. Whelpton, "Population Statistics 1, National Data," National Resources Board, Washington, D.C., 1937, Table 1.

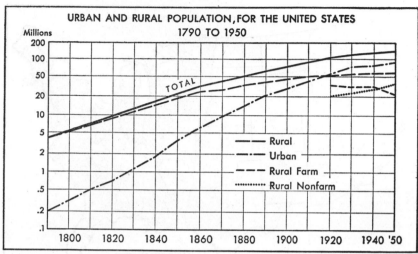

Bureau of the Census

FIGURE 13. *Rural and Urban Growth Curves of the Population of the United States from 1790 to 1950*

explanation of this was, in part: (*a*) many postponed marriages of the 1930's were consummated in the 1940's; (*b*) children of the high-birthrate 1920's came of age in the 1940's; (*c*) war and full employment.

**Geographic distribution.** The westward movement of population has been one of the most important factors in the history of the United States. While this important development will be discussed more fully in Chapter 7, it is well to note here that whereas a century ago the census reported no population in the Mountain and Pacific states, in 1950 there were nearly twenty million people in those states. This was, however, only 13.3 per cent of the total population of the country, and represented relatively low density. The most densely populated sections were the North and East, with the South almost on a par with them. (See Figure 14.)

**Rural-urban changes.** Reference to Figure 13 again will indicate that the urban population has been growing much more rapidly than has the rural. The United States was predominantly rural until about 1920, when the number of urban people exceeded the rural for the first time. The rural-urban distribution at various decades is shown graphically in Figure 15. In 1790 nearly

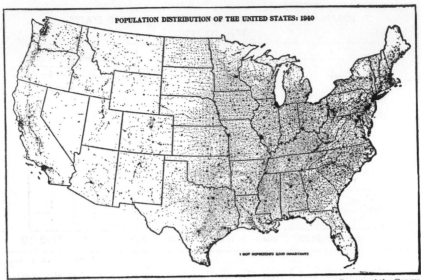

POPULATION DISTRIBUTION OF THE UNITED STATES: 1940

Bureau of the Census

FIGURE 14. *Population Distribution of the United States, 1950*

95 per cent of the population was rural, compared with **43.5** per cent in 1940 and **42.4** per cent in 1950. The ratio of urban and rural has changed but little since 1930. The census figures, however, are not realistic. While cities themselves have not increased greatly, the suburbs have grown but, unless incorporated, are classed as rural.

**The rural-farm population.** In 1920, due to the effective work of C. J. Galpin, then head of the Division of Farm Population and Rural Life Studies in the United States Department of Agriculture, the Census enumerated the rural-farm and rural-nonfarm populations separately. Since that time, annual estimates have been made of the farm population as of January 1. The annual fluctuations are shown in Figure 16.

It will be noted that the numbers fluctuate with the business cycle. When employment opportunities are good in industry, the farm population declines, only to build up again during periods of depression or reduced industrial activity. It is also to be noted that the long-term trend of the farm population is downward. Only in one or two years since 1920 did the numbers reach the figure for that year, and this was during the depression of the early 1930's. In 1945 farm people numbered a little over

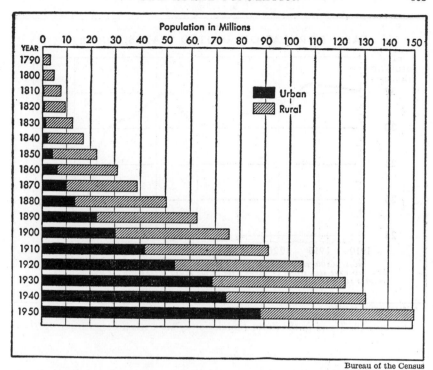

FIGURE 15. *Rural and Urban Proportions of the Population of the United States at Census Periods from 1790 to 1950*

25,000,000, although they produced about a third more than before World War II. After the war the number increased again to an estimated 28,258,000, about 2,000,000 fewer than in 1940. In 1952 the farm population numbered 24,819,000.

**Reasons for decline in the farm population.** Perhaps the main reason the farm population is smaller today in actual numbers than it was a quarter century ago is that technological efficiency has greatly increased. These advances are of several kinds. Those of a *mechanical* nature are most noticeable and no doubt are of greatest importance. The most important single implement introduced into agriculture in this generation has been the gasoline tractor. It has been improved over the years, reduced in cost, and adapted in size to farms of various sorts. In 1953 there were 4,400,000 tractors on farms of the United States, compared with 920,021 in 1930. While 46.9 per cent

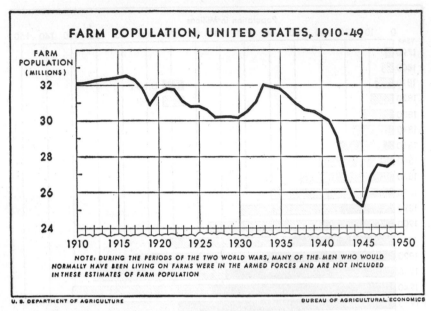

FIGURE 16. *Trend in the Farm Population of the United States Since 1910*

of the farms reported tractors in 1950, only 13.5 per cent did so in 1930. The steady increase in tractors has reduced the horse and mule population accordingly and thus released for human food production additional acres which formerly produced feed for livestock. With the tractor are associated many other machines which *save* human labor: the gang plow, the multiple-row cultivators, the combine harvesters, the two-row corn-picker, and many others now replace scores of thousands of laborers formerly required in agriculture. Practically all crops are yielding to mechanization. A practical sugar-beet harvester which lifts, tops, and loads beets in one operation is now in use. Even cotton, which has been difficult to mechanize, has been conquered. Under the old methods of cotton culture, 160 man hours of labor were required to produce an individual bale. By mechanizing as completely as possible with existing equipment—including the mechanical picker, tractor, multiple-row cultivators, rotary hoe, and flame cultivation —it is now possible to produce a bale of cotton with 20 to

35 hours of man labor, or as little as one eighth of the labor formerly required.[3]

There are also the technical improvements of a nonmechanical nature. The development of higher yielding breeds of livestock and crop varieties, and methods of controlling insects and plant diseases, belong in this class.

The market for agricultural products abroad has had something to do with the trend in farm population also. Since World War I, the foreign market for American agricultural goods has declined because of the increased self-sufficiency of other countries, promoted by the war itself and later by the military leaders as a measure of preparing for the "next war."

The domestic prosperity invoked by World War II has demonstrated, however, the value of the domestic market when incomes of the nonfarm population are sufficient to enable them to buy the things the farmer produces, though up to the present time, prosperity has not altogether eliminated the dependence of many farmers on the export market. Even the fact of adding over 2.5 million people annually to the population has not relieved the pressure on the market of the phenomenal production of the farms. The increase in efficiency on the farms is thus far more rapid than is the increase in population. The immediate outlook, therefore, is for a continued decline in the population on farms, provided always that employment in nonfarm work is at a sufficiently high level to absorb the surplus.

**The rural-nonfarm trend.** The rural-nonfarm population in 1920 was 20,047,000; in 1930 it was 23,663,000; and in 1940 it was 27,095,000. In 1950 the nonfarm population figure was 36,693,358. Thus the center of gravity of the rural population shifted from the farm to the nonfarm segment. From 1940 to 1950 there was a remarkable increase in the population of places from 1,000 to 2,499. Even with the farm population declining, that of the trade centers was strangely increasing. For the nation as a whole, the growth of the rural-nonfarm population is partly due to the growth of the urban fringe, but the fact remains that strictly rural trade centers have also increased. The explanation for this unusual trend requires

[3] Grady B. Crowe, "Farm Mechanization Research in the South," *Agricultural Economics Research*, Vol. III, No. 1, p. 6 (Jan. 1951).

further study, but the following hypotheses are justifiable:
(1) The unparalleled prosperity of agriculture during the decade
along with the rapid mechanization and electrification of farms
created a demand for more services in the villages; (2) the expansion of government services with Federal and State personnel
located in county seat towns; (3) increased number of persons
retiring from farms; and (4) expansion in local industries through
local initiative or through decentralization, or both. The important fact is that farm people are for the first time outnumbered
by their nonfarm neighbors.

### POPULATION VITALITY

In spite of the marked growth of the world population during
the past century and a half, there appears to have been a steady
downward trend in the birth rate. The seeming paradox in
this statement is accounted for by the fact that the death
rate has also declined, so that the *natural increase*—the excess
of births over deaths—has either not declined or has actually
increased. In the United States where birth statistics are available only since 1915, the records show a decline from a rate of
25 per 1,000 in 1915 to 17.3 in 1939. Since 1939 the rate has
risen, reaching 24.6 in 1952. Deaths have also declined, so that
the natural increase is much greater since 1940 than earlier.

The vitality of a population is also measured by the *fertility
ratio*, or the number of children under five years of age per
1,000 women between the ages of 20 and 44 (sometimes the age
used is from 15 to 44). The advantage of using the fertility
ratio is that it makes possible comparisons of trends over a
long period of time—as long in fact as we have census information — as to age and sex distribution of the population. Thus
O. E. Baker,[4] using census data since 1880 and the estimates of
Walter Willcox for decades prior to that time, has indicated
the fertility ratio of the United States population has declined
from 976 children under 5 per 1,000 women 16 to 44 years of
age in 1800, to 479 in 1950. (See Figure 17.)

This decline has been due to many causes. Among the factors
which appear to be associated with the fertility of the population

---

[4] See O. E. Baker, Ralph Borsodi, and M. L. Wilson, *Agriculture in Modern Life*,
p. 118. New York: Harper and Brothers, 1939.

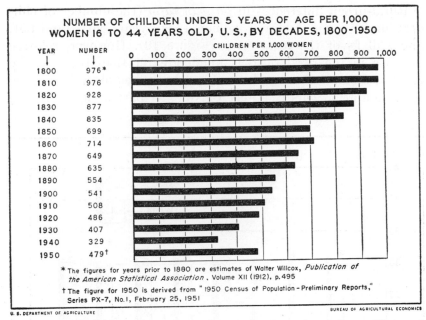

NUMBER OF CHILDREN UNDER 5 YEARS OF AGE PER 1,000
WOMEN 16 TO 44 YEARS OLD, U. S., BY DECADES, 1800-1950

| YEAR | NUMBER |
|------|--------|
| 1800 | 976* |
| 1810 | 976 |
| 1820 | 928 |
| 1830 | 877 |
| 1840 | 835 |
| 1850 | 699 |
| 1860 | 714 |
| 1870 | 649 |
| 1880 | 635 |
| 1890 | 554 |
| 1900 | 541 |
| 1910 | 508 |
| 1920 | 486 |
| 1930 | 407 |
| 1940 | 329 |
| 1950 | 479† |

\* The figures for years prior to 1880 are estimates of Walter Willcox, *Publication of the American Statistical Association*, Volume XII (1912), p. 495

† The figure for 1950 is derived from "1950 Census of Population - Preliminary Reports," Series PX-7, No. I, February 25, 1951

U. S. DEPARTMENT OF AGRICULTURE                    BUREAU OF AGRICULTURAL ECONOMICS

FIGURE 17. *Trend Since 1800 in Vitality of United States Population as Measured by Ratio of Children Under 5 to Each 1,000 Women 16 to 44 Years of Age*

are the following: (*a*) rural-urban residence; (*b*) income and level of living; (*c*) occupation and social class; (*d*) religion; and (*e*) public policies.

**Rural-urban differences.** The rural-urban differences in fertility are shown in Figures 18, 19, and 20. Comparisons are also shown for race by residence and size of place. The urban population has a slightly higher birth rate than the rural according to data in Figure 18. Correction for registration error tends to reverse these figures. Despite this, there is little doubt now that the differences in fertility between rural and urban populations which have been so marked in the past are gradually disappearing. The next point to note is the marked superiority of the non-white rate for all places. Formerly, the Negro race has shown a lower rate in large centers. The dramatic events which took place following 1940 and especially the upheaval during and following World War II have had such impact upon the population as to make any predictions as to future trends very difficult.

Rural-urban differences in *fertility ratio* (the number of children under 5 per thousand women 15–49 years old) stand out, and still favor the rural farm (Figure 19). However, relative increase in the rural ratio is much greater than that for the rural farm, and a spectacular increase has taken place among the rural nonfarm. This last may be due, in part at least, to the

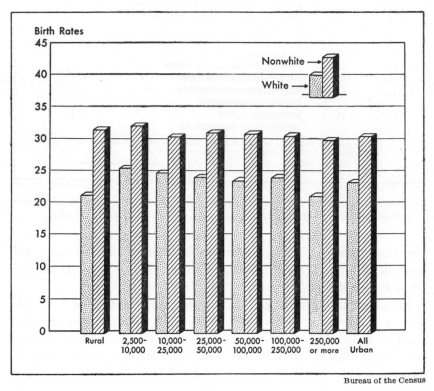

Bureau of the Census

FIGURE 18. *Comparative Birth Rates, White and Nonwhite, by Size of Place, 1950*

growth of the suburban fringe. Such a reversal of a long time trend gives rise to much speculation. Even a decade ago students of population forecast a "plateau" for the United States, that is, a stationary level, to be reached possibly by 1965. When the birth rate rose rapidly during the 1940's it was predicted that it would fall once the large number of war marriages and first and second births had taken place. That this was plausible is suggested by Figure 17 and also by the implications of Figure 20. The downward trend of the fertility ratio has been almost constant since 1800. The special study of human fertility made from the 1940 census showed the extremely high fertility of earlier years; that is, of the women aged 50 to 74 in 1940, who had had their families in the early decades of the century.

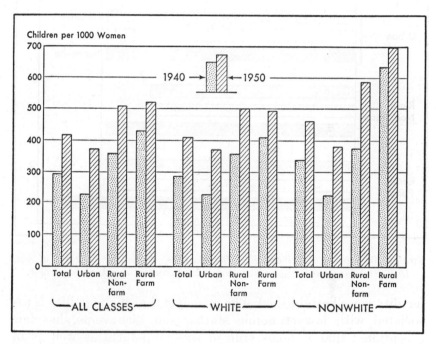

FIGURE 19. *Ratio of Children Under 5 per 1,000 Women Aged 15–49 by Rural and Urban Areas by Color, 1940 and 1950*

In those days, the rural-farm population was indeed the "seed bed" of the nation. It now appears to be taking a back seat, giving place to the ex-service group. The United States birth rate did not decline even after the marriage rate did (about 1950), but continued high to the middle 1950's. This can mean only one thing: the rate is being maintained by second, third, and subsequent births. Truly, the children born in the Quonsets and the "prefabs" have more siblings than their parents.

**Economic status.** The relationship of economic status and

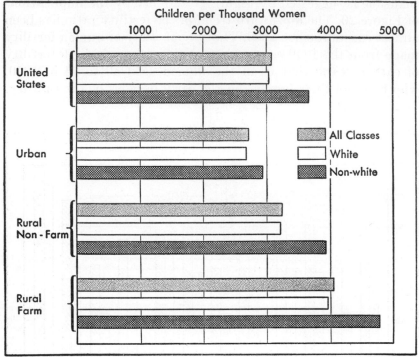

Bureau of the Census

FIGURE 20. *Number of Children Ever Born to 1,000 Women 50–74 Years of Age, 1940.* Standardized for age and marital status, urban, rural, and by color.

fertility is well established. The principle that high fertility is associated with low economic status, and vice versa, has few exceptions; that it holds true in the rural farm as well as in the urban population, is attested by census data (Figure 21) giving fertility ratios by class of farm. Commercial farms are classified on the basis of the value of products sold, from Classes I and II, having $10,000 or more, on down to Class VI with from $250 to $1,200. Note the inverse relation to fertility ratio.

**Religion.** The association of religion with the vitality of the population is clearly demonstrated in but a few studies. G. W. Hill and H. T. Christensen found that the average number of children per family differed as between Lutherans and Catholics in the State of Wisconsin. Catholics had larger families than Lutherans, on the average, although the difference was more marked in those families classified as having high economic

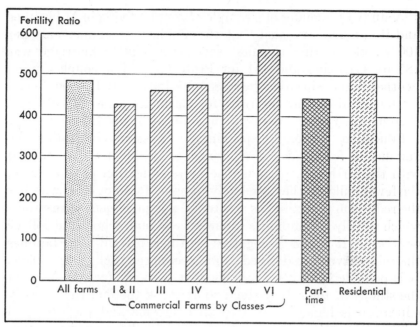

FIGURE 21. *Fertility Ratio by Economic Class of Farms, United States, 1950 (Standardized for Age and Marital Status)*

status.[5] Among those of low economic status the difference was small. Perhaps the most conspicuous demonstration of the role of religion in influencing population growth is found in the case of the Mormons in Utah and adjacent states. W. A. DeHart made a careful study of this group and found a high correlation between fertility ratio and the per cent of the population by counties which were Mormon. When the factors of level of living and urban percentage of the population were held constant, the result was a higher correlation coefficient between the proportion of the population which was Mormon and the fertility ratio.[6] Thus it was clearly demonstrated that religious affiliation was the dominant factor accounting for the differences in fertility.

[5] George W. Hill and Harold T. Christensen, "Some Factors in Family Fertility Among Selected Wisconsin Farmers," *American Sociological Review*, 1942, 7:498–503, p. 501.

[6] William A. DeHart, "The Relation of Religious Affiliation to Population Fertility in Utah and Selected Counties in Adjacent States," M.S. thesis, University of Minnesota, 1941. Also, "Fertility of Mormons in Utah and Adjacent States," *American Sociological Review*, 1941, 6:818–829.

A study by Stouffer of a sample of couples living in Milwaukee and its suburbs revealed that the number of confinements per 100 couples during the first seven years after marriage was 185 for Catholics and 151 for Protestants. For couples living in other Wisconsin cities the rates were 193 and 164, respectively. He found, also, that the rates for Catholics between 1919 and 1926 declined more rapidly than those for Protestants.[7]

**Education.** Generally speaking, in western civilization the amount of formal schooling tends to be inversely associated with the birth rate; that is, the more education parents have, the fewer children they are likely to have. It is not clear whether the reduction in fertility is due to the postponement of marriage which usually accompanies attendance at high school and college or whether it is due to negative attitudes toward large families that may have been derived from experience in school or college. It is possible and even probable that both are factors. Most of the studies of the subject tend to overlook the fact that usually education is highly correlated with income and the observed relationship with fertility may be due to the economic rather than the educational factor.

However, in a study of fertility rates in Kentucky, Merton D. Oyler tested the influence of education by holding constant the factor of income. It turned out that the coefficient of correlation between fertility and education was − .262, which, while not highly significant, no doubt justifies Oyler's conclusion that "high-school attendance, independently of income and communication with which it is so closely associated, has a depressing effect on the specific birth rates of age-groups that have attended high school." [8]

The United States census of 1940 provided some additional data on the subject. The native white women between the ages of 15 and 49 were classified according to several characteristics: amount of education received, whether they resided in rural or urban areas, and the number of children under 5 years of age per 1,000 women. The relation between education and

    [7] Samuel A. Stouffer, "Trends in the Fertility of Catholics and non-Catholics," *American Journal of Sociology*, 1935, 41:143–167, p. 153.
    [8] Merton D. Oyler, "Fertility Rates and Migration of Kentucky Population 1920 to 1940, As Related to Communication, Income, and Education," *University of Kentucky AES Bulletin 469*, November, 1944, pp. 19–20.

fertility was found to be inverse. With only one exception, the women who had no schooling had more children than those who had various amounts of schooling. The exception was among the rural-farm population. Those with from one to four grades of schooling had 716 children per 1,000, while those with no schooling had 713. (See Table 7.) The Table reveals the

TABLE 7. *Fertility Ratio of Native White Women 15–49 in United States Based on Years of Schooling They Received*

| Schooling Completed | Average | Urban | Rural-Nonfarm | Rural-Farm |
|---|---|---|---|---|
| No Schooling | 607 | 477 | 650 | 713 |
| Grades: | | | | |
| 1 to 4 | 612 | 422 | 679 | 716 |
| 5 to 6 | 554 | 411 | 614 | 676 |
| 7 to 8 | 473 | 379 | 536 | 598 |
| High School: | | | | |
| 1 to 3 | 504 | 445 | 561 | 624 |
| 4 | 452 | 399 | 514 | 610 |
| College: | | | | |
| 1 to 3 | 404 | 365 | 430 | 519 |
| 4 or more | 386 | 374 | 415 | 417 |

Source: Sixteenth Census of the United States, *Population: Differential Fertility, Women by Number of Children Under Five Years Old, 1940.*

rural-urban differentials discussed previously. It is interesting to observe also that there was a greater difference between the fertility of the high and low educational groups in the rural-farm population than in either of the other groups. This suggests the possibility that the further diffusion of high school and college learning among the rural-farm population may be a very important depressing factor in the future increase of the farm population. These figures are not to be accepted uncritically as being more than indicative of the relationship. For one thing, income is not controlled. For another, the age of the women is not held constant. Doubtless, more older women are represented in the groups with little or no schooling and more younger women in the better educated groups. The duration of marriage, in other words, has no doubt been much longer for those with little or no schooling.

Some interesting exceptions may be noted to the general rule that the amount of formal schooling tends to depress the birth rate. One of them occurs in China. J. B. Griffing, in a study of education and size of family in China, discovered a positive correlation existed: the more educated parents had larger families.[9] In a study of 428 completed families (families in which the mother had reached the age of 45) residing in two Utah communities, it was found that there was no relationship between the number of children ever born to these couples and the amount of formal schooling of the parents.[10]

In both of these groups there are factors of greater importance influencing the birth rate. For the Utah group it is definitely a matter of religion; and, although statistical demonstration is not available, the same factor may be supposed as a determining one in China.

**Public policies.** It is not too clear that public policies play more than a minor role in connection with the vital trends in the population. The family-building policies introduced by the Nazi Party in Germany appear to have had a definite and immediate result in increasing the birth rate. On the other hand, similar policies introduced in Italy by the Fascists had no such spectacular results. That they may prove effective when other factors are favorable, is likely. The term "family-building policies" refers to the subsidies of one kind or another which are provided by the government for those who undertake the responsibilities of parenthood. For example, the German government under the Nazis provided a marriage loan of 400 marks to a couple; it could be retired by having a specified number of children. In Italy special concessions on rentals were made to families in proportion to the number of children. Other kinds of policies are those which prohibit or promote the dissemination of information regarding birth control techniques, and such indirect measures as the providing of social, health, and educational services at public expense.

## AGE AND SEX COMPOSITION

Having considered the general course of population growth in the United States and the evidence for associating certain

---

[9] J. B. Griffing, "Education and Size of Family in China," *Journal of Heredity*, 1926, 17:331–337.

[10] Lowry Nelson and N. I. Butt, "Education and Size of Family," *Journal of Heredity*, 1928, 19:327–330, p. 330.

socio-economic factors with its growth, we should next consider the age and sex composition as revealed in recent census enumerations. The significance to any society of the changes in age composition is very great. A population characterized by a high birth rate, and consequently a large child population, must invest heavily in schools, children's clothing, toys, books, and equipment, as well as pediatricians, who would be numerous and busy. On the other hand, a society which has a large proportion of aged people must spend heavily for homes for the aged, old-age pensions, hospitals, wheel chairs, and the like. It is important for governmental bodies, such as welfare and educational boards, to know the trend in age composition of the population, in order to make plans to meet the needs of the respective groups.

The proportion of the sexes in the population also has important social consequences. Where there is a disproportion of one or the other, the normal opportunities for marriage are reduced for the majority group. For example, in the rural population of the United States there is a 12 per cent excess of men, while in the urban population there is a 4 per cent excess of women. Considering the total population in 1940 the sexes were about equal in numbers for the first time in the nation's history. In the past, the males have outnumbered the females because of the fact that emigrants from the Old World were predominantly men.

The most useful way of indicating the age composition of a population is by means of the age pyramid. (See Figure 22.) In this manner it is possible to see at a glance the proportionate numbers in each five-year group. In a new country the tendency is for the birth rate to be relatively high, with proportionately fewer persons in the upper ages. In other words, the true pyramid or cone shape is observed. However, the older populations tend to fatten out in the center and towards the top, and to become narrower at the bottom, assuming more the shape of a beehive than a true pyramid. A comparison of the pyramids of the United States population for 1900 and 1940 will readily reveal this difference.

Perhaps the most important fact demonstrated by the United States census of 1930 was that the age group under five years

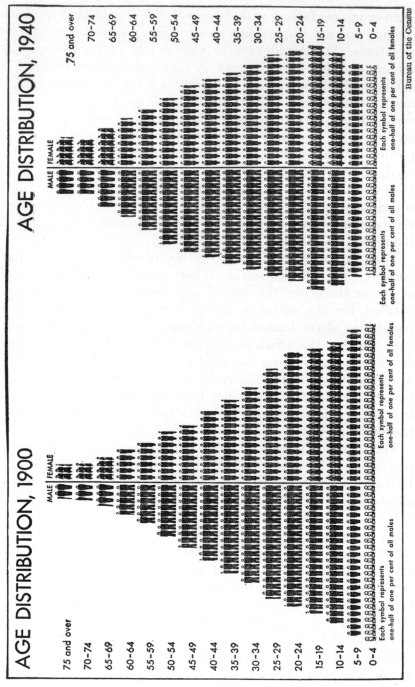

FIGURE 22. *Comparison of Age-Sex Pyramids of United States Population for 1900 and 1940*

was smaller than the group from five to nine years. It was the first time such a situation had come about, foreshadowing far-reaching changes in the "shape" of the population, which in turn have had repercussions throughout community life. From 1935 to 1947 thousands of school desks were placed in storage and many schools closed for lack of pupils. Increased births after 1941 have increased demands on school facilities.

These age characteristics are by no means uniform throughout all segments of the population. There are notable differences, especially between rural and urban groups. The pyramids for the urban, rural-nonfarm and rural-farm groups reveal these points of difference: (a) the urban population contains a higher proportion of people in the age group between 20 and 65 years of age; (b) in the age group 65 and over, urban and rural-farm groups are about equal, while the rural-nonfarm exceeds all others; (c) the rural-farm population contains a greater proportion of persons under 20 years of age than either of the other groups.

The population is growing older. In 1930 only 5.5 per cent of all persons were 65 years or older, while in 1950, 8.2 per cent were in this group. The number in proportion to the total is steadily growing. The significance of the aging of the population is widely recognized. The development of social security plans for the care of the aged, the increasing emphasis on the medical problems of the aged (geriatrics), the employment problems raised by the increasing proportions of the population in the working ages—are some of the social problems created by the changing age composition. (See Figure 23.)

The age pyramids as shown by the five-year groups reveal the differences between the rural and urban population segments. Although the characteristics of the three population groups are as stated above, the differences among them are much less pronounced than they have been in earlier decades, a further indication of the fact that rural and urban people are becoming progressively more alike.

The sex ratios of the various segments of the population are shown in Figure 24. During the decade of the 1930's the farm population increased in the number of males per 100 females, while all other segments of the population—as well as the total

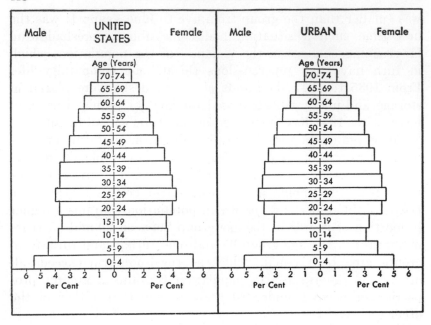

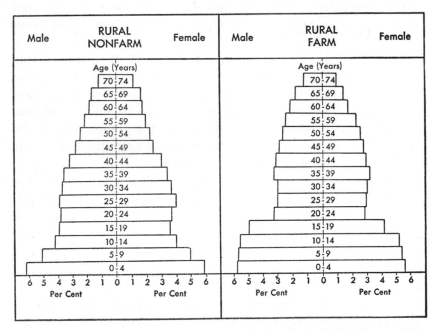

FIGURE 23. *Age-Sex Pyramids for the Population of the United States, 1950*

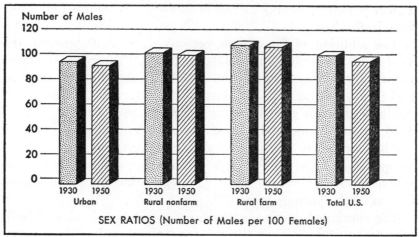

FIGURE 24. *Sex Ratios of Rural and Urban Population, 1940 and 1950*

—declined. The growing disparity in sex ratios of rural farm and nonfarm populations is the result of the excessive migration of women from the farms.

### DISTRIBUTION OF THE RURAL POPULATION

In the United States the rural-farm population is heavily concentrated in the sixteen southern states; in 1940 they contained 53.7 per cent of the total. However, of the rural-nonfarm population the same states contained only 37 per cent. The Northern states, including New England, the Middle Atlantic states, and the Middle West, contained 39.5 per cent of the rural-farm population and slightly over half of the rural-nonfarm. The fifteen western states claimed nearly 8 per cent of the rural-farm and 13 per cent of the rural-nonfarm. The figures for the rural-farm population were approximately the same in 1950. In fact there has been small change in the proportions in the three great rural regions since 1930. In 1950 the rural-farm population was distributed as follows: South, 51.6 (a slight decrease); North, 40; and West, 8.4 per cent. The 1950 distribution of the rural-nonfarm by percentages was South, 39.6; North, 47.6; and West, 12.8. In this group, the South gained a little, the North lost, and the West remained the same.

Urban populations also increased more in the South and West than in the North.

The addition of 20 million persons since 1940 brought the United States population to 150,697,000 in 1950. Since the farm population declined during the decade by 2 million, the urban and rural-nonfarm segments increased by 22 million. The rural-nonfarm group is growing more rapidly than the urban, and in 1950 exceeded in size the farm population for the first time in our history. There are very important differences in sex and age composition of the three groups—rural-farm, rural-nonfarm, and urban. These differences have significance for the social organization of the various areas.

The continued decline in the farm population is viewed both with favor and disfavor. From an economic point of view the transfer of unused manpower out of agriculture to other work adds to the total production of the country, and therefore makes possible improved levels of living not only for those who move but for those who remain. Some advocate the transfer of several additional million of workers out of agriculture. On the other hand, the continued increase in the size of farms as population declines raises serious questions of a social nature. How far should the concentration of land ownership be allowed to go? Is the family farm in danger? Should it be preserved in the face of competition of large-scale agriculture? In short, what kind of rural life do we want in the future?

## QUESTIONS FOR DISCUSSION

1. Highly significant changes have taken place in the world's population since 1800. Discuss these changes. Has there been a significant change in the amount of interest shown in population problems during the same period? Discuss.

2. What is the relationship between a growing population and (1) land values, (2) social stratification, (3) social contacts?

3. Review the changes that have taken place in the proportionate and absolute growth of rural and urban populations in this country since 1790.

4. How is the size of the farm population related to the business cycle? Discuss this relationship with reference to the periods of prosperity and depression since 1920.

5. Cite evidence to show that the increased use of machines in agriculture has resulted in the partial depopulation of farming areas. What

are the probable future trends in the size of the farm population? Would you regard these trends as a cause for alarm?

6. How has the rural-nonfarm differed from the rural-farm population growth trend since 1920?

7. Define and explain the social significance of *natural increase* and the *fertility ratio*. How does the *fertility ratio* differ from the *net reproduction rate?*

8. Discuss and evaluate the importance that may be attached to the present differential fertility of the urban, rural-nonfarm, and farm populations.

9. What evidence is there that church affiliation and education have a bearing on the fertility of a group? Have governmental policies been very effective in changing fertility trends? Discuss.

10. What are the possible social consequences of (1) an aging, and (2) a declining population?

## SELECTED REFERENCES

Landis, Paul H., and Hatt, Paul K. *Population Problems: A Cultural Interpretation*, Chapters 5 and 8. New York: American Book Co., 1954.

Nelson, Lowry. *American Farm Life in the Twentieth Century*, Chapter 3. Cambridge, Mass.: Harvard University Press, 1954.

—————— "Education and the Changing Size of Mormon Families." *Rural Sociology*, 17:335–342. Report of a restudy of families in two Utah villages 25 years after the first study mentioned on page 114.

Thompson, Warren. *Population Problems*, Fourth Edition, Chapters 6 and 15. New York: McGraw-Hill Book Co., 1953.

United States Bureau of the Census. *Differential Fertility, 1940 and 1910.* A series of four reports as follows: "Fertility by States and Large Cities"; "Standardized Fertility Rates and Reproduction Rates"; "Women by Number of Children Under 5 Years Old"; and "Women by Number of Children Ever Born."

Whelpton, P. K., and Kiser, Clyde V. *Social and Psychological Factors Affecting Fertility*. New York: Milbank Memorial Fund. Vols. I and II, 1946, 1950.

## CHAPTER 7

## MIGRATION OF THE RURAL POPULATION

There are two types of social mobility: horizontal, and vertical. Horizontal mobility refers to the movement of persons from one place to another and is ordinarily comprehended under the familiar term *migration*, the subject of this chapter. Vertical mobility refers to the movement from one social status to another, such as from occupation to occupation. Although the two forms of mobility are related, it is most convenient to discuss migration in a general treatment of population and to reserve discussion of vertical mobility for a later section dealing with social processes.

Fundamentally, migration is a change of location of a person or a group in physical space. Ordinarily, not all such changes in location are regarded as migrations. Migration does not include the following sorts of movement: (1) the diurnal routine movements of individuals, such as going from home to place of work; (2) the occasional trips to and from other communities or localities, such as the vacation trip or the Saturday night trip of the farm family to town; (3) change of domicile from one section of a community to another.

On the other hand, migration *does* include the permanent change of residence from one country, state, community or farm to another; or the seasonal movements of people in pursuit of an occupation, such as the "streams" of migratory agricultural workers in the United States. C. E. Lively classifies the movements of people into three categories: "(1) circulation from a fixed domicile; (2) movement of domicile; and (3) transiency." [1] Most of the discussion to follow refers to the second

[1] C. E. Lively, "Spatial and Occupational Changes of Particular Significance to the Student of Population Mobility," *Social Forces*, 1937, 15:351–355, p. 351. See also T. Lynn Smith, "Characteristics of Migrants," *The Southwestern Social Science Quarterly*, 1941, 21:335–350.

type of movement, namely, change of domicile. Beyond these general qualifications, precise definition of migration is difficult, and there is no common agreement among students of the subject on several points. Some of the difficulties of definition become apparent when one considers the questions raised by R. B. Dixon's definition of migration as "the movements of people over *considerable* distances and on a *large* scale with the *intention* of abandoning their former homes for some *more or less* permanent new domicile. . . . "[2] Such a definition, while conveying a general meaning, requires a great deal of refinement for technical use, chiefly by the substitution of more precise terms for those which are in italics. All students of migration have encountered the difficulty of definition, but controversies over technical details need not concern us further in this general survey of the problem.

**Social significance of migration.** The sociologist is interested in migration for the following reasons: (1) it is the means by which the individual finds, or attempts to find, a better adjustment in the social and economic order; (2) it is the means of correcting the unbalance between population and the natural resources; (3) by disturbing the age and sex composition of a particular segment of the population, it affects marriage rates and marriage opportunities; (4) it breaks the social bonds and institutional ties of the *individual*, and therefore influences the church, the school, and other institutions and agencies; (5) it affects the economic order because the movement of individuals involves the movement of economic goods.

FACTORS WHICH INFLUENCE MIGRATION

Numerous factors, singly and in combination, cause, determine, or influence migration. It is important to know the basis of migrations to account for their particular characteristics and their differential effects. Some writers have attempted to classify the factors in migration under two headings: namely, those that tend to *push* and those that *pull*.[3] The push factors, obviously,

---

[2] Roland B. Dixon, "Migrations: Primitive," *Encyclopedia of the Social Sciences*, Vol. 10, p. 420. (Italics are used by Lowry Nelson.)

[3] Or, as Paul H. Landis calls them, forces of "attraction" and "compulsion," in *Rural Life in Process*, p. 191. New York: McGraw-Hill Book Co., 1940.

are those at work in the area of *origin*, while the pull factors are active in the points of *destination*. While this classification is a useful one, it should be fully understood that seldom is either set of factors working independently of the others. Moreover, as will be shown presently, it is difficult to classify some factors as either one or the other in this two-fold plan.

### PUSH FACTORS

**Natural increase.** A high rate of increase in the population of an area is likely to promote outward migration, provided there is not a corresponding increase in the resources. Such a situation creates *population pressure* and while migration may not *necessarily* result, it sets up a favorable condition for it. One expression of this factor—in combination with certain pull factors—is found in the migration from the farm population to cities and towns and in the migration of people from such areas of high natural increase as the southern states and Utah.

**Depletion or exhaustion of resources.** This has special significance in those areas where communities are based upon the mining of ore or the harvesting of the virgin timber crop. When these resources are depleted or exhausted, the population is stranded and must find alternative forms of employment in the area or migrate from it. Land exhaustion is also a basis for forced migration. An excellent example is found in the Near East, where areas which once supported relatively large populations now contain little more than the ruins of the once flourishing communities. The reason for decline has been assigned to soil exhaustion.[4] (See pictures following page 128.)

**Climatic fluctuations.** Periodic droughts and floods are familiar factors which induce migrations of people. Huntington goes so far as to account for the migration of man from his primitive home in Asia to the lands of Europe by proposing as cause the climatic fluctuations in the primitive homeland.[5] But more recent examples are close at hand. During the severest droughts on record in the United States, during the decade of the 1930's, migrations of farm people from the Great Plains took place on

[4] W. C. Lowdermilk, *Palestine, Land of Promise.* New York: Harper and Brothers, 1944.

[5] Ellsworth Huntington, *The Pulse of Asia.* New York: Houghton Mifflin Company, 1907.

a large scale. The only states which actually lost population from 1930 to 1940 were those located in the area most acutely affected by droughts.

**Social maladjustment.** Finally, among the push factors must be mentioned those acute social maladjustments which occur from time to time throughout the world. The settlement of New England in 1620 was an example of the working of this factor. The Pilgrims were in a state of conflict, religious and political, with society in England. They migrated first to Holland and later to the New World. The migration of the Mennonites from Germany to Russia and then to the United States and other countries is another case in point. One of the most dramatic migrations in the history of the United States was that of the Mormons from Nauvoo, Illinois, to the Great Salt Lake valley in 1847, as a result of conflict with their neighbors.

PULL FACTORS

**Discovery and development of new resources.** The settlement of the United States by European peoples during the past three hundred years is a prime example of the role of this factor. The availability of a vast area of fertile land in a suitable climate set up one of the largest migrations in history. Discovery of gold in California and in Alaska also set in motion spectacular migrations of people from all parts of the world.

**New inventions and the industries built from them.** The classic example of the role of this factor is the invention of steam and the rise in England of the factory system, which in turn provided jobs in the cities in which the factories were located. Similarly, in the United States during the decade of the 1920's the rapid expansion of the industrial cities, based particularly on the manufacture of automobiles and electrical goods, attracted migrants in great numbers from the rural sections of the country.

**A favorable climate.** The heavy influx of population to California and Florida from other parts of the United States has been the result of their favorable climatic conditions: individuals have sought the areas because of health, old age, and a general desire to escape from more rigorous climatic zones.

OTHER FACTORS

It is not possible to classify all the factors into the two categories of "push" and "pull" without some qualification. *Technological changes* may act as a push as well as a pull factor. While, as indicated above, the expansion of the automobile industry acted as an attractive force to migrants from rural areas, the technical changes in agriculture itself operated as a push factor on the rural migrant. The introduction of the tractor and related implements, the development of new and higher yielding varieties of crops and breeds of livestock, improved methods of managing farms—all tend to reduce the amount of labor required in agriculture. Technological improvements in agriculture tend to create a surplus population on the land, which cannot be effectively and profitably employed there; they therefore seek opportunity elsewhere. (See Figures 25 and 26.)

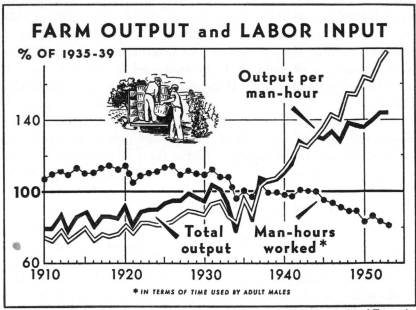

U.S. Department of Agriculture                    Bureau of Agricultural Economics

FIGURE 25. *Trend in Farm Output, Man-Hours Worked, and Production per Man-Hour Since 1910*

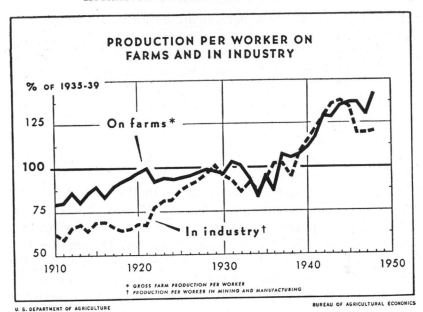

U. S. DEPARTMENT OF AGRICULTURE      BUREAU OF AGRICULTURAL ECONOMICS

FIGURE 26. *Production per Worker, Agricultural and Industrial, United States, Since 1910*

Also, *changes in the market place* may result from lowered demand for products of one region and increased demand for those of another, and thereby set the stage for migration between regions. *Public policies* constitute another factor which influences the redistribution of the population. The AAA acreage reduction program in the 1930's resulted in the displacement of many tenant farmers, many of whom migrated to the Pacific Coast. Settlement laws of the various states, which require several years residence in order to attain eligibility for relief, are designed to deter the indigent from migrating from one state to another. Differentials in the liberality of relief or public assistance benefits may influence migration to some extent.

Finally, there are many *personal factors* which influence migration. Farmers retire and move to town or to a warmer climate because of some reason of health in a great many cases. Others move because they want to provide their families with better social services, education, or other opportunities. There is a strong probability, too, that migration with many people is a *social habit*. It is certainly true of the hobo, who neither has nor wants a permanent domicile; itineracy is his way of life. Besides, it is doubtful whether the large number of moves of tenant farmers is always a matter of deliberate and careful choice of alternatives on their part. Many of them move merely because it is their custom to move every year or two. The story of Thomas Henry Harrison Higginbottom is illustrative of this sort. Moving was apparently no ordeal to him as it often is to many people.

Mr. Higginbottom was interviewed by the Congressional Committee to Investigate the Interstate Migration of Destitute Citizens at its hearings at Los Angeles in 1940. His testimony revealed that during the space of about 25 years in Oklahoma, before he gave up farm operation to join the stream of migratory labor in California, he had made 10 moves. During the first five years he occupied five different farms, spending one year on each. This was during the period before 1920 (dates are not clear in all cases) when agriculture was prosperous. Practically all of his moves were for short distances, except one which was made to Kansas. His longest time on any one farm was 6 years. There is no clear economic or other reason for most of these moves, as the following excerpt from the testimony indicates:

Question: "Well, now, Mr. Higginbottom, how long did you remain there?" (Reference was to Slick, Oklahoma.)

Answer: "We stayed one year."

Question: "Did you make any money there?"

Answer: "Yes; we made a little money. We got ahead. We accumulated a little stuff around us—generally a farmer does—and we moved from there to another farm about 5 miles from there that belonged to a banker. We did extra good there. We hit a good crop.

"From there we moved to Kansas where her folks lived. We had taken—we rented a farm there of about 640 acres. It was mostly in alfalfa and in grass, and raised two or three hundred acres of crop. We stayed one year.

"There was a bunch of wheat growers come in from the West. At that time the war was on pretty good, you know, and so we sold out, sold our stock and went back to Oklahoma. I figured we could do better there; knew our country. We rented a farm down close to Muskogee. We did fairly good. We made a good crop, I guess about the best crop there was in the neighborhood at that time; corn and cotton.

"Then we moved close to Tahlequah, Oklahoma. We stayed there

The mechanical cotton picker (below) can pick about as much cotton in a day as 40 to 60 people can by the hand method (above). The cotton weeder (center) has greatly reduced the cost of weeding per acre.

*The picture below shows how exhausted land may be restored to production through applying fertilizers. Above is a submarginal farm purchased by the Government, to be returned to grazing land.*

on that farm two years and it wasn't large enough, so I moved to another farm and bought a farm at the same time." [6]

Doing well or ill in a place did not seem to have as much to do with Mr. Higginbottom's movement from one farm to another during this period, as did an inexplicable desire to move for the sake of moving.

### SOURCES OF DATA FOR THE STUDY OF MIGRATION

The volume, direction, and characteristics of migration in the United States may be ascertained or estimated in part from the following sources:

(1) *The United States Census of Population*

A. *The birth-residence data.* The census reports the place of birth of each person as well as place of present residence. It is possible to tell from these data how many people living within a state were born in other states or foreign countries and the names of those states or countries of birth; also how many persons born in a particular state are living elsewhere, and the state in which they are living. (See Figures 27 and 28.)

B. *Total population enumerations of areas*—states, counties, townships, etc.—for ten-year intervals, along with the birth and death statistics. By comparing, say, the population of a county in 1930 with that in 1940, and adding the excess of births over deaths, it is possible to compute the total net migration in or out during the decade.

C. *Special census of internal migration from 1935 to 1940.* (See Sixteenth Census of the United States, *Population: Internal Migration 1935 to 1940.*) This volume presents data based upon replies to the question included in the 1940 census: "In what place did you live on April 1, 1935?"

(2) *Special Surveys*

A. *The annual estimates of the farm population.* Based upon a special questionnaire sent annually to a sample of farm people over the United States, the Division of Farm Population and Rural Welfare of the Bureau of Agricultural Economics gives annual estimates of the population as of January 1, the number who left farms for

---

[6] Select Committee to Investigate the Interstate Migration of Destitute Citizens, Los Angeles Hearings, September 20, 1940.

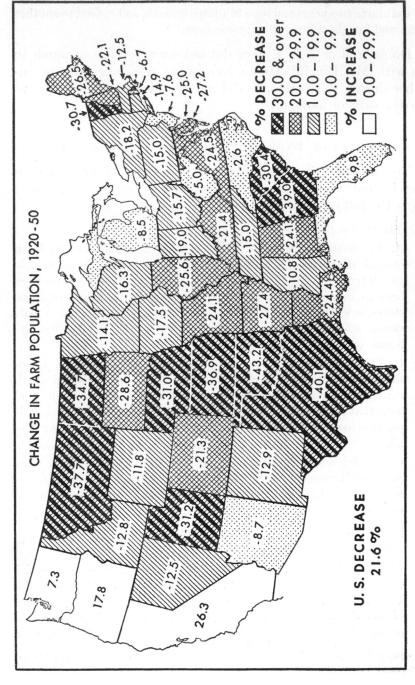

FIGURE 27. *Change in the Farm Population, 1920–1950*

villages, towns, and cities; and the number who came to farms from cities, towns, and villages.

B. *Local studies.* A large number of special studies have been made in various states designed to reveal information on the volume, direction, and characteristics of migrations.

## PATTERNS OF MIGRATION

C. E. Lively has conveniently classified these patterns of migration, so far as the United States is concerned, as follows [7]:

1. The Westward and Eastward migrations
2. The Northward and Southward migrations
3. The rural-urban and urban-rural
4. Migratory labor
5. Transiency
6. Local

**The east-west movement.** The most spectacular population movement in the history of the United States was the movement toward the frontier. Following the Revolutionary War and the establishment of the new nation, the settlement of the western lands went on rapidly. In the space of less than a century practically all of the more suitable agricultural lands were occupied. The migration was composed not only of people from the older American communities along the Atlantic seaboard, but from practically all of the countries of the Old World as well. Everybody, it seemed during this period, was "going West." However, it was not a one-way movement, for migrations are never wholly in one direction. As E. G. Ravenstein puts it in his "laws," "each main current of migration produces a compensating counter current." [8] There was probably a continuous stream of people returning from the frontier throughout the period of early settlement, although the volume was small compared with that moving west. However, the eastward movement has grown steadily in volume. The census provides us the facts in this

---

[7] C. E. Lively, "The Development of Research in Rural Migration in the United States," paper read before the International Population Congress, Paris, July 1937. (mimeo.)

[8] E. G. Ravenstein, "On the Laws of Migration," *Journal of the Royal Statistical Society*, 1885, 48:167–235; and 1889, 52:241–305. See Sorokin, Zimmerman, and Galpin, *A Systematic Source Book in Rural Sociology*, Vol. 3, p. 616.

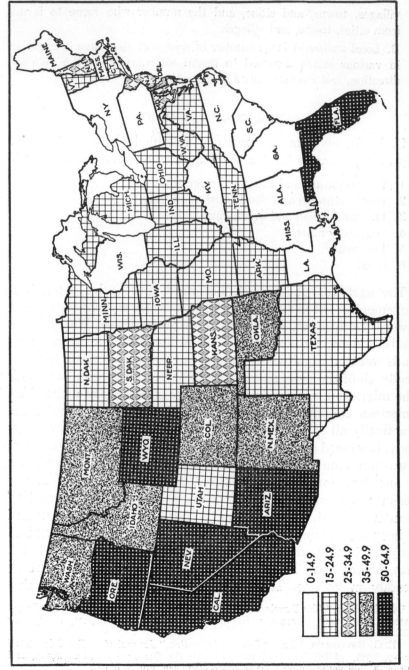

FIGURE 28. *Per Cent of Each State's Population Which Was Born in Other States, 1950*

0-14.9

15-24.9

25-34.9

35-49.9

50-64.9

way: that the number of people born west of the Mississippi River and living east of it increased from 684,000 in 1910 to 2,699,000 in 1950, while the number born east of the river and living west increased only from 5,276,000 to 5,822,000.[9] Clearly, the eastward movement now assumes a volume of great importance. During the 1930's the movement to the West was given new impetus by the drought and the depression, and after 1941, by the war. Previous to these crises the trend had been the other way, with larger volume of migration to the East.

**The south-north migration.** It is an interesting fact that migrations in the United States have been predominantly along the lines of latitude—that is, the east-west direction. The many cultural differences between the South and the North have apparently served as something of a barrier to the interchange of population. During the 1920's, however, the northward movement of population, particularly of Negroes, assumed major proportions. In 1920, there were 780,000 southern-born Negroes in the northern and western states, and in 1950 there were 2,693,125. Negroes migrated from the South in greater proportions to their numbers than did the whites during this period. The movement of whites from South to North, however, was also considerable. There were 4,818,775 persons who were born in the South and living in the North in 1950, compared with the 3,307,070 who were born North and living South. This tends again to show the reciprocal nature of these population movements, although the interchange is not an equal one in numbers. It is more nearly equal for the white population.

**Rural-urban migration.** The movement of people from farms to cities, towns, and villages, and its reciprocal movement, constitute a phenomenon of major social significance. It is a phase of the general process of urbanization. It removes excess population from the land and supplies needed labor for urban industries. From the latter standpoint, it is looked upon as a necessary process in our national economy. On the other hand, those who view with misgiving the urban concentration of the

---

[9] United States Census of Population: 1950. Special Reports: State of Birth. Table 2.

population and the decline, relatively and absolutely, of the farm population, consider the rural exodus as a "menace" to the national welfare. German students have been inclined to speak of the "flight from the land" and the "menace of the rural exodus." "The problem of the rural exodus is surely at present the most urgent social problem of modern agriculture."[10]

The movement of people from farms is of great magnitude in the United States, having risen to its highest peak in the decade from 1940 to 1950. During that period the estimated *net* loss to the farm population amounted to 5.1 million persons. By net loss we mean that there were 5.1 million more persons leaving farms for cities, towns, and villages, than returning to farms from these centers. Actually, according to estimates of the Bureau of Agricultural Economics, there were nearly 9.3 million migrants from farms to nonfarm areas, while the return migration to farms from nonfarm areas amounted to 4,134,000.[11]

The net migration from farms during the 1930's was only about 3½ million, about equal to the natural increase in the farm population during the period. Less than one million of the loss accumulated in the first five years, when the depression was at its worst. (See Figure 29.) In 1932 there was an estimated net migration to farms of 325,000.

It is quite evident that migration from farms is related to the cycle of prosperity and depression. During the prosperous years of the 1920's and 1940's the out-migration of farm people was tremendous. But during the depression years the rate of out-migration was greatly reduced. From 1930 to 1935 the average of 195,000 net migrants from farms was only 30 per cent of the average annual number of 630,000 during the 1920's. During the period from 1935–1939, when urban employment improved somewhat, the average annual net migration from farms reached 550,000.

Counties from which net loss due to migration was heaviest during the 1930's were located chiefly in the Great Plains and

---

[10] See Konrad Meyer, *Proceedings of the International Conference of Agricultural Economists, 1938*, p. 56. London: Oxford University Press, 1939. See also the paper by H. Niehaus in the same volume.

[11] "Farm Population Estimates, Jan., 1949," mimeograph release, Bureau of Agricultural Economics, Washington, D.C., June, 1949.

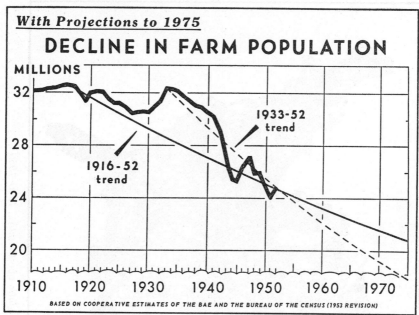

FIGURE 29. *Trend of the Farm Population Since 1910, With Projections to 1975*

in the Southwest where drought was severe during part of the decade. In three fourths of the counties of the nation there was 15 per cent or more out-migration of the rural-farm population. (See Figure 30.) It should be noted that reference is to the loss due to migration "expressed as a percentage of survivors to 1940 of persons living in 1930." [12] Bernert points out that "counties which showed a net loss of rural-farm population through migration at a rate greater than the national average were most heavily concentrated in the states of the West North Central Division and the three Southern Divisions. ... "[13]

Counties showing losses smaller than the national average, according to this analysis, or with actual gains from migration, were located in the predominantly urban counties and states.

[12] Eleanor H. Bernert, "County Variation in Net Migration From the Rural-Farm Population, 1930–40," Bureau of Agricultural Economics, December, 1944. (mimeo.)
[13] *Ibid.*, p. 2.

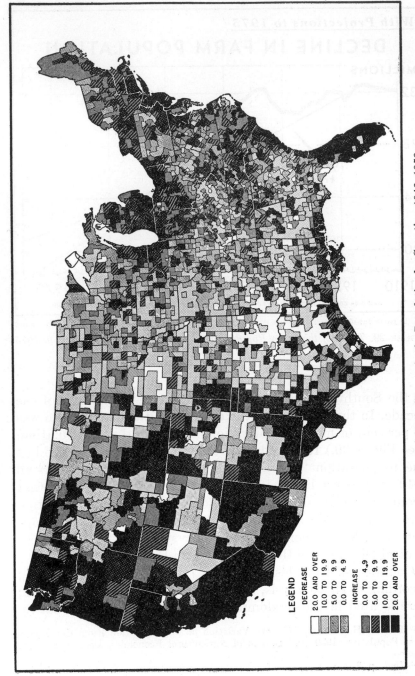

FIGURE 30. *Per Cent Change in the Population by Counties, 1940–1950*

LEGEND

DECREASE
20.0 AND OVER
10.0 TO 19.9
5.0 TO 9.9
0.0 TO 4.9

INCREASE
0.0 TO 4.9
5.0 TO 9.9
10.0 TO 19.9
20.0 AND OVER

This is no doubt a reflection of the suburban trend in these areas. People who build homes on small tracts adjacent to urban centers where they find part-time employment are classified in the farm population.

This migration is, therefore, rather large in volume; it fluctuates with the changes in the prosperity of urban centers; its origin has been predominantly in the South and Great Plains areas.

**Migratory labor in agriculture.** The labor needs of the agricultural enterprise fluctuate widely with the seasons. During the planting and early care of crops and again when the harvest takes place, the demand for labor reaches its peaks. These extraordinary demands occur largely in the areas devoted to specialized crop production, including the wheat, cotton, and fruit and vegetable areas. There was a time before mechanization of the wheat harvest when the demand for harvest hands from the "outside" amounted to upwards of 200,000 or more. There was a heavy seasonal migration from South to North as the crop ripened. But now most of the seasonal labor is recruited from nearby areas, from towns and villages, and from other farms. The total seasonal demand for extra labor in the United States, according to W. T. Ham, ranges between one and two million persons for the entire country.[14]

The number of these workers who are *migratory* is not known. Several local estimates for various parts of the country have been summarized by the Select Committee to Investigate the Interstate Migration of Destitute Citizens as follows: "In the Pacific Northwest, about 75,000; in California, 200,000; in Arizona, for cotton alone, 30,000; in New Mexico, 8,000; in Texas, 325,000; in the Mississippi Valley berry and truck regions, 30,000; in Florida, 60,000; in New Jersey, about 9,000; in the beet field areas throughout the country, 93,000." [15] The report points out that these estimates are only for certain areas of the country, owing to the lack of any basis for estimating the number for the rest of the country. Also it is not known whether

[14] Testimony of William T. Ham, Hearings, Subcommittee on Education and Labor, United States Senate, 76th Congress, Second Session, Washington, D.C., May 9, 1940.

[15] Interstate Migration, House Report No. 369, 77th Congress, First Session, Washington, D.C., 1941, p. 338.

workers employed in packing and processing plants are included or not, for they are temporary members of the migratory labor stream. As to the number who follow the crops as a permanent occupation, the best estimate is between 200,000 and 350,000.[16]

The routes of migratory streams are shown in the accompanying map (Figure 31). All but one of them—that involved in the Florida crops—originate in the South and flow toward the North. This is a consequence of the variation in climate from

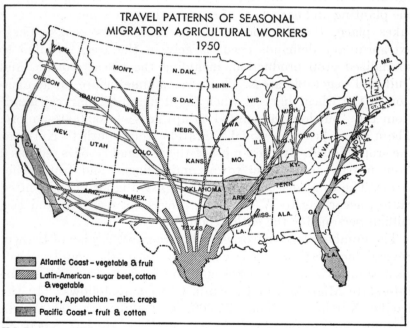

TRAVEL PATTERNS OF SEASONAL
MIGRATORY AGRICULTURAL WORKERS
1950

Atlantic Coast – vegetable & fruit
Latin-American – sugar beet, cotton & vegetable
Ozark, Appalachian – misc. crops
Pacific Coast – fruit & cotton

U.S. Department of Agriculture                    Bureau of Agricultural Economics

FIGURE 31. *Routes of Farm Laborers Following Maturing Crops.* Hundreds of thousands of farm laborers annually move over rather well-established routes mostly from South to North, following the harvest as the crops mature. This map shows the general routes of these migrations and the type of crop involved in each.

South to North, which affects the time of maturing of the crop. The stream in the Plains area is declining in numbers as the mechanization of the harvest approaches completion. An inno-

---

[16] Paul S. Taylor, "Migratory Farm Labor in the United States," *Monthly Labor Review*, 1937, Vol. 44, No. 3, p. 546.

vation in this particular enterprise is the development of the combine harvester crews which contract with the farmers to harvest their crops, very much in the same manner as the old threshing crews contracted to thresh the grain. Those who ply the sugar-beet route may also feel very soon the impact of the newly developed beet harvester with which two or three men may be able to do the work of a dozen. The berry crop begins to ripen in Florida and Louisiana and the large numbers of pickers required move north with the ripening fruit to the Canadian border. Fruit and truck crop streams characterize the Atlantic and Pacific coastal areas.

## MIGRATIONS IN TERMS OF DISTANCE

The census of 1950 provided information regarding those who had moved during the year previous to the census and, by giving the movements between political subdivisions, supplied a very general measure of distances which people move. The data are presented in Table 8.

TABLE 8. *Percentages of Migrants, Rural and Urban, in the United States by Types of Migration, 1949–1950*

| TYPES OF MIGRATION | AVERAGE | URBAN | RURAL-NONFARM | RURAL-FARM |
|---|---|---|---|---|
| All types | 100.0 | 100.0 | 100.0 | 100.0 |
| Same county | 66.7 | 68.3 | 61.7 | 67.4 |
| Within state | 17.9 | 15.2 | 22.2 | 21.8 |
| Between contiguous states | 6.5 | 6.3 | 7.1 | 5.9 |
| Between noncontiguous states | 8.9 | 10.2 | 9.0 | 4.9 |

Source: *Census of Population, 1950*

The important facts to note from the table are these: (1) In all segments of the population the majority of migrants moved within the state; (2) the volume of intrastate movement was proportionately greater in the rural-farm population, with the rural-nonfarm population ranking next; (3) urban migrants showed a tendency to move longer distances—beyond the contiguous states—than the rural groups, while the rural-farm population showed the least tendency toward distant movement.

These data on a national scale tend to confirm the information available from local studies in the United States, as well as another of the Ravenstein laws—that which states that "the great body of migrants proceed only a short distance." It has long been known from local studies, as well as from other data in the census, that a large proportion of the movement of farm people was from farm to farm. Particularly is this true among the tenant farm families. In 1935 the agricultural census reported that in the southern states 44 per cent of the croppers and 37 per cent of the other tenants had been on their farms less than one year. R. T. McMillan, in a careful study of migration in five Oklahoma townships, found that "moves for short distances accounted for the major portion of all migration." [17]

## SELECTIVITY OF MIGRATION

**Age.** All of the available evidence points to the selectivity of migrations on the basis of age. In the case of migrations from the farms to towns and cities, it is the youth who migrate, in disproportionate numbers. Lively and Taeuber found that "almost 45 per cent of the net rural migrants from 1920 to 1930 were 10–19 years of age in 1920. More than 75 per cent of the migrants were persons who were less than 25 years of age in 1920." [18]

The same authors noted a difference in the age of migration between white and colored segments of the population. In the case of the colored migrants, 28.1 per cent were 35 years old or over in 1920, compared with 19.1 per cent of the white migrants.

After analyzing the composition of the migration from the farm during the decade of the 1930's, Bernert concludes as follows:

Migration from the rural-farm population was generally greatest among those aged 15–19 in 1930, who were 25–29 by the end of the decade, ranging from 35 to 43 per 100 persons still living in 1940. After this age, net losses through migration continued, though with a gradual decrease in migration rates, up to the age group of persons 25–29 in 1930, in which net gains generally took place. . . . Though the net

[17] Robert T. McMillan, "Migration of Population in Five Oklahoma Townships," *Oklahoma AES Bulletin B271*, 1943, p. 34.

[18] C. E. Lively and Conrad Taeuber, "Rural Migration in the United States," *Works Progress Administration Research Monograph XIX*, 1939, p. 15.

migration from the rural-farm population between 1920 and 1930 was 74 per cent greater than in the 1930–1940 decade, the age pattern of net migration was similar for both periods. In each period the greatest proportion of net migration from the rural-farm population occurred in the age group 15–19 at the beginning of the decade.[19]

**Sex.** One of the clearest indications of the selectivity of rural to urban migration in terms of sex is the differential sex ratios of rural and urban populations. The fact that in 1950 there were 110 males per 100 females in the farm population and only 94 in the urban can be explained only on the basis of the migration from farms of a disproportionate number of women. That girls leave the farm areas in greater proportions than boys is confirmed by many studies. Lively and Taeuber, for example, say that 'among children 16 years of age and over who were not living at home at the time of the surveys, . . . there were more women than men, the ratio being only 84 men per 100 women. The preponderance of women among the migrants was most marked at the youngest ages, the result of earlier migration of women." [20] That is, women not only migrate in greater proportion from the farms, but they leave at earlier ages.

Bernert, analyzing the 1930–1940 data, again confirms the earlier study of Lively and Taeuber:

As vocational opportunities for women are greater in nonfarm areas than on farm, the net migration from the rural-farm population was greater among females (15.3 per cent) than among males (10.2 per cent). Females tended to migrate at younger ages. Even among those under 10 years of age in 1930 the net migration from rural-farm areas was greater among females. Persons who were under 10 years of age in 1930 accounted for 15 per cent of the female outmigration and only 7 per cent of the male net outmigration. Net migration from the rural-farm population 50 years of age and over was greater among females than among males. The proportionately heavier net outmovement of females in the older age groups reveals, to a large extent, the migration of widows, who are more likely to leave the farms than are male operators who have lost their wives.[21]

---

[19] Eleanor H. Bernert, "Volume and Composition of Net Migration from the Rural-Farm Population, 1930–40, for the United States, Major Geographic Divisions and States," Bureau of Agricultural Economics, 1944, p. 2. (mimeo.)

[20] C. E. Lively and Conrad Taeuber, *op. cit.*, p. 106.   [21] Bernert, *op. cit.*, p. 2.

**Qualitative selectivity.** Aside from sex and age, the evidence of the selectivity of rural-urban migration is not clear. E. A. Ross in 1920 propounded the question thus: "Is it *milk* or *cream* that the cities with their constant suction abstract from the rural population?" [22] His own answer to the question was that people with initiative were leaving the country for the city in disproportionate numbers, resulting in what he termed "folk depletion" in the country. In the quarter of a century since Ross's famous generalization a great deal of research has been carried on to test its validity. The results have not been convincing. Dorothy Swaine Thomas, one of the ablest students of migration phenomena, points out the existence in the literature on migration of four conflicting hypotheses of the selectivity of rural-urban migration as follows: (1) Cityward migrants are selected from the superior elements of the parent population; (2) cityward migrants are selected from the inferior elements; (3) cityward migrants are selected from the extremes, i.e., both the superior and the inferior elements; and (4) cityward migrants represent a random selection of the parent population.

After discussing the various studies bearing on each of these hypotheses, Thomas finds support for all four of them. In conclusion she says:

We have, then, evidence of a sort that migration selects the better elements, the worse elements, both the better and the worse, and also that it is unselective. Even though we may decide that the evidence cited is tenuous, it is not improbable that selection does operate positively, negatively, and randomly, at different times, depending on a variety of factors that, up to the present, have not been adequately investigated. [23]

## MIGRATION AND RURAL–URBAN RELATIONS

Whatever the qualitative selectivity of migration from the farms may be, it is clear that it is quantitatively significant.

[22] E. A. Ross, *The Principles of Sociology*, p. 24. New York: The Century Company, 1920.

[23] D. S. Thomas, "Selective Migration," *The Milbank Memorial Fund Quarterly*, 1938, 16:403–407. For a more extensive examination of the literature see the excellent volume by the same author, "Research Memorandum on Migration Differentials," *Social Science Research Council Bulletin 43*, New York, 1938. Extensive treatment of the subject will also be found in P. A. Sorokin and C. C. Zimmerman, *Principles of Rural-Urban Sociology*, p. 525–607. New York: Henry Holt and Co., 1929.

On the other hand, while the interchange of migrants results in a net loss to the country, there is always a movement of considerable magnitude from the city to farm. The interchange has considerable social significance, particularly the larger movement from farms to cities. In the first place, as we have seen, the sex ratio is disturbed in both segments of the population, resulting in an excess of males in the country and a deficit in the city; an unbalance which is reflected in the marriage rates of the two sexes in cities and on farms. Secondly, the age composition is affected to the disadvantage of the country and advantage of the city, which benefits from a greater proportion of people in the working ages. Thirdly, the migration of people from the farms results in the movement from the country to the city of rural wealth, chiefly in the form of the cost of rearing the farm children who migrate, but also in the form of equities of these migrants as heirs of rural property. There is, of course, a counterflow of wealth from the cities, but of relatively less magnitude. Finally, the interchange of migrants is a factor in breaking down provincialism in both country and city and in lessening the importance of the barriers between city and country which sometimes result in antagonism and conflict. Migration is, in short, one means of making and keeping the unity of national society.

## QUESTIONS FOR DISCUSSION

1. Distinguish between spatial movements that are really migratory and those that are nonmigratory.
2. Cite instances in which exhaustion of natural resources, climatic fluctuations and social maladjustments have resulted in emigration. Give other examples in which *pull* factors appear to have played a dominant role in causing people to migrate.
3. Discuss the factors which inhibit migration, or that tend to keep people where they are.
4. Migratory movements may be viewed from the standpoint of (1) underlying causes, (2) the group that migrates, (3) the time and duration of the migration and (4) the personal and social adjustment of the migrants. Discuss the several movements described in the text from these points of view.
5. Which of the movements would you describe as *distress* migration?

How do the movements compare from the standpoint of number of persons involved?

6. Would you: (1) regard migration as inherently bad and take steps to reduce it to an absolute minimum; (2) regard migration as a necessary and temporary expedient in the lives of people and adopt measures to help those who find themselves in distress; or (3) regard migration as desirable, with efforts made to prepare people to adjust themselves to moving from one place to another?

7. Review the available evidence that migration is selective as to age, sex, and qualitative differences. What are the probable effects of this selectivity on rural and urban welfare?

8. Although the farm population in 1940 was only one fifth of the total for the nation, a much higher proportion of the men in the armed forces reported having had farm experience. How was this possible assuming proportionate drafting of men from urban and rural areas?

9. In 1930 the population of Blank county was 21,560; in 1940, 22,423. Assuming a birth rate of 20 and a death rate of 10 per thousand, calculate the volume of migration during the ten-year period and tell whether it was in or out of the county.

## SELECTED REFERENCES

Andrews, Wade H., and Westerkamm, Emily M. "Population Change and Migration in Ohio, 1940–1950," *Ohio AES Research Bulletin 737.* November, 1953.

Blizzard, Samuel W., and John, Macklin E. "Social Participation Patterns of Husbands and Wives Who Are Migrants in the City," *Pennsylvania AES Paper No. 1922, Journal Series.* February, 1952. (mimeo.)

Dorn, Harold F. "Effects of Rural Urban Migration Upon Death Rates," *Population,* Vol. I, No. 3, November, 1934.

Gist, Noel P.; Pihlblad, C. I.; and Gregory, Cecil L. "Selective Factors in Migration and Occupation: A Study of Social Selection in Rural Missouri." *University of Missouri Studies,* 1943.

Hagood, Margaret Jarman, and others. "Dynamics of the Rural Population" (Report of the Ad Hoc Subcommittee on Population), *Rural Sociology,* 19:73–82, March, 1954.

Hagood, Margaret Jarman, and Sharp, Emmit F. "Rural-Urban Migration in Wisconsin, 1940–50," *Wisconsin AES Bulletin 176.* August, 1951.

Hitt, Homer L. "The Role of Migration in Population Change Among the Aged," *American Sociological Review,* 19:194–200, April, 1954.

U.S. DEPARTMENT OF AGRICULTURE

*Excessive erosion (above) means eventual farm abandonment and migration. Planting of trees (center) prevents floods and dust storms. Terraces, strip crops, and contour cultivation for soil and water conservation (below) preserve basic resources.*

SOIL CONSERVATION SERVICE

U. S. DEPARTMENT
OF AGRICULTURE
FOREST SERVICE

COOPERATIVE

FARM SHELTERBELT

PLANTED
1939

*While most farmers deliver milk to the co-op creamery by truck, a few do not (above). Co-ops are well-managed business enterprises (below).*

FREMONT·COUNTY
DAIRYMENS·CO·OP
Marketing Association
Cream Of Wyoming BUTTER

Hitt, Homer L., and Smith, T. Lynn. "Population Redistribution in Louisiana," *Social Forces*, Vol. XX, No. 4, May, 1942.

*Interstate Migration*. The Select Committee to Investigate the Interstate Migration of Destitute Citizens, House Report 369, 77th Congress, 1st Session.

Jehlik, Paul J., and Wakeley, Ray E. "Rural-Urban Migration in Iowa, 1940–50." *Iowa AES Research Bulletin 407*. April, 1954.

Kraenzel, Carl F. "Farm Population Mobility in Selected Montana Communities." *Montana State College AES Bulletin 371*. April, 1939.

Landis, Paul H. "The Drought Farmer Adjusts to the West." *State College of Washington AES Bulletin 378*. July, 1939.

——— "The Territorial and Occupational Mobility of Our Washington Youth." *State College of Washington AES Bulletin 499*. July, 1944.

Landis, Paul H., and Hatt, Paul K. *Population Problems: A Cultural Interpretation*, Chapters 20, 21. American Book Co. 1954.

Lange, Dorothea, and Taylor, Paul S. *An American Exodus: A Record of Human Erosion*. New York: Reynal and Hitchcock, 1939.

Lively, C. E. "The Development of Research in Rural Migration in the United States." Paper given before International Population Congress, Paris, France. July, 1937. (Mimeographed)

Lively, C. E., and Taeuber, Conrad. "Rural Migration in the United States." *Works Progress Administration, Division of Research, Monograph XIX*. Washington, D.C.: Government Printing Office, 1939.

Loomis, Charles P. "Wartime Migration from the Rural Spanish Speaking Villages of New Mexico." *Rural Sociology*, Vol. VII, No. 4, December, 1942.

McMillan, Robert T. "Migration of Population in Five Oklahoma Townships." *Oklahoma AES Bulletin B271*. 1943.

——— "Migration and Status of Open-Country Families in Oklahoma." *Oklahoma Agricultural and Mechanical College AES Technical Bulletin T–19*. September, 1943.

Ramsey, Charles E.; Orman, Allan E.; and Nelson, Lowry. "Migration in Minnesota, 1940–50." *Minnesota AES Bulletin 422*. January, 1954.

Reuss, Carl F. "Back to the Country—The Rural Trend in Washington's Population." *State College of Washington AES Bulletin 426*. 1942.

——— "Depopulation in a Remote Rural District," *Rural Sociology*, Vol. II, No. 1, pp. 66–75, March, 1937.

Slocum, Walter L. "Migrants From Rural South Dakota Families." (Their Geographical and Occupational Distribution.) *South Dakota State College AES Bulletin 359.* 1942.

Smith, T. Lynn. *The Sociology of Rural Life*, Third Edition, Chapter 9. New York: Harper and Brothers, 1953.

Sorokin, P. A., and Zimmerman, C. C. *Principles of Rural-Urban Sociology*, pp. 525–539. New York: Henry Holt and Co., 1929.

Spaulding, Irving A., and Beers, Howard W. "Mobility and Fertility Rates of Rural Families in Robertson and Johnson Counties, Kentucky, 1918–1941." *Kentucky AES Bulletin 451.* 1943.

Taylor, Paul S. "Adrift on the Land." *Public Affairs Pamphlet 42.* 1940.

Thomas, Dorothy S. "Selective Migration," *The Milbank Memorial Fund Quarterly*, XVI:4, pp. 403–407, October, 1938.

———— "Research Memorandum on Migration Differentials." *Social Science Research Council Bulletin 43.* New York, 1938.

Thompson, Warren S., with the assistance of Minnis, Evangelyn D. *Population Problems*, Chapters 13, 14. New York: McGraw-Hill Book Company, 1953.

United States Bureau of the Census. *Internal Migration 1935 to 1940;* a series of four reports as follows: "Color and Sex of Migrants" (1943); "Social Characteristics of Migrants" (1946); "Age of Migrants" (1946); and "Economic Characteristics of Migrants" (1946). This is by far the most exhaustive report of internal migration ever attempted by the Bureau of the Census. While it is based on 1940 information, it is still a valuable source for the study of migration.

Williams, Robin M., and Beers, Howard W. "Attitudes Toward Rural Migration and Family Life in Johnson and Robertson Counties, Kentucky, 1941." *Kentucky AES Bulletin 452.* 1943.

# PART IV

## SOCIAL INTERACTION IN THE RURAL ENVIRONMENT

## INTRODUCTION

In PARTS II and III we have considered the people and the manner in which they have arranged themselves on the surface of the land. The next step is to consider the people in their personal and group interaction. The responses which persons and groups make to other persons and groups can be classified into patterns. A fist fight or a war represent one such pattern; a husking bee quite another. The first we refer to as *conflict*, and the latter *cooperation*. These are the two basic forms of interaction or process most commonly observed. However, there are others to be considered also. In the chapters to follow, in addition to those on Conflict, Competition, and Cooperation, there are those on Stratification and Social Status, Assimilation, and Social Mobility.

These are universal characteristics of societies whether rural or urban, simple or complex. The particular form of expression within the general patterns will differ somewhat as cultures differ, but the patterns are nonetheless universal.

# CHAPTER 8

# CONFLICT, COMPETITION, AND ACCOMMODATION

Among the social processes there are two which are considered more important than any of the others. These are the various forms of opposition and cooperation. The first, together with accommodation, will be treated in this chapter, and the second, in the chapter to follow. Conflict and competition are so closely related that it is difficult to consider the two processes separately. It is particularly difficult to define the two concepts. In the following introductory comments, therefore, reference is made to both.

Antagonistic effort is one of the most widely observed ways of behaving among both the lower and the higher forms of life. Plants struggle against each other for the limited space, nourishment, and sunshine of a particular location. Animals strive with other animals for the available food supply, in defense of a nest, or of their young. One form of animal life preys upon another form of life, both plant and animal. According to Charles Darwin (1809–1882), the "struggle for existence" and the resultant "survival of the fittest" has been the basis for the evolution of the myriad forms of life.[1] Man himself is in competition with the other forms of life, as well as with his own kind. The farmer struggles to protect his crop against the noxious weeds which threaten it or the insect and animal pests or plant diseases which would destroy it. He is in competition with numerous other farmers to produce his crop at a profit. He strives with the middlemen and other urban interests for a larger share of the consumer's dollar.

Meanwhile, he is also in a state of cooperative effort with his neighbors, whose goals coincide with his own and whose joint

[1] See Charles Darwin, *The Origin of Species*, Oxford University Press, 1902.

efforts are much more effective proportionally than those of several individuals acting by themselves. The two processes have been well defined by Kimball Young: "opposition is a struggle *against* another or others for a good, goal, or value; cooperation is joint striving *with* another or others for a good, goal, or value." [2]

Two forms of opposition are distinguished: conflict and competition. Differences between conflict and competition usually made by sociologists are these: (1) competition is universal and continuous; conflict is intermittent, arising in periods of crisis; (2) competition is oppositional interaction without personal contact; conflict involves contact; (3) competition is more or less unconscious; conflict is conscious interaction; (4) competition does not hamper directly the opponent or necessarily change his relative status; conflict does both.[3] In practice, however, it is difficult to say just where competition ends and conflict begins.

Conflict is related to cooperation in the sense of antithesis. The two forms of interaction might be considered as the extremes on a continuum, with varying degrees of the one or the other in between. The central position on the scale would constitute *neutrality*. Between neutrality and conflict on the one hand would range behavior denoted as *aversion, intolerance, disagreement, controversy, battle of words*, or *name-calling*, and finally, *overt physical conflict*. On the other side of the scale from *neutrality* to *cooperation*, would range varieties of behavior indicated by the terms *tolerance, sympathy, agreement, active application of joint effort*.

## BASES OF STRUGGLE

The general bases for struggle among human beings are the existence of fundamental drives, wants, and needs which require

[2] Kimball Young, *Sociology: A Study of Society and Culture*, Second Edition, p. 641. New York: American Book Co., 1949.

[3] See discussion of the concepts in R. E. Park and E. W. Burgess, *Introduction to the Science of Sociology*, Chicago: University of Chicago Press, 1921; R. L. Sutherland and J. L. Woodward, *Introductory Sociology*, Chicago: J. B. Lippincott Company, 1937; E. A. Ross, *Principles of Sociology*, New York: D. Appleton-Century Co., 1938; E. E. Eubank, *The Concepts of Sociology*, Boston: D. C. Heath and Co., 1932; E. B. Reuter, *Handbook of Sociology*, New York: The Dryden Press, 1941.

satisfaction, and the relative scarcity in goods, services, or other cultural objects which satisfy these drives. The fundamental interests or wants in men are the same in rural as in urban society. The objects are sometimes—though not always —different in that the two cultures are different. The struggle for agricultural land and water, for instance, is a phenomenon of rural society, but strife over wages is characteristic of both urban and rural groups. In both societies, antagonistic effort chiefly arises from diversity in (a) economic and political, (b) religious, or (c) other cultural interests; and (d) race and nationality. In terms of participants, conflict situations may be classified as (a) person *versus* person, (b) person *versus* group,[4] and (c) group *versus* group.

## COMPETITION

Competition in rural as in urban societies is most apparent among individuals and groups in pursuit of some economic end. In order for the farmer to survive, in the economic sense, he must apply a certain minimum of skill, knowledge, industry, and managerial ability to the farm enterprise—assuming a reasonably stable market for farm products and insurance against unusual weather or other crises. (See Chapter 2.) Failure to meet the minimum conditions means financial bankruptcy. That many farmers do not possess the necessary qualities is demonstrated by the number of mortgage foreclosures and forced sales in agriculture, even during years of favorable prices and weather conditions.

**Competition for profits.** There has been a ceaseless struggle among farmers, wherever they are engaged in commercial production of crops and livestock for the market, as distinguished from production for consumption on the farm. Self-sufficing agriculture characterized the American frontier, but has become relatively less important in the face of the steady growth of commercial farming. For commercial farmers, competition for profits is not unlike that which characterizes other business

[4] Person *versus* group conflict includes criminal and other antisocial behavior. This aspect of rural society is not treated in the present volume chiefly because of the absence of available data on the subject. Persons interested in this field will find an excellent brief résumé of the literature in George B. Vold, "Crime in City and Country Areas," *The Annals*, September, 1941.

enterprises. Each one seeks to find more efficient ways to operate his farm, ways to reduce the cost of production and thereby widen the margin of profit. If, for example, one dairy farmer comes into possession of a breed or strain of dairy cows which will produce more milk for the same intake of feed than the cows possessed by his neighbor, he will reap an advantage in the market, other things being equal.

Similarly, the farmer who has a better way of feeding and caring for his cows than has his neighbor or who makes a more effective combination of the various factors of production—land, labor, and capital—widens the margin of gain compared with his neighbor. In order to be able to compete successfully, other farmers will seek to secure similar high-producing cows and to improve their methods of operation. The farmers who fail to take such steps will find themselves progressively worse off and ultimately will be faced with financial failure.

**Competition for ownership and control of land.** This is another expression of the economic struggle among farmers. It also is characteristically continuous, although it flares at times into intermittent conflict. Such competition is illustrated by the tendency toward concentration of land ownership. In the days of feudalism, of course, the ownership of the land was the special privilege of the nobles, both civil and ecclesiastical. There was a monopoly of land ownership by a privileged class and competition did not exist. However, the stage was set for conflicts, as will be indicated presently. After the breakup of the feudal economy, land became more of a marketable commodity, and the distribution of ownership became more widespread.

The discovery of America in the fifteenth century opened a vast territory for settlement by the land-hungry people of the Old World. The continent was practically given away to those who wanted it. While so-called "free land" was not achieved until the passage of the Homestead Act in 1862, land was previously available at a nominal price of a dollar and a quarter an acre. Although each person was entitled to only 160 acres under the provisions of the Homestead Act, unscrupulous individuals found ways to acquire more than the stipulated amount. Without recourse to fraudulent methods still others were able to acquire larger tracts by virtue of their having cash or credit resources greater than others.

From the very beginning of settlement in the United States, the ownership of land has been in a state of continual flux. Many homesteaders sold their quarter sections to neighbors and returned to the eastern or European communities from which they came. Others mortgaged their farms and lost them in one of the recurrent depressions. Some farms have become progressively smaller as they have been subdivided to satisfy the rights of heirs. Others have been increased in size as more efficient owners have sought to find the most efficient size of farm. That the long-time trend has been towards concentration of ownership in relatively few persons, and these not the ones who operate the farms, is shown by census statistics. The Bureau of Agricultural Economics estimates that in 1890 forty-one per cent of the value of farm real estate was not owned by the farm operator, but by 1930 the percentage had increased to fifty-eight.

The land of Cuba passed through an interesting evolution. Until the latter part of the nineteenth century, the ownership of land was rather widely distributed. Although most of the land was divided into large livestock ranches, originally individual grants to persons who applied for them during the two centuries from 1536 to 1729, the possessors of rights in them increased over the generations through the operation of inheritance laws, even though the ranch lands themselves remained undivided. Subsequently, with the expansion of the sugar industry, particularly after 1900, the ownership of vast areas of the best land was acquired by sugar companies, while the former holders of ownership rights became wage workers or tenants. Since 1933 the policy has been toward restriction of the size of holdings and re-distribution among peasants, though little progress has been made in carrying it out.

In part, the competition for land ownership and control is also a struggle between *farming systems*. The opposition between the slave plantation of the American South and the small farm system of the North was one of the irreconcilable conflicts which led to the War Between the States. In Cuba the small farmer producing diversified crops or the livestock rancher could not compete with the sugar *latifundia*, since the latter system of farm organization produced vastly greater income per unit of land than did the prevailing systems.

**Sectarian competition.** The multiplication of religious sects in the rural areas of the United States offers another interesting phase of oppositional interaction among groups. The backgrounds of this sectarian strife will be treated more fully in Chapter 17. It is pertinent here, however, to refer to the fact that there were some 250 different sects and denominations listed in the *Census of Religious Bodies: 1936*. Each one, quite naturally, regards itself as the only true church and, therefore, considers all the others to be in error. In order that the whole of mankind may enjoy the benefits of salvation—according to the "true faith"—each sect carries on missionary work throughout the world, if their resources permit it. Competition among the various denominations has given rise to the practice of subsidizing churches in areas where local support is not sufficient to maintain them. Thus it frequently happens that in a given rural area there may be a half dozen Protestant churches, differing one from another in seemingly minor degree, each one without sufficient members to enjoy self-maintenance, yet unable to come together in a joint congregation. Sometimes a community or federated church emerges, but all too infrequently for the welfare of the rural church as an institution.

Even within the same denomination, schisms and subdivisions occur that occasion community strife. The essentials of the process of intrasectarian strife are well illustrated by the Mennonites of Mountain Lake, Minnesota.[5] About 1800 Mennonites came to this community from Russia during the period 1873–1880. Though they all belonged to the same denomination, they found many points of difference, including mode of dress, form of baptism, details of church discipline and policy, whether there should be musical instruments in the church or part singing as opposed to singing in unison, whether conversion was necessary to become a church member, and whether there should be a Sunday school.

[5] The account is based on Ferdinand P. Schultz, *A History of the Settlement of German Mennonites From Russia at Mountain Lake, Minnesota*, published privately by the author, 1938.

The existing diversities made difficult the organization of any church at all, and it was only after living together for several years that they organized the first church. The new church, however, was by no means representative of the entire community. The man elected elder received only a bare majority of votes. In two years, two additional churches were set up by groups differing on some one or more of the points mentioned above. A few years later the members of the first church organized were unable to agree on the issue of the Sunday school; the result was a three-way division of the congregation and the addition of three more churches to the community. Thus in a brief period of 15 years, what was apparently a single denomination of Christians had split into five different congregations, and as late as 1924 still another group emerged.

Internal strife is not limited among Protestant groups to Mennonites by any means. A glance at the list of sects in the *Census of Religious Bodies* will show the several varieties of Lutherans, Baptists, Methodists, Adventists, and so on.

**Ethnic group competition.** "I do not see what is to prevent all of the land of Blank county eventually falling into the hands of the people of German descent who live there," said a competent observer to the author after he had visited one of the counties in Minnesota. He went on to explain that the German people appeared to be the most successful farmers: more diligent husbandmen, more careful in conserving the soil, and more frugal. Moreover, they are not interested in doing anything other than farming. They like farming, want their children to farm, and are buying land to make this possible. Similar observations about the Amish people have frequently been made. Since there is a tendency for ethnic groups to occupy contiguous areas of land (see Figure 32), any expansion of one group must be at the loss of land ownership by another. To protect the residents against the severe competition of Japanese immigrants in California, alien land laws were enacted which prevented Orientals from owning land. However, it did not stop the latter's descendants born in the United States from becoming landowners. By 1940 there were 5,135 farms operated by Japanese in California, including a total of 236,094 acres. As Carey McWilliams points out, their unusual industry,

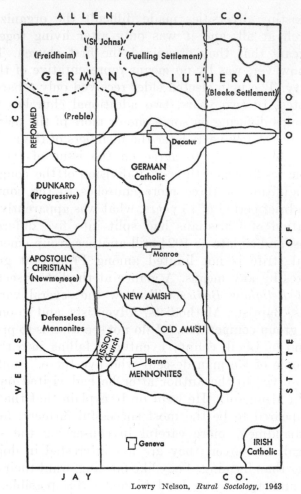

Lowry Nelson, *Rural Sociology,* 1943

FIGURE 32. *Map of Adams County, Indiana, Showing Various Ethnic Groups.*
As each one expands, it seeks to acquire land that adjoins its holdings.

willingness to work hard and long, their skill in reclamation and use of lands previously regarded as of little value, have made them useful members of the California economy,[6] and rather formidable competitors of their American farmer-neighbors.

An interesting case of ethnic group competition is described in a work on rural China. In a "mixed" community of southwest China live the Chinese who at some time in the remote past

[6] Carey McWilliams, *Brothers Under the Skin,* pp. 148, 155. Boston: Little, Brown and Co., 1943.

invaded the region occupied by the native Lolos. The Chinese became the landlords and the natives the workers under a feudal system that prevailed until the natives rose up and drove out the invaders. In the peace settlement following the uprising, the natives were not allowed to take over the land from the Chinese, though they did gain the privilege of buying and own- ing land. In the course of time their holdings have steadily increased at the expense of those of the Chinese landlords. The latter are no longer uniformly rich and the natives uni- formly poor. Many of the latter exceed the former in wealth.[7] The success of the natives in the competitive struggle is due to their willingness to forego the better and more expensive way of living of the Chinese, to work harder, and to make every sacrifice necessary to satisfy their craving for land.

An interesting case of competition between landowners and landless individuals in which ethnic differences are involved is described by Paul S. Taylor. It concerns the economic evolution of Nueces County, Texas, in the early part of the nineteenth century. Most of the land was used for grazing and, although it was largely privately owned, it was not fenced, so that many people who owned no land were able to graze their livestock in the area. In the late 1860's the "enclosure movement" began, which entailed the fencing of property by those who claimed it. Taylor comments as follows:

The fencing of the range during the height of the cattle and sheep raising period brought about most profound social change. It was the change that affected landowners, mostly Americans, by raising the value of their lands and adding to the security of their stock. It affected also, but quite differently, the landless Americans, Mexicans, and a few Negroes, who had been pasturing their own stock on the range: fencing put them out of business or forced them westward until that range, too, was closed by the barrier. As the process of the enclosure advanced, its catastrophic effects on the landless cattlemen, and on smaller owners of land without water, became apparent.[8]

---

[7] Yu-I Li, Hsiao-Tung Fei, and Tse-I Chang, *"Three Types of Rural Economy in Yunnan,"* International Secretariat, Institute of Pacific Relations, New York, 1943, pp. 9, 10.

[8] Reprinted from *An American-Mexican Frontier*, p. 76, by Paul S. Taylor by permission of the University of North Carolina Press. Copyright, 1934, by the University of North Carolina Press.

**Rural-urban opposition.** The opposition of country people to city life and city people is one of ancient tradition. Some of the forms which it takes have already been discussed. In addition there are the old traditional notions which the two groups have about one another. By rural folk the city has long been regarded as a "den of iniquity." City people, so the stereotype has it, are effete, sophisticated, superficial, and corrupt. They are also regarded as parasitic in that they do not produce the means of their own subsistence. Rural people, on the contrary, have always regarded themselves as virtuous, industrious, moral and leading a more natural life. A certain resentment towards the city rankles in the bosom of the ruralite because he is aware that the urbanite regards him as of lower status, as being inferior.[9] Some city people hold certain stereotyped notions of the farmer. He has been called a "rube," a "hayseed," a "clodhopper," or the more specialized names of "hillbilly," "red neck," or "sand-hiller."

While these stereotypes may be archaic and no longer of much significance, there can be little doubt that vestiges of such attitudes persist today. They are by no means universal, though in many communities there are manifestations of antagonism.

The suburban movement brings conflicting ideas and interests of urban and farm people into focus. N. L. Whetten and E. C. Devereux, in describing suburbanization in Connecticut, have this to say:

The suburban families have quite a different point of view towards civic affairs than do the natives. They are not so much interested in preserving the charm of antiquity as they are in having all the familiar conveniences in their country homes. They want electric lights, sewers, sidewalks, water, and roads. They want modern schools and modern homes. They want progress and growth. In short, they are interested in developing Windsor as a modern residential suburb on the order of West Hartford or Scarsdale.

When we consider the setting in which this suburbanization has been taking place it is not surprising that the movement has been accompanied by a certain amount of conflict. Many of the older residents are

---

[9] *Farmers in a Changing World*, Yearbook of Agriculture, pp. 118, 119. Washington, D.C.: United States Department of Agriculture, 1940.

opposed to the suburbanization of the area in so far as this would tend to destroy what they consider to be their priceless heritage, the historical charm of an old New England village. Their Yankee conservatism resents the intrusion of these "outsiders" with their "newfangled" ideas, and resists change. Furthermore, many of the natives resent the increased expenditures for the various public services which suburbanization entails, pointing with alarm at the soaring school budget.[10]

### CONFLICT

All situations described under competition may and do give rise to open conflict, in which the opposing agents are identified and their elimination from the contest is attempted. In the struggle for ownership and control of land the opposing forces have been the landlords on the one hand and the landless peasants on the other.

During the days of feudalism the irksome duties imposed upon the serfs by the landed nobles incited a number of uprisings and peasant revolts. There was a series of revolts in West Frisia in the latter part of the thirteenth century, in West Flanders in the forepart of the fourteenth century, in England in the latter part of the fourteenth century, in Germany in the sixteenth century. There were revolts against the enclosure movement in England during the seventeenth century, the Russian uprising in the latter eighteenth century, the successful revolt of the Negro slaves in Haiti after the French Revolution, and many others on down to the Mexican revolution of 1910. Shays' Rebellion in the United States (1786) might also be regarded as a "peasant revolt" against the high rate of land taxes in Massachusetts, against the cost of litigation, and against the high salaries paid public officials.

Two conflicting value systems regarding property in land are involved. In the peasant tradition land is regarded as more than an instrument of production. Its possession is a value and an end in itself because the land is his home as well as his place of work, a place to live as well as a livelihood.[11] On the other hand, the landlord class regards land primarily as a means of producing wealth or as a symbol of class status. Any particular

---

[10] Nathan L. Whetten and E. C. Devereux, Jr., "Studies of Suburbanization in Connecticut: Windsor," *Storrs AES Bulletin 212*, October, 1936, p. 135.

[11] See Chapter 13 for further discussion.

piece of land is valued not only in terms of its net product, but also in terms of the social prestige it gives the possessor. Often it is not even a place of residence for the owner and his family. The large landowners of various South American countries, as well as many of those in the United States, live in cities and hire managers and overseers to supervise operations. Thus land as a *social* good, around which there are sentiments of attachment, is not part of their value system; the pursuit of profits is the primary interest.

Peasants of Poland, Rumania, and Hungary, as well as of Cuba and other Latin-American countries, have long been restive under governments which deny them ownership of land and which condone the monopoly of ownership by a few. No national uprisings have compelled the redistribution of land in these countries as in Mexico and, in a sense, in Russia.[12] Nevertheless, the political pressures exerted by the peasants are finding expression in land reform legislation.

In his novel descriptive of rural life in the highlands of Peru, Ciro Alegría [13] pictures the conflict between groups based on racial as well as economic differences. On the one hand there is the native Indian community whose lands are held in common; on the other, the "white" *ranchero* who covets not only the land of the community, but also the labor force. He justifies his position on the grounds of "progress" and the ethnic inferiority of the villagers. Because of the influence which the *ranchero* has over the courts, he is able by intimidation and bribery to win his case and secure title to the communal lands. When the villagers decide to resist his occupation of their land, a contingent of militia is sent against them, and they are finally subdued. The ranchero's superior economic position, based upon exploitation of Indian labor, enables him to control political institutions, the press, and the courts of "justice." Periodic uprisings of the peons are ruthlessly suppressed by the military who act in effect as agents of the wealthy landlords.

[12] In Russia, the peasants actually did not get title to the land, which instead was nationalized as property of the Russian state. Whether the peasants are content and satisfied under the present regime is not known definitely from unbiased study and reporting.

[13] Ciro Alegría, *Broad and Alien Is the World*. New York: Farrar and Rinehart, 1941.

In the history of the United States conflicts over the control of land occurred frequently on the frontier. One of the most common was that between the cattleman and the homesteader on the Great Plains and in the Rocky Mountains. The cattleman wanted to keep the range open, free from barbed-wire fences, while the homesteader in pursuit of his own interests fenced in his 160 acres to protect his crops against the herds of livestock. The cowboys cut the wire fences and allowed the cattle to graze on the homesteader's crops; the homesteader retaliated by shooting the cattle. Sometimes both cowboy and homesteader shot it out between themselves.

Another form of competition for land which flared into conflict on the American frontier was that between the cattleman and the sheepman. It did not have its basis in the ownership of the land, since the land in question was the public domain. Rather, it was a question as to whether a particular part of the range was to be used for cattle or for sheep. Since neither the cattleman nor the sheepman had official title to the area, it was a question of either getting to the grazing area first, or making life so intolerable for the other that he would voluntarily withdraw. Thus many cowboys performed acts of sabotage against the sheepman, such as destroying his camp or supplies, if they were left unguarded. Such acts often led to retaliation by the sheepherders. On occasions there were shooting duels.

**Person *versus* person conflict over property.** Many examples are to be found in every community of conflict between persons over disputed property titles. Usually settled in courts of law, such disputes frequently are the basis of long-drawn-out family, interfamily, or interpersonal feuds and strife. In the Far West, where irrigation water is the limiting factor in agricultural operations, numerous conflicts of serious proportions arise between farmers. Many a fistfight or shovel duel has taken place at the headgate of an irrigation ditch between disputants over rights to the use of the water. While most of these encounters result in nothing worse than bruised heads and black eyes, homicide is not uncommon. As late as 1938 in a village in Utah a man shot and killed his brother-in-law and the county sheriff in a dispute over rights to the use of a stream of water.

**Conflict in the marketplace.** Another historic form of struggle as far as rural people are concerned has been centered about their efforts to achieve equality in the marketplace. This has taken the form of movements of protest against the persons and groups identified by farmers as those chiefly responsible for their disadvantaged position. Beginning with the organization of the Grange at the close of the Civil War there has been a succession of movements arising out of agricultural distress and representing protests against the existing situation, usually some economic disadvantage.

The Grange, organized in 1867, rose to its greatest popularity in the early 1870's during a period of extreme depression in the price of farm products. The railroad, the bankers, and the middlemen in general were singled out as the agents responsible for the farmers' condition. The farmers sought to better their condition by establishing their own marketing and purchasing agencies and by exerting political pressure on government to exercise control over the railroads.

Next came the Farmers' Alliance, which began in Texas about 1874 or 1875. It represented an organized attempt to rid the country of landsharks and cattle thieves. Later on the organization took on a more comprehensive character, national in scope, and aimed at rooting out monopolies, limiting the influence of private banks, and providing more circulating medium. It became the basis of a third party movement in 1890, the first and only time the American farmers as a group had formed a political party. Significantly, this movement has been called the Populist Revolt.

The American Society of Equity came into existence about 1902. It too was a protest against what farmers considered to be their exploitation by the middlemen who marketed their products. The simple aim of this organization, therefore, was to get control of the markets. The technique employed was to secure cooperation of farmers in withholding their grain from the market by building granaries and storing the grain on their own farms or to construct cooperative warehouses and elevators for storage purposes. In their efforts to restore the price of Burley tobacco in Kentucky they attempted to organize some 40,000 tobacco growers into an association. Each member of the association would agree not to sell tobacco for less than

11 cents a pound, a price about double that then being paid by the buyers. When some tobacco growers could not be induced to join, members of the association organized the so-called Night Riders, who visited the reluctant farmers and sought to intimidate them. Some tobacco fields were destroyed and lives were lost in the struggle.

The Farmer's Union began in Texas also about 1902. It was a protest against the poverty of the cotton growers and the conditions under which they had to live and work. It also sought to obtain and maintain profitable and uniform prices for grain, cotton, livestock, and other products of the farm.

The Nonpartisan League began about 1916 in the state of North Dakota and flourished during World War I and for a few years after. It was a particularly aggressive movement, aiming to reduce the power of the elevator, railroad, and milling concerns over the price of wheat. To this end their program called for state ownership of terminal elevators, flour mills, packing houses, and cold storage plants, for state inspection of grain and grain dockage, for exemption of farm improvements from taxation, and for the establishment of rural credit banks. They largely succeeded in putting into operation their plan in North Dakota, where they established a state bank and a state flour mill.

During the depression of the early 1930's one of the most radical of farmer movements developed in the Middle West, the Farm Holiday Association. Its objective apparently was to prevent the enforced liquidation and foreclosure of mortgages on farm property. When sheriff's sales were announced for a farmer's property the group would attend the sale en masse, intimidate any "outsiders" who might intend to bid on the property, and finally buy up the property for a nominal sum of a few dollars. The legal formalities of the sale over, the property would be returned to the original owner. The creditors, however, would get nothing. The usual legal processes broke down under this sort of action on the part of the farmers. Violence flared in Iowa when a judge who, according to the judgment of the farmers, was too diligent in performing his duties, was taken out on a lonely road and given a beating.

These and other movements of farmers are all attempts to

redress what they regard as wrongs imposed upon them. Usually, redress is sought in the courts and in the legislatures, but frequently by means of more direct action. As we shall see in the next chapter, a phase of these movements of protest has been the development of cooperative organizations.

**Conflict over wages.** Among farm people there is essentially the same pattern of employee-employer struggle characteristic of urban industry. It is a kind of conflict peculiar to the areas where agriculture is highly industrialized, the so-called "factories in the field" type of farming. It is not a struggle for possession of the land but for distribution of the net product in wages for laborers and profits for management. The agricultural worker in this situation is interested primarily in a reward for his labor. Most of the laborers involved in conflicts are migratory, following the crops. Lack of permanent homes, which the nature of their work makes impossible, leads to a precarious existence, and frequently destitution. The supply of workers sometimes exceeds the available jobs, thus creating unemployment for many and a tendency toward low wages for all.

The operator may be a person, a partnership, or a corporation. In any case, the objective is primarily to secure the largest possible returns from the enterprise. This leads to attempts to reduce costs of production, including wages, to the lowest level possible. The operator's position is also vulnerable and precarious, since agricultural products in these areas are largely fruits and vegetables, and are quickly perishable. The entrepreneur, therefore, is concerned primarily with having an adequate supply of laborers at the time he needs it. He would much rather have too many workers than too few, since, if there are more than he really needs, wages may be lower and at the same time he is sure of enough workers to get his crops in. The crops must be harvested, moreover, within a relatively short period of time, and it is during this crucial period that the operator is most vulnerable and insecure. Any shortage would result in wages being driven up through competitive bidding among employers, and at the same time would threaten the loss of part of the crop through failure to harvest at the proper time. Indiscriminate recruiting of labor over wide areas is therefore the common resort. Word is spread far and wide that work and good wages will be available, and the usual result, particularly during the depression, was to invite the migration of workers greatly in excess of the requirements.

It is obvious that the interests of the two groups are opposed although fundamentally both depend upon the produce of the land for profit: the one receiving it in exchange for his capable management; the other, for his labor and skill. Forced by circumstances to accept low wages, irregular employment, or dependency, the laborer seeks to better his position through collective action. A labor union may be organized, usually under the leadership of individuals outside the ranks of the workers in a particular area. Representatives of the union lay before the employer requests for better pay and working conditions, initiating the negotiation stage or collective bargaining. However, the attempts at bargaining in agriculture have been largely unsuccessful. The last resort is to strike. The time chosen for the strike is naturally set for a period when the labor is most essential to the employer, usually at harvest time. Since agricultural products are highly perishable, such a threat to an enterprise is crucial.

To protect their interests large operators form associations among themselves or set up special agencies which they finance for the purpose of recruiting labor on the one hand, and on the other, for controlling the labor market, dictating wages, carrying on espionage, strike-breaking activities, and the like.[14]

Strikes in agriculture increased from 5 in each of the years 1930 and 1931 to 10 in 1932, 35 in 1933, 27 in 1934, 19 in 1935, and 28 in 1936. The number of strikes, therefore, and also the number of workers involved reached a peak in the depression year of 1933. At that time there were 34,000 workers involved in strikes, representing a loss of 516,900 man-days.[15]

ACCOMMODATION

By accommodation we mean those adjustments among persons or groups which usually follow a conflict experience or the threat

---

[14] For a full description of the situation in California see *Violations of Free Speech and the Rights of Labor*, Report of Senate Committee on Education and Labor, 77th Congress, Second Session.

[15] Lawrence Peterson, *Strikes in the United States, 1880 to 1936*, Bulletin 651, p. 159. Washington, D.C.: United States Department of Labor, Bureau of Labor Statistics, 1938.

of one. As E. B. Reuter puts it, "accommodation is the recognition and acceptance of the relations that define the status of the person in the group or of the group in the more inclusive social organization. The social pattern that accommodation always takes is the subordination of a person or group to another person or group." [16] Like the process of conflict, from which it arises, accommodation is apparent among the lower animals. Within a flock of chickens there develops a "pecking order"; one becomes master of the group and the rest find their respective niches in progressively lower order, until the lowest individual may be unable to survive at all without some outside protection.

### Caste As Accommodation

Among human beings the pattern is much the same, modified here and there by the veneer of civilization which dictates methods of subjugation not so crude as those of the jungle and the barnyard. However, one would not dare press the argument too far. In matters of land distribution, the feudal system is an interesting illustration of accommodation. Each class had its rights and privileges, its duties and responsibilities. The nobles held the land, the serfs and slaves did the work. The latter could not leave the manor without permission of the lord; but neither could the lord deny the serf the means of existence. In other words, the positions of the two were well established and mutually recognized; and while that of the serf was more often than not a humiliating and debasing one, with heavy tasks as his lot, it entailed security not to be had outside the manor.

**The Negro, slave and free.** Negro slavery in the United States was similar to feudalism. The plantation was the property of the white landlord, as were the slaves themselves. It was unthinkable that the slaves should aspire to possess the land or that the landlord would actually pick the cotton. Each had his place, which was mutually recognized. The slave received for his labor the assurance of food to eat, a place to sleep and medical care in case of illness. As the property of the landlord, the slave was well-worth protecting and caring for physically.

Robert E. Park has clearly stated how rigid stratification of society resolves conflict, as follows:

[16] E. B. Reuter, *Handbook of Sociology*, p. 79. New York: Dryden Press, 1941.

From this point of view we may regard caste, or even slavery, as one of those accommodations through which the race problem found a natural solution. Caste, by relegating the subject race to an inferior status, gives to each race at any rate a monopoly of its own tasks. When this status is accepted by the subject people, as is the case where the caste or slavery systems become fully established, racial competition ceases and racial animosity tends to disappear. This is the explanation of the intimate and friendly relations which so often existed in slavery between master and servant. It is for this reason that we hear it said today that the Negro is all right in his place. In his place he is a convenience and not a competitor. Each race being in its place, no obstacle to racial cooperation exists.[17]

After the slaves achieved their freedom, a new "definition of the situation" became necessary. The landlords found themselves in a state of financial ruin as a result of the destruction caused by the war and the loss of the capital which the slaves represented. Yet there remained the land, which would still raise cotton if there were the labor to plant, cultivate, and harvest it. When they had no money to pay the ex-slaves' wages, as their status of freedom required, the landlords promised to give them a share of the crop at harvest time if they would remain on the land and do the work. Meanwhile, the landlord would, as in the days of slavery, provide them with a place to sleep, with food to eat, and with clothes to wear, all of which would be charged against the ex-slave's share of the crop and deducted with interest at the end of the war. Thus emerged the system of sharecropping which has persisted to the present time.

The economic arrangements were only part of the readjustment that had to be made in Negro-white relations after the War Between the States. How was the freed Negro to be regarded by his former master in matters of social relationships? Was he now to vote as the free white men did? Was he to own land, engage in professional occupations, enjoy free schools, move freely from place to place, enjoy equality before the courts, in employment opportunities, in the choice of a vocation? These questions were not settled readily, not without further

[17] Robert E. Park, "Introduction" to Jesse F. Steiner, *The Japanese Invasion.* Chicago: A. C. McClurg and Co., 1917. Reprinted in Park and Burgess, *op. cit.*, p. 620.

shedding of blood. Some have never been settled. The period
of Reconstruction, during which political appointees from the
North dominated the governments of the South, was one of
turbulence, resentment, and intermittent violence. Out of the
strife came the Jim Crow laws providing for segregation of
Negroes. Today the Southern states have separate schools,
churches, hospitals, and other institutions for Negroes. Negroes
must occupy the rear sections of buses and railway cars. Intermarriage with whites is forbidden. More subtle, but no less
important, are the informal patterns of subordination of the
Negro. He must always go to the back door of the house when
calling on a white person. He is not to be addressed by white
men as "Mister," or a Negro woman as "Miss" or "Mrs."
Negroes are addressed by their first names, unless they are
entitled to be referred to as "doctor" or "professor." The question of Negro-white relations is undergoing changes, however
slow. Accommodative adjustments represent an uneasy equilibrium which frequently breaks down into further conflict.[18]

**Mexicans and Anglo-Americans.** A situation similar to that
among Negroes and whites exists in areas where Mexicans and
Anglo-Americans have come into contact. Taylor describes the
situation in Nueces County, Texas, thus:

> In the transition from stock raising to farming, the American whites
> have become farmers. The Mexicans as laborers have cleared the land
> of brush and tended the cotton and vegetable crops. The roles of the
> two races in this development have been sharply distinguished.[19]

**The American Indian.** The accommodative technique used
upon the American Indians has been to segregate them geographically on reservations. Their status has been defined by
the whites as politically inferior. Many of them are not citizens,
but are wards of the state.

To these several illustrations of accommodation between
ethnic groups might be added the cases of several Mennonite
sects, particularly the Amish and Hutteran Brethren, as examples in which the minority group has achieved a state of

[18] See T. Lynn Smith, *The Sociology of Rural Life*, p. 481 f. for a good discussion
of accommodation of this sort.
[19] Reprinted from *An American-Mexican Frontier*, p. 93, by Paul S. Taylor, by
permission of the University of North Carolina Press. Copyright, 1934, by the University of North Carolina Press.

accommodation with the enveloping culture without overt conflict.

**Equalitarian accommodation.** Accommodation does not always take the form of "subordination of one person or group to another person or group."[20] When wage disputes occur, the labor contract developed in the process of collective bargaining represents a form of accommodation in which both parties have made some concessions and neither is subordinated to the other. In agriculture, where few effective unions exist among the workers, this recourse is not as common as it is in industry. In many countries the government has therefore become an active agent in resolving conflicts. In England, for example, there are boards which determine the wages for agricultural workers. In the United States only in the production of sugar beets and cane are wages set by the government; the Secretary of Agriculture does so after holding hearings in various areas at which both employers and workers testify. In Cuba the wages of sugar-cane workers are determined by law. Numerous countries have minimum wage laws, as well as laws setting minimum daily or weekly hours of work, which represent attempts by government to achieve or maintain equilibrium between agricultural employers and employees.

In this chapter we have considered two of the most fundamental forms of social interaction, conflict, and competition. We have also considered the process of accommodation, which represents the adjustments which follow conflict. The source of these actions lies in imperious wants of individuals, wants which call for satisfaction and for which there is a limited supply of goods or services or other cultural means with which to satisfy them. Thus individuals and groups strive for the same area of land, for a limited supply of food, machinery, or other commodities and services. Laborer and employer struggle for their respective shares in the produce of an enterprise. There are opposing interests between the urbanite and the ruralite. Farmer competes with farmer for profits; one ethnic group competes with another for control of land or market; one sect tries to outrival another for the patronage of a limited clientele. When conflict flares it is never of long duration. The participants

[20] E. B. Reuter, *op. cit.*

cannot endure for an extended period the intensity of open combat. There must be a truce, a settlement, under which peaceful life is again possible. The two factions have to accommodate each other. Oftener than not accommodation brings about a stabilization of relations, one individual or group in a position of dominance over the other. Sometimes, as in wage agreements, the participants acknowledge equality; such settlements do not necessarily involve domination and subordination.

## QUESTIONS FOR DISCUSSION

1. Point out the differentiating characteristics of *conflict, competition,* and *accommodation.*
2. Give the two main reasons or factors that explain why human beings oppose one another. Are there rural-urban differences in this regard? Discuss.
3. Why has there always been a basic conflict between landowners and the nonowning tenants and workers? Analyze the two value systems involved in this struggle. Where are conflicts of this kind most serious at present?
4. Summarize the origin, the issues involved, and the outcome of the agrarian protests against urban exploitation, including the Granger, Farmers' Alliance, the American Society of Equity and the Farmer's Union movements. Would you regard these movements as expressions of political radicalism? Explain.
5. Why is the industrialization of agriculture, involving large estates and *factory farms,* almost sure to result in serious social conflict?
6. Agricultural production that is largely dependent on hired workers could not well withstand the effects of periodic strikes. Why?
7. What, according to your view, are the basic causes for conflicts within and among churches?

## SELECTED REFERENCES

Chase, Stuart. *Democracy Under Pressure.* New York: The Twentieth Century Fund, 1945. See especially Chapter 9.

Hardin, Charles H. *The Politics of Agriculture: Soil Conservation and the Struggle for Power in Rural America.* Glencoe, Ill.: The Free Press, 1952.

Kester, Howard. *Revolt Among the Sharecroppers.* New York: Covici Friede, 1936.

McConnell, Grant. *The Decline of Agrarian Democracy*. Berkeley and Los Angeles: University of California Press, 1953.

McWilliams, Carey. *Brothers Under the Skin*. Boston: Little, Brown and Co., 1943.

Myrdal, Gunnar. *An American Dilemma: The Negro Problem and Modern Democracy*, Vol. I, Chapter 27. New York: Harper and Brothers, 1944.

*Report of the President's Commission on Migratory Labor*. Washington: Government Printing Office, 1951.

Saloutas, Theodore, and Hicks, John D. *Agricultural Discontent in the Midwest*. Madison: University of Wisconsin Press, 1951.

Sanderson, Dwight, and Polson, R. A. *Rural Community Organization*, Chapters 4, 10. New York: John Wiley and Sons, 1939.

Taylor, Carl C. *The Farmers' Movement, 1620–1920*. See especially Chapters 7 and 12. New York: American Book Co., 1953.

*Violations of Free Speech and the Rights of Labor*. Report of Senate Committee on Education and Labor, 77th Congress, Second Session, Report No. 1150, Part III. See "The Wheatland Riot," pp. 243–254, and "The Economic, Social, and Political Plight of Labor in California's Industrialized Agriculture," pp. 175–196.

Young, Kimball. *Sociology: A Study of Society and Culture*, Second Edition, pp. 64–69. New York: American Book Co., 1949.

# CHAPTER 9

# COOPERATION

Cooperation and antagonistic effort (conflict and competition) are opposite forms of social interaction. They are, as it were, opposite sides of the same shield. Nevertheless, they operate simultaneously in group action. This is especially manifest in times of war. When nations are engaged in struggle with each other, the intensity of cooperation within the respective groups is at its peak.

The phenomenon, which is referred to as *ambivalence*, is nowhere better illustrated than in the history of farmer movements in the United States. As manifestations of an instrument of conflict between farm and nonfarm groups these various movements were discussed briefly in the preceding chapter. As part of their effort to redress the inequalities which farmers felt between themselves and those identified as their enemies, they began to set up *cooperatives*. That is to say, they were at one and the same time engaged in economic warfare with those whom they regarded as their exploiters and were cooperating with unusual intensity among themselves. What provoked cooperation in the first place was the desire widely felt by farmers to improve their position with respect to the nonfarm group. They realized that the desired objective could not be achieved except through the pooling of their efforts.

## COOPERATION ROOTED IN NATURE

Mutual aid or the joint effort of two or more individuals to achieve some purpose is a pattern of behavior common not only to mankind but to other forms of life as well. Traditional examples from the insect world are the honey bee and the ant, and from the plant world, the lichen. The social insects seem to operate according to a well-organized plan with division of labor among various classes. It is quite natural, viewing the impressive works of the insects, to attribute to them a cooperative instinct; and generally to regard as instinctive the manifestations of cooperation in all forms of life.[1] However, it is equally clear that the form of interaction we call conflict is also universal among plants and animals.

Both kinds of behavior are natural forms of expression, in man as in the other forms of life. Whether they represent inherited or acquired traits has been discussed often; but as with the larger question of heredity versus environment, no final decision can as yet be made. Still, as Kimball Young observes, it is not necessary to explain the traits in terms of heredity; they can be accounted for quite easily in terms of cultural conditioning.[2] For our purposes the genetic aspect of the question is not important. What is of primary interest in the present discussion is to describe the nature of cooperation and to indicate the forms of its expression among rural people, including the principles of organization which have proved effective insofar as contractual cooperation is concerned.

### FORMS OF COOPERATION

**Informal.** The word *cooperative* has become so prominent in the daily speech of peoples the world over as designating a formally organized agency or institution, that it is easy to overlook the less conspicuous but probably more important informal cooperation in which people engage from day to day. The informal sort may involve at one time a simple act of helpfulness for a neighbor in need; another time an agreement to share the work of harvesting crops if it is more efficient to reap together than to reap separately; again, there may be an emergency in the community, such as a fire or flood, which requires that everybody lend a hand to save life and property.

In the history of rural life voluntary acts of helpfulness to achieve a common end are characteristic. In American culture,

[1] The classic work on the subject is that of P. A. Kropotkin, *Mutual Aid: A Factor in Evolution*, Revised Edition. New York: Alfred A. Knopf, 1917.

[2] See Kimball Young, *Sociology: A Study of Society and Culture*, Second Edition, pp. 72-73. New York: American Book Co., 1949.

informal cooperation is most commonly manifested in the exchange of farm work, in the borrowing and lending or sharing of machinery and other facilities. It was also manifested in the house- and barn-raisings of the frontier days, which took on the character of a festival as well as an economic enterprise. Putting up a barn or a house was a difficult matter for a man working alone, but with a few neighbors to help out the work was more than proportionally lightened. Many hands make light work, says the proverb. In Cuba rural people have a counterpart to the American house-raising in the *cobija* or roof-thatching. Practically all houses are thatched with palm leaves, and periodically the roof has to be replaced. But whether it is the roof of a new or of an old house, the *cobija* is an occasion when the neighbors come and help with the work, the owner providing dinner, cigars, and perhaps a little rum to add a festive touch.[3] To mention other characteristic expressions of mutual aid among rural people, there are those acts of helpfulness which neighbors always perform when death or sickness visits a family.

C. P. Loomis has drawn some interesting graphs to show the patterns of informal cooperation in the community of El Cerrito. The diagrams show the extent to which farm implements are lent and work exchanged among the inhabitants. Among other things, they reveal the extent to which kinship groups are involved in mutual aid, a phenomenon which is probably common to many other sections of the world.

Informal cooperation is characteristic of simple primary group societies, and is especially associated with the family and the neighborhood. It occurs most frequently among groups living under frontier conditions with minimum capital and other resources. Weather and personal crises weigh heavily on such individuals, families, and neighborhoods, and the pooling of effort is necessary for success or survival. The passing of the frontier, the increased sense of security of the individual farmer, as well as the capital resources at his command, the increased mobility resulting from rapid and easy communication facilities have brought about a decline in the informal type of cooperation even in the rural neighborhood. Farmers have become more

---

[3] A former resident of Yucatán has informed the author that the *cobija* is common in that region also.

independent and able to get along without calling on the neighbors for help.

**Formal.** Cooperative action beyond the primary group—and more and more within it—takes on the structural form of an institution in which the participants may be personally unacquainted with one another. Close acquaintance is certainly not a necessary precondition for success in the formal sort of cooperative enterprise, although it is a beneficial one. Cooperation institutionalized is in the form of a corporation, legally constituted. Capital is provided through sale of stock, membership fees, or by borrowing, and the returns are measured in dividends or savings. The members are those who have paid their fees, not as in the case of the informal sort merely those who live in a certain neighborhood or family.

Most cooperatives are designed for economic ends: either to lower the cost of purchased commodities or services—consumers' cooperatives; or to increase the profit from the sale of commodities produced by the members—producers' cooperatives. Even the so-called service cooperatives, although distinguished by the United States census from those engaged in buying and selling, have an economic purpose. Examples of service cooperatives are in medicine or hygiene and rural electrification.

### PHASES IN COOPERATIVE DEVELOPMENT

In the United States it is an interesting fact that the formal or what T. Lynn Smith calls the *contractural* sort of cooperation has been pre-eminently a movement among farm people.[4] Isolated cases of farm cooperatives have been noted as early as 1810, but most of the activity in the field has developed since the War Between the States. It was after this war that commercial agriculture assumed major proportions. As long as the self-sufficing economy, characteristic of the frontier, was predominant, cooperative marketing associations had little reason for being.[5] The National Grange, the first of the major farm organizations, imparted considerable momentum during the

[4] T. Lynn Smith, *The Sociology of Rural Life*, p. 458 f. New York: Harper and Brothers, 1940.

[5] B. H. Hibbard, *Marketing Agricultural Products*, p. 3 f. New York: D. Appleton-Century Co., 1921.

1870's to the cooperative movement. It developed some cooperative marketing organizations, established a considerable number of cooperative stores and purchasing associations, and some cooperative banks.[6] Moreover, the Grange, as Ellsworth points out, made an important contribution when it sent a representative abroad in 1875 to study cooperation in European countries.[7] In the same year a set of rules for the organization of cooperative stores based on the famous Rochdale principles was promulgated in the United States. Although most of the Grange cooperatives were short-lived, a few have persisted and the influence of the early Grange activities of two generations ago greatly stimulated subsequent developments. Additional support has been given to the movement by other farm organizations, such as the Farmers Cooperative and Educational Union of America, the American Society of Equity, and the American Farm Bureau Federation.

T. G. Stitts has appropriately divided the history of farm cooperatives in the U.S. into four periods:

. . . The *first* began around 1810, when cheese-making enterprises were cooperatively organized. It ended about 1870, with a record of accomplishment that included formation of mutual insurance and irrigation companies and supply-purchasing cooperatives.

The *second* period began with the rise of the Grange, Patrons of Husbandry. Grange-sponsored cooperatives marketed farm products, bought supplies, and manufactured farm implements. They were short-lived for the most part, but a few continued well into the present century.

The *third* period started in the early nineties and continued about 30 years. It saw the perfection of techniques for operating the various types of local associations, and the development of federations, large-scale centralized associations, and cooperative selling on terminal markets.

It was this third period that merged and developed into the *fourth* period, beginning about 1920. Large-scale cooperative marketing of various commodities reached a high state of development. Committees, councils, and an annual institute were organized to seek out the essentials necessary for continued substantial progress. Numerous Federal and

---

[6] R. H. Ellsworth, *The Story of Farmers' Cooperatives*, pp. 4–7. Washington, D.C.: Farm Credit Administration, 1938.
[7] *Ibid.*

state laws facilitating farmers' cooperative business activities were put upon the statute books.[8]

By 1952 farmers' cooperatives of all kinds enrolled an estimated 7,363,000 members as against about 3 million members in 1932. Since some farmers belong to more than one cooperative, it is impossible to say what the proportion of all member farmers is, but it is well over half, and probably two thirds, of the so-called commercial farmers. In 1950–52 the 10,166 marketing and purchasing cooperatives had a gross volume of business of 12.1 billion dollars.[9] The Interbureau Committee on Postwar Programs summarizes the development in cooperation for the two decades after 1925:

Developments in agricultural cooperation during the last two decades have been characterized by the formation and growth of large-scale cooperative businesses, both in marketing and purchasing, and by the broadening of the services rendered by cooperatives, particularly within the range of related functions. Thus many marketing cooperatives also assist their members in obtaining supplies and special services needed for quality crop production; many purchasing cooperatives add to their original line of goods, such as gasoline and oil, feed and fertilizer, such other lines as farm hardware, farm and household equipment, building materials, groceries, and other consumer goods. In many commodity fields, large-scale marketing associations are now carrying their members' products through to the terminal market and on the way performing the necessary services of grading, processing, and packing. In order to reduce the cost and to improve the quality of farm supplies, large-scale purchasing associations are now operating feed mills, fertilizer factories, petroleum refineries, chick hatcheries, and the like.

The last two decades have been characterized also by many improvements in local cooperatives and expansion of local cooperative services. Many new fields of cooperative activity have been opened, such as cotton ginning, cotton warehousing, forest management, cooperative auctions for various products, rural electric cooperatives, rural health associations, cooperative slaughter houses, cold-storage locker enterprises, artificial breeding associations, and cooperative farm machinery groups.[10]

[8] Tom G. Stitts, in his foreword to R. H. Ellsworth, *op. cit.*

[9] Anne L. Gessner, "Statistics of Farmers' Marketing, Purchasing and Service Cooperatives, 1951–52," p. 14. General Report 2, Farmer Cooperative Service, 1954.

[10] "Agricultural Cooperatives in the Postwar Period," Interbureau Committee on Postwar Programs, United States Department of Agriculture, Washington, D.C., July, 1945, p. 3.

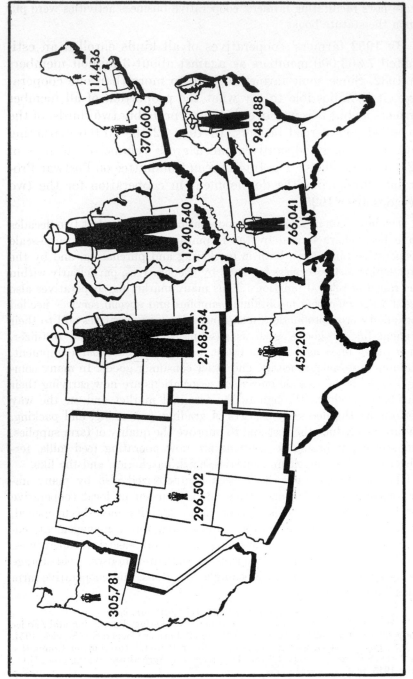

114,436

370,606

948,488

1,940,540

766,041

2,168,534

452,201

296,502

305,781

FIGURE 33. *Membership in Farmers' Cooperatives at Midcentury, by Geographic Divisions*

This growth has by no means been general over the United States. Some sections have responded with more enthusiasm than have others. (See Figure 33.) In the Southern states there were relatively few farmers who reported buying or selling goods or services through cooperatives in 1950. The area which shows the most response in proportion to the number of farmers is the North Central and Far West, especially Minnesota, Wisconsin, Iowa, and Idaho. Regional differences in use of contractual type of cooperation are obviously related to basic cultural differences. Within the. states showing high rates of participation there are differences among ethnic groups and types of farms involved. The ethnic group with the most noted reputation for establishing and working through cooperatives is the Finnish. As we shall see presently, the cooperatives are most numerous in the marketing of dairy products, grain, and fruits and vegetables; and in milk processing plants. These are especially common in the states rating highest. On the other hand, in spite of the national importance of cotton in the nation's agriculture, relatively few cooperatives engage in the marketing or processing of this crop.

## THE PRINCIPLES OF COOPERATIVE ORGANIZATION

Most of the successful cooperatives, whether of the consumer or producer type, operate on the principles developed in 1840 by a group of English textile workers and commonly referred to as the Rochdale principles. They have been conveniently restated by W. W. Fetrow as follows:

1) *Democratic control by members.* This is achieved by the application of the famous Rochdale principle of "one man, one vote." In other words, voting is by members, not by the amount of stock held as is the customary plan in a non-cooperative enterprise. In rare cases voting may be on the basis of the amount of business the individual contributes to the cooperative.

2) *Payment for capital limited to a conservative rate.* The typical cooperative is a non-profit organization, the earnings of which are in reality savings for its members. Therefore it cannot return these profits or savings to holders of capital. Naturally, it must have capital just as any other business enterprise, but it pays for it at a specified rate of interest and not in terms of the earnings of the organization.

3) *Benefits and savings are shared in direct proportion to patronage.*
This means that whatever earnings accrue above the cost of operation
are returned to the patrons in proportion to the amount of business
they have contributed.

For example, [continues Fetrow] the farmer who delivers 10,000
bushels of grain to his cooperative contributed ten times as much to
the business of association as did the farmer who delivered only 1,000
bushels. If the savings amount to 1 cent a bushel the farmer who delivered 10,000 bushels would be entitled to $100 and the other farmer
to only $10.[11]

**General types of cooperatives.** The Bureau of the Census,
in reporting the amount of business done through co-ops by
farmers in 1939, classifies cooperatives into three general
categories: *buying, selling,* and *service.* Buying cooperatives
obviously would include all of those which in more common
terminology are referred to as *consumers'* cooperatives, although
this latter term is applied chiefly to those which have developed
in the urban centers. Among farmers it is more common to
refer to them as cooperative purchasing associations. It is
common practice of farmer cooperatives to combine purchasing
and selling in the same organization to a considerable extent.
That is to say, a cooperative for the marketing of eggs and
poultry products will also purchase feed, young chicks, and other
supplies for their members. The selling cooperatives include
all of those that are customarily referred to as marketing
co-ops. They include a wide variety of organizations, usually
set up around a specific commodity. Service cooperatives include such associations as the mutual telephone companies,
power and light associations, group health associations, and
the like. This breakdown of types of cooperatives as given by
the Census Bureau does not suggest fully the breadth of the
activities of cooperatives; still, census data can be used to
indicate areas where cooperative activity is strong or weak.
It will be noted from Figure 33 that there were ten states, all
in the South and most of them adjacent, of whose farmers less
than ten per cent did business through cooperatives in 1939.
The high ranking states were in the North and were mostly

[11] Ward W. Fetrow, "Three Principles of Agricultural Cooperation," Farm
Credit Administration, Washington, D.C., 1940, pp. 6, 7.

adjacent; they had more than four times as high a proportion
of farmers doing business with cooperatives of all kinds as did
the ten lowest states.

Specific types. There are no accurate figures on the number
of farm cooperatives of all types in the United States, but a
partial list is shown in Table 9.

TABLE 9. *Number of Cooperatives of Various Types and Estimated
Membership at Midcentury*

| TYPE | NUMBER OF ASSOCIATIONS | ESTIMATED MEMBERSHIP |
|---|---|---|
| Marketing | 6,582 | 4,228,556 |
| Beans and peas | 16 | 6,403 |
| Cotton and cotton products | 546 | 388,303 |
| Dairy products | 1,939 | 827,823 |
| Fruits and vegetables | 825 | 138,237 |
| Grain | 2,193 | 906,881 |
| Livestock | 538 | 905,453 |
| Nut | 42 | 43,312 |
| Poultry and poultry products | 144 | 133,774 |
| Rice | 52 | 7,060 |
| Sugar products | 65 | 33,599 |
| Tobacco | 28 | 709,018 |
| Wool and mohair | 116 | 98,855 |
| Miscellaneous | 78 | 29,838 |
| Purchasing | 3,323 | 3,032,541 |
| Service | 261 | 102,032 |
| Total | 10,166 | 7,363,129 |

Source: Anne L. Gessner, *op. cit.*, Table 2.

A mere reading of the list of cooperatives in Table 9 and
the purposes which they serve emphasizes the great diversity
of activities around which such organizations have been formed.
The associations are clearly most numerous for transactions
involving grain, dairy products, and fruits and vegetables. It
will be recalled from the discussion in Chapter 3 that these are
commodities produced mainly in the North and West where,
as the map (Figure 33) reveals, the greatest membership is
found. In membership livestock and tobacco also rank high.

Types according to structure. From the standpoint of organization, cooperatives have been classified into three groups:

1) *Local associations.* These are small community enterprises,
operating independently of other organizations, and with a membership limited to the community concerned. They are usually
formed around the marketing of one commodity.

—

2) *Federated associations.* These are unions of a number of local associations for purposes of increasing their efficiency and quality of service. One of the benefits is the reduction of overhead cost and the ability to employ more capable management. An example of this type is the California Fruitgrowers Association.

3) *Centralized type.* This type of organization is characterized by a rather widely scattered membership interested in the marketing of one commodity. There are no local or regional associations although the association may serve members over a wide area.

### RECENT TRENDS

Most readily discernible trends in farmer cooperatives are shifts from the smaller to the larger and more complex, from country shipping point to city market. The *Farmer Cooperative Service* in 1954 reported 177 federations of cooperatives. Of these, 102 were engaged primarily in marketing, 69 in purchasing supplies for member locals, with locals of the remaining 6 both purchasing and selling for member patrons. Also reported were 175 large-scale organizations operating on a centralized basis, with another 83 associations combining features of the federated and the centralized business structure.

One of the most significant developments in the field of cooperatives in recent years has been the expansion of the purchasing associations and the service cooperatives. As pointed out earlier, the purchasing activities had been largely associated with the selling cooperatives, though not entirely so. This is particularly true in the purchasing of gas and oil, in which the expansion of the cooperative technique has been most rapid. The rapid growth of purchasing as compared with marketing associations in recent years is shown by the estimated membership of marketing and purchasing associations as reported by the Department of Agriculture.[12] (See Table 10.)

The Federal government has had a significant influence on the growth of service cooperatives, through its various agencies. The Farmers Home Administration helped to organize health cooperatives among low-income farmers. At the peak of this

[12] Anne L. Gessner, *op. cit.*, p. 65.

TABLE 10. *Membership in Cooperatives*

| Year | Purchasing | Marketing | Total |
|------|-----------|-----------|-------|
| 1939–40 | 900,000 | 2,300,000 | 3,200,000 |
| 1940–41 | 980,000 | 2,420,000 | 3,400,000 |
| 1941–42 | 1,170,000 | 2,430,000 | 3,600,000 |
| 1942–43 | 1,270,000 | 2,580,000 | 3,850,000 |
| 1951–52 | 3,032,541 | 4,228,556 | 7,250,097 |

program these health organizations existed in 600 counties and served some 80,000 families.[13] Although most have ceased to function, they served as experiments in joint action, and hastened the spread of medical care by other means in rural areas. Also, the FHA, through its community and cooperative services division, promoted thousands of small cooperatives for numerous purposes, including purchasing machinery (such as combines, feed mills, and terracing equipment) and purebred sires.

Another marked advance in the spread of service coops came with the establishment of the Rural Electrification Administration. At mid-century over 900 electrical cooperatives were serving nearly 4 million farms. In 1952 Congress authorized REA to conduct a similar program to bring telephone service to the farm. These were but a few of the types of service cooperatives. Mutual fire insurance companies, mutual irrigation companies, and mutual telephone companies have existed for many years in the United States. These were formed without any government promotion.

## THE SOCIAL ASPECTS OF THE COOPERATIVE MOVEMENT

1) Expansion of the cooperative movement has added greatly to the complexity and the variety of social contacts for rural people. The fact that half of the farmers of the United States belong to cooperatives of one kind or another means that for them, at least, the opportunities for social acquaintanceship have been increased. At the same time, these organizations, representing as they do "interest groups," transcend the old

[13] Farm Security Administration, United States Department of Agriculture, May 1, 1941, p. 14.

neighbor boundaries and constitute a phase of the transition from a primary group to a secondary group rural society.

2) The economic cooperatives, particularly, have greatly enlarged the farmer's social horizons. Through them he has come to learn more of the outline of national and world economy. He has learned that his relationship to the outside world is one of interdependence. His experience in the cooperative has taught him that necessary middleman functions must be performed, and he has learned some of the problems involved in the distribution of his products from the farm to the consumer. It is highly possible too that the farmer's increased knowledge of the services performed by nonfarm people in the cities, towns, and villages has tended to reduce the antagonisms between town and country, which previously were based so largely upon a lack of appreciation, on the part of both groups, of the work and way of life of each other. (See pictures following page 144.)

3) By encouraging specialization in crop production, cooperatives have tended to increase the dependence of the farm family on the outside world. There is a growing awareness on the part of farm people that their welfare is indissolubly linked with the urban world.

4) Since the cooperative movement has always stressed the importance of developing social bonds among the members, it has become a rallying point for many activities other than those involved in its economic functions. These other activities have included especially adult education and recreation.

5) By adding to the income of the cooperating families and by establishing services which otherwise would be outside their reach, the cooperatives have undoubtedly helped to raise the level of living on farms and in rural areas generally. Cooperative associations hold meetings, issue publications, conduct tours and demonstrations, and in numerous ways seek not only to educate the membership in their relations with the organization itself, but also to give them an understanding of their broader relations to the Great Society. They are frequently cited as being among the most important organizations contributing to an understanding of the actual functioning of democracy in present-day society.

## QUESTIONS FOR DISCUSSION

1. Discuss the significance of the decline of mutual aid and the increase in formal cooperation. Relate this trend to the changes in primary and secondary group relations.
2. Account for the comparative lag in development of consumers' and producers' cooperatives among farm people.
3. Can you see any reason or reasons why producers' cooperatives should oppose cooperatives of consumers? Do you know of cases in which *cooperatives* have been a basis for *conflict* in rural communities?
4. Account for the regional differences in cooperative activity in rural America. Why have certain foreign countries, such as Sweden, Denmark, and New Zealand, made such phenomenal progress in cooperative organization?
5. Why do you think there have been so many failures in cooperative farm enterprises?
6. Discuss the proposition that people tend to be more cooperative in times of crisis than at other times.

## SELECTED REFERENCES

Abrahamsen, Martin A., and Searce, Jane L. "Operations of Major Regional Purchasing Cooperatives 1941–1945," *Farm Credit Administration Circular C–148*, Washington, D.C., 1952.

Anderson, W. A. "Farm Cooperatives and Farm Women." *Cornell University AES, Department of Rural Sociology, Mimeograph Bulletin 16.* May, 1945.

Banfield, E. C. *Government Project: An Account of Big Government in Action*, Glencoe, Ill.: The Free Press, 1951.

Beal, George; Fessler, Donald; and Wakeley, Ray E., "Agricultural Cooperatives in Iowa: Farmers' Opinions and Community Relations," *Iowa AES Research Bulletin 379.* 1951.

*Co-ops in Other Lands.* (Reprints from the *News for Farmer Cooperatives.*) Farm Credit Administration, 1952.

Eaton, Joseph W., and Katz, Saul M. *Research Guide on Cooperative Group Farming.* ("A Research Bibliography on Rural Cooperative Production and Cooperative Communities.") New York: The H. W. Wilson Company, 1942.

*Farmers in a Changing World.* Yearbook of Agriculture, 1940. "The Growth of Farm-City Cooperative Associations," pp. 706–720, by Sidney N. Gubin; "Cooperative Marketing by Farmers," p. 705, by E. A. Stokdyk. Washington, D.C.: Government Printing Office.

Fetrow, Ward W. "Three Principles of Agricultural Cooperation," *Farm Credit Administration Circulation E–24*, Washington, D.C., 1940.

Kolb, J. H., and Brunner, E. deS. *A Study of Rural Society*, Fourth Edition, Chapter 9. Boston: Houghton Mifflin Company, 1952.

May, Mark A., and Doob, Leonard W. *"Competition and Cooperation." Social Science Research Council Bulletin 25.* April, 1937.

Sanderson, Dwight, and Polson, R. A. *Rural Community Organization,* pp. 64–71. New York: John Wiley and Sons, 1929.

Smith, T. Lynn. *The Society of Rural Life,* Chapter 21. New York: Harper and Brothers, 1940.

Taylor, C. C. *The Farmers' Movement, 1620–1920.* See especially Chapter 19, "The Cooperative Marketing Movement." New York: American Book Company, 1953.

Young, Kimball. *Sociology, A Study of Society and Culture,* Second Edition, pp. 70–73. New York: American Book Company, 1949.

*CHAPTER 10*

# CULTURE CONTACT, ASSIMILATION, ACCULTURATION

There are several words used to describe various aspects of human behavior resulting from the contact of different cultures. *Diffusion* is one such term and is defined by Herskovits as "that aspect of cultural change which includes the transmission of techniques, attitudes, concepts, and points of view from one people to another; whether it be through the medium of a single individual or of a group, or whether the contact is brief or sustained." [1] *Acculturation* and *assimilation* are used to indicate different types of diffusion. The first refers to "those contacts which are brief and involve no prolonged association between an individual and folk of a different culture—as where, for example, a trait of Polynesian culture is taken over by a Melanesian group visited once by some voyagers from an island far removed. . . . " [2] The second term, assimilation, is "used to designate the process by means of which a synthesis of culture is achieved, whatever the degree of contact or amount of borrowing." [3]

According to this distinction in the meaning of the terms, the reciprocal borrowing of culture traits by two diverse groups (acculturation) may take place without the achievement of synthesis (assimilation). That is to say, two or more diverse ethnic groups may occupy the same general area in a state of peaceful social interaction without either one of them losing its group identity or "social visibility." This is a useful distinction for the student of rural society, because he is everywhere confronted with the fact that complete assimilation has really

---

[1] Melville J. Herskovits, *Acculturation: A Study of Culture Contact*, p. 14. New York: J. J. Augustin, 1938.

[2] *Ibid.*, p. 14.

[3] *Ibid.*, p. 15.

not taken place and that groups of different origins and backgrounds have stubbornly retained in the American environment a sufficient number of their historic traits to make their social identification relatively easy.

Assimilation should be regarded as a *process* as well as an achieved *synthesis*. The measure of assimilation may be conceived of as a continuum between cultural diversity at one end and cultural synthesis at the other. There would, therefore, be *degrees of assimilation*, and conceivably a given cultural group could be placed on the continuum according to its progress toward, or regress from, total synthesis. Thus assimilation is recognized as a dynamic process as well as a condition achieved. It should also be pointed out that the process may work either way; that is, a group may be moving rather far towards assimilation with the larger group, when some event may occur which would retard or even reverse the process. For example, the antisemitism of the Nazi regime undoubtedly reversed the process of Jewish assimilation everywhere its policies took hold.

The conventional definition of assimilation is given by R. E. Park and E. W. Burgess as follows:

Assimilation is a process of interpenetration and fusion in which persons and groups acquire the memories, sentiments, and attitudes of other persons or groups, and, by sharing their experience and history, are incorporated with them in a common cultural life.[4]

## GROUP BEHAVIOR IN CULTURE CONTACT

When diverse cultural groups come into contact with each other, different forms of behavior may result as follows:

1) One group may consciously attempt to assimilate or absorb the other. Such behavior was somewhat typical of the reaction of "American culture" to the immigrant from Europe. Assimilation was attempted through devices of "Americanization" programs, compulsory education, and the like.

2) The minority group, on the other hand, may resist the attempts of the "enveloping culture" to absorb it, consciously adhere to its own values and way of life, and thus become

---

[4] Robert E. Park and E. W. Burgess, *Introduction to the Science of Sociology*, p. 735. Chicago: University of Chicago Press, 1924.

a cultural island. A notable example of this sort of behavior in rural areas is among the Old Order Amish people of Pennsylvania, Ohio, and Indiana.

3) The minority group may consciously seek identification with the enveloping culture. This behavior is especially characteristic of the children of immigrants in the New World who, despite the opposition to their actions by the older generation, often resort to various devices to achieve synthesis, such as Anglicizing foreign names, adopting current modes of dress, etc., which tend to diminish or obliterate their "social visibility." The larger group for its part may, of course, either react favorably, welcoming assimilation, or may resist it.

### DIVERSE CULTURAL GROUPS IN RURAL AMERICA

While the rural population of the United States is not as heterogeneous as the urban, it is by no means homogeneous. The rural South has the most nearly homogeneous population from an ethnic standpoint; the rural North and West the most mixed. The vast majority of non-English immigrants came at a time when new lands were being opened on the frontier region of the North and West, and these areas therefore contain many different ethnic groups. More recent immigrants from Europe have located in large numbers along the North Atlantic seaboard states.

**Distribution.** The number of descendants of various ethnic stocks in the American population is impossible to determine. The census enumerates only the foreign-born and the native-born of foreign or mixed parentage, failing to include the more numerous third and later generations. However, the 1940 census contains data on the mother tongue of the white population, which may be somewhat more indicative of the distribution of ethnic groups than the nativity data. How the non-English speaking groups [5] are distributed in the rural population of the United States is shown in Figure 34.

The concentrations of these non-Anglo elements in the North and East, and in Louisiana, Texas, and New Mexico are clearly

---

[5] "Mother tongue" was defined by the Census Bureau as "the principal language spoken in the home of the person in his earliest childhood." See *Nativity and Parentage of the White Population, Mother Tongue*, United States Bureau of the Census, p. 1.

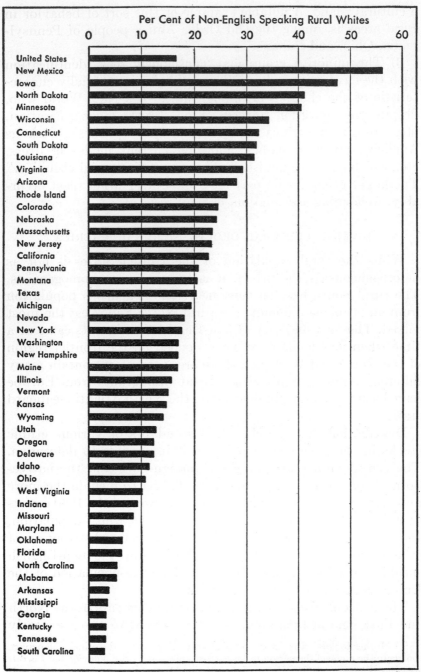

**Per Cent of Non-English Speaking Rural Whites**

| | 0 | 10 | 20 | 30 | 40 | 50 | 60 |
|---|---|---|---|---|---|---|---|
| United States | | | | | | | |
| New Mexico | | | | | | | |
| Iowa | | | | | | | |
| North Dakota | | | | | | | |
| Minnesota | | | | | | | |
| Wisconsin | | | | | | | |
| Connecticut | | | | | | | |
| South Dakota | | | | | | | |
| Louisiana | | | | | | | |
| Virginia | | | | | | | |
| Arizona | | | | | | | |
| Rhode Island | | | | | | | |
| Colorado | | | | | | | |
| Nebraska | | | | | | | |
| Massachusetts | | | | | | | |
| New Jersey | | | | | | | |
| California | | | | | | | |
| Pennsylvania | | | | | | | |
| Montana | | | | | | | |
| Texas | | | | | | | |
| Michigan | | | | | | | |
| Nevada | | | | | | | |
| New York | | | | | | | |
| Washington | | | | | | | |
| New Hampshire | | | | | | | |
| Maine | | | | | | | |
| Illinois | | | | | | | |
| Vermont | | | | | | | |
| Kansas | | | | | | | |
| Wyoming | | | | | | | |
| Utah | | | | | | | |
| Oregon | | | | | | | |
| Delaware | | | | | | | |
| Idaho | | | | | | | |
| Ohio | | | | | | | |
| West Virginia | | | | | | | |
| Indiana | | | | | | | |
| Missouri | | | | | | | |
| Maryland | | | | | | | |
| Oklahoma | | | | | | | |
| Florida | | | | | | | |
| North Carolina | | | | | | | |
| Alabama | | | | | | | |
| Arkansas | | | | | | | |
| Mississippi | | | | | | | |
| Georgia | | | | | | | |
| Kentucky | | | | | | | |
| Tennessee | | | | | | | |
| South Carolina | | | | | | | |

Bureau of the Census

FIGURE 34. *Per Cent of Non-English Speaking Rural Whites, by States, 1940*

indicated. The concentrations in the southern states mentioned are chiefly the French-speaking population of Louisiana and the Spanish-speaking population of Texas and New Mexico. In the North and East the "foreign" tongues include German, Swedish, Norwegian, Danish, Polish, French, Russian, and Czech as the most important groups. In the Southeast section of the United States there are very few non-Anglo peoples.

The retention of non-English tongues by the farm population is greatest in states where French and Spanish predominate. (See Table 11.) Thus, New Mexico, Louisiana, and Maine show unusually high proportions in the third generation or later.

TABLE 11. *Percentage of Rural-Farm Population Reporting Mother Tongue Other Than English Who Were Third Generation or Later*

| STATE | PERCENTAGE | STATE | PERCENTAGE |
|---|---|---|---|
| Louisiana | 94.9 | Maryland | 20.9 |
| New Mexico | 91.2 | Arkansas | 20.4 |
| Maine | 62.7 | North Dakota | 18.6 |
| Indiana | 52.6 | Michigan | 17.1 |
| Texas | 45.5 | Vermont | 13.7 |
| Missouri | 44.7 | Idaho | 12.0 |
| Colorado | 41.6 | New Hampshire | 9.7 |
| Ohio | 38.0 | West Virginia | 9.6 |
| Pennsylvania | 37.7 | Oregon | 7.8 |
| Florida | 33.3 | California | 7.2 |
| Virginia | 31.5 | Massachusetts | 5.9 |
| New York | 31.4 | Rhode Island | 5.4 |
| Kansas | 31.0 | Washington | 5.2 |
| Oklahoma | 30.2 | Connecticut | 3.4 |
| Wisconsin | 29.9 | Delaware | 3.4 |
| Illinois | 29.2 | New Jersey | 2.8 |
| Tennessee | 26.9 | Utah | 2.8 |
| Minnesota | 25.7 | Alabama | None |
| Iowa | 25.6 | Mississippi | None |
| Nebraska | 24.0 | Nevada | None |
| Arizona | 23.1 | North Carolina | None |
| South Dakota | 22.7 | South Carolina | None |
| Kentucky | 22.5 | Georgia | None |
| Montana | 21.7 | District of Columbia | None |
| Wyoming | 21.4 | | |

Source: Sixteenth Census of the United States, 1940, *Population: Mother Tongue by Nativity, Parentage, Country of Origin, and Age.* Table 3.

The high ranking of Indiana in fourth position is due largely to German-speaking inhabitants who belong to such pietistic religious sects as the Mennonites, Amish, Dunkards, and the German-

Lutheran denomination, all of which promote the use of the German language. The rank of Texas in fifth position while due in part to the Spanish and French influence is no less the result of several other groups, including German, Polish, and Czech.

**Ethnic groups differ in persistence.** The "mother tongue" data provides us with information on the persistence of the different languages, as measured by the proportion speaking each language who are native-born of native parentage—that is, third generation or later. The presumption is that if a high percentage of a group is in this third generation or later, there is a tendency for the language to persist.[6] It will be noted from Figure 35 that the French and Spanish groups have the highest persistence rates, followed by German, Czech, Norwegian and Polish. Italian, Yiddish, and Russian have low percentages in the native-born of native parentage group, no doubt because immigration of these groups has been more recent and thus the foreign-born constitute relatively greater proportions.

However, if we take the Swedish and Norwegian groups which were somewhat parallel in time of immigration, we note rather marked differences in their tendency to persist in the New World. It is rather remarkable that the Norwegian tongue shows a persistence rate three times as great as that for Swedish.

### FACTORS IN ASSIMILATION

**Assimilation retarded in rural areas.** The marked differences in the persistence rate of the various tongues in rural and urban areas, with uniformly higher rates in the rural-farm than in either of the other population groups, is also revealed by a study of Figure 35. The "social metabolism" of the city is much more rapid, and there is an apparent tendency for foreign groups to become absorbed by the third generation. Not so in the country. Here the ethnic groups may be located in geographically compact areas, where they are able to continue their old world customs and languages with little inconvenience so far as their relations with the outside world are concerned.

---

[6] The recency of immigration of the particular stock will tend to affect this percentage—or persistence rate—so that the data are not an infallible index of assimilation of the particular groups.

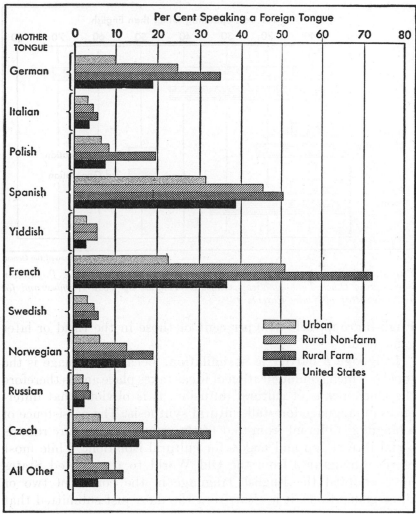

Bureau of the Census

FIGURE 35. *Per Cent of Those Speaking a Foreign Tongue Who Were Native-Born of Native Parents*

This rural-urban difference is further illustrated by the data in Figure 36. These data show, for example, that while the urban centers contained 71.4 per cent of all non-English-speaking peoples, they contained only 43.2 per cent of those who were third generation or later. On the other hand, the rural-farm population which contained only 14.5 per cent of the non-

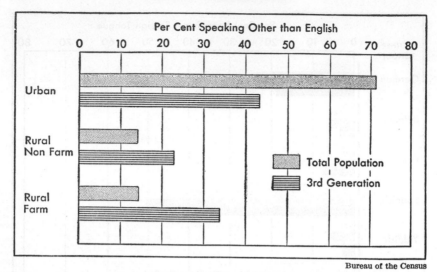

Bureau of the Census

FIGURE 36. *Percentage Distribution, Rural and Urban, of White Population Speaking Other Than English as Mother Tongue, by Total Number and for Native-Born of Native Parents*

English group, held 34.0 per cent of those in the third or later generations.

**Language a barrier to assimilation.** Because language is the tool by which communication of ideas takes place and is therefore the chief means of cultural diffusion, it is obvious that differences in language forestall cultural synthesis. The persistence of a language different from that of the enveloping culture retards social interaction and makes for cultural isolation. While most of the immigrants from the Old World to the United States have adopted the English language in the course of two or three generations, it is clear from the data just submitted that there are significant numbers of people to whom the old language is still the major language and who learn English but little if at all. Even the compulsory attendance of children in the public school is not enough to establish the English language as the tongue in general use in such groups. Thus, among the French-speaking population of Louisiana and the Spanish-Americans of the Southwest, among certain Amish and Mennonite groups, Bohemians, Poles, Italians, and other language groups, children even today come in contact with the English language only in the school after they have reached the age of six years.

In the case of the Spanish-American group in New Mexico, G. I. Sanchez points out that free schools and compulsory attendance have not wrought the miracle of cultural assimilation which many people have erroneously assumed they would. This cultural group had an existence in what is now the United States for two centuries before the intrusion of Anglo-European culture. Priority in time, however, brought no advantages to them; quite the contrary says Sanchez:

The special nature of the problem of educating this cultural minority has never been properly recognized by Federal and State governments. Educational practices in New Mexico have been patterned after those developed in the Middle West and in the East for peoples and conditions vastly different from those obtaining here. The selection of educational officials by popular election is a practice that is particularly incongruous in this situation. So is the district system. The use of standard curricula, books, and materials among these children is a ridiculous procedure.

The language problem illustrates the inadequacy of current instructional practices. Imagine the Spanish-speaking child's introduction to American education! He comes to school, not only without a word of English but without the environmental experience upon which school life is based. He cannot speak to the teacher and is unable to understand what goes on about him in the classroom. He finally submits to rote learning, parroting words and processes in self-defense. To him, school life is artificial. He submits to it during class hours, only partially digesting the information which the teacher has tried to impart. Of course he learns English and the school subjects imperfectly! The school program is based on the fallacious assumption that the children come from English-speaking homes—homes that reflect American cultural standards and traditions.[7]

The limitations upon full participation of this group—or any other which nurtures a tongue different from the official language—is further illustrated by the fact pointed out by G. Grisham who observed that "agricultural extension work has not reached the valley communities [of New Mexico]. Natives, not realizing the benefits they could receive from agricultural workers, have not cooperated to the extent that those in other communities have."[8]

[7] George I. Sanchez, *Forgotten People: A Study of New Mexicans*, pp. 31–32. Albuquerque: University of New Mexico Press, 1940.

[8] Glen Grisham, "Meeting Today's Needs in the Land of Mañana," *Land Policy Review*, United States Department of Agriculture, 1940, 3:32–36.

Grisham points out further that the "natives are still temperamentally much the same as were their fathers. Their culture, modified by the evolution of long isolation and poverty, is still distinctly Spanish in speech, custom, and religion." "Wheat," he says, "is cut by hand. Goats and horses stamp out the grain on mud threshing floors before it is winnowed by hand."

But it is not alone the Spanish-Americans who are prevented from sharing fully in the life of the majority culture. The Amish, who speak German and who refrain from signing any papers, including such documents as membership agreements in agricultural marketing organizations, can participate fully in extension and other activities only if some special effort is made to interpret the program to them and—as in the case of the Amish farmer—to make some concessions to his ancient prejudice against legal papers.

In a study of participation in agricultural extension work in Michigan, Hoffer found a significant correlation between such participation and the percentage of native-born farmers in the population. This lack of participation of the foreign-born, Hoffer rightly says, "may be explained by a failure on the part of the leaders in extension to interpret their programs to them in ways which, from the standpoint of their culture, are meaningful rather than to a lack of interest in the work." [9]

**Religion as a factor in assimilation.** The immigrants to the United States brought their religions and their church organizations with them. Naturally, the literature of the church—Bible, creed, catechisms, hymnals, etc.—was in the native language. Services in the native tongue were conducted in the New World, and inevitably for a considerable time, by ministers who were trained in the Old. The problem involved in adapting the immigrant church to the new conditions is well told by J. P. Johansen:

One of the most important elements in culture is language and every European church in America, save those whose native tongue was English, has been required to make its accommodation to this factor. The language question has been one of the most difficult problems with

[9] C. R. Hoffer, "Selected Social Factors Affecting Participation of Farmers in Agricultural Extension Work," *Michigan State College AES Special Bulletin 331,* June, 1944, p. 25.

which the immigrant churches have had to deal, for it involved the problem of rebirth in a new civilization. Conservatives in these churches have always maintained that the abandonment of the old European tongue and the adoption of English as the language of worship and instruction involved the abandonment of all the ways of the fathers and the introduction of a new "English or American religion." Their intuitions have usually been correct, for the adoption of the native tongue is only the most obvious symptom of the assimilation of the native culture as a whole. Progressive, that is more Americanized, leaders have argued for two centuries in immigrant church after immigrant church that abandonment of the foreign language was essential for the self-preservation of the denomination concerned. Their reasoning has also been sound, for it is a well-known fact that institutions are much more conservative than individuals and that churches will continue to pray, preach and teach in Dutch or German or Swedish long after the major number of their members have dropped these languages in all save religious relations and have raised a generation of children to whom the mother tongue is a foreign sound. The choice betweeen accommodation and extinction finally becomes a forced choice. Though churches may delay the moment of their surrender few elect to perish with their mother tongue.[10]

However, the church has slowly made the transition from the native language to English. But it cannot be said that it has taken the lead in promoting assimilation. Rather it has tended to resist the pressure which has come from the third or later generations to make the change. Says Johansen:

In the history of most foreign congregations one may observe three fairly distinct stages of language usage: the foreign language wholly; both the foreign language and English (American); and the native language. This change of the church language is accompanied by profound spiritual changes in the nature of the service liturgies and hymns are essentially untranslatable. The translations are apt to be clumsy expressions which satisfy neither the foreign-born nor the native-born. There are, of course, available many instances of perfect or near-perfect renderings of foreign hymns in English and the spirit of the music is not difficult to preserve. But when the language of the old country is dropped, the worship of the immigrant churches rapidly changes so as to conform in general pattern with the democratic spirit, the urban-industrial life, and the patriotism of America. The immigrant church has become in

---

[10] John P. Johansen, "Immigrant Settlements and Social Organization in South Dakota," *South Dakota State College AES Bulletin 313*, June, 1937, p. 53.

many ways utterly dissimilar from the mother church from which it sprang.[11] (See Table 12.)

TABLE 12. *Displacement of Norwegian Services by English in Norwegian Lutheran Congregations in South Dakota*

| NORWEGIAN AND ENGLISH SERVICES | 1935–36 | 1925 | 1915 | 1905 |
|---|---|---|---|---|
| Congregations Considered | 272 | 274 | 164 | 120 |
| Reporting: | | | | |
| English only | 125 | 47 | 10 | 1 |
| Both English and Norwegian | 121 | 202 | 86 | 16 |
| Norwegian only | 0 | 12 | 68 | 100 |
| No report | 26 | 13 | 0 | 3 |
| Average Number of Services: | | | | |
| Per congregation having English services | 29.0 | 22.1 | 9.0 | 11.6 |
| Per congregation having Norwegian services | 9.1 | 15.9 | 19.6 | 23.6 |
| Per cent Norwegian services of all services | 13.6 | 37.3 | 78.2 | 93.0 |

Source of data: The parochial reports of the Norwegian Lutheran Church in America, for 1936 and 1926. For 1915 and 1905, use was made of the Norwegian reports of the United Norwegian Lutheran Church in America "Den Forenede Norsk Lutherske Kirke i Amerika."

**Intermarriage as a measure of assimilation.** It seems logical to regard intermarriage as an indication of the degree to which assimilation has taken place. Groups may discard the language of their parents or grandparents in favor of the English tongue. They may assume the standard modes of dress in the new environment, join different churches from those of their forebears and become apparently completely assimilated, except that they choose a mate from their own group. The casual visitor to Wright County, Minnesota, would not be able to detect any apparent difference in behavior among the Finns, Germans, Swedes, French, English, Irish, or old American stock. Yet a survey of the nationality of husbands and wives of 885 farm families revealed that two thirds of them had married persons of the same nationality as themselves.[12]

In the survey from which the data in Figures 37 and 38 were secured, fourteen different nationalities were represented. However, four of them were in such small numbers that they were excluded from tabulations. The large number of ethnic groups involved emphasizes the great heterogeneity of the farm popula-

[11] John P. Johansen, "Immigrant Settlements and Social Organization in South Dakota," *South Dakota State College AES Bulletin 313*, June, 1937, p. 55.

[12] Lowry Nelson, "Intramarriage Among Nationality Groups in a Rural Area of Minnesota," *American Journal of Sociology*, 1943, 48:585–592.

| HUSBANDS Total 885 | German | Swedish | Finnish | French | Irish | Polish | English | Dutch | Norwegian | Bohemian |
|---|---|---|---|---|---|---|---|---|---|---|
| 385 German | 308 | 23 | 4 | 13 | 13 | 4 | 6 | 1 | 10 | 3 |
| 195 Swedish | 35 | 120 | 9 | 4 | 6 | | 4 | 1 | 15 | 1 |
| 83 Finnish | 2 | 4 | 72 | 1 | | | | | 3 | 1 |
| 54 French | 16 | 3 | | 26 | 5 | 1 | 1 | 1 | 1 | |
| 43 Irish | 18 | 6 | 1 | 2 | 10 | 3 | 1 | | 1 | 1 |
| 34 Polish | 6 | | | | 1 | 25 | 1 | | | 1 |
| 27 English | 4 | 3 | | 2 | | | 16 | | 1 | 1 |
| 24 Dutch | 7 | 1 | | | 1 | | 1 | 14 | | |
| 22 Norwegian | 5 | 10 | | 2 | 1 | | | | 4 | |
| 18 Bohemian | 4 | 3 | | 1 | 1 | | | | | 9 |
| WIVES 885 Total | German 405 | Swedish 173 | Finnish 86 | French 51 | Irish 38 | Polish 33 | English 30 | Dutch 17 | Norwegian 35 | Bohemian 17 |

Lowry Nelson, *American Journal of Sociology*, 1943

FIGURE 37. *Distribution by Nationality Groups of Husbands and Wives, Wright County, Minnesota*

tion in this area. The patterns of intermarriage among these groups is shown in Figure 37.

There is considerable difference among the groups in the rates of intramarriage. (See Figure 38.) The Finnish group rated highest with 86.7 per cent of all marriages of husbands being endogamous. Only the Irish and Norwegian fell below 50 per cent for either husband or wife marriages within the group.

It is quite clear that in this area of rural Minnesota, the people are still acutely conscious of nationality background. There was no hesitancy in giving the "nationality" on the schedule; in only 94 cases did the respondents say "American" in answer to the nationality question. The tendency to choose marriage partners along nationality lines is reinforced by

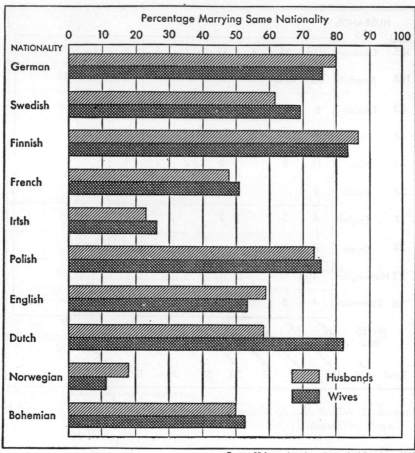

Lowry Nelson, *American Journal of Sociology*, 1943

FIGURE 38. *Percentage of Husbands and Wives Marrying Within the Same Nationality, Wright County, Minnesota*

religious affiliation, which is so often associated with ethnic origins. The tendency also for families with a common nationality background to settle in compact groups on the frontier has abetted the persistence of Old World culture and contributes to the continuation of in-group marriages.

The fusing of peoples through marriage is usually termed amalgamation, rather than assimilation. There are some students who do not regard intermarriage as a crucial test of cultural assimilation. Thus, C. A. Galitzi maintains that "intermarriage is not a condition *sine qua non* of assimilation, as complete assimilation can be achieved without racial amalgamation. It is more of a cultural than a biological process. . . . " [13] She admits, however, that intermarriage "hastens" the process of assimilation. And if this be true, then it must also be that intragroup marriage tends to *delay* the process. The family, which is one of the important carriers of culture, is likely to condition the child in the ancient traditions of the ethnic group if both parents are of the same background; it is less likely to share in the traits of the larger culture. Complete assimilation means that the alien group loses its "social visibility," interacting freely with the larger culture without manifestations of prejudice. So long as a person looking for a marriage partner avoids an individual because he or she is identified with a certain group—German, Irish, Finnish, Swedish, or what not—then the avoided group may not be considered as having been fully assimilated.

### IS ASSIMILATION INEVITABLE?

As pointed out in the beginning of this chapter, assimilation is a process as well as a completed synthesis. As a process it must be regarded conceptually as a continuum, and it is theoretically possible to locate any particular group under study at a particular point on this continuum which would indicate whether it had moved in the *direction of* or *away from* synthesis. That is to say, a group may be moving away from synthesis, moving toward it, or remaining in a more or less static relationship. This conception therefore is not based on the usual assumption that assimilation is inevitable and that all social change is towards synthesis. Donald Young, for example, states the assumption as follows: "It is a truism that two or more peoples living in the same geographical area, participating in the same economic system, no matter how divergent originally in racial or national origin, cannot be kept biologically separate; ultimately they become one stock." [14] Of course, "ultimately" is a long time, but even so, there is reason to doubt the inevitability

---

[13] Christine A. Galitzi, *A Study of Assimilation Among Rumanians in the United States*, p. 168. New York: Columbia University Press, 1929.

[14] Donald Young, "Research Memorandum on Minority Peoples in the Depression," *Social Science Research Council Bulletin 31*, 1937, p. 199.

of this one-way process. Differentiation is taking place as rapidly as is assimilation.

It seems justifiable to say that so long as the in-group marriage rate is at least 50 per cent, it is difficult to see how absorption is going to take place. This or even a smaller percentage of intragroup marriages will tend to maintain a "hard core" of cultural identity. The "melting pot" figure of speech is an unfortunate one to describe what is actually taking place. The melting *pot* so often does not reach the melting *point*. What we have in rural America apparently is not the amalgam suggested by the melting pot idea. It is more like *stew*, in which the separate elements are still identifiable, although each has contributed something of its flavor to the whole.

**Is assimilation necessary or desirable?** As assimilation has been regarded as inevitable, it has also been regarded as "desirable" if not actually "necessary." When one group conquers another, it tries to impose its language and culture upon the conquered. When Macedonia was given to Bulgaria by Hitler in 1941, the Bulgars, it is reported, proceeded to try to make the Hellenic population Slavic by going so far as to alter tombstone inscriptions from Greek to the Bulgar tongue. There are many illustrations, in Europe especially, of similar attempts of one ethnic group to absorb another by imposing its culture upon them. The United States has made one such attempt and failed, in the case of the American Indian. They seem to have succeeded only in part, after three hundred years of contact, in making Europeans out of them. Now, interestingly enough, the Federal policy is to restore something of the aboriginal culture which through the centuries they have tried to destroy. The fact that in the United States there are numerous "minority peoples," that the Spanish-Americans and the French "cajuns," for instance, persist without any marked weakening of the integrity of their cultures, seems to challenge the basic assumption that it is desirable to become synthesized. Rather the notion seems to be gaining headway that a nation can exist, as the United States has existed, without homogeneity being achieved. Perhaps it is only necessary that cultural assimilation be achieved on a certain level, where national unity is necessary, and that below that level, assimilation need not take place. It may even enrich the variety of social experience of all to have diversity persist throughout these levels. We can enjoy the *unity* where unity is needed and *diversity* where unity is not crucial.

**Differences in the assimilative process in rural and urban areas.** It seems apparent from the data submitted that the process of assimilation is much slower in the country than in the city. In fact, there is some question as to whether complete assimilation is likely to occur in some of the rural groupings. This seems especially true of the Canadian-French and the Spanish-Americans. But there are also others who are geographically segregated and whose old cultural characteristics seem to remain through the generations.

Whetten and Green point out that the process in rural areas is characterized by "group assimilation" while in the city it is "individual." [15] Still, it is well to remember that in the city there are cultural islands made up of groups apparently resistant to assimilation: there are the ghettos, the "little Italy's," and other isolated quarters. The anonymity of the city, on the other hand, favors the process of individual departure from the mores and customs of the immigrant community. In rural areas the individual is always identified with his group.

To summarize: the concept of assimilation implies both a process and a state of being. As process it denotes the interaction involved in the mutual acceptance of each other by two groups with different cultures or the merging of two cultures, both tending to lose their "social visibility." As a state of being, assimilation denotes the complete identification and synthesis of different cultures. The rural society of the United States is a mosaic of many ethnic and religious elements, which can be identified by differences in language, customs, and general ways of life. In many instances the melting pot has never reached the melting point. The retention of distinctive group characteristics has a definite relation to the functioning of community institutions. The rate of assimilation is apparently more rapid in the city than in the country, though even in the city there are hard cores which seem to resist the abrasive effect of the enveloping culture.

[15] N. L. Whetten and Arnold W. Green, "Field Research and the Concept of Assimilation," *Rural Sociology*, 1942, 7:252–260, p. 257.

## QUESTIONS FOR DISCUSSION

1. Give the meaning and describe the relationship of the following terms to each other: (a) *diffusion*, (b) *acculturation*, and (c) *assimilation*.
2. Under what circumstances can acculturation occur without assimilation taking place?
3. Distinguish between assimilation considered as a *process* and assimilation when used to designate a *synthesis*. What difficulty arises in connection with the second usage? How can this difficulty be resolved?
4. Relate instances in which a minority group has (a) consciously tried to adapt itself to a majority group or (b) resisted assimilation into an *enveloping culture.*
5. Account for the greater homogeneity in the population of the South as compared with the people in the North, East, and West. Where are non-English nationality groups concentrated?
6. Why may persistence in the use of the "mother tongue" by an immigrant stock and its descendants be taken as an index of non-assimilation? Which nationality groups have been the slowest to assimilate in terms of this index?
7. Three nationality groups whose *mother tongues* are largely of Latin origin, the French, Spanish, and Italians, have shown different rates of assimilation even though the three should have been able to learn English with about equal facility. How do you account for the fact that the Italians have assimilated much faster than the other two?
8. Explain why people in rural areas have lagged behind urban groups in the process of assimilation.
9. Mention some special difficulties that are often encountered by an immigrant church in the process of assimilating American culture? What is likely to happen to such a church if it fails to assimilate?
10. Why may intermarriage of racial or nationality groups be regarded as an *acid test* of the degree to which assimilation has taken place? Cite evidence to show that in-group marriage of nationality and racial stocks in this country continues at a rather high rate. What bearing does this have on the usually accepted view that America is a *melting pot?*
11. Would you regard the complete elimination of cultural and group differences as a desirable social goal? Discuss.
12. According to Whetten and Green, rural assimilation is on a group basis while urban assimilation is on an individual basis. How then

would you account for the *Little Italy's*, the ghettos, and the Negro sections of the large cities?

## SELECTED REFERENCES

Kollmorgen, Walter M. "The German Settlement in Cullman County, Alabama: An Agricultural Island in the Cotton Belt." United States Department of Agriculture, Bureau of Agricultural Economics, Washington, D.C., June, 1941. See also by same author, "A Reconnaissance of Some Cultural-Agricultural Islands in the South," *Economic Geography*, Vol. XVII, pp. 409–430, October, 1941.

Lynch, Russell Wilford. "Czech Farmers in Oklahoma: A Comparative Study of the Stability of a Czech Farm Group in Lincoln County, Oklahoma, and the Factors Relating to Its Stability." *Oklahoma Agricultural and Mechanical College Bulletin, Vol. XXXIX, No. 13.* June, 1942.

Marshall, Douglas. "Nationality and the Emerging Culture," *Rural Sociology*, 13:40–47, March, 1948.

Marshall, Douglas; Sewell, W. H.; and Haller, A. O. "School Attendance of Wisconsin Farm Youth," *Rural Sociology*, 18:257–260, September, 1953.

Myrdal, Gunnar. *An American Dilemma: The Negro Problem and Modern Democracy*, Vol. I, Chapters 3, 4, 5. New York: Harper and Brothers, 1944.

*Understanding Our Neighbors*. A Factual Study of America's Major Race Problem. Atlanta, Georgia: Commission of Interracial Cooperation, Inc., 1940.

Useem, John and Ruth H. "Minority-Group Pattern in Prairie Society," *American Journal of Sociology*, Vol. L, pp. 377–385, March, 1945.

Whetten, Nathan L., and Green, Arnold W. "Ethnic Group Relations in a Rural Area of Connecticut." *Storrs AES Bulletin 244.* January, 1943.

Young, Kimball. *Sociology: A Study of Society and Culture*, Second Edition, pp. 77–79; 273–4. New York: American Book Co., 1949.

## CHAPTER 11

# SOCIAL STRATIFICATION

Traditionally Americans have claimed that equal opportunities exist for all people. When he began his investigations in Plainville, James West observed, "Many, if not most, Plainvillers completely deny the existence of class in their community." [1] Yet when his inquiry got under way there was no difficulty in getting the local inhabitants to classify people according to a "higher" or "lower" status. Obvious inequalities in prestige, power, and the ability to "get ahead" are easily observable in American society and in all societies.[2] The importance of these inequalities hardly needs to be elaborated, but the importance of each is magnified by the fact that one begets the other; for example, institutionalized power (office) begets prestige and the opportunity to achieve important goals.

Three problems will be considered in this chapter. First, how does the farmer compare in inequalities with other social aggregates in American society; second, what are the inequalities within rural society; and third, what meaning does this inequality have for rural institutions?

### STATUS OF THE FARMER IN AMERICAN SOCIETY

In spite of the lip service paid to the farmer as the "backbone" of the nation, "the most important producer," and the "indispensable worker," farming does not rank high in the hierarchy of occupations. Comparisons of the farmer with other

[1] James West, *Plainville, U.S.A.*, p. 115. New York: Columbia University Press, 1945.
[2] This discussion follows the framework suggested in Harold F. Kaufman, Otis Dudley Duncan, Neal Gross, and William H. Sewell, "Problems of Theory and Method in the Study of Social Stratification in Rural Society," *Rural Sociology*, 1953, 18:12–24.

distinguishable groups will be made in terms of prestige, power, style of life, and life chances.

*Prestige or Social Honor.* One of the ways in which prestige has been determined by sociologists is by asking persons to rank occupations according to how they feel or how they think the community feels about the prestige of various occupations. One such study, which was conducted in Kansas with high school and college students, found that among 100 occupations, farm owner-operators ranked fiftieth, farm tenants, seventy-second, and farm laborers, eighty-sixth.[3] Among those occupations ordinarily found in a rural community, that of clergyman, bank cashier, editor-owner of the paper, trained nurse, county sheriff, and hotel-keeper all were ranked above the owner-operator farmer in the order indicated. When the 100 occupations were grouped into 26 categories and the rating averaged, the owner and tenant combined were in twenty-fifth place, only one rank above the bottom. In spite of the obvious difficulties of such research, for example, the connotations of the word one happens to use to describe an occupation, these results were consistent with other studies. (See Table 13 and 14.)

TABLE 13. *Median Years of School Completed of Experienced Male Workers 14 Years of Age and Over in the Labor Force by Major Occupation Groups for the United States*

| TYPES OF WORKERS | SCHOOL YEARS, 1950 |
|---|---|
| Professional, technical, and kindred workers | 16.0 |
| Sales workers | 12.3 |
| Managers, officials, and proprietors (exc. farm) | 12.2 |
| Clerical and kindred workers | 12.2 |
| Craftsmen, foremen, and kindred workers | 9.3 |
| Operatives and kindred workers | 8.7 |
| Service workers (exc. in private household) | 8.7 |
| Farmers and farm managers | 8.3 |
| Laborers (exc. farm and mine) | 8.0 |
| Farm laborers (exc. unpaid) and foremen | 7.1 |

Source: Bureau of the Census: *Census of Population: 1950*, Vol. IV, *Special Report*, Part 5, Chapter B, Education, 1953.

While data from studies made in the United States indicate for farming a relatively low position in the scale of occupations,

[3] Mapheus Smith, "An Empirical Scale of Prestige Status of Occupations," *American Sociological Review*, 1943, 8 : 185–192.

TABLE 14. *Median Income of Experienced Male Workers 14 Years of Age and Over in the Labor Force by Major Occupation Groups for the United States, 1952*

| TYPES OF WORKERS | MEDIAN INCOME, 1952 |
|---|---|
| Professional, technical, and kindred workers | 4,876 |
| Sales workers | 3,662 |
| Managers, officials, and proprietors (exc. farm) | 4,402 |
| Clerical and kindred workers | 3,448 |
| Craftsmen, foremen, and kindred workers | 3,792 |
| Operatives and kindred workers | 3,263 |
| Service workers, (exc. in private household) | 2,516 |
| Farmers and farm managers | 1,642 |
| Laborers (exc. farm and mine) | 2,325 |
| Farm laborers (exc. unpaid) and foremen | 924 |

Source: Data from *Current Population Reports: Consumer Income,* Series P-60, No. 14, December, 1953.

it can be said with some assurance that it rates even lower in many other countries of the world. The word *peasant* applied to the farmers of Europe and Asia is freighted with connotations of a derogatory nature, which trace back to days of slavery and serfdom. *The Man With the Hoe,* as depicted in the famous painting by Millet and the poem by Edwin Markham, represents a stereotype of the farmer which will yet require long generations to change. In addition to the peasants of Europe, China, and India, there may be mentioned as other agricultural groups of low status the *fellahin* of the Near East and the *peon, campesino, guajiro, jibaro, colono,* or *agrigado,* as the ruralite is variously called in Latin-American countries.

**Power.** Power is the ability to influence others. No precise measurement of power in most situations has yet been devised, other than "office," but some kind of common-sense ranking of farmers with other occupational groups is possible. Although not a direct measure of power, the amount of money spent in lobbying activities will indicate comparative rank in attempted power. When lobbies are classified into nine types of groups represented, the farmer lobbies have a variable rank, but they are always rather high in amount of money spent to influence legislation.[4] In 1952 the seven farm lobbies spent over $350,000 as compared with $2,215,000 spent by 96 business lobbies.

[4] *Congressional Quarterly,* Vols. VII–XI, 1950–1953.

In the same year farm lobby groups spent less than the business lobbies, professional lobbies, employees, and combined welfare, civic, and religious lobbies, but more than lobbies trying to influence legislation on foreign policy, reclamation, taxation, and veterans' affairs. In 1951 farm lobbies spent the third largest amount among these same groups (about one and one quarter million dollars); in 1950 they ranked fourth with a similar amount; in 1949, fourth.

When specific lobbies are compared there is an even greater variation, due to the kind of legislation being considered in any given year. In 1952 the first four lobbies in order of expenditures (as reported) were the National Association of Electric Companies, American Medical Association, Association of American Railroads, and National Milk Producers Federation, all of which spent between $200,000 and $480,000. In the same year the American Farm Bureau Federation spent $85,000 on lobbying activities and ranked thirteenth. In 1951, the American Farm Bureau Federation spent $878,813 in lobbying activities and ranked first among the lobbies reporting expenditures. In 1950, the American Medical Association spent over one and one quarter million. The largest amount spent by a farm organization in the same year was slightly over one hundred thousand by the National Council of Farmer Cooperatives. The rank in this case was fifteenth among all the lobbies reporting.

Insofar, then, as lobby expenditures represent attempted power over legislative action the farm organizations rank high when important farm legislation is under consideration. However, there are other smaller groups, such as the American Medical Association in very recent years, which spend more.

More direct expressions of power of farmer organizations are indicated by the history of the Grange and the Farmers Alliance; these did much to establish the Secretary of Agriculture as a Cabinet officer, the Interstate Commerce Commission, and rural free delivery.[5] Generally it may be said that the farm organizations have a considerable power relative to other groups

[5] For an excellent account of the rise and development of these and other farm organizations, see Carl C. Taylor, *The Farmers' Movement, 1620-1920*, especially Chapters 6-11, inclusive. New York: American Book Co., 1953.

in American society, although they tend to represent interests of larger, commercialized farmers.

**Style of life.** Style of life has two major subheadings, material possessions and nonmaterial culture. The former has received much attention from researchers while the latter has received little study except for some of the more obvious characteristics. However, throughout the book there are many aspects of the subculture of rural people which may be interpreted in the terms of the present problems.

From the point of view of material culture, farmers have, in the past, lived under somewhat substandard conditions if compared with the modern conceptions of what is material necessity.[6] The farmer has lagged behind the city in electrification, running water in the home, proper sewage disposal, and commercialized entertainment in the home. The same has been true of the rural-nonfarm population. The gap has been narrowing in recent years even to the point of equality in some areas near cities. Generally, however, the farmer group is still behind nonfarm occupational classes in such developments.

In nonmaterial culture the problem is more difficult because there is less agreement on what is desirable. Differences may be pointed out, however, and the ranking may be left to future research on desirability.

Traditionally the farmer is believed to be more religious and familistic, less inclined to finish high school and college, and more economically individualist (even though poorer) than members of nonfarm groups. Of particular importance has been the nature of the family as a work unit with little division of labor. Many of the stereotypes of the farmer's life have been wrong and those which were correct formerly are becoming less so. Isolation, which doubtless gave rise to many of the differences between the farmers and others, has been breaking down, and compulsory education and commercialized farming have helped to eliminate differences.

**Life chances.** Opportunity, both to achieve goals and to avoid misfortune, is a crucial factor in stratification. In achieving goals valued in American society the farmer ranks higher in

[6] See Chapter 16 for a full analysis of level of living and its importance in rural life.

some respects than other groups and lower in others. In longevity and in probability of suffering some kinds of diseases the farmer has some advantage.[7] The mortality rate generally, and particularly death rates due to cancer, tuberculosis, diabetes, circulatory diseases, and rheumatic fever all favor farmers over the combined nonfarm occupations. Part of this may be due to differences in accuracy of diagnosis, but other factors are lack of crowding and less exposure to communicable diseases and perhaps less anxiety than urban occupational groups experience. However, the shortage of hospitals and a tendency to avoid physicians' care make for a higher rate of death due to influenza and pneumonia in the rural area.

In other eventualities which may occur in an individual's career the farmer also enjoys some advantages. For example, temptations to commit delinquent acts are believed to be less frequent; it is a fact that juvenile delinquency is lower among farm groups than many city groups. Crime rates for adults are also lower.[8]

There are many personal and social characteristics which affect life chances. In some of the factors the farmer ranks very low. Reference to Tables 13 and 14 reveals the fact that in amount of education as well as income, farmers and farm laborers rank at the bottom of the scale.

Measured intelligence is a basis for life chances because with it increases the number of occupational alternatives open to the individual. It therefore has often been used as a basis of comparison among groups. On such comparisons farmers have consistently ranked lower than other occupational classes. This has been so whether the samples were school children, armed service draftees, or other adults.

M. E. Haggerty and H. B. Nash,[9] in a study of over six thousand village children in New York State, found the median I.Q.'s varied directly with the occupations of the fathers, from the professional category at the top "downward" through busi-

[7] Louis I. Dublin, *The Facts of Life from Birth to Death*, Chapters 8–13. New York: The Macmillan Company, 1951.

[8] Donald R. Taft, *Criminology, A Cultural Interpretation*, pp. 159, 171, and 350. New York: The Macmillan Company, 1950.

[9] M. E. Haggerty and H. B. Nash, "Mental Capacity of Children and Paternal Occupation," *Journal of Educational Psychology*, 1924, 15 : 559–572.

ness and clerical, skilled and semiskilled wage earners, farmers, and unskilled wage workers, in the order named. Other studies show similar gradations.[10]

C. D. Clark and N. P. Gist,[11] in a study of 2,423 graduates of rural high schools in Kansas, whose intelligence quotients were available, determined the occupations in which these individuals were engaged some thirteen years after graduation. In terms of their "occupational choices" the mean I.Q.'s of these individuals were as follows: professional, 100.82; clerical, 100.00; teachers, 99.28; salespeople and proprietors, 96.6; skilled workers, 96.18; housewives, 95.44; semiskilled and unskilled, 93.28; farmers, 92.75; housekeepers and unemployed, 91.38. However, over one sixth of the farmer category scored higher than the mean for professional strata.

In a study of Missouri high-school students who had attended rural high schools mostly between 1923 and 1927, N. P. Gist, C. I. Pihlblad and C. L. Gregory [12] found gradations according to occupational choice of these young people as represented by the occupations they were in at the time of the study (1938). Their results were similar to those of the Kansas study. These authors used scholastic ratings given students by their teachers on subjects taken in high school, rather than intelligence tests, as the basis of measurement of mental ability. Of the 2,142 males in the sample the following mean scholastic indexes were reported by occupations: teachers, 109.74; professional, 104.14; clerical, 102.08; business, 92.00; farmers, 89.47; unskilled, 88.79; skilled, 86.27. The gradations are not uniform with those of the Kansas study, which was based upon intelligence tests; still, they are similar. Both studies place farming well down

---

[10] E. S. Dexter, "The Relation Between Occupation of Parent and Intelligence," *School and Society*, 1923, 17 : 612–614; J. E. Collins, "The Intelligence of School Children and Paternal Occupation," *Journal of Educational Research*, 1928, 17 : 157–169; F. L. Goodenough, "The Relation of the Intelligence of Pre-School Children to the Occupation of Their Fathers," *American Journal of Psychology*, 1938, 40 : 284–294; J. W. Bridges and L. E. Coler, "The Relation of Intelligence to Social Status," *Psychological Review*, 1917, 24 : 1–31; Stuart M. Stoke and Harvey Lehman, "Intelligence Test Score of Social and Economic Groups," *School and Society*, 1930, 31 : 372–377.

[11] Carroll D. Clark and Noel P. Gist, "Intelligence As a Factor in Occupational Choice," *American Sociological Review*, 1938, 3 : 683–694.

[12] Noel P. Gist, C. I. Pihlblad, and Cecil L. Gregory, "Selective Factors in Migration and Occupation," *University of Missouri Studies*, Vol. XVIII, No. 2, 1943.

towards the bottom of the hierarchy of occupations in rating the intelligence of those who entered it.

## STRATIFICATION IN RURAL SOCIETY

While students of rural life have paid little attention to power, except as it is reflected in participation in organizations, and to life chances as such, they have been much interested in prestige, material style of life, and at least two of the "objective

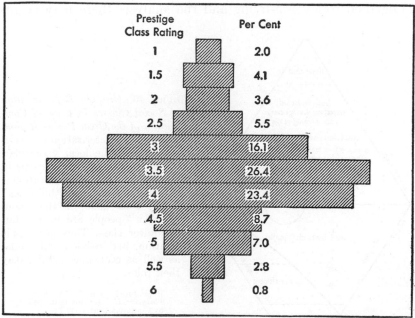

Prestige Class Rating | Per Cent

| Prestige Class Rating | Per Cent |
|---|---|
| 1 | 2.0 |
| 1.5 | 4.1 |
| 2 | 3.6 |
| 2.5 | 5.5 |
| 3 | 16.1 |
| 3.5 | 26.4 |
| 4 | 23.4 |
| 4.5 | 8.7 |
| 5 | 7.0 |
| 5.5 | 2.8 |
| 6 | 0.8 |

H. F. Kaufman, *Cornell University AES Memoir 260*, 1944

FIGURE 39. *Class Structure in Macon Community, New York.* Note the general "diamond shape" and the marked concentration of population in the three middle classes.

indices" of stratification, income, and tenure status. These will be analyzed in turn.

**Prestige.** Many researchers have discussed the "shape" of stratification, and one such scheme is presented here to demonstrate the prestige inequalities that do exist. Kaufman's [13] diagrammatic representation of prestige in Macon Community in New York is shown in Figure 39, and that of James West

[13] Harold F. Kaufman, "Prestige Classes in a New York Rural Community," *Cornell University AES Memoir 260*, March, 1944, p. 10.

in Figure 40. The results are based on actual rankings by the people themselves. The extreme groups are much smaller in number than the middle groups, but nice distinctions are made between groups by people of the communities when called upon to do so.

**Material Style of Life.** The material style of life in rural society is usually measured either by the level of living index or the Sewell socioeconomic scale.[14] A large part of a later chapter is devoted to level-of-living and the analysis there may be in-

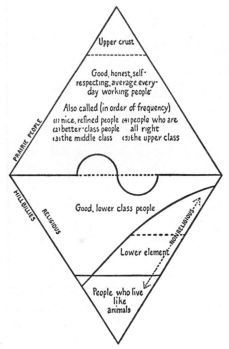

FIGURE 40. *Graphic Representation of Social Classes in a Rural Community of the Great Plains Region.* This is a characterization of classes in terms of the local vernacular. Note the separation of groups in terms of geographic location— "prairie people" and "hillbillies" —and that none of the "non-religious" people are in any but the lower class. Thus geographic location, and religious affiliation, as well as economic criteria, play their roles.

Reproduced from James West, *Plainville, U.S.A.* Copyright, 1945 by Columbia University Press.

terpreted in the present frame of reference. The concept underlying the Sewell scale may be defined as "the position that an individual or family occupies with reference to the prevailing

[14] W. H. Sewell, "The Construction and Standardization of a Scale for the Measurement of the Socio-economic Status of Oklahoma Farm Families," *Oklahoma Agricultural and Mechanical College AES Technical Bulletin 9*, April, 1940. See also by the same author, "A Short Form of the Farm Family Socioeconomic Status Scale," *Rural Sociology*, 1943, 8:161–170. J. C. Belcher and E. F. Sharp, "A Short Scale for Measuring Farm Family Level of Living: A Modification of Sewell's Socio-Economic Scale," *Oklahoma Agricultural Experiment Station AES Bulletin T-46*, September, 1952.

average standards of cultural possessions, effective income, material possessions, and participation in the group activities of the community." [15]

The usual form of the scale ("short form") has 13 items. In most samples families are found to vary in score from 0 through 13. The following list of the items which make up the score will indicate the inequalities that exist in material style of life in rural society: construction of house, room-person ratio, lighting facilities, water piped into house, power washer, refrigerator, radio, telephone, automobile, daily newspaper, wife's education, husband's education, husband attends church or Sunday School, and wife attends Sunday School. Some changes were made in a recent study of the scale, principally consisting of dropping the last two social participation items. [16]

The importance of socioeconomic status for rural life is well indicated by the fact that the Sewell scale has been included in so many studies in rural life in recent years.

Otis Dudley Duncan and Jay W. Artis, [17] in studying a Pennsylvania community, found that families with higher socioeconomic scores participated more in formal organizations and in informal visiting than those with lower scores. In a study of a rural Minnesota community, Forsyth found families having higher scores were less favorable to the relief program in the late 1930's. [18] More will be said of the importance of this factor later.

**Income.** Income inequalities are basic to many stratification factors, including style of life, power, and life chances. That great inequalities do exist in rural society is apparent from Figure 41. Notable is the fact that nearly one fourth of the farmers had total money incomes of less than $500, and over one third less than $1,000, while about two per cent had incomes of over $10,000.

The low-income groups are most heavily concentrated in the southeastern portion of the United States, with secondary concentrations in the cut-over area of the Lake States and in the

[15] Sewell, *op. cit.*, p. 20.

[16] Belcher and Sharp, *op. cit.*

[17] Otis Dudley Duncan and Jay W. Artis, "Social Stratification in a Pennsylvania Rural Community," *Pennsylvania State College AES Bulletin 543*, October, 1951.

[18] F. H. Forsyth, "Social Crisis and the Social Attitude Toward Relief," *Journal of Social Psychology*, 1943, 18:55–69.

New Mexico and Arizona region. However, they occur in practically every section of the country and in every community. Low income is, of course, associated with a low level of living, and with heavy rates of migration. Also, a characteristic configuration of attitudes and income has been indicated by L. S. Bee [19] in his study of a New York community. Higher incomes were associated with favorable attitudes toward the community and greater economic conservatism, which in turn were strongly associated with offices held, memberships in organizations, and meetings attended.

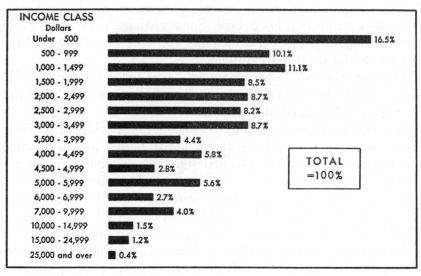

FIGURE 41. *Percentage Distribution of Families by Total Money Income Group for 1952 of Farmers and Farm Managers*

**Land tenure.** That ownership of land carries prestige is a matter of common observation and requires no special proof. Its significance as a criterion of social status in American rural society will vary in different areas of the country and at different times. In the ante-bellum South, for example, the planter, or plantation owner, was at the apex of the prestige or class pyramid. As W. E. Moore and R. M. Williams [20] point out, "The cue to understanding one of the main elements of social strati-

[19] L. S. Bee, "Attitude Differentials in a New York Rural Community," *State College of Washington Research Studies*, 1941, 9:37–48.

[20] Wilbert E. Moore and Robin M. Williams, "Stratification in the Ante-Bellum South," *American Sociological Review*, 1942, 7:343–351, p. 344.

fication in this society is given by the high prestige accorded to slave ownership and the possession of a landed estate. The evidence is substantial that the planter-pattern stood as an end or standard of achievement and that the attainment of such a status was typically an effective desire among a large portion of the white population." The diagrammatic representation of the class and caste lines in the prewar South is shown by these authors in Figure 42.

William Alexander Percy [21] and many others confirm this judgment as to the superior rank of the plantation owner in Southern society. But below the top class there were the other

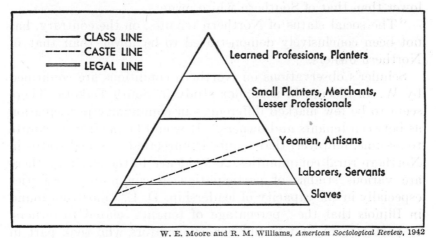

W. E. Moore and R. M. Williams, *American Sociological Review*, 1942

FIGURE 42. *Diagrammatic Representation of Class, Legal, and Caste Lines in the Ante-Bellum South*

groups ranging downward to the base of the pyramid. As Moore and Williams [22] put it, the "poor whites" were at the bottom of the social scale among the whites or "dominant caste." Above this group was the class composed of the independent nonslaveholding farmers, who, while not the equal of the slaveholding class,. were nevertheless "respectable and respected members of the community." Next higher were the "small planters, merchants, and professionals" who constituted the upper middle class. Occupying an anomalous position in the social scale, by virtue of relatively high economic standing on

[21] W. A. Percy, *Lanterns on the Levee*. New York: Alfred A. Knopf, 1941.
[22] Moore and Williams, *op. cit.*, p. 344.

the one hand and low moral standing on the other, were the slave traders and overseers.

The situation in the South is still marked by the caste line between the black and white peoples, with laborers, croppers, tenants, and farm owners ranking in about that order from low to high. E. A. Schuler, in a study of the social correlates of land tenure, found that tenure differences in the South were more important as criteria of status than in the North. Some of his conclusions are as follows:

"The preponderance of evidence seems to demonstrate conclusively that the social status of Southern white tenants is lower than that of Southern white owners.

"The social status of Northern tenants, on the contrary, has not been conclusively demonstrated to be lower than that of Northern owners." [23]

Schuler's observations on Northern conditions are confirmed by W. L. Slocum in a similar study in South Dakota. There seem to be few marked differences in community participation as between tenants and owners.[24] It would be far from accurate to assume, however, that tenure is unrelated to social status in Northern rural communities. As evidence to the contrary there are various studies of participation in community activities especially in the capacity of leadership. D. E. Lindstrom found in Illinois that the "percentage of tenants related to owners, to part owners, and to full owner-operators who took part in programs was significantly higher than the percentage of unrelated-to-owner tenants who took part. Almost 70 per cent of the laborer-members took no part in the activities of organizations, not even paying dues. . . ."[25] E. L. Kirkpatrick and others in Wisconsin found that the "average number of affiliations (with organization) for the owner families is almost two times as high as for the tenant families." [26] Evidence could be

[23] E. A. Schuler, "The Present Social Status of American Farm Tenants," *Rural Sociology*, 1938, 3:20–33, p. 32.

[24] W. L. Slocum, "The Influence of Tenure Status Upon Rural Life," *South Dakota AES Circular 29*, May, 1942.

[25] D. E. Lindstrom, "Forces Affecting Participation of Farm People in Rural Organization," *University of Illinois AES Bulletin 423*, May, 1936, p. 109.

[26] E. L. Kirkpatrick, J. H. Kolb, Creagh Inge, and A. F. Wileden, "Rural Organizations and the Farm Family," *University of Wisconsin AES Research Bulletin 96*, November, 1929, p. 18.

added from other studies, though the same story is told, namely, that the tenant families show generally lower rates of social participation when compared with owner families.[27]

On many other points tenure differences appear. The fertility of farm laborers is higher than that for tenants, while the latter exceed the farm owners in this respect. Notestein has also noted differences in the age at marriage. The average age at marriage of women of native white parentage, who were under 40 years of age at the time of marriage and who were living with their husbands at the time of the census of 1910, was for tenure classes as follows: farm owners, 22.3; farm renters, 20.9; and for farm laborers, 20.1.[28] Sewell and Ellenbogen in Wisconsin found mean measured intelligence of children to decrease with tenure status of father.[29]

**Farm laborers.** Among the most unfavorably situated groups is the farm laborer, who is lowest in the social scale. His life is characterized by economic and social insecurity, a low level of living, excessive mobility, and lack of association with the permanent institutions of the community. His annual income is the lowest in the scale of occupational groups reported in the United States Census for 1950. This income, low when compared with other economic groups, is attested by numerous local studies. As a rule, the laborer has poor housing, and his work is uncertain and subject to wide seasonal fluctuations. As C. C. Taylor and his associates remark: "The farm laborer is on the bottom rung of the so-called agricultural ladder and many farm laborers, apparently an increasing number, are destined never to rise above farm-labor status." [30] His future is made all the more uncertain by the steady progress of agricultural technology which is tending to reduce the number of workers needed in the agricultural enterprise.

---

[27] See also W. A. Anderson, "The Membership of Farmers in New York Organizations," *Cornell University AES Bulletin 695*, April, 1938.

[28] Frank W. Notestein, "Differential Age at Marriage According to Social Class," *American Journal of Sociology*, 1931, 37:22–48, p. 40.

[29] W. H. Sewell and B. L. Ellenbogen, "Social Status and the Measured Intelligence of Small City and Rural Children," *American Sociological Review*, 1952, 17:612–616.

[30] Carl C. Taylor, Helen W. Wheeler, and E. L. Kirkpatrick, "Disadvantaged Classes in American Agriculture," *Farm Security Administration and Bureau of Agricultural Economics Research Report VIII*, Washington, D.C., 1938, p. 5.

The relationship between social class in rural society and the tenure of land is perhaps more clearly marked in other countries of the world than it is in the United States. In Cuba, for example, the opportunities for owners of small and medium-sized farms have not been favorable; most typically, the owner has large holdings and many renters, sharecroppers, or laborers. The big owner may or may not live on his land. If he lives in the city, as is often the case, he will be represented on the farm by a *mayoral* or manager. This situation is common also in the British West Indies, as well as throughout South America.

In Cuba, where much of the land is owned by the sugar companies, it is common practice to rent holdings in rather large blocks to *colonos*. They are large operators as a rule, who are in reality entrepreneurs dependent upon the company, usually for capital to finance the crop, and upon hired labor to grow it. Many of them are wealthy men.

In the tobacco-producing areas of Cuba the landowner is definitely at the pinnacle of the social pyramid. Next to him is the cash-renter (*arrendatario*) who pays a specified amount of rent for the use of the land. Below him is the share-renter (*partidario*). He may rent either from an owner or from a cash-renter; in the latter case he might be regarded as a subrenter. In practice, he has about the same status as a laborer paid in cash. Frequently he is a single man who boards at the table of the *arrendatario* and has sleeping space in part of some rude hut also used as a storage shed for corn, vegetables, or machinery.

The situation in areas which produce coffee is about the same as that in the tobacco areas. The landowner is at the top of the pyramid, the day-laborer at the bottom (corresponding to the sharecropper's position in tobacco), with the cash and share-renters in between.

## SIGNIFICANCE OF STRATIFICATION FOR RURAL INSTITUTIONS

Social institutions and organizations in the community are affected by social stratification. Some churches are popular among the upper classes; neighborhoods tend to be made up of people of comparable social status. Schools patronized by the "lower classes" are avoided insofar as possible by the "upper." Then, of course, in the southern United States there is the practice of segregation of Negroes and the rigid separation of the races in the schools, churches, and many other community enterprises.

**The church.** An example of the selectivity of church membership on the basis of socioeconomic status is reported by Goldschmidt [31] in his study of a community in the San Joaquin Valley of California. Located in an area characterized by highly commercialized farming, the community during the depression years received a heavy influx of migrants from the southern states, both Negro and white; Mexicans were also represented in considerable numbers. These "outsiders" participated little or not at all in the established community functions which were carried on by the older settlers whom Goldschmidt refers to as the "nuclear" group. The Mexicans and Negroes formed subcommunities of their own, while the white newcomers attempted to become part of the nuclear group.

Ten churches served the whites in the community, nine of of them Protestant. The Catholic Church represented a cross section of the population more nearly than the Protestant. Of the Protestant churches five represented the "nuclear" population: Christian Science, Congregational, Methodist, Baptist, and Seventh Day Adventist. The "outsiders" made up the membership of the Nazarene, Assembly of God, Church of Christ, and Pentecostal churches.

Among the Protestant churches there was clearly a selectivity of membership in terms of social (occupational) class. The older (nuclear) churches contained very few of the unskilled laborers, one of them scarcely any at all. On the other hand, only one of the "outsider" churches contained any professional, managerial, or entrepreneurial members, and it had only a few.[32] (See Figure 43.)

Kaufman found similar selectivity in church membership in New York. Only 11 per cent of the members of the Presbyterian Church were from the four lower prestige groups, while 41 per cent of the members of the Federated Church and 61 per cent of the Oldland Evangelical Church were from these classes.[33]

[31] Walter R. Goldschmidt, "Class Denominationalism in Rural California Churches," *American Journal of Sociology*, 1944, 49 : 348–355.

[32] *Ibid.*, p. 350.

[33] Kaufman, *op. cit.*, p. 16.

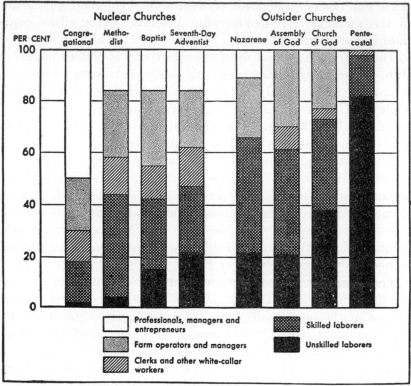

W. R. Goldschmidt, *American Journal of Sociology*, 1944, University of Chicago Press

FIGURE 43. *Differences in Occupational Composition of Membership of Eight Protestant Churches in a Community in the San Joaquin Valley, California.* The "nuclear" churches were those which existed in the community for a long time and served chiefly the older settlers. The "outsider" churches were those which served the new influx of agricultural workers, Mexicans, Negroes, and whites.

Similar results were obtained by Duncan and Artis in Pennsylvania.[34]

**The school and class structure.** An interesting practical situation arising from stratification in the state of Arkansas came to the writer's notice. On one plantation of 35 square miles owned by a single individual there were the customary separate schools for the colored and the white children. The white people were predominantly the small businessmen operating the various trade and service enterprises of the village center and those in

[34] Duncan and Artis, *op. cit.*, pp. 45–46.

charge of the administration of plantation affairs. The Negroes were sharecroppers and tenants. Here color as well as tenure status largely coincided, because there were no white tenants or sharecroppers. The white school was therefore almost entirely made up of children of the middle or upper classes, when the Farm Security Administration purchased a tract of land from the plantation and settled a number of "low-income" white families on it. The children of these families naturally went to the white school. But between them and the other children there was a social gulf, of which both groups were conscious. The white school population was no longer composed of a homogeneous class; it had become stratified. Class consciousness, according to the teachers of the school, was expressed in many ways on the playground and in the schoolroom.

But the school itself tended to implement the social differences rather than to attenuate them, because the school term was adapted to the needs of the upper-class children. It began in September and ran until June, and there was nothing to interfere seriously with the attendance of the upper-class children. Children of the low-income group above the fourth grade at least were kept out of school to pick cotton in the fall of the year, and usually did not get started until after January 1. Then in April they would be taken out of school again to help with the cotton chopping. Thus they were bound to become progressively more retarded in school, and the differentiation between them and the other more fortunate students would be increasingly apparent. Yet the teachers were trying to make the best of a very difficult situation.

In a study of a midwestern community Hollingshead found not only that the school was controlled mainly by upper status citizens, through the school board, but that discipline was somewhat discriminatory in favor of upper status children.[35] Duncan and Artis found that semiformal participation, much of which concerned attendance of adults at school functions, increased among the higher status group.[36]

Stratification, in summary, refers to inequalities. In compar-

[35] A. B. Hollingshead, *Elmtown's Youth*, especially pp. 121–128. New York: John Wiley and Sons, 1950.
[36] Duncan and Artis, *op. cit.*, p. 39.

ing the farmer with other social aggregates it was found that the farmer is very low in prestige, style of life, and on the bases of life chances such as measured intelligence, income, and educational attainment. In some life chances, such as longevity of life, probability of death due to most dread diseases, and crime rates, the farmer ranked above combined nonfarm occupations. In power, those farmers who belong to organizations appear to be well off, as evidenced by expenditures for lobbying activities and in the history of legislation concerning farm problems.

The inequalities within rural society were shown to be greater than is ordinarily believed. The inequalities in prestige, style of life, income and tenure status were shown to be of considerable importance in social participation, attitudes, measured intelligence, and institutional behavior.

## QUESTIONS FOR DISCUSSION

1. Explain, using examples, the interrelationship between prestige, style of life, power, and life chances.
2. Under what circumstances or in what social groups would each of the following factors be important criteria of social strata: income, occupation, family background, race or nationality, folkways, religion, pattern of living, personal qualities?
3. Give specific examples of how some stratification factor blocked people you know from attaining important goals.
4. The Mapheus Smith study indicates that farming as an occupation has little prestige. Is this status explainable in terms of income, education, and mental-test results? Discuss.
5. Point out regional differences in the status attached to various levels of land tenure. How do tenure groups differ from the standpoint of social participation?
6. What are the social disadvantages associated with the status of being a farm laborer?
7. How do you account for the fact that Kaufman's diagram illustrating social prestige in a rural community has a diamond shape?
8. Why is it reasonable to suppose, as the findings show, that there would be more stratification among the Protestant churches than within the Catholic Church?
9. Draw a diagram illustrating the relationship between class structure and the color-caste system of the South.

SELECTED REFERENCES

Bee, Lawrence S. "Attitude Differentials in a New York Rural Community," *State College of Washington Research Studies*, Vol. IX, pp. 37–48, 1941.

Bendix, Richard, and Lipset, Seymour M. *Class, Status, and Power.* Glencoe, Illinois: The Free Press, 1953.

Duncan, Otis Dudley, and Artis, Jay W. "Social Stratification in a Pennsylvania Rural Community." *Pennsylvania State College AES Bulletin 543.* October, 1951.

Forsyth, F. Howard. "Social Crisis and the Social Attitude Toward Relief," *Journal of Social Psychology*, 1943, 18:55–69.

Hollingshead, August B. *Elmtown's Youth.* New York: John Wiley and Sons, 1950.

Hughes, Everett C. "Position and Status in a Quebec Industrial Town," *American Sociological Review*, Vol. III, No. 5, October, 1938.

Kaufman, Harold F. "Prestige Classes in a New York Rural Community." *Cornell University AES Memoir 260.* March, 1944.

Kaufman, Harold F.; Duncan, Otis Dudley; Gross, Neal; and Sewell, William H. "Problems of Theory and Method in the Study of Social Stratification in Rural Society," *Rural Sociology*, Vol. XVIII, No. 1, March, 1953.

Moore, Wilbert E., and Williams, Robin M. "Stratification in the Ante-Bellum South," *American Sociological Review*, Vol. VII, No. 3, June, 1942.

Sewell, William H. "The Construction and Standardization of a Scale for the Measurement of the Socioeconomic Status of Oklahoma Farm Families," *Oklahoma Agricultural and Mechanical College AES Technical Bulletin 9.* 1940.

Useem, John; Tangent, Pierre; and Useem, Ruth. "Stratification in a Prairie Town," *American Sociological Review*, Vol. VII, No. 3, pp. 331–342, June, 1942.

Warner, W. Lloyd, and Lunt, Paul S. *The Social Life of a Modern Community*, "Class and Social Structure," Chapter 6. New Haven: Yale University Press, 1941.

Young, Kimball. *Sociology: A Study of Society and Culture*, Second Edition, Chapter 28. New York: American Book Co., 1949.

CHAPTER 12

# SOCIAL MOBILITY

There are two aspects to social mobility. One of them—the movement of persons or groups in geographic space—has been discussed in Chapter 7, dealing with migration. It is usually called *horizontal* mobility. The other aspect, which is referred to as *vertical* mobility, is concerned with the movement of persons or groups from one *class* to another, either upward or downward. It is the latter aspect which will be discussed in the present chapter.

Vertical mobility constitutes a test of the "elasticity of the group's structure." [1] If there is comparatively free movement from one stratum in the social order to another, vertical mobility can be said to exist and the "social metabolism" of society can be considered relatively rapid. American society generally is characterized by comparatively free and rapid vertical mobility.

A *caste* society, on the other hand, is characterized by a very small degree of mobility. Theoretically there is none at all. In practice, however, there are always persons in a caste society who find it possible to escape from their hereditary social position. Mukerjee commenting on the relaxing of caste lines in the Deltaic districts of India has this to say:

Here well-to-do members of the lower caste can obtain admission into a caste of higher rank; not all at once, but by change of surname, association with members of the better caste and judicious expenditure, recognition is obtained in the course of time. [2]

Mukerjee even notes the movement of entire groups (castes) up the social status scale:

[1] P. A. Sorokin, C. C. Zimmerman, and C. J. Galpin, *A Systematic Source Book in Rural Sociology*, Vol. 1, p. 305. Minneapolis: University of Minnesota Press, 1930.

[2] R. Mukerjee, *Man and His Habitation*, p. 167. London: Longmans, Green and Company, 1940. The author further observes (p. 180) that "mobility becomes the solvent of tradition, caste, and ancient social functions and institutions."

226

Agricultural labourers, artisans, peasants, traders, and priests represent the order of social stratification, which in large measure approximates to economic status and scale of living. There is neither inelasticity in the caste structure, nor a rigid fixation of rural wages and services. Artisan groups, which show an upward economic movement and improve their income, art, and skill, obtain social recognition by gradually crystallising themselves into new castes. . . . [3]

**Vertical and horizontal mobility related.** Since one of the motivations for migration is the desire to improve one's social and economic position, it is inevitable that horizontal and vertical mobility should be related. One of the most impressive examples of their relationship is found in the great migrations from Europe to the United States in the eighteenth and nineteenth centuries. This phenomenon of concurrent vertical and horizontal mobility was observed by an early reporter of the American scene, the Frenchman St. John de Crèvecœur. He entered the English colonies about 1760, after service in the French army in Canada under Montcalm, and wrote down his observations on American frontier life in a series of *Letters* published in 1782. He thought he saw a new race of people emerging from the American soil, due to the transformation which took place in the emigrants from the Old World once they became transplanted. "Men are like plants: the goodness and flavor of the fruit proceeds from the peculiar soil and exposition in which they grow. We are nothing but what we derive from the air we breathe, the climate we inhabit, the government we obey, the system of religion we profess, and the mode of our employment." [4] In his opinion the emigrants were selected by circumstance from the middle and poor classes of Europe:

Formerly they were not numbered in any civil list of their country, except in those of the poor; here they rank as citizens. . . . An European, when he first arrives, seems limited in his intentions, as well as in his views; but he very suddenly alters his scale . . . he no sooner breathes our air than he forms new schemes, and embarks in designs he never would have thought of in his own country. There the plenitude of

[3] *Ibid.*, pp. 105, 106.
[4] St. John de Crèvecœur, *Letters From an American Farmer*, p. 56. New York: Fox, Duffield and Company, 1904.

society confines many useful ideas, and often extinguishes the most laudable schemes which here ripen into maturity.[5]

He begins to feel the effects of a sort of resurrection; hitherto he had not lived but simply vegetated; he now feels himself a man, because he is treated as such; the laws of his own country had overlooked him in his insignificancy; the laws of this cover him with their mantle. Judge what an alteration there must arise in the mind and thoughts of this man; he begins to forget his former servitude and dependence, his heart involuntarily swells and glows; this first swell inspires him with those new thoughts which constitute an American. . . . From nothing to start into being, to become a free man, invested with lands, to which every municipal blessing is annexed! What a change indeed! It is in consequence of that change that he becomes an American.[6]

**The poor move more often.** A recent study in the United States calls attention to an inverse relationship existing between the amount of migration and socioeconomic status. "Movements in geographic space and in social space tend to be complementary," says R. T. McMillan. "An improvement in tenure or wealth status generally reduces the amount of moving but losses of status increase the migration rates sharply."[7] B. O. Williams, in a study of farmers in South Carolina, found a similar relationship between poverty and mobility, and concluded that "farmers who had moved the most had the lowest socioeconomic status and vice versa."[8] His statement is not intended to suggest that people who move do not improve their socioeconomic status, but simply that those low in economic status tend to move much more than those in the higher strata.

Vertical mobility, it must be kept in mind, may be either up or down. It is by no means true that all people who migrate improve their socioeconomic position, that is, move up the scale. In other words a migrant may, in terms of his socioeconomic position, move up or down the scale or remain in about the

---

[5] St. John de Crèvecœur, *Letters From an American Farmer*, p. 19. New York: Fox, Duffield and Company, 1904.

[6] *Ibid.*, p. 20.

[7] Robert T. McMillan, "Migration and Status of Open Country Families in Oklahoma," *Oklahoma Agricultural and Mechanical College AES Technical Bulletin T-19*, September, 1943, p. 73.

[8] B. O. Williams, "Occupational Mobility Among Farmers," *South Carolina AES Bulletin 296*, June, 1934, p. 73.

same relative position he held before migrating. On the other hand it is obvious that vertical mobility is not dependent upon horizontal mobility. An individual may rise in the socioeconomic scale and remain within his community.

## MOBILITY AS A FUNCTION OF AGING

In an open-class system any individual is likely to move through several levels in the hierarchy of occupations as he advances in age. To begin "at the bottom and work his way up" is a common expression of this phenomenon. The young man may begin as a common laborer and as he gains experience and skill move into the category of skilled laborer. Then he may become in successive stages, foreman, superintendent, general manager, and proprietor. There are many stories in business lore of individuals who have "risen" from office boy to general manager.

This movement upward on the occupational scale with advancing age is demonstrated by the age composition of the labor force in the United States. (See Table 15.)

TABLE 15. *Per Cent Distribution of Males in the Experienced Labor Force [a] According to Socioeconomic Class, for Various Age Groups, United States, 1940*

| | 14 and over | AGE GROUP | | | | | | |
|---|---|---|---|---|---|---|---|---|
| | | 14–24 | 25–34 | 35–44 | 45–54 | 55–64 | 65–74 | 75 and over |
| ALL CLASSES | 100.0 | 100.0 | 100.0 | 100.0 | 100.0 | 100.0 | 100.0 | 100.0 |
| Professional persons | 5.2 | 2.5 | 6.6 | 6.1 | 5.1 | 4.9 | 5.3 | 6.4 |
| Farmers | 13.4 | 5.0 | 9.8 | 12.7 | 16.8 | 22.0 | 32.2 | 41.9 |
| Proprietors,[b] managers, officials | 9.1 | 1.9 | 7.0 | 11.4 | 13.1 | 12.5 | 12.4 | 13.6 |
| Clerks and kindred workers | 12.5 | 14.6 | 14.3 | 12.7 | 10.8 | 9.5 | 8.0 | 7.6 |
| Skilled workers | 15.6 | 7.6 | 14.3 | 18.8 | 19.9 | 18.4 | 13.9 | 9.0 |
| Semiskilled workers | 15.6 | 20.0 | 19.4 | 15.3 | 12.1 | 9.8 | 7.7 | 5.5 |
| Farm laborers | 8.2 | 23.0 | 7.2 | 4.2 | 3.6 | 4.4 | 4.9 | 4.1 |
| Other laborers | 12.5 | 15.2 | 13.6 | 11.6 | 11.5 | 11.3 | 8.3 | 5.0 |
| Servant classes | 4.3 | 5.0 | 4.1 | 4.0 | 4.0 | 4.2 | 4.6 | 4.4 |
| All others | 3.6 | 5.2 | 3.7 | 3.2 | 3.1 | 3.0 | 2.7 | 2.5 |

[a] Excluding persons on public emergency work.
[b] Excluding farm proprietors.

Source: *Statistical Bulletin*, p. 6. New York: Metropolitan Life Insurance Company, June, 1944.

The category "farmers" in Table 15 refers to all farm operators including owners, tenants, and farm managers. As the age
increases there is a steady increase in the proportion of farmers
in the labor force. Their preponderance in the groups 65 years
and older is no doubt due to the tendency for people in other
occupations to retire at the age of 65, whereas farmers continue
on the job in greater numbers. On the other hand, the proportion
of the labor force which farm laborers constitute shows a tendency to decline with advancing age. They are numerically
the most important single occupational class in the age group
14–24, but drop sharply in the succeeding age group. It is well
known that a considerable portion of farm laborers become
tenants and even owners after 25 years of age. This movement
up the agricultural ladder continues through subsequent years.
The movement is not, however, solely in an upward direction.
There are many cases of farm laborers in the upper age groups
who have sometime previously been tenants or owners.

Table 15 indicates that other classes move according to
various patterns. The professional group reached its highest
proportions in the age groups from 25 to 44; skilled workers
in the age group 45 to 54; laborers and the semiskilled groups
showed rather consistent declines with increasing age, as did
the clerical and kindred workers. Proprietors, managers, and
officials generally increased in relative numbers with advancing
age, while there was little change throughout the age groups
in the proportion of servant classes. The last group probably
comes closest to approximating a "caste" group in our society.

### MOVEMENT OF FARM PEOPLE OUT OF AGRICULTURE

Technological improvements in agriculture have resulted in a
decline in the number of farms and farm operators, as well as
reduced demand for farm labor. At the same time there is a high
rate of natural increase in the farm population. This chronic
surplus of the farm labor force has to be continually redistributed among other occupations and siphoned off the farms.
Retirement, death, and departure from agriculture create nowhere near enough vacancies to take care of 350 to 400 thousand
young people, the natural yearly increase in the farm population

annually. It is apparent, therefore, that fewer than half of the young men reaching maturity on farms are needed for replacements among the farm operators. Of course, a considerable number of them will find work as farm laborers, but it is well to keep in mind that the demand for farm labor is steadily declining. At the same time there are people moving into agriculture from nonfarm occupations, reducing still further the opportunity of farm-reared boys to become farm operators.[9]

The surplus of young men in the farm population find their way through migration into villages, towns, and cities and perforce into other occupations than farming. The specific occupations into which they move will depend upon a number of factors. One of these is the availability of jobs in particular industries, the rates of pay and opportunities for employment in the professional fields. As we have noted in the previous chapter, the intelligence of the individual also plays a role. Studies by Clark and Gist and others have shown that those with greater measurable intelligence find their way into the professional and clerical occupations, while the less gifted move into manual work.[10]

*Ethnic* and *cultural* backgrounds influence to some extent the rate of movement away from the farms so far as particular groups are concerned. For example, the Old Order Amish people strongly discourage their children from entering any occupation other than farming. When an Amish farmer in Indiana was asked by the author, "Why don't you send your children away to college to prepare them as doctors, teachers, and clerical workers?" his reply was, "That is not for Amishmen." By contrast, Finnish immigrants have a strong enthusiasm for education and are contributing heavily of their numbers to the nonagricultural occupations.

Hill and Christensen found significant difference between farm people of German and those of Scandinavian descent in Wisconsin in the proportions of the third generation who were

[9] P. G. Beck found that over one fourth of the farmers in three areas of Ohio had entered farming from nonfarm occupations. *Bimonthly Bulletin*, Ohio Experiment Station, November–December, 1929, p. 205.

[10] N. P. Gist and Carroll D. Clark, "Intelligence As a Selective Factor in Rural-Urban Migration," *American Journal of Sociology*, 1938, 44:36–58. N. P. Gist, C. I. Pihlblad, and C. L. Gregory, "Selective Aspects of Rural Migrations," *Rural Sociology*, 1941, 6:1–15.

in nonfarm work. "In the trend toward occupational mobility
. . . Scandinavian farmers have moved more rapidly than German farmers." [11]

These authors also find that movement into nonfarm occupations was proportionately higher in those groups with low
economic status. In the larger families there was also a higher
percentage of the adult males who went into the nonfarm
occupations. J. Wargelin observes that while the Finns entered
the mining occupation in the New World, they moved from that
into timber and agriculture, and many third generation or
later Finns found their way into higher occupational strata,
due chiefly to their passion for education.[12] In this connection
it is well to point out that the spread of high-school education
in rural areas in the recent decades has stimulated the movement of farm children out of agriculture.

**The transmission of farming as an occupation.** Although,
as we have seen, a large portion of the farm youth find their
way into nonfarm occupations, it is a characteristic of farming
that it is transmitted from one generation to the next more
commonly than other vocations. This fact is attested by the
study of W. A. Anderson in New York State. According to
his findings, "farming is self-perpetuating, being carried on
from generation to generation chiefly by the sons of those already
engaged in it. There is some shifting to farming from other
occupations but not to a large extent." [13] Anderson further
found that the oldest son tended to inherit the farm, though
it does not seem to be so in all areas. Hill and Christensen in
Wisconsin reported a greater tendency for the middle son to
take over the farm. The oldest son was less likely to become
the farm operator than was the youngest.[14] This logically

[11] George W. Hill and Harold T. Christensen, "Some Cultural Factors Related
to Occupational Mobility Among Wisconsin Farmers," *Rural Sociology*, 1942,
7:193–200, p. 196.

[12] J. Wargelin, *The Americanization cf the Finns*, p. 69 ff. Hancock, Michigan:
Lutheran Book Concern, 1924.

[13] W. A. Anderson, "The Transmission of Farming As an Occupation," *Cornell
University AES Bulletin 768*, October, 1941, p. 18. The statement regarding the shifting to farming from nonfarming occupations as unimportant would not agree with
the findings of P. G. Beck in Ohio. Obviously, such shifting will vary with the section
and with economic conditions. Beck found nonfarm people were coming into agriculture in large numbers around industrial centers.

[14] Hill and Christensen, *op. cit.*, p. 200.

would seem to be a likelier tendency. A farmer, for example, who has a son born when he is 25 years of age would scarcely be ready for retirement at the time his son reaches the age of 25 since the farmer himself would be only 50 years of age. A first-born son is more likely to try to get a farm of his own or enter some other occupation than is a second or later son who would come to maturity at more nearly the normal retirement age of the father.

### MOBILITY WITHIN AGRICULTURE

One of the favorite symbols of vertical mobility in the United States is the "agricultural ladder." The figure of speech refers to the traditional steps by which the young man rises to the position of farm ownership. The "rungs" on the ladder are as follows: (a) hired man, (b) farm tenant, (c) part owner, and (d) full owner. A young man begins his career in agriculture by working as a hired man, perhaps for a neighbor. After a few years in this position he accumulates enough capital to purchase a team of horses and some equipment which makes it possible for him to become a tenant. After a few years as a tenant he buys a small piece of land and rents enough additional to make up a farm. Finally, in the process of climbing the ladder he is able to become a full owner, at first with a mortgage on the place and, finally, free from any encumbrance.

That this system worked for a large proportion of farmers in the past there can be no doubt. Not always, of course, did they pass through all of these steps or stages, but the "ladder" did provide opportunity for vertical movement. In the past quarter of a century, however, it has become increasingly difficult for men to achieve farm ownership in the traditional way. The chief impediment to movement up the agricultural ladder is the increased amount of capital required for successful farm operation. The average price paid for a family farm under the farm ownership program of the Farmers Home Administration is approximately $8,000. The cost varies considerably from state to state, from approximately $3,500 in some of the southern states to $12,000 in the North and West. These figures are for family-size farms and represent only the cost of land and buildings. In addition the farm operator will need to have $2,500 to $3,000 worth of stock, tools, and equipment, if he is planning operation of a Midwestern diversified wheat or corn-hog farm; and upwards of $1,000 to $1,500 for a poultry farm or for a dairy farm of 15 cows in the Southern states. In addition, about the same amount of money is necessary for investment in livestock, as well as $1,000 or so for feed, seed, fertilizer, and labor each year.[15] This means that it will require a great many years for a hired man starting out to acquire enough capital; and in most cases he will never make it.

Apparently sensing the growing difficulty of vertical mobility in land tenure, the President's Committee on Farm Tenancy had this interesting paragraph in its report[16]:

Should the rungs of the agricultural ladder become rigid bars between classes, an American ideal would be lost. In a community of rigid groups, normal democratic processes are unable to function.

**Regional differences.** The agricultural ladder seems never to have operated as successfully in the South as it has in the North. The plantation system during the time of slavery and after was essentially feudal in character and did not provide opportunity for ownership on the part of more than a small minority of the total group engaged in agriculture. What is needed in this system is large numbers of field workers. These are usually tenants, sharecroppers, or wage hands rather than owners and their families as in the North. In ante-bellum days, of course, they were slaves.

Even outside the plantation economy the system seems to have worked only partially. C. H. Hamilton, in a study of tenure in North Carolina, found that very few farm laborers had become owners during a 15-year period; mostly the laborers shifted into the sharecropper group and got no further. "The fact is," he says, "that most farm laborers become croppers if and when they have a large number of children or other

---

[15] "Shall I Be a Farmer?" United States Department of Agriculture, Washington, D.C., July, 1944. For further discussion of the problem see John D. Black and Charles D. Hyson, "Postwar Soldiers Settlement," *Quarterly Journal of Economics*, 1944, 59:1-35.
[16] *Farm Tenancy*, Report of the Committee, p. 7. Washington, D.C.: Government Printing Office, February, 1937.

persons in their household who can function as unpaid family workers." [17]

Within a limited range of circulation, movement is both up and down, according to Hamilton. Referring to the farm labor class as the "catch-all for displaced owners, tenants, and croppers" he states that "approximately 60 per cent of the farm laborers in the five rural areas have at one time or another been croppers, 20 per cent have been tenants." [18]

With respect to limited range of circulation, these results confirm the earlier findings of B. O. Williams in the neighboring state of South Carolina. Williams traced the occupational history of over 1,830 farmers, of whom 1,046 were white and 744 colored. Two fifths of the white owners and over one fifth of the colored had always been owners. Seventy per cent of the white tenants and 78 per cent of the colored had always been tenants. Obviously, there had been some vertical mobility, since 60 per cent of the white owners and about 80 per cent of the colored had had other than ownership experience, chiefly, it was found, as tenants. On the other hand, very few of the group had begun as farm laborers. There was, in other words, only a limited range within which movement took place.[19]

Recent data from a sample of Minnesota farmers indicate that 53 out of 174 full owners began as hired men. Twenty-five out of the 53 went from hired man to tenant to owner status, while 15 went *directly* from hired man to owner status. Forty-nine of them had been owners from the beginning of their careers; twenty-six began as part owners, 29 as tenants. These were farmers who, in 1944, were 55 years of age or over but still actively engaged in farming. In a sample of retired farmers in the same study only 19 out of 88 owners had begun as hired men, 36 had always been owners, 16 began as tenants, and the balance were distributed in other tenure combinations.[20] For that generation several alternative ways were open to achieve ownership.

[17] C. Horace Hamilton, "Recent Changes in the Social and Economic Status of Farm Families in North Carolina," *North Carolina State AES Bulletin 309*, May, 1937, p. 72.     [18] *Ibid.*, p. 87.

[19] B. O. Williams, "Mobility and Farm Tenancy," *Journal of Land and Public Utility Economics*, 1938, 14:207–208.

[20] Lowry Nelson, "Farm Retirement in Minnesota," *Minnesota AES Bulletin 394*, May, 1947.

Because of the apparently increasing difficulty of movement up the tenure scale, the hypothesis seems justified that tenure status, whether owner or tenant, seems to be increasingly transmitted by inheritance. Increasingly, the children of owners will be the owners of tomorrow and the children of tenants will be tomorrow's tenants.

B. O. Williams, in the previously mentioned study of 1,830 South Carolina farmers, states that the agricultural ladder from lower to higher rungs was negotiated more frequently by the children of owners than by the children of tenants. The latter seldom got beyond the tenant class.[21]

The chances for vertical mobility in a rural society characterized by concentration of land ownership are extremely limited. Those at the top who possess the land are few, and those at the bottom who work the land are many. The number of laborers who can aspire to the top is negligible. In many of the countries of the world such a situation prevails. Up to the close of World War II, in Poland, in Hungary, in Rumania, in England, and throughout most of Latin America the ownership of land had been highly concentrated and social mobility quite limited. In a number of these countries there has been peasant agitation to have the lands redistributed. For many years in Mexico such a process of parceling out small tracts from large holdings has been going on. While official declarations were not made, news accounts from Eastern Europe after the end of World War II mentioned the breakup of large estates as part of the postwar plan. By the exercise of public authority to hasten the dissolution of large holdings, the rate of vertical mobility may thus be accelerated.

By way of summary the following conclusions seem to be justified with reference to rural vertical mobility:

1) The rate of movement out of farming as an occupation has been increasing because of (a) the relatively high fertility of the farm population, (b) decline in the number of operated farms, and (c) technological improvement which reduces the number of workers needed.

2) Vertical mobility on the agricultural ladder is becoming

---

[21] B. O. Williams, *op. cit.*

more difficult due to the increased capital necessary for successful operation of highly mechanized farm enterprises.

## QUESTIONS FOR DISCUSSION

1. How can social class and caste be distinguished from the standpoint of social mobility?
2. What appears to be happening to the caste system of India?
3. In what way, according to St. John de Crèvecœur, was the migration from Europe to America selective? What effect did he think that American life and culture had on European immigrants?
4. Point out exceptions to the rule that persons of low status migrate the most.
5. Account for the fact that the proportion of the total labor force who are farm operators increases as their age increases, while an opposite tendency is true with respect to farm laborers.
6. What are the chances that the average farm-reared boy will become a farm operator? What factors will affect his adjustment if he migrates to the village or city to find work?
7. Review the results of research related to the social mobility of various racial and nationality groups.
8. Why is it logical to assume that a *middle* son is more likely to replace his father on the farm than the oldest son?
9. Why has movement up the agricultural ladder been slowing down during recent years? Point out the bearing this trend has on the *American ideal*.
10. Describe and explain regional differences in the operation of the agricultural ladder.

## SELECTED REFERENCES

Anderson, W. A. "The Transmission of Farming as an Occupation." *Cornell University AES Bulletin 768.* October, 1941.

Smith, T. Lynn. *The Sociology of Rural Life*, Third Edition, Chapter 24. New York: Harper and Brothers, 1953.

Sorokin, P. A. *Social Mobility*, Chapter 2. New York: Harper and Brothers, 1927.

Sorokin, P. A.; Zimmerman, C. C.; and Galpin, C. J. *A Systematic Source Book in Rural Sociology*, Vol. 1, Chapter 8. Minneapolis: University of Minnesota Press, 1930.

Williams, B. O. "Occupational Mobility Among Farmers." *South Carolina AES Bulletin 296.* Clemson College, 1934.

# PART V

## *RURAL SOCIAL INSTITUTIONS*

## INTRODUCTION

OUT OF THE PROCESS of living together, of interacting through the various forms discussed in the chapters immediately preceding, there have developed certain well-established ways of acting together, which are stable and permanent and which are found universally among peoples throughout the world. These basic institutions of society, the family, the school, the church, the government, and the economic agencies connected with the production and distribution of the physical means of existence, are treated in this section. We will also discuss those agencies which have come into special prominence in the United States in recent years, the agencies having to do with health and social welfare.

The first two chapters to follow deal with two economic institutions, property in land and farming systems. It may be noted that property as an institution differs from the school, family, church, or state, in that there is no formal organization, no officers, no headquarters. Like language, art, or the system of numbers, it is a *diffused* institution, while the others mentioned are *nucleated*.* All of the institutions discussed in the ensuing section, except property, are of the nucleated type.

* A distinction made by F. S. Chapin, *Contemporary American Institutions.* New York: Harper and Brothers, 1933.

# CHAPTER 13

# PROPERTY IN LAND

Social behavior and social organization are profoundly influenced by the manner in which people provide for their physical maintenance. This statement should not be interpreted to mean that economic factors *determine* other phases of culture, for the other phases may and do influence the forms of economic activity. Culture is a unity of which economic activities are an organic part, and it is only for purposes of analysis and understanding that we for the moment consider them independently of the others. It is our purpose, however, to attempt an analysis of only two of the more basic, rural, economic institutions: property in land, and systems of farm organization.

**Property in land.** In a peculiar sense, rural people relate themselves directly to the land. While the urban dweller is only indirectly aware of the importance of the soil to his well-being, the farmer is always conscious of his immediate dependence upon it. He and the members of his family have planted, nurtured, and harvested from his own acres the food on his family table. The fuel which warms his house most probably has been secured from the farm woodlot. In many sections of the earth today, and in all sections at one time or another, the clothes worn by the family are of wool or cotton grown on the farm and made into cloth at the spinning wheel and family loom.

It should elicit no surprise therefore to learn that land to the farmer-peasant takes on the character of something sacred. Only where there is the development of highly commercialized agriculture does the worker on the land lose this emotional attachment. At all times, however, property in land looms as an all-important holding to rural people. Its social significance lies primarily in the effect which it has on the social status of people, upon the degree of stratification of rural society, and upon social mobility. Generally speaking, those societies in which the land is owned by those who till it are less likely to be characterized by considerations of differences in social status. Moreover, ownership contributes to the development of a more stable and less mobile population and thereby gives greater stability to the various social institutions.

## MEANING AND KINDS OF PROPERTY

A simple definition of property is "the exclusive right to the control of an economic good." *Private property* is "the exclusive right of a private person to control an economic good." [1] R. T. Ely and G. S. Wehrwein point out that "property implies (1) owner, (2) the property object, (3) the State to protect the owner in his rights over the property object." [2] Without the third factor—the protection of the State—private property could scarcely exist, unless the "owner" himself were sufficiently powerful to maintain possession against the encroachment of others. Property, therefore, as we know it, is a right granted to the individual by society which guarantees the right.

*Common property* is an economic object whose ownership and use are shared equally by all members of the group. Pastures and woodlands of the New England towns in the early period are examples. The tribal lands of the American Indians were also common property. Until the remaining areas of public domain were withdrawn from further settlement and unrestricted use, they were treated as common property and were open to use by anyone without let or hindrance. Before the Forest Service was created in 1905, the forest lands were similarly regarded.

*Public property* is that which is held by the government for the use of all the citizens; it differs from common property in that it is subject to certain restrictions as to use. The national forests, parks, and grazing districts are examples. Theoretically, a citizen is entitled to use these lands, provided he conforms to stated regulations. In the case of grazing lands, both on the national forests and in the grazing districts (on what was pre-

[1] R. T. Ely, *Property and Contract*, Vol. 1, p. 101. New York: The Macmillan Company, 1922.
[2] R. T. Ely and G. S. Wehrwein, *Land Economics*, p. 75. New York: The Macmillan Company, 1940.

viously public domain) stockmen are restricted to certain numbers of livestock; each is given a "permit" to graze a specified number of sheep, cattle, horses, etc., and may not use the grazing lands except within time limits set by the Government.

**The "bundle of rights" concept.** If we follow the definition of property given above as the right to the use of something, it is clear that such a right is often shared by others than the owner himself. That is, the owner may *contract* part of his right to someone else, as is done in the case of the landlord-tenant relationship. The idea of property as a complex—or "bundle"—of rights is useful in this connection. Thus, while the owner retains some of the rights to his farm, he may grant others to a tenant for a temporary period. During such a period, the tenant can exercise the right of using the land and buildings, growing such crops as he desires (unless otherwise stipulated in the contract), and sharing in the produce.

## SPECIAL CHARACTERISTICS OF LANDED PROPERTY

Because it is the immediate source of the essentials for sustaining life, the possession of land has always been associated with *security*. To have a piece of land on which to grow food, obtain fuel, and if need be, fiber for clothing, is even today regarded by many people as the ultimate in economic security. Moreover, land is tangible, *real* property; it is immovable. Those who want to "hedge" against inflation seek to invest money in land or in other tangibles, rather than in the paper certificates of property.

What land means to the peasant is poignantly expressed in the following excerpts from a letter from an East Frisian mother to her son in Illinois:

You say that you have all the papers for the land now? Please put them where they will not take them back. When they try to take your land you can show them the papers. Be sure to take care of them. If you have land you are as a king. Land is everything. One cannot move land away from you and if one has the land by a paper, one cannot be made to leave the land. [3]

[3] E. T. Hiller, Faye E. Corner, and Wendell L. East, "Rural Community Types," *University of Illinois Studies in the Social Sciences*, Vol. XVI, No. 4, p. 25.

To this the son replied in part:

"When I am plowing I can shut my eyes and smell the dear land under me and say it is mine, mine, all mine. No one can take it away. I am king as you said . . . [4]

There was a time before the rise of our commercial-industrial society when land was the chief form of property. It was true in the days of feudalism. The ownership of land meant power to control the economic and political life of the time. And even though the values of commercial and industrial enterprises now vastly exceed those of land, ownership of the latter still carries with it some of the ancient prestige. The possession of land, in other words, is still associated with relatively high *social status*.

Land ownership is also characterized by emotional or sentimental values not common, at least in the same degree, to other forms of property. Perhaps it is due in part to the fact that the home of the farmer is on the land. The land on which he lives is identified with "home," and therefore associated with the sentiments that inhere in that word. Moreover, the land is the nexus between the generations that have gone and those that are to come. The nonmaterial aspect of land as property is well indicated by A. I. Tannous in his description of a Lebanon village, as follows:

One cannot possibly overestimate the vital significance of land, the life-giving soil, to the Bishmizzeen villager. To him, land cannot be conceived of as a piece of property, worth so much in cash money to be bought today and sold tomorrow. Its significance goes far beyond that. From the beautiful gifts of the soil he satisfies his primary needs, the starting points of his whole existence. For generations, through the long line of his ancestors, he has become conscious of this vital fact, and land has become intimately bound up with his life. Working the land is his primary and almost sole occupation. To this occupation any other in which he may engage is secondary and subsidiary.

More than that, for several generations the land, the same land, has been handed down to him through a continuous line of ancestors. It represents to him these ancestors in a living and realistic manner. He toils on it as they toiled. He is generously rewarded by it as they were. He handles it through the same type of activities as they handled it

[4] *Ibid.*, p. 27.

before him. As a result the land never failed them, and they lived happily. The same land shall not fail him, and he shall live happily too. As the center of such consciousness of such realization in the mind of the villager, the land stands as a major value, a major symbol of identification, which ties him, in an organic manner, with a large group of fellow human beings, those who passed before him and those who come after him. He feels stable, integrated and secure.[5]

A similar expression is found in a recent study of rural life in China:

Land is inherited from one's ancestors, and the inheritor has the obligation to hand it down to his descendants. The individual is only a temporary custodian of the property. If one is not able to keep the land of the family, he will be condemned in public opinion. Selling land is the last resort that a financially hard-up peasant can think of. Rather, he will try to raise a loan even at a suicidal rate of interest.[6]

Such attitudes are very important in consideration of land as property. They probably account for much of the reputed conservatism of farm people and they unquestionably have much to do with the persistence of the peasant peoples of the world in their struggle to get title to the land. There is a principle of immediacy involved, a juxtaposition of owner and owned, which makes the one an expression of the other. Stocks and bonds by contrast are merely evidences of property, not the thing itself. The landowner is "aware" of his property: it has reality and substance, its own peculiar shape or contour and other visible features become identifying marks by which it is familiarly different from the property of others.

The quotations given above refer to another element in land property which is distinctive, namely, the idea of *stewardship*. This idea is very old. "The earth is the Lord's and the fulness thereof," sang the Psalmist. Men are only God's stewards and land takes on an aura of the sacred. "The farmer . . . must first build up within himself an appreciation of his high calling. It is a sacred calling. In his work he is a partner of God. The

[5] Afif I. Tannous, *Trends of Social and Cultural Change in Bishmizzeen, An Arab Village of North Lebanon*, Ph.D. thesis, Cornell University, June, 1940.
[6] Yu-I Li, Hsiao-Tung Fei, and Tse-I Chang, *Three Types of Rural Economy in Yunnan*, International Secretariat, Institute of Pacific Relations, New York, 1943, p. 23.

land which he tills is 'holy land.' The soil has been committed to him as a sacred heritage." [7]

One might ask why the owner of land should be charged with a "sacred" responsibility or why property in land should be considered any more "holy" than other forms. Why does not the banker, or the merchant, or the industrialist also carry a "sacred" responsibility? Why not refer to one's "dear" stocks and bonds, or "dear" bank, as well as the "dear land"? But such questions emphasize the fact that there is in the human tradition a different psychological content associated with property in land, a fact which conditions very significantly the social life of rural people throughout the world.

## CHANGING CONCEPT OF PROPERTY

While there can be no doubt that, historically, property in land has carried with it distinctive values, including those of a sentimental nature, it cannot be said that farmers themselves always and equally cherish these values. In the United States until about 1890 there was an abundance of land; there developed a carelessness and wastefulness in its use which would not derive from a "love of the soil." Title to land is given in *fee simple*, which carries with it no limitations of the use to which the land is put. The owner may abuse it by overgrazing or overcropping and allow severe erosion to carry the topsoil away. There is no authority to restrain him. As a consequence of unwise use of the soil, millions of acres have been rendered practically valueless for agriculture by erosion, and other millions are in advanced stages of destruction.

The American public became acutely conscious of the need for soil conservation during the drought of the early 1930's, and, responding to an obvious need, Congress enacted legislation looking towards the establishment of better land-use practices. Under legislation, soil-conservation, demonstration areas were established in severely eroded areas, in which farmers and the government cooperated to build erosion dams and terraces, and develop contour farming. Also, through the Agricultural Ad-

[7] "Rural Life in a Peaceful World," The National Catholic Rural Life Conference, Des Moines, January, 1944, p. 14.

justment Administration farmers were paid benefits for carrying out cropping practices which would limit the acreage of surplus crops and encourage the planting of such crops as grass, alfalfa, clover, and others which would reduce erodibility and at the same time improve fertility.

More direct action has been taken in some respects. Most of the States have enacted weed laws, under the terms of which certain weeds may not be allowed to grow on privately owned land. That is, the landowner is expected to kill such weeds himself, or failing to do so, the local government authority may go on the premises and kill the weeds and add the expense of doing it to the farmer's taxes. The zoning ordinances which have been passed in a number of states forbid the use for agriculture of lands that have been classified as more suitable for other purposes. Finally, the Soil Conservation Districts, which are now organized in most of the states, have authority to establish land-use practices which farmers within the district may be compelled to follow. In actual practice compulsion is seldom if ever resorted to, the aim being to achieve the objective by enlisting the active cooperation of every inhabitant in the district.

There is no doubt that in the decade of the 1930's the American people came to realize more fully the dependence of all upon the basic resource of the land. The principle of social control over its use was more widely discussed and accepted than at any previous time in history. Through education and demonstration, or through "benefit payments" if possible, or through use of the police power if need be, some limitations of "rights" in the use of land appear to be inevitable.

**Changes in Russia.** In contrast with the rather slight modifications of property in land which have developed in the United States, those imposed by the Russian Revolution have been drastic. For the first time in history on so large a scale the Russians attempted the abrogation of private property and the assumption of ownership by the State. The original program not only involved the elimination of private property in land, but also provided for the breakup of the large estates and the distribution of the land among the peasants. However, the new regime "regarded the peasant, not as a proprietor of the

land, but as a workman operating government-owned land." [8]
Since under the communistic system all were to share and share
alike, the peasants might have only such produce as they needed
for their own maintenance; the balance was to be given to the
state. The understanding was that clothing and other goods not
produced on the farm would be distributed free of charge.
That such a change in their relationship to the land did not
satisfy the peasants is evident from the drastic decline in agricultural production and ultimately from the uprisings which
occurred during 1920 and 1921.[9] Although vigorously suppressed
by the government, they were no doubt in large measure responsible for the change to the new communistic program known
as the New Economic Policy. Important concessions were made
to the peasants. They no longer had to surrender all the surplus
of their produce. They were now required to pay taxes instead.
"At first this was a tax in kind, principally grain, but later it
became a tax in money. . . . The Soviet Government promised
the peasants that it would take only a definite proportion of
the produce of their labor in the form of a tax, and not the
whole surplus in excess of their immediate needs. The peasants
received the right to dispose of the surplus as they wished—
that is, to sell it in the open market." [10]

The change affected only the farmer's property in the produce
of the land, not his relation to the land itself. The land code of
1922 merely granted the free use of the land, not a title of
ownership. Moreover, the small individual peasant enterprises
were discouraged by policies which set up agricultural cooperatives and state-owned farms. The government enterprises represented an attempt to modify the historic peasant tradition
that possession of land "by a paper" was the supreme good.
Sentimental attachment to a particular piece of land could
not be compatible with the Soviet policy. While there is no
reason to suppose that in a generation or two the typical
peasant attitude toward property cannot be changed—such
attitudes being culturally, not biologically determined—it is
yet too early to judge the success of the Russian experiment.

[8] George Vernadsky, *A History of Russia*, p. 277. New Haven: Yale University
Press, 1929.
    [9] *Ibid.*, p. 281.          [10] *Ibid.*, pp. 281–282.

The initial response of the peasantry to the communization of property entailed a disastrous decline in agricultural production, the slaughtering of livestock rather than giving the animals to the government, and finally open revolt. The response of the government was at first cruel suppression of the uprisings, then the making of concessions to peasant demands, and later the development of "incentives," in the nature of rewards for merit, partially to substitute for the loss of the incentive of profit.

### THE DISTRIBUTION OF PROPERTY IN LAND

In considering the distribution of land reference will be made only to the United States in illustrating two dimensions of property distribution. The first of them we shall call the *vertical* distribution and the second, the *horizontal*. The two concepts will become clear as we proceed.

**Vertical distribution.** We have reference to the distribution of the "rights" to the land, conceived as a "bundle." The occupants and workers of the land may be thought of as being distributed on a vertical continuum, from those at the top who hold all the rights in the bundle to those on the bottom who hold very few. Usually it has been the practice to classify farm people in the terminology of land tenure as (*a*) owners, (*b*) part owners, (*c*) tenants, (*d*) sharecroppers, and (*e*) wage workers. We are compelled here to use this classification, although in the present frame of reference, considering the innumerable variations within each group, it is theoretically possible to distribute them on a continuous scale in terms of the rights which they have to the land.

**Meaning of the tenure classes.** A farm owner is one who has a title in fee simple to all the land he operates. The land may either be free from mortgage or mortgaged; he is still classed as an owner. The part owner is one who owns—whether mortgaged or not—some of the land which he operates, and rents some in addition. He is both owner and renter. The tenant is one who rents his farm from a landlord; he may pay cash, a specified *amount* of crops, or a specified *share* of the crops grown. The sharecropper, classified as a tenant in the census, is in reality a laborer who is paid in kind (a share of the crop) rather

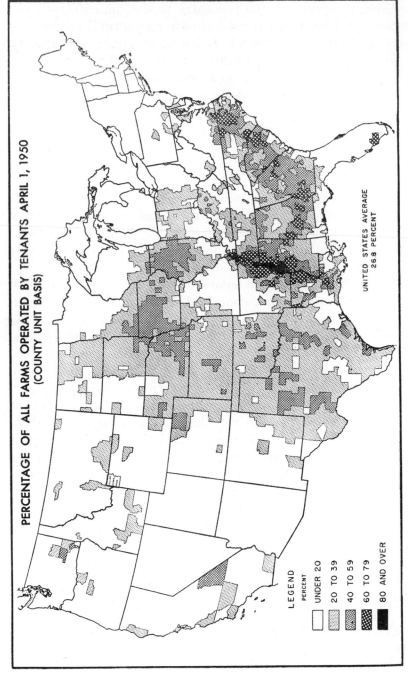

PERCENTAGE OF ALL FARMS OPERATED BY TENANTS APRIL 1, 1950
(COUNTY UNIT BASIS)

UNITED STATES AVERAGE
26.8 PERCENT

LEGEND
PERCENT

UNDER 20
20 TO 39
40 TO 59
60 TO 79
80 AND OVER

FIGURE 44. *Percentage of All Farms Operated by Tenants*

TABLE 16. *Tenure Groups in the United States, 1940 and 1945*

| TENURE CLASS AND YEAR | | UNITED STATES | NORTH | SOUTH | WEST |
|---|---|---|---|---|---|
| All Operators | 1945 | 5,859,169 | 2,483,578 | 2,881,135 | 494,456 |
| | 1940 | 6,096,799 | 2,579,958 | 3,007,170 | 509,670 |
| Per cent change | | −3.9 | −3.7 | −4.2 | −2.9 |
| Full Owners | 1945 | 3,301,361 | 1,460,320 | 1,509,056 | 331,985 |
| | 1940 | 3,084,138 | 1,437,958 | 1,327,690 | 318,490 |
| Per cent change | | 7.0 | 1.5 | 13.7 | 4.2 |
| Part Owners | 1945 | 660,502 | 384,551 | 193,607 | 82,344 |
| | 1940 | 615,039 | 322,618 | 216,607 | 75,814 |
| Per cent change | | 7.4 | 19.1 | −10.6 | 8.7 |
| Tenants | 1945 | 1,858,421 | 621,410 | 1,165,279 | 71,732 |
| | 1940 | 2,361,271 | 803,426 | 1,449,293 | 108,552 |
| Per cent change | | −21.3 | −22.7 | −19.6 | −33.9 |
| Managers | 1945 | 38,885 | 17,297 | 13,193 | 8,395 |
| | 1940 | 36,351 | 15,957 | 13,580 | 6,814 |
| Per cent change | | 6.9 | 8.4 | −2.8 | 23.2 |

Source: United States Census of Agriculture, 1945.

than in money. He furnishes none of the equipment or livestock; the landlord provides them for his use. The latter also "furnishes" him with subsistence for himself and his family, including the use of a house, until the crop is harvested. He is in a different situation from that of the wage laborer in that he shares to some extent in the risk of the enterprise. If the crop is good, he gets more for his season's labor; if it is bad, he gets less. The usual share received is 50 per cent of the crop. The wage laborer is paid in cash and perquisites in the form of board, housing, the use of a garden plot, etc. Arrangements with respect to perquisites vary with the individual farm and in different sections according to local custom. (See Figure 44.)

Changes in the tenure classes from 1940 to 1945 by areas of the United States are shown in Table 16. Full owners have increased in all areas; part owners have increased in the North and West but decreased in the South; tenants are fewer in all parts; and managers have declined in the South but increased in the North and West. Mechanization has been a potent factor in bringing about these changes in tenure. Total operators are fewer, which means an increase in the average size of farm.

Another factor in changing the tenure status has been the increased prosperity of agriculture during and since World War II.

While the improved ownership status of American farmers is a gratifying trend, it needs to be noted that the increase in the average size of farm is entirely due to the enlargement of farms operated by part owners and managers.

The tenancy rate has declined since 1930 until it seems to have reached a point not much higher than it was in 1880. The decline in tenancy, while general, has been most marked in the South. (See Figure 45.)

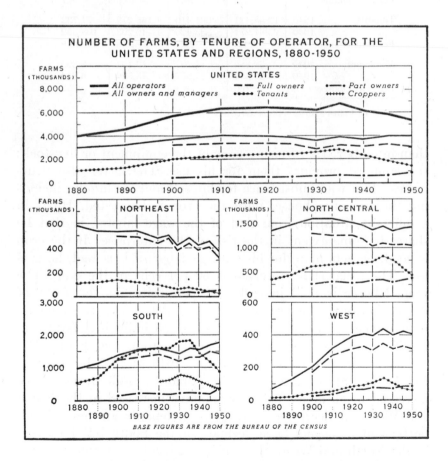

FIGURE 45. *Number of Farms, by Tenure of Operator for the United States and Regions, 1880–1950*

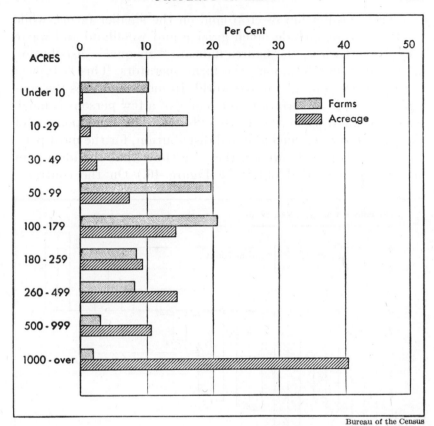

FIGURE 46. *Percentage Distribution of Farms and Farm Acreage by Size of Farms, 1950*

**Horizontal distribution.** About 60 per cent of the two billion acres of land surface in the United States is in farms. The 1.1 billion acres of land in farms in 1950 were distributed among approximately 5.3 million farmers. While these figures would make the average farm approximately 215 acres, there is a wide range in size. (See Figure 46.) While two thirds of the farms are in the groups from 10 to 180 acres, they contain less than 23 per cent of the acreage. The 5.7 per cent of all farms which are over 500 acres in size contain over half (53.5 per cent) of the acreage in farms. It should be kept in mind that the figures refer to all land in farms, and include not only the crop acreage, but pasture, grazing, woodlands, and waste, as well. Naturally there is a larger proportion of crop land on the smaller farms, while the large farms include much grazing and woodland and waste area. Nevertheless, the figures indicate "unequal" distribution of the land surface among the farm operators. This is typical of agriculture throughout the world. In most countries the concentration of land surface in the hands of a few persons is much greater than it is in the United States. The land policies of this country were aimed at equal distribution, for the most part, in 160-acre tracts. However, the data show that the ideal plan has not been carried out. (See Figure 46.) On the contrary,

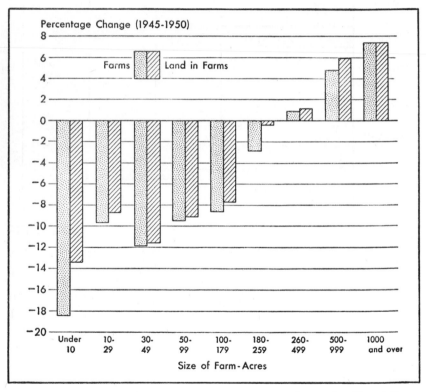

FIGURE 47. *Percentage Change in Farms and Land in Farms by Size of Farm, 1945–1950*

we discover that the tendency has been toward further concentration of acreage in large holdings. Reference to Figure 47 will reveal the changes that have taken place since 1945. All farms under 260 acres declined, as did also their total acreage.

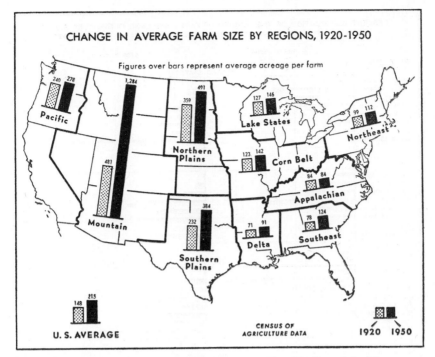

FIGURE 48. *Sectional Change in Acreage Showing Growth in West*

Figure 48 shows the change in the average acreage per farm over the thirty-year period from 1920 to 1950. It will be noted that the most marked increases have taken place in the Great Plains and the Mountain States. There was no change in the average size in the Appalachian area, and only small increases in other parts of the South, in New England, and in the Lake States and the Corn Belt. An examination of the Census of Agriculture shows that farms over 1,000 acres increased in all states of the Union. The census further reveals that in the North the decrease by size of farm from 1920 to 1950 was most marked in the group from 100 to 174 acres, the class that contained the "old homestead." [11] (Figure 49) Reference to Figures 50 and 51 reveals clearly that the trend towards concentration of land ownership was accelerated during World War II. Thus the data for 1945 demonstrated that the concentration continued over

[11] Paul S. Taylor, "Good-bye to the Homestead Farm," *Harpers Magazine,* 1941, 1092 : 589–597.

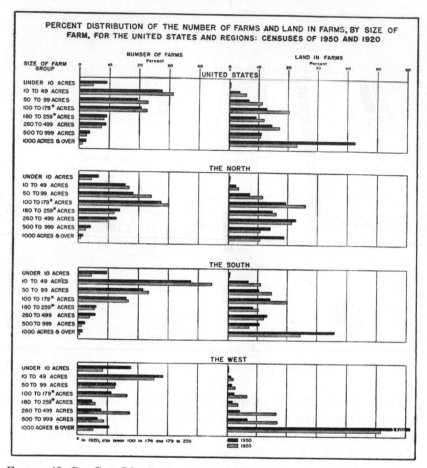

FIGURE 49. *Per Cent Distribution of the Number of Farms and Land in Farms by Size of Farm, for the United States and Regions: 1920–1950*

the past thirty years. Farm efficiency has increased with larger farms. Careful students, however, question the desirability of reducing the number of middle-sized farms and increasing the number of very large and very small units.

**Demands for redistribution.** In practically all countries there has been a demand by the agricultural class to have the land "returned" to them. Frequently bloody revolutions are fought to achieve an equitable distribution of the land. The question of land is a primary cause of political unrest in several Latin-American and European countries, as well as in China.

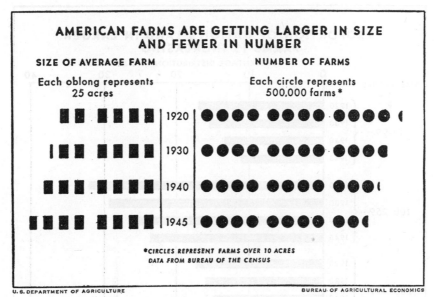

FIGURE 50. *Size and Number of Farms in United States, 1920–1945*

In the United States there has been some agitation for setting a limit on the amount of land any one individual may operate, although there has been no official action. North Dakota in 1933 passed legislation prohibiting corporations from owning land and granting them ten years in which to dispose of the land they held at the time the act was passed.

The most important steps taken recently to redistribute land were (*a*) Government purchase and retirement from agricultural use of submarginal land, and (*b*) the purchase and resale of farm land under the Farmers Home Administration and its predecessor agencies. The most important is the FHA program. Under its provisions the Government may purchase farms from nonoperating farm owners and sell them to tenants. Or it may purchase large tracts (such as plantations), subdivide them, and resell to farmers who are now tenants or laborers. This program is of relatively small significance in terms of the large number of landless farmers in the United States, but is a step in the direction of redistributing the land. The farms handled by FHA must not exceed a certain value—about $12,000—which automatically sets a limit on the size of the

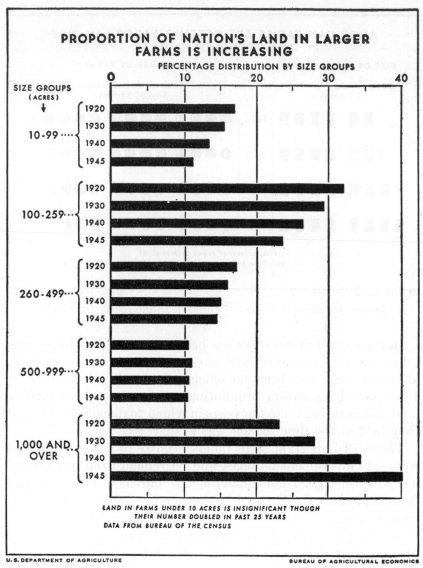

FIGURE 51. *Percentage Distribution by Size Groups of Land in Farms in United States*

property. The average loan for these farms in 1944 was about $6,000.

Another public policy adopted in some states which is aimed at discouraging the concentration of land in the hands of nonoperators is Homestead Tax Exemption. The differential in favor of the operator-owner is ordinarily not great and it cannot be regarded as an effective measure by itself in discouraging absentee ownership of land. However, it points in the direction of such a goal. A regressive land tax to discourage large holdings has been proposed at various times.

However, the American people are probably not in a mood as yet to adopt drastic measures to inhibit further concentration of land ownership or to bring about forcible redistribution. The FHA program is widely criticized and has difficulty obtaining appropriations with which to operate. There is strong opposition in various quarters to direct action on the part of government. (See pictures following page 264.)

**Significant trends.** In this chapter there is shown the special character of property in land and what it means to the people who live upon it; also, the forms in which land is distributed among the people, on the vertical as well as horizontal planes. Greater control by society over the uses to which land is put to the end that it will be properly conserved for the future appears as a current trend. Rights to land on the part of those who operate farms have been declining up to recent times. Some gain in farm ownership was noted during World War II, while the mortgage debt of owners was greatly reduced, thus indicating a reversal of previous trends. The distribution of the land area, however, has been increasingly concentrated in fewer hands. Farms have been declining in number while total area has remained about the same. The increase in farms of 1,000 acres and over has been steady since 1920, while the number of acres in farms smaller than this has declined.

## QUESTIONS FOR DISCUSSION

1. It has sometimes been argued that the primitive form of all property was communal and that private property is either (a) a degenerate, or (b) a more advanced form. From what you know of primitive peoples, is the first part of the generalization true or false? In other words, do primitive groups tend to be communal property holders? Do you regard private property as superior to communal property, inferior to, or no difference? Give reasons.

2. Why does tenancy often give rise to soil wastage? Is it tenancy *per*

*se* which is to blame, or the particular system of tenancy which fails to provide feelings of security to the tenant family?

3. Can the farm owner afford to practice soil conservation? If the answer is *yes*, why has he failed to conserve the soil in the United States? If the answer is *no*, how can society achieve the desirable goal of conserving the soil?

4. Does the contemporary farmer in the United States manifest any such sentiment towards the soil, as the author indicates for certain other groups?

5. Have you observed any difference in soil practices among different nationality groups in an area with which you are familiar? What are they? How would you account for any such differences that may exist?

6. In terms of the *bundle of rights* concept of property, would you say that the farm laborer has *property* in the farm on which he works? Discuss.

7. What significance do you attach to the increasing size of farms in America? What is happening? What does it imply in terms of the number of farm people we will have in the next few decades? What will it mean to the social institutions of education, religion, etc.? What will be the consequences to the village and the small town?

## SELECTED REFERENCES

Carroll, Thomas F. *Report on the Latin American Seminar on Land Problems.* Rome: Food and Agriculture Organization. 1953.

"Cooperative Reports," Bureau of the Census and the Department of Agriculture: 1. *Agriculture, 1950;* 2. *Farm Tenure, 1950;* 3. *Economic Class and Type of Farm, 1950;* 4. *Farms and Farm People, 1950.*

Ely, R. T., and Wehrwein, George S. *Land Economics.* New York: The Macmillan Company, 1940.

*Farmers in a Changing World. Yearbook of Agriculture, 1940.* Washington, D.C.: Government Printing Office.

Gras, N. S. B. *A History of Agriculture in Europe and America,* Chapter 11. New York: F. S. Crofts and Co., 1925.

*Progress in Land Reform.* New York: United Nations, 1954.

Sorokin, P. A., and others. *A Systematic Source Book in Rural Sociology,* Vol. I, pp. 636–645. Minneapolis: University of Minnesota Press, 1930.

Shepard, Ward. *Food or Famine: The Challenge of Erosion,* Chapter 3. New York: The Macmillan Company, 1945.

# CHAPTER 14

# FARMING SYSTEMS

The manner in which the agricultural enterprise is organized is important to the social structure of rural life. This fact will become clear as the discussion proceeds, but at this point it may be well to illustrate the generalization by calling attention to the contrast between two systems of farming, the family farm and the corporation farm. In the former, the family occupies a relatively small tract of land, provides the capital for its operation out of savings and borrowings, undertakes the function of management and direction of operations, and usually performs most of the labor involved. A community based upon family farms is characterized by a maximum degree of social homogeneity—which means a minimum of social stratification— and usually provides a greater number of people per unit of land.

In contrast, the corporation farm is much larger. Capital is provided through sale of stock or bonds and through borrowing; management is hired, and the manager may or may not have any ownership in the land himself. Labor is usually hired on a wage basis, although the plantation with its sharecropper class may be considered a partial exception. The laborers, therefore, like the manager, have no ownership in the land. The sole purpose of the corporation farm is to make profits, like any industrial enterprise. While the family farm likewise seeks profits as a primary goal, it is also a home for the family. It is to the family farm that the statement, "farming is more than an occupation, it is a mode of life," would especially apply. A community built around a system of corporation farming is characterized by a greater degree of social stratification, giving rise to conflicting interests as between labor and management. Social institutions are influenced by the system, as will be shown later.

**Factors in farm organization.** Like all economic enterprises, agricultural production results from the organization and utilization of capital, labor, and land. The entrepreneur is the agent who brings the other three factors into combination in such a way as to produce goods and services. The essential difference between the agricultural and nonagricultural enterprise lies largely in the relative importance of the land factor. The factory must have land on which to operate, but the major part of the total enterprise is represented in the factory itself, that is, in the building and mechanical equipment. By way of contrast, in agriculture approximately 80 per cent of the capital investment is represented in the land itself.

**The agricultural plant.** Our agricultural plant in the United States consists of approximately 1.1 billion acres of land in farms (which is just over 50 per cent of the total land area of the nation) and the buildings, implements, livestock, and other capital goods. In 1945 the agricultural enterprise consisted of 5,859,169 farms, with an average of 195 acres per farm. There is a wide range in the size of farms—from less than 3 acres to more than a million. There were 262 farms with 100,000 or more acres in 1945. As a general rule, the larger places are devoted to livestock production, the land being used for grazing.

The area of the "land in farms" on which crops were harvested in 1944 was 352 million acres. The balance of the land is classified as woodland, pasture, crop land idle or used only for pasture, and waste land. The remainder of the land area of the country—not included in farms—is occupied by cities, industrial establishments, roads, parks, national forests, mountains, grazing districts, and other public reserves. Much of the area in the forests of the West and in the grazing districts constitutes a part of the productive enterprise of agriculture, even though not privately owned. Stockmen graze their livestock on these areas, and a large part of the financial returns credited to farms is really derived from the use of the public lands.

In 1950 the assets of American agriculture amounted to 127 billion dollars, distributed as follows:

|  | Billions | Increase over 1940 |
|---|---|---|
| Real estate and stored crops | 71.3 | 97 per cent |
| Livestock | 13.2 | 157 per cent |
| Machinery and motor vehicles | 14.3 | 358 per cent |
| Household furnishings, equipment | 6.5 | 152 per cent |
| Deposits, currency, bonds, etc. | 21.8 | 296 per cent |

The labor force. In agriculture the labor force consists of the operators, the wage laborers, and unpaid family workers. Their distribution is shown in Table 17. The table shows the downward trend in numbers of the farm labor force.

TABLE 17. *Types of Workers on Farms at Times of Enumeration, 1935–1950.*
(numbers are in thousands)

| TYPE OF WORKER | 1950 No. | 1950 PER CENT | 1945 No. | 1945 PER CENT | 1940 No. | 1940 PER CENT | 1935 No. | 1935 PER CENT |
|---|---|---|---|---|---|---|---|---|
| All workers | 8,538 | 100.0 | 8,373 | 100.0 | 9,694 | 100.0 | 12,407 | 100.0 |
| Family workers | 6,983 | 81.8 | 7,625 | 91.1 | 7,941 | 81.9 | 10,762 | 86.7 |
| Operators | 4,246 | 49.8 | 4,978 | 58.5 | * | | * | |
| Unpaid family workers | 2,737 | 32.0 | 2,647 | 31.6 | * | | * | |
| Hired workers | 1,555 | 18.2 | 748 | 8.9 | 1,754 | 18.1 | 1,646 | 13.3 |

Source: U. S. Census of Agriculture, 1950. Vol. II.
* Not reported separately.

## CLASSIFICATION OF FARMS

The simplest classification of farms for our purposes is (a) the family farm and (b) the large-scale farm. Within these broad classes many variations occur, and it is always difficult to tell where one class merges into the other. When the question is asked, "How large is a 'large-scale' farm?" there is always difficulty in finding a suitable answer. The usual resort is to set some arbitrary standard, based upon income or value. Thus D. C. Mumford defined a large-scale farm as: "A single farm or group of farms under one closely controlled and supervised management, if the size of its total farm business was at least five to eight times as large as the typical farm business in the same locality producing the same kinds of products." [1] The Bureau of the Census issued a special monograph on large-scale farming based on the 1930 census, and used as the criterion of "large" a gross value of products of $30,000 or more in the year 1929.[2]

Fortunately, the Bureau of the Census in 1950 adopted a classification which gives a much clearer idea than we have had

[1] D. Curtis Mumford, "Large-Scale Farming in the United States," Bureau of Agricultural Economics, Washington, D.C., April, 1938, p. 2.
[2] R. D. Jennings, "Large-Scale Farming in the United States, 1929," United States Bureau of the Census, Washington, D.C., 1933.

before of farms by economic class and the characteristics of each. The criteria for classification are mainly the value of products sold and the number of days the operator worked off the farm during the year previous to the census. The classification is as follows:[3]

| Type | Number (000's) | Per cent | Value of products sold (dollars) |
|---|---|---|---|
| I. Commercial farms: | 3,706.4 | 68.9 | 250–25,000 |
| Class  I | 103.2 | 1.9 | 25,000 |
| II | 381.1 | 7.1 | 10,000–24,999 |
| III | 721.2 | 13.4 | 5,000–9,999 |
| IV | 882.3 | 16.4 | 2,500–4,999 |
| V | 901.3 | 16.8 | 1,200–2,499 |
| VI | 717.2 | 13.3 | 250–1,999  (operator works off less than 100 days) |
| II. Other farms: | 1,672.8 | 31.1 | |
| Part-time | 639.2 | 11.9 | 250–1,199 (and more than 100 days off-farm work) |
| Residential | 1,029.3 | 19.1 | Less than 250 |
| All Farms | 5,379.2 | 100.0 | |

Even this classification is only partly satisfactory for our purposes in that it fails to take into account the manner in which the farm is organized. There is, for example, a considerable difference between a large-scale farm operated by a corporation and one which is operated by a cooperative whose members are also the workers on the land. For this reason, we need to indicate some of the types of large-scale farms from the standpoint of the way in which they actually function. But first it is well to say something about the family farm.

[3] *1950 Census of Agriculture*, Vol. II. The geographic distribution of some of these classes is shown on maps facing p. 264.

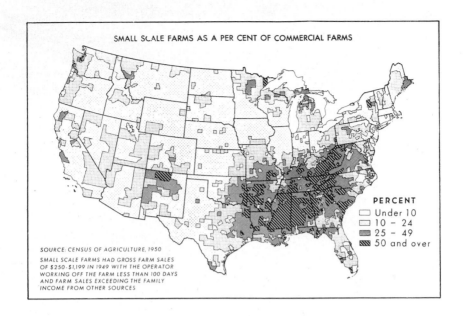

SMALL SCALE FARMS AS A PER CENT OF COMMERCIAL FARMS

PERCENT
☐ Under 10
☐ 10 – 24
■ 25 – 49
▨ 50 and over

SOURCE: CENSUS OF AGRICULTURE, 1950

SMALL SCALE FARMS HAD GROSS FARM SALES
OF $250-$1,199 IN 1949 WITH THE OPERATOR
WORKING OFF THE FARM LESS THAN 100 DAYS
AND FARM SALES EXCEEDING THE FAMILY
INCOME FROM OTHER SOURCES

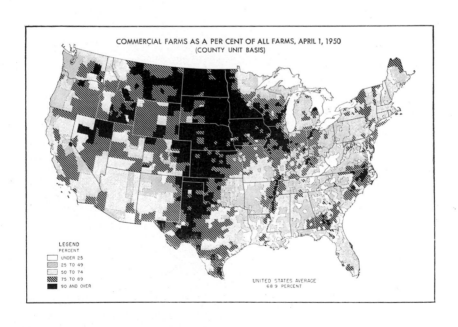

COMMERCIAL FARMS AS A PER CENT OF ALL FARMS, APRIL 1, 1950
(COUNTY UNIT BASIS)

LEGEND
PERCENT
☐ UNDER 25
▨ 25 TO 49
☐ 50 TO 74
▨ 75 TO 89
■ 90 AND OVER

UNITED STATES AVERAGE
68.9 PERCENT

*Careless farming in Ventura County, California, (above) resulted in destruction of this farm. Soil-conserving practices (below) protect the farmer and the community.*

## THE FAMILY FARM

By family farm we mean that type or system of farm organization in which the family performs the function of management, provides its own capital from savings or borrowings, and furnishes a large, if not the major, part of the labor. The concept itself is susceptible to wide variations and cannot be precisely defined. For example, there may be cases in which a major part of the labor is hired, though from the standpoint of management and control of capital and size of the enterprise, it would still be classified as a family farm. Despite the numerous variations and the difficulty of precise definition, the term "family farm" is in general use and there is a common understanding as to its meaning. That common meaning would conform roughly to the definition given above.

**Variations in type.** The family farm varies widely over the United States. There are, for example, the relatively large farms of the wheat-growing areas, most of them highly mechanized; the mixed livestock and crop farms, the truck farms located chiefly in the areas adjacent to metropolitan centers, and the so-called "subsistence" farms. While the latter are found in various sections of the country, they are notably common in the Southern mountain regions and the Great Lakes cutover area. It is impossible to say precisely what portion of the six million farms of the country would be classified as family farms, but it is certain that the vast majority should be included. For example, over 95 per cent of all farms in the United States are under 500 acres in size. While not all of such farms would be classified as family farms, the overwhelming proportion of them would be. Similarly, there would certainly be many farms larger than 500 acres which would classify as family farms. Thus family farms vary markedly in size and in the type of enterprise carried on. It will be noted in the classification given above only about 1 per cent are listed as large scale. This percentage does not include plantations as a rule, since the census enumerates sharecropper allotments as "farms" instead of considering the plantation as a unit.

The family farm can be said to represent the "American ideal" of farm organization. It was the only system of farming visual-

ized by the founding fathers as the universal pattern for the
people of the United States. It was expected that the family
occupying the farm would also be the owners of it. As is well
known, this part of the ideal has not been fully realized. It
should be borne in mind, by the way, that in talking about the
family farm we consider tenant-operated as well as owner-
operated farms as falling within the classification.

The commercial family farm, numbering approximately three
million farms, is one on which the income is sufficient to support
the family at a satisfactory level of living and to enable the
farmer to maintain improvements and the productivity of the
soil. These "family commercial farms," it will be noted, represent only about half of all the farms in the United States.
Almost as large a number of farms fall below the level of income necessary to support a family satisfactorily. About half
of these are farms which are classified as *part-time*, including
those indicated as "residential"; that is, those whose owners
earn part of the family income from off-farm work. The remainder are farms which are too small to provide a decent
living for the family. The people who occupy them are among the
most impoverished in our society. Unable to supply themselves
with more than the bare essentials to keep body and soul together, they cannot afford to maintain, in addition, the social
institutions and other cultural advantages which are commonly
associated with the phrase, "the American standard of living."

The social significance of the family farm cannot be overestimated. It was the system around which the communities of
the country have arisen, and social institutions organized. It
was out of this system that were developed the typical rural
schools, the rural churches, the local government, and above all,
the type of family that characterizes rural America. The family
farm, especially when owned by those who till its soil, provides
a degree of social stability far greater than has usually been
achieved under conditions of large-scale commercialized farming.

The primary social fact about the family-farm system is that
it makes possible a maximum degree of homogeneity in the
population. Since the family is at the same time capitalist,
laborer, and entrepreneur, there is no ready economic basis

for class interests to emerge. Moreover, it makes possible the identification of the family with a specific area of land as operator if not proprietor. Mobility is therefore much less than in those enterprises in which labor is on a wage basis, and year-round employment for the great masses of those engaged in farming is impossible. The attitudes developed toward the land as property include not only those associated with the pursuit of profits, but also those associated with the land as habitation—as "hearth and home." Such attitudes are of supreme importance in determining the characteristics of rural society.

### THE LARGE-SCALE FARMS

While the number of these farms is comparatively small (perhaps amounting in the aggregate to not more than 80,000, when the plantations are included) [4] they exercise considerable influence because of their concentration in given areas of the country. They are most numerous in California, in the cotton South, and along the Atlantic seaboard. They are of various types, some of which will be described briefly in the following paragraphs.

**The plantation.** "A plantation," says T. J. Woofter, "may be defined as a tract operated by one owner or manager with five or more resident families. These may include the landlord, and laborers, share tenants or renters. Except in the case of renters the landlord exercises close supervision over operators, and except in the case of wage laborers each family cultivates a separate piece of land." [5]

According to the publication from which this quotation was taken, the typical plantation had 14 families residing on it. The average size of the 646 plantations surveyed was 907 acres: the usual amount cultivated by a sharecropper family was 20 acres, although the wage hands averaged 45 acres and the tenants about 25. The layout of the typical plantation is shown in Figure 52.

[4] Estimate given by the Committee on Postwar Agricultural Policy of the Association of Land-Grant Colleges and Universities.

[5] T. J. Woofter, Jr., "Landlord and Tenant on the Cotton Plantation," *Works Progress Administration Research Monograph V*, Washington, D.C., 1936, p. xix.

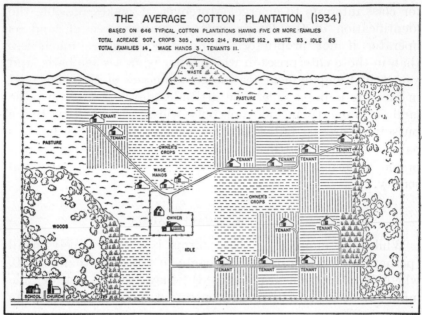

THE AVERAGE COTTON PLANTATION (1934)

BASED ON 646 TYPICAL COTTON PLANTATIONS HAVING FIVE OR MORE FAMILIES
TOTAL ACREAGE 907, CROPS 385, WOODS 214, PASTURE 162, WASTE 83, IDLE 63
TOTAL FAMILIES 14, WAGE HANDS 3, TENANTS 11.

Federal Works Agency—Work Projects Administration

FIGURE 52. *Layout of Average Cotton Plantation*

The plantation is usually under the control of an individual landlord, although corporations and partnerships are not uncommon. In the beginning practically all plantations were family enterprises. Through periods of depression and the attendant foreclosures, many plantations have come into the hands of banks, insurance companies, and other corporations. Mumford found in his study that control by individuals was higher in the South than in other sections of the country and corporation ownership correspondingly lower.[6]

The organization is very elaborate on the large plantations, with provision for departments representing specific activities and a closely knit plan for supervision of the workers. (See Figure 53.) In the period before the War Between the States the plantation was practically a self-contained community with its own "spinning rooms, slaughter and storage houses, gins, grist mills, and other minor processing units."[7] The class lines

[6] Mumford, *op. cit.*, p. 22.
[7] Woofter, *op. cit.*, p. 26.

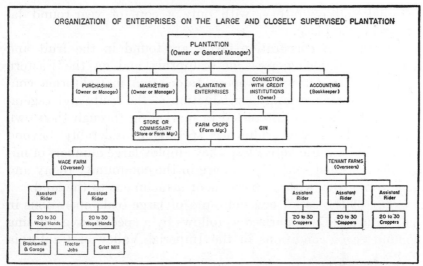

FIGURE 53. *Organization of Enterprises on a Large Plantation*

are particularly marked in the plantation community as between the managerial group and the land workers. The latter may be either colored or white, but the managing group is always white. The large concentration of control of the land in a few hands in the plantation belt gives to the owner-group great power over the political, economic, and social life of the area.

**The corporation farm.** An agricultural enterprise owned by a corporation does not differ markedly in its organization from any other corporate enterprise. The corporation employs a manager who is made responsible for the details of operation and is responsible to the board of directors. The capital is supplied by the corporation through the sale of stocks or bonds, or through current borrowings from banks or other financial agencies. The labor is hired as a rule, although there are cases in which the land is leased to tenants. Most of the corporation farms, or "factories in the fields," are devoted to the production of some crop specialty, such as fruits and vegetables, as is the case with the plantation devoted to cotton or tobacco. The aim, the sole aim, is the profits that can be made in the enterprise. Neither the hired manager nor the hired labor is interested in the farm as a permanent home; the labor force is likely to be seasonal and migratory, with only a core of year-round laborers on the place.

Examples of corporation farms are found in the fruit and vegetable producing areas of California and on the Eastern seaboard. The Grower-Shippers Association in California controls large areas of land in production of the fruits and vegetables which they are interested in marketing through their own agencies. Thus their influence spreads considerably beyond merely agricultural activities. They employ large numbers of migratory seasonal workers, who are in the community today and gone tomorrow, with no permanent attachment to the land.

Some of the social concomitants of large-scale operations in agriculture are summarized as follows by a special investigating committee of conditions in the Imperial Valley of California in 1934:

This vast vegetable acreage is operated in part by owners or lessees of relatively small farms who reside in the Valley and in part by corporations or companies who lease much of the land they farm, hire all labor, and operate with paid managers and superintendents. The major part of the total vegetable production of lettuce, cantaloupes, carrots, etc., is contributed by the large-scale corporate type of farming and but a minor part by operators who own or lease the holdings that they farm. The major portion of the pea and tomato output, however, appears to be produced on the smaller farms. In general, the corporate type of farming is of greatest importance from the standpoint of acreages farmed and value of outputs.

This difference in the prevailing types of agriculture creates dissimilar problems. Operators of relatively small farms do not appear to have problems that are identical with those of the so-called "grower-shippers." The latter group because of its influence largely determines the course of action pursued by the smaller growers. The problems, therefore, tend to be those incident to the concentration of an industry in relatively few hands, working with the better class of lands, operating on a relatively large scale, leasing much of the land that is thus farmed, planned, and directed by nonresident managers, financed with considerable borrowed capital, conducted with paid resident farm managers, superintendents, and farm hands. The goal is one of profit-making, accompanied by a lack of permanency inherent in a combination of leased lands and salaried positions. The growing of vegetable crops, therefore, is largely of a speculative nature (in so far as marketing is concerned) and every effort is directed to producing crops as economically as possible and marketing them to the best of the operators' abilities in order to produce as wide a margin of profit as may be possible.[8]

**Chain farming.** This is a type of corporation farm which consists of a number of separate tracts operated as one enterprise under a central corporate management and control. The separate tracts composing such farms have been acquired through the purchase of former average-sized, or family farms. Thus the Collins Farms Company of Cedar Rapids, Iowa, in 1931 consisted of 150 of such units scattered in 31 counties; the total holdings in 1931 amounted to 30,000 acres. In describing this enterprise, O. M. Kile [9] says:

The first thing the Collins Company does on acquiring a farm is to make a survey and map of it showing particularly any existing tile drains, the natural drainage courses, etc. Next all fences are torn down except, of course, line fences separating neighboring farms from those operated by the Collins Company. Since the usual purpose is to make one or two big fields of each farm and since no livestock is kept, there is no need for fences. Elimination of fences not only adds considerably to the cultivatable area, but enables the tractors to plow right up to the edge of the road right-of-way. Furthermore, elimination of fence rows means a big reduction in the weed nuisance. Eventually the soil in some of the larger farms will probably become entirely weed free.

Each unit of 5 to 10 farms within a radius of a few miles of a central point is placed under the management of one person who lives not on the farm but in the trade center. Under the manager is a working foreman, usually a well-trained individual and frequently a former county agricultural agent, who assumes direct charge of operations. One set of equipment serves the various tracts, being moved from one tract to another as it is needed. All the labor is hired, and part may occupy some of the farm buildings on the units. Other workers, particularly those needed only during the busy season, live in towns and villages. Since there is no livestock kept, the number of year-

---

[8] Report of the Senate Committee to investigate violations of free speech and rights of labor, 77th Congress, Second Session, Report No. 1150, pt. 3, p. 166.

[9] O. M. Kile, *The New Agriculture*, pp. 91–92. New York: The Macmillan Company, 1932.

round workers needed is small. Central machine shops for
repairing and maintaining the equipment are characteristic of
the system. It appears to be efficient from the economic standpoint, but obviously it is a far cry from the traditional type of
rural life in the United States.

**The cooperative farm.** This may also be regarded as a "corporation" farm; it differs from other types in that the control is
vested in the people who live and work on the land. There have
been many attempts throughout American history to establish
cooperative farming, though with indifferent success. The Owen
and Fourier communities during the first half of the nineteenth
century in most cases disappeared within one or two years.
Recent attempts have been made through the Farmers Home
Administration (successor to Resettlement Administration and
Farm Security Administration) to develop cooperative farms.
It is probably too early to say what success may be achieved,
but upward of 25 such communities have been established.

The cooperative farm has the obvious merit of combining the
economic advantages of large-scale operation, without at the
same time creating a landless proletariat. The workers are
owners who have combined their property in order to achieve
the benefits of unitary operation. Moreover, on the cooperative
farm the dwellings can be grouped in one area, bringing the
advantages which accrue from such grouping. The difficulties
arise from the so-called "human factor." People usually have
difficulty in working out their social relations in such a way as
to prevent the enervating frictions that make life intolerable.
Disagreements over sharing the labor and the products are
many. Some members of the group attempt to avoid performing their due share of the work through feigned illness and
other excuses. One such group had serious internal friction over
the question as to whether a small family should have as many
eggs from the common poultry house as the large family. And
so it goes without end: the little things make tempers short
and in the end all too frequently frictions add up to failure.
Nevertheless, the obvious advantages still exist. That failures
have happened in the past is no reason to assume that they
have to happen in the future.

The Jews in Palestine have apparently made a success of

the cooperative farm. Over 100 of them now exist and from reports of observers they are working out satisfactorily.[10]

**Cooperative leasing.** A variant of the cooperative farm has developed among tenants in some sections of the United States. Under the encouragement of the Farmers Home Administration cooperatives composed of tenant families have been organized under state laws for the purpose of leasing and operating plantations. Mr. R. W. Hudgens reported in 1940 that 31 plantations were under lease in Arkansas, Mississippi, and Louisiana, involving 1,700 families, 950 Negro and 750 white, with a total acreage of 94,600. He describes the situation as follows:

To form a land-rental cooperative, the tenant farmers with the aid of the Farm Security Administration, draw up a charter and by-laws, subscribe $1 each for a share of stock, elect a board of directors, and organize under the laws of the State. Then, in the name of the association, they lease a plantation from its owner for a period of usually 5 to 10 years, and agree to pay a yearly cash rental for the land and buildings.

Often the arrangement includes an option for eventual purchase. In the lease either the owner or the association agrees to place the existing buildings in adequate repair, and the cash rent is adjusted to credit whichever one does this work. The association also agrees to operate the farm under sound soil-conserving practices.

In operation, the cooperative fills the position usually held by the plantation owner. It subleases individual tracts to each one of its members on a rental basis, and operates all of the usual plantation enterprises such as grist mills, commissaries, gins, tractors, and other large-scale machinery. In some cases, where the association members lack the skill needed to operate their individual tracts on a rental basis, the association sets them up as sharecroppers. . . .

The management of the enterprises of the cooperative is in the hands of a trained farm manager appointed by the board of directors. The manager is responsible for such enterprises as the commissary and gin, and supervises generally the farming operations on the individual tracts.[11]

Enough has been said to make it clear that farming in the United States is carried on under a wide variety of systems of

[10] See W. C. Lowdermilk, *Palestine: Land of Promise.* New York: Harper and Brothers, 1944.

[11] R. W. Hudgens, *Land Policy Review*, Bureau of Agricultural Economics, United States Department of Agriculture, November, 1940.

| | | ARVIN<br>(LARGE FARMS) | DINUBA<br>(SMALL FARMS) |
|---|---|---|---|
| | POPULATION | 6,300 | 7,800 |
| | TRIBUTARY<br>TRADE AREA<br>(APPROX.) | 70,000<br>ACRES | 77,000<br>ACRES |
| | BANKS | NONE | TWO |
| | NEWSPAPERS | ONE | TWO<br>(one vigorous, a real<br>force in the community) |
| | ALL BUSINESS<br>ESTABLISHMENTS | 60 | 156 |
| | SCHOOLS | ONE GRAMMAR SCHOOL<br>(no high school) | Four grammar schools<br>(one high school) |
| | LOCAL<br>GOVERNMENT | COUNTY ONLY | Incorporated, elects own<br>local officials |
| | SERVICE AND<br>COMMERCIAL CLUBS | TWO | FIVE |
| | FRATERNAL AND<br>WOMEN'S CLUBS | NONE | SEVEN |
| | VETERANS'<br>ASSOCIATIONS | NONE | TWO |
| | CHURCHES | SIX<br>(only three<br>are adequately housed) | Fourteen<br>(mostly substantial<br>and in good condition) |
| | HOUSING | Very poor; houses badly<br>crowded on small lots;<br>very few brick or other<br>permanent buildings | Modest but generally<br>adequate; most houses<br>on lots of 50x120 ft.;<br>lawns, trees, etc. |
| | YOUTH AND<br>JUVENILE<br>DELINQUENCY | Fairly serious, few<br>recreational opportunities | Almost nonexistent;<br>numerous recreational<br>facilities |

Reprinted by courtesy Public Affairs Committee, Inc. From pamphlet No. 100, *Small Farm and Big Farm*, by Carey McWilliams.

FIGURE 54. *Social and Economic Differences Between a Community of Large Farms and One of Small Farms*

organization and management. By far the most common is the family farm. As we have seen, the term covers a large range of situations, from the profitable commercial farm to the impoverished units commonly referred to as "subsistence." On the other hand are the large-scale enterprises of various types. The rise in importance of the latter, with the great number of migratory laborers dependent upon them and representing about the lowest stratum in American rural life, has prompted a great deal of discussion and concern for the future. The Senate of the 74th Congress passed a resolution authorizing a subcommittee of the Committee on Education and Labor to investigate "violations of free speech and the rights of labor," and in the course of its investigations the subcommittee spent a great deal of time on the migratory labor problem of California agriculture. The House of Representatives, for its part, established the Tolan Committee to investigate the "interstate migration of destitute citizens." Its voluminous hearings were largely centered about the problem of agricultural labor associated with the large-scale farming enterprises.

The question is whether this type of enterprise should be encouraged or whether it should be discouraged by public policy. The larger question is, "what kind of rural life can we look forward to" with the "passing of the Old Homestead?"

A recent survey by Walter R. Goldschmidt [12] points up dramatically some of the social and economic differences in community life in a large and small farm area. For the purpose of the study two California communities were selected, one of which represented a large-farm economy and the other the small-farm system. The conclusions of Goldschmidt's study have been arranged by Carey McWilliams [13] making possible a ready comparison between the two communities. (See Figure 54.) Efficiency in production can apparently be greater for large-scale enterprises. But social considerations may weigh more heavily than the strictly economic when and if a decision has to be made between the two. There would be few people in

[12] Walter R. Goldschmidt, "Large Farms or Small: The Social Side," paper prepared for the annual meeting of the Western Farm Economics Association, 1944. (mimeo.)

[13] Carey McWilliams, "Small Farm and Big Farm," *Public Affairs Pamphlet 100*, Public Affairs Committee, 1945.

America today who would not agree, along with the Committee on Postwar Agricultural Policy of the Association of Land-Grant Colleges and Universities, that "the family-type farm should remain the basis on which American agriculture typically is organized. Although there is no reason to standardize all farms, because of differences in agricultural requirements and in the managerial abilities of farmers, the best interest of the country will be served when a majority of farms are of a type on which the operator, with the help of his family and perhaps a moderate amount of outside labor, can make a satisfactory living and maintain the farm's productivity and assets." [14]

The way in which the farm is organized as an enterprise is clearly related in a basic manner to the organization of rural society itself. Around the family farm is polarized the kind of rural life with which North Americans are most familiar. The large-scale enterprise, the *latifundium*, involves a class structure and other features quite different from those of the small-farm system. In the former the class lines are more clearly marked, the land as property carries less sentimental overtones, and the institutional structure is less elaborate. The gulf between rich and poor is usually less in the society based upon the family farm. However, the large-scale enterprise permits the more efficient utilization of labor and capital and the effective exercise of the managerial function.

### QUESTIONS FOR DISCUSSION

1. What are the factors associated with the increasing size of farms in the United States?
2. If large-scale farms are more efficient economically than small ones, are there any reasons why as a matter of national policy, we should not encourage the formation of more and more large-scale enterprises?
3. Discuss the advantages and disadvantages of the cooperative farm. Why have most of the *experiments* in cooperative farming ended in failure? Can the *mistakes* be prevented?
4. Discuss critically the definition given for *family farm*.
5. Discuss the impact of technological changes on our farming systems. Does improved technology necessarily mean larger farms?
6. How might the economic efficiency of the small farm be improved?

[14] "Postwar Agricultural Policy," Association of Land-Grant Colleges and Universities, p. 30. Distributed by the University of Minnesota.

## SELECTED REFERENCES

Ackerman, Joseph, and Harris, Marshall (eds.) *Family Farm Policy*, Chapter 3. Chicago: University of Chicago Press, 1950.

Brunner, Edmund deS. "Case Studies of Family Farms," New York: Columbia University Seminar on Rural Life. Undated.

*Economic Class and Type of Farm: A Graphic Summary*. Washington, D.C.: Government Printing Office, 1952.

Jennings, R. D. *Large-Scale Farming in the United States*. Fifteenth Census of the United States: 1930. Census of Agriculture. Washington, D.C.: Bureau of the Census, 1933.

Johnson, Sherman E. *Changes in Farming in War and Peace*. United States Department of Agriculture, Bureau of Agricultural Economics, Washington, D.C., June, 1946.

—— and Associates. *Managing a Farm*, Chapter 2. New York: D. Van Nostrand Company, 1946.

Jones, Lewis W., and Neal, Ernest W. "The Cotton Community Changes," *Tuskegee Institute Rural Life Information Series Bulletin 4*, 1951.

Maris, Paul V. *The Land is Mine: From Tenancy to Family Farm Ownership*. Washington, D.C.: Government Printing Office, 1950.

McPherson, M. D. "Critical Appraisal of Family Farms as an Objective of Public Policy," *Journal of Farm Economics*, 34:310–24, August, 1952.

Nelson, Lowry. *American Farm Life in the Twentieth Century*. Cambridge: Harvard University Press, 1954. See especially Chapters 2 and 3.

Rohwer, Robert A. "Family Farming as a Value," *Rural Sociology*, 16:330–339, December, 1951.

Smith, T. Lynn. *The Sociology of Rural Life*, Third Edition, Chapters 13 and 14. New York: Harper and Brothers, 1953.

Sorokin, P. A.; Zimmerman C. C.; and Galpin, C. J. *A Systematic Source Book in Rural Sociology*, Vol. I, pp. 387–396. Minneapolis: University of Minnesota Press, 1930.

Wayland, Sloan R. *Social Patterns of Farming*. New York: Columbia University Seminar on Rural Life, 1951.

# CHAPTER 15

# MARRIAGE AND THE RURAL FAMILY

The family differs from other associations in the fact that it is basically a biological unit. Its peculiar composition, organization, and patterns of interaction are directly related to the physical processes of birth, maturation, and aging of the human organism.

The family, however, is much more than a biological group; it is a cultural unit. It is the basic cell of society. It is the first group with which the newborn individual has contact and during the years of infancy and early childhood it is almost the only one. The significance of this fact in determining personality —in so far as it is molded by the environment—can scarcely be overestimated. It is in the family that the basic elements of the culture are transmitted to the new generation. The child learns such elementary traits as eating and dressing and communicating with others by gesture and language. He learns all the elemental folkways as well as those forms of behavior which are regarded as right and wrong or approved and prohibited. Moreover, it is in the period of infancy that the bond of affection between parents and children and among siblings is developed.

It is clear from the previous paragraph that the family performs many different functions. There is the basic function of human reproduction, but there are also many others. The helplessness of the human infant over such a long period of time requires provision of sustenance, shelter, and other physical needs. Similarly, the family has historically provided the protective care needed by its members who are dependent and disabled, including the aged. The educational function of the family has already been referred to and it is quite obvious that the family is excelled by no other agency in its conditioning influence upon the person. The religious function of the family also is well known. Children from earliest childhood are usually

278

indoctrinated with the religious ideology of the parents and the doctrines of the church their parents attend. A good deal of ritual of a religious character has always been a part of family life.

## SIZE AND COMPOSITION

**Size.** The size of the family is largely a function of the birth rate. On the whole, as the birth rate declines the average number of persons per family in a given population likewise declines; as birth rate increases size of the family tends to increase. The size of the family in the United States has been declining rather steadily for over 150 years. This decline has continued over the last decade in spite of an increase in the birth rate. As noted in Chapter 6, in 1800 there were 976 children under 5 per 1,000, women 16 to 44 years of age in the United States. By 1940 this ratio of children to women had declined to 329, but rose to 472 by 1950. It is estimated that the average size of the family has also dropped from approximately 6 persons in 1790 to 3.89 in 1940 and 3.53 in 1953.

This decline in family size has been continuing in spite of rising birth rates since the 1933 record low (16.6 per thousand population). After 1933 there was a slow rise in the rate to around 20 between 1942 and 1945, but in 1947 it rose to the highest recorded rate, 25.8. During the 1940–50 decade the rural birth rate increased 28 per cent, while the urban birth rate probably increased faster.

Thus, while absolute figures on average size of family continue to decline, younger families are larger than a generation ago. The reports of the National Office of Vital Statistics show consistent and sizable increases in number of second through fifth children born per 1,000 women between 1940 and 1950. At the same time, the number of very large families has tended to decrease.

Another indication of the sizes of rural and urban families is the average number of persons under 18 years old. The average for urban families was 1.11; rural nonfarm, 1.40; and rural farm, 1.65; all as of April 1, 1953.[1]

---

[1] "Household and Family Characteristics: April, 1953," Bureau of the Census, *Current Population Reports, Series P–20, No. 53*, April 11, 1954.

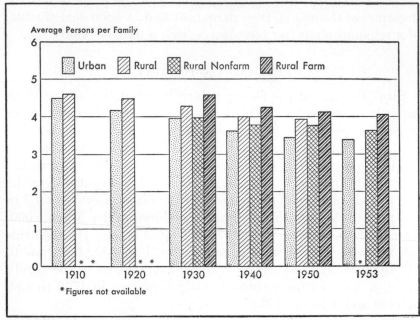

Bureau of the Census

FIGURE 55. *Trend in Average Number of Persons per Family, Rural and Urban, 1910–1953*

Changes in the size of families are shown in Figure 55. The downward trend in the averages continued to 1953 in all categories, although the change after 1940 was moderate, in part because of changes of definitions. Larger families are still more common in the rural population in spite of the relatively greater upsurge in the urban birth rate.

**Definitions.** The 1950 census defines certain types of families as follows: *family,* "a group of two or more persons related by blood, marriage or adoption, and living together"; *primary family,* "head of a household and all other persons in the household related to the head"; *secondary family,* "a group of mutually related persons . . . either in households or quasi-households who are not members of a primary family"; *household,* "all persons who occupy . . . a dwelling unit." Bachelors living alone are no longer counted as families.[2]

[2] United States Bureau of the Census, "Marital Status," *Population Special Reports, P.E., No. 20.*

The effect of this change is to increase the average size of the urban family, by virtue of the elimination of the large number of single-person "families" from the calculation. Another change in the census which affects the statistics is the inclusion of suburban population in the urban. These changes in definition must be taken into account in speaking of social change, particularly if the emphasis is on the rate of change. The change in classifying the suburban population, for example, is actually twofold: *from* rural nonfarm *to* urban.

**Family composition.** Customarily, we think of a family as a husband and wife and their children. Such a concept, however, would exclude from consideration as family members such individuals as aged parents or other relatives who may be living with the family. Neither would it take into account the situations in which there is only one parent present or in which there are a husband and wife but no children. There are vast differences, obviously, between the various family groups. The usual concept of the family as consisting of a husband and wife and their children may be referred to as a *normal* family. The family in which one or another of the parents is absent may be regarded as a *broken* family. In Western society the families which contained dependent aged individuals would undoubtedly still be classified as normal families.

In Oriental society, however, the family consists of all the living generations with the eldest living male the recognized head of the household. This is sometimes called the *great* or *joint* family. A. I. Tannous described such a family in the Near East as "consisting of the grandparents, their unmarried sons and daughters, their married sons with their wives and the children of these." [3]

Whether or not there are other members in the household besides the husband and the wife and their children is determined to a large extent by cultural norms. For example, among the Amish people there is a strong sense of responsibility for the care of aged parents. They will not accept relief or public assistance as do other groups in American rural life and consequently the aged parents are likely to be found under the same roof with the family of one of their children. Among other groups the

[3] Afif I. Tannous, "Rural Problems and Village Welfare in the Middle East," *Rural Sociology*, 1943, 8:269–280, p. 273.

development of public assistance programs for the aged seems to have facilitated the separation of dependent aged from their reliance upon sons or daughters for support and makes possible the maintenance of separate households. Among Negro families in the South it has been found that individuals not related to the husband and wife were found more commonly in the household than is true in white households. A. F. Raper, for instance, found only 4.4 per cent of the white families had children living with other than their own parents, compared with 13.4 per cent of the Negro families. He attributes the higher rate for Negroes to greater migration, higher death rates, particularly in middle aged groups, and illegitmacy; all tend to create broken homes and larger proportions of dependent children. Also, there is less provision for dependent children in the form of orphanages for Negroes, and as a result families take them in. As he says, "The Negro mother or grandmother bears the brunt of the family's reverses. If mother, sister, or daughter dies she takes the small children and rears them." [4]

Rural-urban differences in marriage are shown in Figure 56. Of all males over 14, a higher proportion of the rural nonfarm and urban are married than of the rural farm. Among women the opposite is true. Of rural farm men 63.6 per cent, and of urban 68.7 per cent, report living with their wives; while 67.9 per cent of the farm women and 61.0 of the urban women report their husbands present. Higher proportions of both urban men and women are widowed, divorced, or separated. On the whole, rural nonfarm men and women fall between the other two groups. [5]

In spite of the higher proportion of persons married in 1953 than in 1940, the proportion separated because of marital difficulties remains small, especially for rural men and women. Separated and divorced persons are about twice as common among the urban as in the rural population. The rural farm group leads in the proportion of widowers, while the urban and rural nonfarm are well ahead in number of widows.

The assumption that rural families tend toward "normality" is supported by the data of Figure 57. In rural areas, husband-wife or other family types with the male head present are more

[4] Arthur F. Raper, *Preface to Peasantry*, p. 68. Chapel Hill: University of North Carolina Press, 1936.
[5] *Current Population Report*, P–20, *No. 53*, Bureau of the Census, April 11, 1954.

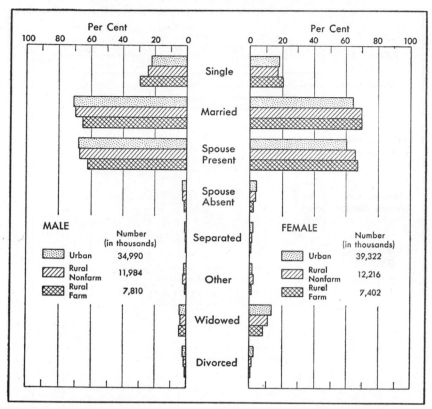

FIGURE 56. *Marital Status of Persons 14 years old and over for the United States Civilian Population. April, 1953*

common than in urban populations. Parent-child groups with their own households occur less often in the farm than in other residence groups. A widow or widower with one or more minor children, in the farm area, would be more likely to share a household with others, as is indicated by the more frequent occurrence of subfamilies in the farm group.

## ORGANIZATION OF THE FAMILY

There is of course no formal organization in a family group, such as one finds in most other associations. Nevertheless there is a definite pattern of authority and differentiation of function. Families in which the authority resides in the husband-father are called *patriarchal*. Those in which the wife-mother

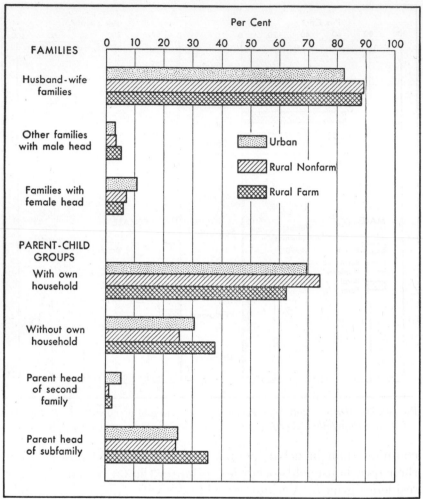

Bureau of the Census

FIGURE 57. *Families and Parent Child Groups, by Type, for the United States, Urban and Rural, April, 1953*

is the recognized head are called *matriarchal*. In Western civilization and throughout most of the world the patriarchal type is dominant. It is a matter of common observation, however, that in Western culture the trend has definitely been away from the absolute form of patriarchal family. In other words, the rule of the father has been challenged. Women are no longer regarded as the property of the husband; they share equally in the family property and generally are to a large extent emancipated from the rule of the husband.

Yet in actual practice the husband and father is considered the head of the household. The persistence of the patriarchal form of family organization is especially to be noted in rural-farm areas. Although changes in our culture over the past half century have greatly lessened the paternal authority over the rural family, it is still strong by comparison with the urban or even the town family.

In his study of farm-family organization in New York State, Foster identified and described two types, the Xa and the Ya. The Xa family organization is characterized by (1) joint control of all phases of family life, (2) attachment of children to parents jointly, (3) labor divided, (4) the family acting together within the home, (5) much ritual within the home, (6) the families having active participation in a few organized activities outside the home.

The Ya type possessed the following characteristics: (1) male dominant, (2) attachment of children to parents divided, (3) labor divided as in Xa, (4) individual and few activities within the home, (5) little ritual, (6) inactive or infrequent participation outside the home.[6]

It will be noted upon careful examination of the traits of these two types that the Ya represents typically the patriarchal family in which the male parent dominates the scene. The Xa represents the emerging type in which control is shared, at least by the mother-wife, and in many cases by the older children as well. The Ya might be called an *authoritarian* type of organization and the Xa *democratic*. Certainly the Xa type is the one which is coming to be recognized as the normal and generally approved type in American society.

**Specialization of function.** From the standpoint of differentiation of function in the farm family the major division of labor is based upon sex differences. The father has responsibility for labor in the field and with his sons performs it to the practical exclusion of the wife and the daughters. The mother has responsibility for the management and performance of work

[6] Dwight Sanderson and Robert G. Foster, "A Sociological Case Study of Farm Families," *The Family*, 1930, 11:107–114, p. 112.

in the home and, in addition, usually assumes responsibility for the feeding and care of the poultry and frequently of the hogs as well. Mother and daughters usually care for the family garden. When dairy cows are kept, milking and other chores associated with the care of the cows are frequently shared by both the men and women.

These generalizations regarding the differentiation of work in the farm family are not to be taken as absolute. There are many exceptions. For example, 19 per cent of the married rural farm women living with their husbands were in the labor force in 1953. This compares with 28 per cent for urban women of the same marital status, and 13 for rural nonfarm women.

In a study of 357 Minnesota families in 1926, C. C. Zimmerman found that about 80 per cent of the women "helped with the farm work in one way or another, with milking, separating milk, cleaning poultry utensils, tending poultry, or other chores, or with the actual field work." [7] On 202 diversified farms in Alberta, Canada, Helen C. Abell found 94 per cent of farm women performing some agricultural work. Jobs and percentages of women habitually doing them were: care of poultry, 78; gardening, 72; cleaning milk equipment, 69; milking, 61; field work, 49. [8] Under conditions of mechanized farming it is possible that many more women will participate in the actual field work on the farm. The trend seems definitely toward the sharing of certain responsibilities which were previously allocated on a sex basis. [9]

Further differentiation of tasks is based upon age. Children, whether boys or girls on the farm, are assigned tasks or chores at very early ages. Certain of these tasks come to be known among the children themselves as "boys' work" and "girls' work." Farm boys are not expected to wash dishes and would be rather humiliated if compelled to do so. On the other hand, boys learn to drive the team, handle livestock, and operate the tractor and other machinery at early ages. It is the farm boy's ambition to be able to do "men's work" as early as possible.

[7] C. C. Zimmerman, "How Minnesota Farm Family Incomes Are Spent," *University of Minnesota AES, Bulletin 234*, June, 1937, p. 48.

[8] Helen C. Abell, "The Women's Touch in Canadian Farm Work," *The Economic Annalist*, 1954, 24:4.

[9] Zella and Howard Forsyth, "Trend Toward Sex Equality in Homemaking," *Journal of Home Economics*, 1939, 31:249–257.

Girls for their part are expected to help in the house, with the small stock, and with the family garden—in other words, to be of assistance to the mother.

## THE FARM FAMILY AND ITS WORK

The farm family has a relationship to its occupation which is unique. As a rule, the farm home is located on the farm itself, meaning that the family day or night is never completely separated from its work. A farmer may be awakened in the night by some unusual disturbance in the barnyard which may require his attention. During the day his barn and his fields are seldom out of sight. There is practically no other family situation in modern society comparable to this. By contrast, the urban family may be separated several miles from the place of work of the family members.

Another peculiar occupational factor regarding the farm family is that *all of the members are engaged in the same occupation and the same enterprise.* Whereas the working members of an urban family may be engaged in widely different pursuits and are thus separated from each other during working hours, the men, women, and children of the farm family not only take part in the same sort of work, but also they work together.

**The farm workday.** The length of the farmer's workday is not limited by any arbitrary restrictions such as those which have been established in industry. The main reasons for this are the following:

1) Farming for the most part has as its main labor supply the operator and his family. Since the family members have a common interest in the profit of the enterprise, all of them do whatever tasks need to be done regardless of the amount of time required each day. Their interest is therefore not in the amount of pay for a set number of hours or days per week, but in the total income which the farm will produce in a year.

2) Farming is closely geared to biological processes and to the weather. Many farm tasks cannot wait, but have to be done at the propitious time if disaster is not to ensue. Cows have to be milked twice a day; all livestock has to be fed regularly; when the planting season arrives, crops must be planted

within a limited length of time; likewise, harvesting must be done at the right time, or irretrievable losses will occur.

3) Farming has not been a very profitable enterprise throughout most of its history. Its bargaining power in the markets has been low, and such returns above costs as have been made are the result of the long hours and hard work which the family has been able and willing to put in.

4) As far as the farm wage workers are concerned, they have largely been unsuccessful in such attempts as have been made to limit the hours of work. This has been due largely to lack of organization for increasing their bargaining power and to low returns of agriculture which do not enable farmer-employers to afford the luxury of labor standards such as characterize industrial workers.

If you were to ask a farmer how many hours he works each day, he would be likely to tell you 12 to 16. In making this reply he probably is thinking of the fact that he gets up around 4:30 or 5:00 o'clock in the morning and usually does not get his chores done until 8 or 9 o'clock at night. But he is forgetting the time taken out for meals, visiting with neighbors, resting, reading, and making trips to town. Moreover, he would probably be thinking of the busiest time of the year rather than the slack periods. Even so, the available data on the number of hours worked per day indicate that the farm workday is over the usual eight-hour standard for industry. Table 18 shows the average number of hours worked by farm operators and their families by type of farm.

It is not easy to reduce these total annual hours to daily units, but it has been found by farm management studies in Minnesota that farmers work nine to ten hours on week days and about four hours on Sundays and holidays, a total of 3,000 to 3,300 hours a year.[10] Time for meals, visiting, and the like is not included. About one in four worked eleven or more hours a day and about the same number eight or less. Mechanization has not apparently brought much more leisure time.

It will also be noted from Table 18 that there is considerable variation among types of farming. This variation is also

[10] S. A. Engene and Niels Rorholm, "The Farmer's Work," *Minnesota Farm and Home Science*, Vol. XI, No. 1, Oct., 1953.

in the study by Engene and Rorholm,[11] which shows that longer days are characteristic of dairy farming than of cattle feeding and other types, the least time being required in grain farming.

It is important to note that the workday seems to be getting longer rather than shorter. It might be assumed that increased efficiency would bring shorter workdays to the farmer.

TABLE 18. *Operator and Family Labor Used on Commercial Family-Operated Farms, 1951*

| TYPE OF FARM AND LOCATION | HOURS PER FARM |
|---|---|
| Corn Belt farms: | |
| Cash grain | 3,499 |
| Hog-beef fattening | 3,499 |
| Hog-beef raising | 3,499 |
| Hog diary | 3,499 |
| Diary farms: | |
| Western Wisconsin | 3,892 |
| Eastern Wisconsin | 4,099 |
| Central Northeast | 4,116 |
| Tobacco-livestock farms: | |
| Kentucky Bluegrass | 2,802 |
| Cotton farms: | |
| Southern Piedmont | 2,884 |
| Delta of Mississippi | 2,827 |
| Black Prairie, Texas | 2,903 |
| Southern Plains | 2,444 |
| Winter wheat farms (So. Plains): | |
| Wheat | 2,725 |
| Wheat-grain sorghum | 2,700 |
| Spring wheat farms (No. Plains): | |
| Wheat-corn-livestock | 3,270 |
| Wheat-small grain-livestock | 2,665 |
| Wheat-roughage-livestock | 3,219 |
| Sheep ranches: | |
| Northern Plains | 4,320 |
| Intermountain region | 4,023 |
| Cattle ranches: Intermountain region | 4,020 |

Source: *Agricultural Statistics 1952*, p. 640. U. S. Dept. of Agriculture.

Mitchell reports for Wisconsin, "Farm operators with tractors worked somewhat longer hours than farmers without tractors."[12]

In an earlier Minnesota study, G. A. Sallee and G. A. Pond reviewed farm records for 35 years and found the workday had

[11] *Loc. cit.*

[12] D. R. Mitchell, "Time for Work and Leisure," *Proceedings of the American Country Life Conference.* New York: American Country Life Association, 1930.

increased. The increase was greater for the winter and summer months. They cite the following reasons for the increase:

1) An increase in the amount and quality of livestock production. This has tended to increase the average length of workday largely by providing more work during the winter and therefore a more uniform distribution of work, rather than by increasing the length of day in the busy season.

2) An increase in the number of tractors, automobiles, and trucks. These can be used continuously whereas there is a limit to the number of hours per day horses can be worked.

3) A decrease in physical effort needed for much of the work because of the adoption of tractors, trucks, automobiles, and other modern machinery and equipment. This tends to permit an increase in number of hours of work without a corresponding increase in fatigue.

4) Greater difficulty in obtaining satisfactory hired help when needed at wages the farmer feels he can afford to pay. This has tended to lead farmers to increase the number of hours they work in order to reduce hired labor to the minimum.[13]

**The daily routine.** Following are descriptions of the daily routine of farm work in two different American farm communities, the Old Order Amish of Pennsylvania and New Englanders of Landaff, New Hampshire. Walter M. Kollmorgen describes the Amish day as follows:

Franklin's maxim about early to bed and early to rise is well observed by the Amish farmer. All members of the family except the smallest children arise between 4 and 5 o'clock in the morning. Milking and other chores require from 1 to 2 hours depending on the number of cows that are to be milked and the number of hands available. Between 5:30 and 6 o'clock, breakfast is served. If milk is sold, it is hauled to the station just before or after breakfast. Shortly after 6 o'clock, the day's operations are begun. Field work receives most attention in spring and summer, and stripping tobacco and hauling manure are the important tasks in the winter.

Work in the barns or fields continues until 11 o'clock, which is dinner time. If the weather is not too disagreeably hot, field work is resumed shortly after 12 o'clock. On hot days, a rest of 30 minutes to an hour may be taken. Supper on the Amish farm is served between 4 and 5 o'clock, usually about 4:30. Chores come immediately after supper. During the rush season, one or several men may again work in the

[13] G. A. Sallee and G. A. Pond, "The Farmer's Work Day," *Minnesota AES Farm Business Notes*, October, 1938.

field after supper until dark. Between 8:30 and 9 o'clock, most of these people go to bed." [14]

K. M. MacLeish and Kimball Young give the following account of the daily routine in Landaff, New Hampshire:

. . . the daily round of life varies from one farm to another, even as to times of eating and getting up in the morning. It also varies from winter to summer in the same families. On one of the larger farms a typical winter's day might run as follows: At 5:30 the wife gets up and starts breakfast while her son and husband go to the barn to milk. Breakfast is at 7 o'clock, after which the men return to the barn to feed the stock and clean out the stables. One drives to the station with the milk, then comes back to the barn to go on with the work which will keep both busy until 11 o'clock. Before dinner one of a dozen odd jobs might be done and some wood is carried from the shed to the kitchen.

Dinner is at noon. Shortly afterward, the men go out and work on the buildings or on some broken tool or machine. Later if there is time, one does some of the heavy work in the house. The milking is done just before supper, which is at 5:30; after supper the cattle are given hay again and the stables are cleaned. By 8 o'clock the work is finished unless some harness needs repairing or there is bookkeeping to be done.

In summer the rising hour is earlier, and the cows are grained, milked, and turned out to pasture. During the morning, after the milk has been taken to the village, there is plowing to be done or manure to be spread. Later in the season the garden needs hoeing and the hay is cut or carried to the barn as time and circumstances dictate. If the haying is over and there is no cultivating to do, the ever-present odd jobs will take up the time of the farmer and the son. In the evening the cows come in and are milked after supper, but the barn need not be cleaned again; this leaves part of the evening for whatever work there is to be done. [15]

The significance to agriculture, to the rural community, and to the farm family, of a more rational organization of work on the farm and in the farm home lies in the possibility of making farming more attractive for both old and young. Young people especially are often glad to escape from farming to other occupations, because in the latter they are able to find more

[14] Walter M. Kollmorgen, "The Old Order Amish of Lancaster County, Pennsylvania," *Rural Life Studies 4*, United States Department of Agriculture, Bureau of Agricultural Economics, Washington, D.C., September, 1942, pp. 43, 44.

[15] Kenneth M. MacLeish and Kimball Young, "Culture of a Contemporary Rural Community: Landaff, New Hampshire," *Rural Life Studies 3*, United States Department of Agriculture, Bureau of Agricultural Economics, April, 1942, p. 41.

leisure time which can be utilized for education, self-improvement, recreation, and other activities. All of these satisfactions could and should be found in country life, if people did not allow the imperious work demands of farming to claim too much time and attention. The extremely high rate of migration of young women from farming areas—accentuated during the 1930's—is probably not unrelated to the conditions of work there.

## CHARACTERISTICS OF SUCCESSFUL FAMILIES

Unfortunately very little research has been carried on which might reveal the patterns of interpersonal relations and activities in the family that make for happiness. Of the few such studies, one of the earliest was by Mildred Thurow, working at Cornell University. She used in her research the autobiographies of 200 college students. On the basis of their analysis she concluded that the following characteristics were associated with the most successful families: (1) *little* tension in the home, (2) *much* family affection, (3) *much* entertaining of friends and relatives in the home, (4) *much* entertaining of children's friends in the home, (5) *much* joint attendance of husband and wife at social functions, (6) high-school education or more for parents, (7) consensus of parents on discipline, (8) *little* dominance of the father in the home, (9) *moderate* to *much* family counseling, preferably *much*, (10) *little* to *moderate* discipline in the home, preferably *little*, (11) *moderate* supervision of children's activities by both parents, (12) *moderate* to *much* confidence of the children in the parents, preferably *much*.[16]

Howard Beers, also working at Cornell University, secured data by interview from 85 families. On the basis of his general impressions of the 85 families, Beers gave each family a rating as to the degree of family integration which existed. He also constructed an index of shared activities. These shared activities consisted of such items as the demonstration of affection, husband and children help in the home, the family members attend church with equal frequency, reading aloud, family picnics, and the like. Each family was given an index of shared

---

[16] Mildred B. Thurow, "A Study of Selected Factors in Family Life As Described in Autobiographies," *Cornell University AES Memoir 171*, February, 1935, pp. 48, 49.

activities. This index was rather positively correlated with his integration rating, with the proportion of those with other children home visiting, sex instruction at home, wife's leadership record, and show of affection. It was negatively correlated with families where the husband alone decides about crops or insurance, or the wife alone supervises schoolwork, and with the age of the oldest child.[17]

Leland H. Stott conducted a number of studies of child adjustment in farm families in Nebraska, and concluded that:

Some of the more important characteristics of the successful farm family from the standpoint of the personal development of the boy and the girl . . . are roughly . . . as follows:

|  Boy  |  Girl  |
|---|---|
| 1. An attitude of welcome on the part of parents toward the child's friends in the home. | 1. An attitude of welcome on the part of the parents toward the child's friends in the home. |
| 2. Frequently to have enjoyable times in the home as a group. | 2. Infrequent punishment. |
| 3. Infrequent punishment. | 3. Nothing in the behavior of the mother which she particularly dislikes. |
| 4. An affectionate relationship between the boy and his mother (expressed by frequently kissing mother). | 4. A minimum of participation of the mother in the work outside the home. |
| 5. A minimum of nervousness manifested in the mother. | 5. A confidential relationship between the girl and her father. |
| 6. A minimum of nervousness in father. | 6. An affectionate relationship between the girl and her mother (frequently kisses mother). |
| 7. Nothing in the behavior of the mother which he particularly dislikes. | 7. A confidential relationship between the girl and her mother. |
| 8. Nothing in the behavior of the father which he particularly dislikes. | 8. Frequent family excursions (picnics, visits, church, etc.) in which she participates.[18] |

[17] H. W. Beers, "Measurements of Family Relationships in Farm Families of Central New York," *Cornell University AES Memoir 183*, December, 1935.

[18] Leland H. Stott, "The Relation of Certain Factors in Farm Life to Personality Development in Adolescence," *University of Nebraska AES Research Bulletin 106*, October, 1938, pp. 45, 46.

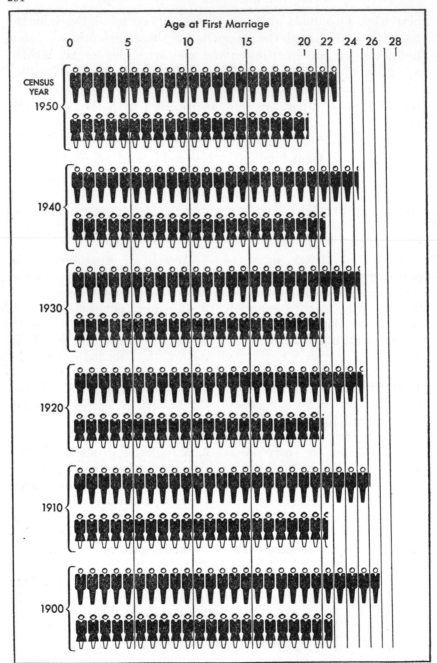

FIGURE 58. *Median Age at First Marriage for Men and Women*

## CONDITIONS AFFECTING MARRIAGE RATES AND THE FORMATION OF FAMILIES

**Age at marriage.** The median age of marriage has been declining over the past fifty years for both men and women. (See Figure 58.) There are considerable differences in the ages of marriage between rural and urban people, among regions of the country, and between men and women. Census data warrant the following observations: (*a*) women marry earlier

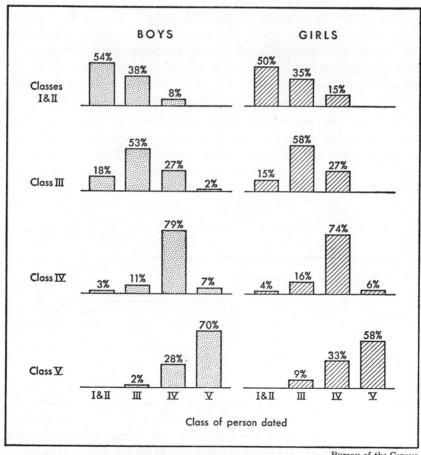

Bureau of the Census

FIGURE 59. *Trend of Dating Along Class Lines by High School Students in Elmtown, 1949.* (From A. B. Hollingshead, *Elmtown's Youth*, John Wiley & Sons, 1949.)

than men in general, (b) women marry younger in farm areas than in either urban or rural-nonfarm, there being very little difference between the latter two groups, (c) rural-nonfarm men marry younger than either the farm or urban, while urban men marry later than any; the difference between urban and farm men is less than that between rural-nonfarm and farm, (d) both men and women marry at earlier ages in the South than in any other region, and this is true for urban and rural groups, (e) in the North Central and Western states farm men marry later than the urban.

**Sex ratios in relation to marital status.** The proportion of men and women 15 years old and over who were married in 1950 was definitely related to the proportion of the sexes in the population. Where there is an excess of males, as in the rural-farm areas, the percentage of women married is high and that of men, low. In the cities, where there is an excess of females, the proportion of women married is low and that for men is high. In the rural-nonfarm population, where the proportions of the sexes are more nearly equal, there is scarcely any difference in the proportions which are married. (See Table 19.)

TABLE 19. *Sex Ratios and Proportion of Married White Men and Women 15 Years Old or Over, Rural and Urban, 1940 and 1950*

| RESIDENCE | SEX RATIO | | PER CENT MARRIED | | | |
| | | | MALE | | FEMALE | |
| | 1940 | 1950 | 1940 | 1950 | 1940 | 1950 |
| --- | --- | --- | --- | --- | --- | --- |
| Urban | 95.8 | 92.5 | 61.9 | 69.0 | 58.2 | 64.0 |
| Rural-nonfarm | 104.2 | 103.1 | 63.0 | 67.7 | 64.9 | 69.9 |
| Rural-farm | 112.1 | 113.7 | 58.3 | 64.5 | 66.7 | 71.9 |

Source: Bureau of the Census.

If the sex ratios for the rural-farm population for the 48 states are correlated with the per cent of the rural-farm females who are 15 years of age or over, one finds a positive correlation, that is, that the higher the sex ratio, the higher the proportion of females married. On the other hand, the reverse is true when the sex ratio is correlated with the percentage of males who are married. The states which ranked highest in the sex ratio for the farm population were Nevada, Montana, Wyoming, North

Dakota, Minnesota, California, Vermont, Oregon, Nebraska, Colorado, and Washington, in that order, all of which had more than 115 males per 100 females. Those with the lowest sex ratios were Mississippi, South Carolina, Alabama, North Carolina, Georgia, Tennessee, Louisiana, Virginia, Arkansas, and Florida, all below 108 males per 100 females. In those states with high sex ratios the marriage opportunities of the young men are greatly reduced, and those for the women correspondingly increased. These high sex ratios probably account in the main for the younger age at marriage for women and the generally later age for the men, although economic conditions probably play a role here also.

**Who marries whom.** This question is determined by several factors, but one of the most important of these is *propinquity*. It has long been recognized and studied as a factor in determining mate selection in cities, but only two studies of rural populations have been reported.[19] H. Y. McClusky and A. Zander, in a study of Branch County, Michigan, found that 46 per cent of the couples applying for marriage licenses in that county gave the same post-office address, with an additional 12 per cent reporting post-office addresses within the county.[20] D. Mitchell, in examining the marriage applications in Scott and Carver counties Minnesota, found that 42.2 per cent in Scott, and 43.2 per cent in Carver gave the same post-office address, while 17.8 and 26.6 in the two counties respectively gave other post offices within the county as their addresses. It is apparent that in all cases about 60 per cent or more of the couples were from the same county. Only 13 per cent in one county and 5 in another were couples of whom one came from more than 50 miles from the county of residence of the other.[21]

In addition to locality as a determinant of mate selection, there are many other factors operative. Chief among these is the practice of *endogamy* in certain ethnic and religious groups. For example, among the various nationality groups in Wright

[19] See J. H. S. Bossard, "Residential Propinquity As a Factor in Marriage Selection," *American Journal of Sociology*, 1932, 38:219–224, for a report on his study of 5,000 applicants for marriage licenses in Philadelphia.

[20] Howard Y. McClusky and Alvin Zander, "Residential Propinquity and Marriage in Branch County, Michigan," *Social Forces*, 1940, 19:79–81.

[21] Donald Mitchell, "Residential Propinquity and Marriage in Carver and Scott Counties, Minnesota," *Social Forces*, 1941, 20:256–259.

County, Minnesota, it was found that 68.2 per cent of a sample of 885 marriages were within the same nationality. The nationalities varied somewhat, with the Finns having the highest percentage, the German group next, followed by Poles, Swedes, English, Dutch, Bohemian, and French, in that order. There appeared also to be some evidence that the percentage marrying within the same religious groups was higher than that for nationality alone. The percentage of Catholic husbands married to wives of the same religious group was nearly 90, while the same men were married to wives of the same nationality in only 76 per cent of the cases. Protestant husbands were married to Protestant wives in 92.9 per cent of the cases, although they were of the same nationality to the extent of only 70 per cent.[22]

Racial lines, particularly those between whites and Negroes, are observed in choosing mates. In 1939, out of 597,749 marriages reported to the Census in 25 states, 524,845 were white, 71,141 were Negro, and only 1,763 were given as "mixed."

Social class is also a consideration in the choice of mate, although it is not usually a matter of very great importance in rural communities. One frequently hears expressions, such as "he (or she) is marrying beneath him," or "she (or he) is throwing himself or herself away." A "good match" is generally regarded as one which is between people of about the same economic or social class.

In his study of Elmtown, a Midwestern trade center, Hollingshead found over half of all dating among young people to be within class lines. (See Figure 59.) Hollingshead has also studied the relative importance of race, age, religion, ethnic origin, and social class in mate-selection, finding race and religion to be the most formidable barriers to free choice.[23] Ruby Jo Reeves Kennedy, in a similar study comes to the conclusion that religious factors are more important than age, propinquity and nationality.[24]

[22] Lowry Nelson, "Intermarriage Among Nationality Groups in a Rural Area of Minnesota," *American Journal of Sociology*, 1943, 48:585–592.

[23] August B. Hollingshead. *Elmtown's Youth.* New York: J. Wiley and Sons, 1949. See also his articles, "Age Relationships and Marriage," and "Cultural Factors in the Selection of Marriage Mates," *American Sociological Review*, 16:492–499, and 15:619–627, October, 1950.

[24] Ruby Jo Reeves Kennedy, "Single or Triple Melting Pot," *American Journal of Sociology*, 49:331–339, January, 1944.

In conclusion, the farm family is larger on the average than either the village or the city family. It lives with its work as does no other family in society, the farm being not only the place for work but also the location of the home. Like few other family situations, the farm-family members all work in the same enterprise. There is some differentiation of function between the sexes and between young and old, but the lines are not rigidly drawn and there is a tendency toward mutual sharing of both farm and household duties. Moreover, while the organization of the farm family may still approximate more closely the patriarchal type than that of either the town or city family, the tendency is away from a father-dominated situation toward one in which both parents, and sometimes the older children, share in making important decisions. The lower percentages of broken homes in rural as compared with urban areas indicate greater stability in the former. The daily routine of farm work is geared to the seasons, to the growth cycle of plants and animals, and to custom. Hours of work are long as compared with urban occupations and unregulated by legislation; the farm family has less time for leisure activities. This chapter discussed rates of marriage as adversely affected by unequal sex ratios, and propinquity and group attitudes as important factors influencing the choice of a marriage partner.

### QUESTIONS FOR DISCUSSION

1. Discuss the significance to rural society of family size; for example, its effects upon the school, the church, land tenure, etc.
2. Compare the status of women and children on farms with that in the towns and cities.
3. How do you account for the high proportion of men in the farm population? Discuss its significance to the family.
4. Give examples of *urbanization* of the farm family.
5. Discuss the significance of the rising divorce rate. Is it a symptom of more basic maladjustments; or is divorce itself an evil that should be restricted?
6. How might parent-child conflict in the farm family be reduced?
7. How might the workday on the farm be regulated to lessen family tensions?
8. Discuss the significance of what the Forsyths call the *trend toward sex equality in home-making*. Is there really such a trend?

SELECTED REFERENCES

Arensberg, Conrad M., and Kimball, Solon T. *Family and Community in Ireland.* Cambridge, Mass.: Harvard University Press, 1940.

Brown, James S. "The Farm Family in a Kentucky Mountain Neighborhood," *Kentucky AES Bulletin 587.* 1952.

Burgess, Ernest W., and Locke, Harvey J. *The Family,* Second Edition, Chapter 3. New York: American Book Co., 1953.

Dinkel, R. M. "Parent-Child Conflict in Minnesota Families," *American Sociological Review,* 8:4, August, 1943.

Edwards, Florence M. "Farm Family Living in the Prairie Provinces," Ottawa, Canada: *Department of Agriculture Technical Bulletin 57.* 1947.

*Farmers in a Changing World.* Yearbook of Agriculture, 1940. "Patterns of Living of Farm Families," pp. 848–869, by Day Monroe. Washington, D.C.: Government Printing Office.

Green, James W. "Social Factors in Farmhouse Planning," *North Carolina AES Progress Report RS–11,* 1951. (Process.)

Landis, Paul H. *Rural Life in Process,* Second Edition, Chapter 21. New York: McGraw-Hill Book Co., 1948.

Loomis, Charles P., and Beegle, J. Allen. *Rural Social Systems,* Chapters 2, 3, and 4. New York: Prentice-Hall, Inc., 1950.

Monahan, Thomas P., and Kephart, William M. "Divorce and Desertion by Religious and Mixed-Religious Groups," *The American Journal of Sociology,* 59:453–465, March, 1954.

Sirjamaki, John. *The American Family in the Twentieth Century.* Cambridge: The Harvard University Press, 1953.

Sorokin, P. A.; Zimmerman, C. C.; and Galpin, C. J. *A Systematic Source Book in Rural Sociology,* Vol. II, Chapter 10. Minneapolis: University of Minnesota Press, 1931.

Stott, Leland H. "The Relation of Certain Factors in Farm Life to Personality Development in Adolescence." *University of Nebraska AES Research Bulletin 106.* October, 1938.

Thurow, Mildred B. "A Study of Selected Factors in Family Life as Described in Autobiographies." *Cornell University AES Memoir 171.* February, 1935.

Wilkening, Eugene A. "Adoption of Improved Farm Practices as Related to Family Factors," *Wisconsin AES Research Bulletin 183.* December, 1953.

# CHAPTER 16

# LEVELS OF FAMILY LIVING

The phrase "standard of living" is one which is frequently on the lips of the American people. For the American labor movement the phrase has become a slogan and a tool which they have been able to use successfully in bargaining for higher wages. Politicians, when it meets their purposes, like to refer to the "American standard of living." Such usage brings to the minds of people the existence of a norm which is somewhat above the average. A standard refers to something which may or may not be attained but which is rather a goal to be striven for.

The phrase "level of living" is a more meaningful one to use in reference to actual conditions. Among students of the subject it is rapidly replacing the phrase, "standard of living," which still persists in the popular mind. In general, the "level of living" is denoted and measured by material possessions, although it is quite obvious to anyone that nonmaterial considerations are also an important part of the content of family living. It is in fact difficult, if not impossible, to make a sharp distinction between material and nonmaterial things, or to assign relative values to each. There is, rather, a definite reciprocal relationship between the material and nonmaterial elements.

The status of the family from the standpoint of its material possessions tends to be related to the morale, degree of satisfaction, social adjustment and general psychological well-being of family members. This statement is especially confirmed by the studies of L. H. Stott and E. C. McVoy. In his studies of Nebraska farm families Stott found that . . .

. . . material prosperity is of some importance to the psychological well-being of farm people, both parents and children. The effects of this factor may come about in any of a variety of ways. It is quite likely for example that young folks in some instances are affected directly

301

in their development by the relative lack of cultural advantages in the home. In other instances a sense of insecurity might develop from the economic failure of the family, or a feeling of social inferiority might arise from an unfavorable relative economic level. It is also probable that youngsters often are affected indirectly through their parents' reactions, attitudes, and adjustments to unsuccessful farming operations, financial difficulties, and relatively poor living conditions. An economically-poor, farm-family situation need not necessarily result in personal maladjustments in family members, but apparently it might operate as an unfavorable factor. Likewise, farm-family prosperity can by no means insure optimum psychological adjustments within families, but it definitely may be regarded as one condition conducive to such a desirable outcome.[1]

McVoy, in a study of farm and village families in Isanti County, Minnesota, found a relatively high coefficient of correlation between socioeconomic status and satisfactions in various items of family living (food, clothing, housing, education, health, recreation, etc.), and general social adjustment.[2] The coefficient of correlation between dissatisfaction and socioeconomic status scores was $r = -.73$. The relationship is shown graphically in the scatter diagram, Figure 60.

## FACTORS INFLUENCING LEVEL OF LIVING

**Money income.** The level of living, as measured in terms of such items as housing, food consumption, clothing expenditures, and so on, is definitely related to the income of the family. This fact was recognized and formulated into a "law" by Ernst Engel, published in 1895. Studies among the workers in Belgium on which his generalizations were based were made earlier. Engel's law, as quoted by C. C. Zimmerman, is as follows:

The poorer a family, the greater is the proportion of the total outgo which must be used for food.

The proportion of the outgo used for food, other things being equal, is the best measure of the material standard of living of the population.[3]

---

[1] Leland H. Stott, "Family Prosperity in Relation to the Psychological Adjustments of Farm Folk," *Rural Sociology*, 1945, 10:256–263, p. 263.

[2] Edgar C. McVoy and Lowry Nelson, "Satisfactions in Living: Farm versus Village," *Minnesota AES Bulletin 370*, June, 1943, pp. 6, 7.

[3] Carle C. Zimmerman, *Consumption and Standards of Living*, p. 99. New York: D. Van Nostrand Company, 1936.

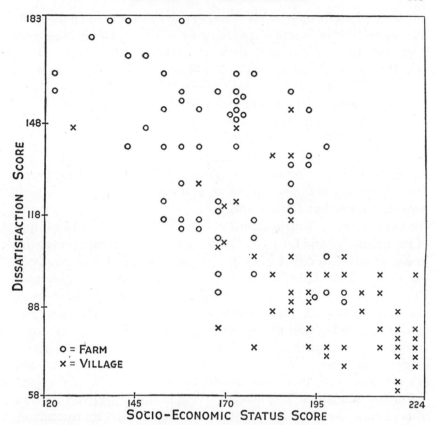

FIGURE 60. *Relation Between Socioeconomic Status and Dissatisfaction, With Reference to General Living Conditions.* The higher the score on the socioeconomic scale, the lower the dissatisfaction score.

This law is well demonstrated in the various studies that have been made of rural families in the United States. The most exhaustive survey and analysis of expenditures by American families is that known as the Consumer Purchases Study.[4] This study included urban, village, and farm families in various regions of the United States. The analysis was by family types—according to number and age of family members—

[4] This study was conducted under the auspices of the Work Projects Administration and under the technical direction of the Bureau of Home Economics of the United States Department of Agriculture. The results have been published in a series of bulletins by the Department of Agriculture. See especially Hazel K. Stiebling and others, "Family Food Consumption and Dietary Levels," *Miscellaneous Publication 405,* United States Department of Agriculture, 1941.

and by various income levels. The survey was made in 1935–1936. The operation of Engel's law may be illustrated from the proportions of family expenditures which were spent for food by two income-level groups in the Pennsylvania-Ohio sample of farm families. For the income class $250–499 the value of the food consumed by the average family amounted to 43 per cent of the value of all family living, while for the income group $1,500 to $1,750 the corresponding percentage was 39.

During 1941 and 1942 the Bureau of Nutrition and Home Economics of the United States Department of Agriculture conducted a study of family spending and saving in wartime, which presents somewhat similar and more recent material concerning the expenditures of rural families. The data for the entire sample of rural families and for two selected income groups are presented in Figure 61. The differences in the proportions of income spent for the various items between the two groups are significant. First to be noted is the higher proportion of the expenditures of the lower-income group which went for food, housing, and clothing. The higher-income groups spent more for furnishings, transportation, medical care, gifts, and welfare. It is quite evident, therefore, that the variation in the amount of income is associated with modifications in the pattern of family living.

**Formal education.** The level of living is not entirely a function of economic factors. Indeed, it is not clear that the amount of income is the most important influence in the level of living. We do not know whether the amount of income is a cause or simply a correlate of the level of living. The amount of formal education has been found to be definitely associated with income and with the level of living. In his pioneer study of farm families living in New York State, E. L. Kirkpatrick found the following relationships: ". . . among the farm families studied the extent of education received by the heads of families bears a direct relation to the standard of living, by whatever method the latter is measured. Those with more education are spending more money and a larger proportion of it for the less immediate needs, and they are living in more valuable and better-furnished houses." [5]

[5] E. L. Kirkpatrick, "Family Living in Farm Homes," *Department Bulletin 1214,* United States Department of Agriculture, January, 1924, p. 31.

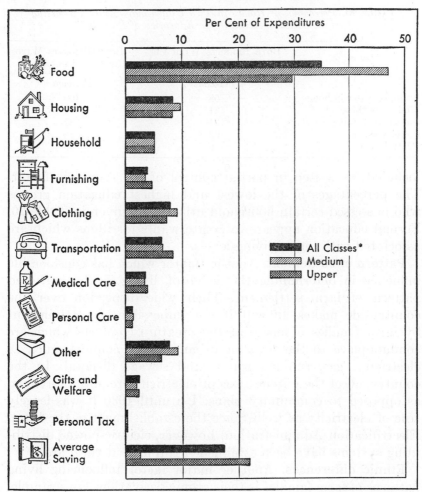

Bureau of Agricultural Economics

FIGURE 61. *Expenditures of Rural-Farm Families for Various Items of Family Living, 1941.* (*All classes include the income groups falling above or below the two given.)

The same relationship between education and living level was found also in a survey of 871 families in two Utah rural communities—including both farm and nonfarm families.[6] Only those families whose heads were over 30 years of age were

[6] Lowry Nelson and N. I. Butt, "Influence of Formal Schooling on Consumptive Tendencies in Two Rural Communities," *Publications of the American Sociological Society*, Vol. XXIII, p. 257.

TABLE 20. *Percentage of Homes in Two Utah Communities Possessing Certain Utilities, According to Education of Parents*

| ITEM | BOTH PARENTS WITH ELEMENTARY EDUCATION ONLY | BOTH PARENTS WITH COLLEGE EDUCATION |
|---|---|---|
| | Per cent | Per cent |
| Running water in home | 58 | 100 |
| Modern bathroom | 31 | 94 |
| Indoor flush toilet | 31 | 81 |
| Power washer | 62 | 88 |
| Central heat | 6 | 50 |

included, as a step in partial control of the economic factor. The percentages of the lowest and highest education groups who possessed certain household utilities are given in Table 20. Formal education appears to create wants for items which are associated with higher living levels.

**Pattern of settlement.** Another factor which has considerable influence in determining the level of living is the scattered pattern of farm settlement. Their wide dispersion over the countryside makes difficult if not impossible the attainment by farm families of many of the creature comforts which are commonplace to the town or urban family, comforts such as electricity, gas, running water, and sewage disposal. In the country, all of these items, except electricity, require individual as opposed to community plans. Up until 1930 it was largely true of electricity as well. Since the establishment of the Rural Electrification Administration, however, electric-power distributing systems have been established throughout rural areas.

**Ethnic differences.** Another major factor influencing living patterns of farm families is their ethnic derivation. For example, differences may be noted in the design of farmhouses among the Canadian-French in Louisiana when compared with that among the rural peoples of Anglo-American descent. Among the Spanish-Americans of the Southwest also, a characteristic pattern of housing is found, along with distinctive food habits. For instance, O. Leonard and C. P. Loomis observed that bread is still baked outside in large ovens, a custom which has persisted for many generations.[7] Again, the homes of the Old

[7] Olen Leonard and C. P. Loomis, "Culture of a Contemporary Rural Community: El Cerrito, New Mexico," *Rural Life Studies I*, Bureau of Agricultural Economics, November, 1941.

Order Amish follow a distinctive pattern, differing in several respects from the homes of their neighbors. Their homes are large because they are used as places of religious worship for the community Sunday services which rotate from home to home. Their standards also prohibit commercially-made carpets or other elaborate furnishings. Their clothing also follows a special pattern imposed upon all members of the community.[8] Among practically all of the ethnic groups that compose the rural population there are culture traits persisting from previous generations involving food, clothing, housing, education, recreation, and the like.

**The life cycle of the farm family.** Finally, the way of life of a particular family is determined in part by the "stage" of its life cycle. Unlike most other social institutions or associations, the family has an inevitable life cycle—inevitable because it is associated with the biological factor of aging in the human organism. Other institutions may in the course of events have a beginning and an end, but not necessarily so. A church— any particular church—may exist for hundreds of years, and there is no inherent reason why it should not persist indefinitely. Only the shifting of population away from a particular location or changes in the religious convictions to which the institution itself does not adjust may cause it to disappear. The same thing is true of other social institutions. We know that thousands of business units go out of existence every year and new ones appear; but again it is not due to any organic and imperious factor in the nature of the institution itself.

The family is subject to the biological processes which control the living organism. Men and women marry predominantly in their youth, rear children, grow old and die. The children grow up and they themselves marry, have children and grow old, and thus the process is repeated over and over. Family relationships as we know them are transitory for every individual family. Individual associations come and go; only the form persists.

Interest of American students in the study of the family

8 Walter M. Kollmorgen, "Culture of a Contemporary Rural Community: the Old Order Amish, Lancaster County, Pennsylvania," *Rural Life Studies IV*, Bureau of Agricultural Economics, September, 1942.

cycle was stimulated by the publication of *A Systematic Source Book in Rural Sociology*.[9] The authors presented a classification of stages apparently suggested by papers of two Russian scholars, A. V. Tschaianoff and N. P. Makaroff. The stages given in the *Source Book* are shown along with those of other investigators, in Table 21.

O. D. Duncan made a survey of farm families in Oklahoma, using the age of the oldest child as a measure of the duration of family life. He found that there was a steady increase in the number of children at home until the twentieth year, when decline set in and continued from then until the children were all gone at the fifty-fifth year. (See Figure 62.)

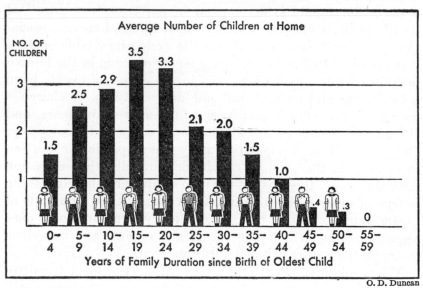

O. D. Duncan

FIGURE 62. *Average Number of Children ot Home in Oklahoma Farm Families, by Duration of Family.* (Adapted from O. D. Duncan, *Analysis of Farm Family Organization in Oklahoma*, Ph.D. thesis, Louisiana State University, 1941. Unpublished study, made in 1932–1933.)

The family cycle, of course, is a continuum but it may be divided logically into various phases or stages. On the basis of his own data, Duncan [10] postulated four stages as follows:

[9] P. A. Sorokin, C. C. Zimmerman, and C. J. Galpin, *A Systematic Source Book in Rural Sociology*, Vol. II, p. 30 ff. Table 2 in unpublished study. See reference under Figure 62. Minneapolis: University of Minnesota Press, 1931.

[10] Table 2, in unpublished study. See reference under Figure 62.

*Stage I.* The period immediately following marriage while there were no children yet born.

*Stage II.* The period of constant increase in the number of children at home. In this study it was from birth of the first child to its fifteenth birthday.

*Stage III.* The period in which the older children were leaving home (a) about as rapidly as others were being born; (b) more rapidly than others were born.

*Stage IV.* The period beginning when the number of children in a home had decreased to the nearest point to the same level as at the beginning of Stage II (at about 35 years in this study) and continues until all have departed.

TABLE 21. *Stages in the Family Cycle as Described by Various Investigators*

| FAMILY CYCLE PHASE | SOROKIN, GALPIN, ZIMMERMAN | LOOMIS | KIRKPATRICK ET AL | DUNCAN |
|---|---|---|---|---|
| I | Married couple just starting independent existence | Childless couples of child-bearing age | Children under 6 years of age | Married couple — no children |
| II | Couple with one or more children | Oldest child not over 14 years of age | Children 6 to 13 years of age | Constant increase in number of children at home |
| III | Couple with one or more adult self-supporting children | Oldest child over 14 but not over 35 (no broken families included this stage) | Children 14 to 18 years of age | Children leaving home (a) as fast as others born; (b) faster than births |
| IV | Couple becoming old; some children marry, separate from the family, and start as an independent couple (enter Stage I) | Families over 35 years of age as calculated from the birth of the oldest child, and broken families with husband, if living, over fifty, and wife, if living, over forty years of age | All adult; children 19 years or older | Begins when number of children at home had declined to about same level as beginning of stage II. (approx. 35 years after birth of first child). Continues until complete disintegration of parental household (approx. 50 years for tenants and 55 years for owners after birth of first child) |

C. P. Loomis,[11] using a somewhat more arbitrary system of classification, also derives four stages based upon the age of the oldest child. The first stage is similar to that of Duncan, described as "childless couple of childbearing age." The second includes families in which the oldest child is not over fourteen years of age; the third, those in which the oldest child is over fourteen but under thirty-five; the fourth, those families (a) over thirty-five years of age as calculated from the birth of the oldest child and (b) all broken families, with husband (if living) over fifty and wife (if living) over forty years of age. E. L. Kirkpatrick, R. Tough, and M. L. Cowles [12] arrive at a similar classification of stages based upon school ages of children. They indicate the stages as Preschool, Grade School, High School, and All Adult.

The proportion of families in a population which fall within each stage is shown in a study made by Gordon W. Blackwell of 1,653 farm families on relief in North Carolina in 1934.[13] Following with slight modification (in the form of subgroups) the classification into stages used by Loomis, he found only 2.6 per cent of the families in Stage I, and 1.0 per cent in Stage IV. The modal group was in the beginning of Stage III, with the oldest child 15 to 19 years of age. The number and percentage of families in various stages of development are shown in Table 22.

Blackwell appropriately observes that since familism is still strong in Southern agricultural regions, the number of families in Stages I and IV are very few. Young couples do not wait long before having a child, and it is still rather common for aged parents to be cared for in the homes of their children. Both of these tendencies, however, seem to be declining.

It should be pointed out that these phases are postulated on the basis of the classification of groups of families included in field surveys. The categories represent what Loomis calls a cross-sectional analysis. He suggests that a more accurate

[11] C. P. Loomis, "Growth of the Farm Family in Relation to Its Activities," *North Carolina AES Bulletin 298*, June, 1934.

[12] E. L. Kirkpatrick, Rosalind Tough, and May L. Cowles, "The Life Cycle of the Farm Family," *University of Wisconsin AES Bulletin 121*, September, 1934.

[13] Gordon W. Blackwell, "Correlates of State of Family Development Among Farm Families on Relief," *Rural Sociology*, 1942, 7:161–174.

TABLE 22. *Stage of Family Development of 1,653 Farm Families*
*on Relief in North Carolina in 1934*

| STAGE OF DEVELOPMENT | No. FAMILIES | PERCENTAGE DISTRIBUTION |
|---|---|---|
| Total | 1,653 | 100.0 |
| I. Before Children | 43 | 2.6 |
| II. Oldest Child under 5 | 184 | 11.1 |
| Oldest Child 5–9 | 253 | 15.3 |
| Oldest Child 10–14 | 382 | 23.1 |
| III. Oldest Child 15–19 | 450 | 27.2 |
| Oldest Child 20–24 | 253 | 15.3 |
| Oldest Child 25 and over | 72 | 4.4 |
| IV. Final Stage, No Children | 16 | 1.0 |

method of studying the life cycle would be the historical approach, which would involve the study of the life histories of individual families.[14] Together with C. Horace Hamilton, he made a study using a sample of 14 Negro families, which they compared with the results of a cross-sectional analysis of 153 Negro families. While the size of the samples was admittedly small, the investigators came to the opinion that "a relatively accurate picture may be secured by the makeshift method—the cross-section analysis." [15]

**Social significance of the family cycle.** As it waxes and wanes, the family must make many adjustments. Especially important are those of an economic nature. C. P. Loomis found in North Carolina that farm acreage changed according to the stage of the cycle. The acreage is smallest in the first stage, increases during the second stage, reaches its largest size in the third, and declines in the fourth.[16] Similarly, total cash income varied with stages, reaching its highest point in Stage III, and its lowest in Stage IV.

Even among relief families Blackwell found similar differentials in economic condition. The lowest net wealth occurred in

[14] C. P. Loomis, "The Study of the Life Cycle of Families," *Rural Sociology*, 1936, 1:180–199.
[15] C. P. Loomis and C. Horace Hamilton, "Family Life Cycle Analysis," *Social Forces*, 1936, 15:225–231.
[16] Loomis, *op. cit.*, p. 21.

Stage II, especially in the first subgroup (oldest child under 5). In succeeding Stages, the net wealth steadily increased to the last subgroup in Stage III, then levelled off to Stage IV. Net cash income per consumption unit, however, was highest in Stage I, and declined with successive stages until the middle of Stage III, where it rose slightly in the subgroup with the oldest child 25 or over, and then fell to its lowest level of all in Stage IV. Federal aid per consumption unit was highest in Stage IV, although Stages I and II were higher than Stage III.

Stages II and IV, as already indicated, represent periods of greatest economic insecurity and vulnerability to economic crises. Families which are in these stages are the ones most likely to be in need of public assistance. On the basis of data secured in the survey of consumer incomes and expenditures in 1935, D. S. Martin and others [17] compared relief and non-relief farm families as to persons per family and the average number of persons under 16 years of age. The data cover the states of New Jersey, Pennsylvania, Ohio, Michigan, Wisconsin, Illinois, Iowa, and Vermont. The number of relief families was small, only 280 out of a total of 7,545 families in the survey. The differences between relief families and nonrelief families are uniform in all state samples. In every state the relief families were larger on the average than the nonrelief, and contained more persons under 16 years of age. The conclusion seems to be warranted that the relief families were predominantly from families in Stage II of the life cycle. Admittedly there are other factors involved in dependency, but at least this is an important one, and one not commonly appreciated.

In numerous other ways the community relations of the family will fluctuate with the cycle. The orientation of family interest regarding the school, the church, and other agencies will inevitably change with the stage of its development. It is of considerable importance to community leaders, such as teachers, ministers, social workers, and physicians, to be aware of the cyclical changes. In planning for the future, prudent parents always take these stages into account.

[17] Dorothy S. Martin, Day Monroe, Dorothy S. Brady, and Elizabeth Phelps, "Family Income and Expenditures: Middle Atlantic, North Atlantic, and New England Regions," *Miscellaneous Publication 383*, United States Department of Agriculture, 1940, pp. 177–178.

## THE PROBLEM OF RURAL HOUSING

The material aspects of rural family living present many problems of interest to the student of society. Some of them have been indicated in other sections of the text, including the chapters on education, health, welfare, and stratification. Obviously, in a general survey it is impossible to give them the intensive treatment they deserve. There are the questions of the "ill-fed, ill-clothed, and ill-housed" segments of the population, about which so much has been said during the crises of depression and war. The problem of housing is considered to be of such significance socially that it has been selected for somewhat more extensive analysis here. It is socially significant because it is doubtful if there is any other material trait in our culture which has so much influence on the status relations of families in the community.

Kirkpatrick found that even a subjective rating of the exterior of house and grounds by field interviewers bore a rather close relationship to the level of living as measured by schedules providing data on family expenditures.[18] F. S. Chapin and others have used the living room and its furnishings as the basis on which to construct socioeconomic status scales. This is done on the assumptions expressed by Chapin that

(1) the living room is the room most likely to be the center of interaction of the family; (2) it reflects the cultural acquisitions, the material possessions, and the socioeconomic status of the family; (3) the attitude of friends and other visitors, and hence social status, may be advantageously influenced by the selection and proper display of cultural objects in the living room.[19]

Farm housing in the United States is notoriously substandard in certain areas and among certain classes. There are other areas, on the other hand, where housing is conspicuously adequate, and is not to be criticized either on grounds of design or roominess. The colonial houses of New England, the Middle States, and the Middle West, and the plantation homes of the

[18] E. L. Kirkpatrick, "Rating Marginal Homes From Observation," *Rural Sociology*, 1937, 2:51–58, p. 51 ff.

[19] F. Stuart Chapin, *Contemporary American Institutions*, p. 375. New York: Harper and Brothers, 1935.

*ante-bellum* South represent high-water marks in rural housing in the United States. At the other extreme are the small frame shacks of the Great Lakes cut-over areas and the cabins of the Southern sharecropper.

Several factors have influenced the standard of housing in rural United States. In the first place, the recency of pioneering is still revealed in the quality of contemporary dwellings. The first houses on the frontier were, of necessity, temporary and make-shift. Some were no more than "dug-outs" or holes in the earth with a dirt roof over them. In the Great Plains the initial houses were built of sod. In the forested areas they were made of logs. In most cases these primitive houses gave way to more per-manent abodes, perhaps within a year or two after settlement. However, the second-stage houses also were rather simple in design and construction, since the fortunes of the pioneering family had not yet reached the stage where more adequate homes could be built. As the wealth of the family increased, quite often the "second-stage" house would become the granary, tool house, or even part of the barn, while the family would have a more commodious and permanent home. There are many farms in the United States, however, which have not been able to advance in the matter of housing beyond the second stage—some indeed are still in the primitive stage of the frontier. The low incomes in farming which have prevailed since 1920 have arrested the development of rural home con-struction. Under conditions of economic stress the surplus of the family has to be invested in land and equipment, where it will be productive. Capital invested in housing for the family cannot yield a tangible return. Thus it often happens that the livestock is more adequately housed than is the family and the barn more modern in design and equipment than the farm home.

Tenancy and the high mobility associated with it also tend to degrade the quality of housing. The landlord complains that tenants take no interest in maintaining the house—that they tear up the floor boards and use them for fuel, break the win-dows and refuse to replace the glass, and so on. The tenant who reckons with the prospect of moving next year is not likely to make any improvements in the house even of a minor nature, since he will not be there to benefit from them and existing tenant agreements do not provide for his being compensated for such improvements upon his departure. Meanwhile he complains that the landlord will not fix up the house and becomes resentful at having to live in the kind of house provided for him. Thus, among the sharecroppers of the South occur the pitiful little cabins with leaky roofs, often without doors or windowpanes. Only a cotton bag or quilt hung to the window or the doorway marks these apertures.

Finally, inferior housing—as with other culture patterns— tends to be socially "inherited." The pattern of the frontier housing, in which a generation of children grew up, is bound to affect the quality of housing for several generations. The first generation on the frontier usually knew better housing in their childhood, and as far as they were able to do so they modeled their houses of the second and third stages after those of the communities from which they came. If, however, their fortunes did not permit the fulfillment of their ambitions for better homes, their children knew only the kind of housing of the frontier, and thus became a sort of "lost generation" so far as housing design was concerned. Therefore, in certain sections of the country, we have the bad housing of the frontier persisting as the contemporary pattern. Children who grow up in such environments are not likely to do much about improving them, unless aid should come in from the outside.

**Value of housing.** The average value of owner-occupied farm dwellings in the United States was less than a third that of urban. (See Table 23.) It will be noted also that there is a very great variation among the different regions of the country, with the lowest valuations occurring in the South, the next lowest in the West, and the highest values in the North. The uniformly lower valuation of houses of nonwhites as compared with whites is an additional fact to be noted. While the valuation of tenant-occupied dwellings is not given in the 1940 census, the rural-urban, regional, and racial differences in rentals parallel those for the valuation of owner homes. In 1930 the valuation of farm homes by tenure groups was as follows: owners, $1,421; tenants, $702; and sharecroppers, $283. It will be noted that the differences in values are in geometric ratio.

**Size of house in relation to family.** The size of a house has

TABLE 23. *Median Value of Owner-Occupied and Rental of Tenant-Occupied Dwellings by Regions and Race, Rural and Urban, 1940*

| AREA AND COLOR | TOTAL | | URBAN | | RURAL NONFARM | | RURAL FARM | |
|---|---|---|---|---|---|---|---|---|
| | Owner (value) | Tenant (rental) | Owner (value) | Tenant (rental) | Owner (value) | Tenant (rental) | Owner (value) | Tenant (rental) |
| United States | 2,377 | 18.22 | 3,501 | 24.60 | 1,715 | 10.08 | 1,028 | 4.72 |
| White | 2,486 | 20.07 | 3,595 | 25.98 | 1,834 | 11.10 | 1,102 | 5.61 |
| Nonwhite | 615 | 6.22 | 1,288 | 12.59 | 427 | 3.99 | 316 | 2.70 |
| North | 2,851 | 23.33 | 3,712 | 26.96 | 2,068 | 12.79 | 1,450 | 8.47 |
| White | 2,874 | 23.62 | 3,744 | 27.48 | 2,091 | 12.87 | 1,455 | 8.55 |
| Nonwhite | 1,675 | 19.42 | 2,123 | 20.28 | 675 | 8.45 | 517 | 4.23 |
| South | 1,250 | 6.99 | 2,730 | 15.13 | 1,119 | 6.02 | 600 | 3.51 |
| White | 1,451 | 9.94 | 3,123 | 19.45 | 1,368 | 7.17 | 645 | 4.07 |
| Nonwhite | 525 | 4.43 | 947 | 8.27 | 406 | 3.73 | 332 | 2.65 |
| West | 2,491 | 20.82 | 3,389 | 25.06 | 1,596 | 13.69 | 1,084 | 9.20 |
| White | 2,536 | 21.07 | 3,408 | 25.36 | 1,638 | 13.80 | 1,163 | 9.27 |
| Nonwhite | 513 | 15.80 | 2,437 | 18.44 | 293 | 8.61 | 213 | 7.83 |

Source: United States Bureau of the Census, Sixteenth Census, *Housing*, Vol. II, General Characteristics — Part 1, United States Summary, p. 45.

significance only in relation to the number of persons who live in it. The farm homes of the United States are not only somewhat smaller than the urban and rural-nonfarm homes, but the number of persons in the family is larger on the average. This means that, when measured in terms of the number of persons per room, the farm homes compare unfavorably with either urban or rural-nonfarm groups. The urban population is better housed than is the rural. (See Figure 63.)

It will be observed that three times as large a proportion of the farm homes have over 1.5 persons per room as do the urban homes. Overcrowding, in other words, is a phenomenon preeminently of the rural areas, rather than of the urban. As Howard R. Cottam observed in regard to rural housing in Pennsylvania, "housing is clearly related to the size of the family, although the relationship was in reverse order to that which is commonly advocated by child welfare workers. That is, the largest families had the poorest housing." [20]

**Modern conveniences.** Not only is overcrowding more serious in rural-farm than in urban areas, but also there are fewer

[20] Howard R. Cottam, "Housing and Attitudes Toward Housing in Rural Pennsylvania," *Pennsylvania State College AES Bulletin 436*, December, 1942, p. 15.

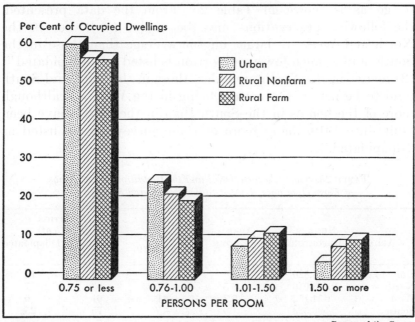

Bureau of the Census

FIGURE 63. *Per Cent of All Occupied Dwellings by Number of Persons per Room, Rural and Urban, 1950*

of those facilities which, if present, might mitigate to some extent the disadvantages of lack of space. Farm families made marked progress in obtaining these facilities during the decade of the 1940's, as Table 24 shows.[21]

TABLE 24. *Per Cent of Rural-Farm and Urban Homes Possessing Certain Conveniences*

| ITEM | RURAL-FARM | | URBAN | |
|---|---|---|---|---|
| | 1940 | 1950 | 1940 | 1950 |
| Electric lighting | 32 | 78 | 96 | 99 |
| Running water | 18 | 43 | 94 | 96 |
| Mechanical refrigerator | 15 | 63 | 56 | 86 |
| Private flush toilet | 11 | 28 | 83 | 87 |
| Private bath | 12 | 30 | 78 | 84 |

At this rate of progress it will not be long before farm housing with respect to some conveniences will approach a par with that of the urban population. However, there is still some distance

[21] United States Bureau of the Census, *Housing*, 1940 and 1950.

to go as is shown in Table 25. From the data presented, the following observations may be made: (1) houses in the North and West are larger on the average than those in the South, and a much lower proportion is listed as "dilapidated"; (2) houses in the North are older, those in the West and South tend to be newer, the newest being in the West; (3) although more of the houses in the South than in the North have been built since 1919, many more of those surveyed were listed as "dilapidated."

TABLE 25. *Some Characteristics and the Condition of Dwellings of Farm Operators, United States, North and South, 1950*

| AREA | NUMBER REPORTING | AVERAGE ROOMS | PER CENT BUILT BE- FORE 1919 | CONDITION (*Per Cent*) Not di- lapidated | Dilapidated |
|---|---|---|---|---|---|
| United States | 5,278,820 | 5.6 | 52 | 84 | 16 |
| North | 2,228,016 | 6.5 | 77 | 93 | 7 |
| West | 454,152 | 5.2 | 41 | 91 | 9 |
| South | 2,598,523 | 4.9 | 45 | 75 | 25 |

Source: Bureau of the Census, *Farms and Farm People — Population, Income and Housing*, 1952. For definition of *dilapidated* see page 7.

The criteria used by the Census in rating a dwelling "dilapidated" were several. In general, a place was so rated if it had holes, open cracks, rotted, loose or missing materials over much of the foundation, walls, roof or ceiling; or had substantial sagging of floors or walls, or had been extensively damaged by storm or flood, and so on. The fact that one sixth of all farm dwellings— nearly a million—were so classified, is a measure of the task of farm house-construction facing the nation. Some improvement in rural housing is being made. James E. Montgomery reports that rural people are thinking in terms of "open planning" (i.e., opening of interior by reduction of weight bearing walls).

It is pointed out further that the problem of poor housing is "most acute on class VI commercial farms. These are the farms that had from $250 to $1,200 worth of farm sales, on which operators had less than 100 days work off the farm . . . and other income did not exceed the value of farm sales. Two thirds . . . had family income under $1,000. . . ." [22]

[22] Bureau of the Census, *Farms and Farm People*, 1952, p. 69.

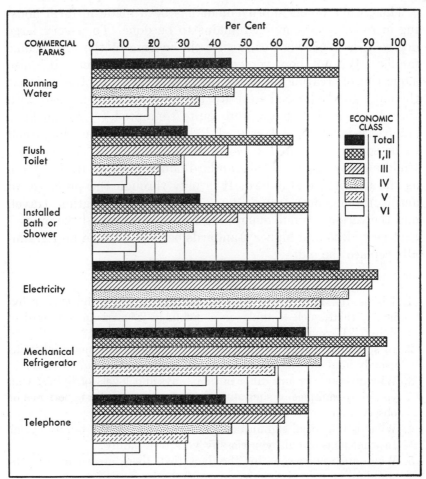

FIGURE 64. *Percentage of Commercial Farms by Economic Class with Indicated Equipment, United States, 1950*

Class VI farms had fewer conveniences installed in farm homes (Figure 64). It is clear from this chart that the better farms (Classes I and II, income $10,000 or better) are fast approaching complete satisfaction of their wants as far as these facilities are concerned. As we saw earlier in this work, the Class VI farms are highly concentrated in the South. However, they exist in all parts of the country as well.[23]

[23] See Chapter 14.

Thus, while much improvement has been made in farm housing in recent years, much remains to be done. To a very large degree it is a problem of raising the income of the low-income families. It is not, however, entirely a financial problem. It is also a question of creating the desire to improve. Cottam observed that the most poorly housed were for the most part dissatisfied with their houses, "but a few were quite contented." [24] As we have emphasized before, patterns of living, including housing, tend to be socially inherited because they are part of the culture. Children growing up in substandard homes come to regard them as the acceptable standard. It is only through the processes of acculturation—accelerated by means of formal education, travel, and the various stimuli emanating from the radio and the press— that new ideas and higher standards become diffused and gradually replace the old.

### QUESTIONS FOR DISCUSSION

1. Discuss the difference in meaning between *standard* and *level* of living. Is there such a thing as a definable "American standard of living?" If your answer is affirmative, what then is it?
2. In speaking of level or standard of living, why are material items usually implied? Are there not nonmaterial items also? Discuss.
3. Why do ethnic groups differ in their ways and levels of living? Can you give examples of such differences from your own experience or observation?
4. What is the social significance of the changes in the family cycle? In what phase would you classify your own family?
5. What are the reasons for the fact that there are so many substandard houses on American farms?
6. Discuss the quality of housing in Latin America; in Europe; in Asia.
7. What role should government play in the development of adequate housing, rural and urban?
8. What are the reasons that mass production techniques have not been applied to the manufacture of houses?
9. In regard to nutrition, what determines the food habits of people? Why, for example, is rice so important in the Cuban diet, and relatively unimportant in the Iowa diet?
10. How do you account for the fact that so many United States farm people are inadequately nourished?

[24] Cottam, *op. cit.*, p. 63.

SELECTED REFERENCES

Anderson, W. A. "Rural Social Participation and the Family Life Cycle," *Cornell University AES Memoir 318*. January, 1953.

Cowles, M. F. "Changes in Family Personnel, Occupational Status, and Housing Occurring over the Farm Family's Life Cycle," *Rural Sociology*, 18:35–44, March, 1953.

Davies, Vernon. "Farm Housing Needs." *Minnesota AES Bulletin 393*. March, 1947.

Dickins, Dorothy, and others. "Family Consumption in Three Types of Farming Areas of the South," *Southern Cooperative Series Bulletin 7*. June, 1950.

*Farmers in a Changing World*. Yearbook of Agriculture, 1940. "Patterns of Living of Farm Families," pp. 848–869, by Day Monroe. Washington, D.C.: Government Printing Office.

Flagg, Grace L., and Longmore, T. Wilson. "Trends in Rural and Urban Levels of Living," *Agricultural Information Bulletin No. 11*, Washington, D.C.: Government Printing Office, December, 1949.

Garnett, William E. "Farm Housing in Virginia." *Virginia AES Bulletin 417*. October, 1948.

Kolb, J. H., and Brunner, E. deS. *A Study of Rural Society*, Fourth Edition, Chapter 17. Boston: Houghton Mifflin Company, 1952.

Lionberger, Herbert F. "Low-Income Farmers in Missouri." *Missouri AES Research Bulletin 441*. May, 1949.

Longmore, T. Wilson, and Taylor, Carl C. "Elasticities of Expenditures for Farm Family Living, Farm Production, and Savings, United States, 1946." *Journal of Farm Economics*, 33:1–19, February, 1951.

Mangus, A. R., and McNamara, Robert L. "Level of Living and Population Movements in Rural Areas of Ohio, 1930–1940." *Ohio AES Bulletin 639*. March, 1943.

Taves, Marvin J. "Farm Versus Village Living: A Decade of Change," *Rural Sociology*, 17:47–55, March, 1952. A re-study of families in the area previously studied in 1940 and referred to on page 302.

Zimmerman, C. C. *Consumption and Standards of Living*. New York: D. Van Nostrand Company, 1936.

# CHAPTER 17

# RELIGION AND THE RURAL CHURCH

## THE NATURE OF RELIGION

Religious behavior appears to grow out of a recognition by man of the existence of supernatural powers in the universe and of his own hope or aspiration for perpetuity as an individual. Human life is characterized by great uncertainties and many frustrations. There are many phenomena, not understood or perceived by the senses, which therefore cannot be controlled. The nature and origin of life and death and what happens after death still are supreme mysteries. Yet human beings live their lives in the presence of these and other unknowns, which they cannot explain in everyday words, but to which they constantly must *adjust* their lives.

At the same time, such adjustment involves some explanations which the prophets, seers, and philosophers have provided. These explanations usually comprehend (a) the origin and purpose of human existence, (b) the existence of spiritual beings who cannot ordinarily be perceived by earthly beings, but who exercise a potent influence—for good or ill—over their lives, and (c) the continued existence of persons after death. Neither the truth nor the falsity of these formulations can be demonstrated in the laboratory, nor by any "scientific" technique yet devised, but the fact remains that they are widely accepted in substance and they govern a large portion of the daily behavior of human beings. It is this behavior, rather than attempts to test the hypotheses, which is the concern of the sociologist. And from such a standpoint, religious behavior is *socially* significant and must be considered in any treatise on social organization. That is to say, the church is a *social* institution in practice, howsoever its origin and destiny may be regarded.

**Religious attitudes.** From his contemplation of the universe and his aspiration to understand its operation, mankind has universally accepted the explanations of the "unknown" given by the prophets. Such acceptance induces the emotions of *awe* for the nonunderstandable forces that are manifest; *reverence* for the spiritual beings who are the repositories of the power, and whom it is important to propitiate, if conceived to be good, or to avoid, if conceived to be evil; and *devotion* to the recognized "power" and the accepted human mediators of that power.

**Ethics and religion.** Most religions have developed sanctions concerning the behavior of man to man, defining certain acts as "right" and others as "wrong." These do not constitute the "essence" of religion itself, but flow directly from the religious conceptions listed above. For example, one can "serve God" by serving his fellowman. If he is a true believer he will want to "please" God and he will want salvation in the world to come. These ends are best secured through living the "good life" and doing "good" to others. His own good deeds to others become the visible expression of his inner thoughts. But all these actions toward his fellow human beings are in the realm of ethics. There are many religious sects which emphasize merely the individual's acknowledgment of God as sufficient for salvation, but even these would not tolerate antisocial behavior. Rather, they would expect the "saved" to live a righteous life as further evidence of his having been "saved." Thus ethics are involved in practically all religious systems.

**Religion and rural life.** It has been frequently observed that the great religions have had their origin and growth among rural folk. The Bible is written in the language and imagery of rural pastoral peoples. Farming as an occupation is so largely dependent for success upon the forces over which the worker has no control that dependence upon the benignity of these forces is a natural consequence. It was particularly so before the development of modern science, with the increased knowledge of nature which has come as a result. Still, as Warren H. Wilson has observed, "Religion is native not to the world of measurement but to that experience of mankind in which he walks all his days on the edge of the abyss of mystery. Its roots are in awe; its fruits are the moral ventures of faith." [1]

---

[1] Warren H. Wilson, *The Farmers' Church*, p. 53. New York: The D. Appleton-Century Co., 1925.

**Importance of the church in rural life.** No other agency in which membership is voluntary provides as many social contacts for rural people as does the church. It is revealed in study after study that membership and attendance at a church provide rural families with the vast majority of their opportunities for social intercourse. For instance, a survey of farm and village families in seven rural communities of Minnesota in 1934 showed that about 70 per cent of the total social participation of these families in the course of the year was provided by church organizations. Clearly, students of rural life should come to understand something of the role which this institution plays in the lives of people.

It is well to remind ourselves too that religious interest is shared by urban and rural people alike. Indeed, while the church as a social agency functions differently in urban and rural environments, it is a part of the national culture and cuts across urban and rural divisions of the population. Both rural and urban people in America derive their religious heritage predominantly from the European Judean-Christian tradition. While some denominations may be more predominant in cities or in the country, most of the major ones are represented in both areas. There are rural as well as urban Methodists, Catholics, Baptists, Presbyterians. Both rural and urban representatives make up the local conference bodies. Indeed, many farm people are more and more aligning themselves with urban churches, and drive to town each Sunday to attend services with their urban brethren.

In spite of the common elements in rural and urban religions there are distinctive features of the rural church which are derived from *historical developments* and from *ecological factors*. It is important for a full understanding of the contemporary rural church problem in America that these conditioning influences be reviewed.

### HISTORICAL BACKGROUNDS OF THE AMERICAN RURAL CHURCH

There are four historic influences which cast their shadows over the contemporary rural scene: (1) the Protestant tradition of dissent, (2) the religious revivals of the early nineteenth

century, (3) congregationalism, and (4) the diverse racial and
nationality backgrounds of the population.

**"The dissenting tradition."** Religion in America is dominantly
Protestant, particularly in rural areas, where the Catholic church
reports only about 20 per cent of its total membership. Jewish
congregations are less than 1 per cent rural. This situation traces
back to the original settlement of New England by the Puritans
and the Separatists. Says W. W. Sweet: "the one fact, more
than any other, which explains American religion in the period
of the colonies is that the colonial churches were largely planted
by religious radicals." [2] The early colonists were no less religious
dissenters than they were political dissenters. As such they
opposed the state churches of the Old World and suffered the
inevitable persecutions which forced them to leave their home-
lands and flee to the New World. In 1677 Increase Mather
declared, "there never was a generation that did so perfectly
shake off the dust of Babylon, both as to ecclesiastical and civil
constitution, as the first generation of Christians that came to
this land for the Gospel's sake." [3] Protestantism of one brand or
another, therefore, became the initial and what might be called
the native religion in America. This Protestantism was, of
course, the product of the social ferment associated with the
breakdown of feudalism, the rise of capitalism, the influence
of the new geographic and scientific discoveries, the invention
of printing, and the discovery of the learning of the ancient
Greeks—to mention some of the more important developments
of a remarkably creative period of history.

American religion received its impetus from this intellectually
fertile, though very confused, period. It was the suppressed
minorities of the Old World, religious, political, and economic,
which found their way to America and the freedom they so
much desired. Once in the new country, they established
religious organizations which were free from the restraints
imposed in the country of origin. Once the new bodies were
established, however, they became in themselves as arbitrary
and conservative as were the churches in the old country. The

[2] William Warren Sweet, *The Story of Religions in America*, p. 2. New York:
Harper and Brothers, 1930.
[3] Quoted by Sweet, *op. cit.*, p. 3.

Puritans of New England, for example, were exceedingly intolerant of the nonconformist. But the ferment of dissent was a virile force; the intolerance of the Puritans only served to give the germ a new vitality, and thus to produce new schisms and new separatist movements. Ironically, the Puritans who had fled the persecutions of Elizabethan England banished Roger Williams, who founded the colony of Rhode Island and with his associates formed the first Baptist Church in the New World.

**The religious revivals.** The revivals of the late eighteenth and early nineteenth century are historically important in the present context because they stimulated anew the trend toward multiple-sectarianism. They were Protestant, and primarily a phenomenon of the rural frontier. They constitute one of the most interesting happenings in the history of America. It is not easy to account for them, but among the various reasons given are the following:

1) The Bible was about the only familiar book most of the settlers had; they were strong believers in its being the "word of God."

2) The new settlers had been without the services of regularly organized religion, such as they had enjoyed in the older communities from which they came. Consequently, they responded with enthusiasm to the itinerant preachers who came among them.

3) The frontier community was characterized by social instability and an uncontrolled sense of freedom.

4) The rigors of frontier life produced much frustration and failure, and led many to seek solace and expression in religion.

5) The revival message was one of extraordinary excitement, based as it was upon the re-establishment of the early Christian experiences of a Pentecostal character and the imminence of the Second Coming.

The religious revivals were related to other social developments in the new nation. There was the general social, economic, and political aftermath of the Revolutionary War. A new nation was being born and a new national consciousness with it. No longer was it tied to the apron-strings of the mother country.

V. L. Parrington, commenting on this period, calls it "The Romantic Revolution," "a period of extravagant youth, given over to a cult of romanticism that wrought as many marvels as Aaron's rod. In the South, in New England, on the western front it laid hold of men's minds, consuming the stubble of eighteenth-century harvests, sweeping away the drab realisms of a cautious past, and offering in their stead more alluring ideals." [4] Parrington's volume has sprinkled through its pages such phrases as: "loosening of ancient ties," "drastic over-turnings of the customary and familiar," "a gusty generation, sensitive to every storm on the far horizon," "that changing generation," "confused generation," "wreck of old standards," and "bold adventuring upon new worlds."

John R. Commons has also phrased a cogent characterization of this period. Says he: "Men's minds had become unsettled. Visions of a new moral world had come down upon them. Tradition had lost its hold, and transition its terrors." Referring to what he calls the "unbounded loquacity" of the period, Commons says:

The columns of advertisements in a newspaper might announce for Monday night a meeting of the anti-slavery society; Tuesday night, the temperance society; Wednesday night, the graham bread society; Thursday night, a phrenological lecture; Friday night, an address against capital punishment; Saturday night, the "Association for Universal Reform." Then there were all the missionary societies, the woman's rights societies, the society for the diffusion of bloomers, the seances of the spiritualists, the "associationists," the land reformers— a medley of movements that found the week too short. A dozen colonists of idealists, like the Brook Farm philosophers, went off by themselves to solve the problem of social existence in a big family called a phalanx. The Mormons gathered themselves together to reconstitute the ten lost tribes. Robert Owen called a "world's convention" on short notice, where a dozen different "plans" of social reorganization—individualistic, communistic, incomprehensible—were submitted in all solemnity. It was the golden age of the talkfest, the lyceum, the brotherhood of man—the "hot air" period of American history.[5]

[4] V. L. Parrington, *Main Currents in American Thought*, Vol. II, *The Romantic Revolution in America*, p. iii. New York: Harcourt, Brace and Co., 1927.

[5] Reprinted by permission of the publishers, The Arthur H. Clark Company, from *Documentary History of American Industrial Society, 1649–1880*, edited by John R. Commons and others, Vol. 7.

It was a period of great expectations. When William Miller predicted the end of the world for the Spring of 1843, there were untold thousands who sincerely believed him and who on the appointed date were prepared to be taken up into Heaven. Transcendentalism and Unitarianism, theologies of a more intellectual sort, took root in the same period.

An extensive list of new indigenous religions date from this period of revivals. Among those most familiar to us today are the Mormons, Adventists, Spiritualists, and the Disciples of Christ. All of these strictly native religious movements were added to the already complex sectarian composition of the rural areas.

**Congregationalism.** While the term is applied to a particular denomination, in a generic sense it refers to a type of church organization in which the autonomy of the local church is fundamental. The theory of congregationalism had its origin in the Protestant reformation. The practice of congregationalism had its beginning in Leyden, Holland, where a group of English radical "Puritans," the Scrooby congregation, had emigrated in 1609 under the leadership of John Robinson. In the freer atmosphere of Holland they became more definitely separated from the Anglican church. "It was this little band of radicals, despised by all parties among their own countrymen, which was destined to lay the foundations of New England, and to furnish the model of church government which was afterwards to be accepted and developed by the far more numerous and influential Puritans, the founders of Massachusetts Bay." [6]

The Puritans who settled Salem, Boston, and the other Massachusetts colonies were in rather sharp contrast with the Pilgrims, both in the matter of greater numbers and economic resources, as well as in attitudes towards the mother church. The Puritans loudly proclaimed their loyalty. In view of their attitude it is interesting that the congregationalism of Plymouth became the pattern of church organization in the Bay colonies. "This," remarks Sweet, "is one of the most important developments in the history of New England and marks a turning point of vast significance." [7]

Sweet goes on to explain how it came about. Apparently the

[6] Sweet, *op. cit.*, p. 67.    [7] Sweet, *op. cit.*, p. 73.

two groups of colonists had little intercommunication. Severe sickness in the Salem community during its first winter, brought a call for Dr. Samuel Fuller of Plymouth, the only physician on the New England coast at the time. Fuller's ministry among the colonists of Salem and his general attitude mollified the prejudices of Governor Endicott, who previously had been suspicious of his neighbors. In 1629 Salem chose a minister by vote of its male members. "Thus," comments Sweet, "was the congregational principle, that every Christian congregation has the right to choose and ordain its own officers, inaugurated in Massachusetts Bay colony." [8]

The social significance of the congregational principle lies in the freedom which it provides for dissident groups to organize new churches (congregations). It is thus one of the factors responsible for the contemporary problem of "over-churching," even within the same denomination.[9] It also provides the basis for the organization of entirely new sects.

**Diverse origins of the population.** It will be readily appreciated by any student of religion in America that the present diversity of sects and denominations derives in part from the heterogeneous origin of the population. Coming from all of the countries of the world, the immigrants brought with them the traditional religions of their place of origin. While the dissenters from traditional churches of the Old World constituted the vanguard of the transoceanic migration, they were soon followed by the nondissenters. From Catholic Bavaria; from Protestant Prussia; from Lutheran Scandinavia; from Episcopal England; from Catholic Ireland, Poland, Italy, and France; from Orthodox Russia, Greece, Rumania, and the Balkans; even from the non-Christian countries of India, Japan, China, and elsewhere, came the waves of immigrants who today constitute the rural population of America. Living side by side on their new homesteads in the West were Danish, Norwegian, Swedish, German, and Finnish Lutherans; and French, Irish, German, Polish, and Italian Catholics. Each group established its own churches with its own particular brand of the Protestant

[8] Sweet, *op. cit.*, p. 75.
[9] See the discussion of the Mennonite divisions in Mountain Lake, Minnesota, in Chapter 8.

or Catholic faiths, importing from its respective homeland the Bibles, hymnals, and other religious books and pamphlets in its own mother tongue. And to add a final complication, the American Negro had to set up separate church organizations because of the existence of the "color line."

This brief recital of certain historical circumstances in the settlement of America should be sufficient to indicate the roots of the present mosaic of rural religions in America. Practically all of them are Christian in their fundamental conceptions, yet each of them finds some basis for differing from the others. The total picture is one of religious sectarianism, setting the stage for interdenominational competition, community strife, and generally inadequate rural churches with small membership, and leadership poorly trained and underpaid.

### ECOLOGICAL FACTORS AFFECTING THE RURAL CHURCH

In addition to the historical background of the present religious situation in rural America, still further complication proceeds from the manner in which the farm population has arranged itself over the countryside. In an earlier chapter the various patterns of settlement were described. The prevailing system of isolated farmsteads means that in a given area only a limited number of families are available to support the institutions of the community. Even when all of the families are willing to sustain a given institution, the numbers are often too few for the purpose. When, as in the case of the church, there is a high degree of heterogeneity, the problem is doubly serious. For example, the average township in the Middle West will contain approximately 150 to 200 families, some more and some less. If all of these families belonged to the same church they would be no more than sufficient to maintain adequately a church organization. However, it would be rare chance indeed if such a degree of religious homogeneity were to be found. Most likely in such an area as a township there would be several different denominations dividing the population.

Raymond Hatch, reporting a rural church survey in Kingsbury County, South Dakota in 1940, found that 11 open-country churches averaged only 24 families per church and all but one of them had no resident pastor. There were 40 churches in the county, including both town and country, when, on the basis of the recommended norm of one church per thousand people, 11 churches would have been sufficient. Situations similar to this could be found in practically every county of the nation.[10]

The open-country church has been, and still is, a neighborhood institution. This fact decrees for any individual church a comparatively small congregation and therefore limited financial resources and an itinerant and poorly paid minister. Brunner and Lorge, in their study of 140 villages, found, for instance, that the average membership per village church was 171 compared with 93 for those in the open country.[11]

The small geographic-social base results in a comparatively high mortality among open-country churches. Brunner and Lorge found also that between 1930 and 1936 one in eleven village churches died, compared with one in five for the open country.[12] The mortality was found to be higher outside the Southern states. The persistence of open-country churches in southern areas is attested by Hoffsommer. In a study of the rural church in Covington County, Mississippi, he found that, while the school and the country store had enlarged their areas of service, the "church attempts to cling to . . . its former position." [13] There were 42 of the 50 open-country neighborhoods which had one or more churches, several containing as many as three. By contrast, only six of the neighborhoods have not consolidated their schools. In other words, while other social organizations are tending to become village-centered, the church remains as a neighborhood institution in this area. "Rural crossroads stores have succumbed, schools have been consolidated or abandoned, but there are no abandoned churches in Covington County." [14]

This persistence of the church as a neighborhood institution

[10] Raymond Hatch, "The Rural Church in One Dakota County," *Land Policy Review,* United States Department of Agriculture, 1941, 4:25–28, p. 25 ff.

[11] Edmund deS. Brunner and Irving Lorge, *Rural Trends in Depression Years,* p. 301. New York: Columbia University Press, 1937.

[12] *Ibid.,* p. 299.

[13] Harold Hoffsommer, "The Relation of the Rural Church to Other Rural Organizations," *Social Forces,* 1941, 20:224–232, p. 226.

[14] *Ibid.,* p. 227.

in the South may be a reflection, on the one hand, of the failure, or at least the unwillingness, of the church to adapt itself to changing conditions and, on the other hand, a manifestation of the vitality of neighborhoods as social entities. Changes in wants may bring changes in the local store, outside pressures may result in school consolidation, but the church is one institution over which the local group has practically absolute control. It may therefore be reluctant to relinquish this remaining center of its social life.

The church, because of denominational rivalry, has difficulty in making adjustments to its geographic base. Occasionally "consolidation" with adjacent units is possible, though the more common development, where an open-country church has been closed, is for the former members of the congregation to affiliate themselves with a church of the same denomination in the village. Brunner and Lorge found that the percentage of village church members from the open country increased from 35.5 in 1930 to 38.2 in 1936.[15]

### MEETING THE PROBLEM OF THE UNDERSIZED CHURCH

The usual methods of keeping "alive" churches which are too small for autonomous existence is for the parent denomination to provide part of the funds for its maintenance or for the congregation to share a minister with one or more other churches. Both methods leave the basic problem unsettled, which is the provision of a sufficiently broad base in the population to make possible a fully functioning church. Some other methods, involving chiefly the technique of interchurch union or cooperation, are being tried and deserve special mention.

**What is an "undersized" church?** It is not an easy matter to say just how large a church should be to maintain adequate services for the congregation at a cost which the members can afford. For one thing the number will vary with the denomination. Churches which do not pay their ministers a salary, such as the Mennonites and the Mormons, will obviously be able to maintain their church organization with a comparatively small membership. Moreover, in those churches such as the

---

[15] E. deS. Brunner and Irving Lorge, *op. cit.*, p. 307.

the ones in which the local parish has relatively little autonomy and the priest or minister is paid largely if not entirely from a central fund, making unnecessary financial reliance upon the local parish, smaller memberships may suffice to justify maintaining a congregation—smaller, that is, than in those churches where local autonomy and local responsibility are practically complete. As a rough measure of adequacy, so far as size is concerned, it is usually considered that a church for each 1,000 people would approximate an ideal minimum.

Since a large proportion of churches have less than 1,000 as a basis for support, attempts have been made to enlarge the congregations. Several plans have been devised to this end, which can be classed under two main headings: (1) the union of existing congregations, and (2) the resettlement of a given area by members of a single denomination.

**United churches.** Elizabeth Hooker [16] distinguishes four types of united churches: (a) the federated church, (b) the undenominational church, (c) the denominational united church, and (d) the affiliated church. They are defined as follows:

A federated church is composed of two or more organized churches differing in denomination which have entered into an agreement to act together as regards local affairs. The denominational units retain their own rolls, usually keep in the hands of their own trustees their separate property, and almost always continue to send benevolences to their separate denominational boards. They combine in calling and paying a minister, hold services of worship in common, almost invariably conduct a common Sunday school, and frequently join in other local activities.[17]

The undenominational united church is "an organized church not connected with any denominational body." [18]

The term "denominational united church" signifies a church connected with a single denominational body that has definitely undertaken, or had allocated to it responsibility for the religious needs of a public not confined to one denominational group, and that includes in its membership—whether regular or associate—elements of different denominational origins. Members received from other than the official

---

[16] Elizabeth R. Hooker, *United Churches*, p. 35. New York: George H. Doran Co., 1926. Used by permission of Harper and Brothers.
[17] *Ibid.*, p. 36.      [18] *Ibid.*, p. 61.

denomination are not required to surrender creed, form of baptism, or denominational loyalty. Denominational United Churches, being easily distinguished in this way from the numerous denominational churches of the traditional kind, have received a large proportion of their members by letter from churches of other denominations. . . . [19]

The affiliated church is one

that in freedom to form its own constitution and control its own local affairs resembles the undenominational church, but that is connected with a denominational body for certain specific purposes, usually including ministerial supply and distribution of benevolences. Persons from other denominations are received to full membership with equal voting powers . . . [20]

The importance of the movement for federation or union among churches is indicated by the Census of Religious Bodies as reported in statistical information for 1926 and 1936. Comparative data are shown in Table 26.

TABLE 26. *Number and Membership of Federated Churches by Rural and Urban Areas, 1926 and 1936*

| YEAR AND AREA | NUMBER OF CHURCHES | MEMBERSHIP | AVERAGE MEMBERS PER CHURCH |
|---|---|---|---|
| 1926 | 361 | 59,977 | 166 |
| Urban | 60 | 16,336 | 272 |
| Rural | 301 | 43,641 | 145 |
| | | | |
| 1936 | 508 | 88,411 | 174 |
| Urban | 82 | 26,027 | 317 |
| Rural | 426 | 62,384 | 146 |

Source: United States Bureau of the Census, *Census of Religious Bodies*, 1926 and 1936.

While the number and membership of federated churches are not large relative to the totals for the country, it is clear that the movement is growing. In the 10-year period the membership increased by 47.4 per cent. In 1936, federated churches were reported in 42 states. The Northern and Eastern states contain the vast majority of them. New England alone, with 175 federated churches, had over a third of the total. Vermont

[19] Elizabeth R. Hooker, *United Churches*, p. 80. New York: George H. Doran Co., 1926. Used by permission of Harper and Brothers.
[20] *Ibid.*, pp. 100–101.

led all states with 54; Massachusetts had 52 federated churches; New York, 50; Ohio, 37; Maine, 32; Iowa, 30; and Illinois, 29. Only a few of the total number were located in the South and West, although California ranked relatively high with 22 churches.

Nearly three fourths of the total number of units of all federated churches studied, reports the Census, belonged to four denominations—Congregational and Christian, Methodists, Presbyterian, and Baptist. It is worthy of note also that the vast majority of the churches were located in rural areas where the need for church federation is greatest.

**Consolidation of village and open-country churches.** In addition to the union of diverse denominational groups, the undersized church may move towards consolidation with a neighboring congregation of the same faith. Such union may take the form of a consolidation of two open-country congregations. The most common tendency, however, is for an open-country church to unite with a village church. The latter is a trend of considerable importance. E. deS. Brunner and others, in their study of 140 villages in 1920, 1930, and 1936, found a marked and somewhat steady increase in the percentage of village church membership which came from the open country. In 1920 only 22.6 per cent were from the open country, compared with 40 per cent in 1936.[21]

**The larger parish.** This is another kind of church cooperation designed to enhance the services of the rural church to its membership. Definitions of the larger parish are many and mostly lacking in specificity.[22] The objective, however, is to create a more effective service for the people in a given area. It is to be accomplished through the pooling of financial resources and the centering of administration in a larger Parish Council. It makes the community the focus of attention rather than the individual church. By combining their resources several or all of the churches in a particular area may be able to employ not only a full-time minister but also certain specialized personnel, such as a director of religious education, director of recreation, or a director of women's work.

[21] J. H. Kolb and E. deS. Brunner, *A Study of Rural Society*, p. 498. Boston: Houghton Mifflin Company, 1940.

[22] E. deS. Brunner, *The Larger Parish*, p. 4 ff. New York: Institute of Social and Religious Research, 1934.

**Resettlement.** This method may be applied in two ways. The church body may purchase outright a tract of land and settle upon it only its own members. An example is the purchase by the Mormon Church of the 4,000 acre Keogh ranch in Idaho, which was resold to members of the Mormon Church in small family-sized units.[23]

The other method is a gradual infiltration into a heterogeneous church area, of members of one of the denominations, until other sects are largely displaced. The Catholic church is in some measure following this plan. The process is simple: if a non-Catholic farmer within the area of a Catholic parish should decide to sell or rent his farm, the parish priest will endeavor to secure a Catholic family as purchaser or renter; the church itself has a fund from which the Catholic family may borrow if need be to make the purchase. The social advantages of the resettlement method lie in creating a church unit of sufficient size for effective functioning. The disadvantages lie in the possibility of creating "cultural islands." It may promote rather than allay sectarianism. It may bring about interarea conflicts between opposing "islands," each of which may be seeking to expand at the expense of the other. Competition for land in such areas may drive land prices up. The possibility of political conflict among such groups is also readily seen.

### THE CHURCH IN RELATION TO ITS SOCIAL ENVIRONMENT

The church, like all social institutions, faces the problem of adapting itself to its social environment. This environment is in a constant process of change. Unless the church also changes with the larger culture, maladjustment occurs. The church, being an essentially conservative institution, tends to lag behind the changes in the culture about it. The extensive discussion of the problem of the rural church is itself evidence that such maladjustment exists.

In his excellent study of urban churches, H. Paul Douglass takes as his central hypothesis that the "city church is an evolved rural church. What it has come to be is the result of an

[23] Charles Morrow Wilson, *The Landscape of Rural Poverty: Corn Bread and Creek Water*, p. 38 ff. New York: Henry Holt and Co., 1940.

evolution from a rural parent stock."[24] On the basis of his hypothesis he classified urban churches according to the extent of adaptation to the urban environment. In other words, the problem of the city church was to cast off its rural characteristics and take on those forms more suitable to an urban society. But the country and the city are not isolated from each other, and the process of social interaction is continuous. If the city church has the task of adapting its rural tradition and organization to the urban environment, so also does the rural church have to adapt itself to the influences of urban civilization which penetrate to the country.

The impact of urbanism is manifest in many ways, one of the most significant of which is the development and dissemination of scientific thought. With the growth in knowledge about the universe, some of the old mysteries which found explanation in the supernatural no longer hold attention as objects of religious awe. An outbreak of insect pests is no longer to be treated as a divine punishment which can be expiated through some religious ritual. The new method is to apply an insecticide. Thus as human knowledge gradually "replaces" supernatural explanations, skepticism grows even in relation to the as yet unexplained mysteries. As doubts arise, so also does the demand for new interpretations of the ancient dogmas.

However, a religion based upon revelation—such as Christianity—has difficulty making adaptations to the growth of secular knowledge. The revelation is written; it is the word of the Almighty; therefore, it is unchangeable. Thus the doctrines of the church can be changed only in the face of overwhelming scientific evidence. Often this is accomplished by finding new interpretation of the revelation. Reinterpretation of doctrines remains one of the inherent problems in the social adaptation of the church.

**The sacred and the secular.** Another philosophical problem in the contemporary church is the traditional dualism which distinguishes between the sacred and the secular. That man is composed of a body and a spirit is an ancient belief in Western religious culture. The body, according to the tradition, is prone

[24] H. Paul Douglass, *One Thousand City Churches*, p. 83. New York: George H. Doran Co., 1926.

to do evil, while the spirit is capable of good. The body is of the earth, the spirit is divine. The notion has resulted in a clear cleavage between what is spiritual or sacred and what is secular or of the earth and the flesh. *Church* and *state* are themselves expressions of this dualism; the one sacred, the other secular.

The practical result, so far as the social organism of religion is concerned, is to bring about a large measure of isolation—or insulation—of the church from the affairs of the community. The church, some people hold, cannot concern itself with economic matters, for that would mean engaging in secular activities. It would be equally inappropriate for the church—or the minister—to engage in political activity, for that concerns the state. The church may not undertake recreational activities of certain kinds, since they represent distinctly human activities and are of the "flesh." Thus, adaptation to the other agencies in the community is inhibited by this concept of the role of the church.

**Growing concern for the secular.** Some leaders of the Christian churches are taking a deliberate stand that the traditional distinction between the sacred and the secular is unfortunate. They argue that the person behaves as a unity, not as a "body" on weekdays and as a "spirit" on Sunday, and that the church is obliged to try and see that religion functions in the life of the individual at all times. In other words, they would "forget" the distinction between sacred and secular and dedicate the church to service of man in all his activities. A. D. Mattson suggests "it is not a matter of secularizing the church; it is a question of spiritualizing the secular. . . . The rural church ought to be interested in social problems because it ought to be interested in human welfare. Nothing human ought to be foreign to the interests of the church. . . . Soil conservation, for example, is of direct concern to the church. People cannot live the abundant life on depleted land and they cannot support the church on such land. . . . " [25]

**Need for redefinition of function.** The church is faced continuously with the need to define its function in relation to the state. This is especially so in the field of social welfare. Histori-

[25] A. D. Mattson, "A Study of the Mid-West Rural Churches," pp. 26, 27. Rock Island, Illinois: Augustana Book Concern, Rock Island, Illinois, 1943.

cally, the church has performed many welfare functions. It has helped the aged, the poor and the needy, the widow and the orphan. The recent vast expansion of state welfare services has confronted the church with the problem of where its functions end and where those of the state begin.

A similar development has occurred in the pursuit of recreation and leisure time. Should the church expand or contract its services here? The rise of the public high school in recent years and the expansion of extracurricular activities have provided for a great deal of the leisure time of rural youth. In fact, in some areas where the church had a rather elaborate recreational program, something of a crisis has arisen as to a division of time between the high school and the church. Often the same young people are participating in a high-school play at a time when the church desires them to take part in something else. The duplication of function by high school and church is a serious problem in such areas. In sections where the rural church has little or no youth program it may find itself losing control of its young people whose activities are centered in the high school. The sense of competition with the high school may lead to the setting up of a church-sponsored program which in a measure would duplicate that of the high school.

Such statements merely raise the question and do not answer it. There is no simple answer: it must be sought through community discussion and group decision. The main points of this discussion are (*a*) that the church does not exist in a social vacuum, (*b*) that it is organically related to the other segments of culture and to other institutions in the community, and (*c*) that the arbitrary distinction between sacred and secular results in a futile insulation of the church from the affairs of the community.

The contemporary ecclesiastical scene in rural America, characterized by a multiplicity of sects, has its background in the historical development of the country. The chief factors have been the Protestant tradition of dissent, the heterogeneous origins of the population, and the rise of native American sects, especially during the religious revivals of the nineteenth century. The problem of supporting the churches arises not only from the numerous sectarian divisions, but also from the pattern of open-country settlement which severely limits the number of potential members.

## QUESTIONS FOR DISCUSSION

1. Discuss the importance of religion as (a) a means of adjustment to the unknown, (b) an organization of values, (c) an expression or release of emotions and (d) an authoritative source of sanctions determining what is right and wrong in the way of personal and social conduct.

2. In what way can membership in one of the established denominations aid in the adjustment of the rural-urban migrant?

3. List some of the favorable and unfavorable results of the Protestant tradition of dissent, considered from a long-range social point of view.

4. Frontier life was apparently conducive to the expression of revivalism in religion. Why? Would you consider revivals to be democratic? Discuss.

5. Where and among whom did congregationalism have its origin? How has it contributed to over-churching in rural America?

6. Point out the relationship between population composition and sectarianism in rural areas.

7. What are the criteria that should be considered in determining the optimum size of a church unit or parish?

8. Give the distinguishing characteristics of (a) a federated church, (b) a nondenominational, united church, (c) a denominational, united church, and (d) an affiliated church. What have been some of the recent trends in the development of such churches in rural regions?

9. What are the essential features of the larger parish movement? Would you say that this movement offers any solution to the problem of over-churching? Discuss.

10. Describe the resettlement program now being utilized by the Roman Catholic church.

11. Thousands of open-country churches have been closed since the turn of the century. This phenomenon is unquestionably related to population density and mode of settlement. Why?

12. Can you present reasons why the open-country church in the South shows a superior ability to persist? Discuss.

13. Describe some of the problems currently faced by the rural church in its adjustment to (a) urbanization, (b) the growth of secularism, and (c) the expanding social functions of government and its institutions.

## SELECTED REFERENCES

Clark, Elmer T. *The Small Sects in America*, Revised Edition. New York and Nashville: Abingdon-Cokesbury Press, 1949.

Hollingshead, A. B. "The Life Cycle of Nebraska Rural Churches," *Rural Sociology*, Vol. II, No. 2, pp. 180–191, June, 1937.

Hooker, Elizabeth R. *United Churches*. New York: Harper and Brothers, 1926.

Loomis, C. P., and Beegle, J. Allan. *Rural Social Systems*, Chapter 12. New York: Prentice-Hall, 1950.

Niebuhr, H. Richard. *The Social Sources of Denominationalism*, Chapters 3, 4. New York: Henry Holt and Company, 1929.

Parrington, V. L. *Main Currents in American Thought:* Vol. II, *The Romantic Revolution in America*. New York: Harcourt, Brace and Co.. 1927.

Schneider, Herbert W. *Religion in Twentieth Century America*. Cambridge: Harvard University Press, 1952.

Sweet, William Warren. *American Culture and Religion*. Dallas: Southern Methodist University Press, 1951.

——— *Revivalism in America*. New York: Charles Scribner's Sons, 1944.

Williamson, Ralph L. "Federated Churches," *Town and Country Church*, No. 92, November, 1953, pp. 1–2.

Wilson, Warren H. *The Farmer's Church*. New York: D. Appleton-Century Co., 1925.

## CHAPTER 18

# THE CHURCH AS A SOCIAL INSTITUTION

As already indicated, the church must be considered as a social institution in much the same manner as we consider the school or local government. As a social institution its elements are: (a) a system of doctrine or beliefs with reference to God and the unseen world; (b) a set of ceremonies and rituals appropriate to these beliefs; (c) a body of members who have subscribed to the creed; (d) a pattern of organization, involving both lay and professional leaders, with specific duties and responsibilities; (e) physical facilities to carry on its functions, including houses of worship, and recreational and educational facilities.

**Functions of the church.** Broadly speaking, the church is an instrument through which concepts of religion are inculcated and practiced. Specifically, the church has a *teaching* or indoctrinating function. The systems of belief concerning God are taught the neophyte before he formally assumes the status of member. Thereafter he is continually reminded of these concepts and of their significance to his daily life and behavior; he is encouraged to live his life in accordance with them. This is a matter of constant *exhortation*, which becomes another function of the church, particularly as it is exercised by the minister. Demonstration that he is living his religion is usually by the overt observance of certain established rituals of the church. They vary with different denominations, from the simple to the very elaborate, but some forms of ritual are common to all.

The member is expected to attend regular weekly services of *worship*, and it becomes a function of the church to provide the place of worship—the chapel, the meetinghouse or the synagogue.

Because of its emphasis upon the fellowship of man with

342

man, the church has· historically maintained certain responsibilities for human welfare, for the ill, the comfortless, and the needy. The church, therefore, has a *welfare* function. Some churches, in their desire to create a wholesome social environment for their young people, have undertaken to provide *recreational* facilities. Moreover, most ministers in the daily performance of their duties advise their members on a great variety of personal problems. Such *personal counselling* may become an increasingly important function in a complex society like ours, where the possibilities of personal maladjustment are omnipresent. Obviously, this point has significance for the training of ministers in the techniques of personal guidance.

Finally, the church is one of the most potent agencies for *social control* in our society. Being a voluntary agency, not subject to the control of the state, it can act as critic of public policies. It can, and does to a considerable extent, resist the invasion of individual rights by an overambitious government, and becomes therefore a possible instrument for the preservation of democratic controls. But perhaps the church's most important influence in the field of social control is exercised over its members in the maintenance of the traditional mores. Especially does it concern itself with the maintenance of the stability of the family, exhorting its members to obey the laws of the country, to be good neighbors and good citizens.

In summary, the functions of the church today may be listed as follows: (1) to teach religious doctrines, (2) to exhort its members to obedience to and practice of the precepts, (3) to provide the physical facilities for communal religious activities, including worship and ritual, (4) to carry on welfare and recreational activities, (5) to counsel members on personal problems, and (6) to serve as an agency of social control.

## CHURCH POLITY AND ORGANIZATION

Churches are organized according to three general patterns: the *congregational*, the *episcopal*, and a *combination* of both forms. Under the congregational system, ecclesiastical control is vested in the local congregation which chooses its own minister, decides upon its local budget, determines how the money is to be raised, and generally makes all other decisions respecting the operation of the church. Local authority is delegated to an elected board which acts for the congregation in administrative matters. In matters of common interest affecting the denomination as a whole, the local bodies unite on state, regional, and national levels. In doing so, however, they lose none of their powers of independent action. Examples of denominations which are organized on this pattern are the Congregational and Christian Churches, the Baptists, Plymouth Brethren, Mennonites, Disciples of Christ, and the Unitarians.

Under the episcopal system the control of the denomination is vested in a body of bishops. In the Roman Catholic Church control is vested in a Pope, whose authority is supreme in matters of faith and in the conduct of the affairs of the church. Under the Pope is the College of Cardinals whose members act as his advisers. In case of the death of the Pope the Cardinals elect his successor.

A form of organization partaking of the nature of both congregational and episcopal types is found in the Protestant Episcopal Church. The head of the church is the Presiding Bishop, who since 1919 in the United States is elected by the House of Bishops, subject to the approval of the House of Deputies composed equally of laymen and clergy elected from the dioceses. The Methodist Church has a similar form of church polity.

These forms of organization, it will be noted, have their counterparts in the field of government. The polity of the Roman Church was undoubtedly influenced by the pattern of organization in the Roman Empire, during which it had its rise.[1] The revolts against political absolutism in the modern period of history were reflected in the religious revolts against highly centralized authority in the ecclesiastical realm. Certainly, the rise of American democracy has left a profound imprint upon the organization of churches in the New World.

This point is well illustrated in the case of the Protestant Episcopal Church of America. Although it may be considered as a "daughter" of the Church of England it differs from the

---

[1] See H. Richard Niebuhr, *The Social Sources of Denominationalism*, p. 207. New York: Henry Holt and Co., 1929.

latter in its church polity. According to Howard Chandler Robbins,

... it's diocesan bishops and their coadjutors and suffragans are elected, not appointed; their powers are strictly limited and defined by a written constitution; and the laity are given a large place in the management of church affairs. The constitution of the church was adopted in general convention in 1789. Among the deputies to this convention were men who drafted the constitution of the United States. The provisions for representative government are strikingly similar. Vestries are to be elected by congregations; they in turn elect the rector of parishes; and rectors and other clergy together with elected delegates represent the parishes in diocesan conventions which correspond to state legislatures. Diocesan bishops are elected by these clerical and lay delegates, who vote separately by orders, their concurrence being necessary for an election. Once in three years the bishops of the church and clerical and lay deputies elected by diocesan conventions or representing missionary jurisdictions meet in general convention, where the House of Bishops, sitting as a separate body, corresponds to the Senate of the United States, and the House of Deputies, to the House of Representatives. Legislation may be initiated in either House, but concurrent action is required to make it effective.[2]

The influence of political democracy upon the development of democratic procedures in the church can be further illustrated by the Lutheran immigrant churches. In the Old World the church followed in its own structure the monarchical forms of the political states, authority being organized from the top downward. In America the same denominations have assumed more and more democracy in church government, with a high degree of congregational control prevailing at the present time. The congregation is the primary authority and elects representatives to the state and national governing bodies.

The social significance of these various forms of church polity lies primarily in the opportunities for participation of laymen in church affairs—with such benefits to the development of personality as accrue from such activities—and in the control, or lack of it, over denominational segmentation. In the latter

[2] H. C. Robbins, "Principles of the Protestant Episcopal Church and Community Religion," in J. R. Hargreaves and others, *Community Religion and the Denominational Heritage*, pp. 110 ff. New York: Harper and Brothers, 1930.

instance the congregational type exercises virtually no control, and tends towards increasing subdivision. Highly centralized control, on the other hand, sets rigid limits to cell-division within the general denomination. As we have noted,[3] the practice of local autonomy is one important factor in the excessive sectarianism in the United States.

**Local church organization.** In a church which generally follows the democratic type of structure, the organization begins with the congregation. This body elects a *board* from among its members, very much as the electorate creates a board of education. This board is charged with the general responsibility of operating the affairs of the church. They appoint a minister, often with approval of higher denominational authority, and subject to the confirmation of the congregation. They are responsible for approving and collecting the funds for the church budget.

The *minister*, as the professional paid leader of the congregation, is primarily charged with the executive functions of church government in addition to his usual functions of preaching, pastoral service, and the like.

**Auxiliary organizations.** It is common in the Protestant churches to conduct a Sunday school. This organization, for which the minister assumes general responsibility, is usually presided over by a layman who acts as the superintendent. In the case of a graded school, the teachers who conduct the classes are also laymen chosen from the congregation. As stated, the Sunday school is especially common among the Protestant bodies, although 43.7 per cent of the Roman Catholic and 27.6 per cent of the Jewish congregations reported having Sunday schools in 1936.[4] Out of the total of 244,319 local churches, 162,233 reported Sunday schools. Of these 36.2 per cent were urban and 63.8 per cent were rural. It is interesting, as showing the extent of lay-leader participation, that there were 2,261,740 officers and teachers, or about 14 per church, concerned with the operation of the Sunday school. Over 18 million "scholars" were enrolled, of whom 10,455,919 were urban and 7,933,082 were rural. The average number of "scholars" per church was 113,

---

[3] See the preceding chapter.
[4] *Census of Religious Bodies, 1936*, Vol. I.

with the urban churches averaging 178 and the rural 77. In the rural Sunday schools the average number of scholars ranged from 205 for the General Conference of the Mennonite Church of North America to only 24 for the Church of Christ, Scientist.

Besides the Sunday school, churches usually have special organizations for women such as the Ladies Aid or Women's Auxiliary, as well as special youth groups. Among the latter are such well-known organizations as the Christian Endeavor Society, the Epworth League, and various groups by different names according to the denomination concerned, all functioning primarily for young people.

## CHURCHES AND CHURCH MEMBERSHIP

Membership in a church is voluntary. In this respect the church group differs from the family, the school (up to a prescribed age), and the State. In these latter institutions the individual has no choice. However, in actual practice, membership in a church tends to be socially inherited, since in most instances the child is baptized at an age when he has little or no choice. But at any time in his adult life he may withdraw from membership or fail to participate in church activity.

Perhaps the voluntary aspect of membership has contributed to the idea of "fellowship" which is associated with a church body. Extending the "right hand of fellowship" is a common religious rite. The idea of fellowship implies a community of interest and intimacy of interpersonal relations which characterize few associations to the degree realized in a church body. In this respect, the church ranks next to the family among the major social institutions. Members regard their church as a fraternal group, and it is a practice in many Protestant churches to address fellow members as "brothers" and "sisters."

The feature of close interpersonal relations is especially characteristic of the rural church, because of the dominance in rural society of primary group relations. In the urban church, where mobility of membership is high and secondary group relations characterize society in general, the church itself takes on the nature of a secondary group. Members lack intimate personal relations with one another. Unlike rural congregations, the urban congregations, especially the large ones, seldom linger after the service to visit and discuss the affairs of the week.

Whether the individual may or may not choose to join a church, membership is by no means automatic. The element of choice is assumed in the majority of churches, and the process of becoming a member is surrounded with considerable ceremony. The person is first indoctrinated with the religious beliefs and practices, involving in many churches his attendance for a specified period at a special class where such instruction is given. The individual has then publicly to acknowledge his acceptance of these beliefs. By thus subscribing to the doctrines the individual is considered eligible for the important rite of *baptism*, which in most Christian churches is a requirement to joining. The further ritual of *confirmation* completes the process. Few other organized groups or major social institutions require such elaborate steps in admittance to membership. The social consequence is a strengthening of the bond that unites members in a common fellowship.

**Church membership in the United States.** While the Bureau of the Census has compiled a decennial census of religious bodies since 1906, the reliability of the results leaves much to be desired. The inadequacy grows out of the necessity of depending upon reports in the form of questionnaires sent to each of the local ministers in the United States. Not only was the compilation of a complete mailing list virtually impossible, but also not all of those to whom the schedules were sent cooperated by filling them out accurately and returning them. Nevertheless, in spite of its many inadequacies, the *Census of Religious Bodies* is the only available source of information on many features of religious organization in this country. Consequently, we are compelled to rely heavily upon the data reported therein for broad analysis of the ecclesiastical situation.

According to the 1936 census, the total membership reported by 256 denominations was 55,807,366. Of the total, 38,519,170 were urban (that is members of churches located in incorporated places of 2,500 or more people, and 17,084,410 were rural.[5] The

---

[5] Several other estimates of total membership by denominations are made periodically, notably by the *Yearbook of American Churches.*

comparable figures for the 1926 census were as follows: number of denominations, 212; total membership, 54,576,346; urban members, 35,126,927; rural, 19,386,734. Undoubtedly the increase in church membership was much greater during the decade than these figures appear to indicate. For some reason the returns on the 1936 questionnaire were much less satisfactory than those on the 1926 questionnaire. B. Y. Landis has estimated that possibly 45,000 local churches failed to report in 1936.[6] On the basis of his own survey of information, secured directly from the statistical officers of various bodies in 1940, Landis estimated the church membership for the United States as of that year to be 64,501,594, with 250 denominations and 244,319 local churches. His figures are undoubtedly much more accurate than are those of the official census. Subsequent editions of the *Yearbook of Churches* report annually the membership of American churches by denominations without giving numbers for states or other local units. The total membership for 1952 was 92,277,129 in 251 religious bodies and 285,277 local churches. It is a very interesting fact that the membership of churches is increasing more rapidly than the population.

**Regional distribution of membership.** The number of local churches in relation to population and the total reported membership by different regions is given in Table 27. The important facts in the Table are those concerning the ratio of churches to the population and to the membership. In considering these data it is important to bear in mind the fact that one church per 1,000 population is usually the accepted optimum ratio. Even with the assumed underenumeration of local churches in 1936, it will be noted that the average population per church amounts to only 643 for the country as a whole and the average membership only 280. On the basis of the Landis estimates, the population per church in 1940 would be 540 and the membership per church, 264. These data serve to emphasize the degree of overchurching in this country.

The ratio of population per church falls especially low in the Southern states, but is also below the national average in the West North Central and Mountain areas. Only in New

---

[6] B. Y. Landis, ed., *Yearbook of American Churches*, p. 163. New York: Yearbook of American Churches Press, 1941.

England, the Middle Atlantic, and the Pacific regions does the ratio approximate the optimum figure of 1,000. The regions show about the same variations in members per church. A notable exception is the Pacific Coast which ranks first in population per church, but is fourth in the average size of membership.

TABLE 27. *Number of Churches, Population, and Membership per Church, by Regions, United States, 1936*

| | | | | AVERAGE PER CHURCH | |
| REGION | CHURCHES | POPULATION | MEMBERSHIP | POPULA- TION | MEM- BERSHIP |
| --- | --- | --- | --- | --- | --- |
| United States | 199,302 | 128,053,180 | 55,807,366 | 643 | 280 |
| New England | 8,022 | 8,408,038 | 4,854,270 | 1,048 | 605 |
| Middle Atlantic | 27,720 | 27,332,303 | 14,920,179 | 986 | 538 |
| East No. Central | 33,309 | 25,960,278 | 11,234,047 | 780 | 337 |
| West No. Central | 25,844 | 13,600,063 | 5,684,981 | 526 | 220 |
| South Atlantic | 39,386 | 16,742,053 | 6,449,736 | 425 | 164 |
| East So. Central | 25,864 | 10,374,330 | 3,751,627 | 401 | 145 |
| West So. Central | 24,049 | 12,694,572 | 4,592,733 | 528 | 191 |
| Mountain | 6,606 | 3,938,757 | 1,571,032 | 596 | 238 |
| Pacific | 8,502 | 9,019,913 | 2,544,975 | 1,061 | 299 |

Source: *Census of Religious Bodies*, 1936, Vol. I.

**Urban-rural differences in size of membership.** The small churches are found predominantly in rural areas, due to two factors: the pattern of rural settlement, which makes for small population per institution; and the denominational competition among Protestant churches in rural sections. The rural population of the country is approximately three-fourths Protestant.

**Distribution of members by denominations.** The distribution of the 1953 membership by major denominational groups is shown in Table 28.

TABLE 28. *Distribution of Membership by Major Denominational Groups, 1953*

| DENOMINATION | MEMBERSHIP |
| --- | --- |
| Buddhist | 73,000 |
| Old Cath. and Polish Nat'l. Cath. | 366,956 |
| Eastern Orthodox | 2,353,783 |
| Jewish Congregations | 5,000,000 |
| Roman Catholic | 30,253,427 |
| Protestant | 54,229,963 |

It will be noted that over 55 per cent of the total membership is in the Protestant Church. A larger proportion—59 per cent—was reported by Landis for 1940.[7]

The non-Protestant bodies are overwhelmingly urban. The Roman Catholic Church membership is less than 20 per cent

TABLE 29. *Proportion of Church Membership Which Was Rural, by Denominations With 100,000 or More Members, 1936*

| DENOMINATION | MEMBERS | PER CENT RURAL |
|---|---|---|
| American Baptist Association | 115,022 | 84.2 |
| Norwegian Lutheran Church | 516,400 | 70.0 |
| Church of the Brethren | 153,156 | 63.4 |
| Methodist Protestant | 148,288 | 63.0 |
| Southern Baptist Convention | 2,700,155 | 62.1 |
| Colored Methodist | 269,915 | 57.4 |
| Churches of Christ | 309,551 | 57.2 |
| American Lutheran | 1,424,442 | 56.3 |
| M. E. Church South | 2,061,683 | 53.9 |
| United Brethren in Christ | 376,905 | 52.6 |
| Negro Baptist | 3,782,464 | 50.5 |
| Latter Day Saints | 678,217 | 49.5 |
| Lutheran Synod of Wisconsin | 235,402 | 49.5 |
| African Methodist E. Zion | 414,244 | 48.3 |
| Christian Reformed | 107,993 | 46.2 |
| Evangelical Church | 212,446 | 44.4 |
| Evangelical Lutheran | 1,463,482 | 42.1 |
| African M. E. Church | 493,357 | 42.0 |
| Lutheran Synod of Mo. and Ohio | 1,192,553 | 40.9 |
| Methodist Episcopal | 3,509,763 | 38.3 |
| Evangelical and Reformed | 723,877 | 37.8 |
| Disciples of Christ | 1,196,315 | 37.8 |
| Assemblies of God | 148,043 | 37.3 |
| Reformed Church in America | 184,536 | 36.3 |
| Lutheran Augustana Synod | 327,472 | 35.9 |
| Congregational and Christian | 976,388 | 32.1 |
| United Lutheran | 1,286,612 | 30.0 |
| Church of the Nazarene | 136,227 | 28.9 |
| Seventh Day Adventist | 133,254 | 27.6 |
| Northern Baptist Convention | 1,329,044 | 27.4 |
| Roman Catholic | 19,914,937 | 19.4 |
| Protestant Episcopal | 1,735,335 | 15.5 |
| Church of Christ, Scientist | 368,915 | 5.1 |
| Salvation Army | 103,038 | 1.6 |
| Jewish Congregations | 4,641,184 | 0.9 |
| Greek Orthodox | 189,368 | 1.5 |
| Total | 53,559,983 | |

Source: *Census of Religious Bodies*, 1936, Vol. I.

[7] B. Y. Landis, *op. cit.*, p. 136.

rural, while the Jewish Congregations report less than 1 per cent. The 36 major religious bodies shown in Table 29 account for about 96 per cent of the total church membership of the country, the remaining 4 per cent being distributed among the 220 lesser groups, ranging in number of members from fewer than 100 to 93,000.

The churches vary widely in average size among denominations. The Roman Catholics, with nearly 2,000 members per church, head the list, with the Jewish Congregations next with 1,300 members. Among the church bodies showing high rural averages per church were the Roman Catholic with 382 and the Latter Day Saints with 346. At the other extreme was the Free Methodist Church, whose 600 rural churches averaged only 23 members each.

The small average membership for the rural churches, resulting from the low density of population in rural areas and the sectarianism in the Protestant group which predominates in the country, lays a heavy burden upon the rural people. Their churches are, as a result, poorly supported financially, poorly staffed, and unable to provide the variety of services which characterize urban churches.

### FINANCIAL SUPPORT OF CHURCHES

Considering its importance in the social organization of the American community the church receives a comparatively small fraction of the national income. Since support is on a voluntary basis, the church must rely upon free-will contributions of its members. C. L. Fry estimated that in 1926 total expenditures of, or contributions to, the religious bodies of the United States amounted to about 1 per cent of the national income for that year.[8] B. Y. Landis estimated the corresponding support for 1940 at slightly less than 1 per cent of the national income [9]; it probably did not exceed $600,000,000, or an average of less than $2,500 per church. Of course many churches had very much less than that amount, while others exceeded it.

[8] C. Luther Fry, *The U.S. Looks at Its Churches*, p. 88. New York: Institute of Social and Religious Research, 1930.
[9] B. Y. Landis, *op. cit.*, p. 138.

The *Census of Religious Bodies* reported total expenditures of $519,000,000 in 1936, but as previously noted this does not represent a complete report. The average amount per church in 1936 was $2,750. Here again there was wide variation among churches, with the Catholic and Jewish congregations reporting higher average expenditures per church.

In rural areas, because of the simplicity of the church organization, the small average size of the congregation, as well as the low cash income of farm people, the average expenditures per church are much less than in the urban areas, where on the contrary congregations are larger, there is a greater number of services offered, and at the same time incomes are higher.

E. deS. Brunner and J. H. Kolb [10] in their study of 140 American villages found the average expenditures per village church to be about $2,300 in 1924 and $2,400 in 1930. Comparable figures for open-country churches for the respective years were $650 and $700. The contributions per member were about the same for the two years, $17 for the villagers and $8 for open-country members. In 1936, when the same villages were re-surveyed, Brunner and Lorge [11] found that expenditures for the village churches had declined to $1,900 and those of the open-country churches to $560. Average contributions for village members had declined to $10 and those for the country members to $5.60.

The Consumer Purchases Study, based upon data for the fiscal year 1935–1936, showed that for comparable income groups in village and farm areas the contributions per family did not vary significantly. In the income group $1,000 to $1,249 the average contribution for villagers was $13 and for the farm, $16; in the group with incomes from $2,000 to $2,449 the church gifts of villagers amounted to $34, and those for farmers to $27. There are wide variations among the different regions of the country in the average contributions per farm family, from as little as $2.22 per family among white sharecroppers in Georgia and Mississippi to $25 among the farm families included in the

[10] E. deS. Brunner and J. H. Kolb, *Rural Social Trends*, p. 231. New York: McGraw-Hill Book Co., 1933.

[11] E. deS. Brunner and Irving Lorge, *Rural Trends in Depression Years*, pp. 307–309. New York: Columbia University Press, 1937.

California sample.[12] The financial problem of rural churches is obviously the consequence of the low incomes of rural people and the small average membership per church, and not of any unwillingness to contribute.

## THE CLERGYMEN

From a sociological point of view the clergyman stands in a relationship to the church similar to that occupied by the teacher in relation to the school. The clergyman is the leader whom the congregation employs to carry out the functions associated with the office of minister or priest. He is the professional leader of the group.

**Age-sex characteristics.** As an occupation it has been and is today largely a man's world. In 1950, of the 160,694 persons who reported that they are employed clergymen, only 6,777 were women, amounting to but 4.1 per cent of the total. In the preponderance of males the ministry is similar to the professions of law, medicine, and engineering. Among the major professions, teaching is the only one which has become increasingly a woman's world. While there are a number of well-known women evangelists in the country, they are for the most part associated with the newer sects. Most of the older denominations do not yet extend equal opportunity to women in the ministry. For this reason it is not likely that the proportion of women will change very much in the near future.

The ministry is a profession, moreover, in which mature and older men generally predominate. Among the employed men in this field in 1950, about 48 per cent were 45 years old or over, compared with 44 per cent of the physicians and only 31 per cent of the teachers. (See Figure 65.) The preponderance of older people in the ministry is partly to be accounted for by the fact that salaries are so low on the average that it is difficult if not impossible for ministers to make financial provision for retirement and that there are comparatively few churches having effective and satisfactory retirement plans for superannuated clergymen.

[12] Day Monroe, Dorothy S. Brady, Edith D. Rainboth, and Ellen D. Riley, "Family Expenditures for Personal Care, Gifts, Selected Taxes, and Miscellaneous Items," *Miscellaneous Publication 455*, United States Department of Agriculture, Washington, D.C., 1941.

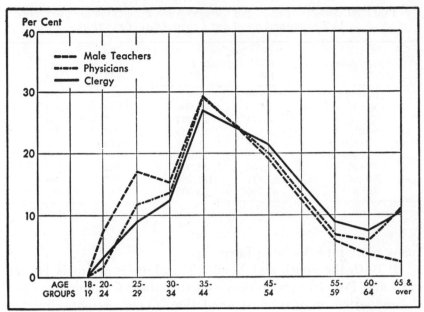

Bureau of the Census

FIGURE 65. *Comparative Age Distribution of Male Teachers, Clergy, and Physicians (Employed Males Only) in the United States, 1950*

**Distribution of clergymen.** The distribution of the 160,694 male clergymen by regions and by rural and urban areas is shown in Table 30 on the following page. The table also shows the number of people 14 years old or over per minister for 1940 and 1950. The important points to note in regard to the data are these: (1) there were more ministers in relation to the population in the year 1950 than in 1940—ministers increased by 19 per cent and the population by 14 per cent; (2) the South led in the number of ministers relative to population in both years, with the North Central next; (3) there were more people per minister in 1950 than in 1940 in the West and in the case of the nonwhite South; (4) relative to population, ministers were fewer in the Northeast and West and in rural areas; (5) finally, all of the regions except the West and the nonwhite South had fewer persons per minister in the year 1950 than in 1940.

**Explanation of differences noted.** (1) 1940 represented the tag end of the depression of the 1930's, when many ministers were unemployed. The increased prosperity of the 1940's brought

TABLE 30. *Number of Employed Clergymen and Population per Clergyman, by Regions and Rural and Urban Areas, 1940-1950*

| AREA | NO. OF CLERGYMEN | | POPULATION PER MINISTER | |
|---|---|---|---|---|
| | 1940 | 1950 | 1940 | 1950 |
| United States | 135,090 | 160,694 | 967 | 938 |
| Northeast | 33,235 | 37,093 | 1,084 | 1,064 |
| North Central | 43,774 | 52,223 | 917 | 851 |
| South | 45,951 | 58,555 | 907 | 806 |
| White | 32,449 | 46,514 | 976 | 792 |
| Nonwhite | 13,448 | 12,041 | 744 | 859 |
| West | 12,130 | 18,906 | 981 | 1,034 |
| Urban | 81,184 | 107,286 | 917 | 899 |
| Rural | 53,906 | 53,408 | 1,062 | 1,015 |

Source: Bureau of the Census.

many more into the labor force.

(2) Both the South and North Central areas are more largely rural and Protestant with the result that there are more sects and denominations in relation to population. There are more churches to be staffed even though the membership per congregation is small.

(3) The increase in the population per minister in the West and the nonwhite South is probably the result of migration. It is a well known fact that Negroes have migrated from the South in greater proportion than have whites. Apparently the ministers did not move with them. The migration to the western states during and following the war was tremendous, and, again, it seems the clergy did not move with them at the same rate.

(4) One main reason why the population per minister is high in the Northeast is that there is a predominance of Roman Catholics and of Jewish congregations, both of which have large congregations per church. In the West, there is a large Mormon population which employs no professional ministry. Moreover, the heavy migration mentioned above doubtless results in a large unchurched population.

(5) The rural-urban differences are due to a number of factors among which the following may be mentioned: (a) there are probably many ministers who live in places of 2,500 population or more yet serve rural churches; thus, the ministers would be enumerated as urban even though working for rural people; (b) the

scattered pattern of rural residence is an impediment to social participation of farm people in general. There is some evidence that closing of open-country churches has reduced participation.

**Number of points served.** The small size of many congregations makes it impossible for them to pay the salary of a full-time minister. It is customary in such cases for several congregations of the same denomination in a given area to share a minister among them. Since small congregations are especially common in rural areas, the "subdivided" minister is primarily a rural phenomenon. According to an analysis of the 1926 *Census of Religious Bodies* made by C. Luther Fry, only about one third of the rural ministers, contrasted with 85 per cent of the urban ministers, served one congregation. About one fifth of the ministers and priests served two congregations, while there were over 10 per cent who served five or more. (See Table 31.)

TABLE 31. *Per Cent of Churches Whose Ministers or Priests Reported Serving Specified Number of Points, 1926*

| DENOMINATION AND AREA | \multicolumn{7}{c}{NUMBER OF POINTS SERVED} | | | | | | |
| --- | --- | --- | --- | --- | --- | --- | --- |
| | 1 | 2 | 3 | 4 | 5 | 6 | 7 or more |
| 17 White Protestant | 48.2 | 20.0 | 12.7 | 9.0 | 5.0 | 2.8 | 2.3 |
| Urban | 84.2 | 11.4 | 2.8 | 1.0 | 0.3 | 0.1 | 0.2 |
| Rural | 37.5 | 22.6 | 15.7 | 11.4 | 6.4 | 3.5 | 2.9 |
| Catholic | 52.5 | 19.6 | 9.4 | 5.8 | 3.4 | 2.1 | 7.2 |
| Urban | 82.9 | 9.4 | 3.2 | 1.6 | 1.0 | 0.5 | 1.4 |
| Rural | 31.8 | 26.6 | 13.7 | 8.6 | 5.0 | 3.1 | 11.2 |
| 3 Negro churches | 56.6 | 26.2 | 11.9 | 4.0 | 1.0 | .3 | |
| Urban | 83.0 | 12.8 | 3.1 | .8 | .2 | .1 | |
| Rural | 49.6 | 29.7 | 14.3 | 4.9 | 1.2 | .3 | |

Source of data: C. Luther Fry, *The U.S. Looks at Its Churches*, pp. 164–175. Copyrighted by Institute of Social and Religious Research, 1930. Used by permission of Harper and Brothers.

For the rural churches of 17 white Protestant denominations an analysis by different regions of the country revealed considerable variation. Rural churches of New England and the Pacific Coast were able in almost two thirds of the cases to provide a full-time minister. The South Atlantic area, on the other hand, reported only one fourth of its ministers serving one congregation. For the country as a whole these 17 major churches had 63 per cent of their ministers serving 2 or more congregations—one fourth of them serving 4 or more! (See Figure 66.)

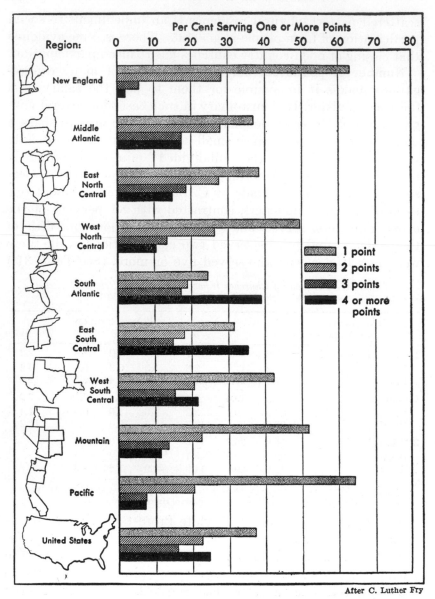

FIGURE 66. *Per Cent of Rural Churches of 17 White Protestant Denominations Whose Ministers Reported Serving One or More Points, by Regions, 1926*

The chief consequence of the part-time minister is, naturally, part-time service. Visits to the congregations are at intervals of two weeks, or frequently longer, and then only on Sunday for formal church services. Those functions associated with the phrase "pastoral service" are hardly performed at all. Unless there is considerable initiative among the laymen themselves, such churches have a strong likelihood of passing out of existence.

**The salary of the minister.** On this mundane question it is very difficult to get general and reliable information. Churches seem peculiarly reticent about giving such information, and when figures are reported they are difficult to evaluate because of the fact that the parsonage is frequently provided in addition to the reported salary. Moreover, ministers derive fees for such services as conducting funerals and performing marriages, which are not reported as part of the salary. There are, moreover, a great many so-called clergymen who have simply "felt the call" to preach, who take up collections at their preaching services as the only pay they receive from the church.

There are a few sources of information for deriving some rough estimates of ministers' salaries. The United States Census in 1950 reported the median income of male clergymen as $2,412. Eighty-five per cent fell below the mark of $4,000. This median compares with $1,200 reported in 1940, although the latter figure included only wage or salary income, while that for 1950 included all sources. Even so, it is clear that there has been a marked improvement in the incomes of clergymen since 1940.

In the *Census of Religious Bodies* for 1936 the total amount paid for salaries is reported by various denominations. Since the number of churches reporting expenditures for pastors' salaries is also given, it is possible to derive the average amount paid by all local churches for this purpose. There were 120,145 rural churches reporting expenditures of approximately $50,000,000 for pastors' salaries, an average of $413. The comparable average paid by the urban churches was $1,208. These figures represented church contributions for payment of salaries. But since nearly two thirds of the rural churches shared their minister with at least one other church, the salary of the minister would on the average considerably exceed this amount.

Certain regional differences are revealed by the 1950 census. The averages of the salaries reported in the respective regions are: North Atlantic, $2,362; East North Central, $2,560; West North Central, $2,432; South Atlantic, $2,436; South Central, $2,082; Western, $2,473. Urban and rural are not reported separately, but for the 11 major cities, the average was $2,395. Thus, the lowest salaries on average are in the South Central and the highest in the East North Central region. Except for the South Central, however, there is not very much variation.[13]

**Training of ministers.** The prevailingly low salaries paid to ministers are reflected in the comparatively poor training received. In the study by Brunner and Lorge it was found that in the 140 rural communities nearly a third (31.5 per cent) of the ministers were neither graduates from college nor seminary; only 44 per cent had had both college and seminary or Bible school training. These figures for 1936, however, did represent some slight improvement over those for 1930 and 1924.[14] Over half of the nonresident pastors had had no professional training.

In the proportions of trained ministers in rural areas there is wide variation among states and among denominations. In 1926 there were 11 southern states in which more than 60 per cent of the rural Protestant ministers of 17 white religious bodies did not claim to be graduates of any higher institution of learning. In two states the proportion exceeded 75 per cent. The percentage of Catholic priests with no formal training was very much less, averaging only about one eighth that for the 17 Protestant denominations.[15]

Among the Protestant bodies those which reported the lowest proportions of untrained rural ministers were: Evangelical Synod of North America, 4.8 per cent; United Lutheran Church in America, 5.6 per cent; Reformed Church in the U.S.A., 6.5 per cent; Evangelical Augustana Synod of North America, 7.3 per cent; Presbyterian Church in the U.S.A., 19.6 per cent.

The low pay also contributes to a high degree of mobility among ministers. Not only do they move from one church to another, in an effort to improve their economic situation, but

[13] *1950 Census of Population*, Vol. II.
[14] E. deS. Brunner and Irving Lorge, *op. cit.*, p. 319.
[15] C. Luther Fry, *op. cit.*, pp. 71–72.

many of the younger men after a discouraging experience in the ministry decide to leave the profession for more lucrative employment in other fields. A considerable number decide to go back to school and prepare themselves for some other profession. At all events, the more promising rural ministers accept town and city charges when such opportunities present themselves, because of the more satisfactory income prospects. As an example of the tenure situation, E. R. Hooker found in the case of the United Churches that the average pastorate had extended over only 2.7 years.[16]

### THE ROLE OF THE MINISTER

The religious leader stands in a peculiar relation to the group. His authority is derived from extrahuman sources, and he often transcends in power that of any other sort of leader. In many primitive groups, for example, the performer of magic— the "medicine man"—is the most powerful individual in the community. Even in the more civilized societies the man accepted as one who can "speak as one having authority" wields an influence far beyond that of the functionary who derives his authority only from the group itself. Nevertheless, in actual practice, the Christian minister is to a large extent regarded as a creature of the group itself. He is subject to critical evaluation by the group. People recognize "good" and "poor" ministers, incompetent and able, mediocre and superior.

There are, in general, two types of religious leaders. There is the *prophetic* type, characterized by the individual who initiates new movements, depending solely on his own personal power and his claims to divine authority as the basis of his leadership. Then there is the *institutional functionary*, who derives his authority by virtue of the position he holds, rather than by personal characteristics or any special claim to divine authority alone. The one is a creator of new social organizations, the other merely functions in an established medium. It is primarily with the latter type that we are concerned here.

In the Judeo-Christian tradition there is a broad basic agreement upon the role of the minister. He is the spiritual shepherd

[16] Elizabeth R. Hooker, *United Churches*, p. 201. New York: George H. Doran Co., 1926. Used by permission of Harper and Brothers.

of the flock. He is the acknowledged and authorized interpreter of the doctrines of the church. He is the exhorter, praising the virtuous, upbraiding the wicked. He is the official comforter in the time of trouble. But within these general concepts there are many particular notions on which there is considerable variation. There is on the one hand the community concept of the ministerial role and on the other hand the concept held by the minister himself. These are not always in agreement, although in general they tend to correspond.

**The community conception of the role of minister.** While the community is not often explicit in expressing itself as to what it expects of its minister, its conception is implied in many ways. Often this implication comes in a negative manner in the form of expressed criticism of the minister. The community may criticize the minister for being too conservative or too liberal, for being a "backslapper" or not a good mixer; or for any number of other characteristics which he possesses or does not possess, or for things which he does or fails to do.

A positive expression of the community concept of the role is found in a report by Mark A. May and others on *The Profession of the Ministry*, a study sponsored by the Institute for Social and Religious Research.[17] The investigators secured 150 letters written by pulpit committees of Protestant churches setting forth qualifications of ministers from the standpoint of the local congregation. The letters came from both rural and urban churches. Essentially, these letters represent the qualities desired in a prospective minister.

Nearly all of the letters mentioned *personality*, which stood first on the list of desirable qualities. "When a church says it wants a man with a pleasing, or an attractive, or a forceful personality, it means it wants a man who is poised and socially at ease, who has self-assurance, spontaneity, a balanced enthusiasm, a man who can get along with people, and more particularly with young people." [18] Other personal qualities mentioned in the letters, although by only a minor fraction of the replies, were "athletic build (mentioned three times but always in

---

[17] Mark A. May, and others, *The Education of American Ministers*, Vol. II, *The Profession of the Ministry*. New York: Institute of Social and Religious Research, 1934.
[18] *Ibid.*, p. 131.

connection with directors of religious education); virile or vigorous (mentioned twice each); well-built, militant type (mentioned once); commanding presence (mentioned once)." [19]

These correspondents also stated they wanted a man who would be a *good pastor*. He must be "vitally interested in people," "consecrated to his task and to the Christian way of life." [20]

About one fourth of the replies mentioned "evangelistic zeal," which implied the ability to attract people, especially young people, to his church. "Adaptability" was mentioned by one fifth of the letters as a desirable quality in the minister, meaning "ability to work with people." [21]

A considerable number mentioned "organizing ability," and "executive ability" was mentioned by about one third of the replies. This involves ability to get others to work, possession of initiative, ability to work hard, efficiency, and resourcefulness. [22]

Most of those who expressed a preference in age and education favored a seminary graduate between thirty and thirty-five. None of them asked for women.

In regard to these statements of expectations of local churches concerning their ministers, May says:

> The work that the minister performs is influenced in many ways by what his people expect him to do. Here we find an endless variety of expectations both within a single denomination and within a single parish. Some members want one thing and others want another. But laying aside for the moment the differences of opinion that often arise within a given parish, we find great varieties among parishes. Some want a minister who is primarily a pastor; others want a "pulpiteer"; others want a money raiser; others a promoter; others a patron of the arts; and so it goes. Many parishes are dominated by the modern psychology of business success. They want a winner, not only of souls, but also of dollars and of prestige. In small towns there is often intense rivalry among local churches, each wanting its pastor to outshine his fellow-pastors in the community. [23]

And again the minister

> . . . is expected to preach, to make pastoral calls, to conduct services of worship including special and seasonal services, to officiate at weddings,

[19] *Ibid.*, p. 131.  [21] *Ibid.*, p. 131.  [23] *Ibid.*, pp. 130–131.
[20] *Ibid.*, p. 131.  [22] *Ibid.*, p. 132.

funerals, and baptisms, to persuade men and women to join the church and support it financially, and to lead a good and exemplary life. In short he is expected to "fit in," which means that he must adapt his preaching, teaching, and personal conduct to the moral and social standards of his community. He may preach against sin in the abstract; but he must be careful not to offend too many of his members, especially his church officials.

He is expected to play the role of peacemaker. He must be compromising and conciliatory, especially in dealing with local reforms. He must avoid taking sides in local issues, especially those of a political or business nature. His business is to build up his church and make it strong in the community. The church is regarded as the community's bulwark of strength against the forces of evil, however ill-defined these forces may be. It is assumed that if the church has a large membership and a large budget, the community will be somehow better off.

Thus the majority of local churches want a priest or an administrator and not a prophet. As long as the minister plays the role of the priest and the friendly pastor, as long as he offends no one, he is held in esteem. It is when he attempts the role of the prophet that he gets into difficulties. True prophets have always been unpopular. The young minister of today who tries to follow the example of Amos or Hosea finds great difficulty in holding a church.[24]

**The minister as "holy man."** Some laymen regard the minister as possessed of a degree of "holiness" which places him above criticism. On the other hand, his behavior is carefully watched and he is expected to live a life which symbolizes all of the group virtues. This conception of the role of ministers leads often to the toleration of incompetence in the minister. Provided he leads a "good life," people are willing to have him preach on Sunday, conduct funerals, and perform weddings, even though they may not consider him their educational or social equal. However, any departure from the established norms in his personal life, or that of his family, causes loss of prestige.[25] In the rural community gossip about the minister and his family is common, related chiefly to any moral shortcomings

[24] Mark A. May, and others, *The Education of American Ministers*, Vol. II, *The Profession of the Ministry*, pp. 141–142. New York: Institute of Social and Religious Research, 1934.

[25] See, for example, the book by Hartzell Spence, *Get Thee Behind Me*. New York: McGraw-Hill Book Co., 1942.

that may become apparent or which may be invented by the purveyors of such gossip.

In his description of the religious life of a rural New York community in the early history of its development, J. M. Williams indicated the qualifications required of a minister in these words:

> . . . The minister was not only the leader in worship but the exemplar of righteousness. He must be consistent in everything. He was, like the farmer, primarily a man of action, not of thought. His business was to declare dogma and the Christian standards of conduct and to practice what he preached. The preferred type of minister was the "straightforward man," erect in bearing, unequivocal in thought, frank even to bluntness in expression, consistent in thought and action. There must be no compromise with worldliness. The minister must believe not only in temperance but in total abstinence and "come out fair and square for it." . . . [26]
>
> The minister was expected to exemplify in his words and manner the spirit of unworldliness. His black apparel, dignified mien and "set" facial expression evidenced self-restraint . . . [27]

Unless the minister exemplified all of these virtues, Williams points out, "his intercessions for the beneficent intervention of providence would not be successful." It was therefore a matter of "public concern" how the minister lived and behaved. But by the same token, "the minister was regarded with awe" because he "stood thus near to God." [28]

**The pastor's concept of his role.** That there is a general pattern in Christian culture as to the role of the minister has already been indicated in the previous discussion of what the community expects of him. Basically his function is to preach, administer the ordinances of the church, and perform pastoral services, including the personal counselling of members and giving assistance to the poor and troubled.

In general, the minister tends to conform to the established pattern laid out for him in the group tradition. Not infrequently, however, he finds his own conception of his role somewhat at variance with that prescribed by the group. Thus one young

---

[26] James M. Williams, *Our Rural Heritage*, p. 144. New York: Alfred A. Knopf, 1925. Used by permission of F. S. Crofts and Co., copyright owner.
[27] *Ibid.*, p. 145.   [28] *Ibid.*, p. 145.

minister, known to the author, desired to undertake in a rural parish a number of pastoral and community activities outside the conventional pattern in that community and found himself "up against a stone wall." "They call me the preacher," he said, "and do not expect me to do anything besides preach to them on Sundays." Fresh out of college and the seminary, he was full of enthusiasm to engage in many community activities which the group considered "secular" in nature and therefore not proper for the minister. Another minister reported that he would like to inaugurate in his church a recreational program for young people, but, as he put it, "the congregation won't let me."

Still other ministers suffer considerable frustration in the knowledge that, because of their superior intellectual training as compared with that of the congregation, their interpretation of the doctrines of the church, if honestly presented, would not conform to that of the people whom they serve. Rather than "shock" the congregation, they conform their sermons to the conventional pattern or frequently move to some other charge where the intellectual environment is more congenial.

Conflicting conceptions of the role of the minister are inevitable between the congregation and the pastor, but have undoubtedly been amplified by the rapid changes in the general culture to which the church as an institution is slow to adjust. Patience, tolerance, and the general diffusion of enlightenment are called for on the part of both pastor and congregation. The primary responsibility will naturally rest upon the professional leader. It is his task to take his congregation from where they are to where he would like them to be.

**What the minister does.** A specific "job description" of the position of minister reveals a long gamut of tasks outside those which might ordinarily be included in the broad categories mentioned. H. Paul Douglass lists sixty activities of urban churches, though not all of them may be performed by any one minister and though there is variation among different areas.[29]

On the basis of a series of interviews with rural ministers

[29] H. Paul Douglass, *The Church in the Changing City*. New York: George H. Doran Co., 1927.

in Windham County, Connecticut, and McHenry County, Illinois, May divides the work of the minister under the following headings: (1) propagation of the message, (2) work with individuals, (3) activities connected with organization and administration of the parish, and (4) community and interdenomination activities.[30]

Under propagation of the message are included such activities as conducting church services; officiating at baptisms, weddings, and funerals; general reading and study; preparation of sermons, lectures, and addresses. Some of them gave considerable time to scouting, leading discussion groups, supervising daily Bible schools, teaching confirmation classes, supervising Sunday school, and so on.

In the work with individuals were included such functions as pastoral visits, emergency calls, social calls, conferences on intimate personal matters, and pastoral attendance at church meetings and social gatherings.

Under the general heading of administrative duties were listed such activities as planning the work of the church, correspondence, supervising church activities, conferences with staff members, financial plans and budget work, and getting out calendars and bulletins.

Community and civic work involved the ministers in community chest drives, young people's club work, and other social service work. Most of the ministers participated regularly in collecting goods and clothing for the poor.

What a rural minister actually does is well illustrated by the following report of one day's activities of one of those interviewed. When asked what his regular duties were he said:

At my graduation from the seminary I could have very well described how I would spend a typical day in the parish; but experience has changed that. In my ideal picture, I was to give the mornings to study and the afternoons to calling. But things don't work out that way.

I have so much fiddling around to do that it is hard to say where my real work begins and my chores leave off. Preaching is my most important work; but just to give you an idea of what we small-town clergymen face, I will tell you what I did yesterday. Let's see—yes, I guess yesterday would be as nearly a typical day as I could select.

[30] Mark A. May and others, *op. cit.*, p. 151 ff.

I really started before the day began. Our baby was not well and, since we have three children and a limited budget, I have to play nurse-maid no little part of the time. The church people call on my wife for a certain amount of her time, and she has to have help. As I started to say, I was up with the baby quite a good deal last night. We got everything cleared away and the children off to school at nine o'clock. After that I took fifteen minutes to prepare my church notices for Sunday and then delivered them to the editor's office. I met some of my men and they wanted to talk about first one thing and another. I got home about ten-thirty. I started to read an article in the ——— Herald. This was a very good article about a minister who worked out a stunt to get a crowd out for services. But about the time I got well started, Mrs. ——— called and wanted to discuss the midweek prayer topic. The topic for this month is on the book of Revelation, and there has been considerable difference of opinion about the meanings of the dragons. We have only a few of the older people at the meetings, but a fellow has to chew the rag with them. They have always had prayer meetings, and I guess they always will. After finishing with Mrs. ——— I had a meeting with the Scout executive (I am assistant scoutmaster) and finished up with a short talk to the Kiwanis Club. (I once was president.) I got home at 1:30 and took a short nap. . . . I helped the wife with some washing and cleaning. By this time some of the boys had come in for their work at the church play-shop. I gave a few minutes with the boys and then spent an hour with the church treasurer trying to get some of our back pledges on the church budget. I got back to the house at 5:30. Mrs. ——— from the Ladies' Aid was there, and we worked on plans for the bazaar and picked out some songs for a funeral I am to hold on Friday. I helped the wife get the children ready for bed. In the evening I went to the Masonic meeting. I belong to this outfit. A fellow more or less has to pull wires in a town like this. Well, this is about the way I spend most of my time. I don't get leisure for study. I read mostly from the church papers and daily press.[31]

From this statement of a day's work in the life of the minister, it is to be noted that much of his time is spent in purely routine activities as getting out church notices, planning for prayer meetings and funerals, consideration of church budget and collections, attending and speaking at meetings, and planning for the bazaar. The confession that he has no leisure for study is significant indeed. In a rapidly changing world one would expect that keeping abreast of these changes should

[31] *Ibid.*, pp. 145, 146.

occupy a good deal of the minister's time. Nevertheless, the minister works long hours, reported by the survey as around 11 hours a day including Sunday.[32]

## SUMMARY

1) Functions of the church include teaching, exhortation, provision for communal religious activities, welfare and recreation, personal counselling of members, and acting as one of the agencies of social control.

2) There are three general forms of church organization: the congregational, the episcopal, and a combination of the two. Certain social consequences derive from each form.

3) Membership in a church is voluntary, in contrast with membership in most other major institutions.

4) The number of denominations and sects increased from 212 in 1926 to 256 in 1936; but 96 per cent of the total church membership is contained in 36 denominations with 100,000 or more members each.

5) Average membership per church was 280 in 1936, with regional variations from 145 in the East South Central States to 605 in New England.

6) Protestant churches predominate in rural America; Catholic Churches are only 20 per cent rural; and Jewish congregations are less than 1 per cent.

7) Financial support of churches is voluntary and varies widely between rural and urban groups and with general economic conditions. Rural churches are, generally speaking, inadequately financed. Ministers are poorly paid.

8) The clergy of rural churches frequently serve more than one congregation and often four or more.

9) The conflicts which often occur between members of the community in their concepts of the role of the minister and the concept which the minister himself has of his functions, sometimes lead to subtle difficulties of a social psychological nature. This is an area which calls for further study. Pastors need more leisure and opportunity for study in order to keep up with developments in a changing world.

[32] *Ibid.*, p. 144.

## QUESTIONS FOR DISCUSSION

1. Analyze your own church with reference to the five elements indicated in the first part of the chapter.
2. Give illustrations other than those listed in the text of churches which would classify in each of the three types of organizations, i.e., congregrational, episcopal, and combination of the two.
3. Can it be successfully argued that the relatively large number of churches in relation to population in the Southern states is evidence of greater religiosity of the people in that area? Why or why not?
4. In the training of rural ministers is it (a) unimportant, (b) desirable, or (c) necessary that they have some knowledge of technical agriculture, that is, of the processes of plant and animal production? Why?
5. If you were made a member of a committee of a church to assist in the selection of a minister, what criteria would you use in judging various applicants?
6. Should the community expect the minister to participate in the secular affairs of the community, or should he more properly spend his entire time in strictly church activities? Give reasons.
7. Church membership in the United States has been growing more rapidly than the population. What explanation do you suggest for this trend?
8. Consult the library regarding the best-selling books of the past ten years and find out how many deal with religious subjects. Account for your findings.

## SELECTED REFERENCES

The latest statistical information regarding churches published by the United States Census is that contained in the *Census of Religious Bodies: 1936*. Congress failed to appropriate funds for the 1946 or the 1956 censuses. Data on membership of the major bodies are published annually along with some other information in the *Yearbook of American Churches*, published by the National Council of Churches, 297 Fourth Avenue, New York.

Anderson, W. A. "Social Participation and Religious Affiliation in Rural Areas," *Rural Sociology*, 9:242–250, 1944.

Fry, C. Luther. *The U.S. Looks at Its Churches*. New York: Institute for Social and Religious Research, 1930.

Goldschmidt, Walter. *As You Sow*, Chapter 5. New York: Harcourt, Brace and Company, 1947.

Hamilton, C. Horace, and Ellison, J. M. "The Negro Church in Rural Virginia." *Virginia AES Bulletin 273.* June, 1930.

Hoffer, C. R. "Activities of Churches in Town-Country Communities." *Michigan AES Special Bulletin 226.* August, 1932.

Hostetler, John A., and Mather, William G. "Participation in the Rural Church," *Pennsylvania AES Paper No. 1762 Journal Series.* 1952.

Kaufman, Harold F. "Religious Organization in Kentucky," *Kentucky AES Bulletin 524.* 1948.

Kolb, J. H., and Brunner, Edmund deS. *A Study of Rural Society,* Fourth Edition, Chapter 20. Boston: Houghton Mifflin Company, 1952.

Kumlein, W. F. "The Social Problem of the Church in South Dakota," *South Dakota AES Bulletin 294.* May, 1935.

Landis, Benson Y. *Rural Church Life in the Middle West.* New York: George H. Doran Co., 1923.

Leiffer, Murray H. *The Layman Looks at the Minister.* New York: Abingdon-Cokesbury Press, 1947.

Mather, W. J., Jr. "The Rural Churches of Allegheny County." *Cornell University AES Bulletin 587.* March, 1934.

Myrdal, Gunnar. *An American Dilemma: The Negro Problem and Modern Democracy,* Vol. 2, Chapter 40, "The Negro Church." New York: Harper and Brothers, 1944.

Nelson, Lowry. *American Farm Life in the Twentieth Century,* Chapter 8. Cambridge: Harvard University Press, 1954.

Sanderson, Dwight. *Rural Sociology and Rural Social Organization,* Chapter 15. New York: John Wiley and Sons, 1942.

Smith, Rockwell. *The Church in Our Town.* New York and Nashville: Abingdon-Cokesbury Press, 1945.

Sneed, Melvin W., and Ensminger, Douglas. "The Rural Church in Missouri." *University of Missouri AES Research Bulletin 225.* June, 1935.

Sorokin, P. A.; Zimmerman, C. C.; and Galpin, C. J. *A Systematic Source Book in Rural Sociology,* Vol. II, pp. 343–357; 373–385. Minneapolis: University of Minnesota Press, 1931.

*The Catholic Digest,* St. Paul, Minn. Various issues commencing in November, 1952.

# CHAPTER 19

# THE RURAL SCHOOL: I

Some form of instruction for the young is one of the basic characteristics of human societies, whether primitive or advanced. While a great deal of education is informally or casually acquired, we are concerned here with the formal and institutionalized arrangements which society provides.

## ROLE IN SOCIETY

**The transmission of culture.** The school is a prime instrument by which elements of the group culture are transmitted to the new generation. Obviously, the school shares this function with other institutions and agencies. The family group plays a particularly important part in passing on to the newcomer the folkways and mores, for it is the first group with which the child has any experience. The family provides the environment in which the child acquires ability to communicate through language, learns the simpler habits of living such as eating and dressing, and is taught the approved and disapproved patterns of behavior. The associations of the child in the neighborhood play group and in the church also contribute to the transmission of culture. Nevertheless, the school bears a major responsibility in this respect, particularly in teaching the basic skills of reading, writing, and the use of numbers, which are virtually indispensable to full and satisfying participation in the group life.

**An instrument of social progress or "image" of culture.** There is a strong tendency to regard education as an all-important means of "reform," a device for bringing about desirable changes in society. One hears education discussed as the means of solving such problems as crime and delinquency, the low standard of living, malnutrition, disease, inefficiency in the labor force, and the preservation of democracy. Says Clark Wissler:

. . . the fact is that we seek to solve every difficulty by education. . . . No matter what it may be, the combating of disease, the inauguration of a new public service, the appreciation of art, dress reform, or anything of that kind, we look to education to make it universal and popular.[1]

That education can contribute greatly to these ends is undeniable, but it must be borne in mind that the school itself is a creature of the group and as such is inevitably a reflection of group sentiments and ideals. The school does not exist in a social vacuum, an institution apart and insulated from the community itself. This idea is magnificently expressed by Durkheim as translated and quoted by White:

. . . [Education] is only the image, the reflection of society. Education imitates society and reproduces it in abridged form, but it does not create it. Education is healthy when the nation itself is in a healthy state, but, not having the power of self-modification, it becomes corrupt when the nation decays. If the moral milieu as it is experienced by the teachers themselves is corrupt, they cannot fail to be affected by it; how then can they impress upon those whom they train an outlook that differs from the one they have received? Each generation is brought up by the previous generation and it is necessary therefore to reform the latter if it is to improve the one which follows it. We go around in circles. At long intervals it may well happen that someone may come along whose ideas and aspirations are in advance of those of his contemporaries, but the moral constitution of a people is not made over by those isolated individuals. No doubt it pleases us to believe that one eloquent voice is sufficient to transform the social fabric as if by magic, but here as elsewhere, something is not produced from nothing. The strongest wills cannot create out of nothing forces which do not exist, and failures in experience always come to dispel these easy illusions. Besides, even though a pedagogical system could succeed by an incomprehensible miracle in establishing itself in antagonism to the social system, it would have no effect by reason of this very antagonism. If the collective organization (society) is maintained from which the moral state that one wishes to combat is derived, then the child cannot fail to be influenced by it from the moment he comes into contact with it. The

---

[1] Clark Wissler, *Man and Culture*, p. 7. New York: The Thomas Y. Crowell Company, 1923. Quoted by permission. See also an excellent statement by Leslie A. White, "Education: America's Magic," *School and Society*, 61:1588, June 2, 1945, p. 353.

artificial milieu of the school can only protect him for a time and then but feebly. In proportion as the real world takes greater hold of him, it will destroy the work of the educator. Thus education cannot reform itself unless society itself is reformed. And in order to do that we must go to the causes of the malady from which it suffers.[2]

Faith in education as a panacea for our ills tends to impose upon the schools and the teaching profession a responsibility which they should not be expected to bear alone. What the schools do and what they can do is determined by the temper, the tradition, and the will of the entire community, of which the schools are only a part.

### FACTORS IN RURAL SOCIETY AFFECTING THE SCHOOL

**Pattern of settlement.** The rural school, and characteristically the one-room school, developed from the isolated farmstead pattern of settlement of the land. (See Chapter 4.) The wide dispersal of families on separate farms made it impossible to have more than a small number of pupils per school. The lack of roads which were passable the year around made it mandatory that the schoolhouse be located within walking distance of the homes of the students. Thus the rural school was in the beginning, and remains largely so today, a neighborhood institution maintained by a small number of families within easy physical access to it. This also made for the creation of local areas of administration, and as a result we have today the numerous small school districts throughout rural America.

**The seasonal character of agriculture.** The occupation of agriculture requires much labor in the planting and harvesting season, with a consequent demand for the help of children of farm families in the fall and spring. This fact has made it difficult to maintain a school term of a length which is desired by educators and readily achieved in town and city schools. In 1940, there were 18 states which reported less than 170 days of school for their rural schools, although in every case except one they had more than 170 days of school for urban children.[3] In

---

[2] Leslie A. White, *op. cit.* The quotation is from Emile Durkheim, *Le Suicide,* Paris, 1897, pp. 427, 428.

[3] "Statistics of State School Systems, 1939–40 and 1941–42," p. 126. United States Office of Education, Government Printing Office, 1944.

Mississippi the rural schools had only 125 days, although the urban schools had 175. Alabama reported 129 days for its rural schools and 173 for its urban schools.

**Inadequate tax base for school support.** The wealth and income of rural people is inadequate to support rural schools on a level of efficiency comparable with that of the city. Although most of the states now provide some additional support for rural schools from state funds, the tradition of local responsibility for financing schools still leaves the major burden to be borne by the local residents. In 1939–1940, 61.3 per cent of revenue receipts came from the local districts. The small size of the average rural school district and the necessary dependence upon revenue from taxes upon farm land in most cases, results in generally inadequate financial support. The low salaries of teachers and their poor technical preparation for the job, and other unfavorable conditions are the inevitable results. The shorter school term is also partially a consequence of this situation, as well as that noted above.

**Population factors.** Since the size of the school enrollment depends upon the number of children born into the population, the relatively high birth rate in the farm population means a heavier educational responsibility than is carried by urban groups. The comparison in terms of proportions of children in the rural and urban groups is shown in Figure 67. While it will be noted that the proportion of school-age children has declined in all population segments during the ten-year period, the decline has not altered the relative position of the rural groups to the urban.

In connection with population factors, the excessive migration of rural people in certain rural areas, particularly those where high rates of tenancy exist, poses an additional problem for the school. The children of tenant families in the South, for example, are frequently taken out of school in the late winter when the family moves to another farm located in another school district. The result is retardation of the child and consequent discouragement. In the case of the seasonal migratory wage workers in agriculture the problem is aggravated because the family is required to move several times during the harvesting and planting seasons.

**Ethnic composition.** Another factor of great importance in the

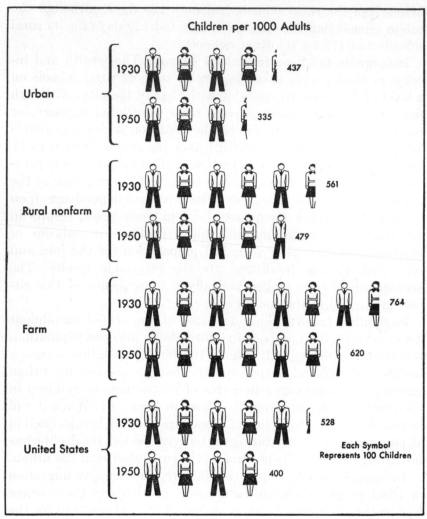

Children per 1000 Adults

Urban
1930    437
1950    335

Rural nonfarm
1930    561
1950    479

Farm
1930    764
1950    620

United States
1930    528
1950    400

Each Symbol
Represents 100 Children

Bureau of the Census

FIGURE 67. *Number of Children of School Age (5 to 19 Years) per 1,000 Persons of Working Age (20 to 64 Years) for Urban and Rural Populations, 1930–1950*

rural South is the existence of two races, which by virtue of the traditions of racial segregation requires the maintenance of two sets of schools in the same area, where otherwise one school would suffice. It happens to be true, also, that the South is predominantly rural and the total wealth available for the support of schools is grossly inadequate. Where wealth must be shared by duplicate sets of institutions, the result is merely a sharing of poverty. Usually, if not always, the Negro schools suffer most, receiving only a fifth or a fourth as much per capita school support as the whites.

There can be little doubt, too, that rural schools in certain areas are heavily influenced by the persistence of Old World traditions in certain ethnic groups. It is well known, for example, that some branches of the Mennonite Church have pronounced negative attitudes towards the secular education of their children. They resist especially education beyond the eighth grade and accept it under considerable duress. In this respect, the Old Order Amish sect is a notable instance, though the Hutterian Brethren have somewhat similar attitudes. The low ranking in school attendance of farm boys and girls of a number of northern states—notably Minnesota, Wisconsin, and North Dakota—is in all probability a reflection, in part, of the attitudes of certain ethnic groups which compose the population.[4]

**Rural attitudes towards education.** While in general the people of rural America have shown considerable devotion to education for their children, the fact remains that there has been in various times and places more or less indifference. One instance is the opposition to compulsory school-attendance laws, an opposition based on the fear that the farmer would be deprived of the labor of his children during the busy seasons on the farm. Moreover, there has been misgiving on the part of farm people that the school would "educate their children away from the farm" or indeed away from all liking for manual labor. M. T. Matthews reports the following reaction of a local leader of a community in the Tennessee mountains:

> After the school has teached 'em all it knows, they ain't fittin' for nothin' any more. You couldn't git one of 'em in twenty feet of a plow. And if you did, they wouldn't know "Gee" from "Haw." They won't tech nothin' but easy jobs, and there ain't none of *them* any more. All they want to do is play basketball an' chase up an' down the road yander. I'll tell you what the school does to them. It makes 'em plum p'nt blank lazy.[5]

[4] See Lowry Nelson, "Education of Minnesota's Farm Population," *Minnesota AES Bulletin 377*, June, 1944.

[5] M. Taylor Matthews, *Experience Worlds of Mountain People, Contributions to Education 700*, p. 19. New York: Teachers College, Columbia University, 1937.

The criticism of education by farm people, however, usually is not directed at the whole establishment, but at particular aspects of it. They have frequently expressed mild disapproval of the addition of certain subjects to the curriculum and the maintenance of a too-elaborate program of extracurricular activities. For example, farm people have been known to suggest that farm boys and girls should get their physical exercise doing useful jobs around the farm and home outside of school hours. There has been opposition to the building and equipping of gymnasiums for physical education programs. Such subjects as art and music are frequently regarded as "frills" and not a proper part of the school program.

While critical attitudes towards education undeniably exist in rural sections, one must not lose sight of the fact that by and large it has been farm people who have supported public education in this country. The school was always one of the first institutions, if not the first, established by the settlers on the frontier. While its standards of performance have not attained those achieved by urban schools, the rural school has steadily improved in several respects. The proportion of children attending has increased, as has also the average length of the school term. There have been steady improvements in the school curriculum and in the training required of teachers, although on both these counts the rural school still lags far behind the urban.

## THE SCHOOL AS A SOCIAL INSTITUTION

As a social group the school is an association of teachers and students. It is an institution formally created by society for the purpose of assisting the young in learning the cultural traditions of the group, including the effective use of the fundamental tools of reading, writing, and the use of numbers. The membership of the association is made up of children of "school age." At least up to the age of 14, membership in a school group is compulsory in all states of the United States and in most countries of the world. In several states of the Union the compulsory age of school attendance is 16 and in some 18. The school, therefore, is an institution in which the membership has had nothing to say about policies, structure, or program, nor are they expected to have. They *accept* the school as given. Attendance being compulsory under edict of the state, parents are liable to penalty under the law for failure to send their children to school. In a sense, parents themselves may be involuntary participants.

**The teacher as leader.** The leader in this social group is the teacher. Before the days of universal public education, the organization of a school was usually the result of the initiative of the teacher who hung out his shingle, as it were, and announced that he was prepared to conduct a school for the community. This is still the practice in some aspects of contemporary education, especially in the field of the arts—music, painting, and the like. Today, however, the teacher in the public school is employed by the local board of education, after having satisfied the minimum requirements of the state for certification. She is therefore a leader only in the sense of being the holder of a position created by the public and in which she is installed. She is the supreme authority in the school group. The students *have* to come to her. She is not dependent upon them for her authority or election to the position. Yet the teacher does not function without limitations on her authority. She is restricted in many ways, both by formal regulations and by mores of the community.

However, an effective teacher does not rely wholly upon her status as *nominal* leader, exercising dominance over the pupils and enforcing discipline like a policeman. Rather, she attempts to develop for herself *real* leadership status through activating those processes of social interaction between the individual and the group by which such leadership is established. The fact remains, however, that as a social group the school is a somewhat unusual one, as regards membership and the relation of leader to the led.

**Interaction between teacher and student.** The nature of the interaction between student and teacher varies greatly among schools. It is largely a function of the personality of the teacher, and the relations will vary as the individuality of teachers varies. There will be found, on the one hand, teachers who rely for the maintenance of order on the strict enforcement of rules and regulations and punishment of offenders against disciplinary rules. On the other, are resourceful teachers who secure discipline in less suppressive ways, through making the subject matter interesting, establishing close personal rapport with pupils, and by various means stimulating each pupil to achieve his maximum performance. With such a teacher, discipline in the usual sense is no problem because it is maintained automatically by the students themselves. It is obvious, however, that within these extremes there are innumerable variations in the "tone" of school groups.

Within the involuntary pattern of the school group other and more spontaneous subgroups arise. Students have the prerogative, and are usually encouraged, to form voluntary associations to express various interests. Thus, there may be literary societies, debating clubs, music clubs, and game groups of various kinds. In the formation of such groups the teacher may act as catalytic agent or advisor, but since the organizations themselves are usually regarded as effective auxiliary aids to the education of the future citizens of the nation, the ideal is to grant as much freedom of action and expression and to assign as much responsibility as possible. To this extent the school group is a microcosm of the Great Society, in which are manifested all of the social processes of competition and conflict, dominance and subordination, acculturation, assimilation, cooperation, and the rest.

The school—in F. S. Chapin's classification [6]—is a "nucleated" or "localized" institution. As such it has certain "material culture traits" associated with it. It has, for example, a school building in which to conduct its activities. It has varying amounts of equipment in desks, books, and other essentials.

Also, schools come to possess certain culture traits of symbolic significance in the form of school colors, pennants, class pins, and the like. These attributes are not so common in the simpler elementary schools of the countryside, but are practi-

[6] See F. S. Chapin, *Contemporary American Institutions*, pp. 15–16. New York: Harper and Brothers, 1935. The author classifies social institutions as diffused or generalized and nucleated or localized. Examples of the first sort are art, language, and numbers; of the second, school, church, family, and government. Upon further analysis he found institutions to be composed of four kinds of attributes: material culture traits (buildings and other property), symbolic culture traits (flags, banners, shields, emblems), common reciprocating attitudes, and a written code, creed, or constitution.

cally universal at the high-school and college levels, where school hymns and other songs also accumulate as part of the school tradition. In upper school levels, also, students are organized under constitutions and bylaws, and manifest attitudes of loyalty and patriotism.

## SCHOOL ADMINISTRATION UNITS

The pattern of organization of the school has already been indicated, in general. It should be specified, however, that a particular public school has back of it, or above it, an organized school district, which has certain relationships to the county and to the state. In some states the county itself is the local school district. Most of the affairs of the local school district are administered by the board of trustees, chosen by the people at an election held for the purpose. In those states where the county is the local unit, a county school board is elected by the people. It employs a county superintendent, who administers the schools and is responsible to the county board.

In the states where the local school districts prevail— including most of the United States—the local board of trustees determines the amount of the tax to be levied in the district, employs the teachers, and, in general, administers school affairs. County superintendents are usually elective officials, with specific responsibility as a rule for the assembling and keeping of records of the various schools and for making periodic reports to the state department of education. In many states they are little more than statistical clerks, while in others they are expected to approve appointments of teachers.

The number of school districts in the United States in 1940 amounted to the staggering total of 115,384. By 1952 the number had dropped to 67,346, and was still going down. The drastic reductions had taken place in those states which had previously had over 10,000 districts. Illinois reduced the number from 12,138 to 3,484. Nebraska led the states in 1952 with 6,392, followed by Minnesota with 6,227. The Middle West remains the favorite habitat of the small school district. A number of states are on the county-unit system, having no more districts than there are counties. The trend throughout the nation is definitely towards enlarging the school administration area.

| | ONE-TEACHER SCHOOLS, 1950 AND 1941-42 | | |
|---|---|---|---|
| | 1950* | 1941-42** | Decrease |
| Iowa | 5,249 | 8,182 | 2,933 |
| Nebraska | 4,378 | 5,495 | 1,117 |
| Wisconsin | 4,143 | 5,408 | 1,265 |
| Minnesota | 4,132 | 6,008 | 1,876 |
| Missouri | 3,788 | 6,504 | 2,716 |
| Illinois | 3,767 | 8,927 | 5,160 |
| Kentucky | 3,127 | 4,158 | 1,031 |
| South Dakota | 3,122 | 3,787 | 665 |
| Kansas | 3,090 | 5,894 | 2,804 |
| Michigan | 3,000† | 5,261 | 2,261 |
| North Dakota | 2,848 | 3,280 | 432 |
| Pennsylvania | 2,431 | 4,402 | 1,971 |
| West Virginia | 2,390 | 3,090 | 700 |
| Mississippi | 1,821 | 2,684 | 863 |
| Tennessee | 1,674 | 2,425 | 851 |
| Georgia | 1,390 | 2,215 | 825 |
| Arkansas | 1,214 | 2,342 | 1,128 |
| Oklahoma | 1,188 | 2,400 | 1,212 |
| New York | 1,100 | 3,414 | 2,314 |
| Virginia | 985 | 1,738 | 753 |
| South Carolina | 980 | 1,110 | 130 |
| Montana | 862 | 1,980 | 1,118 |
| Alabama | 814 | 1,508 | 694 |
| Colorado | 719 | 1,384 | 665 |
| Maine | 676 | 1,146 | 470 |
| California | 618 | 1,384 | 766 |
| Louisiana | 669 | 986 | 317 |
| Vermont | 506 | 772 | 266 |
| Texas | 486 | 2,125 | 1,639 |
| North Carolina | 459 | 848 | 389 |
| Wyoming | 406 | 907 | 501 |
| Ohio | 348 | 732 | 384 |
| Oregon | 302 | 788 | 476 |
| Florida | 262 | 608 | 346 |
| New Mexico | 241 | 454 | 213 |
| Indiana | 240 | 871 | 631 |
| Washington | 166 | 379 | 213 |
| Maryland | 165 | 306 | 141 |
| Idaho | 139 | 601 | 462 |
| New Jersey | 130 | 123 | +7 |
| Massachusetts | 100† | 176 | 76 |
| New Hampshire | 99 | 288 | 189 |
| Nevada | 90 | 113 | 23 |
| Connecticut | 86 | 172 | 86 |
| Arizona | 80 | 136 | 56 |
| Delaware | 42 | 81 | 39 |
| Utah | 31 | 47 | 16 |
| Rhode Island | 25 | 41 | 16 |
| | 61,247 | 107,692 | 46,445 |

*Data for 1950 from Francis L. Chase, "Rural Education Today," *Education in Rural Communities,* Chap. IV; Fifty-First Yearbook of the National Society for the Study of Education, Part II. Chicago: University of Chicago Press (to be published), 1952. Quoted by permission of the Society

**Data for 1941-42 from the U. S. Office of Education

†Estimated

FIGURE 68. *Number of One-Teacher Schools, by States, 1950 and 1941-42*

## TYPES OF RURAL SCHOOLS

**Elementary ungraded.** The little red (usually white) school-house, fabled in song and story, is the typical rural school in America. There are 60,000 of these one-room structures scattered over the countryside in every state of the Union. There is one in the District of Columbia! Standing isolated in the open country, the one-room school was built by the pioneers at a location where it would be most accessible to the largest number of families in the neighborhood.

Figure 68 shows the number of one-teacher schools by states. It will be seen that the greatest concentration of this institution is in the upper Middle West, and, in general, the Mississippi Valley. Outside of this region, New York and Pennsylvania are the only states with any large number. Utah, with the fewest of any of the states except Rhode Island, was settled according to the farm-village pattern, so that the rural people have had graded schools from the beginning.

The number of one-teacher schools has been declining steadily over the years. This decline is due to a number of factors, including the following: (*a*) the decrease in the farm population as a result of enlargement of farms and increased technological efficiency, (*b*) the decline in the birth rate, and (*c*) the school consolidation movement, made possible by the automobile and the construction of all-weather roads throughout farm areas.

The extent of this decline since 1909–1910 is indicated in Table 32. Note that the 212,448 one-room schools then constituted 80 per cent of all school buildings in the country, while thirty years later they were less than half of the total. They have been disappearing at the average rate of about 3,800 per year. So steady and continuous a decline over the years seems to point to still further reduction, and focuses attention on certain inherent weaknesses and disadvantages.

**Disadvantages of the one-room school.** One of the most obvious disadvantages is the *small average enrollment*. The average enrollment in all rural schools in 1939–1940 was 63, compared with 353 for urban schools. But the national average obscures the wide variation among the states from 21 in the state of Maine to 156 in the state of New Jersey. Moreover,

TABLE 32. *Trend in Number of One-Room Schools in United States Since 1909–1910*

| YEAR | ALL BLDGS. IN USE | ONE-ROOM SCHOOLS | |
| --- | --- | --- | --- |
| | | NUMBER | PER CENT OF TOTAL |
| 1909–10 | 265,474 | 212,448 | 80.0 |
| 1919–20 | 271,319 | 187,948 | 69.3 |
| 1927–28 | 255,551 | 153,306 | 60.0 |
| 1929–30 | 248,117 | 148,712 | 59.9 |
| 1931–32 | 245,941 | 143,445 | 58.3 |
| 1933–34 | 242,929 | 138,542 | 57.0 |
| 1935–36 | 237,816 | 130,708 | 55.0 |
| 1937–38 | 229,394 | 121,178 | 52.8 |
| 1939–40 | 226,762 | 113,600 | 50.1 |
| 1941–42 | 222,660 | 107,692 | 48.4 |
| 1943–44 | 209,309 | 96,302 | 46.0 |
| 1945–46 | not rep'd | 86,563 | |
| 1947–48 | not rep'd | 75,096 | |
| 1949–50 | not rep'd | 60,000 | |
| Decline for period | 57,165 | 152,165 | |
| Average loss per year | 1,681 | 3,804 | |

Source: "Statistics of State School Systems—1947–48," United States Office of Education, Washington, D.C. Figure for 1949–50 estimated.

within the states there is even greater range of variation. In the state of Minnesota in 1938 there were 57 schools enrolling from 1 to 4 pupils, 783 had from 5 to 9, and 1,668 had from 10 to 14. Over 35 per cent of all ungraded schools had fewer than 15 pupils.[7] Similar conditions existed in other states.[8]

Obviously, a school maintained for fewer than five pupils is a very expensive institution on a per capita basis. Even with 15 pupils the cost per capita is high if the teacher is paid anywhere near a reasonable salary. But the small enrollment has also a social disadvantage in that the pupils are not of sufficient number to provide a stimulating and satisfactory group experience. Often there is only one or at most but few individuals in a grade; thus the stimulus of rivalry is largely absent.

[7] Minnesota Department of Education, *Bulletin 10*, 1938.
[8] See for example, "Still Sits the Schoolhouse by the Road," p. 35, Committee on Rural Education, Chicago, 1943.

**The quality of instruction is lowered by the impossibility of teacher specialization.** The rural teacher in a one-room school must be a "jack-of-all-grades" and subjects. Yet it is generally accepted as a principle that competence in teaching requires special training according to both grade and subject. It is therefore considered unfair to expect that a teacher can teach all grades with equal competence. Specialization in subject matter, while more common in the high school than in the elementary, is possible to some extent in the latter, particularly in such subjects as art, music, and physical education. The one-room teacher cannot hope to specialize in one or a few subjects, but must be prepared to teach them all *to all.*

**The teacher must also be the janitor.** In an institution as small, as simple in structure, and supported by as few people, as is the one-teacher school, no differentiation of function is possible. It usually devolves upon the teacher to start the fires in the building in the morning, to see that a supply of drinking water is brought in, and to sweep out the schoolroom after the school day ends. Sometimes one of the older students may be paid a little by the school board to do the janitor work, but not infrequently these tasks fall to the teacher. When added to the demands made upon her in the teaching function itself, these tasks make the job add up to something approaching the burdensome. At least this point has been raised often by teachers themselves as a disadvantage which they have and which their urban sisters do not.

There are some advantages claimed for the one-room school. The small enrollment gives it a tutorial character, in that the teacher shares her attention with only a few pupils and can give much individual attention to each. The charge that the ungraded school throws together pupils of various ages, to a disadvantage, is met by defenders with the argument that it therefore conforms more nearly to the family group—and nobody has criticized the family on this ground. The age differential among pupils, moreover, provides opportunity for older ones to help the younger, and both learn something in the process. In other words, the imputed disadvantage may become an educational resource under the guidance of a skillful teacher.

Besides, the very absence of regular janitorial service provides an opportunity for sharing by students of the responsibility for upkeep of the school building. Older students, especially, may be given responsibility for cleaning blackboards, building fires, getting in wood and water. Such assumption of responsibility by students is certainly not unrelated to the training for citizenship which is one of the aims of education.

The advantages and potentialities of the one-room school might well be given more serious consideration by educators, since nearly half our schools are of that sort. However, the educators have seemingly been convinced for some time that the one-room school was on the way out, and that it was merely a matter of time until it would completely disappear. This is an unwarranted assumption, as many educational leaders are coming to recognize, and definite experimentation is going forward in some states—notably in the South—looking toward the development of better methods of teaching in these small units.

### THE CONSOLIDATED SCHOOL

The merging of these small units into larger ones, or consolidation, is the answer proposed to the disadvantages listed above. It increases the number of students per school and enlarges the basis for financial support. Other advantages of the consolidated school may be listed as follows:

1) By enlarging the size of the student body, consolidation greatly increases the range and variety of social contacts for the pupil.

2) Pupils can be organized into age groups, thereby providing the younger boys and girls with opportunity for leadership and self-expression often denied when the school group is dominated by the older pupils.

3) The grading of pupils allows for the specialization of the teaching staff according to grade levels and to some extent in subject matter.

4) Buildings and equipment are more adequate and more effectively used.

5) The cost per pupil, for comparative efficiency, is less. The actual expenditure may be more than in the one-room school, but infinitely more service is purchased with the funds.

6) Better teachers can be secured by a consolidated school because of its many attractions.

7) Specialized services can be made available in the consolidated school, such as health, vocational guidance, art, and music. Extracurricular activities can be more varied and interesting because of the larger number of students.

8) The consolidated school is a *community* rather than a *neighborhood* school, and its creation will contribute an additional bond to the others which are operating to bring an effective rural community into existence.

9) On the administrative side, the consolidated district evens out the financial inequalities previously existing among small districts.

But the consolidated school is not a perfect social instrument. A number of disadvantages may be listed:

1) Being more distant from the farm home, the child is absent from the family for a longer period during the day.

2) Because of the necessity of maintaining bus schedules, and the demands of farm parents to have their children home early, the farm children are denied participation in many of the school activities which come in the late afternoon or evening.

3) Some parents fear the physical and moral risk involved in the transportation of pupils. Some drivers become careless and wrecks occur; the bus may be uncomfortably cold, or too crowded and so provide a means of spreading infectious diseases; or moral supervision may be lax.

4) Consolidation almost inevitably involves new expenses for the construction of central school buildings, to which many people object. Also, because of the added services the taxes in consolidated districts frequently are higher.

There can be little sound argument against consolidation as a general technique of improvement. There is no doubt that there are too many small inefficient educational units in the country. But farm people yield to the movement with considerable reluctance. Their opposition is due mainly to the fear that they are losing control of the school by becoming part of a larger unit, and due also to the traditional sentiment which they attach to the little school in the neighborhood. They do not like to have their children transported to a distant center. Or to put it another way, they like to have the school within easy walking distance, so that the children do not have to leave too early in the morning and arrive home too late at night.

The opposition, in short, centers mainly around the closing of *attendance units*, suggesting that farm people and educators might well consider consolidation not as a single but as a multiple proposition. It is possible to consolidate all of the small *administrative districts* in a county without closing a single school. That is, consolidation might be achieved in stages. It would likely be true most often that there is more advantage to be gained through the consolidation of *administrative* rather than *attendance units*. Yet it is of the latter that greatest discussion occurs and from which opposition to consolidation mostly develops.

To summarize: the rural school in the United States functions in an environment of great complexity, economically, socially, and ethnically. The settlement pattern of dispersed farmsteads which prevails throughout most of the country, the rural neighborhoods based partly on ethnic groups, the dual racial composition of the South—these and other factors constitute the matrix in which the one-room school was formed. This is the typical American rural school, but the number of this type is steadily declining in the face of population changes and the movement toward school consolidation. The latter is still opposed by many farm people throughout the country, partly because they are reluctant to yield the direct control of school affairs which the small school district makes possible. There are other reasons for the opposition but this is a major one. The disadvantages and advantages of the one-room and of the consolidated school need to be carefully weighed by any community considering a change.

## QUESTIONS FOR DISCUSSION

1. Discuss the proposition that "education is only the image, the reflection of society." This being true, how can education be an instrument of progress?
2. Give examples of family or community differences in attitude towards education. What explanation might be made of these differences?

3. What are the historical and geographic factors which have influenced the number and character of school administrative units in the United States?
4. Discuss the effect of World War II on the reorganization of school administration in your state.
5. Discuss the possible effect of school consolidation upon the rural community. For example, how might the enlargement of the school-attendance area influence the area of association in other aspects of community life?
6. The one-room school is frequently the sole remaining institution in the open-country neighborhood, and this is used as an argument by local people against consolidation. Discuss the merits of this argument.

### SELECTED REFERENCES

Butterworth, Julian, and Dawson, Howard A. *The Modern Rural School.* See especially Chapters 1, 2, 7, 8, and 9. New York: McGraw-Hill Book Company, 1952.

Dawson, Howard A.; Reeves, Floyd W.; and others. *Your School District.* Washington: National Education Association, 1948.

Fotzwater, C. O. "Selected Characteristics of Reorganized School Districts." *Office of Education Bulletin, 1953, No. 3.* Washington, D.C.: Government Printing Office, 1953.

Gaumnitz, Walter H., and Blose, David T. *The One-Teacher School: Its Mid-century Status. Office of Education Circular 318.* 1950.

Henry, Nelson B. (ed.) *Education in Rural Communities.* Fifty-first Yearbook of the National Society for the Study of Education, Part II. See Chapters 2, 4, and 7. Chicago: University of Chicago Press, 1952.

Isenberg, Robert M. (ed.) *The Community School and the Intermediate Unit.* 1954 Yearbook of the Department of Rural Education. Washington, D.C.: National Education Association.

Kreitlow, Burton W. *Rural Education: Community Backgrounds.* New York: Harper and Brothers. 1954.

*Rural Teachers in 1951–52. National Education Association Research Bulletin,* Vol. XXXI, No. 1, February, 1953.

Strang, Ruth, and Hatcher, Latham. *Child Development and Guidance in Rural Schools.* New York: Harper and Brothers, 1943.

Weber, Julia. *My Country School Diary.* New York: Harper and Brothers, 1946.

# CHAPTER 20

# THE RURAL SCHOOL: II

The preceding chapter dealt mainly with the one-room school, the problems associated with it, and with some of the proposed solutions to those problems. But, important as it is, the one-room school is by no means the only rural scholastic institution of significance, nor are the problems related to it the only ones which rural people have to face in the matter of education. There remain to be discussed the high school, the educational personnel and its problems, the question of what the schools should teach and, finally, the school in relation to the community.

## THE RURAL HIGH SCHOOL

The rise in importance of the public high school since World War I has had a profound effect upon the rural community. Since 1920 enrollment in public high schools of the country has trebled and the number of high schools almost doubled. Over 70 per cent of the population of high-school age are enrolled. However, the percentage of rural youth attending high school is considerably lower than that of urban young people. For 1950 the United States Census reported that for youths of 16 and 17 years, 78.8 per cent of the urban, 70.2 per cent of the rural-nonfarm, and 67.2 per cent of the rural-farm were attending school.

The importance of the high school to the rural community arises from the fact that the attendance area corresponds very closely to the trade area, or natural community. It brings farm and village populations into contact on the basis of one of the most important of community interests. The high school, as the nexus between town and country, may serve to reduce the possibilities of friction and conflict and to contribute to the emergence of the true rural community.

Several problems exist. One of the most important is that in many sections of the United States the rural high school is legally a village or town institution. That is, the village is also the school district which assumes responsibility for the maintenance of a high school which serves not only the trade center itself, but the surrounding farm area as well. The outlying farm sections, however, are not organically—legally—a part of the district, have little or nothing to say about how the school is operated, and are merely in the position of buyers of a village commodity. Usually, the village, in order to attract the farm students to the high school, will provide appropriate courses for farm boys and girls. But the fact remains that the farm people officially have very little to say about high-school education. There is, therefore, need for consolidating the farm areas and the village into a common high-school district.

**Rural high schools too small.** Another problem connected with the rural high school lies in the large number of such schools with very small enrollments. In a study of rural high schools made in 1926, W. H. Gaumnitz found that out of 14,143 schools, 43 per cent had fewer than 50 pupils and about 76 per cent had fewer than 100. Only 8 per cent of the urban high schools had fewer than 100 pupils.[1]

As late as 1952 there were 824 high schools with from 10 to 24 pupils and nearly one third of all high schools in the United States had fewer than 100. Although the schools are not reported as urban or rural, it is safe to assume that the vast majority of the small ones are rural. (See Table 33.)

The small school cannot offer an attractive curriculum to the student, and thus attendance of rural boys and girls is discouraged. The wide range in response to high-school education in the United States is indicated in Table 34, showing the percentage of farm boys and girls 16 and 17 years of age who were attending school.

**Meeting the small high-school problem.** One of the most important suggestions as to how this problem can be met has come from the state of Wisconsin. In 1935, the State Superintendent of Public Instruction appointed a committee on small

[1] W. H. Gaumnitz, "The Smallness of America's Rural High Schools," p. 7, *Bulletin 13*, United States Office of Education, 1930.

TABLE 33. *Public High Schools, by Size and Number, 1930-1952*

| ENROLLMENT | 1930 | | 1938 | | 1952 | |
|---|---|---|---|---|---|---|
| | NUMBER OF SCHOOLS | PER CENT | NUMBER OF SCHOOLS | PER CENT | NUMBER OF SCHOOLS | PER CENT |
| TOTAL | 22,237 | 100.0 | 24,590 | 100.0 | 23,746 | 100.0 |
| 10–24 | 2,077 | 9.4 | 1,372 | 5.6 | 824 | 3.5 |
| 25–49 | 3,866 | 17.4 | 2,643 | 10.7 | 1,896 | 8.0 |
| 50–74 | 3,521 | 15.8 | 3,051 | 12.4 | 2,311 | 9.7 |
| 75–99 | 2,543 | 11.4 | 2,661 | 10.8 | 2,086 | 8.8 |
| 100–199 | 4,603 | 20.7 | 6,407 | 26.1 | 6,025 | 25.4 |
| 200–299 | 1,633 | 7.3 | 2,561 | 10.4 | 3,103 | 13.0 |
| 300–499 | 1,478 | 6.7 | 2,271 | 9.2 | 3,106 | 13.1 |
| 500–999 | 1,421 | 6.4 | 1,940 | 7.9 | 2,757 | 11.6 |
| 1,000–2,499 | 934 | 4.2 | 1,444 | 5.9 | 1,536 | 6.5 |
| 2,500 or more | 161 | .7 | 240 | 1.0 | 102 | .4 |

Source: "Statistics of Public High Schools," Office of Education, Federal Security Agency, Washington, D.C.

high schools. This committee selected seven communities where local committees were created to make a self-analysis, with the aid of the state committee, of the local high school and its problems. The state committee formulated several considerations which guided them in their work. Among these considerations were the following:

1) Rural schools have too long been planned as imitations of the "superior" urban schools.

2) The children of rural people are attending high school in increasing numbers, a fact which in itself has focused interest upon problems of rural high-school education.

3) This increased attendance means that a larger proportion of high-school graduates will remain on farms and in villages, although many will continue to migrate to the city.

4) The growth of the importance of high schools as a division of formal education makes highly necessary the integration of elementary education with that offered on the high-school level.

5) The total educational structure should be more effectively related to the interests and needs of the rural community in order to achieve the goal of "better education for rural living."

These statements constitute an excellent summary of the conditions facing rural secondary education.

TABLE 34. *Rank of States in the Percentage of Rural Farm Boys and Girls 16 and 17 Years Old Who Were Enrolled in School in 1950 Compared with the Rank for 1940.*[1]

| STATE | PER CENT ATTENDING SCHOOL IN 1950 | RANK 1950 | RANK 1940 | POINTS GAINED OR LOST (−) | STATE | PER CENT ATTENDING SCHOOL IN 1950 | RANK 1950 | RANK 1940 | POINTS GAINED OR LOST (−) |
|---|---|---|---|---|---|---|---|---|---|
| Utah | 90.5 | 1 | 1 | 0 | Wisconsin | 70.9 | 25 | 44 | 19 |
| Oregon | 85.2 | 2 | 4 | 2 | Florida * | 70.7 | 26 | 32 | 6 |
| Washington | 84.1 | 3 | 2 | −1 | South Dakota | 70.3 | 27 | 33 | 6 |
| Idaho | 83.7 | 4 | 5 | 1 | Pennsylvania | 69.5 | 28 | 30 | 2 |
| Nevada | 83.3 | 5 | 6 | 1 | New Mexico | 69.1 | 29 | 20 | −9 |
| Kansas | 82.2 | 6 | 7 | 1 | Missouri | 68.4 | 30 | 35 | 5 |
| California | 81.0 | 7 | 3 | −4 | Louisiana * | 67.7 | 31 | 36 | 5 |
| Connecticut | 79.9 | 8 | 12 | 4 | Maine | 67.1 | 32 | 22 | −10 |
| Ohio | 79.4 | 9 | 8 | −1 | Texas * | 67.1 | 33 | 26 | −7 |
| Iowa | 79.3 | 10 | 21 | 11 | Rhode Island | 65.2 | 34 | 27 | −7 |
| Oklahoma * | 78.4 | 11 | 18 | 7 | North Carolina * | 65.1 | 35 | 37 | 2 |
| Massachusetts | 77.8 | 12 | 15 | 3 | North Dakota | 64.4 | 36 | 41 | 5 |
| Michigan | 77.7 | 13 | 29 | 16 | Delaware | 63.8 | 37 | 31 | −6 |
| Indiana | 77.4 | 14 | 11 | −3 | Vermont | 63.7 | 38 | 38 | 0 |
| Colorado | 76.2 | 15 | 17 | 2 | Arkansas * | 63.5 | 39 | 43 | 4 |
| Montana | 75.7 | 16 | 10 | −6 | Alabama * | 61.8 | 40 | 34 | −6 |
| Nebraska | 74.8 | 17 | 19 | 2 | South Carolina * | 61.7 | 41 | 33 | −8 |
| New Jersey | 74.8 | 18 | 24 | 6 | Maryland | 60.2 | 42 | 45 | 3 |
| Mississippi * | 74.5 | 19 | 14 | −5 | Tennessee * | 60.1 | 43 | 46 | 3 |
| Wyoming | 74.4 | 20 | 9 | −11 | Virginia * | 59.9 | 44 | 39 | −5 |
| Illinois | 74.2 | 21 | 28 | 7 | West Virginia | 59.1 | 45 | 47 | 2 |
| New York | 74.2 | 22 | 13 | −9 | Arizona | 58.7 | 46 | 25 | −21 |
| New Hampshire | 74.0 | 23 | 16 | −7 | Georgia * | 58.5 | 47 | 42 | −5 |
| Minnesota | 72.1 | 24 | 40 | 16 | Kentucky | 50.0 | 48 | 48 | 0 |

* Does not include nonwhites. Computed from Table 62, *Census of Population*, 1950.

[1] The report of the Bureau of the Census on the matter of school attendance is not strictly comparable for 1940 and 1950. Three changes were made for the 1950 enumeration as follows: 1) the question was asked of only every fifth household; 2) the word "enrollment" was used instead of "attendance"; 3) the question asked whether the child had been enrolled as of February 1 instead of March 1, as in the 1940 enumeration. It is difficult to say how much the changes in method of taking the census have influenced the differences in ranking as well as in absolute figures. Another matter should also be mentioned: the 1940 census reported percentages for the "native white population," whereas the 1950 census reported the figure for the total population. In the comparison of the rankings of the states in this table, the "nonwhite" population was subtracted from the total in the case of twelve states in the South and the percentages calculated for the white population.

## PROBLEMS TO BE MET

The following problems of rural education were recognized by the Wisconsin Committee on Rural Community High Schools:

1) The school curriculum must be made applicable to local conditions and to the present and the future needs of pupils. It is especially necessary to provide for the young people who will not go to college; about four out of every five will not do so. The village boy, in particular, is the "forgotten boy" in the public schools of Wisconsin.

2) Relations between the school and the community need to be improved. Often the community does not understand the school. The school has not found its proper place as a community institution; the school does not make proper use of community resources; the school must do more in developing community vocational and recreational activities.

3) The small rural high school in Wisconsin is generally the center of an educational area much larger than the village in which it is located. In many cases two thirds of the high school pupils come from outside the village. Many high-school pupils come from parochial elementary schools. Close cooperation between independent school districts and parochial schools is needed so that the whole twelve years of the transferring pupil's education may be properly coordinated. Plans must be developed for educational areas rather than for school districts.

4) The education, the selection, and the retention of teachers present many problems. In the past, teacher education has been too specialized and not sufficiently related to living in a small community. Teachers now in service must be helped in self-improvement, and teacher-education institutions must be shown how to change their programs. Salaries and living conditions must be made attractive enough to hold superior teachers in the rural schools.

5) The small school must learn to take full advantage of its strong points, especially the possibility of close acquaintance between parent, teacher, and pupil and the keen social consciousness that may be found in a small unified community.[2]

## TEACHERS IN THE UNITED STATES

The teaching profession is predominantly an occupation for women. Of the 1,120,605 employed teachers reported in the

[2] C. E. Ragsdale, "Rural Community High Schools Face Their Problems," *Bulletin 2*, Committee on Rural Education, Chicago, April, 1942, pp. 3–5.

1950 census, about three fourths were women. The United States Office of Education in 1950 reported 913,671 teachers, of whom 78 per cent were women. Since these figures represented all teachers of elementary and secondary schools, rural and urban, they obscured the fact that the proportions of women are much greater at the elementary level and in rural areas. A study made by the National Education Association in 1952 revealed that only 12 per cent of the rural teachers were men, a drop from 15.8 per cent reported in 1937. There is a strong likelihood that the increase in average salaries will attract more men to the profession, but the increase is too recent to have had much effect. In general, states which have a high percentage of male teachers are those which pay better salaries.

The proportion of males has been declining more or less steadily since 1880, when men constituted 43 per cent of all teachers. The lowest percentage was reached in 1920, when, obviously as a result of World War I, only 14 per cent of all teachers were men. Since that time the percentage has risen slowly to its 1940 ratio of 22.6. It declined to 20.4 in 1950.

Until World War II teachers were predominantly youthful. However, there was a wholesale desertion from the profession during the war. Moreover, the ban against employing married teachers was removed, thus permitting more older women to teach. The median age of women rose from 34 to 41.2 and that of men from 34 to 38.4 during the decade. (See Figure 69.)

**Marital status.** Not only has there been a marked change in age of teachers; their marital status has also changed. In 1939, only 26.6 per cent of teachers in one-teacher schools were married compared with 74.4 per cent in 1952.[3] School boards, as previously indicated, were glad to recruit married women during World War II and subsequent years. With the current teacher shortage school boards may be forced to relax their standards permanently with regards to married women.

If conditions similar to those which prevailed in the 1930's should return at some future time, it is probable that the employment policies would again discriminate against married women.

[3] "Rural Teachers in 1951–52," *National Education Association Research Bulletin,* Vol. 31, No. 1, February, 1953, p. 9.

396

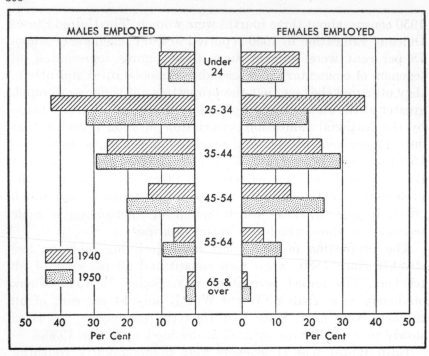

FIGURE 69. *Sex and Age Characteristics of Employed Teachers in United States, 1940 and 1950*

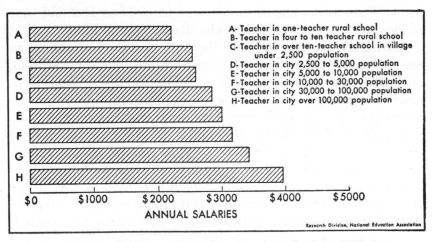

FIGURE 70. *Annual Salaries of Classroom Teachers, 1952*

**Mobility.** About 20 per cent of teachers have to be replaced annually. Mobility is related to a) amount of training, b) age composition, and c) salary level in relation to alternative job opportunities. A study of over ten thousand Arkansas teachers who left positions between terms of 1951–52 and 1952–53 showed that 46 per cent of those with one year of college moved, a rate more than twice as high as any of the higher levels of training. The older average age of the profession as well as higher salaries should reduce mobility.

**Salary of teachers.** The average salaries of teachers have risen sharply since the 1930's, when rural teachers were paid $844 and urban teachers got $1,874 per year. By 1948 rural teachers aver-

TABLE 35. *Average Salaries of Rural Teachers by Size of School*

| Type of School | Average Salary |
|---|---|
| Elementary: 1-teacher | $2,208 |
|      2- and 3-teacher | 2,423 |
|      4- to 10-teacher | 2,538 |
|      Over 10-teacher | 2,581 |
| Secondary: 10 or fewer teachers | 2,866 |
|      Over 10 teachers | 2,987 |

[4] *National Education Association Research Bulletin*, Vol. XXXI, p. 40.

aged $2,086, and urban, $3,174. For all teachers, the average salary in 1950 was $3,010, an increase from $1,441 in 1940. States differ widely in average salaries. In 1950, the average in California was $4,268 compared with an average of $1,416 paid by Mississippi. In general, the states which rank high on other educational indices, such as school attendance and median grades completed by the adult population, are paying better salaries. With the prospect of adding between 2 and 3 million children to the schools, from the high birth rates during and following World War II, the demand for teachers bids fair to exceed the supply. The increase in salaries, which since 1940 has made teaching a more inviting profession, is almost certain to be continued over in the next few decades. There is also the possibility that the differential in salaries between the states will be narrowed over the next twenty years.

The salary of teachers is associated with a number of factors including (*a*) sex, (*b*) size of school, (*c*) color, (*d*) state or region, and (*e*) amount of training and experience. In a survey made in 1952 the National Education Association [4] reported median salaries by size of school, as shown in Table 35.

In 1940, Negro teachers' salaries were little more than half those paid white teachers. However, remarkable progress has been made toward equality. By 1952, the gap was almost closed in all southern states except Mississippi and South Carolina. (See Table 36.) Indeed, in four states the salaries of Negro teachers were higher than those of whites. Salaries are geared to the amount of college training the teachers have had, consequently, the equalization of salaries reflects also the improved preparation of Negro teachers.

TABLE 36. *Salaries of Negro Classroom Teachers As a Percentage of White Salaries in Twelve Southern States, 1940–1952*

| STATE | NEGRO SALARIES AS PERCENTAGE OF WHITE | | | | |
|---|---|---|---|---|---|
| | 1952 | 1940 | | 1950 | 1940 |
| Twelve States | 87 | 54 | | | |
| Alabama | 93 | 47 | North Carolina | 103 | 73 |
| Arkansas | 79 | 59 | Oklahoma | 100 | 97 |
| Florida | 91 | 52 | South Carolina | 75 | 43 |
| Georgia | 93 | 45 | Tennessee | 105 | 76 |
| Louisiana | 86 | 37 | Texas | 96 | 61 |
| Mississippi | 51 | 30 | Virginia | 103 | 61 |

Source: Harry S. Ashmore, *The Negro and the Schools*, p. 159. Chapel Hill: University of North Carolina Press, 1954.

There has traditionally been a difference in salaries paid to men and women teachers. In recent years the profession has campaigned for equal pay for equal jobs. Moreover, school boards have found it necessary to bid high to get Winnie to leave her welding job. Differences in salaries based upon sex are gradually disappearing. In April, 1952, the National Education Association announced that about 20 per cent of the urban school districts covered by their inquiry pay men more than they pay women. Nine per cent pay Negroes less than white teachers. In all cases the smaller the urban center the larger the proportion reporting these discriminations. None of the larger cities reported any variations in pay by sex or color.

In addition to increased income, teachers have been the recipients of more fringe benefits. Most states have retirement provisions for teachers, as well as regulations governing tenure, which protect against unjust dismissal.

**Preparation.** Fifty years ago the average teacher in the elementary school had less than a high-school education. Since that time the standards for certification of teachers have steadily risen until today there are comparatively few teachers who have not had at least one year of preparation beyond high school, and in the vast majority of instances, two or three years. The National Education Association reports that 77 per cent of teachers in 1-teacher schools have had at least 2 years of training beyond high school. In city schools a higher per cent would fall in this group. Most urban schools not only meet the minimum standards set for certification, but frequently go beyond them in requiring additional preparation by the teachers whom they employ. Rural schools have difficulty meeting the minimum standards; during the emergency of World War II large numbers of rural teachers were employed under "emergency certificates" which did not meet the state standards. In the matter of teaching experience, also, the rural schools fall below the urban schools. In the 1-room schools the median years of experience of teachers was 5, compared with 7 years for the two-teacher rural and the village schools, and from 9 to 16 years for urban schools, depending on the size of the community in which the schools were located.[5] (See Figure 72.)

**Rural-urban distribution of teachers.** If we use the statistics of the United States census for 1950, we find that 66 per cent of all teachers are residing in urban areas. The proportion is slightly higher than that for the women. About 30 per cent of men teachers reside in the rural-nonfarm population (chiefly villages of under 2,500), compared with only 22 per cent of the women. A higher proportion of the women than of the men are living in the rural-farm areas. The large proportion of men in the rural-nonfarm group is no doubt due to the fact that the high schools are located in these centers, and their faculties usually contain a larger proportion of men than do

---

[5] "The Status of the Teaching Profession," *National Education Association Research Bulletin,* Vol. XVIII, No. 2, March, 1940, p. 55.

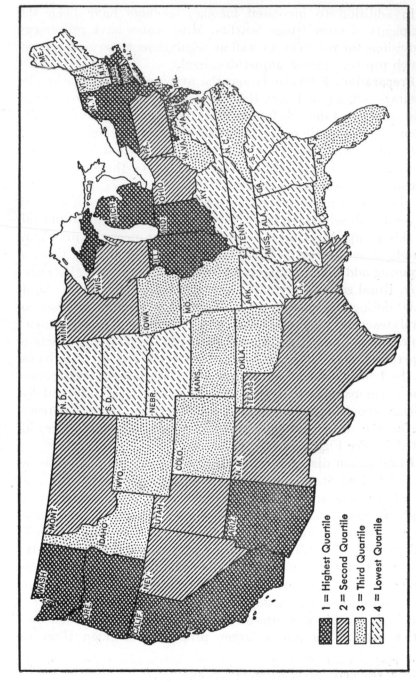

FIGURE 71. *Variations in Average Salaries of Teachers, Supervisors, and Principals, by States Grouped in Quartiles, 1950*

1 = Highest Quartile
2 = Second Quartile
3 = Third Quartile
4 = Lowest Quartile

FIGURE 72. *Years of Experience of Teachers by Size of Location*

the rural elementary schools. (See Table 37.) The Office of Education data allocate teachers according to place of employment and its figures present a different picture of rural-urban distribution, with more than half of all teachers classed as rural.[6] It is obvious from these figures that the country has more teachers in proportion to population than does the city.

TABLE 37. *Rural-Urban Distribution of Teachers, 1950*

| SEX | UNITED STATES | | URBAN | | RURAL-NONFARM | | RURAL-FARM | |
|---|---|---|---|---|---|---|---|---|
| | No. | Per cent | No. | Per cent | No. | Per cent | No. | Per cent |
| Total | 1,127,854 | 100.0 | 754,039 | 66.0 | 270,452 | 24.0 | 112,354 | 10.0 |
| Male | 288,009 | 100.0 | 178,840 | 62.1 | 84,605 | 29.4 | 24,564 | 8.5 |
| Female | 839,836 | 100.0 | 566,199 | 67.4 | 185,847 | 22.1 | 87,790 | 10.5 |

Source: *Census of Population, 1950*, Vol. II, Part I.

**Rural-urban inequalities.** Despite the general assumption that we provide education for everyone, there are sharp differences between the rural and urban sections and between the various states in the amount and the quality of education offered the young. The accompanying Table 38 compares rural and urban education on a number of factors. The rural schools

[6] "Statistics of State School Systems, 1935–36," United States Office of Education.

TABLE 38. *Comparison of Rural and Urban Public Schools, 1950*

|  | URBAN | RURAL |
|---|---|---|
| Population 1950 | 88,927,460 | 61,769,897 |
| Population 5–17 years | 17,186,000 | 13,548,000 |
| Per cent of total | 19.3 | 21.9 |
| Pupils enrolled, 1950 | 14,350,000 | 10,954,000 |
| Per cent | 83.5 | 80.9 |
| Average length of school term | 183 | 172 |
| Per cent of pupils in average daily attendance | 85.7 | 86.9 |
| Average salary of instructors | $3,174 | $2,056 |
| Current expenditures per pupil | $206 | $173 |
| Capital outlay per pupil | $12 | $19 |
| Per cent male teachers | 22 | 18 |
| Number pupils per teacher | 24.5 | 21.9 |

Source: Population and enrollment figures from *Census of Population 1950;* other data from Rose Marie Smith, "Education in Rural and City School Systems: Some Statistical Indices for 1947–48," *United States Office of Education Circular No. 329,* 1951. (Based on reports from 36 states.)

exceed the city only in the proportion of children to be educated, the percentage of attendance, and capital outlay.

Some inequalities among states undoubtedly still exist in per-pupil expenditures for education. (See Figure 73.) In large measure this variation is also a reflection of rural-urban inequalities, since it is in the more largely rural states that expenditures are least. Federal grants-in-aid are the only way of leveling out such differences. In general, it may be said that rural-urban differences are diminishing rapidly.

## THE RURAL SCHOOL CURRICULUM

What the rural schools should teach is a matter of continuing controversy among educators and among school patrons. There are those who think the school should not go beyond teaching children the three R's. Others argue for the enrichment of the school curriculum by adding additional subjects such as music, art, and conservation. Still others say the rural school curriculum should emphasize the virtues of rural life in contrast with city life and should aim to prepare the pupils for life on the farm.

Back of the curriculum discussions lie the great changes in the larger society, which those responsible for the schools, including parents, should always keep in mind. Among the larger trends of paramount importance is population migration.

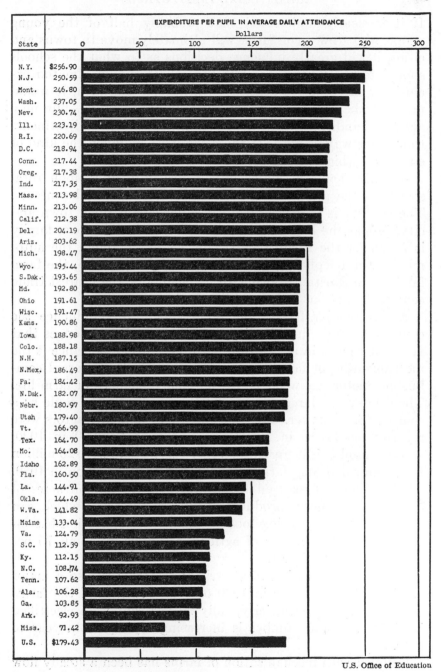

| State | Expenditure |
|---|---|
| N.Y. | $256.90 |
| N.J. | 250.59 |
| Mont. | 246.80 |
| Wash. | 237.05 |
| Nev. | 230.74 |
| Ill. | 223.19 |
| R.I. | 220.69 |
| D.C. | 218.94 |
| Conn. | 217.44 |
| Oreg. | 217.38 |
| Ind. | 217.35 |
| Mass. | 213.98 |
| Minn. | 213.06 |
| Calif. | 212.38 |
| Del. | 204.19 |
| Ariz. | 203.62 |
| Mich. | 198.47 |
| Wyo. | 195.44 |
| S.Dak. | 193.65 |
| Md. | 192.80 |
| Ohio | 191.61 |
| Wisc. | 191.47 |
| Kans. | 190.86 |
| Iowa | 188.98 |
| Colo. | 188.18 |
| N.H. | 187.15 |
| N.Mex. | 186.49 |
| Pa. | 184.42 |
| N.Dak. | 182.07 |
| Nebr. | 180.97 |
| Utah | 179.40 |
| Vt. | 166.99 |
| Tex. | 164.70 |
| Mo. | 164.08 |
| Idaho | 162.89 |
| Fla. | 160.50 |
| La. | 144.91 |
| Okla. | 144.49 |
| W.Va. | 141.82 |
| Maine | 133.04 |
| Va. | 124.79 |
| S.C. | 112.39 |
| Ky. | 112.15 |
| N.C. | 108.74 |
| Tenn. | 107.62 |
| Ala. | 106.28 |
| Ga. | 103.85 |
| Ark. | 92.93 |
| Miss. | 71.42 |
| U.S. | $179.43 |

EXPENDITURE PER PUPIL IN AVERAGE DAILY ATTENDANCE

U.S. Office of Education

FIGURE 73. Expenditure per Pupil in Average Daily Attendance, 1947–1948

If it is clearly understood that probably half of the young people who grow up on farms will ultimately move to towns and cities, it will greatly influence decisions as to what the schools should teach. If, for example, the school should aim too exclusively to teach students how to live on the farm, it would naturally benefit those who remain in the country, but may actually handicap those who leave and must make adjustments to another way of life. Yet these too must be given the kind of education which will be most helpful to them.

Another factor of major importance impinging upon rural society is the rapid expansion of the range of social contacts. The country is in a very real sense dependent upon town and city, just as the latter are dependent upon it. The farm family is no longer the isolated unit it once was. Through the automobile, the telephone, the newspaper and the radio, the farm family is in constant touch with its neighbors, the nearest trade center, the nation, and the entire world.

A third major factor which must inevitably influence the content of rural education involves the numerous changes that are taking place in agriculture itself. Of chief importance is the mechanization of farming. The invention of the internal combustion motor has wrought revolutionary changes in farm life. The tractor has largely displaced the horse and the mule as a source of farm power. Over one and a half million tractors were reported on farms in 1940 compared with 246,000 in 1920, and the number is increasing year by year. There were 25 million horses and mules on farms in 1920, and only 7 million in 1950. This decline has released the use of over 50 million acres of crop land, formerly producing feed for livestock, which can now be used for growing food for man. Mechanization has increased the productivity of agricultural labor by about 75 per cent since World War I.

The recent extension of electricity to farms is also a major consideration. Whereas in 1930 only 13 per cent of the farms were served with electricity, fully 90 per cent were electrified by 1954, and the number is increasing rapidly from year to year.

Coupled with mechanization of farms has been a steady flow of other improvements in agricultural technology. New and

higher-yielding strains of plants and animals have been introduced, more effective methods for the control of plant and animal
diseases have been found, and better methods of farm management developed. All of these developments make agriculture
an increasingly complex and difficult occupation requiring ever
greater degrees of skill and managerial efficiency. Surely the
rural schools cannot avoid recognition of these developments
in planning the educational program for the future.

**The curriculum should be dynamic.** As life is never static,
so education, if it is to be related to life, cannot remain fixed.
It must change as life and society change. This is not to say
that certain elements of the curriculum do not or should not
persist. There will always remain the necessity of teaching pupils
the fundamental skills and tools of the culture. They must learn
to read, to write, and to use numbers. They must learn history
and literature, how people live and make a living. These fundamental elements remain, but the approach to the teaching of
them and the emphasis will change as conditions change.

**Education related to life.** Perhaps one of the most vital
devices for the teacher is to try and relate subject matter to
the life-experiences of the pupils. Most textbooks used in rural
schools have been written with urban students in mind, and
the rural child finds difficulty in understanding this point of
view. Yet if the teacher uses a little ingenuity, arithmetic,
reading, and writing can be taught in terms of average daily
experiences of the rural child. Farm records and accounts can
be used as a basis for the arithmetic lesson just as well as or
better than some problem from the remote urban world.
Similarly with the other subjects the approach can be made in
terms of rural experiences. This is not to say that the child is
to be taught only in terms of rural life. It means merely that the
approach will be through common experiences that have meaning and understandability for the pupil. From such a beginning
a transition to learning of more remote situations can be made.

**The addition of new subjects.** With the typical American
faith in the magic of education have come demands at various
times to add subjects to the curriculum. "Cooperation" is one
of these; "conservation," another. Both are defensible topics
to teach rural pupils. Some states have required by statute

that "cooperation" be taught in the schools, that is, cooperative marketing, cooperative purchasing, and the like. If it is added as a formal subject to the curriculum, it obviously creates a problem in the organization of the school day by the teacher. In a one-room school with six grades, a teacher, who has to allocate a certain amount of time to each of six or more subjects to each of the grades, finds herself confronted with not less than 36 class periods during the day. The addition of another subject only adds to the complication.

One teacher in Minnesota confronted with such a problem, decided to organize a miniature cooperative in the school. As a matter of fact the students took the initiative in suggesting it. The cooperative was organized according to the state laws; each pupil became a member in the approved manner. They elected a board and a manager, who bought and sold school supplies. This wise teacher used the device as a means of teaching arithmetic, writing, and reading, not to mention the lessons in citizenship which the experience provided.[7]

Another teacher in the state of Michigan was ingenious enough to teach the principles of soil conservation to her school by having the pupils observe the gullies which water had made in the road leading up to the schoolhouse and learn how to prevent further erosion by the use of check dams and the planting of grass and shrubs.[8] In similar ways other topics can be covered in the rural school curriculum, without cluttering up the daily program. What is required is a large measure of ingenuity and ability from the teacher. An able teacher will not need to worry unduly about how to get the topics covered. Incidentally, she will not need to worry about getting or keeping a teaching job and at good pay.[9]

**Vocational training.** One of the dominant trends in American education in recent years is the vocational education movement. It has taken hold in rural as well as urban schools. In 1918 Congress passed the Smith-Hughes Act, which provided grants-

[7] Leone Davison, "Consumers' Cooperative of Centerville," *Progressive Education*, April, 1942:203–206.

[8] Iman E. Schatzmann, *Country School at Home and Abroad*, p. 167 ff. Chicago: University of Chicago Press, 1942.

[9] When the Michigan teacher referred to was offered a job elsewhere at double her salary, the school board promptly decided to match the outside offer.

in-aid to the states for introducing vocational courses in the schools. In rural schools this meant primarily high-school courses in agriculture, home economics, and mechanical arts. Teachers are employed on a year-round basis. The purpose of this steady employment is to enable them to instruct students during the school year in the "book learning" in the respective fields and then during the summer to supervise the carrying out of specific projects.

One of the problems which has been troublesome is that of getting farm boys to enroll in the first place, and then getting them to enter agriculture after the course is over. Many students who take the agricultural course go on to college for further specialization and frequently wind up as county agricultural agents or Smith-Hughes teachers themselves. Farmers, therefore, complain that for a student to take the high-school course in agriculture is tantamount to bidding him good-by so far as his becoming a future farmer is concerned. Other boys who take the course subsequently decide to go into some other occupation unrelated to agriculture. This also gives rise to rather unjust local criticism of the program, unjust because the purpose of the program in the first place was in part to provide opportunity for the student to make some vocational exploration. If, after taking the agricultural course, he decides to choose another vocation, it may be assumed that the purpose of the program has been served.

## RELATING THE SCHOOL TO THE COMMUNITY

There has been a growing consciousness among professional educators that the school has somehow become isolated from the community of which it is, in theory, an organic part. In various ways attempts have been and are being made to make the school articulate more closely with the community. One such device is the initiation by the school of community activities in which many people of the community can participate. Thus, the school comes to be a community school, one which maintains close relations with the other institutions in the community and elicits active support and participation of the adult population in its activities. It is one in which the educational process is related to the dynamic life of the community and which changes as the life of the community changes. It is a "life-related" school.

**The community project.** In initiating a community project careful planning is an indispensable prerequisite to success. There are a few simple rules which have been found helpful to teachers and others. These are listed without elaboration:

1) The project must be related to a problem of which the community is, or can easily be made, aware.
2) The project should be planned and fully discussed at various stages by representatives of the community other than the school teachers.
3) The school authorities themselves should play the role of instigator, scene-shifter, and prompter, not the main actors.
4) The project selected should be (*a*) modest in cost and effort, (*b*) productive of tangible results, (*c*) one that will arouse little opposition.
5) More pretentious projects should be undertaken only gradually and after some experience has been gained in simpler undertakings.

Some schools begin with such simple undertakings as beautification of the school grounds, equipping the building with screens, painting and redecorating the schoolhouse, and similar projects.[10]

To summarize: the rural high school, like the one-room rural school, is handicapped by its small size. Its curriculum is limited, it cannot command the better type of teacher, and the teacher is handicapped by having to cover an unreasonable range of subjects. The answer to the problem would appear to lie in consolidation of the smaller units. The teachers in the United States are predominantly single women and conspicuously youthful. Salaries are modest, men get more than women, white teachers more than colored. The rate of pay is roughly proportional to the training and years of service, but within a narrow range of incomes. There is a high rate of departure from the profession, due in part to the low salaries and in part to the fact that teachers in large numbers marry during the first few years of their careers. Rural schools compare unfavorably with the urban on almost every count. Population changes, mechanization of farming, the rapidly expanding world of rural interaction—all make it imperative that the school curriculum be flexible and adaptable to the changing social scene. Above all, the school should be functionally related to the community.

[10] See the story of Rose Dill in I. E. Schatzmann, *op. cit.*, p. 167 f.

## QUESTIONS FOR DISCUSSION

1. Some of the states which reported high rates of high-school attendance rank relatively low in ability to support education. How would you explain the differences in the *willingness* of states to support schools?
2. Why do farm girls exceed farm boys in attending high school?
3. How would you explain the fact that schoolteaching has become increasingly a profession for women in the United States?
4. Schoolteaching as an occupation appears to command greater respect in foreign countries than in the United States. (In China the scholar ranks first in prestige.) What explanation can you give for the differences?
5. One of the objections raised by teachers is that the community expects them to conform to higher standards of conduct than is the case with other public employees. Is the community justified? Compare the social roles of the teacher, the minister, the social worker, the employees in the county courthouse.
6. Suggest a number of projects which a school might sponsor in your community as devices for integrating school and community.

## SELECTED REFERENCES

Ashmore, Harry S. *The Negro and the Schools*. Chapel Hill: University of North Carolina Press, 1954.

*Biennial Survey of Education*. Washington, D.C.: United States Office of Education.

*Education for Rural Wisconsin's Tomorrow*. Committee on Rural Community High Schools, Madison. August, 1946.

Nelson, Lowry. *American Farm Life*, Chapter 7. Cambridge: Harvard University Press, 1954.

Stromberg, E. T. "The Influence of the Central High Schools on Community Organization." *Cornell University AES Bulletin 699*. 1938.

*The Federal Government and Education: A Summary of Findings and Proposals of the Advisory Committee on Education*. Washington, D.C.: Government Printing Office, 1938.

Works, George A., and Lesser, Simon O. *Rural America Today: Its Schools and Community Life*, Chapters 4, 7, 16. Chicago: University of Chicago Press, 1942.

# CHAPTER 21

# OTHER RURAL EDUCATIONAL AGENCIES

While the school has a formal assignment to educate the youth of the land, there are many other agencies in the community which play important roles in this activity. The family itself is, of course, an important agency for transmission of culture. The church has its own program of teaching—quite often both religious and secular—while such institutions and agencies as the newspaper, library, and radio are continuously conveying information and ideas to the rural population. These agencies, and others to be treated presently, are especially important at the adult level. Before discussing them specifically, it may be of value to see what the present educational achievement of the adult population is.

## EDUCATION OF THE ADULT RURAL POPULATION

In 1940, for the first time in the history of the United States Census, data were secured showing the amount of schooling which had been received by the adult population, by rural and urban segments and by other categories. In Table 39 is shown the percentage of rural and urban white populations who had had any high-school education.

TABLE 39. *Per Cent of White Population, Male and Female, Aged 25–29, and 45–49, Who Had Completed One or More Years of High School, Urban and Rural*

| AREA | 25–29 YEARS | | | | 45–49 YEARS | | | |
|---|---|---|---|---|---|---|---|---|
| | Male | | Female | | Male | | Female | |
| | 1950 | 1940 | 1950 | 1940 | 1950 | 1940 | 1950 | 1940 |
| United States | 74.2 | 61.9 | 78.8 | 66.6 | 46.0 | 33.7 | 51.8 | 38.6 |
| Urban | 80.4 | 70.4 | 83.4 | 71.4 | 52.0 | 38.0 | 55.4 | 41.5 |
| Rural-nonfarm | 65.2 | 57.6 | 72.0 | 64.2 | 39.4 | 33.5 | 47.9 | 39.4 |
| Rural-farm | 52.8 | 40.3 | 62.1 | 51.1 | 27.2 | 20.7 | 38.6 | 27.9 |

Source: Bureau of the Census.

It will be noted that (*a*) the urban population greatly exceeds the rural groups—particularly the rural-farm—in the proportions in both of the age groups and shows to especial advantage in the younger group, (*b*) there is a markedly high proportion of those aged 25–29 who have had some high-school education, and (*c*) more females than males have had high-school education.

There is, moreover, a wide variation among states in amount of high-school education of the adult white population twenty-five years or older. The ranking of states in this respect is shown in Table 40. (See also Figure 74.) Not only are there wide differences among states, but data for counties within states also show great variation in the proportion of the adult farm group with any high-school education. For example, in the eighty-seven counties of Minnesota there was a range from 7.1 per cent in the lowest county to 21.4 per cent in the highest.[1]

**Reasons for variations in education.** There can be little doubt that one reason for nonattendance of rural youth is the relative inaccessibility of rural high schools. For most farm young people, getting to high school involves transportation daily to and from their homes. Not all states or local districts arrange transportation at public expense, and the family is frequently unable to provide it. Still, the lack of transportation facilities in a given area is in large measure due to the failure of parents to take the necessary steps to secure it. In the last analysis, attendance or nonattendance of children at high school depends upon the value system of the community. If high-school education ranks high in the hierarchy of the values cherished by the group, provision somehow will be made to make it available and parents will see to it that their children attend.

The comparatively poor educational status of rural-farm adults is the result of the failure of their parents to encourage them to attend school and to make the facilities for education available. As we have seen in the previous chapter, the present generation of farm youth is also shown at a disadvantage when compared with urban. Because their parents had not received high-school education they are less likely to be enthusiastic about providing it for their children.

[1] Lowry Nelson, "The Education of Minnesota's Farm Population," *Minnesota AES Bulletin 377*, 1944, p. 12.

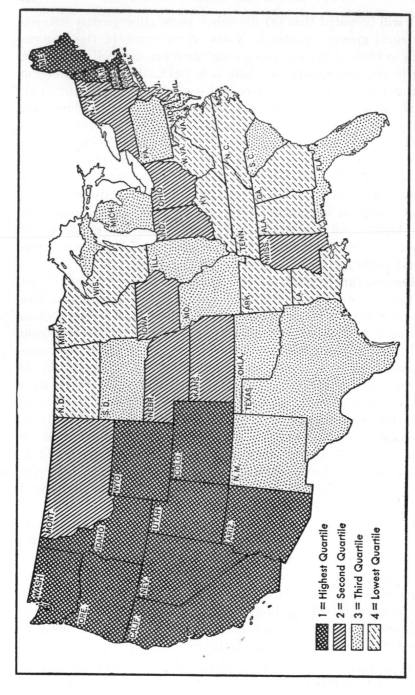

FIGURE 74. *Rank of States in Proportion of White Farm Population 25 Years Old or Over, With Any High-School Education, 1950*

1 = Highest Quartile
2 = Second Quartile
3 = Third Quartile
4 = Lowest Quartile

TABLE 40. *Percentage of the Rural-Farm White Population 25 Years Old or Over With 9 Years or More of Schooling and the Ratio of This Percentage to That for the Urban Population by States, 1940 and 1950*

| STATE | PER CENT RURAL-FARM ADULTS WITH 9 OR MORE YEARS, AND RANK OF STATE | | | | RATIO OF RURAL-FARM TO URBAN PERCENTAGE | | CHANGE 1940–1950 |
|---|---|---|---|---|---|---|---|
| | 1950 | | 1940 | | 1950 | 1940 | |
| | % | Rank | % | Rank | | | |
| Alabama | 28.5 | 40 | 22.4 | 41 | 46.4 | 45.4 | 1.0 |
| Arizona | 47.8 | 11 | 41.5 | 10 | 81.6 | 59.8 | 21.8 |
| Arkansas | 26.7 | 44 | 19.4 | 45 | 43.3 | 38.9 | 4.4 |
| California | 50.4 | 10 | 45.4 | 6 | 74.7 | 65.5 | 9.2 |
| Colorado | 47.5 | 12 | 38.1 | 15 | 74.6 | 73.1 | 1.5 |
| Connecticut | 46.7 | 14 | 44.3 | 7 | 70.6 | 88.7 | −18.1 |
| Delaware | 40.0 | 25 | 29.2 | 28 | 65.0 | 62.9 | 2.1 |
| Florida | 36.7 | 30 | 28.6 | 29.5 | 55.6 | 53.4 | 2.2 |
| Georgia | 18.8 | 47 | 25.9 | 33.5 | 31.7 | 54.1 | −22.4 |
| Idaho | 53.7 | 5 | 42.0 | 9 | 82.4 | 79.1 | 3.3 |
| Illinois | 37.1 | 28 | 26.3 | 31 | 68.3 | 66.2 | 2.1 |
| Indiana | 43.5 | 22 | 30.0 | 27 | 76.3 | 70.6 | 5.7 |
| Iowa | 44.7 | 18.5 | 34.0 | 21 | 74.0 | 70.6 | 3.4 |
| Kansas | 46.8 | 13 | 33.6 | 23 | 75.1 | 72.0 | 3.1 |
| Kentucky | 18.7 | 48 | 13.2 | 47 | 36.9 | 34.9 | 2.0 |
| Louisiana | 27.5 | 43 | 25.1 | 35.5 | 49.5 | 49.1 | 0.4 |
| Maine | 52.8 | 7 | 45.8 | 5 | 91.8 | 90.9 | 0.9 |
| Maryland | 35.8 | 32 | 25.1 | 35.5 | 65.6 | 63.2 | 2.4 |
| Massachusetts | 35.6 | 2 | 48.4 | 3 | 91.3 | 87.3 | 4.0 |
| Michigan | 39.4 | 26 | 31.0 | 25 | 66.4 | 62.3 | 4.1 |
| Minnesota | 27.6 | 42 | 21.2 | 43 | 47.8 | 41.7 | 6.1 |
| Mississippi | 40.9 | 24 | 33.9 | 22 | 57.2 | 49.0 | 8.2 |
| Missouri | 30.9 | 36 | 21.9 | 42 | 60.1 | 57.1 | 3.0 |
| Montana | 44.7 | 18.5 | 36.8 | 17 | 73.5 | 67.1 | 6.4 |
| Nebraska | 44.9 | 16.5 | 34.6 | 20 | 70.7 | 67.6 | 3.1 |
| Nevada | 54.6 | 3 | 49.5 | 2 | 78.9 | 70.5 | 8.4 |
| New Hampshire | 54.3 | 4 | 46.2 | 4 | 105.2 | 101.2 | 4.0 |
| New Jersey | 41.8 | 23 | 33.1 | 24 | 80.2 | 74.5 | 5.7 |
| New Mexico | 35.5 | 33 | 26.0 | 32 | 58.9 | 53.3 | 5.6 |
| New York | 44.9 | 16.5 | 34.8 | 19 | 85.5 | 91.8 | −6.3 |
| North Carolina | 29.0 | 38 | 25.9 | 33.5 | 49.2 | 60.1 | −10.9 |
| North Dakota | 30.3 | 37 | 24.9 | 37 | 53.7 | 45.3 | 8.4 |
| Ohio | 44.2 | 21 | 30.6 | 26 | 76.1 | 69.6 | 6.5 |
| Oklahoma | 34.6 | 35 | 23.7 | 39 | 55.4 | 50.7 | 4.7 |
| Oregon | 51.1 | 8 | 40.4 | 13 | 78.3 | 73.9 | 4.4 |
| Pennsylvania | 35.0 | 34 | 23.2 | 40 | 66.7 | 55.4 | 11.3 |
| Rhode Island | 44.3 | 20 | 40.7 | 12 | 86.9 | 90.7 | −3.8 |
| South Carolina | 36.5 | 31 | 36.7 | 18 | 60.8 | 58.4 | 2.4 |
| South Dakota | 36.9 | 29 | 28.6 | 29.5 | 61.5 | 55.0 | 6.5 |
| Tennessee | 24.1 | 45 | 19.3 | 46 | 41.1 | 46.2 | −5.1 |
| Texas | 38.6 | 27 | 36.9 | 16 | 64.2 | 73.5 | −9.3 |
| Utah | 65.7 | 1 | 53.1 | 1 | 91.3 | 90.2 | 1.1 |
| Vermont | 46.2 | 15 | 40.1 | 14 | 76.9 | 74.1 | 2.8 |
| Virginia | 27.8 | 41 | 24.3 | 38 | 43.4 | 45.1 | −1.7 |
| Washington | 50.8 | 9 | 41.4 | 11 | 77.1 | 70.9 | 6.2 |
| West Virginia | 19.6 | 46 | 12.3 | 48 | 36.6 | 27.9 | 8.7 |
| Wisconsin | 28.7 | 39 | 20.7 | 44 | 53.4 | 48.8 | 4.6 |
| Wyoming | 52.9 | 6 | 44.0 | 8 | 79.2 | 78.1 | 1.1 |

Source: Bureau of the Census.

## AGRICULTURAL EXTENSION SERVICE

The Smith-Lever Act, passed by Congress in 1914, brought the Agricultural Extension Service into formal existence. However, as is always the case in the development of institutions, the formal act of their creation was preceded by a period of preliminary preparation.

**Historical background.** As early as 1862, Congress, by passage of the Morrill Act, provided for the establishment of colleges of agriculture in the various states of the Union. They were endowed by the grant of title to certain lands on the public domain, and this land grant was supplemented by an annual grant of money from the Federal treasury. In some states these colleges were set up as separate institutions, while in others they became a part of the state universities. Another event of great significance to agricultural education was the passage of the Hatch Act in 1887, which provided for the establishment of agricultural experiment stations to be attached to the land-grant or agricultural colleges. Under the act, Congress authorized an annual grant-in-aid of $15,000 for carrying on agricultural research; the Adams Act of 1906 provided an additional grant of $15,000; the Purnell Act of 1925 an additional $60,000; while the Bankhead-Jones Act of 1936 supplemented previous grants by various amounts depending upon the proportion of rural people in the respective states. The Morrill, Hatch, and Adams acts set the stage for the establishment of the Extension Service, which was designed to carry the results of agricultural research to the farm people.

Previous to the formal creation by Congress of the Extension Service, the colleges of agriculture and state boards of agriculture had conducted what were known as farmers' institutes. These institutes would last for a day or two, during which members of the staffs of the colleges would visit local communities and give lectures and demonstrations on better methods of farming. At the same time, the colleges and experiment stations published and circulated widely among farm people bulletins and pamphlets reporting the results of research.

Some of the states, following the lead of New York in the year 1894, appropriated money for the agricultural colleges to carry on extension work. But the most notable action in this direction came in 1906 when the United States Department of Agriculture provided for the employment of county agricultural agents in the state of Texas as a means of teaching cotton farmers how to combat the ravages of the boll-weevil. The moving spirit was Seaman A. Knapp, and due to his activity—coupled with the urgency of the boll-weevil crisis—the work spread rapidly throughout the South. By 1911 when the first northern agents were appointed (in Broome County, New York, and Uintah County, Utah), there were 580 county agents in the cotton country. By 1914, when the Smith-Lever Act was passed, there were 1,350 men and women agents employed in county extension work in 42 of the 48 states.[2]

In 1908 President Theodore Roosevelt appointed the Commission on Country Life. Headed by Dean L. H. Bailey of Cornell University, this Commission held hearings throughout the entire country. In its final report the Commission recommended, among other things, the establishment of a national agricultural extension service; after five years of discussion, Congress, in 1914, passed the Smith-Lever Act creating it.

**Financial support.** The purpose of the act was "to aid in diffusing among the people of the United States useful and practical information on agriculture and home economics and to encourage the application of the same through field demonstrations, publications, and otherwise. . . . " To implement the objectives, annual appropriations to the several states were authorized, to be matched by equal amounts appropriated by state legislatures. The administration of extension work was to be primarily the responsibility of the state agricultural colleges. The funds were to be used for the employment of county agricultural agents, home demonstrators, and boys' and girls' club directors. The work of the county agents is supplemented by the employment of a staff of specialists attached to the state Extension Service office. At the present time the work covers practically every agricultural county in the nation, and Hawaii, Alaska, and Puerto Rico.

The original Smith-Lever Act has been supplemented by

additional acts of Congress which have authorized further grants of money to the states without the requirement that the states match them dollar for dollar. Thus in 1937–1938, a sample prewar year, the Federal appropriations amounted to $18,300,000, and those of the states, $14,100,000. In some states more than in others, counties are called upon to make substantial appropriations for the support of the work; and in a few states the Farm Bureau itself is a contributor to its support.

**Leadership.** Both professional and nonprofessional leaders are involved in extension work. The professional leadership is provided by a body of men and women known as county agricultural, home-demonstration, and club agents, as well as by administrators and subject-matter specialists. As a general rule these individuals are graduates of agricultural colleges. Typically, the county agricultural agent, while at college, did most of his academic work in the fields of crop and animal production. The home-demonstration agent, naturally, is a major in home economics. The club agents, if men, will have had training similar to that of the county agricultural agents, and, if women, their training will have been in home economics.

The county agents are usually regarded as regular staff members of the agricultural college or state university under which they work. Their appointments are made by the boards of these institutions in the same manner as those of the resident staffs. Many institutions also grant the privileges of sabbatical leave to the agents, many of whom have taken advantage of this opportunity to do graduate work and achieve an advanced degree. However, the work is so pressing that not more than a very small proportion of them are able to leave for further study.

That demand for the service is growing is indicated by the one-third increase in personnel in the categories following:[3]

|  | *1942* | *1950* |
|---|---|---|
| County agricultural agents and assistants | 4,125 | 5,239 |
| County home-demonstration agents and assistants | 2,421 | 3,613 |
| County club agents and assistants | 338 | 667 |
| Administrators and supervisors | 628 | 772 |
| Subject-matter specialists | 1,686 | 2,108 |
| Total | 9,198 | 12,399 |

[3] Information supplied by the Agricultural Extension Service, U.S.D.A.

Whether the kind of training the county agents have been receiving is that which will best fit them for the work they actually perform has been a subject of considerable controversy in recent years. Since 1933, especially, county agricultural agents have been asked to spend a great deal of their time—amounting to close to half of it—in administrative work connected with the various programs of the Federal government. Beginning with the AAA program in 1933, the county extension staffs have been asked subsequently to assist with setting up programs in soil conservation, drought relief, land-use planning, and, during the war, with food production and farm labor recruitment and distribution.

This has meant that a county agent, trained for his work by specializing in crop and animal production, has been made into a public administrator, for which he has not had special preparation. In effect, he is now a social engineer, organizing social groups and motivating them to action; he is an educator, particularly an adult educator; he is a trainer of leaders. He is all these things—much more than he is a specialist in crop and animal production. Yet a county agent's training is still based, so it is charged, on the unwarranted assumption that he will spend his time as a specialist in purely agricultural pursuits.

The lay leaders in extension work are the contact persons for the county agents in the local community. Thus the county agricultural agent has a local township or neighborhood leader of a farm group to whom he can communicate instructions with the prospect that they will be relayed to other farmers in the locality. The home-demonstration leader has local neighborhood groups of women, whose leaders may come to a central point in the county, receive instruction, and impart it to their respective local groups on their return. With club work there are volunteer leaders who assume responsibility for guiding local clubs. It is a rather impressive fact that in 1941 there were nearly 600,000 voluntary local leaders who assisted with the "adult extension" program and an additional 156,000 who assisted with the "junior extension" work among farm boys and girls, chiefly through the 4-H clubs. The increase in the number of volunteer leaders from 1924 to 1940 is shown in Figure 75.

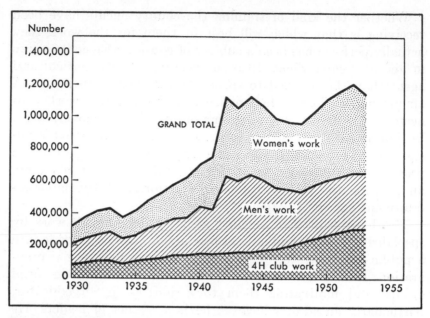

FIGURE 75. *Number of Voluntary Local Leaders in Agricultural Extension Work,
1930–1953*

**Extent of contact.** Some idea of the magnitude of this program
may be had from the report of extension activities during a
single year. In 1950, for example, the county agents made over
3,750,000 farm and home visits; received nearly 90,000,000
office calls and nearly 9,000,000 telephone calls; published over
900,000 news articles; wrote over 8,000,000 letters; distributed
over 21,000,000 bulletins; held nearly 800,000 demonstration
method meetings which, together with all other meetings held,
amounted to 1,600,000. The combined attendance at all meetings was over 61,000,000.[4] (See picture following page 424.)

The response of farm people to the agricultural extension
program varies throughout the country. The Extension Service
has been charged by some critics as reaching only the upper
third of the farmers. Such a general criticism, however, is not
justified. It is by no means the intent of those in charge of the
program that it be in any way limited in participation. Still,
there is no question that certain farmers and their families

[4] *Agricultural Statistics, 1952,* United States Department of Agriculture, p. 849.

are more active in taking advantage of the benefits of extension work.

The extent of participation of farmers appears to be definitely related to tenure. Generally, farm owners participate in larger proportions than do tenants. C. R. Hoffer found in the state of Michigan that there was a significant correlation between the percentage of farm ownership and participation in extension work.[5] Tenure has been found by others to be related to social participation in general.[6] M. C. Wilson reported in 1941, on the basis of a sample study in 16 states, that "77 per cent of tenant families and 81 per cent of owner families were reached by Extension, an advantage of 4 per cent in favor of the owner-operator group." [7] In its 4–H Club work, Wilson states that Extension is reaching "45 per cent of the children of tenant farmers and 56 per cent of the children of farm owners." [8]

That participation in Extension work is also related somewhat to the level of education is indicated by Wilson. He says:

Data on file with the Division of Field Studies and Training reveal that in seven sample areas of six states, 78 per cent of the farmers with eighth-grade school or less were reached in contrast to 88 per cent of the farmers with high-school but no college training. Similar data for nine areas of eight states show 35 per cent of the farm women with eighth-grade schooling or less reached in contrast to 58 per cent of the farm women with high-school but no college training.[9]

Differences are also noted between whites and Negroes (in which the latter compare unfavorably), and in the lower percentages of small as compared with large farmers reached by extension activities. However, in areas of large numbers of disadvantaged rural people—notably the South—the Extension

[5] C. R. Hoffer, "Selected Factors Affecting Participation of Farmers in Agricultural Extension Work," *Michigan State College AES Special Bulletin 331*, June, 1944, p. 23.

[6] See D. E. Lindstrom, "Forces Affecting Participation of Farm People in Rural Organization," *University of Illinois AES Bulletin 423*. W. A. Anderson and Hans H. Plambeck, "The Social Participation of Farm Families," *Cornell University AES Mimeograph Bulletin 8*, March, 1943.

[7] M. C. Wilson, "How and to What Extent Is the Extension Service Reaching Low-Income Farm Families," *Circular 375*, United States Department of Agriculture Extension Service, December, 1941, p. 12.

[8] *Ibid.*, p. 13.

[9] *Ibid.*, p. 12.

Service, as Wilson concludes, "is organized to render, and is rendering, the same educational service . . . as to the other parts of the Nation." [10]

**Community relations.** As an institution, the Extension Service faces the same necessity of adapting to the larger community as does any other institution. One of the most important problems which it has faced, and is still facing, is that of adjusting its program to that of the school. For instance, at the high-school level, another Federally supported program parallels to some extent the work of the Extension Service. The Smith-Hughes Act of 1918 provides Federal grants-in-aid to states for the purpose of developing and expanding vocational education in agriculture, home economics, and mechanical arts. The instructors are hired on a yearly basis and during the summer months supervise project work of the students. Such project work is scarcely distinguishable from that offered through the 4–H Club program of the Extension Service, a fact which gives rise to some interagency disputes and obvious questions from the community as to "what is going on."

Moreover, the Smith-Hughes teachers of agriculture and home economics conduct regular evening classes for adults in these fields, in a sense duplicating the work of the Extension Service. One of the more interesting and important controversies concerns the relation of the 4–H Club to the rural school. There are many educators who hold to the opinion that club work should be an integral part of the country school. It should be, they say, the means by which the work of the country school is brought closer to the lives of boys and girls and of their parents. The rural school teacher, the argument continues, should be trained as a potential club leader as a regular part of her pre-service training and should be employed for the full year, with the expectation that she would devote her summers to supervision of club work with her pupils.

There are many objections raised by the partisans of the existing system. One of these is that the rural teachers sometimes are individuals with no conception of rural life, having lived and been trained in urban situations. It is feared that the rural teachers would have little interest in the program

[10] *Ibid.,* p. 20.

and that it would decline in importance if turned over to them. As a positive argument for the present system, its proponents say that it is an advantage to the school to have an outside agency working with the youngsters, in that it is a challenge to the school to adopt new methods or revise old ones. It keeps them from getting in a rut. Thus, the question of relationships is under constant scrutiny in the Extension Service and among those outside of it who are interested in the general program of education in the country.

The church is another agency with which the Extension Service needs to accommodate itself. In general, the county agents are rather wary about being identified with any one of the usually numerous church organizations in their counties. The reasons are easy to understand. Denominational rivalry being what it is, a county agent might easily alienate support or interest of a large part of the farmers in the county if it should be charged against him that he is partial to this or that sect. An unfortunate consequence is that the Extension agents do not feel it wise to use one of the most important resources in the community. Comparatively few ministers, for their part, take an aggressive attitude in trying to facilitate the work of the Extension Service. After a considerable effort, Rural Life Sunday has finally become established as a regular annual event in a great many states of the Union. This is a definite step in the direction of identifying the church with extension service, particularly as it relates to the welfare of rural youth.

In several of the states, the Extension Service is identified legally with the Farm Bureau, often to the embarrassment of the Service. This relationship developed from the fact that the Extension Service was instrumental in organizing the Farm Bureau in the various states, as an educational adjunct to its work. Following World War I, the Farm Bureau declared its independence from the Extension Service and decided to operate as a private farm organization—comparable to the Grange and the Farmer's Union. But legislation had already been passed in about a dozen states making the Farm Bureau a party to the arrangement by which extension work is locally supported, financially and otherwise. Arrangements differ among the states, but in all of them the other farm organizations justifiably complain that the Farm Bureau is receiving an advantage over them. Because of the advantages, the Farm Bureau itself is loathe to initiate the repeal of the legislation and the tendency therefore is for the present situation to continue.

Another problem of adaptation confronting the Extension Service is a question of emphasis. Traditionally, major attention has been given to the techniques of production of crops and livestock. Getting farmers to grow better varieties of crops and raise more efficient breeds of livestock, developing techniques of disease and pest control, introduction of new and more efficient types of farm machinery—these and other technological problems have been the first concern of the county agent. However, it has been more than evident since the end of World War I that ability to produce food and fiber in quantities adequate for the demand was one of the most conspicuous achievements of the American farmer. The question was now one of markets at adequate prices for his surplus products and of the utilization of increased productivity for better living. Gradually, the relationship of farm prosperity to urban prosperity came to be recognized, and the interdependence of the two was emphatically demonstrated. Other discoveries about farm life have been made. Among these is the painful fact that perhaps one third of the farm population is undernourished. The people who produce the food so abundantly are not getting enough to eat. Also, the people who plant, hoe, and pick the cotton are among the most poorly clothed people in the entire economy. Moreover, in the rich bottom lands of the Mississippi River—some of the most fertile land in the world—there exists such human poverty as can be found in few other sections of the earth. Farm housing is definitely substandard throughout many agricultural areas of the nation. The level of living, in short, is far below what it ought to be and could be. The question is therefore pertinent whether the emphasis of agricultural extension work should not be shifted to economic, social, and "cultural" aspects of rural life. This is not to say that continuing effort should not be made to improve the efficiency of agriculture to produce. However, it is evident that a more balanced program is needed.

## THE RURAL LIBRARY

The library is primarily an educational institution. As such, it is comparable in some respects to the school. The public library is an aspect of local government. It is maintained from the public treasury for all the people, and exists for the purpose of making books available to people who desire to read them and who cannot afford or may not want to purchase individually the books and magazines desired. It is, in short, a managed collection of books which can be borrowed for a limited time by authorized borrowers.

There are as many types of libraries as there are types of library sponsorship. There are, for instance, private libraries maintained by individuals or groups for their own purposes. The majority of libraries in the United States are public libraries, supported by a unit of government. These range from the town or township libraries found in some states, through the municipal libraries, those of the school district, the community, the county, and the state. There is also a Federal library, the Library of Congress. Of greatest importance to the rural population are the libraries located in accessible towns and villages and the traveling libraries which are frequently supported by the state.

**Distribution of libraries.** As is true in the case of many other educational facilities, libraries either do not exist in rural areas, or are inadequately supported. This is due in part to the general problem affecting all rural institutions, namely, the difficulty of access to central services—a difficulty imposed by the dispersed pattern of settlement. In spite of the developments in transportation, distance continues to be an important if not a decisive factor in library use. Regional differences are very great. Taking the total population as the base, H. W. Odum found the Southeast particularly deficient in libraries, with the Southwest next lowest, and the Northwest next. In other words, the areas where library service is most highly developed are the Far West and the Northeast.[11] The principle still holds true in midcentury that the greater the proportion of rural people in a given area, the less chance that there will be public

[11] Howard W. Odum, *Southern Regions of the United States*, pp. 118–119. Chapel Hill: University of North Carolina Press, 1936.

library service. It is important to note also that there are factors other than distance which retard the development of library service. Especially important is the level of formal schooling, which as we have seen, is lower in rural than in urban areas. Leisure is another factor, and something farm people have lacked.

**Standards of adequacy for libraries.** The American Library Association has repeatedly set forth the goals and the standards of library service. A recent pronouncement of this organization states: "The public library is one of America's great contributions to civilization. It endeavors to make easily accessible to people of all ages and all levels of educational attainment the best of the world's knowledge as recorded in print, and guidance in its use. At its best, it serves the cultural, educational, and leisure-time needs of the community without compulsion, censorship, or bias, at low cost." [12] In order that these goals might be achieved, the American Library Association has set up the following standards of adequacy:

1) An annual income of not less than $25,000. In relation to population there should be $1 per capita for limited or minimum service; $1.50 per capita for reasonably good service, $2 per capita for superior service.

2) A book collection of 3 volumes per capita for 6,000 to 10,000 people; $2\frac{1}{2}$ volumes per capita for 10,000 to 35,000; 2 volumes per capita for 35,000 to 100,000; and $1\frac{3}{4}$ to 1 volume per capita for larger populations. A minimum stock of 6,000 volumes is necessary regardless of population.

3) Twenty to 40 per cent of the population 15 years of age and over and 35 to 75 per cent of the population from 5 through 14 years of age should be registered borrowers.

4) Three to 10 volumes per capita for the population 15 years and over and 10 to 30 volumes per capita for the population 5–14 years old should be borrowed each year.

5) The library should ordinarily be governed by a board of trustees who would be responsible for policy but should leave administration to the librarian.

6) The library should be administered by a librarian with professional

[12] "A National Plan for Libraries," *American Library Association Bulletin*, February, 1939.

*The county fair (above) is an important educational influence. Traveling libraries in Louisiana (below) distribute books to readers in isolated spots.*

*Farmers are gathered for a farm bureau meeting in a community in New Mexico (above). A tenant farmer (below) stands in front of his squalid hut, in Arkansas.*

training and ability, who together with the staff should be certificated under state law as to minimum qualifications.[13]

Many small libraries now existing in townships and in small towns and villages would have considerable difficulty in achieving these standards, and for many the standards would be impossible. It is suggested, therefore, that library services be unified and integrated throughout a state or region of a state, so that the resources of each become in a sense the resources of all. Unification can be achieved under a state library commission, with state and Federal financial support provided for local units. In other words, what is called for is the integration and extension of facilities.

**The county or regional library.** One of the best devices for achieving adequate size and support and for extending service to rural areas is the county or the regional library. As the name implies, the county library is an agency of the county from which it receives at least a part of its financial support, and it is under obligation to make library service available to all the people of the county. The county library may be set up independently of any existing library service, although usually it is created by entering into contractual relations with existing village, town, or city libraries, under terms whereby the county agrees to make an annual appropriation to the library or libraries now extant. In return the libraries agree to make their service available without special charge to the people who live outside the corporate limits of the municipality. The county library may be the recipient of state aid through the loan of books from the state collection, or actual grant of funds, or both. Most of the states of the Union have passed enabling acts which provide for the creation of county libraries. The growth in numbers of such libraries has been steady. In 1944 there were 651 in the United States compared with 225 ten years earlier.[14]

The regional library is another way in which the area of support and service of a library can be enlarged. It is set up by two or more counties agreeing to cooperate in the maintenance of

[13] "Standards and Planning for Public Libraries," American Library Association, undated.
[14] "Library Extension and Postwar Planning," *American Library Association Bulletin*, October 1, 1944.

library service for all people in the area. There are many types of these regional libraries. In California one county contracts with the county library of an adjacent county to furnish library service to its inhabitants. The Tennessee Valley Authority has been instrumental in establishing regional service in some of the areas in which it carries on educational activities. In Louisiana the State Library Commission sponsored a tri-parish library and supported it financially to the extent of $25,000 while also providing it with books from its own collection.[15]

**Traveling libraries.** The introduction and use of parcel post has proved to be of great advantage in getting books circulated in rural areas. In those states which have created state library commissions and provided for the acquisition of state collections of books, the circulating package library has become an important method in getting books into remote areas. Such services are also frequently provided by the regional library and by the extension divisions of the state universities.

The ideal scheme of organization of library service is one which will integrate the basic resources of an entire area—whether county, district, or state—in such a way that they will be pooled and made available to all. Out in the rural areas there will be the small branch libraries—which may be housed in a store, barber shop, or other accessible establishment—to which books will be sent from the central reservoir. Or, the bookmobile may make periodic visits to various remote points where isolated families may come on specified days and withdraw books. (See picture following page 424.) More elaborate collections of books may be maintained in village centers, but these too would be able to call upon the central collection. The same would be true of school libraries. The program of expansion of library facilities now proposed by the American Library Association and other interested groups ultimately looks toward making service free and universally available to the population. Experience has shown that this goal can be achieved most effectively if library facilities can be planned for an entire state with counties grouped into districts which have sufficient population and taxable resources to insure adequate support and use.

[15] Julia Wright Merrill, "Regional and District Libraries," American Library Association, 1942. (mimeo.)

**Proposed Federal support.** A significant recognition of the importance of the library as an educational institution was the recommendation of the President's Advisory Commission on Education that the Federal government make grants-in-aid to states for the purpose of promoting expansion of library service. These appropriations from the Federal government were to be a part of the over-all Federal plan of supporting public education in the United States. The proposed grants were incorporated in bills introduced into Congress but which have not yet been made into law. The Federal grants would be based upon the proportion of the state population which was rural, since they were intended primarily as a means of expanding the services for rural people.

Another significant step taken by the Federal government was the creation in 1938 of a Library Service Division in the United States Office of Education. Its functions are "to make surveys, studies, investigations, and reports regarding public, school, college, university, and other libraries; to foster coordination of public and school library service; to coordinate library service on a national level with other forms of adult education; to develop library participation in Federal projects; to foster nation-wide coordination of research materials among the more scholarly libraries, interstate library cooperation, and the development of public, school, and other library service throughout the country." [16]

### THE PRESS

The country weekly, the daily metropolitan press, and the agricultural journal are all important media for the communication of ideas in rural areas. The habitat of the country weekly is, naturally, the small town and village. It is more common in the North, where the number in proportion to population greatly exceeds that of the Southern states. Even so, there were fewer weekly papers in the United States in 1954 than there were in 1900. At that early date there were 16,000. They declined to 13,000 in 1929, 10,860 in 1940, and 9,184 in 1954.[17] The

[16] "A National Plan for Libraries," *American Library Association Bulletin,* February 1939.

[17] Figures from N. W. Ayer and Son's, *American Newspaper Annual and Directory.*

decline in number of weeklies continued to 1946 when only 10,424
were reported. This was partly due to wartime shortages of
labor and materials. Increased availability of these items, however, accounted for the slight gain in 1947.

The county seat is a particularly favorable location for the
weekly paper, and the number located in these centers actually
increased from 2,926 in 1943 to 2,940 in 1944, although there
was a decline to 2,916 in 1947. The weekly paper located in the
county seat is the beneficiary of county government activities
in many ways. In the first place, much of the news is "made"
there—the kind of news in which the country weekly is interested. The official advertising, while usually not given exclusively to the county-seat paper, is an important source of
revenue. Also, the job printing for the various county offices
goes in large measure to the county-seat publisher.

As an institution the weekly newspaper is to a large extent
the reflection of the personality of the publisher. For the
metropolitan press, the era of "personal journalism"—of the
Greeley's, the Reid's, and the Dana's—seems to have passed.
But in the country weekly the personality of the editor-publisher
is manifest today as much as at any time in the past. From the
publisher's point of view, the paper is an economic or business
enterprise. Revenue is derived from the sale of advertising and
subscriptions. Approximately 85 per cent of the income is from
advertising, which occupies from one third to one half of the
space in the paper. This is the financial basis on which the paper
must exist. It is obvious that a country weekly must have such
a base of support before it can perform its other functions,
including that of education.

From the standpoint of the community, the paper is a
source of information, on the one hand, and a voice or representative of the community, on the other. The first function
is performed through the publication of factual matter concerning the community, its members, and its major interests.
This is its function described by the phrase, "reporting the
news." The American standard of news reporting is that it
be presented in the news columns without bias and without
comment, and that all sides of a question be fairly presented.
On the editorial page the editor may express his own opinion

on the significance of the news. He is therefore a guide or leader in the formation of public opinion. He is also something of a conscience for the community. The thoughtful and sensitive editor is a reflector of the community mores. He voices the convictions of the group.

The country paper has changed considerably over the years. Before the more rapid means of disseminating spot news were developed, the weekly was the main source of information concerning current events in the world. However, the daily press and the radio have taken over so completely—even in rural areas—the distribution of spot world news, that the country weekly contains very little of such items. It specializes rather in the local community, including the neighborhoods of the open country adjacent to the trade center, in which it is edited and published. It reports the goings and comings of persons in the locality; in fact, some country editors aim to get the name of every subscriber into their columns some time during every year. The Agricultural Extension Service furnishes a great deal of information on agriculture and rural living, usually by means of a weekly letter written by the county agricultural agent or the home demonstration agent. The country paper, as M. M. Willey points out, is a local institution. "It is printed for a relatively homogeneous constituency. It cannot afford, or hope to compete with the highly organized city press. . . . Its very life depends upon its being a community paper; this is its function." [18] After a detailed study of the content of weekly papers in Washington, C. F. Reuss confirms this statement by Willey in the following words:

News in the country weekly is chiefly news about people and the home community, and secondly, of important local social institutions such as the government, the school, and the church.[19]

And again:

News in the weekly paper was primarily of the type of which conversations are made wherever people come into direct contact—of

[18] Malcolm M. Willey, *The Country Newspaper*, p. 13. Chapel Hill: The University of North Carolina Press, 1926.
[19] Carl F. Reuss, "Content of the Country Weekly," *Rural Sociology*, 1939, Vol. 4, no. 3, p. 336.

people and of events in the environment. Personal news occupied one-third of the news space.[20]

The expansion of the metropolitan daily into rural areas is principally a development of the period between World Wars I and II. The improvement of delivery systems in rural areas at great distances from the place of publication placed the farmer in daily contact with the news, there being only a small time lag between distribution of newspapers in the city and in the country. Newspapers from Chicago, for example, are distributed daily over an area with a radius of 500 miles. Delivery by air now makes it possible for New York daily papers to be delivered within a few hours after printing at any place on the continent. Rural people are subscribing to metropolitan papers in increasing numbers and depend upon them almost completely for news of daily happenings outside their home communities.

The *agricultural papers*, with their extensive circulation, have long been conceded an important educational function in rural America. At one time or another almost every state in the Union has had a farm paper, with some states supporting several. Thus, there is the *Wisconsin Farmer*, *The Farmer* (St. Paul, Minnesota), the *Iowa Homestead*, the *Utah Farmer*, and so on. In addition, there are several farm papers which have assumed national stature and circulate in every state. Examples are *The Country Gentleman* and *The Farm Journal* and *Farmer's Wife*. Others have regional importance, such as *Progressive Farmer* in the Southern states and *The Prairie Farmer* in the Middle West. In addition there is a considerable number of specialized farm papers which are devoted to some special type of agriculture, and which have national distribution. Examples are *Hoard's Dairyman* and the *Breeder's Gazette*.

Historically, these journals have mainly devoted themselves to the improvement in the technology of American agriculture. They have promoted the idea of better seeds and livestock, improved barns and farm machinery, the use of commercial fertilizers, and the like. In recent years these journals have also given increasing attention to the social and economic

[20] Carl F. Reuss, "Content of Washington Weekly Newspapers," *State College of Washington AES Bulletin 387*, 1940, p. 44.

problems of rural life. Today, for example, one will find extensive discussions in the pages of the farm journals of problems of rural health, social security, rural education, the rural church, and other community problems.

The discussion of international problems also appears rather frequently in the pages of these journals. This is an indication of the expanding world of the farmer. He can no longer be unconcerned with developments outside his community and his nation. The events of the 1930's and particularly of the war years have impressed upon him the necessity of understanding his relations to the world at large. Foreign trade has come to have a very important and intimate significance to the American farmer. He knows that his prosperity is geared to the prosperity of other groups in society. Thus the media of communication are carrying more and more discussion related to these larger questions.

## FARM ORGANIZATIONS

All of the major farm organizations carry on active and rather extensive educational programs. The Grange, which is the oldest of the organizations, has from its beginning in 1867 been devoted to educational activity as one of its major tenets. The "lecturer" is one of the most important of its local officials and the "lecture hour" one of the most important items on the regular program. These lecture periods are sometimes devoted to forum discussions, as well as to the straight presentation of topics by one individual. Members are therefore given opportunity for self-expression. The topics cover the range of rural interest, and in recent years, have been devoted increasingly to the consideration of the social, economic, and political problems of agriculture.

The Farm Bureau, like the Grange, began its existence with a primary commitment to education. Indeed, it was organized by the Agricultural Extension Service in the various counties as a means of facilitating the dissemination of agricultural and home economics information. After the locals were organized, the State and National Federations came into being, and they declared their independence from the Extension Service. Their basic educational goals, however, were never forsaken, even though the organization came to take an active part in developing cooperatives and in securing state and national legislation for the benefit of the farmer. (See picture following page 424.)

The Home Bureau, or women's division of the Farm Bureau, has been especially active in the field of education. In Iowa, for example, a rather elaborate handbook for the discussion of current problems is issued for the guidance of the township chairmen in conducting discussion groups. The 1941 handbook was in the form of a packet containing six pamphlets. The first pamphlet in the series was entitled "Iowa Farm Bureau Women's Program," and under "program" were listed the following topics: (a) home project work, (b) 4–H Club support, (c) music, (d) health, (e) libraries ("each county to have a library chairman to stress extension of rural libraries"), (f) schools, and (g) discussion ("to promote a state-wide program for the training of leaders in discussion techniques"). The packet contained a special pamphlet on library extension and one on rural schools.

The Farmer's Union also has a very active educational program. Considerably more "liberal" in its social and economic principles than either the Grange or the Farm Bureau, it is characterized by a rather crusading attitude in behalf of its principles. It seeks to promote the interests of the small farmer for whom it claims to be the spokesman and to encourage the cooperation of organized labor and organized agriculture. It is committed to the principle that the farmer must control the buying and selling organizations. Through these, as well as through the organization itself (which remains technically independent of the cooperatives), an aggressive educational program is carried on every year.

### THE COOPERATIVES

No inventory of rural educational agencies would be complete that did not include the rural cooperatives. This means particularly the cooperative marketing organizations, though in recent years the buying cooperatives have also assumed considerable importance. From the beginning of the movement in the United

States it has been recognized that success rested very largely in the degree to which the membership of cooperative enterprises could be kept informed of their purposes, organization, and functioning. Therefore, in practically every cooperative, there is provision for setting aside a certain amount of the annual earnings for the purpose of carrying on an "educational" program. While such a program will necessarily be concerned predominantly with the affairs of the cooperative itself, it does not mean that it is thus limited. For example, the controversy over whether or not the cooperatives should be taxed in the same manner as other corporations has brought discussion of the entire tax structure into prominence and practically compelled local groups to consider the broader relations. But the work of the cooperatives has mainly been teaching farmers the methods and fruits of cooperation. Through these activities farm people have come to know more than they previously did about the steps involved in the marketing process. They have learned that middleman services must be performed by someone, that you do not eliminate these services when you eliminate the middleman. They have come to understand that their relations to the ultimate consumer must be on a basis of honesty and integrity, and that the improvement and the maintenance of quality in a product is the best guarantee of a market.

The educational work of the cooperatives has been more important than perhaps any other factor in bringing the farmer into understanding relations with urban society. Since there has been a close relationship maintained between the cooperatives and the Agricultural Extension Service, these organizations might be regarded in part as auxiliary agencies to the work of the Extension Service. This would be true particularly of the marketing cooperatives.

The buying or consuming cooperatives have, as a rule, developed independently of the Agricultural Extension Service. Even the farm organizations, with the exception of the Farmer's Union, have been less concerned about this aspect of cooperative development than with the marketing aspect. Nevertheless, their rapid growth in recent years has brought consumers' cooperatives into national prominence. Their educational programs are given an important place in their organization and budget. For example, the Midland Cooperative Wholesale headquarters in Minneapolis has an "educational department" with a competent staff and ample budget to maintain an active educational program throughout the area which it serves.

It is clear from the discussion in this chapter that there are important agencies other than the school at work in the field of education. This is especially true in the matter of adult education. There are wide differences among the states in the levels of education among adults. Among the agencies which cover the nation in this field are the Agricultural Extension Service, the libraries, newspapers and magazines, the farm organizations, and the cooperatives.

## QUESTIONS FOR DISCUSSION

1. Why would it be unrealistic to think of public and private schools as the only institutions or agencies engaged in the process of education?
2. Point out and discuss the significance of differences in the educational status of (a) age groups and (b) residents of urban, rural-non-farm, and rural-farm areas.
3. Can you derive any regional patterns from the data on the ranking of states according to educational status? Discuss.
4. What would appear to be the fundamental reason why a considerable proportion of the young people in certain rural areas fail to complete their high-school education?
5. Summarize the essential provisions and historical significance of (a) the Morrill Act, (b) the Hatch Act and (c) the Adams, Purnell, and Bankhead-Jones acts.
6. Describe the circumstances surrounding the original employment of county agents.
7. Explain the origin and significance of the Commission on Country Life.
8. Outline the important features of the law passed by Congress in 1914 which created the Agricultural Extension Service. What types of personnel are now engaged in this service?
9. Is there any criticism which can be made with respect to the kind of training received by county agents? Discuss.
10. How is the amount of participation in extension activities on the part of farmers related to (a) tenure, (b) years of schooling, and (c) race?

11. Point out ways in which there is a lack of coordination between the program of the Agricultural Extension Service and other agencies or institutions, including Smith-Hughes work, the rural school, and the rural church.

12. How did the present relationship between the Extension Service and the Farm Bureau happen to develop? Criticize or appraise this relationship.

13. Mention certain social problems in rural areas which are receiving inadequate attention by the Agricultural Extension Service. How might the Extension Service deal more effectively with these problems?

14. Why should the library be regarded as an essential educational institution? What proportion of the rural population in this country is without library service? Point out regional differences in the adequacy of this service.

15. Summarize the standards of adequacy advocated by the American Library Association. Describe the kind of organization which would appear to be necessary in order to provide library service in rural areas that would meet these standards.

16. Describe some plans which have been put into operation in various parts of the country as a means of improving rural library service.

17. How does the present compare with the past with regard to the number and distribution of country weeklies? Why have county-seat papers more than held their own in the struggle for survival? Mention some important functions performed by these weeklies.

18. Give the names of the agricultural journals which you have read. Is it your opinion that some of them have a definite propaganda slant? Discuss.

## SELECTED REFERENCES

Note to the student. If you live in a community in which the county extension agents, or any of the other Federal agencies, such as the Soil Conservation Service, have their offices, they can be interviewed for special information about their work. Representatives of farm organizations, cooperatives, the local paper, radio stations, and the like are also excellent sources of information regarding current developments in adult education.

Baker, Gladys. *The County Agent*. Chicago: University of Chicago Press, 1930.

Brunner, Edmund deS., and Hsin Pao, E. *Rural America and the Extension Service*. Teachers' College, Columbia University, 1949.

Brunner, E. deS.; Sanders, Irwin T.; and Ensminger, Douglas. *Farmers of the World*. New York: Columbia University Press, 1945.

Ekstrom, George F., and McClelland, John B. *Adult Education and Vocational Agriculture*. Danville, Illinois: Interstate Printers and Publishers, 1952.

*Farmers in a Changing World*. Yearbook of Agriculture, 1940. "Public Information and the Preservation of Democracy," pp. 1075–1080, by Alfred D. Stedman. Washington, D.C.: Government Printing Office.

Kolb, J. H., and Brunner, E. deS. *A Study of Rural Society*, Fourth Edition, Chapter 19. Boston: Houghton Mifflin Company, 1952.

Loomis, Charles P., and others. *Rural Social Systems and Adult Education*. East Lansing: Michigan State College Press, 1953.

Reck, Franklin M. *The 4–H Story*. Ames: Iowa State College Press, 1951.

Smith, C. B., and Wilson, M. C. *The Agricultural Extension System of the United States*. New York: John Wiley and Sons, 1930.

"The Contributions of Extension Methods and Techniques toward the Rehabilitation of War-Torn Countries." A Conference Report. United States Department of Agriculture, Extension Service and Office of Foreign Agricultural Relations, Washington, D.C., October, 1945.

## NEWSPAPERS

Clark, Thomas D. *The Rural Press and the New South*. Baton Rouge: Louisiana State University Press, 1948.

Hoffer, C. R. "Interests of Rural People As Portrayed in Weekly Newspapers." *Michigan State College Special Bulletin 298*. February, 1939.

Mott, Frank Luther. *American Journalism*. New York: The Macmillan Company, 1947.

Reuss, Carl F. "Content of the Country Weekly," *Rural Sociology*, 4:3, September, 1939.

Willey, Malcolm M. "Community, Socialization, and the County Newspaper—A Study of Newspaper Content," *Proceedings American Sociological Society*, Vol. XXXII, 1926.

————— *The Country Newspaper*. Chapel Hill: The University of North Carolina Press, 1926.

## LIBRARIES

Anderson, C. Arnold, and Gross, Neal C. "Can Iowa Have Better Public Library Service?" *Iowa AES and Agricultural Extension Service, Cooperating Bulletin P50*. January, 1943.

Humble, Marion. *Rural America Reads.* New York: American Association for Adult Education, 1938.

Joekel, C. B. *Library Service.* Study No. 11, The President's Advisory Committee on Education. Washington, D.C.: Government Printing Office, 1938.

Johnsen, Julia E. *County Libraries.* The Reference Shelf, Vol. VI, No. 7. New York: The H. W. Wilson Co., 1930.

Leigh, Robert D. *The Public Library in the United States.* New York: Columbia University Press, 1950.

Nason, Wayne C. "Rural Libraries." *United States Department of Agriculture Farmers Bulletin 1847.* 1940.

*The Library's Public.* Report of the Public Library Inquiry. New York: Columbia University Press, 1949.

Wilson, Louis R. *The Role of the Library in Adult Education.* Chicago: University of Chicago Press, 1937.

———, and Wight, E. A. *County Libraries in the South: A Study of the Rosenwald Library Demonstration.* Chicago: University of Chicago Press, 1935.

# CHAPTER 22

# LOCAL GOVERNMENT

What we usually have in mind when we use the word "government" is an institution, or institutions, which will do for all of us at least two things: establish and maintain law and order, and provide certain necessary services. John R. Commons was no doubt thinking of the first function when he defined an institution "as collective action in control of individual action," although he was seeking a definition of all institutional behavior.[1] It is true that we think of government as essentially the agency through which rules and regulations are established and the infractions of the rules penalized. It is the one institution which exercises control over life and property and may deprive the individual of both under certain conditions. It is an association to which everyone "belongs," with no voluntary act on his part. He is born into citizenship. Not only is membership involuntary, but so also are certain aspects of participation. For example, the individual *must* pay taxes and obey numerous laws—or pay the penalty.

He is not compelled to vote in elections, to attend public hearings, to come to the town meetings, or to participate in many other activities which are his privilege and his responsibility. But whether he participates actively in these affairs or not, his life is affected by some government regulation in innumerable ways. The electric light which he switches on and off comes from a company that is under the regulation of the public utilities commission. The food which he eats at breakfast has passed the inspection of sanitary departments of government. The water which flows from the tap in his house is provided by the municipal government. The highway over which he rides to town is built and maintained by a governmental

[1] John R. Commons, *Institutional Economics*, p. 69. New York: The Macmillan Company, 1934.

agency. So is the school which he passes on the way. Thus at every turn of the road the individual meets up with government in some manifestation.

## LEVELS AND UNITS OF GOVERNMENT

Rural government in the United States involves the following entities: the *county*, the *township*, the *incorporated village*, the *school district*, and *special districts*. Except for the Federal and state governments, all the units may be called "local." In 1942 and in 1952, units of government in the United States, distributed by type, were as follows [2]:

|  | 1942 | 1952 | PER CENT CHANGE |
|---|---|---|---|
| Federal | 1 | 1 | 0.0 |
| States | 48 | 48 | 0.0 |
| Counties | 3,050 | 3,049 | 0.0 |
| Townships or towns | 18,919 | 17,202 | —9.1 |
| Municipalities | 16,220 | 16,778 | 3.4 |
| School districts | 108,579 | 67,346 | —38.0 |
| Special districts | 8,299 | 12,319 | 48.4 |
| Total | 155,116 | 116,743 | —24.7 |

These numbers compare with over 175,000 units estimated by Anderson ten years earlier.[3] The decrease during the period was chiefly in school districts and in the townships and towns.

## THE COUNTY

With the exception of those residing in New England, this is by far the most important form of government with which rural people in the United States have to deal. In New England the township supplants the county in importance. However, the county exists in some form in all of the 48 states. The county as an area is ordinarily an arbitrary unit bearing little relation in its boundaries to physical features or to the natural social groupings in the population. In the areas surveyed according to the rectangular pattern adopted in 1785, the counties tend to be shaped into squares and oblongs, depending on the number and arrangement of the townships included within them. They are by no means uniform in size. The largest county in

[2] "Governments in United States in 1952," United States Bureau of the Census, p. 1.
[3] William Anderson, "The Units of Government in the United States," *Public Administration Service Publication 42*, Chicago, 1934.

area is San Bernardino in California, with 20,175 square miles. It is as large as the five New England states of Vermont, New Hampshire, Connecticut, Massachusetts, and Rhode Island combined. The smallest county is Arlington, Virginia, with only 25 square miles.[4]

**Size in population.** As the counties vary in area, so do they in population. The frequency distribution by population for 1940 and 1950 was as follows:

|  | *1940* | *1950* |
|---|---|---|
| Under 5,000 | 236 | 254 |
| 5,000–10,000 | 466 | 508 |
| 10,000–25,000 | 1,255 | 1,171 |
| 25,000–50,000 | 669 | 640 |
| 50,000–100,000 | 253 | 252 |
| 100,000–250,000 | 114 | 147 |
| Over 250,000 | 57 | 77 |
| Total | 3,050 | 3,049 |

It is clear that the functioning of government is going to be quite a different matter in the smallest as compared with the largest county. Moreover, there were 547 counties in which there were fewer than 10 people per square mile; and 70 per cent had fewer than 50 per square mile, which is about the average density of population in the United States.

The county is a creature of the state and legally "but an agent of the state with little or no discretion as to the selection of the duties which it will discharge."[5] The officers, their duties, responsibilities, rates of pay, methods and times of election, and the like, are all prescribed by statutes of the state. The county levies and collects taxes for the state; it enforces state laws, and, in a legal sense, its sheriff and attorney are officers of the state.

However, it is in practice a unit of *local* government. The county officers are elected by the people of the county, not appointed by the state. In practice the county frequently exercises some discretion as to choice of methods in discharging functions. For example, in some states there are counties in which the welfare program for direct relief is handled by the county board and in others it is the responsibility of township boards. There are then two points of view from which to regard

[4] Anderson, *op. cit.*, p. 16 ff.
[5] Lane W. Lancaster, *Government in Rural America*, p. 56. New York: D. Van Nostrand Company, 1937.

the county: (*a*) as an agent of the state, and (*b*) as a unit of local self-government. It is perhaps reasonable to say that while *legally* it is an arm of the state government, in *reality* it is a self-governing unit which has considerable powers of its own and a great deal of administrative freedom in interpreting state laws.

Its functions are the familiar ones, having to do with enforcing the laws (police function); administering public welfare, health, and, in some places, educational services; maintaining and constructing roads and highways; assessing and collecting taxes; and various miscellaneous services, depending on local variations.

The administration of public welfare has in recent years become the most important activity of county government, when measured in terms of money expended. Expenditures for roads rank next in importance. The latter function, however, is more and more being absorbed by the state.

County government varies considerably among the states. Some states have the commissioner form, with from three to ten commissioners. In most of the states these members are elected at large, while in others they are elected by districts. In six Northern states the boards are larger, consisting of one representative from each township or urban ward. These boards vary in size from about fifteen to fifty members, though in a few populous counties they may be larger. In several Southern states the county boards are also large, and represent districts. Examples are the county courts of justices of the peace in Kentucky, Tennessee, and Arkansas.

These differences in the constitution of the governing boards of counties are essentially nominal and do not alter the general similarity of functions performed. Every county has a sheriff and a court clerk or county clerk who is usually secretary of the county board. Most of them have a prosecuting officer, called by various titles including "county attorney," "state's attorney," "district attorney," and "prosecuting attorney." Most counties also have a county or probate judge, a county treasurer, a county recorder or register of deeds, a coroner, an auditor, a surveyor, and a superintendent of schools.

**Is the county a social group?** The counties were laid out in most cases as land *areas*, to be constituted as local units of government after settlement had reached a certain development. As such, they are arbitrary units, and are not designed to represent the natural areas of community life. They had to be small enough in the early period to make the county seat accessible to the population by means of horse-and-buggy, but otherwise there was little or no concern for the social groupings within its boundaries. However, the fact that it was the main form of local government has meant the development of some community consciousness. In the first place, the *county name* became a means of identification. To the question, "where are you from?" comes the reply, "Crawford County," more often than the name of the trade center through which the farmer gets his mail.

The people of a county elect a representative to the state legislature to "look after our interests." Moreover, there are many nongovernmental activities which are conducted on a county basis and which tend to reinforce the community consciousness of the county. Among these activities are the county fair, which encourages a community pride in the achievements of the *county*, and the Farm Bureau, one of the most important of the farm organizations, which is organized on the basis of the county as the unit. Professional societies, doctors, lawyers, and teachers, are also organized in county chapters, societies, or associations. Political parties organize committees in each of the counties. Thus in various ways the county has come to act as a community and to develop a "we-feeling," in spite of the fact that it was not originally designed to be a natural social area.

Among the purely local (county) activities which have come into prominence in recent years especially are the construction and maintenance of county hospitals, libraries, parks, and airports. The county poor farm is another institution maintained independently of the state, and is of long standing.

### THE TOWNSHIP AND TOWN

There are 22 states in which the town or township is a unit of local government. These are all Northern states and, except for Washington, all lie east of the Mountain States. (See Figure

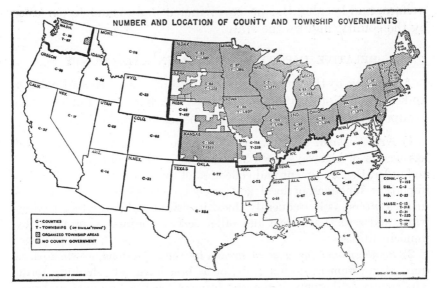

FIGURE 76. *Distribution by States of the Number of County and Township Governments*

76.) They fall roughly into two types: those in New England, and those in the other states. The New England towns (i.e., townships) are much more densely populated than the civil townships of the other states. The latter are almost entirely rural, the incorporated towns and villages being usually independent. The New England towns are so populous as to be practically urban units of government. They also perform most of the functions which elsewhere are discharged by the counties. The New England county has but few functions.

Outside of New England and the Middle States, the political township is usually coextensive with the six-mile square surveyor's township. The offices of these units usually consist of a town board of supervisors (usually 3), an overseer of highways, a clerk, a treasurer, justices of the peace, and constables. The townships vary considerably from state to state in functions, but they are generally limited to poor relief, road maintenance, and fire protection. In some states the assessing of property for tax purposes is done by township assessors. The townships in those states where the county is relatively strong appear to be declining steadily in importance. Responsibility for roads, for welfare, and keeping the peace, is increasingly being taken over by the county, and by the state.

## RELATIVE IMPORTANCE OF TOWN AND COUNTY

According to the relative importance of township and county and the relationship between the two, Kirk H. Porter [6] has grouped the states into four divisions, as follows:

1) *New England.* The town is more important than the county and has charge of highways, poor relief, schools, the maintenance of law and order, the assessment and collection of taxes, and most of the other important functions of local government. Where the town embraces urban centers, as it frequently does, it also undertakes street paving, water and sewage systems, and other services ordinarily provided by municipalities.

2) *Southern and far western areas.* In these sections, townships as units of government do not exist, or at best have only shadowy form. The county is the only important form of local government and performs all of the functions for the local people, outside the incorporated towns, villages, and cities. The township, where it exists at all, is a means of describing property, or may be a voting precinct, a magistrate's district, or a road district.

3) *The township-county or supervisor type* is found in the states of New York, New Jersey, Michigan, Illinois, Wisconsin, and Nebraska. The county board under this system is made up of the administrative officers (supervisors) of the townships. It is therefore a large county board of from 15 to 50 members. The significant aspect of it is that the county is "run" by the townships or representatives of the townships. Such an organic relationship emphasizes the importance of the township. The county unit, however, is very important; still, the system tends towards greater duplication of governmental machinery.

4) *The county-township or commissioner type* is found in the states of Pennsylvania, Ohio, Indiana, Minnesota, Iowa, Missouri, North Dakota, South Dakota, Kansas, and Oklahoma. There is no organic connection between the county and the township, the county being controlled by a board elected usually at large or, if not, from districts which are independent of townships. The townships are in turn governed by boards of supervisors which are independent of the county board. The township is definitely subordinate to the county, the latter greatly overshadowing it in importance.

[6] Kirk H. Porter, *County and Township Government in the United States*, Chapter IV. New York: The Macmillan Company, 1922.

## THE INCORPORATED VILLAGE

The majority of the people of the United States who are classified as rural-nonfarm are able to have more or less effective local government by incorporating villages under the various state laws. Of the 16,677 incorporated cities, towns, or villages (in 1950 Census), 13,235 were rural—that is, under 2,500 population. The incorporation of villages is apparently of greater popularity in the North than in the South, for a very large proportion are found in the northern states. The form of organization for municipalities is defined by the state legislatures of the respective states or by constitutional provision. The power which can be exercised by a municipality is expressly stated in its charter. Thus, the incorporated village, town, or city is authorized to levy and collect taxes, to pass ordinances which have the force of law within its borders, to bond itself and borrow money for improvements of various kinds. It can acquire property and hold it for the use of the people of the community, and do many other things. It is about the most significant type of local government in rural America, from the standpoint of the services which it can perform for its citizens and the degree of local autonomy which it enjoys.

Unlike the township or the county, the incorporated village or town represents a natural social grouping. In fact, it developed into a *community* before it became a unit of government, whereas the reverse was usually true in the county and township. Moreover, the village is a unit in which are combined a number of functions. It is not only a municipality for the exercise of the powers of police and other means of social control, but it is also the school district, the library district, and the unit of other social services as the people may decide.

## SPECIAL DISTRICTS

These include districts created for specific and limited purposes, such as drainage, irrigation, fire service, highway development, cemetery maintenance, soil conservation, and the like. About a third of all special districts reported in 1952 were drainage and SCS districts; highway districts were also very

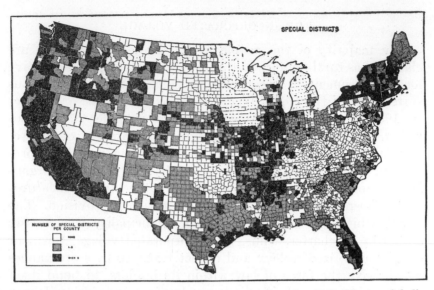

FIGURE 77. *Distribution of Special Districts by Counties, 1942.* The special districts include such units as drainage districts, irrigation, fire service, and soil-conservation districts.

important. (See Figure 77.) Districts in 1952 were as follows:[7]

| TYPE | NUMBER | PER CENT | TYPE | NUMBER | PER CENT |
|---|---|---|---|---|---|
| All kinds | 12,319 | 100.0 | Housing | 863 | 7.0 |
| Fire | 2,272 | 18.4 | Drainage | 2,174 | 17.6 |
| Highways | 774 | 6.3 | Soil conservation | 1,981 | 16.1 |
| Health and | | | Irrigation and | | |
| hospitals | 371 | 3.0 | water conservation | 641 | 5.2 |
| Sanitation | 429 | 3.5 | Cemeteries | 911 | 7.4 |
| Nonhighway | | | Urban water supply | 665 | 5.4 |
| transportation | 159 | 1.3 | Other | 1,079 | 8.8 |

One, and perhaps the main, aspect of special districts is that they are usually able to levy taxes or special assessments for the purposes for which they are created. For example, once an irrigation district is created, bonds may be issued and sold against the property included in the district, and taxes or assessments may be made and collected with which to pay interest and provide a sinking fund to retire the bonds.

One of the most important types of special districts for rural people is the soil-conservation district. Practically all of the

[7] "Governments in the United States, 1952," United States Bureau of the Census, p. 5.

states have now passed enabling acts which permit the formation of these districts for the purpose of effecting a soil-conservation program on the farms included within the district. Such districts are created under the act when a majority of the landowners within a given area (which may be parts of several counties or all or part of one county) request that a district be established. Once it is created, officers are elected in a specified manner, and the district may vote to have certain land-use regulations put into force in the district. These regulations, like the ordinances of a city or of a county, carry the force of law. The district, once created, may also enjoy the helpful cooperation of experts in agronomy, soil management, erosion control, and farm management, who are employed and paid by the United States Soil Conservation Service.

### CRITICISMS OF AMERICAN LOCAL GOVERNMENT

The political scientists and others have levied many severe criticisms against local government in the United States. Among these are the following:

1) There is an excessive number of units, often overlapping in function. Specifically, there are too many school districts, townships, and counties, with power to levy taxes and often, as in the case of counties and townships, performing like functions (road construction and maintenance, poor relief, etc.).

2) The units are frequently too small in population numbers and inadequate in taxable wealth to perform effectively the services expected of them. Attention is called to the large proportion of counties with fewer than 5,000 people. It is stated that there should be 35,000 people in a county as a minimum. There should be taxable wealth to the amount of $20,000,000 at least. R. R. Renne reported that of 56 Montana counties, 36 had a taxable valuation of less than $6,000,000— six of them had fewer than 2,500 people.[8] Carl F. Reuss found that 26 of the 39 counties in Washington fell below 35,000 population and the $20,000,000 assessed valuation standard.[9]

[8] R. R. Renne, "Montana County Organization, Services and Costs," *Montana State College AES Bulletin 298*, 1935, p. 97.

[9] Carl F. Reuss, "County Government in Washington," *State College of Washington AES Bulletin 400*, 1941, p. 49.

Or, if more liberal minimum standards are set, as indicated by
Reuss at 20,000 residents and an assessed valuation of
$10,000,000, then 20 of the 39 counties fell below the population
minimum and 12 below the valuation standard. Well over half
the counties fell below the population standard.

3) In the county government there are too many elective officers
with coordinate rank. This means there is no one of them who
is responsible for the "running" of the county. The commissioners cannot supervise the clerk, the treasurer, the auditor,
the attorney, or the coroner, because they too were elected by
the people and are responsible only to the people.

### SOME REFORMS PROPOSED

To meet these various problems it has been proposed that
states modify the laws governing the structure of county
government, so that there may be fewer elective officials, and
a centralization of authority and responsibility in one officer
or at least in a board. Under this responsible authority there
could be organized a hierarchy of officials who would be subject
to its direction and control. Moreover, the number of officers
should not be specified. It is obviously ludicrous to require of
a county with no more than 2,500 people that it have the same
number of elected officials as a county with half a million. One
person might perform with ease all of the functions required
of an auditor, clerk, treasurer, and recorder; yet under the
existing system these must be separate elected officials, whether
the county be small or large. In some states where the number of
local units of government is great, the number of elected officials
is baffling to the voter. (See Figure 78.)

Another reform proposal is that the county boundaries be
redrawn in such way as to create more nearly natural social
areas. Some counties have no possibility of achieving any unity,
because so many segments of their areas belong to the trade
areas of communities located in other counties.

The small size of the units can be met only by outright consolidation of two or more counties. This has been widely discussed and the idea promoted by interested students of county
government. In one state (Utah) 5 counties were proposed

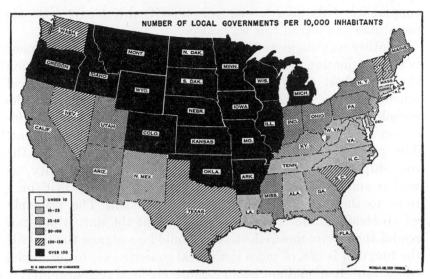

FIGURE 78. *Number of Local Governments per 10,000 Inhabitants*

for the existing 28.[10] In Minnesota, William A. Anderson suggested 35 counties in place of the existing 87. Similar proposals for consolidation of units have been made in several other states including Texas, Colorado, Montana, Washington, and Arkansas. In spite of the obvious advantages in favor of consolidation, there are very few instances where it has been achieved. The reason seems to be social-psychological. An excellent case can be made out for consolidation on grounds of governmental efficiency, economy, and considerations of distance or area. But, as Euler points out, "county consolidation has been retarded not so much by economic factors as by the fact that such socio-psychological factors as the habits, the attitudes, the customs, and the traditions of the people concerned have not been given serious consideration." [11]

To some extent counties are cooperating for the support of certain services which are beyond the capacity of each one separately to maintain. An example of this is the district library, where two or more counties form a working relationship to

[10] George H. Hansen, "A Regional Redistricting Plan for the State of Utah," *Brigham Young University Studies 5*, 1937.

[11] H. L. Euler, "County Unification in Kansas," *Contribution to Education 645*, Columbia University, 1935, p. 82.

support it.   Jails, poor farms, and public health departments are sometimes handled in this way, also.

Another way suggested for improvement of local government is the elimination of overlapping jurisdictions. This suggestion carries with it the proposal of complete elimination of local school districts in favor of a unified county system and the complete elimination of the townships. It means also a reallocation of functions among the various units of government. The process has been going on to some extent among the townships, which have lost some functions to the county, as well as among the counties, which have lost some of their functions to the state and the Federal government. The principle which should guide this reallocation is that the unit which can render the service most effectively should be assigned the task. If the function is one of more than local concern—as, for example, education—it should not be an exclusively local responsibility.

However, if the townships are abandoned, the farmers would then have no purely local instrument of government. The point can be made that in 36 states no such units of government exist now, and farmers seem to survive their absence. Furthermore, in those states where townships do exist, they are not to be regarded as effective instruments of government. This is all quite true, and the question is whether farmers can or cannot enjoy the advantages of a local mechanism of government. C. J. Galpin pointed out many years ago that the "farmers of the United States have no effective local municipalities." [12] He proposed an "alliance of city and farm" through the establishment of a single municipality composed of the villages and the surrounding farm people tributary to it. Galpin would incorporate the villagers and farmers in one legal entity, abolishing the present townships (for farmers) and the village corporations with their small areas. The new legal corporation —call it city, town, or village—would be coextensive with the trade-area community. The advantages would be many, not the least of which would be the tying together in the municipality of all occupations, instead of segregating the farmers from nonfarmers as happens in the present township and

[12] C. J. Galpin, *Rural Social Problems*, p. 213.   New York: D. Appleton-Century Co., 1924.

village system. It would have the further advantage that the municipality itself would correspond to a natural social area for trading relations, and as a rule would represent rather closely the attendance area of the local high school. It could serve effectively as the local school district, and also discharge other local governmental functions.

The chief disadvantage probably lies in the possibility of conflict between the farmers and nonfarmers, between the "village core" and the "farming fringe," to use Galpin's phrase. Obviously, the interests of the two differ at many points, even though it is recognized that they have many basic interests in common. For example, people who live in the village core are able to have sewage and water systems and other services not now practical to extend to open-country dwellers. Should the open country pay the same amount of taxes as the villagers when these services are not enjoyed by them? Galpin recognizes the difficulty, and suggests a system of zoning. Zone 1 would be the "city core," zone 2 would be a concentric belt around the village about two miles wide, and zone 3 would be the remainder of the area. He envisioned an area about 15 miles square.

The merits of Galpin's proposal are many, but the prospects of its general adoption do not seem promising. After a quarter of a century since the idea was first enunciated by Galpin, there appears to have been no practical application of it. Perhaps, like any reform, the movement needs an effective promoter.

It has been frequently observed by students of local government that county government is one of the most conservative of institutions. As one surveys the many obvious weaknesses of the county system and considers that practically no changes have occurred since the foundations of the various states, there is cause for wonder at its constancy.

The shortcomings of the county and the township as governmental units have been exposed by numerous studies and by many competent observers. However desirable they may have been in the early period of land settlement, these units have failed to adapt to changing conditions. For the people who reside on farms, neither the county nor the township constitutes an effective and serviceable unit.

## QUESTIONS FOR DISCUSSION

1. Recount historical instances in which families, churches, and business groups have exercised important governmental functions. What objections might be raised to having either of the latter two institutions take over the reins of government at present?
2. Set forth ways in which a person's relationship to government is similar and also dissimilar to his relationship to other institutions.
3. Can you perceive a possible relationship between the manner in which New England was settled and the fact that townships are of more importance than counties as governmental units in that area?
4. In what ways should the functional relationship between the county government and the average citizen differ in a very large as compared with a small county?
5. Characterize the status of the county as (a) an agent of the state and (b) a self-governing unit. Is there any evidence that the county is becoming more and more an agent of the state? What bearing do present trends have on the persistence and vitality of the democratic process on the local level?
6. The text presents evidence in support of the view that the county is a social unit or group. Would you agree, on the basis of your knowledge, that your home county is a social group with a consciousness of unity?
7. Treat the township as a local governmental unit from the standpoint of (a) spatial distribution, (b) official personnel, and (c) customary functions.
8. Point out regional differences in the relationship between the county and township. Which of the various arrangements possesses the greatest merit according to your view? Discuss.
9. How does an incorporated village differ from one that is unincorporated?
10. What needs have been satisfied through the organization of special districts? Give the advantages that might accrue from the organization of soil-conservation districts.
11. Review the main criticisms of local government as it exists in rural America.
12. Present reasons for believing that consolidation of counties should result in greater economy and increased efficiency.
13. Appraise Galpin's proposal that villages and their tributary farm population be incorporated into single functional units.
14. Account for the fact that proposals for reform of local units of government have rarely gone beyond the "talking" stage.

## SELECTED REFERENCES

Anderson, William. "The Units of Government in the United States," Public Administration Service Publication 42. Chicago, 1934.

Anderson, William, and Weidner, Edward W. *State and Local Government in the United States.* New York: Henry Holt and Co., 1951.

Bates, F. G. "Village Government in New England," *American Political Science Review,* August, 1912.

Brannen, C. O. "Characteristics and Costs of County Government in Arkansas." *University of Arkansas AES Bulletin 338.* 1937.

Fairlie, John A. *Local Government in Counties, Towns, and Villages.* New York: The Century Co., 1906.

"Governments in United States in 1952." Washington, D.C.: United States Bureau of the Census, 1953.

Klemmedson, G. S. "The Cost of Local Government in Larimer County, Colorado." *Colorado State College AES Bulletin 361.* 1930.

Kumlien, W. F. "Basic Trends of Social Change in South Dakota: Local Government." *South Dakota State College AES Bulletin 347.* 1941.

Lancaster, Lane W. *Government in Rural America,* Second Edition. New York: D. Van Nostrand Company, 1952.

Loomis, Charles P., and Beegle, J. Allan. *Rural Social Systems,* Chapters 17, 18, 19. New York: Prentice-Hall, Inc., 1950.

Manny, Theodore B. *Rural Municipalities.* New York: The Century Co., 1930.

Moore, H. R. "Local Government in Two Rural Ohio Counties." *Ohio AES Bulletin 597.* November, 1938.

Porter, Kirk H. *County and Township Government in the United States.* New York: The Macmillan Company, 1929.

Snider, Clyde F. "American County Government: A Mid-Century Review," *American Political Science Review,* 46:66–80, March, 1952.

Spicer, G. W. "Ten Years of County Manager Government in Virginia," *University of Virginia Ext. Bulletin, Vol. XXIII, No. 3,* September, 1945.

Wager, Paul W. (ed.) *County Government Across the Nation.* Chapel Hill: University of North Carolina Press, 1950.

Weidner, Edward W., and Preiss, Jack. "Rural Local Government and Politics and Adult Education," in *Rural Social Systems and Adult Education.* East Lansing: Michigan State College Press, 1953.

*CHAPTER 23*

# FARM PEOPLE AND THE FEDERAL GOVERNMENT

Throughout American history the farmer has faced a series of problems with which he could not deal successfully at the local community level and has therefore sought their correction through action of the Federal government. Very early in the history of the nation the settlers on the frontier importuned the Federal government to grant them the land free. For nearly half a century before the Homestead Act was finally passed in 1862, this issue was hotly debated in Congress. After the War Between the States came the rapid settlement of the trans-Mississippi West, the building of the railroads throughout the continent, and the extensive exploitation of the timber, mining, and other resources of the new land.

## TRANSPORTATION PROBLEMS

Farm people generally discovered that the achievement of free land under the Homestead Act did not by any means solve all of their problems. The rapid expansion of the acreage sown to crops as a result of the accelerated rate of settlement, particularly in the Great Plains, brought about serious overproduction. To the farmers, however, the problem was not so much one of overproduction, as they saw it, but the failure of the system of distribution. In some cases it was a question of a lack of transportation facilities. In other cases, where the railroads had penetrated, it was a question of excessive freight rates. In short, the farmers blamed the railroads for their economic distress. Says F. A. Shannon:

When the farmers of Iowa, Nebraska, or Kansas complained that it took the value of one bushel of corn to pay the freight on another bushel, or when the Minnesota or Dakota farmers said the same of wheat, often this was no exaggeration and sometimes it was an understatement.[1]

It was out of the period of economic distress following the War Between the States that the Granger Movement arose and this had as one of its main purposes the securing of Federal regulation over the railroads. The final passage of the Interstate Commerce Commission Act in 1887 has always been claimed as a victory for the Grange.

As a matter of fact, transportation has been one of the serious problems in American agriculture from the very beginning. The country is so vast that the provision of railroads and highways came slowly and at great cost. The government subsidized the railways with huge grants of public lands and subsequently appropriated money from the national treasury for the development of a national-state system of public highways. Grants of public land also were made for the construction of wagon roads and canals at the time land grants were made for the railroads. Farm organizations were active in promoting such Federal legislation, particularly the National Grange.

### CREDIT AND INTEREST RATES

Besides transportation, a major complaint of the American farmer has been credit. Until 1916 the farmer had difficulty in getting capital even at the exorbitant rates of interest which he had to pay. Farm organizations have therefore advocated Federal intervention in the matter of credit for many years—at least since the 1880's. It was not until 1916, however, that such intervention came. The Farm Loan Act of that year provided for the creation of twelve regional land banks under the supervision of the Farm Loan Board. Loans were to be made to farmers for the purchase of land, equipment, or livestock, or for retirement of an existing mortgage. The loans were to run for a period of as many as 34 years at 5 per cent interest—later reduced to 4 per cent.

The Farm Credit Acts of 1933 and 1937 have considerably enlarged the Federal credit facilities available to the farmers.

[1] Fred A. Shannon, *The Farmer's Last Frontier*, pp. 295, 298.   New York: Farrar and Rinehart, 1945.

In addition to the 12 land banks, the system now includes
12 Production Credit Corporations and their constituent cooperative Production Credit Associations, 12 Federal Intermediate Credit Banks, and one central and 12 regional Banks
for Cooperatives. Certain emergency credit facilities—such as
Land Bank Commissioner loans, feed and seed loans and the
Federal Farm Mortgage Corporation—are designed to aid
farmers who are unable to supply first-class security.

Farm credit is also available from the Farmers Home Administration to farmers who are unable to secure credit elsewhere.
Designed to rehabilitate farmers who were on relief rolls during
the depression years, this organization has assisted upward of
a million farm families who have participated in its rehabilitation program. It has 2,000 county offices throughout the nation,
and employs a large staff of regional, state, and county personnel.

### PRICES AND MARKETS

Prices and markets have likewise been concerns of farmers
and have led them to bring pressure upon Congress for special
legislation. In the '80's and '90's farmers regarded the problem
of prices chiefly as one of manipulating the money of the
country. The Populist Movement favored the free and un-
limited coinage of silver along with gold as a chief means of
solving the economic problems of the farmer. However, the
Populist Party was unsuccessful in getting its program adopted
even though it was supported by the Democratic Party under
the leadership of William Jennings Bryan.

**The Agricultural Marketing Act, 1929.** The main achievement in legislation affecting farm prices has come about since
1929. In that year Congress passed the Agricultural Marketing
Act. This act provided for the promotion and financing of
cooperative marketing organizations under the Federal Farm
Board, and for the maintenance of prices through purchases
by government-sponsored stabilization corporations of those
products which existed in surplus amounts. When the prices of
wheat or cotton began to decline on the market, the stabilization corporation would begin purchasing in the hope of
bringing the price up again. Surplus production proved to be

so great, however, that the efforts of government to maintain prices by this device proved futile, for by 1932 they had fallen to disastrously low levels.

**Legislation of 1933 and after.** In 1933 began the series of Congressional acts looking toward the improvement of agricultural prices. As general background for what happened during the Roosevelt administration it is important to realize that American agriculture had been in a depressed condition since 1920 and had seen its most profitable years during the first two decades of the century. Following World War I the price level fell drastically and remained comparatively low throughout the decade of the 1920's, despite the unparalleled industrial prosperity. It was inevitable, therefore, that during this period there would arise from the farm population a demand that agricultural prices be placed on an equality with industrial prices. At no time during the 1920's did the index of prices of farm products in the United States rise to a position of equality with industrial prices. The farmer's dollar, therefore, was worth consistently less than 100 cents in terms of the goods and services which he had to buy. Throughout the period of the 1920's the demand for "farm relief" was spearheaded by the Farm Bloc in Congress and actively supported by the American Farm Bureau Federation. The McNary-Haugen Bill was the main point of controversy. It provided that farm prices should equal the world price of the particular commodity plus the amount of the tariff for that portion of each crop which was sold in the United States. Surpluses would be exported at whatever price could be obtained and the loss would be paid from a fund secured by levying an equalization fee on each commodity. This bill was twice passed by Congress and twice vetoed by President Coolidge. The next step of the farm organization was to secure commitments from the leading political parties and candidates in the election campaign of 1932, and the winning candidate, Franklin D. Roosevelt, agreed after his election to be guided by the farm group themselves in setting up a national program.

**Parity with industry.** Immediately after the inauguration of Roosevelt, Secretary of Agriculture Wallace called the farm leaders of all of the main farm organizations together and they agreed upon certain principles which were incorporated in the 1933 Agricultural Adjustment Act. In signing the measure, President Roosevelt, on May 12, 1933, approved the declared policy of Congress to "give agricultural commodities the purchasing power with respect to articles farmers buy, equivalent to the purchasing power of agricultural commodities in the base period 1909–1914." Thus was voiced by the President of the United States the battle cry of the farmers throughout the previous decades for equality with industry. "Parity" became the new slogan and the basis of the new price program.

After the new administration had committed itself to raising the income of farmers, its first move was to reduce the surplus of farm products, which was depressing prices, by setting up controls over production. The Agricultural Adjustment Act of 1933 provided that farmers be compensated for voluntarily reducing the acreage of those crops of which there was a surplus. The funds for compensation were to be derived from a tax levied upon the processors of the crops concerned, such as the millers, brewers, and textile manufacturers. The AAA represented a new sort of intervention of the Federal government in agricultural affairs. It meant doing for agriculture through government influence what certain branches of industry had done voluntarily. In so far as price is a result of the ratio of supply to demand, it is possible to affect price by controlling supply. If the supply of farm products could be restricted, in other words, the price would automatically rise. Such was the reasoning back of the Act of 1933.

It was, however, challenged in the courts and finally declared unconstitutional in 1936. The legislation which followed the court verdict, seeking the same end by only slightly different means, emphasized soil conservation as a basic measure. Farmers were compensated for carrying out certain soil-conserving or soil-building practices; the funds came directly from the public treasury rather than from a processing tax. Thus a farmer who planted more of his acres in soil-conserving crops, such as grass, or in soil-building crops, such as alfalfa and clover, or who terraced his land, built check dams in ravines, or performed other acts looking to conservation of the soil, would be paid a specified sum per acre for doing so. Crops like wheat, cotton, corn, or other row crops were not regarded as soil building or conserving, since they tended to promote rather than retard erosion. Consequently, a certain shifting of crops, from those which were in surplus to those which were not and yet to those still considered beneficial to the soil, was achieved by a more indirect approach. As D. C. Blaisdell points out, the change in approach did not affect materially the practical operation of the program, for "soil conservation was never absent from the first phase of the farm program, nor was production control, at least indirectly, absent from the second phase." [2]

Supplementing the soil-conservation technique were several other programs which constituted a part of the total attack on the price problem. Among them were marketing programs for fruit, vegetables, and dairy products, besides Federal purchase of surplus crops for free distribution among people on relief.

**Attempt to secure local participation of farmers.** As if realizing the momentous centralization of power in the Federal government which the new program entailed, the leaders were from the beginning eager to secure local participation of the farm people themselves. The question of centralization will be discussed presently, but it is of interest to observe in passing that the agricultural officials were well aware of the criticism which would be leveled at them because of the unprecedented extension of Federal authority which the legislation involved. Local participation was promoted through the setting up of township and county committees of farmers, who were to decide in their respective jurisdictions the allotments of acreage of various crops to which each farmer was entitled under the law. Since most of the more than 3,000 counties in the United States are agricultural and since there would be at least as many county committees as agricultural counties, the total number of county committees would be nearly 3,000—not to mention the innumerable township or other related committees.

**Act of 1938.** By 1937 the drought had run its course and favorable weather had brought farm production back to levels where surpluses were of such magnitude that they could not

---

[2] D. C. Blaisdell, *Government and Agriculture*, p. 48. New York: Farrar and Rinehart, 1940.

be handled by the old program. Farm prices were again falling below the parity level. This situation brought renewed pressure from farm organizations for a long-range program which would guarantee farmers their share of the national income. The result was the passage of the Agricultural Adjustment Act of 1938. Its general purposes were to conserve the soil resources and use them efficiently, to assist in marketing farm products at home and abroad, to regulate interstate and foreign commerce in cotton, wheat, corn, tobacco and rice, and to protect consumers by maintaining adequate reserves of food and feed.

To achieve these ends the new law authorized continuation of payments of cash benefits to farmers for carrying on good farm practices as determined by the Secretary of Agriculture. It also provided that the Secretary of Agriculture might set acreage allotments for certain crops, and farmers who keep their plantings within the allotments qualify for benefit payments under the conservation program. Farmers who do not stay within their allotments have benefit payments withheld and lose eligibility for maximum commodity loans and parity payments. In addition, the bill provided for setting up the Commodity Credit Corporation which is authorized to make loans on any agricultural commodity with the commodity itself as security. When supplies of the given crop rise beyond certain levels specified or when prices fall below certain levels, the corporation may make advances on a specified percentage of the parity price to farmers who have planted within their acreage allotments. The effect is to put a floor under prices and prevent their collapse. Furthermore, the government protects itself by providing marketing quotas to prevent the dumping of surpluses on the market. These various provisions referred to as soil conservation, ever-normal granary, and income-protecting features are supplemented by several other provisions which give the government broader powers of action in the field of agriculture than it has ever had before.

**The war and its effects.** The outbreak of World War II created an extraordinary situation in which all limitations on agricultural production were lifted. There was a phenomenal increase in total production in 1942, 1943, and 1944, about 35 per cent above the average production from 1935 to 1939, inclusive. This expansion in the volume of farm products was achieved in spite of the decline of approximately 5,000,000 in the farm population. While the demands of World War II disposed of even the increased produce at high prices, the demonstrated productivity foreshadows serious difficulty in maintaining prices after the effects of the war have disappeared. A renewed call for government action may be expected at such a time.

## CENTRALIZATION OF GOVERNMENT

The present brief review of the more recent developments in agricultural legislation emphasizes one of the most notable changes in the relation of the American farmer to the national government, namely, the unprecedented centralization of rule. It is not a trend peculiar to the United States; it is practically world-wide and involves far more than control of agriculture. The recent flowering of dictatorships in various countries of the world is an extreme aspect of the general trend. In other countries there has been less spectacular, though no less real, transference of function from the local to the national level of government.

The rise of the all-powerful state and the decline of local autonomy were accelerated by the world-wide depression of the 1930's, but it would be a mistake to regard the depression as the chief factor involved. Such a development must be considered against the background of the expanding area of social interaction resulting from the rapid and easy means of communication. Also to be considered are the changing and expanding needs of people for services which local units of government are unable to supply. The far-reaching developments of Federal intervention in agriculture, it should be noted, came about mainly as an answer to the demands of farmers themselves expressed through the large farm organizations.

**Social effects of centralization.** The transfer of functions from the local to the central government, together with the addition of many activities to the central unit, not previously part of either it or the local unit, could not but affect fundamentally the life of the rural community. The extent and nature of the changes that have occurred in the local community, it is impossible to judge with assurance at the present time, since the problem has not been carefully studied. But some of the immediate effects of the extension of Federal power into the local community, which are readily observable, include the following:

1) The creation of a large number of local committees, particularly in connection with the agricultural program, whose function is mainly to put into effect policies determined at the national level.

2) The decline in voluntary committee service in which members pay their own expenses and contribute their time, in favor of committee service for which the Federal Government pays "per diem," including some compensation for the time spent and complete coverage of expenses.

3) Responsibility for making decisions as to policy was held by the Federal authority, although the local committees made decisions within the general rules laid down in Washington.

4) "Working for the Government" became an occupation for a considerable number of additional people in the community. The "government man" was no longer an unusual or rare individual.

5) With all these developments, the Federal government is no longer the rather remote entity "down in Washington," as it has been traditionally considered by farmers in the past.

In discussing the social significance of centralization of political power, C. C. Zimmerman has the following to say:

Most of the agents of the government become clerical employees responsible directly to the centralized authority. This bureaucracy, with its good and bad features, grows in power. Where local government exists, a citizen represents a vote, a neighbor, and a physical acquaintance. The town official tends to be very considerate of him. But the civil service bureaucrat in the centralized government feels impelled to listen only to those who have the rare privilege of speaking directly to the central authorities. Consequently, the lower classes, when more and more they become physical wards of the central government, lose a friendly psychological relation with its agents. A poverty-stricken individual in this typical village may live in a mediocre house practically given to him by the central government. But his chances for securing

kind neighborly recognition when he approaches a bureaucratic clerk
are by no means so great as under localized control. The bureaucrat is
forever concerned with keeping his job or gaining promotion. Consequently, he tries to avoid any action where responsibility may be
charged against him, and he acts only under direct orders from above.
He always says "Maybe," or "Do you have permission?" or "Come
again and I will see," rather than "Yes." [3]

This statement probably paints the situation in darker hue
than it would appear in reality. For example, the employee of
a central government, who works in a local community, is not
likely to be as "hard-boiled" and callous to the needs of people
as the author infers. It is likely that in his efforts to secure and
maintain his status as resident of the community he would
strive for friendly and sympathetic relations between himself
and the other residents. It seems improbable that a central
government would consider a person an effective employee who
could not maintain reasonably good relations. Even a highly
centralized and autocratic government cannot ignore public
opinion. Nevertheless, Zimmerman has stated some of the
unfavorable possibilities that may arise in connection with the
centralization of government.

Perhaps more important as a social concomitant of the
centralization of authority is the decline in local interest and
participation in public affairs. Zimmerman also comments on
this point:

The local people lose interest in community affairs and become im-
mersed primarily in private doings. Local government tends to become
a matter of petitions which are directed only at the more obvious
(objective) "injustices." The intangible things in government cannot
be clarified by petition since the bureaucrats generally do not know the
local situation. Government passes more and more from subjectivity
to objectivity, and from the hands of thoughtful people to the peti-
tioners.[4]

In England, where the growth of the central authority has
all but obliterated local self-government, participation in parish

[3] C. C. Zimmerman, *The Changing Community*, p. 650. New York: Harper and
Brothers, 1938. See also by the same author, "Centralism vs. Localism in the Community," *American Sociological Review*, 1938, 3:155–166.
[4] Zimmerman, *op. cit.*, p. 651.

meetings and parish councils has fallen to a very low level. In a report, *Country Planning*, published in 1944, the Agricultural Economics Institute of Oxford University stated that "it is a far cry to the days when parochial government was a reality in which everyone took an active part," when "people controlled their own affairs, social and industrial, by a scheme of administration maintained by the consensus of public opinion, without recourse to the law of the land and at very small cost." [5]

All this has changed and . . . instead of this personal participation in the active administration of his parish, the rural dweller today can do no more than cast a vote for the election of someone to represent him on a larger local administrative unit, the executive functions of which are carried out by salaried officials. After holding up his hand at a Parish Meeting, or making a cross on a ballot paper, the man in the field has no further part nor lot in the administration of his countryside.[6]

Later on in the report the authors made the general observation that "local government in those villages of the survey area with only a Parish Meeting is nearly everywhere a farce." [7] They were of the opinion, however, that the Parish Meeting could "be made to work," because they had seen examples where it had worked.

### THE DILEMMA

There can be no doubt that the centralization of authority is accompanied by certain trends which are disquieting to those who would maintain local self-determination. In the United States, where the democratic tradition glorifies the principal of local autonomy and regards the central government with some distrust lest it encroach upon local prerogatives, the recent trend toward centralization is viewed by many with misgiving. There is fear expressed that the democratic United States we have known may be moving towards the sort of totalitarianism which has characterized Italy and Germany. At the same time, it is not easy to see how the local units of government can

[5] *Country Planning*, a staff report by the Agricultural Economics Research Institute, p. 89. Oxford: Oxford University Press, 1944.
[6] *Ibid.*, p. 89.
[7] *Ibid.*, p. 93.

perform effectively the functions which the people are asking government to do. The dilemma therefore is this: How can the increased services demanded of the Federal government be secured, without losing the sense of local responsibility and local self-determination?

**Old political devices inadequate.** The New England town meeting, in which all the citizens meet once a year and agree upon policies, plan future activities, hear reports from the elected officers, and elect new officers, has been idealized if not romanticized in the American tradition. It symbolizes local self-determination, the participation of all, the real rule of the people. However, such a mechanism, while suited to small units—neighborhoods, primary groups—is not practicable for larger population units. Representative government has to supplant the direct action by the voters themselves, especially when the number of citizens is so large that they could not possibly be accommodated in the largest available meeting place. In spite of the patent inadequacies of the town meeting as a means of government for large units of population, people who have witnessed it operate on a small scale are reluctant to substitute representative devices in its stead and grant powers which cannot be easily and readily recovered if abused.

Undoubtedly, much of the criticism of central government expansion in the United States is the result of comparing it, always unfavorably, with the town meeting. Usually, too, it is a romanticized version of the town meeting, such as children read about in their history books or which is presented pictorially in *Life* magazine about once a year. The town meeting is a part of the political folklore of the United States and stands as the yardstick by which other forms of political organization are judged—and usually found wanting.

It is futile to expect that the vast functions of the Federal government in the United States can be operated on any such simple plan. They must be carried on by salaried civil servants who, as far as possible, are chosen because of their special competence to do the tasks assigned them. This means bureaucracy. No government can operate without a bureaucracy. There may be evils inherent in such a government, but "bureaucrats" are indispensable. There must be, therefore, a frank acceptance of the necessity of centralization of government and the accompanying mechanics of organization.

Another point which needs to be mentioned is the inevitability of combining local and national interests. The farmer's social horizon is becoming ever broader. No longer can he confine his concerns solely to his own farm or his own community. He is coming more and more to realize that his interests are bound up with those of the national, even the world, community. What happens in the rest of the country or the world may affect him vitally. In his own interest, therefore, he cannot well avoid joining hands with those outside his locality. Such cooperative action can be implemented on the larger scale only by the extension of the functions of the central government.

### POSSIBLE MEANS OF BETTERMENT

The social crises of recent decades have thrown into relief the inadequacies of the old local structures of government by making demands upon them which they could not fulfill without help from the outside. But, since centralization of authority is so vigorously opposed by many people, the problem of finding a solution is extremely difficult. Clearly, the old forms do not meet the demands of modern life. There is need for change, and change actually is taking place. The decline of local autonomy is everywhere apparent.

The question seems to be not whether to go back to local institutions, but rather how to mediate central authority at the local level in such a way as to mitigate its unfavorable aspects. It is not realistic to try to undo what has been done over a period of at least two decades, to take away functions from the central and return them to the local unit, or to try otherwise to pump new life into what appears to be moribund. As a starting point in considering the possible solution of the problem it is well to ask and answer the questions of whether the imputed evils of centralized government set forth in previous paragraphs are inherent in the institutional form itself, and whether that form might be adapted and adjusted in such a manner that the needs of local communities could be met without atrophy of local responsibility and decline of local participation.

Perhaps nobody at present can give final answers to these questions. Answers will be produced in the crucible of experience during the coming years. However, it ought to be clear to the student of social history that institutions, being the creatures of men, can be molded and fashioned to meet human needs. The United States government represented at its founding a rather new experience in the history of mankind. The Russian government of communistic origin is also a new experience. Both new forms were the result of revolution; both have undergone a great deal of evolution since their beginnings. As the modern state undergoes its transition from a loose aggregation of local self-governing units to a highly centralized organization there will, no doubt, be more experimentation and more planning. Always there is the possibility that the unusual might happen and that a method of government be invented and applied to meet the needs of the new situation.

**A new technique of administration.** Meanwhile, until a more desirable form is developed, we should consider the possibility of evolving administrative methods within the old forms that will help to cope with changing conditions. That is, in accepting the necessity for centralized government, people should insist its administration be directed to the end that (*a*) services needed and required by the public should be efficiently provided, and that (*b*) a maximum of local responsibility and participation should be encouraged. Such a method would primarily involve a new conception of the role of the Federal agent: that he would act in large part as if locally employed and that his duties would require of him a high degree of training in the art of public administration.

The point might be illustrated by the example of the Land Use Planning program of the United States Department of Agriculture.[8] It was based upon a cooperative agreement between the states and the Federal government, under which the latter would furnish at its expense one or more experts in land utilization, while the former would organize state, county, and township committees to work with the Federal delegate. The

[8] As a Federal program it was abolished by the Congress in 1942 by means of refusing to appropriate money for its continuance. However, its fate does not invalidate its use as an illustration of the possible relations between the various levels of government.

immediate purpose of the program was to develop a wise policy
of land use in the various counties where readjustments apparently needed to be made. A long-term aspect was the coordination at the local level of the various Federal agencies devoting
themselves to agriculture. The work involved making a map
of the county, showing areas suitable for agriculture, forestry,
fish and game reservations, or recreational uses; and ultimately
securing the passage of an ordinance by the county governments
to prohibit future settlement in areas marked as unfit for agricultural purposes.

Obviously, the work could have been performed by experts
without the aid of local committeemen, had this been the
method decided upon. It was done differently, however. Township and county committees were consulted from time to time
and many actually made the major contribution in delineating
lands suitable for the various purposes. The expert checked the
results carefully; where necessary the original judgments of the
committee were revised. He did not assume final authority, however, for ultimate approval remained with the committee.

**The grant-in-aid.** Another device in common use in the
United States, which goes far to meet the new situation, is
the grant-in-aid. Under this system the Federal government
provides funds for specific purposes, supplementing those available at the local level; the administration, however, is left to
the local unit. Examples are numerous. A notable one is in agriculture in the extension services and experiment stations. For
both programs each state receives a certain amount of money
yearly under very general stipulations as to what it may be
spent for or how it may be disbursed. The programs are administered entirely by the states, with the Federal government
making annual inspections to see that the minimum conditions
prescribed in the laws and regulations have been met. They
have the virtue of providing the additional funds that may be
necessary to enable the local unit to meet the demands of its
citizens and, at the same time, leaving the local unit free to
administer them in accordance with local conditions. The
general program is open to the objection that there are serious
inequalities and inefficiencies in the handling of funds, resulting
in forty-eight programs of action instead of one. In the case of

public assistance, for example, the amount of monthly grants to the aged varies widely among the states.

To summarize the chapter briefly: We have noted the long history of the appeals farm people have made to the Federal government for the solution of problems which could not be dealt with at the local level, including the problems of transportation, credit, and prices. Federal legislation during the 1930's placed in Federal agencies unprecedented powers and set up a large number of local organizations. The effect of centralization upon the local community is a decline in local participation and in assumption of responsibility. At the same time, the local units proved inadequate to meet the demands of their people for assistance and for service. The assumption of many functions by the central government seemed, therefore, inevitable. In seeking a solution to the problem of preserving a sense of local responsibility and at the same time providing the services which people demand, it is futile to consider a return to the old system. Rather, some means must be found to mitigate whatever evil effects of centralized administration there may be. The development of a new method of administration and a new kind of administrator is suggested as a possible help, and the further use of the grant-in-aid principle as another.[9]

## QUESTIONS FOR DISCUSSION

1. What were the main causes of agrarian discontent during the last half of the nineteenth century? To what extent did farmers' complaints appear to be justified?
2. Mention the issue or issues involved in the conflict which culminated in the passage of the Homestead Act of 1862.
3. Describe the role played by the Grange and the Populists in helping farmers in their struggle to eliminate abuses by urban interests.
4. Were there any precedents for what the New Deal did by way of giving direct financial aid to farmers? Discuss.
5. List the specific types of financial aid given to farmers by the Federal government from 1933 to the present, along with the objectives that were expected to be achieved through each type of assistance.

[9] For further discussion of this problem see Kimball Young, "Society and the State: Some Neglected Areas of Research and Theory," *American Sociological Review*, 11:137–146, April, 1946.

6. How did American agriculture respond to World War II demands for increased production? On the basis of what has happened in the past, can you predict some of the problems that are likely to arise from the increased productivity? Discuss.

7. If you have resided in a rural area during recent years give your impression as to how people that you know feel about Extension, AAA and FHA officials and committees and their activities.

8. What dilemma has resulted from the expansion of Federal functions to include cooperation with state and local governments in furnishing direct aid to needy individuals and families? Do you regard this dilemma as very serious? Discuss.

9. Mention the traits of the "bureaucrat" considered as a stereotype. Account for the widespread criticism of this stereotype. Do you agree with Zimmerman's criticism? Discuss.

10. Suggest means of minimizing the danger of government personnel acting arbitrarily and of people on the local level losing their interest and sense of responsibility in government.

### SELECTED REFERENCES

Blaisdell, Donald C. *Government and Agriculture.* New York: Farrar and Rinehart, 1940.

Gross, Neal C. "A Post-Mortem on County Planning," *Journal of Farm Economics,* Vol. XXV, No. 3, August, 1943.

Hardin, Charles M. *Soil Conservation and the Struggle for Power in Rural America.* Glencoe, Ill.: The Free Press, 1952.

Lilienthal, David E. *Democracy on the March.* New York: Harper and Brothers, 1944.

MacIver, R. M. *The Web of Government.* New York: The Macmillan Co., 1947.

Selznick, Philip. *TVA and the Grass Roots: A Study in the Sociology of Formal Organization.* Berkeley: University of California Press, 1949.

Taylor, Carl C. *The Farmers' Movement: 1620–1920.* New York: American Book Co., 1953.

Walker, John O. *Grass Roots.* Washington, D.C.: Council on Intergovernment Relations, 1946.

Young, Kimball. "Society and the State," *American Sociological Review,* Vol. XI, No. 2, pp. 137–146, April, 1946.

Zimmerman, Carle C. "Centralism Versus Localism in the Community," *American Sociological Review,* Vol. III, No. 2, pp. 155–166, April, 1938.

# CHAPTER 24

# RURAL WELFARE AND ITS AGENCIES

Formally organized welfare is a comparatively new institution in rural areas. In spite of its recent development, however, it has assumed such importance in the rural community that it deserves special treatment.

The word "welfare," like the words "society" and "culture," has two different usages: the one, general; the other, specific. In the general sense it refers to the condition of society in terms of its well-being, such as the state of prosperity, health, security, or happiness. In the specific sense it refers to those acts, procedures, and organizations in society which are intended to assist individuals or groups out of trouble. It involves the correction of social ills, the alleviation of such pathological states as poverty, unemployment, family disorganization, crime, and delinquency. Formerly such activities were referred to as charity and correction, but such words, though still in use, are gradually being replaced by the words "welfare" or "social welfare."

The object of social welfare institutions is to provide an effective means by which the risks of life can be shared by the community and the burden on the individual accordingly lightened. The modern conception is much broader than the giving of charity or alms to the poor. It regards poverty, crime, or prostitution as social ills which may be prevented, treated, or cured. For example, it considers the individual who is unable to support his family as needing rehabilitation. The basic principle on which modern welfare work is grounded is that socially pathological states are not necessarily inevitable. It has substituted for the fatalistic view implied in the dictum of Jesus of Nazareth, "for ye have the poor always with you" (Matt. 26:11), the more hopeful view that social ills are susceptible of successful treatment.

471

In this chapter it is not intended to deal with all the various ills of society and their methods of treatment. Only the problem of economic dependency will be discussed. From the standpoint of its cost and the number of persons concerned, it is the most important of the various problems mentioned. The question of health organization will be treated in the chapter following.

### HISTORICAL BACKGROUND

Like other contemporary institutions, welfare has its historical roots in human needs and in the mores and folkways which developed from experience in simple, primary, group relations. The primitive welfare institution is the family, which even in modern times is important in this respect. In the simpler societies the family or the clan is the chief and, often the only, support for individuals in need of aid. The formal organization of welfare came about as a result of the growth of cities and towns, where family or neighbors were often unable to care for the increased number of dependent persons. Charity, in the sense of almsgiving, is an old pattern of assistance to which reference is made in the pre-Christian literature of Greece, Rome, and Judea. However, while the interpretations of charity by the Jewish and later by the Christian writers established the principle of extrafamilial responsibility for the poor and needy, the development of community agencies specifically dedicated to their service is a development since the early Christian era and especially of the past 300 years. They developed first in the urban centers as private philanthropic efforts rather than functions of government. The church was one of the first to engage in organized welfare work. St. Gregory, in 590 A.D., divided Rome into districts and parishes, with a deacon in each district whose responsibility it was to care for the poor, widows, orphans, wards, and old people.[1] During the Middle Ages, the Christian monasteries became centers of relief, collecting funds

---

[1] Charles Stewart Loch, "Charity and Charities," in the *Encyclopædia Britannica*, Thirteenth Edition, Vol. 5, p. 872. New York: The Encyclopædia Britannica Company, 1926.

For a more adequate treatment of the historical background of present welfare institutions, see S. A. Queen, *Social Work in the Light of History*, Parts 2, 3, 4. Philadelphia: J. B. Lippincott Company, 1922.

*Family planning for farm and home program, in Missouri (above). Farm families canning home-grown vegetables and fruits at a community center, in Virginia (below).*

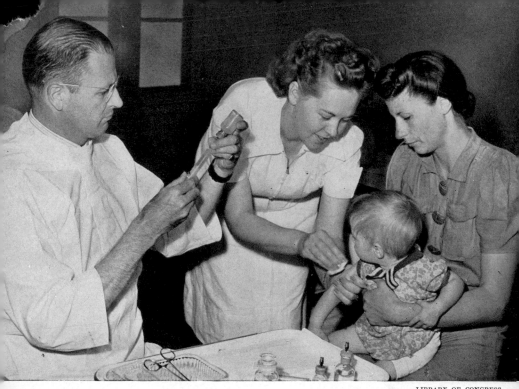

*Getting ready for vaccination at a clinic at a farm labor camp, in Idaho (above).
Migrant high-school students arriving home from school, in California (below).*

from those able to give and dispensing them to the poor, the beggars, the aged, sick, infirm, or disabled. The beginning of governmental assumption of responsibility for relief and welfare was the English Poor Law enacted in 1601 during the reign of Queen Elizabeth. Under its provision each parish was authorized to raise by taxation, by gift, or by both, the necessary funds for relief of the needy. The principle of responsibility for the poor at the local level of government, as well as support of the program from the public treasury, dates from this time.

## TYPES OF WELFARE INSTITUTIONS

Welfare agencies may be classified as *public* or *private* and *generalized* or *specialized*. The *private* institution is the result of the voluntary association of people having the desire and the means to contribute to the solution of a social problem. Such an institution is chartered by the state and incorporated as a nonprofit organization. It has a membership composed of individuals who sympathize with its objectives and to whom its officers are responsible. The officers ordinarily are a board of directors who employ a paid staff of professional workers. Funds for its purposes are derived mainly from free-will contributions of persons or groups in the community and from the income of endowments. It is common practice in the United States to coordinate the solicitation of funds for financing private organizations in a single drive sponsored by the Community Council of Social Agencies, known as the Community Chest or Fund.

The *public* agency is an aspect of government and is similar in its design to the public school or the public library. Typically, at the local level of government there is a welfare board. Almost universally in the United States the local unit is now the county, except, of course, in the New England states where it is the town. In a few states outside of New England the township boards still function in matters of direct relief. In addition, there is the State Board of Public Welfare which decides policies governing the expenditure of state funds and acts as a general coordinator of County Welfare Board activities.

The *general* welfare agency is designed to cover more than

one form of social need; that is, it may not only treat cases in
need of old-age assistance, but also those of child or mother
dependency, the blind, the transient needy, or those temporarily
in need of help. Such an agency is the typical county welfare
department in the United States. *Specialized* institutions are
those which are devoted to the treatment of special cases.
Examples are the Travelers Aid Society, which maintains its
agents in the chief railway and bus stations of the country to
provide assistance to travelers who need help; and the Red
Cross, which specializes in war and disaster relief. Also there are
welfare associations which perform rather general services, primarily for special groups. The Catholic and Jewish welfare
associations are examples.

**Federal-state-local organization of public welfare.** Public
welfare in the United States since 1935 has been largely on a
cooperative basis among the Federal, state, and county governments, representing a new development in organization and
financial responsibility. Before the depression of the 1930's,
public welfare was almost entirely a local matter, from the standpoint of both financial support and administration. However,
the severity of the depression, combined with the great drought
over most sections of the nation, created a relief burden much
greater than the local units of government could carry. The
Federal government was asked to help and the result was a
series of acts of intervention by the Federal government cul-
minating in the passage of the Social Security Act in 1935.

One of the first significant acts of Federal assistance came in
1927 when Congress appropriated six million dollars for the
relief of the population affected by the great Mississippi flood
of that year. Funds were to be lent to farmers for purchasing
seed, feed, and fertilizer, and were not intended as grants. Four
years later another disaster in the form of drought overtook
the nation. On August 14, 1931, President Hoover called a
conference of the governors of the drought-stricken states and
as a result sixty-seven million dollars were made available to
the Department of Agriculture to lend to farmers in the affected
states, in order that they might buy feed, seed, and fertilizer.
However, the depression soon reached such a critical state that
more general action became imperative, and in July, 1932,

the Reconstruction Finance Corporation was organized with authority to lend up to 300 million dollars to the states for emergency relief. At the same time the Red Cross was called upon to arrange the distribution of the wheat and cotton holdings of the Federal Farm Board to needy sections of the population. These commodities were given away.

In 1933, the Roosevelt administration began a national program of direct relief, using Federal funds. The Civil Works Administration, in the summer of 1933, set up machinery for the direct disbursement of Federal funds in the states and counties of the nation. It was succeeded in late 1933 by the Federal Emergency Relief Administration, which, while operating primarily on Federal funds, sought and usually received some state support. It provided for decentralized administration in the various states. The FERA handled not only all means of direct public assistance, but also organized work projects on which able-bodied persons on relief were assigned jobs.

In 1935 the decision was made to return to the states and their local subdivisions all responsibility for what was termed direct relief. At the same time, however, provision was made to supplement the state funds for the care of the aged, the blind, and dependent children; and to provide also a strictly Federal program of public works. Thus the Social Security Act of 1935 provided for grants-in-aid to the various states for the three categories of public assistance indicated above, the Federal funds amounting to half the total amount spent, up to a specified maximum, and the states and counties making up the other half. The Works Progress Administration, operating on Federal funds, provided work for the able-bodied.

The Social Security Act specifically designated the county as the local unit through which public assistance funds were to be administered. Since in a number of the states the distribution of relief funds was a function of the local township boards, this provision was a rather drastic change. In some states, such as Minnesota, compromises were agreed upon in some counties under which the townships retained the function of dispensing direct relief not subsidized by the Federal government, while the county handled only the cases coming under the subsidized program. The removal from the township of the major responsibility for relief and the recognition of state and Federal financial responsibility represented a sharp break with the tradition established by the Elizabethan Poor Laws, a tradition which was a most potent factor in the early development of welfare agencies in America.

## DIRECT FEDERAL ACTION AT THE LOCAL LEVEL

**Old-age insurance.** In addition to the grants-in-aid for public assistance, the Social Security Act provided for old-age and survivors insurance, which is administered directly, not through state or local agencies. While farmers or farm laborers were exempted from the social insurance program, it is expected that they will eventually be included. The program is compulsory, except for the exempted workers. It is financed by a pay-roll deduction each month, amounting originally to two per cent of the worker's salary, half of which is charged to him and half to the employer. The act provided that the percentage would be increased every few years until a maximum of six per cent was reached. However, Congress has been loath to make increases so long as the insurance fund appears ample to meet current needs. At the retirement age of 65, the worker will begin to receive monthly benefits based upon his average monthly wage and the number of years worked. When his wife reaches 65, the amount of the monthly benefit is increased by 50 per cent. In case the insured dies before reaching age 65 the survivors may benefit in two ways. If there are children under the age of 18 a monthly allowance is provided until the youngest is 18. When the widow reaches the age of "retirement," she will receive a monthly benefit. Congress has modified the act several times, and will no doubt make other changes.

**Problems in extending social insurance to farmers.**[2] The arguments against extending social insurance to farm people have been based upon the difficulties involved in administration. Such was the main reason for their specific exemption in the original Social Security Act. The anticipated problem of collecting pay-roll taxes from farmers appeared an insurmountable

[2] For an excellent discussion of the various aspects of this question see Murray R. Benedict, "Retirement System for Farmers," *Planning Pamphlets 49*, National Planning Association, Washington, D.C., January, 1946.

difficulty in the early stages of the general program. It was decided, therefore, that it would be wise to establish the program for industrial laborers before venturing into agriculture. Another objection to social insurance in general, and one which farmers have raised specifically, is its compulsory nature. However, all social insurances are made compulsory in order that there will be universal participation and that those who need the coverage most will get it. Still another objection to the old-age and survivors' insurance program is that farmers have come to regard old-age assistance as a pension to which they are entitled as a matter of right and they feel no embarrassment in accepting it, even though it is granted on the basis of a means test.

The advantage of social insurance from the standpoint of the public is that it greatly reduces the burden upon the public treasury. Through the organization of pressure groups in various states the aged have been able to increase the so-called pensions to a point where they seriously endanger the ability of the states to support other necessary activities. For instance, in the month of April, 1945, the average monthly payment to recipients of old-age assistance in the state of California was $47.31. The total amount paid to recipients in that month was $7,450,000. This was almost double the amount paid out in any other state in the Union.[3] Payments to the aged on the Old Age Assistance program will diminish as the Old Age and Survivors Insurance (OASI) takes effect. Each year more and more of those reaching retirement age will receive benefits under the insurance program. In theory, it should be possible to eliminate the OAA program, but this can happen only if Congress extends OASI coverage to the entire labor force. The lawmakers have shown a tendency to increase the number of industries and workers covered.

From the standpoint of the individual, social insurance has the advantage that it is not received on the basis of a means test, but as something to which a person is entitled because he has in reality purchased it. There is no degradation of status in receiving it.

Administrative objections to extending social insurance to farm people are fast being overcome. Experts advise the use of the

[3] *Social Security Bulletin*, 8, June, 1945.

stamp plan of collecting social security taxes. Under this system the farm laborer would carry a stamp book in which both he and his employer would paste revenue stamps each time he received his wages. While, undoubtedly, many farmers will object to this as being troublesome, they will become accustomed to it in the course of time.

**The Farmers Home Administration.** This agency of the Federal government deserves special treatment because of the unprecedented character of its program and the magnitude of its operations. It was unprecedented in that it not only represented direct Federal intervention in what had previously been a local responsibility, but also in that it was exclusively designed to facilitate the rehabilitation of farm people on relief. The latter point itself deserves a little elaboration. Why should people on the land require the services of a relief agency? This question was asked by many people during the depression of the 1930's, particularly when in 1935 there were two and a half million rural families on relief.[4] The answer was not a simple one. In the background of the difficulty was the evolution of American farm life from the self-sufficient status of frontier times to the very highly commercialized economy which developed especially during the half century preceding 1930. Farmers had become dependent upon a money economy. They had grown progressively less self-sustaining. They needed money to purchase innumerable articles in daily living which in earlier times they either did not require or were able to provide themselves. They were therefore almost as vulnerable to depressions as were the urbanites.

The more specific reasons for the necessity of assisting farm people are implied in the listing of groups considered to be insecure by the President's Committee on Farm Tenancy. They classified them as follows:

1) *Tenants.* Family incomes as a class are below those enjoyed by owners. They are economically vulnerable, particularly in the South, because of their excessive mobility, lack of security in the occupancy of the land, and many associated social disabilities such as inferior

---

[4] T. J. Woofter, Jr., and Ellen Winston, *Seven Lean Years*, p. 11. Chapel Hill: The University of North Carolina Press, 1939.

educational opportunities and chances for full participation in the life of the community. (See picture following page 424.)

2) *Croppers.* There were about half a million in 1940. They occupy a lower status than that of the other tenants. In recent years many of them have been converted into wage laborers and made dependent on casual employment.

3) *Farm Laborers.* The migratory workers are perhaps the most insecure group in rural farm areas because of their low annual wages, excessive migration in pursuit of employment, seasonality of work, and lack of group organization for their self-protection.

4) *Families on Submarginal Land.* Estimated by the President's Committee at about one half million.

5) *Families on Holdings of Inadequate Size.* This group includes a large number of home owners and tenants endeavoring to support themselves by full-time farming on farms so small that they will not provide for an adequate standard of living. They are concentrated heavily in the Lake States Cutover, the Appalachian-Ozark region, and the Great Plains.

6) *Owner Families Hopelessly in Debt.* This group which was of considerable importance during the recent depression has had its economic position greatly improved during the war years. However, if speculation in land should force land values to inflated heights, it is easily possible that another group of insecure landowners burdened with heavy mortgages may be the result.

7) *Farm Young People Unable to Obtain Farms.* During the depression years when migration to towns and cities of the surplus farm population was largely stopped there was a large number of young people unemployed and underemployed on farms. This is a chronic situation and may recur if industrial activity slows down to a level comparable with that of the early 1930's.[5]

The program of the Farmers Home Administration [6] is broad and flexible. It is authorized to make small loans to farmers who cannot secure credit from any other source; it can purchase farms and resell them to tenants, allowing forty years to repay the loan on which the interest rate is only three per cent; it employs both agricultural and home agents to assist families in drawing up farm and home plans as bases of their future

[5] *Farm Tenancy,* report of the President's Committee, pp. 4, 5. Washington, D.C.: February, 1937. See also Woofter and Winston, *op. cit.,* Chapter 3.

[6] The official name of the agency, formerly the Farm Security Administration, was changed to Farmers Home Administration in 1946.

operations and to guide them in executing the plans. (See picture following page 472.) It can make loans to small cooperatives of farmers for purchasing pure-bred sires, farm machinery, or for organizing health associations. It can build and maintain camps for farm laborers in sections where they are needed.

The method of operation of the rural rehabilitation program as distinct from the others is of special interest. Whether FHA continues as an agency of the Federal government or not, its experience in dealing with farm families on an individual basis should be carefully examined and its value appraised with a view to applying its techniques in other services. To begin with, the farmer makes his application for a loan at the Farmers Home office of the county in which he resides. If he is considered eligible for a loan, his next step is to make a farm plan showing how he expects to operate his farm during the coming year. In common practice, the making of this rather intricate plan falls largely to the FHA supervisor. The guiding principle involved is, nevertheless, that the FHA supervisor should keep himself in the background as much as possible and shift as much of the responsibility upon the family as it will assume. In other words, when the plan is made, it should be the plan of the family and not that of the FHA supervisor. Psychological rehabilitation could not be achieved if the initiative and responsibility were carried wholly by the supervisor. (See picture following page 472.)

The next step, one that properly goes along with the farm plan, is making a plan for operating the household. The FHA home supervisor assists in the task. Farm and home are regarded as inseparable units and it is recognized that no matter how successfully the farm plan may work out, rehabilitation of the family would not be achieved if the household were managed in a careless and wasteful manner.

Another principle is that the money be regarded as a loan and not as a grant. It is true that grants may be made to a family to tide it over until a crop is made, but in such cases the family well understands that this aid is for emergencies only and that further grants may not be made. Rehabilitation loans are secured by chattel mortgages on articles purchased. That is, if the farmer buys a cow, or a team of horses, or implements with the money lent him, the government takes a mortgage on them as security for the loan. The loans carry five per cent interest and run for about five years or for the life of the article bought. In the case of seed, feed, and fertilizer loans, the money is supposed to be repaid at the end of the year.

From 1934 to 1944 the organization had made about one million loans for rehabilitation purposes, the average loan amounting to about $400.[7] The total amount loaned during this period was 868 million dollars.

The other main aspect of the program, the purchase of farms for resale to tenants, requires considerable follow-up activity on the part of the organization after the original contract is signed. The purchaser is selected on the basis of his recognized ability as a farmer and of his reputation for integrity. However, during the first three years especially, he is given assistance in making farm and home plans and keeping accounts.

A word should be added concerning the phase of the FHA program having to do with farm labor. This group is one of the most disadvantaged in American rural society and is extremely vulnerable to the impact of economic depressions. In 1933–1934 there were tens of thousands of them on the highways, bound for California or the Pacific Northwest in search of a means of livelihood. Many were unable to find work after they arrived. They were without adequate shelter, often camped along the roadside, on vacant lots near the towns, or along canal banks. Their plight was truly critical. The Emergency Relief Administrations of the various states were trying to see that nobody starved, but it was obvious that a special program was needed.

Early in 1935 the Federal government[8] authorized the construction of two camps for migratory laborers as an experiment. The results were so successful that others were built, not only in California, but also in Arizona, Idaho, Oregon, Washington, Texas, Florida, Arkansas, and other states where migratory workers are a regular part of the agricultural industry and where adequate housing facilities do not exist. (See pictures following page 472.)

[7] *Agricultural Statistics, 1944*, p. 485. Washington, D.C.: United States Department of Agriculture.
[8] Colonel Lawrence Westbrook, director of the Rural Rehabilitation Division of the Federal Emergency Relief Administration gave the authorization. Paul S. Taylor of the University of California deserves most of the credit for initiating the program.

The camps varied in elaborateness. In some, floors were provided on which families could pitch their own tents. In others there were finished cabins or tents. In most of them, there were not only minimum sanitary facilities, but also health clinics, day nurseries, and community halls in which recreational and other social activities could be carried on. The camps, accommodating about 200 families each, were administered by employees of the FHA. No rent was charged for their use, but each family was asked to contribute about ten cents a day to a camp fund, disbursed jointly by a campers' committee and the FHA camp manager for minor improvements around camp and to help families which were particularly in need. In addition to this contribution, each family was expected to give two hours of work a week for cleaning up the camp, maintenance of sanitary buildings, planting grass, and the like. Legislation passed in 1947 provided for the liquidation of the camps, although some might be donated to public or nonprofit institutions for housing agricultural workers.

The functions of FHA have been modified by Congress from time to time. While it no longer operates migratory labor camps or cooperative settlements, its loan authority for farm housing was recently greatly expanded. It also makes disaster loans and grants in addition to its major activities of assisting farmers to get re-established in farming and helping tenants to become owners.[9]

In the administration of welfare in rural areas there are, then, certain agencies operated exclusively by the Federal government, notably the FHA; agencies which represent joint responsibility of Federal, state, and local governments, including the public assistance programs provided by the Social Security Act; and agencies which are either state or local or a combination. In the state-provided group are the various state institutions, including hospitals, reformatories, and sanatoriums. Responsibility for direct relief of those who cannot qualify for the Federally supported public-assistance programs rests jointly upon the state and county as a rule, although there are variations in policy among the states.

[9] The story of FHA has been well told by Paul V. Maris, *The Land Is Mine: From Tenancy to Family Farm Ownership.* Washington, D.C.: U.S. Government Printing Office, 1950.

## PROFESSIONAL SOCIAL WORKERS

As a profession, social work is comparatively new and its personnel rather small. There were in 1950 approximately 91,533 "social, welfare, and recreational" workers employed, compared with 69,677 in 1940. The 1950 figure is probably ten times that of 1930. The expansion of welfare activities as a result of the depression and the war created an extraordinary demand for trained social workers. It is a profession predominantly of women who outnumber the men two to one. There are nearly four times as many people per social worker in rural areas as in urban (Table 41). The disparity was even greater in 1940.

TABLE 41. *Social, Welfare, and Recreation Workers, 1940 and 1950*

| AREA | TOTAL | MALE | FEMALE | PERSONS PER WORKER |
|------|-------|------|--------|--------------------|
| United States | | | | |
| 1950 | 91,533 | 32,616 | 58,917 | 1,650 |
| 1940 | 69,677 | 24,868 | 44,809 | 1,890 |
| Urban | | | | |
| 1950 | 79,359 | 27,934 | 51,425 | 1,210 |
| 1940 | 58,418 | 20,527 | 37,981 | 1,270 |
| Rural | | | | |
| 1950 | 12,174 | 4,682 | 7,492 | 4,490 |
| 1940 | 11,169 | 4,341 | 6,828 | 5,120 |

Source: Bureau of the Census

**Geographic distribution of workers.** In proportion to population the states which are highly urban are better supplied with workers than those which are predominantly rural. (See Figure 79.) The main concentration is in those highly urban states of New York, Illinois, California, Massachusetts, Connecticut, Pennsylvania, and other states containing metropolitan centers. Salaries do not vary much in the states (Figure 80). However, one notes a differential pay rate in favor of men. It may be explained in part by the tendency to employ men in administrative positions to a greater extent than women, since such positions usually carry larger salaries.

**Training.** The standard training required or recommended for the professional social worker is two years of graduate study beyond the four-year preparatory course. The demand for

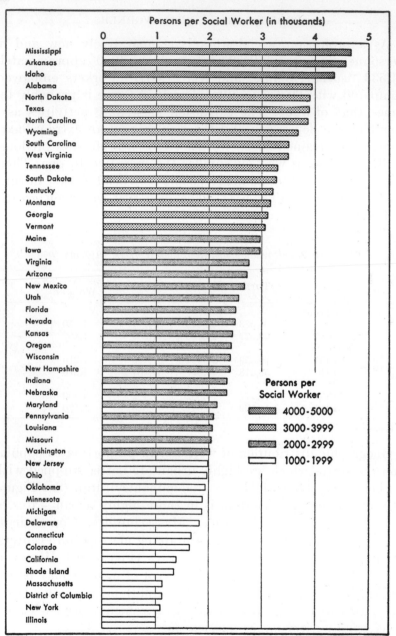

FIGURE 79. *Rank Order of States by Persons per Social Worker, 1950*

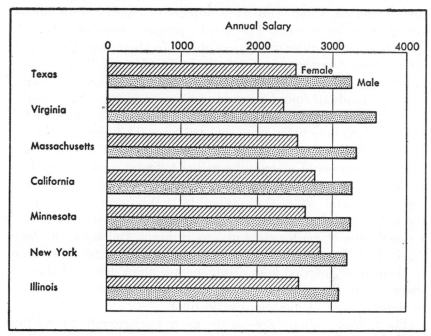

Bureau of the Census

FIGURE 80. *Median Income of Social Workers, Male and Female, for Selected States, 1950*

workers during recent years has been so great, however, that there have not been enough people with so much training. States, too, vary in their standards of requirements as to training for social work positions. Some, more lenient than others, will employ people of less than college training and with only a smattering of technical course work, or even none at all. Other states, however, have higher standards, and aim to raise them gradually as the better-trained personnel becomes available. The two-year, graduate course involves field training in addition to the professional academic courses.

**The application of social-work techniques in the rural community.** The acceptance of public charity has traditionally been something to be avoided by every means possible, and only the direst necessity could justify it. Of course, there were always those in every community who were on the town (or county), and those who had to be helped. But except for the widow and the orphan, whose acceptance of aid had religious and scriptural sanction, those who were objects of charity were generally held in low esteem. The word "pauper" was frequently—though perhaps unjustifiably—applied to them, and they were often called "no accounts," "beggars," and so on.

During the severe crisis of the 1930's, many formerly high-status individuals found themselves in need of assistance. Early in the period the needy were referred to as the "unemployed," a term which bore little or no social stigma. This group certainly was not like the traditional recipients of help. They were not paupers, they could scarcely be called indigent; ordinarily, they would not even classify among the "poor." Yet here they were "in need." Were they "eligible"? Who was to determine the eligibility of an applicant? Under the RFC program, it was a committee of one's neighbors, as it were. And some of these "neighbors" could hardly believe that applicants who came to them really needed help. More people than deserved it were suspected of trying to get something they were not entitled to, or hoping to get something for nothing.

These observations are made as a background to raising certain questions regarding social work in rural areas. One very large question is how a trained social worker—who is paid a salary from relief funds—can get herself accepted in a rural community as a justifiable expense. In a community where public aid has been administered by volunteer committees or by township or county officials as one of many other functions they performed, it is not easy to accept the idea of paying "relief money" as salary to a person whose job is to disburse relief funds, especially, as is often so, a person who is "sent in from the outside." "Why can't one of our own people look after it?" is a question frequently asked in the rural community.

The profession of social work rightly maintains that the adequate analysis, diagnosis, and treatment of a person or family in trouble is an art requiring skill, training, and experience. Against the background of the rural mores, it is not an easy task to convince a rural group. The local pressure is to have the county give that job to Mrs. Blank, "she's a widow and needs the work." In the local judgment any "good, sympathetic person" can do social work.

Another question which arises is how a social worker can

avoid subjecting a rural family to the destructive effects of neighborhood gossip. It is one thing to do case work in an urban community, where individuals and families enjoy a great deal of anonymity; it is quite another to make contact with a needy family in a rural neighborhood, where everybody knows nearly everything about everybody else.

A social worker among farm people can scarcely do an intelligent job of case analysis, diagnosis, and treatment, who does not know something of farming and of how farm people live and make a living. Moreover, the resources for social work in a rural community are vastly different from those in a city. Often they are completely lacking, a fact which should be recognized by institutions which train social workers for rural positions. Also, many of the problems of economic security are bound up in national agricultural programs which aim to raise the general level of farm income throughout the whole country. Some familiarity with these programs should be part of the equipment of any rural social worker. The agricultural organizations or agencies at work in the rural community, whether Federal, state, or local, should be known to the worker and working relationships developed with them. The agricultural agencies, for their part, should likewise know the social welfare worker and, as far as possible, the objectives and nature of the welfare program.

By way of summary these points may be made:

1) Welfare work as a formal activity had its origin in the attempts to meet social problems which arose with the growth of cities. In simpler societies, aid to the helpless and dependent was a function of the primary groups, family, clan, or neighborhood.

2) Rural welfare in the United States was a function of the family and neighborhood until the depression of the 1930's. Such welfare as was carried on outside these units was the responsibility of the local county or township. The system was little changed from that established in England in 1601 and brought to the American colonies shortly after their settlement.

3) Since 1935 the system of support and administration has assumed three different aspects: (*a*) full local responsibility for

direct relief, (*b*) Federal-state-county responsibility for old-age assistance, grants to the blind and to dependent children, and (*c*) direct Federal administration of old-age and survivors' insurance, and of the Farmers Home Administration.

4) The rapidity of expansion of welfare work has made it impossible to provide adequately trained personnel to supply the need. Moreover, at least in rural areas, there is a lack of appreciation of the need of specialized training in this field. Historically, such aid has been given by neighbors or by people with little or no special training; the public has not been convinced that it is a job for professionals.

5) The application of social-work techniques in rural areas should be modified appropriately to meet the conditions of primary group relations. The social worker needs to be aware of the fact that, in the rural neighborhood, relations among people are more intimate than in the city, and should adopt techniques which will damage as little as possible the status of the person or family.

6) The professional schools of social work have a responsibility to give more attention to the training of personnel for rural agencies.

7) Finally, it is clear that the changes in methods of administering welfare programs, as well as the expansion of the programs themselves, denote certain basic cultural changes which have been observed in other aspects of contemporary life. It was made evident by the crises of the 1930's that the presumed security which had always been associated with farming was to a large extent fictitious. While in an absolute sense it might well be true that a farmer has a better chance of survival than a nonfarmer, events have demonstrated that in the United States, at least, farmers fared but little if any better than others during the depression. This state of affairs was partly due to the long and gradual transition which had taken place from a self-sufficing to a cash economy. The crisis only threw into bold relief the outline of cultural changes which had been slowly, almost imperceptibly, taking place. The inadequacy of local government units to cope with a major economic crisis is also made clear. State and nation must also provide help in time of distress.

## QUESTIONS FOR DISCUSSION

1. Farm prosperity may be said to be a function of such factors as the processes of nature, technological "know-how," and market prices. In what way was each of these three factors affected by the agricultural depression of the 1920's and 1930's?
2. Identify and mention the essential purpose of each of the following: RFC, FERA, WPA, RA, CCC, SSA, and FHA.
3. What new element of social stratification was introduced into American society during the recent depression? Is it your impression that the social status of those who accepted aid has been permanently affected or has the reception of relief undergone a redefinition?
4. Mention the specific disabilities suffered by each of the following: farm tenants, sharecroppers, farm laborers, farm operators on submarginal land and inadequate-sized holdings, mortgaged owners, and unemployed or underemployed farm youth.
5. Which of the groups mentioned in the preceeding question received help from the Farmers Home Administration? In what way did the aid given migrant farm laborers differ from the assistance given others? Has the work of the FHA been in any way a duplication of what the Grange, Farm Bureau, and the Farmer's Union have set out to do? Discuss.
6. Point out regional differences in the training and salary status of professional social workers.
7. Why did the employment of professional, salaried, social workers in rural areas set up certain "stresses and strains" in rural culture?
8. Why was the farm population neglected under the provisions of the Social Security Act? To what extent would the Murray-Wagner-Dingell Bill remove this discrimination?
9. Mention some factors which are likely to render difficult the acceptance of an old-age and survivors' insurance system by farm people?
10. Describe the method which has been suggested as a means of facilitating the collection of social security taxes from farm laborers.
11. Outline the provisions of the Social Security Act which are related to the improvement of health conditions.

## SELECTED REFERENCES

"After the War—Toward Security." National Resources Planning Board. September, 1942.

Browning, Grace. *Rural Public Welfare.* Chicago: University of Chicago Press, 1941.

*Farm Tenancy.* Report of the President's Committee. Washington, D.C.: Government Printing Office, February, 1937.

Farnham, Rebecca, and Link, Irene. "Effects of the Works Program on Rural Relief." Washington, D.C.: Government Printing Office, 1938.

Folsom, Josiah C. "Social Security for Farm People," an annotated bibliography. *Library List No. 50.* Washington: Department of Agriculture, 1949.

Harper, Ernest B., and Gibson, Duane L. "Reorganization of Public Welfare in Michigan," East Lansing: *Michigan AES Special Bulletin 318.* 1942.

Hayes, Wayland J. "Public Welfare in Rural Areas," *Rural Sociology,* Vol. 6, No. 1, March, 1941.

Kolb, J. H., and Brunner, E. deS. *A Study of Rural Society.* Fourth Edition, Chapter 23. Boston: Houghton-Mifflin Company, 1952.

Landis, B. Y. *Rural Welfare Services.* New York: Columbia University Press, 1949.

Lerrigo, Ruth, and Bradley, Buell. "Social Work and the Joneses." *Public Affairs Pamphlet 97.* 1944.

McKain, Jr., Walter C.; Baldwin, Elmer D.; and Ducoff, Louis J. "Old Age and Retirement in Rural Connecticut," *Storrs AES Bulletin 299.* 1953.

Sewell, William H.; Ramsey, Charles E.; and Ducoff, Louis J. "Farmers' Conceptions and Plans for Economic Security in Old Age," *Wisconsin AES Research Bulletin 182.* 1953.

Smith, Marjorie J. *Rural Casework Services.* New York: Family Public Welfare Association, 1943.

Taylor, Carl C.; Wheeler, Helen W.; and Kirkpatrick, E. L. "Disadvantaged Classes in American Agriculture." *United States Department of Agriculture Social Research Report VIII.* April, 1938.

Wilson, M. L. "Farm People and Social Security," *Extension Circular 458,* Washington, D.C., 1949.

Woofter, T. J., Jr., and Winston, Ellen. *Seven Lean Years.* Chapel Hill: University of North Carolina Press, 1939.

# CHAPTER 25

# HEALTH AND HEALTH AGENCIES

Problems of health are for the most part continual and inevitable. The so-called conquest of disease is an unending battle, the outcome of which is only partial and approximate, never decisive. The contest is always joined; we are always trying to do something to forestall or to cure disease. It is one of the major preoccupations of human beings from childhood to the grave.

**Health a social concern.** Our point of view in regard to health has undergone considerable change throughout history. Time was when sickness was considered largely a matter of concern for the affected individual and those upon whom he was immediately dependent. The discovery of the germ theory of certain diseases made people aware that the diseased individual was a threat to the well-being of others, and they set up regulations to restrict his activities. In other words, his health became a matter of *social* concern. Gradually we have come to accept the social significance of health and disease from many other angles. Ill-health, in general, is a social burden; good health, a social asset. On the basis of the National Health Survey in 1937, it was estimated that "on an average day of the year, 4 million or more persons in the United States are disabled by illness. Every year 70 million sick persons lose more than 1 billion days of work. The total cost of illness and premature death in this country is approximately 10 billion dollars a year. This estimate includes only those factors which can be expressed in dollar values—the cost of health services and medical care, the loss of wages through unemployment resulting from disability, and the loss of potential future earnings through death."[1]

It might be added that the national health survey was based

---

[1] *National Health Conference Proceedings*, 1937. Statement of Josephine Roche, p. 2.

on an urban sample of 740,000 families, with only 36,000 rural families represented. No account was taken of disability due to hookworm infection, malaria, and pellagra. All of these diseases impose a heavy draft on the bodily energy of the rural population in the South. All are preventable. If rural rehabilitation is to be achieved in the South, the improvement of the health of the population must be a primary consideration. Yet, speaking generally, we pay little attention to the prevention of disease. We spend every year about three billion dollars for medical care, but devote only one dollar out of every 30 to prevention.

The burden of ill-health, so long carried by the family members, has come more and more to be recognized as a responsibility to be shared by the community. Thus we have provided many health services at public expense, and, for a considerable portion of the population, we have assumed practically the entire financial responsibility. On the other hand, in recognition of the advantage to society of good health, we have been placing increasing emphasis on prevention of disease and the education of the population in ways of living which will keep them in a state of physical well-being. The demands for manpower during World War II especially brought to the attention of the public the necessity of health conservation as one of the important means of waging a successful war.

Moreover, the health of the individual is affected by the environment in which he lives and for which society is at least partly responsible. It is then a matter of public concern that unhealthful living conditions be removed. Not wholly is it the obligation of society to protect itself against the diseased individual, but also to protect the individual against disease-ridden surroundings. The realization that ill-health is a concern not only of the individual, the family, and the neighborhood, but also of the community and the nation has focused attention upon efforts to find the most feasible and desirable means by which society can collectively conserve and improve its physical and mental well-being. Many questions are raised. Granting the postulate that health is a social concern, is society, whether through the state or through private means, to assume the responsibility for seeing that everyone is provided with needed medical care? Or should the individual retain the responsibility, purchasing such care as he is able and when he thinks he needs it? Should the insurance principle be applied to the risk of ill-health? In short, what kind of social organization will best meet the need? Medical care is now being referred to as a right to which every individual in the nation is entitled. Are we ready to accept this as a principle, as we have accepted the principle of universal education?

## PROBLEMS OF RURAL MEDICAL CARE

**The high cost.** One of the chief impediments in the way of an adequate system of medical care for farm people is the high cost of service. Farm people have especially low annual cash incomes. The median income of farmers in 1952 was $2,226, compared with $4,249 urban, and $3,721 rural nonfarm. In a family in the "lower half," a surgical operation for one of its members would take as much out of the budget as is normally spent on clothing for the entire family in a year. Moreover, the farm family living in the open country is many miles from a doctor, necessitating payment for mileage on the doctor's car, in addition to the regular service fee. It is understandable, therefore, that people are very cautious about calling a doctor and usually do so only in extreme emergency.

The average amount which rural families actually spend for medical care does not represent what they should spend to secure adequate treatment; yet such data are of value in indicating the general situation. Fortunately, there are several studies which provide information. O. D. Duncan has assembled the pertinent data from a number of studies in different parts of the country, which are presented in Table 42. They show a wide variation among regions in the actual amount spent and in the proportion of the family budget the expenditure represents.

More recent data than from any of the studies collated by Duncan is found in the Consumer Purchases Study for 1935–1936. In that year farm families spent for medical services an average of $39, which was 6 per cent of all expenditures for family living. When the cost of drugs, medicines, health and accident

TABLE 42. *Comparative Health Cost per Family in Various States*

| AREA OF STUDY | Agric. Exper. Station Bulletin Number | Name of Investigator | Date Published | Average Health Expenditure per Family | Health Cost, Per Cent of Total Family Living Costs |
|---|---|---|---|---|---|
| Minnesota farms | 255 | C. C. Zimmerman | 1929 | $108 | 9.7 |
| Minnesota farms | 246 | Zimmerman and Black | 1928 | 72 | 8.7 |
| Minnesota farms | 234 | Zimmerman and Black | 1927 | 79 | 8.4 |
| Minnesota farms | 240 | Zimmerman and Black | 1927 | 77 | 7.6 |
| Wake Co., North Carolina | 269 | W. A. Anderson | 1929 | 56 | 6.5 |
| Oklahoma, eleven counties [1] | | Duncan and Sanders | | 61 | 5.5 |
| Green Co., Wisconsin | 106 | Kirkpatrick and McNall | 1931 | 89 | 5.4 |
| Dane Co., Wisconsin | 106 | Kirkpatrick and McNall | 1931 | 87 | 5.3 |
| Iowa farms | 238 | J. F. Thaden | 1928 | 84 | 5.0 |
| Groton, New York | 431 | C. V. Noble | 1924 | 71 | 4.3 |
| Urban Virginia | 6 [2] | Gee and Stauffer | 1929 | 103 | 3.9 |
| Laurel Co., Kentucky | 301 | Merton Oyler | 1930 | 16 | 3.8 |
| Minnesota villages and towns | 253 | C. C. Zimmerman | 1929 | 90 | 3.6 |
| Eleven states | 1466 [3] | E. L. Kirkpatrick | 1926 | 62 | 3.5 |
| Iowa farms | 237 | G. H. Von Tungeln, et al | 1928 | 85 | 3.5 |
| Minnesota cities | 255 | C. C. Zimmerman | 1929 | 122 | 3.1 |
| Rural Virginia | 6 [2] | Gee and Stauffer | 1929 | 53 | 3.1 |
| Vermont (survey) | 294 | Muse and Brooks | 1929 | 54 | 1.8 |
| Vermont (from records) | 294 | Muse and Brooks | 1929 | 36 | 1.7 |

Source: O. D. Duncan, "Some Social and Economic Aspects of the Problem of Rural Health in Oklahoma," *Experiment Station Circular No. 78*, Stillwater, Oklahoma, September, 1931, Table IV, p. 11.

[1] Unpublished Study, Oklahoma Agricultural and Mechanical College.
[2] Institute Monograph, University of Virginia.
[3] United States Department of Agriculture, Department Bulletin.

insurance, and other medical costs are added, the total comes to $51 per family and amounts to 8 per cent of family expenditures.

During the war year of 1942 an estimate of the amount spent for medical care for all families of the United States by income levels, made by the Office of Price Administration, placed the average amount per family at $90, which was about 3.5 per cent of the family budget. However, for the low-income group—in which many farm families would fall—the expenditure per family was only $26, though nearly 8 per cent of the budget. (See Table 43.)

**Scattered homes.** Another important aspect of the problem of providing medical service to rural-farm people is the factor of distance. While the automobile, good roads, and telephones

TABLE 43. *Medical-Care Expenditures of All Families and Single Consumers in the United States, by Money-Income Level, 1942*

| MONEY-INCOME LEVEL | AGGREGATE EXPENDITURES | AVERAGE EXPENDITURES | PER CENT OF INCOME |
|---|---|---|---|
| | (millions) | | |
| Total | $3,710 | $90 | 3.5 |
| Under $500 | 91 | 26 | 7.9 |
| 500–1,000 | 261 | 39 | 5.1 |
| 1,000–1,500 | 375 | 57 | 4.6 |
| 1,500–2,000 | 413 | 69 | 4.0 |
| 2,000–2,500 | 404 | 87 | 3.9 |
| 2,500–3,000 | 341 | 104 | 3.8 |
| 3,000–4,000 | 596 | 129 | 3.7 |
| 4,000–5,000 | 428 | 163 | 3.7 |
| 5,000–7,500 | 390 | 205 | 3.3 |
| 7,500–10,000 | 143 | 228 | 2.8 |
| 10,000 and over | 268 | 340 | 1.6 |

Source: *Civilian Spending and Saving, 1941 and 1942,* Office of Price Administration, Division of Research, Consumer Income and Demand Branch, March 1, 1943. Estimates cover all civilian consumers except those in institutions.

help to mitigate the matter of distance, they by no means eliminate it. Except in crises, a farm family living five to ten miles from the doctor's office is unlikely to ask for his services, when it is known that the mileage charge is 50 cents. Then, too, the time taken in getting to a doctor or a hospital is crucial. This scattered pattern of rural dwellings makes it important that consideration be given to the possibility of providing certain minimum services in small centers where they do not now exist.

**Persistence of medical folkways.** There exist in all rural areas certain traditional ways of treating disease, which may or may not have any valid scientific basis, but which are nevertheless part of the folkways. They persist often in the face of the demonstrated lack of scientific validity. The people have faith in them, which often transcends their faith in the doctor. For example, I. C. Wilson and W. H. Metzler found the following remedies used in the Ozark area of Arkansas: for appendicitis—"hot turpentine on cloths, enemas of olive oil and castor oil"; for cancer—galangal root, powdered bloodroot, and chloride tincture; for diphtheria—tea of dog fennel bloom; for cough—slippery elm tea; for tuberculosis—strong tea of sage and persimmon bark and a little piece of alum.[2] The investigators listed many more home remedies, but these examples indicate the dependence as late as 1938 in this area on remedies, few, if any, of which modern medical knowledge would approve and some of which would be considered actually harmful. The problem of getting more modern medical care to rural people is, in part, one of breaking down the reliance on home remedies and self-medication. This can best be done by providing modern service on a basis which they can afford, and by conducting an effective educational program to increase the confidence of the people in more scientific care.

### THE HEALTH OF RURAL PEOPLE

The comparative health of rural people may be judged by the use of death rates, life tables, and the incidence of disease as revealed in special surveys. In using mortality statistics the student should be aware of certain limitations and inadequacies in them. One is the fact that not until 1933 were all of the states included in the so-called registration area; that is, the area from which vital statistics are gathered. In the second place, the completeness of reporting is seldom 100 per cent. That is to say, deaths occur which do not get reported to the state department of health. Moreover, since the rate is the number of deaths per thousand population, it cannot be computed with accuracy except for the census years. This is especially true for any segment of the population, and for any subdivision below the state level. Under-reporting of deaths is more common in rural than in urban areas, although these differences are becoming less. Yet it is still true that the states with a high proportion of rural farm people can be expected to be under-reported not only on deaths but on births. Nevertheless, with the growing tendency of farm people to use more fully the available hospital facilities, under-reporting will soon be eliminated.

Another point of importance in considering death rates is that prior to 1939 deaths were reported as of the place of occurrence and not by place of residence of the deceased persons.

---

[2] Isabella C. Wilson and W. H. Metzler, "Sickness and Medical Care in an Ozark Area in Arkansas," *University of Arkansas AES Bulletin 353*, April, 1938, pp. 16–17.

Thus a person from a rural area who died in an urban hospital would be recorded as of the city rather than the country. Finally, it must be noted that prior to 1939 the figure 8,000 was used as the dividing line between rural and urban instead of 2,500, which has been used since that year. The responsibility for collecting, analyzing and publishing vital statistics is borne by the Department of Health, Education, and Welfare established in 1953.

**Trend of mortality downward.** For the United States as a whole, and for the rural and urban segments of it, the mortality rate has declined rather steadily since 1900. There have been fluctuations but the general trend has been downward. In 1900 the death rate for the registration area was 17.6 per 1,000, and for 1950 the rate had declined to 9.6 per 1,000. Death rates have always been lower for the rural population. In 1920 the respective rates for rural and urban populations were 11.9 and 14.2; by 1950, they were 8.3 and 10.5. All data show conclusively that mortality rates are lower in the rural than in the urban population. Not only are mortality rates different in rural and urban areas, but they will vary from state to state.

The influence of two additional characteristics on mortality, sex, and race, is shown in Figure 81. The nonwhite group consists mainly of Negroes. While the difference between the rates for the two races is small as of 1950, it still favors the whites as it has done consistently since 1900.[3] However, the fact that then the rates were 17 for whites and 25 for Negroes indicates how far they have come towards equality on this score. Negroes in larger cities seem to suffer greater health hazards than do whites. (See Figure 82.)

Women have always had a lower death rate than men in the United States. This is true for both races and for rural and urban populations. Moreover the favorable rate for women is true at all ages.

As the population ages, it is possible for the crude death rate to increase, even if the average length of life should also increase. This is due to a "bulge" in the late-middle-age group in our country.

[3] *Historical Statistics of the United States, 1789–1945.* Washington, D.C.: Government Printing Office, 1949.

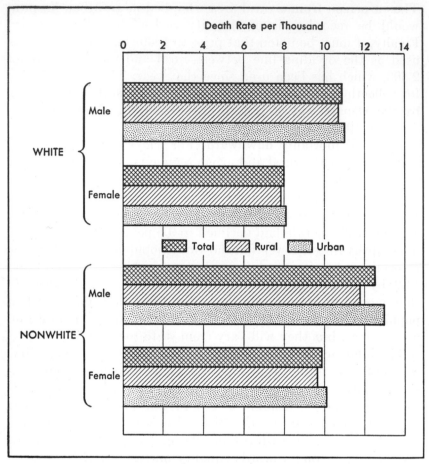

FIGURE 81. *Crude Death Rates by Sex, Race, and Residence, 1950*

It remains to point out the effect of age composition on mortality rates. Comparative rates for 1940 and 1950 by age groups are shown in Table 44. It is interesting to note that there was a greater percentage decline during the decade in the rural death rate than in the urban. Indeed, the difference seems to be greater in favor of the rural population. In part, this is due to the fact that the huge wave of immigrants reaching this country around the 1920's are now reaching the "dying age group." By and large, these migrants were city dwellers, the impact of the foreign born on the rural death rate has declined. Of course, other factors are involved as, for example, the difference in birth rates and migration patterns.

**Morbidity rates.** While we have reasonably good data on death rates for the various states and by specific causes, the

TABLE 44. *Number of Deaths per 1,000 Population by Age in Rural and Urban Communities, and Percentage Decrease in Death Rates, 1940–1950*

| AGE | 1940 | | 1950 [1] | | PERCENTAGE DECREASE 1940–1950 | |
|---|---|---|---|---|---|---|
| | RURAL | URBAN | RURAL | URBAN | RURAL | URBAN |
| 0–4 | 12.3 | 13.5 | 7.0 | 8.0 | 43.0 | 48.1 |
| 5–14 | 1.0 | 1.0 | .6 | .6 | 40.0 | 40.0 |
| 15–24 | 2.1 | 2.0 | 1.4 | 1.2 | 33.3 | 40.0 |
| 25–34 | 3.1 | 3.1 | 1.8 | 1.8 | 41.9 | 41.9 |
| 35–44 | 4.7 | 5.5 | 3.1 | 3.9 | 34.0 | 29.0 |
| 45–54 | 8.9 | 11.7 | 7.0 | 9.5 | 21.3 | 61.5 |
| 55–64 | 18.6 | 24.8 | 15.8 | 21.1 | 15.0 | 14.9 |
| 65–74 | 42.7 | 52.1 | 35.6 | 43.9 | 16.6 | 15.7 |
| 75 and over | 126.1 | 131.5 | 103.8 | 113.5 | 17.6 | 13.6 |
| All ages: crude | 9.8 | 11.5 | 8.3 | 10.6 | 15.3 | 7.8 |

Source: *Vital Statistics of the United States* and the United States Census of Population, 1940 and 1950.
[1] Based on the old urban definition.

same cannot be said of the rates for disabling diseases which do not eventuate in death. On this point our data are limited to special surveys and estimates. For instance, the Committee on the Costs of Medical Care found that during a consecutive twelve-month period, 52 per cent of all persons were sick one or more times with an illness sufficiently serious to be reported. The annual rate was 823 illnesses per 1,000 persons observed. The rate of disabling illnesses, which caused persons to lose one or more days from their work, or other activities, was 492 per 1,000. The rate of bed cases was 414 per 1,000 persons.[4] The National Health Survey made in 1937 found that on any winter day there are six million persons incapacitated by illness and accident from carrying on their accustomed duties. In a year over a billion man-days of work are lost. The average time lost is about 8 days. At an average wage of $5 per day, this would

[4] Selwyn D. Collins, "The Incidence and Causes of Illness at Specific Ages," *The Milbank Memorial Fund Quarterly*, Vol. XIII, No. 4, pp. 325–326.

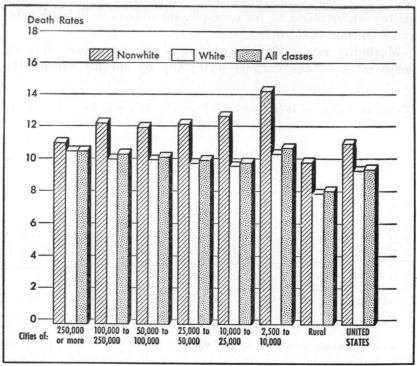

Bureau of the Census

FIGURE 82. *Death Rates by Color and by Place of Residence, 1950*

amount to over five billion dollars worth of time lost and yet would not include the expense of medical treatment nor loss of earning power due to premature death or disability, in themselves items of great consequence.

About half of the disabilities result from diseases of the respiratory system, mostly the "common cold," according to the tabulation by the Committee on the Costs of Medical Care. Next three in order were diseases of the digestive system, acute communicable diseases, and injury from external causes.

Illness rates for preventable diseases are higher in rural than in urban areas. Fred A. Mott wrote:

. . . As of 1940 we find that the infectious and more or less preventable diseases take larger rural tolls. If we consider the most rural state and the most urban state in each of the nine census regions we find that, as a group, the most rural states had higher case rates in 1942 for chickenpox, whooping cough, mumps, scarlet fever, diphtheria, septic sore throat, malaria, bacillary dysentery, typhoid and paratyphoid, tularemia, and smallpox. Trends show that tuberculosis and syphilis may soon become primarily rural.[5]

Illness rates, as shown in Table 45, are related to age, sex, and place of residence. Considering the two sexes combined, the rates are a little higher in the rural population, with variations among the age groups.

TABLE 45. *Estimated Percentage of Persons with a Disabling Illness or Condition in the Civilian Noninstitutional Population, by Age, Sex, and Place of Residence, United States, February, 1949 and September, 1950, Combined*

| SEX AND PLACE OF RESIDENCE | | AGE | | | | | | |
|---|---|---|---|---|---|---|---|---|
| | | 14–64 | 14–19 | 20–24 | 25–34 | 35–44 | 45–54 | 55–64 |
| Both sexes | Urban | 4.17 | 2.61 | 2.93 | 2.53 | 3.47 | 5.24 | 8.97 |
| | Rural-nonfarm | 3.92 | 2.04 | 1.79 | 2.36 | 3.34 | 5.47 | 10.32 |
| | Rural-farm | 4.65 | 2.51 | 3.71 | 3.27 | 3.56 | 5.95 | 9.77 |
| Male | Urban | 4.47 | 2.73 | 2.77 | 2.16 | 3.06 | 5.78 | 11.43 |
| | Rural-nonfarm | 4.50 | 2.52 | 1.74 | 2.25 | 3.77 | 5.76 | 13.42 |
| | Rural-farm | 5.12 | 2.44 | 2.56 | 3.55 | 3.97 | 6.40 | 12.14 |
| Female | Urban | 3.90 | 2.52 | 3.07 | 2.87 | 3.83 | 4.72 | 6.65 |
| | Rural-nonfarm | 3.36 | 1.57 | 1.82 | 2.46 | 2.89 | 5.17 | 7.35 |
| | Rural-farm | 4.14 | 2.60 | 4.69 | 3.01 | 3.15 | 5.45 | 6.92 |

Source: Theodore D. Woolsey, *Estimates of Disabling Illness Prevalence in the United States.* Public Health Monograph No. 4, p. 2, Table 1. Washington, D.C.: Public Health Service, 1952.

In a survey of rural areas in Missouri, R. B. Almack found that 509 of 1,121 persons included had been ill during the year. Some had been ill more than once, however, so that the total illnesses amounted to 600.[6] In Virginia, L. B. Tate reported that of 984 families 29 per cent had members sick and in bed an average of 15 days or more for a period of a year, and that another 25 per cent had members who were ill as long as 2 weeks without staying in bed.[7]

[5] Fred A. Mott, "A Public Health Program for Rural Areas," *Journal of the American Medical Association*, 1946, 131:554–555.

[6] R. B. Almack, "The Rural Health Facilities of Lewis County, Missouri," *University of Missouri AES Research Bulletin 365*, 1943, p. 16.

[7] Leland B. Tate, "The Health and Medical Care Situation in Rural Virginia," *Virginia Polytechnic Institute AES Bulletin 363*, October, 1944, pp. 17, 18.

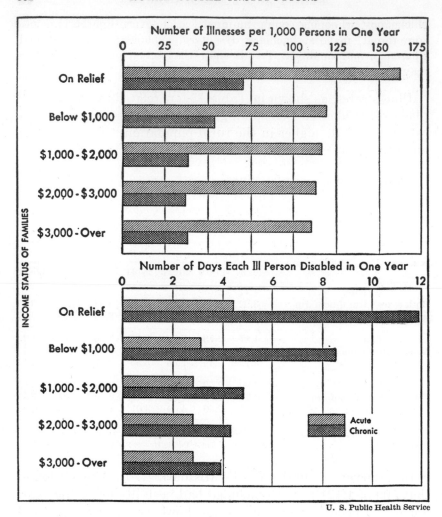

U. S. Public Health Service

FIGURE 83. *Illness and Income.* Based on a survey of 2,308,588 persons in 81 cities in 1935–1936.

**Illness and economic status.** It is at least partly true to say that good health can be purchased. While ill-health is associated also with ignorance, personal neglect, and other like characteristics, the fact that the incidence of disabling illness is proportionately higher among the low-income groups indicates a clear association between economic factors and sickness. The National Health Survey revealed that "in large and small cities in all regions of the country, and in the rural areas, the frequency and severity of illness was uniformly higher in relief and marginal-income families than in any other income class. . . . In the relief population the annual period of disability per capita amounted to 16 days; in the marginal-income class, to 12 days; among persons in the highest-income class, the rate was only 7 days per capita." [8] In other words, the poor are not only sick more often, but their sickness also lasts longer. (See Figure 83.) In a study of medical care and cost in California in 1934, Margaret Klem found also that illness rates varied inversely with income in both urban and rural areas.[9]

Moreover, the poor receive less attention. The National Health Survey revealed that families in the income class "under $1,000" were attended by a physician in 72 per cent of the cases, with 4.6 calls per case. Those in the income class over $3,000 were attended by physicians in 83 per cent of the cases, and had 5.7 calls per case.[10] The following summary of the situation, from the official bulletin, would indicate that within certain obvious limits health appears to be a purchasable commodity:

Not only do relief and low-income families experience more frequent illness during a year than their more fortunate neighbors, but their illnesses are, on the average, of longer duration. Thus, the average case of disabling chronic illness among persons in the relief families was 63 per cent longer in duration than the average case in the group with incomes of $3,000 and over. Coupled with the higher frequency of chronic illness in the relief group, this gives rise to an annual per capita volume of disability in the relief group that is three times as great as among the upper-income families—11.9 days as compared with 3.9 days per person.[11]

**The incidence of physical defects in the rural population.** Data from local studies indicate the very wide incidence of

[8] Report of the Interdepartmental Committee to Coordinate Health and Welfare Activities, National Health Conference, Washington, D.C., 1938, p. 51.

[9] Margaret Klem, "Medical Care and Costs in California Families in Relation to Economic Status," State Relief Administration of California, San Francisco, 1935, p. 80.

[10] "Illness and Medical Care in Relation to Economic Status," *Bulletin 2*, National Health Survey, 1938, p. 2.

[11] *Ibid.*, p. 3.

physical defects among the rural population. For example, the Farmers Home Administration, in 1940, examined 7,500 persons in 21 rural counties in 17 states and found only 4 out of every 100 persons in prime physical condition. In other words, 96 per cent had significant physical defects, with an average of about 3½ defects per man, woman, and child examined. Other significant results of these examinations were the following: 70 per cent had bad teeth; 40 per cent of the wives and 35 per cent of the husbands had defective vision; 1 out of every 12 heads of white families had hernia; 1 per cent of the heads of white families and their wives, and 12 per cent of the heads of colored families and their wives, had syphilis; while 1 child out of every 12 under 15 years of age suffered from malnutrition, and 1 out of every 17 children had rickets or the after-effects of rickets. The official FHA announcement, dated December 22, 1941, contained the following statement:

The arresting fact about the conditions found in this survey is that the great majority of them are preventable or remediable. Adequate medical care would go far toward solving the problem but medical care alone is not enough. There must be more public health work, more emphasis on nutrition, more education.

L. B. Tate in Virginia, reporting results of the inspection of school children by teachers and others, found defects of teeth, throat, vision, speech, hearing, and weight more common among rural than among urban school children.[12]

**Data from life tables.** Life tables are estimates of the probability of survival at various ages. They have as their basis the death rates by specific years of age. Knowing the prevailing death rate for people of various ages, classes, and sexes, it is possible to estimate the average life expectancy for each group. The life expectancy of urban males at birth in 1901 was about 44 years and for rural areas (places under 8,000 population) it was 54. By 1930 these figures had risen to 56.7 years for the cities and 62.1 for the rural. The life expectancy for females is uniformly and consistently higher than that for males, and the same rural-urban differences exist.[13]

---

[12] Leland B. Tate, *op. cit.*, p. 15.
[13] T. Lynn Smith, *The Sociology of Rural Life*, p. 156. New York: Harper and Brothers, 1940.

It is to be regretted that the United States Census does not report vital statistics by occupational groups, but a few special analyses have been made that indicate a more favorable mortality and survival rate for people engaged in agriculture. Thus Jessamine S. Whitney, in an analysis of data for 10 states, reported death rates for agricultural workers to be lower than those of the other major occupational groups. Next to them were professional men, followed by clerks and kindred workers, with unskilled workers having a higher rate than any.[14] Titze, reporting vital data on English occupational groups, found that farmers, gardeners, and agricultural laborers had a life expectancy in 1930 to 1932 of 63 years. They were exceeded only by the professional class, having 63.1 years.[15] One is forced to the conclusion, therefore, that the rural population shows to rather definite advantage when compared with the urban on death rates and life expectancy. Still, there is some evidence that the illness rate is at least as high, if not higher, than the urban, and the incidence of physical defects seems to be greater.

## THE MEDICAL ESTABLISHMENT

**Private practitioners.** The healing of the sick in the United States is largely in the hands of practitioners whose services are paid for by the patient on what is commonly called a fee-for-service basis. Fees are established for general consultation at the doctor's office or for a home call and for each type of surgery or other treatment that might be involved, as for setting a limb, for removal of tonsils, for an appendectomy, and so on. The schedule set up is usually on a minimum basis, the physician being free to levy larger fees at his discretion. The Mayo Clinic, for example, aims to charge according to the principle of "ability to pay." The bills are payable at the time service is rendered or within a reasonable time thereafter. Each individual is free to choose among the physicians available in the area. It is customary to speak of "my" physician, meaning that a person has retained a physician for his own private

---

[14] See *Problems of a Changing Population*, p. 188. National Resources Committee, Government Printing Office, 1938.

[15] Christopher Titze, "Life Tables for Social Classes in England," *The Milbank Memorial Fund Quarterly*, 1943, 21:182–187.

care. The close relationship of the patient and the physician, corresponding to that of client and lawyer, is regarded by some as peculiar to the private—as opposed to the social—practice of medicine. It might be argued, of course, that under private practice the individual shares "his" physician with the rest of the community as truly as though the physician himself were employed by the community on a salary basis to minister to the health needs of the citizens. Nevertheless, the principle of privacy is jealously guarded by the majority of members of the medical profession, as is also the principle of freedom of choice of a physician.

**Characteristics and distribution.** Since the private practitioner is the central figure in the treatment of disease in our society, it is of interest to note some of his characteristics. In the matter of training the standards are comparatively high. Entrance to the four-year medical course requires two years of college work. Before the M.D. degree is granted, one year must be spent in interneship at an approved hospital or clinic. After that, the requirements set up in the state in which the individual hopes to practice must be met before license to practice is granted. The number of students entering the various medical schools is sharply limited, and candidates for admission are carefully selected on the basis of scholastic ability, aptitude for the profession, and general character.

**Rural-urban distribution.** There is wide variation in the distribution of physicians throughout the country. For the country as a whole in 1940 there were 164,649 physicians for 132 million people or one physician for every 800 people. However, the distribution was uneven. The state of New York, for example, had one doctor for every 487 people, while South Carolina had one for every 1,506 people. The maldistribution between rural and urban populations is indicated by the fact that the cities have one doctor for every 580 people and the rural areas one for every 1,336. The disparity between urban and rural concentrations of doctors has been increasing over a long period. For instance among the rural population of Minnesota in 1912 there was one physician for each 1,443 people, while in 1936 the number had increased to 1,814. Meanwhile, during the same period the ratio of population per physician in urban areas declined from 632 to 434. Of the physician population as a whole in 1912, 38 per cent were in rural communities, compared with 23.8 per cent in 1936.[16] The data for Minnesota are typical of trends for the United States as a whole.[17]

**Age.** Older physicians predominate in rural areas. According to Stern, "thirty-five years ago one half of young medical-school graduates established themselves in places of less than 5,000 population, by 1923, less than one quarter, and by 1931, less than one fifth, although such areas include 48 per cent of our whole population." [18] The prevalence of older physicians in rural areas has significant implications for the quality of medical service available through them. The Procurement and Assignment Service for Physicians for army service considers physicians in civil practice over 65 years of age as one-third effective and all others equal in skill.[19]

**Mobility.** Rural physicians are more mobile than are those in the cities. In Minnesota, for the period 1931–1936, the average annual turnover rate in communities of under 500 people was 31.1, compared with 18.1 for places of 10,000 and over.[20] The instability of residence of rural physicians is undoubtedly associated with economic factors. The physician moves about in search of more favorable locations in which he can improve his income. Mountin, Pennell, and Nicolay found that the proportion of doctors in the population increased with the increase in per-capita income.[21]

**Other professional personnel.** The most important medical professional group, other than the physicians, are the nurses. In 1940 the census reported 371,066 "trained nurses and student

[16] Lowry Nelson, "Distribution, Age, and Mobility of Minnesota Physicians, 1912–1936," *American Sociological Review*, 1942, 7 : 792–801.

[17] See R. G. Leland, *Distribution of Physicians in the United States*, American Medical Association, Chicago, 1936; and Joseph W. Mountin, Elliott H. Pennell, and Virginia Nicolay, "Location and Movement of Physicians, 1923 and 1938," *Public Health Reports*, September 11, 1942, and December 18, 1942.

[18] Bernhard J. Stern, *American Medical Practice*, p. 70. New York: The Commonwealth Fund, 1945.

[19] *Ibid.*, p. 71.

[20] Harold Maslow, "The Characteristics and Mobility of Rural Physicians," *Rural Sociology*, 1938, 3 : 267–278, defined "Turnover rate" as the annual number of changes during a period, divided by the average annual number of doctors.

[21] *Public Health Reports*, Vol. 57, p. 1946. December, 1942.

nurses" in the labor force (exclusive of new workers), an increase from 294,189 in 1930. The number reported for 1950 was 474,680. (See Table 46.) That the number of nurses increased more rapidly than the population is indicated by the decline in the population per nurse from 370 in 1940 to 317 in 1950. Note especially the reduction for the rural population from 1,106 to 836. Professional nurses receive their training in nursing schools of which there were 1,155 in 1952, with an enrollment of 102,000.

TABLE 46. *Employed Trained Nurses and Student Nurses by Rural-Urban and Regional Distribution, 1940 and 1950*

| AREA | 1950 | | 1940 | | POPULATION PER NURSE | |
|---|---|---|---|---|---|---|
| | No. | Per Cent | No. | Per Cent | 1950 | 1940 |
| United States | 474,680 [1] | 100.0 | 355,786 [2] | 100.0 | 317 | 370 |
| Urban | 398,129 | 85.9 | 304,062 | 85.6 | 241 | 245 |
| Rural | 65,366 | 14.1 | 51,764 | 14.4 | 836 | 1,106 |
| Northeast | 162,699 | 34.3 | 132,625 | 37.3 | 243 | 271 |
| North Central | 134,189 | 28.3 | 103,135 | 29.0 | 331 | 389 |
| South | 105,352 | 22.2 | 72,559 | 20.4 | 448 | 574 |
| West | 12,440 | 15.2 | 47,467 | 13.3 | 270 | 292 |

Source: Census for 1940 and 1950.
[1] Includes 11,185 male nurses not reported by rural-urban residence.
[2] Does not include 13,501 experienced nurses reported as "seeking work" in 1940.

Nurses, like doctors, are concentrated in the urban centers because that is where the hospitals are mostly located. This applies especially to the nurses in private employment. Public health nurses are distributed more in accordance with population. In total numbers, they have increased from 19,939 in 1937 to 25,788 in 1952.[22] Federal grants-in-aid to the states for maternal and child health are provided for in the Social Security Act and have made it possible to expand public health work greatly in other respects as well. Since some of the most serious public health problems existed in rural areas at the time the act was passed, special emphasis was given to the expansion of rural services.

It is interesting to note from the census that the number of

[22] See *America's Health Status, Needs and Resources*, Vol. III of "A Report to the President by the President's Commission on the Health Needs of the Nation." Government Printing Office, 1952.

dentists remained about the same at 70,000 during the period from 1930 to 1940, then shot up to 87,000 in 1950. The distribution of dentists according to rural or urban residence follows about the same pattern as that of physicians. A special tabulation made for the President's Commission on the Health Needs of the Nation shows that in 1949 there were only 13 dentists per 100,000 population living in places under 2,500, compared with from 74 to 90 in places of urban size.[23]

## HOSPITALS

At midcentury, hospital facilities were more generally available to the rural population than they had ever been. For example, in 1942 only 44.8 per cent of rural births took place in hospitals, whereas in 1950 the percentage had risen to 78. The comparable urban percentages were 84.4 and 95. Thus, the rural and urban groups are fast approaching "parity" in this respect. Rural people seem to have overcome a long-standing prejudice about going to the hospital, something traditionally done only in the direst emergency.

While hospitals are inevitably located in urban centers in most cases, yet access to them by rural people has been greatly facilitated by improved roads and vehicles. It is still possible to refer to the large number of counties which have no hospital, but the truth is that a hospital is not necessary in every county. Naturally, it is a great convenience to have the hospital as near as possible to the people in terms of distance, but this is not always possible from a financial standpoint.

The unmet need for hospital beds at midcentury was estimated by the Public Health Service at 640,000.[24] Nearly half of these are needed in the South. This estimate is based on the need for all purposes, including mental illness, and tuberculosis, as well as general use. Rapid progress is being made toward meeting this need under the impetus of Federal grants-in-aid to the states provided by the Hospital Survey and Construction Act. The law requires each state to submit a plan for hospital construction for the approval of the Surgeon-General of the Public Health Service.

[23] President's Commission, *op. cit.*, p. 177.
[24] *Ibid.*, p. 234.

The law also encourages the construction of hospitals in rural areas. Typically, these state plans are patterned somewhat after the army system, in which the first-aid stations are close to the front line, and other stations of increasing complexity in point of services offered, farther back until the base hospital is reached. Clinics, mobile or stationary, might be made accessible to rural people in remote hamlets. They would be prepared to take care of most of the medical needs of the population, including physical examinations of the simpler kind, treatment of common and less serious ailments and injuries. Those requiring more extensive treatment or diagnosis would be referred to the next hospital, perhaps in a town of 5,000 people, and such cases as required more specialized treatment would be referred farther to the large and elaborate hospitals in the bigger cities. When the system is developed and operated as a unit, it will mean many things. In the first place, many of the cases which now go to the large city hospital would be handled by the clinic or small hospital. In the second place, the services will be more immediate to rural people in point of distance. Finally, and of very great importance, it will mean a redistribution of physicians, dentists, and nurses in the rural areas.

## PUBLIC HEALTH SERVICES

One of the cardinal principles of any good health program is that emphasis should be placed on prevention. The system of medical care based upon the private practitioner does not properly stress it. The physician has a vested interest in the ill-health of the population. He is not paid for keeping people well, but for curing them after they get sick. If there is no sickness, the doctor cannot make a living. To supply the service for disease prevention and to perform other important functions, there have been established the public health services of the Federal and state governments. The recognized functions of a public health service, as summarized by the Committee on the Costs of Medical Care, are as follows:

(a) The collection and analysis of vital statistics; (b) the control of water, milk, and food supplies; (c) the control of sanitation; (d) the control, through quarantine and supervision, of communicable disease; and (e) the provision of laboratory services. In addition to these, the

Committee believes that the following activities are also proper public health activities: (*f*) the promotion of maternal, infant, and child hygiene, including medical and dental inspection and supervision of school children; (*g*) popular health instruction; (*h*) the provision of preventive dental care of children, and (*i*) the provisions of special services for the prevention, diagnosis, and treatment of patients with tuberculosis, venereal diseases, malaria, hookworm, or any other disease which constitutes a special health problem in the community that cannot be solved adequately and effectively by the other available medical and health agencies.[25]

At the Federal level the functions are implemented through the Public Health Service of the Department of Health, Education and Welfare. The major responsibility for administration rests upon the states, through their departments of health. These bodies, in turn, share responsibility with the county, city and town or village boards of health. The program is financed largely from funds appropriated by the states and subdivisions thereof, although the Federal government is taking on increasing responsibility in this respect.

**Health provisions of the Social Security Act.** Federal aid to states and local areas in the enforcement of quarantine laws and health regulations has been an established principle for over 100 years. But not until the passage of the Social Security Act in 1935 did the Federal government accept anything like an adequate share of responsibility in health maintenance. Under the provision of Title VI of the Social Security Act, authority is granted for (1) an annual appropriation not to exceed $8,000,000 for the purpose of assisting state, counties, health districts, and other political subdivisions of the states in the establishment and maintenance of adequate health services, including the training of personnel for state and local health work; and (2) an annual appropriation not to exceed $2,000,000 to the Public Health Service for research activities of the Service and for the expense of cooperation with the states in the administration of the Federal funds granted for aid in the establishment and maintenance of state and local health services.

[25] *Medical Care for the American People,* p. 43. Chicago: University of Chicago Press, 1932.

The grants-in-aid are conditioned upon two factors: (*a*) the state or territory must have an adequately organized public health program, and (*b*) must use the Federal funds as supplemental to its own appropriations and not to displace state or local funds. "Adequate" organization is interpreted to involve the following:

(*a*) A qualified full-time state or territorial health officer.

(*b*) Adequate provision for the administrative guidance of local health services.

(*c*) An acceptable vital-statistics service. This should include an approved plan for the registration of births and deaths and the prompt forwarding of information relative thereto to the Public Health Service.

(*d*) An acceptable state public health laboratory service.

(*e*) Adequate services for study, promotion, and supervision of maternal and child health.

(*f*) Special services for the study, promotion, and guidance of local activities for the control of preventable diseases and for health promotion. This should include an approved plan for the collection of reports of notifiable diseases and the prompt forwarding of information relative thereto to the Public Health Service.

(*g*) Services for study, promotion, and supervision of environmental sanitation.[26]

In addition to the funds made available to the Public Health Service under Title VI of the Social Security Act, as indicated above, appropriations were authorized for the expansion of maternal and child health and for aid to crippled children. These activities are administered by the Children's Bureau in the Department of Labor. The amount of the appropriations authorized at present is $5,820,000 for maternal and child-health services, $3,870,000 for crippled-children services, and $1,510,000 for child-welfare services. Part of the funds must be matched by the states before they can be made available for use in the states. All states are now cooperating in all three programs. The funds are used to conduct prenatal clinics in both rural and urban counties, to employ public-health nurses, to pay for services of local practicing physicians in connection

[26] "The Public Health Program," *Public Health Service Supplement 126*, 1937, p. 3.

with mothers' and children's clinics, to purchase medical and hospital care for maternity patients and children who otherwise would be unable to receive such care, to provide home nursing care in maternity cases and other health services for medically needy mothers and children. According to the Secretary of Labor, in the year 1939–1940:

Approximately 2,000 of the 3,050 counties in the United States have public-health nurses supervised by the health departments, who include maternity service in their nursing program. In far too many of these 2,000 counties, however, one public-health nurse is attempting to serve thousands of families for all types of public-health-nursing care. More than 1,000 counties have no public-health nurses under State health department auspices rendering any type of service to maternity patients.

In 1939 there were 6,080 public-health nurses rendering services under the maternal and child-health programs, including 418 supervisors or consultants, and 5,662 staff nurses.[27]

Since the Social Security program began to function, the number of public-health nurses in the United States has increased from 19,939 (January, 1937) to 23,705 (January, 1940).[28]

. . . The maternal mortality rate for 1938 was 11 per cent lower than for 1937, 23 per cent lower than for 1936, and 25 per cent lower than for 1934, the year prior to the passage of the Social Security Act by Congress.

The infant mortality rate for 1938 was 6 per cent lower than that for 1937, 11 per cent lower than that for 1936 and 15 per cent lower than that for 1934. . . . Decreases in infant mortality are evident in both cities and rural areas and for both white and Negro infants.[29]

### PROPOSALS FOR IMPROVING HEALTH SERVICES

The proposals and experiments or demonstrations for the improvement of the social mechanism for distributing medical care may be classified under the following headings: (a) the medical cooperative composed of consumers of medical services and under their direction, (b) physician-controlled prepayment plans, (c) compulsory social insurance, and (d) "state medicine."

[27] Annual Report of the Secretary of Labor, 1939–1940, p. 162.
[28] *Ibid.*, p. 163.
[29] *Ibid.*, p. 165.

**The medical cooperative.** This is simply a nonprofit cooperative whose members decide to pool their "health money" and engage physicians as needed and pay them from the joint fund. It is of course a prepayment plan, each family or person contributing so much a month or a year whether services are needed or not. It has been promoted most widely in rural areas by the Farmers Home Administration. According to one of the reports of that organization, "on June 30, 1943, there were FHA medical-care groups active in 1,009 counties in 41 States and Puerto Rico, with a total membership of 90,111 borrower families, or 470,836 persons." The plans cover general physician services and many provide surgery as well. Dental care was included in 129 of the counties and hospitalization in 531. Plans are worked out in cooperation with the county Medical Association, whose physician members agree to provide the service at fees somewhat less than the standard rate.

Under the cooperative plan, hospitalization groups have been more widely developed than have those which provide physician services. Under the designation of the Blue Cross Hospital Plan, groups have been organized in practically all of the states and in the Canadian provinces, with a 1947 membership of about 30 million persons. The growth has been little short of phenomenal since its beginning in 1929 in Baylor, Texas. In several states the farm organizations have actively promoted the organization of group hospital plans among farm families. While it is a commendable advance over the previous system of "paying when you have to," the plan is open to the criticism that it will not reach all of those who need it. The low-income groups will not likely be reached.

**The physician-controlled prepayment plans.** The most noted example is the Ross-Loos clinic in Los Angeles, which contracts with patients to provide medical care of specified character for a set monthly fee paid in advance.

**The social insurance plan.** Social insurance was first introduced in America to cover disability due to accidents in industry. All 48 states and the Federal government have had such plans in force for many years. Not until 1935, however, was the insurance principle applied to other hazards, when the Social Security Act provided for old-age and survivors' insurance and unemployment compensation. It is now proposed to add sickness insurance. The principle involves compulsory contributions from employee and employer in the case of wage workers; the self-employed will be required to pay the full amount of the premium. The proposed plan would cover the doctor's bill, hospitalization, and compensation for loss of time.

The objections to compulsory sickness insurance are chiefly these: (*a*) there is a decided tendency to object to anything that is compulsory; (*b*) the physicians object that it may mean the control of the medical profession by politicians; and (*c*) the plan might promote malingering—a lot of people would insist upon services beyond their actual needs. The arguments for social insurance usually boil down to these: (*a*) the compulsory feature would make family heads, who otherwise would not do so, provide security for their families; (*b*) it spreads the risk over the entire population and reduces total costs, at the same time making for improved services; (*c*) improved services result from ability to plan services on a national or state, rather than a local community, basis; (*d*) administrative cost is reduced below that of the cooperative, in that less expense is involved in securing members; and (*e*) it guarantees comprehensive coverage because benefits are not limited to the prosperous, the foresighted, and the frugal.

**State medicine.** This phrase has become a catchword and synonym for many evil things proposed for medical care. Indeed, this phrase or "socialized medicine" is thrown at any proposal to reform the present system. State medicine already is in force in the United States for a large part of the population, including the armed forces and to some extent their dependents, the population of state hospitals, penitentiaries, and other institutions, veterans, the population on relief, and, of course, those affected by the public-health program. State medicine involves the payment of all the costs of medical care from the public treasury.

What we have then at present is not a single system of medical care, but many systems. Since 1930 we have developed a vast number of experimental plans involving all of the types enumerated above. We are moving toward a greater degree of public responsibility for medical care. Whether we go as far as we have in education is a matter for future determination.

In the field of health there is further convincing evidence of the trend away from primary group to secondary organization and control. The orientation of rural life is becoming more and more like that of urban society. The transition is well symbolized in the passing of the horse-and-buggy doctor and the apparent decline of his successor, the general family physician with an automobile. In prospect now is the clinic, mobile or stationary, with its staff of specialists. Relations between patient and doctor will become less personal and continuous, though the new service may be more efficient. These are indications of the fundamental social changes taking place in rural society.

## QUESTIONS FOR DISCUSSION

1. Why is it no longer feasible or desirable to consider the maintenance of good health a purely individual concern?
2. The results of several surveys are available bearing on the health of the nation as a whole. Briefly review these data from the standpoint of (a) the incidence of illness and premature deaths, (b) the economic and social costs of preventable sickness and deaths, and (c) the costs of health services.
3. What are some of the advantages as well as disadvantages of the farm family with respect to health and the availability of medical care?
4. Evaluate the use of death rates as a measure of health conditions. What inference can be made from the fact that rural death rates are generally lower than urban?
5. Compare and discuss the significance of urban and rural morbidity rates.
6. How are health and health care related to differences in income?
7. Account for the interest the Farmers Home Administration has shown in improving rural health organization? Describe what the FHA has done to meet the health needs of its clients?
8. Point out the essential characteristics of private medical practice as it exists in rural America at present. Show how rural areas occupy an inferior position with regard to (a) the distribution of physicians, nurses, and hospitals, (b) the quality and tenure of physicians, and (c) the adequacy of public-health services.
9. Discuss the adequacy of present health-insurance plans from the standpoint of (a) coverage of various income groups, (b) coverage of various kinds of illness, and (c) recognition of the principle of "ability to pay."

SELECTED REFERENCES

Almack, R. B. "The Rural Health Facilities of Lewis County, Missouri." *University of Missouri AES Research Bulletin 365.* May, 1943.

Bird, Bedford W. "Prepaid Health Insurance for Farm Families." *State College of Washington AES Extension Bulletin 316.* May, 1953.

Dickinson, Frank G. *Medical Service Areas.* Bureau of Medical Economics Research Bulletin 80. Chicago: American Medical Association, 1951.

Goldstein, Marcus S. "Longevity and Health Status of Whites and Nonwhites in the United States," *Journal of the National Medical Association,* 46:83–104, March, 1954.

Hamilton, C. Horace. "Normal Occupancy Rate in the General Hospital," *Hospitals,* September, 1946.

Hay, Donald G., and Larson, Olaf F. "Medical and Health Care Resources Available in Cortland County, New York." *Cornell University, Department of Rural Sociology, Bulletin 24.* (mimeo.) 1950. See also by the same authors, Bulletins 25, 27, 29, and 30 in this series.

Hepple, Lawrence M. "Selective Service Rejectees in Rural Missouri, 1940–43." *Missouri AES Research Bulletin 439.* 1949.

Hoffer, C. R. "Health and Health Services for Michigan Farm Families." *Michigan AES Special Bulletin 352.* 1948.

Kaufman, Harold F. "Extent of Illness and Use of Medical Services in Rural Missouri." *University of Missouri AES Progress Report 5.* April, 1945.

Klem, Margaret C. *Medical Care and Costs in California Families in Relation to Economic Status.* San Francisco: State Relief Administration of California, 1935.

Lively, C. E. "Rural Health and Medical Service in Missouri." *Missouri AES, Department of Rural Sociology.* October, 1943.

Lively, C. E., and Lionberger, Herbert F. "The Physical Status and Health of Farm Tenants and Farm Laborers in Southeast Missouri." *Missouri AES, Department of Rural Sociology, Preliminary Reports 2 and 3.* July, 1942.

Mangus, A. R. "Health and Human Resources in Rural Ohio," and "Health Defects of Selective Service Registrants in Rural Ohio." *Ohio State University, Department of Rural Economics and Rural Sociology Bulletins 176 and 178.* 1944. (mimeo.)

Mott, Frederick D., and Roemer, Milton I. *Rural Health and Medical Care*. New York: McGraw-Hill Book Company, 1948.

North Carolina Medical Care Commission, *Report for 1949–51*. 1951.

Pink, Louis H. "The Story of the Blue Cross." *Public Affairs Pamphlet 101*. 1945.

*Report of the President's Commission on the Health Needs of the Nation.* Vol. V, Washington: Government Printing Office, 1952.

Roemer, Milton I. "Rural Programs of Medical Care," *The Annuals*, 273:160–168, January, 1951.

*State Cash Sickness Plans, 1949*. Chicago: Research Council for Economic Security, 1949.

Stern, Bernard J. *American Medical Practice*. New York: The Commonwealth Fund, 1945.

Tate, Leland B. "The Health and Medical Care Situation in Rural Virginia." *Virginia Polytechnic Institute AES Bulletin 363*. October, 1944.

Wilson, Isabella C., and Metzler, William H. "Sickness and Medical Care in an Ozark Area in Arkansas." *University of Arkansas AES Bulletin 353*. April, 1938.

Winslow, C. E. A. "Health Care for Americans." *Public Affairs Pamphlet 104*. 1945.

# CHAPTER 26

# THE OUTLOOK FOR RURAL LIFE

It should now be abundantly clear to the reader that mid-century rural life in the United States has recently undergone and is undergoing social changes of very great moment. What seemed the most important of these changes have been indicated. It is appropriate in this final chapter to call attention to the probable future trends. While it is given to no mere man to see into the future and delineate its course, it is possible to gain some idea of what to expect by merely projecting the trends already in evidence.

## SOME MAJOR FORCES OF CHANGE

Among the dynamic forces which are causing rural social readjustments on a rather large scale and at the same time increasing the tempo or rate of change, are the new technological and population changes.

**The march of technology.** The technological revolution which has come about with the invention of the internal-combustion engine and its use in the automobile, tractor, truck, and airplane, has wrought profound changes in the societies where these inventions have been widely used. Take the United States, as an example.[1] Only a generation ago a large part of the rural population was isolated during several months of the year, owing to impassable roads. Even in more favorable seasons communication with the world was slow and infrequent. But, today, there are few farms that do not possess a truck or automobile or which do not otherwise have ready access to towns by an all-weather road. In addition to the rapid communication made possible by the automobile and truck—the airplane is of minor though growing significance to the farmer as yet—the

---

[1] Canada might as easily serve as an illustration because conditions there are similar.

gasoline tractor has wrought its own revolution on the organization of the American farm. With the many laborsaving attachments which go with it, the gasoline tractor has reduced the man-labor requirements for the production of crops and thus set the stage for a series of social readjustments, including increased migration of farm people, unemployment and underemployment, and changes in farm-management procedures.

Along with these basic implements must be mentioned the development of such laborsaving devices as the two-row mechanical corn picker, the improved combine harvester, the mechanical sugar-beet harvester, and the cotton picker. These implements are adding to the efficiency of production of the American farmers, but at the same time they are obviously creating social changes of great importance.

Other technological improvements which have already had a marked effect upon rural life in America are the radio and rural electrification. With the latter go many gadgets and machines which greatly alter the shape of rural living, among which may be mentioned refrigeration, lighting, power-driven washing machines, grinders, and so on.

Of great significance, also, are the developments in scientific agriculture other than those of a mechanical character. The plant and animal breeders, the farm economists, the entomologists and pathologists—all have contributed and are contributing to the growing efficiency of agricultural producers.

But the United States and Canada are only part of one continent and represent only a small fraction of the total rural population of the world. What about South America, Asia, eastern Europe, and Russia? How are mechanical and other technological changes affecting them? In Russia, the collectivized farms and the tractor and machine stations have contributed greatly to the mechanization of farming in that country. In the rest of eastern Europe, in Hungary, Rumania, and Czechoslovakia, mechanization is still in its very early stages. In Asia, South America, and the Caribbean, farming is either carried on by the hoe or with methods only a step more advanced. Yet in all these countries there is evidence of further steps in mechanization. On the island of Trinidad in early 1946 the author observed that the large, unwieldy two-wheeled oxcarts were being replaced by rubber-tired carts, although the tractor had not supplanted the oxen. In Puerto Rico not only were the rubber-tired carts in use but they were being pulled by tractors. Oxen will eventually give way entirely to the tractor, at least on the large estates throughout the Caribbean area. There is no need further to amplify this point that mechanization and other technical improvements of agriculture are one of the pronounced trends of the times.

**Population changes.** A second major trend of basic importance are the changes in population. These changes are of two kinds, namely, the change in numbers and the change in composition. The change in number of people, in turn, is to be regarded in two aspects, that for the total population and that for the rural. The total population of the world is increasing, and throughout the nonindustrialized areas of the world—such as Asia and parts of Latin-America, for example—the increase is quite largely in the rural population. If a world population of two and one half billion persons is assumed, with a natural increase rate of ten per thousand, the annual increment is 25,000,000. This sheer increase in total numbers, whether in rural or urban areas, is bound to add to the complexities of existence. As was pointed out in Chapter 6, the growth in number of people within a given space affects society in many ways. Institutions are modified and social processes accelerated or slowed down as populations grow or decline. In the industrialized nations rural populations are either not increasing at all, are growing more slowly than the urban, or are actually declining. In the United States there appears to be a tendency for rural population to remain stationary, or to decline slightly. The trend is affected by technological changes which are being introduced into agriculture. This differential growth of the urban and rural segments in the industrial nations presents the possibility of ever greater urban influence on rural culture, if not actual economic and political domination.

With the steady advance in the mechanization of agriculture, and the continued growth of industrial cities and towns, it is to be expected that the balance of population will continue to shift away from rural areas. Even in so rural a nation as China it is expected that industrial development will absorb some of the current excess of people on farms in that country. As industrial growth proceeds in China and other countries where there has been little such development up to the present time, the further urbanization of the population of the world can be safely forecast. The land suitable for agriculture is practically all occupied, and further growth in the rural population of the world will take place only if the opportunity for migration to cities is lacking.

Changes in composition of the population are among the fundamental dynamic factors in social change. The social impact of these changes was pointed out in Chapter 6. From the world viewpoint, it is to be expected that changes will differ in different areas and countries. In more highly industrialized areas, urban and rural segments will continue their differential rates of growth, with rural sections losing their youth to the cityward migration. In those countries which are on the threshold of industrial development, the population pyramids will come to have shapes similar to those of the United States and other industrialized nations. The introduction into the more backward countries of better medical care will result in marked temporary increase in the rate of population growth, and in time will mean the lengthening of the life span to a point comparable to those of the United States, Canada, and western Europe. Thus the aged can be expected to make up increasing proportions of the populations of most of the countries of the world. The increase in total number of people, the changing ratios of rural and urban segments—with the urban gaining and the rural losing in importance, the increasing proportions of aged in the population, the temporary, at least, increase in children as improved medical practice is extended to areas now suffering from high infant mortality—all are population changes which are clearly manifest in the contemporary world and which may be expected to continue.

## THE SECULARIZATION OF RURAL LIFE

These factors of technological and population changes foreshadow many readjustments in rural society throughout the world. For want of a better word, these changes may be included under the general heading of *secularization*.

By *secularization* is meant the evolution toward a complex, sophisticated, and secondary-group society, away from the simple folk society characterized by a high degree of informal and intimate personal relations. The old dependence for social satisfactions upon the primary group of family and neighborhood is gradually giving way before the new social independence born of the automobile, the paved highway, the radio, and the other means of rapid movement and communication. The one-time intimate personal relations among neighbors and among family members become less intimate as the individual is freed from the locality group for his contacts and is able to choose from an infinitely larger number of human beings the companionship he wants.

**Changes in attitude toward farming.** Farming is becoming increasingly a business rather than a mode of life. While it would be a mistake to assume that there will be an absolute change in the nature of farm life, the trend is in the direction indicated. Secularization of farm life means further advance towards a cash economy, with a much more careful scrutiny by the farmer of his earnings' record. Attitudes of farm people toward the land as property which were discussed in Chapter XIII may be expected to change and to become more like the attitudes associated with other forms of property. In terms of a folk society, which rural society approximates in character, the farmer and his family are content to go along from year to year without keeping books, or counting up the costs and computing their profits. It is sufficient for them if at the harvest, the barns and bins are filled, the fuel supply ample for the winter, and the livestock comfortably quartered against the storm and the cold. While not without a definite interest in dollars and cents, the farmer-peasant's preoccupation is not to amass large gains but to live comfortably and securely. And security means above all things a clear title to his land.

These historic peasant attitudes are giving way before the pressure of ideas emanating from the urban-industrial world. The advertising campaigns of the farm-machinery manufacturers, the fertilizer dealers, the makers of electrical gadgets and machines, with their emphasis on "costs of operation," "greater economy," "efficiency"; the unimpeachable arguments based on "careful records" and the like, are having their effect. The Agricultural Extension Service itself is devoted to the objective of improving the efficiency of the farmer, making him a better "businessman," helping him to keep farm accounts. The farm organizations are bombarding their members with propaganda about cost of production, about parity, about wage legislation, and similar phrases and words which characterize a businessman's approach to farming. It seems inevitable that the time is not far distant, in the United States at least, when the farm will no longer be facetiously referred to as the "only business that can continuously be operated at a loss." When the bookkeeping farmer collectively appears on the scene, he is likely to demand prices sufficient to keep his books balanced, at least, if not to show a profit.

**Pattern of rural-urban opposition.** Thus secularization may bring into sharper outlines the pattern of rural-urban conflict. While the developments briefly sketched above will tend to lessen the observable differences between country and city, with the attitudes of rural people becoming similar to those of the city with respect to many things, and the standard of rural and urban living approaching more nearly a state of equality, the new requirements of country living in terms of expendable cash will mean higher prices for farm products, and will produce counteraction on the part of the city population. Urbanites are accustomed to getting food at relatively low prices because of the chronically depressed market resulting from overproduction on the farms. The farmer, for his part, has been able to survive under these conditions only because of the non-cash returns secured from the farm. These latter are likely to figure less and less in his calculations in the future. Thus the increased prices that urbanites may be asked to pay for food in order that farmers may have parity of income with them will most likely cause friction and conflicts which will require real statesmanship to resolve.

The role of central governments in all this will naturally be an important one. Farmers everywhere during World War II came to rely upon the authority of government to decide prices, and prices were generally rather favorable in order to stimulate production. In the face of the poorly organized condition of farmers generally and their consequent weakness in collective bargaining, they are likely to continue to look to government to function in their behalf.

**The family.** The rural family in the new *milieu* produced by these forces will seem to lose some of its apparent stability and integrity, as the children and parents alike find their social life individually more and more outside the home in clubs and organizations and in community-wide activities. Aged parents, under the benefits provided by the welfare state, will reside in homes for the aged or in their own homes supported by a pension, rather than with the families of their sons or daughters. The trend is definitely towards individual release from the ancient locality bonds of the family and the neighborhood. The new conditions will test the real integrity of the family as its chief and almost only bond will be that of affection, rather than authority of parents or the need of protection of the individual. Protection will be provided by secondary agencies. This new family need not be any less satisfying to the individual than the old, and may provide improved conditions for the growth of personality.

**The church.** Under the impact of these forces the church will also undergo changes. Certainly, with the steady rise in the level of education of country people, with the spread of scientific knowledge, and with the competition of other institutions in the community for the attention of the members, the church may witness a decline in the effectiveness of its ancient sanctions in invoking obedience and conformity. This trend may be interpreted by some as a decline in the religiosity of the community. It may also be regarded merely as a modification in the form of religious expression. A more highly educated and sophisticated rural population is likely to be impatient with the multiplicity of creeds bearing the same general stamp and differing only in minor interpretations of doctrine. Finally, the rural clergy, to bear the respect of the community, will need to be carefully chosen and well trained.

**Social stratification.** As the farmer-peasant gains more ready access to the outside world and forms his contacts more and more on the secondary level, moving away from the primary, social stratification may increase and approach more nearly the characteristics of the city. In the drive for social status, possession of an electric refrigerator or a television set may carry more prestige than the ownership of land did in the simpler community. The expanded demands for money income which have characterized farm life in the United States since World War I, and which will become more pronounced both here and throughout the world, almost certainly will mean increased emphasis upon income as a measure of status. Especially will stratification increase if the "factory in the field" type of farm organization expands.

**Status of labor.** One of the most significant effects of the application of the new technology to agriculture concerns the *latifundia* or large-scale enterprises. These effects have already been manifested in the United States to some extent, especially in cotton production. Mechanization has reduced the amount of human labor needed in cotton culture, causing thousands of workers to migrate, while the status of the workers who remain has been changed from that of sharecroppers to wage hands.

In other countries proposals to mechanize the latifundia have aroused much misgiving and opposition on the part of labor. In Cuba, the workers on the sugar plantations have opposed the introduction of mechanical harvesters because of the threat to their employment and security. What will become of them if the machine takes their jobs away? In countries like those of the Caribbean, where mineral resources are meager and industrial possibilities therefore limited, the dilemma posed by the new technology is baffling indeed. How to enjoy the benefits of the new technology without hazarding the economic and social security that the present world provides is the question which these countries would like to have answered.

This naturally raises the large question as to whether limits will be imposed upon the technological advance in other countries. Is there a point beyond which it is undesirable to go in the march toward efficiency or toward secularization of life? If so, where is that point? How can these forces be controlled? Will there arise a generation of Rousseaus or Thoreaus who will try to find a simpler life by going back to nature? These are interesting questions but the student of social history will be very skeptical about any answer which would postulate a rever-

sal of the basic trends. There have always been attempts by
small groups and by individuals to counter the major trends of
society, to withdraw from the world and create a society more
to their hearts' desires, but they have affected the general
drift but little, if at all.

These general statements are but hypotheses as to the future
of rural life. In a word, what is happening and what appears
likely to continue to happen, is the urbanization (considered
in its broadest aspect) of the countryside. Rural life is expanding
and its social horizons receding. As the effective area of social
interaction of the ruralite increases, it intersects that of the
urbanite, and the two come to have a common social world.

It is not to be expected, however, that in the *rapprochement*
of the urban and rural worlds there will be a coalescence of the
two, and that each will therefore lose its distinguishing features.
Rural people and rural living will take on many of the characteristics of urban people and urban living, but the two ways of
life will still be inevitably different for reasons set forth in
Chapter 2. It should also be recognized that in this sharing of
a common culture the urban world will be influenced by the
rural as well as the other way about. That is, there will be as
there has always been, a reciprocal relation between city and
country.

As things look in the United States at present rural and urban
differences will be based more on occupation. Whether one lives
inside the city limits or in the country will make little difference
for material considerations. But farmers' interests are tied up
with the fortunes of agriculture as an industry, and these interests
will be reflected in their social life; in the education they want
for their children, the way they vote, and the public policies which
they will approve.

The student, however, should not assume that these changes
are coming everywhere in the world at the same time or at the
same rate. He should not assume either that the changes indicated will be rapid in any case. Social change is likely to be
slow, scarcely perceptible, if short periods of time are taken.
But over longer periods of time change is observable even in
the areas where the tempo of life and change is extremely slow.
For of all things, change is the most constant and inevitable.

# APPENDIX A

## TOPICS FOR TERM PAPERS AND SPECIAL REPORTS

1. On the basis of data available in the United States census reports, make a study of the population trends in your home county, or in a county in which you are interested.
2. Population displacements in Europe incident to World War II. (Consult publications of International Labor Office and the *Population Index.*)
3. The extent of migration from the rural sections of the United States to industrial centers during the period from 1940 to 1950.
4. Choose one of the following countries and make a report on recent population changes, with special reference to total numbers, rural-urban ratios, age composition, etc.: (a) Soviet Russia; (b) Canada; (c) Mexico; (d) Cuba; (e) Puerto Rico.
5. Review of the theories of the relation between culture and the geographic environment.
6. Types of settlement in Colonial America. (Student may choose to treat this topic in connection with some other country: Brazil, Argentina, Palestine, etc.)
7. Settlement patterns in Europe.
8. Origin of the line village among the Canadian French.
9. Social classes on the medieval manor.
10. A case study of social stratification in a rural community.
11. Description of a rural cultural island (e.g., some minority ethnic group).
12. Assimilation or accommodation of an ethnic group, (Japanese, Indian, Polish, French, German, Swedish, etc.)
13. Social effects of the mechanization of agriculture.
14. The systems of farming in Soviet Russia. (Student may also choose some other country such as Brazil, Argentina, Germany, France, England, Rumania, Hungary, etc.)
15. Description of a community situation in which religious differences cause conflict.
16. A description of community conflict growing out of differences in interests of agricultural and nonagricultural groups.
17. Select a cooperative enterprise in some community and write a description of its origin, development, and the results attained. Give

attention to the background forces which produced it, the role of leaders in its evolution, etc.

18. Regional cultural differences in rural America.
19. Study of rural survivals in urban culture.
20. Survey of recent studies related to the morale of rural people.
21. The spread of urban-culture traits into rural areas.
22. Survival of American-Indian traits in contemporary rural culture.
23. The importance of the village trade-center in American rural society.
24. Origin of utopian rural communities in America.
25. National origins of the American population, or of the state or county.
26. Construct age-sex pyramids for 1940 and 1950 for your state (county or community) and for urban and rural farm populations. Account for the differences.
27. The survival prospects of the rural neighborhood.
28. The farm village versus the trade-center-dispersed-farmstead rural community: a study of relative advantages.
29. The relationship of voting behavior to rurality of population in a selected state, in a Presidential election year.
30. Differential characteristics of rural and urban families.
31. An evaluation of family-cycle theories.
32. Interview the county agricultural agent and prepare a description of his work.
33. Using the annual reports of your religious denomination, describe its work in your state during a decade.
34. Comparison of cooperative and corporate organizational differences, with social implications.
35. Describe the various functions of a local church.
36. Interview a local minister and write a job description of his position.
37. Rural-urban differentials in crime or juvenile delinquency.
38. Review of the development of Social Insurance for farm people.
39. The present status of migratory agricultural workers.
40. Problems incident to the education of migratory workers' children.
41. Describe the present program of price supports and acreage control of farm commodities. Choose one commodity.
42. History and achievements of the Soil Conservation Service.
43. The farmer and the labor unions: mutual and conflicting interests.
44. Community relations of the migrant farm family.
45. Social implications of differences in age distribution of urban, rural-nonfarm and rural-farm families.
46. Critique of recent efforts to measure or delimit social status and social stratification in rural society.

47. Migratory movements of individuals and families from a small rural community, 1940 to 1950.
48. A history of three generations in your own family. Pay special attention to changes in occupation and economic and social status, standards of living, family organization and integration, size, and migration.
49. The development of the Blue Cross Hospital Plan among farm families in your state or in some other area.
50. Present status of cooperative health associations among farm families.
51. Marital status of rural and urban populations 15 years of age and over, by states, 1940 and 1950. (Source: Census, Vol. II.)
52. Family life in some special religio-ethnic group (such as Amish, Polish, Jewish, Catholic, Protestant, and the like).
53. Effects of suburban movement upon rural social organization in areas involved.
54. Changes in sex ratios from 1940 to 1950 by age groups in the farm population, and its probable effect upon rural social institutions.
55. Some explanations of lower high-school attendance among farm youth as compared with urban.
56. A review of a selected, politically radical movement among farmers such as The Nonpartisan League, Farm Holiday Association, Farmers' Alliance, and the like.
57. A critique of the township as a unit of local government.
58. A description of organization and functions of the soil-conservation district.
59. Some proposals for reform of county government in the United States. (Include a summary of weaknesses which the proposals are intended to correct.)
60. Choose one religious denomination and find data on (a) trends in total membership, (b) distribution of members by states, (c) rural and urban churches and church membership; (d) sex distribution of membership; and other facts available in the *Census of Religious Bodies* for 1916, 1926, and 1936.
61. Distribution by counties of your state of number of churches and members of a selected denomination. (See *Census of Religious Bodies*.)
62. Trends in farm-family expenditures. (Consult extension agents.)
63. Deficiencies in rural housing in a selected state as revealed in the *Census of Housing*.
64. An evaluation of the techniques of adult education as used by the Agricultural Extension Service.
65. The place of the weekly newspaper in the rural community, with emphasis on recent trends.

66. Present status of rural library services in the United States (or a particular state).
67. The social concomitants of the large-scale farm enterprise.
68. Choose some foreign country in which you are interested and describe the land tenure systems and the distribution of land.
69. Describe the organization and functioning of some cooperative, either producers' or consumers'.
70. Definitions of the family farm, and significance of the family farm to social organization of rural life.
71. Church denominations, membership, and ministerial services in my home community.
72. The relation of the rural church to recreation. Describe the recreational functions performed by a church with which you are familiar.
73. The Rural Electrification Administration. History, how it functions, and an evaluation of its significance to rural social institutions.
74. Discussion of proposed changes in the Social Security program as applied to rural society.

# APPENDIX B

## BIBLIOGRAPHY

I. *UNITED STATES AND CANADA*

A. TEXTBOOKS

Galpin, Charles J. *Rural Life*. New York: D. Appleton-Century Co., 1918.

—— *Rural Social Problems*. New York: D. Appleton-Century Co., 1924.

Gillette, John M. *Constructive Rural Sociology*. New York: Sturgis and Walton Co., 1913.

—— *Rural Sociology*. New York: The Macmillan Company, 1936.

Hawthorne, H. B. *The Sociology of Rural Life*. New York: D. Appleton-Century Co., 1926.

Hayes, A. W. *Rural Sociology*. New York: Longmans, Green and Co., 1929.

Hoffer, C. R. *Introduction to Rural Sociology*, Revised Edition. New York: Farrar and Rinehart, 1934.

Holmes, Roy H. *Rural Sociology*. New York: McGraw-Hill Book Co., 1932.

Kolb, J. H., and Brunner, E. deS. *A Study of Rural Society*, Fourth Edition. Boston: Houghton Mifflin Company, 1952.

Landis, Paul H. *Rural Life in Process*, Second Edition. New York: McGraw-Hill Book Co., 1948.

Loomis, Charles P., and Beegle, J. Allan. *Rural Social Systems*. New York: Prentice-Hall, 1950.

Lundquist, G. A., and Carver, Thomas Nixon. *Principles of Rural Sociology*. Boston: Ginn and Company, 1927.

Sanderson, Dwight. *Rural Sociology and Rural Social Organization*. New York: John Wiley and Sons, 1942.

Sanderson, Dwight, and Polson, Robert A. *Rural Community Organization*. New York: John Wiley and Sons, 1939.

Sims, Newell L. *Elements of Rural Sociology*. New York: The Thomas Y. Crowell Company, 1946.

Smith, T. Lynn. *The Sociology of Rural Life*, Third Edition. New York: Harper and Brothers, 1953.

Sorokin, P. A., and Zimmerman, C. C. *Principles of Rural-Urban Sociology*. New York: Henry Holt and Co., 1929.

Sorokin, P. A.; Zimmerman, C. C.; and Galpin, C. J. *A Systematic Source Book in Rural Sociology*. Minneapolis: University of Minnesota Press, 1930–1932. 3 vols.

Taylor, Carl C. *Rural Sociology*. New York: Harper and Brothers, 1933.

Taylor, Carl C., and associates. *Rural Life in the United States*. New York: Alfred A. Knopf, 1949.

Vogt, Paul L. *Introduction to Rural Sociology*. New York: D. Appleton-Century Co., 1918.

B. SOME GENERAL REFERENCES

Chapin, F. Stuart. *Contemporary American Institutions*. New York: Harper and Brothers, 1935.

Cooley, Charles H. *Social Organization*. New York: Charles Scribner's Sons, 1909.

533

Eubank, Earle E. *The Concepts of Sociology.* Boston: D. C. Heath and Co., 1932.

Gide, Charles. *Communist and Cooperative Colonies.* New York: The Thomas Y. Crowell Company, 1928.

Gras, N. S. B. *An Introduction to Economic History.* New York: Harper and Brothers, 1922.

Harrison, Shelby M., and Andrews, F. Emerson. *American Foundations of Social Welfare.* New York: Russell Sage Foundation, 1946.

Herskovits, Melville J. *Acculturation: A Study of Culture Contact.* New York: J. J. Augustin, 1938.

Kropotkin, P. *Mutual Aid: A Factor in Evolution.* New York: McClure, Phillips and Co., 1902; Revised Edition, Alfred A. Knopf, 1917.

Semple, Ellen Churchill. *American History and Its Geographic Conditions.* Boston: Houghton Mifflin Company, 1903.

Sorokin, P. A. *Contemporary Sociological Theories.* New York: Harper and Brothers, 1928.

———— *Social Mobility.* New York: Harper and Brothers, 1927.

Sumner, W. G. *Folkways.* Boston: Ginn and Company, 1907.

Sydenstricker, Edgar. *Health and Environment.* New York: McGraw-Hill Book Co., 1933.

Zimmerman, C. C. *Consumption and Standards of Living.* New York: D. Van Nostrand Company, 1936.

Zimmerman, C. C., and Frampton, Merle E. *Family and Society: A Study of the Sociology of Reconstruction.* New York: D. Van Nostrand Company, 1935.

C. FICTION WITH RURAL LIFE SETTING

Caldwell, Erskine. *Tobacco Road.* New York: The Viking Press, 1934.

Carroll, Gladys. *As the Earth Turns.* New York: The Macmillan Company, 1933.

Cather, Willa. *My Antonia.* Boston: Houghton Mifflin Company, 1926.

Garland, Hamlin. *Son of the Middle Border.* New York: The Macmillan Company, 1923.

Quick, Herbert. *Vandemark's Folly.* New York: A. L. Burt Co., 1922.

———— *The Hawkeye.* Indianapolis: Bobbs-Merrill Co., 1923.

Rawlings, Marjorie Kinnan. *The Yearling.* New York: Charles Scribner's Sons, 1938, 1940.

Roberts, Elizabeth Madox. *The Time of Man.* New York: The Viking Press, 1926.

Rolvaag, Ole Edvart. *Giants in the Earth.* New York: Harper, 1927.

———— *Peder Victorious.* New York: Harper and Brothers, 1929.

Sandoz, Marie. *Old Jules.* Boston: Little, Brown and Co., 1935.

Steinbeck, John. *The Grapes of Wrath.* New York: The Viking Press, 1939.

Suckow, Ruth. *The Folks.* New York: Farrar and Rinehart, 1934.

D. RURAL LIFE AND INSTITUTIONS

a. *Books*

Adams, Herbert B. *The Germanic Origin of New England Towns.* Baltimore: Johns Hopkins Press, 1882.

Anderson, Wilbert L. *The Country Town.* New York: Baker and Taylor Co., 1906.

Bailey, L. H. *The State and the Farmer.* New York: The Macmillan Company, 1908.

Bidwell, Percy W., and Falconer, John I. *History of Agriculture in the Northern United States, 1620–1860.* Washington, D.C.: The Carnegie Institute of Washington, 1935.

Branson, E. C. *Farm Life Abroad.* Chapel Hill: University of North Carolina Press, 1924.

Brunner, E. deS. *Village Communities.* New York: George H. Doran Co., 1927.

Brunner, E. deS.; Hughes, Gwendolyn S.; and Patten, Marjorie, *American Agricultural Villages.* New York: George H. Doran Co., 1927.

Brunner, E. deS., and Kolb, J. H. *Rural Social Trends.* New York: McGraw-Hill Book Co., 1933.

Brunner, E. deS., and Lorge, Irving. *Rural Trends in Depression Years.* New York: Columbia University Press, 1937.

Brunner, E. deS.; Sanders, Irwin T.; and Ensminger, Douglas. (eds.) *Farmers of the World.* New York: Columbia University Press, 1945.

Buck, Solon J. *The Granger Movement.* Cambridge: Harvard University Press, 1913.

Burr, Walter. *Small Towns: An Estimate of Their Trade and Culture.* New York: The Macmillan Company, 1929.

Butterfield, Kenyon L. *Chapters in Rural Progress.* Chicago: University of Chicago Press, 1908.

Carrier, Lyman. *The Beginnings of Agriculture in America.* New York: McGraw-Hill Book Co., 1923.

Cook, Katherine M. *Review of Conditions and Development in Education in Rural and Other Sparsely Settled Areas.* Washington, D.C.: Government Printing Office, 1937.

Daniels, John. *Cooperation: An American Way.* New York: Ccvici Friede, 1938.

Davis, Allison; Gardner, Burleigh B.; and Gardner, Mary R. *Deep South: A Study of Social Class and Color Caste in a Southern City.* Chicago: University of Chicago Press, 1941.

Dollard, John. *Caste and Class in a Southern Town.* New Haven: Yale University Press, 1937.

*Economic and Social Problems and Conditions of the Southern Appalachians.* United States Department of Agriculture Publication 205. 1935.

Fairlie, John A. *Local Government in Counties, Towns, and Villages.* New York: The Century Co., 1906.

Felton, Ralph A. *Local Church Cooperation in Rural Communities.* New York: Home Missions Council, 1940.

Fry, C. Luther. *American Villages.* New York: Doubleday, Doran and Co., 1920.

——— *Diagnosing the Rural Church, A Study in Method.* New York: George H. Doran Co., 1924.

Galpin, Charles J. *My Drift into Rural Sociology.* Baton Rouge: Louisiana State University Press, 1938.

Gee, Wilson. *The Social Economics of Agriculture,* Third Edition. New York: The Macmillan Company, 1954.

Gray, L. C. *History of Agriculture in the Southern United States to 1860.* Washington, D.C.: The Carnegie Institute of Washington, 1933. 2 vols.

Hardin, Charles M. *Politics of Agriculture.* Glencoe, Ill.: The Free Press. 1952.

Harris, Marshall. *Origins of the Land Tenure System.* Ames, Iowa: Iowa State College Press. 1953.

Hibbard, B. H. *A History of the Public Land Policies.* New York: The Macmillan Company, 1924.

Hicks, Granville. *Small Town.* New York: The Macmillan Company, 1946.

Hicks, John D. *The Populist Revolt.* Minneapolis: University of Minnesota Press, 1931.

Johnson, Charles S. *The Shadow of the Plantation.* Chicago: University of Chicago Press, 1934.

Kester, Howard. *Revolt Among the Sharecroppers.* New York: Covici Friede, 1936.

Kile, O. M. *The Farm Bureau Movement.* New York: The Macmillan Company, 1921.

Kirkpatrick, E. L. *The Farmer's Standard of Living.* New York: The Century Co., 1929.

Loomis, C. P. *Studies of Rural Social Organization in the United States, Latin America and Germany.* East Lansing: Michigan State College Book Store, 1945.

Loomis, Charles P., and others. *Rural Social Systems and Adult Education.* East Lansing: Michigan State College Press. 1953.

MacLear, Anne B. *Early New England Towns.* Columbia University Studies in Economics, History and Public Law. New York: Longmans, Green and Co., 1908.

Miner, Horace. *St. Denis: A French-Canadian Parish.* Chicago: University of Chicago Press, 1939.

Munro, William Bennett. *The Seigneurs of Old Canada.* Toronto: Brook and Company, 1922.

Myrdal, Gunnar, and others. *An American Dilemma: The Negro Problem and Modern Democracy.* New York: Harper and Brothers, 1944.

Odum, Howard W. *Southern Regions of the United States.* Chapel Hill: University of North Carolina Press, 1936.

Plunkett, Sir Horace. *The Country Life Movement in the United States.* New York: The Macmillan Company, 1910.

Porter, Kirk H. *County and Township Government in the United States.* New York: The Macmillan Company, 1929.

Powdermaker, Hortense. *After Freedom.* New York: The Viking Press, 1939.

Raper, Arthur. *Preface to Peasantry.* Chapel Hill: University of North Carolina Press, 1936.

——— *Tenants of the Almighty.* New York: The Macmillan Company, 1943.

Sanderson, Dwight. *The Farmer and His Community.* New York: Harcourt, Brace and Co., 1922.

Sanderson, Dwight. *The Rural Community: The Natural History of a Sociological Group.* Boston: Ginn and Company, 1932.

Shepard, Ward. *Food or Famine: The Challenge of Erosion.* New York: The Macmillan Company, 1945.

Sims, Newell L. *A Hoosier Village.* New York: Longmans, Green and Co., 1912.

―――― *The Rural Community: Ancient and Modern.* New York: Charles Scribner's Sons, 1920.

Taylor, Carl C. *The Farmers' Movement, 1620–1920.* American Book Company, 1953.

Taylor, Paul S. *An American-Mexican Frontier.* Chapel Hill: University of North Carolina Press, 1934.

Terpenning, Walter A. *Village and Open-Country Neighborhoods.* New York: D. Appleton-Century Co., 1931.

Treat, Payson Jackson. *The National Land System, 1785–1820.* New York: E. B. Treat and Co., 1910.

Turner, Frederick Jackson. *The Frontier in American History.* New York: Henry Holt and Co., 1921.

Vance, Rupert B. *Human Factors in Cotton Culture: A Study in the Social Geography of the American South.* Chapel Hill: University of North Carolina Press, 1929.

Wager, Paul W. (ed.) *County Government Across the Nation.* Chapel Hill: University of North Carolina Press. 1950.

Webb, Walter Prescott. *The Great Plains.* Boston: Houghton Mifflin Company, 1936.

Weeden, William B. *Economic and Social History of New England, 1620–1789.* Boston: Houghton Mifflin Company, 1891.

West, James. *Plainville, U.S.A.* New York: Columbia University Press, 1945.

Willey, Malcolm M. *The Country Newspaper.* Chapel Hill: University of North Carolina Press, 1926.

Williams, James M. *American Town.* Waterville, N.Y.: R. W. Williams, 1906.

―――― *Our Rural Heritage—The Social Psychology of Rural Development.* New York: Alfred A. Knopf, 1925.

―――― *The Expansion of Rural Life—The Social Psychology of Rural Development.* New York: Alfred A. Knopf, 1926.

Wilson, Louis R. *The Geography of Reading.* Chicago: American Library Association and University of Chicago Press, 1938.

Wilson, Warren H. *Quaker Hill.* Brooklyn, N.Y.: W. H. Wilson Company, 1907.

―――― *The Farmer's Church.* New York: D. Appleton-Century Co., 1925.

Woofter, T. J., Jr. *Races and Ethnic Groups in American Life.* New York: McGraw-Hill Book Co., 1933.

Works, George A., and Lesser, Simon O. *Rural America Today: Its Schools and Community Life.* Chicago: University of Chicago Press, 1942.

Zimmerman, C. C. *The Changing Community.* New York: Harper and Brothers, 1938.

b. *Monographs, Bulletins, Articles*

Allen, R. H.; Cottrell, L. S., Jr.; Troxell, W. W.; Herring, Harriet L.; and Edwards, A. D. "Part-Time Farming in the South East." Washington, D.C. *Division of Social Research, Works Progress Administration, Research Monograph IX.* 1937.

Anderson, W. A. "Rural Youth: Activities, Interests, and Problems—I and II." Ithaca. *Cornell University AES Bulletins 649 and 661.* May, 1936; January, 1937.

Anderson, W. A., and Korns, Willis. "Interests, Activities and Problems of Rural Young Folks.—II. Men 15 to 29 Years of Age." Ithaca. *Cornell University AES Bulletin 631.* May, 1935.

Anderson, W. A., and Loomis, C. P. "Migration of Sons and Daughters of White Farmers in Wake County, North Carolina, 1929." Raleigh. *North Carolina State College AES Bulletin 275.* June, 1930.

Andrews, Charles M. "The River Towns of Connecticut." Baltimore. *Johns Hopkins University Studies in Historical and Political Science, Seventh Series VII–IX.* 1889.

Asch, Berta, and Mangus, A. R. "Farmers on Relief and Rehabilitation." Washington, D.C. *Division of Social Research, Works Progress Administration, Research Monograph VIII.* 1937.

Beck, P. G., and Forster, M. C. "Six Rural Problem Areas." Washington, D.C. *Federal Emergency Relief Administration Research Monograph I.* 1935.

Beers, Howard W. "Measurements of Family Relationships in Farm Families of Central New York." Ithaca. *Cornell University AES Memoir 183.* December, 1935.

Beers, Howard W.; Williams, Robin M.; Page, John S.; Ensminger, Douglas. "Community Land-Use Planning Committees." Lexington. *Kentucky AES Bulletin 418.* 1941.

Brannen, C. O. "Characteristics and Costs of County Government in Arkansas." Fayetteville. *University of Arkansas AES Bulletin 338.* 1937.

Brooks, Robert Preston. "The Agrarian Revolution in Georgia, 1865–1912." Madison. *University of Wisconsin Historical Series III.* 1914.

Brunner Edmund deS., and Smith, T. Lynn. "Village Growth and Decline, 1930–40," *Rural Sociology,* IX, 1944.

Burt, Henry J. "Contacts in a Rural Community." Columbia. *University of Missouri AES Research Bulletin 125.* August, 1929.

Dickey, J. A., and Branson, E. C. "How Farm Tenants Live." Raleigh. *University of North Carolina Extension Bulletin,* Vol. II, No. 6, November 16, 1922.

Dickins, Dorothy. "Family Living on Poorer and Better Soils." State College. *Mississippi State College AES Bulletin 320.* 1937.

——— "Occupations of Sons and Daughters of Mississippi Cotton Farmers." State College. *Mississippi State College AES Bulletin 318.* May, 1937.

Egleston, Melville. "The Land System of the New England Colonies." Baltimore. *Johns Hopkins University Studies in Historical and Political Science, Fourth Series XI–XII.* 1886.

Elting, Irving. "Dutch Village Communities on the Hudson River."

Baltimore. *Johns Hopkins University Studies in Historical and Political Science, Fourth Series I.* 1886.

Felton, Ralph A., and Beal, Marjorie. "The Library of the Open Road." Ithaca. *Cornell University Extension Bulletin 188.* November, 1929.

Ford, Amelia Clewley. "Colonial Precedents of Our National Land System As It Existed in 1800." Madison. *University of Wisconsin History Series II, Bulletin 352.* 1910.

Frame, Nat. T. "Focusing on the Country Community." Morgantown. *West Virginia University, College of Agriculture, Extension Circular 211.* July, 1918.

Frame, Nat. T., and Rapking, A. H. "Helping the Country Community Saw Wood on Its Community Program." Morgantown. *West Virginia University, College of Agriculture, Extension Circular 265.* January, 1925.

Galpin, Charles J. "The Social Anatomy of an Agricultural Community." Madison. *University of Wisconsin AES Research Bulletin 34.* 1915.

Gaumitz, Walter H. "Availability of Public-School Education in Rural Communities." Washington, D.C. *United States Office of Education Bulletin 24.*

Geddes, Joseph A. "Farm Versus Village Living in Utah, Plain City—Type 'A' Village." Parts III and IV. Logan. *Utah AES Bulletin 269.* March, 1936.

Halbert, Blanche. "Hospitals for Rural Communities." Washington, D.C. *United States Department of Agriculture, Farmers Bulletin 1792.*

Hall, R. B. "Some Rural Settlement Forms in Japan," *Geographical Review XXI,* 1931.

Hamilton, C. Horace. "Recent Changes in the Social and Economic Status of Farm Families in North Carolina." Raleigh. *North Carolina AES Bulletin 309.* May, 1937.

Hamilton, C. Horace, and Garnett, W. E. "The Role of the Church in Rural Community Life in Virginia." Blacksburg. *Virginia AES Bulletin 267.* June, 1929.

Hammar, Conrad H., and Barton, Glen T. "The Farmer and the Cost of Local Rural Government in Missouri." Columbia. *Missouri AES Bulletin 385.* 1937.

Harris, Marshall. "Agricultural Landlord-Tenant Relations in England and Wales." Washington. *Land Use Planning Publication 4. Resettlement Administration.* 1936.

Hay, Donald G. "Social Organizations and Agencies in North Dakota, A Study of Trends, 1926 to 1936." Fargo. *North Dakota Agriculture College AES Bulletin 288.* July, 1937.

Hayes, Augustus W. "Community Value of the Consolidated Rural School: A Study in Rural Community Organization." New Orleans. *Tulane University Research Bulletin 2.* 1923.

Hill, George W.; Slocum, Walter; and Hill, Ruth C. "Man-Land Adjustment, A Study of Family and Inter-Family Aspects of Land Retirement in the Central Wisconsin Land Purchase Area." Madison. *University of Wisconsin AES Research Bulletin 134.* 1938.

Hummel, B. L. "Community Organization in Missouri." Columbia.

*University of Missouri College of Agriculture Extension Circular 183.*
September, 1926.

Hurd, T. N. "Local Government in Tompkins County, New York."
Ithaca. *Cornell University AES Bulletin 657.* 1936.

Hypes, James L. "Social Participation in a Rural New England Town."
New York. *Teachers College, Columbia University, Contributions to
Education 258.* 1927.

Hypes, James L., and Markey, John F. "The Genesis to Farming Occupations in Connecticut." Storrs. *Storrs AES Bulletin 161.* 1929.

Johansen, John P. "Immigrant Settlements and Social Organization
in South Dakota." Brookings. *South Dakota State College AES
Bulletin 313.* 1937.

―――― "Immigrants and Their Children in South Dakota." Brookings.
*South Dakota State College AES Bulletin 302.* 1936.

―――― "The Extent of Dependency Upon Old Age Assistance in South
Dakota." Brookings. *South Dakota State College AES Bulletin 318.*

Kaufman, Harold F. "Extent of Illness and Use of Medical Services in
Rural Missouri." Columbia. *University of Missouri AES Progress
Report 5.* April, 1945.

Kemp, Louise, and Smith, T. Lynn. "Health and Mortality in Louisiana." Baton Rouge. *Louisiana AES Bulletin 390.* 1945.

Kirkpatrick, E. L. "The Farmer's Standard of Living; A Socio-economic Study of 2886 White Farm Families of Selected Localities in
11 States." Washington, D.C. *United States Department of Agriculture,
Department Bulletin 1466.* 1926.

―――― "The Standard of Life in a Typical Section of Diversified Farming." Ithaca. *Cornell University AES Bulletin 423.* July, 1923.

Kirkpatrick, E. L.; Kolb, J. H.; Inge, Creagh; and Wileden, A. F.
"Rural Organizations and the Farm Family." Madison. *University
of Wisconsin AES Research Bulletin 96.* November, 1929.

Kirkpatrick, E. L.; McCall, P. E.; and Cowles, May L. "Farm Living
in Wisconsin." Madison. *University of Wisconsin AES Research
Bulletin 114.* January, 1933.

Kirkpatrick, E. L.; Tough, Rosalind; and Cowles, May L. "How Farm
Families Meet the Emergency." Madison. *University of Wisconsin
AES Research Bulletin 126.* January, 1935.

―――― "The Life Cycle of the Farm Family." Madison. *University of
Wisconsin AES Research Bulletin 121.* September, 1934.

Kolb, J. H. "Rural Primary Groups." Madison. *University of Wisconsin
AES Research Bulletin 51.* 1921.

―――― "Service Institutions for Town and Country." Madison.
*University of Wisconsin AES Research Bulletin 66.* December, 1925.

―――― "Service Relations of Town and Country." Madison. *University
of Wisconsin AES Research Bulletin 58.* December, 1923.

Kolb, J. H., and Wileden, A. F. "Special Interest Groups in Rural
Society." Madison. *University of Wisconsin AES Research Bulletin 84.*
December, 1927.

Kumlien, W. F. "The High School Education of Farm Boys and Girls
in South Dakota." Brookings. *South Dakota AES Bulletin 250.*
March, 1930.

Kumlien, W. F. "The Rural Health Situation in South Dakota." Brookings. *South Dakota AES Bulletin 258*. 1931.

—— "The Social Problem of the Church in South Dakota." Brookings. *South Dakota State College Bulletin 294*. May, 1935.

Landis, Paul H. "Rural Population Trends in Washington." Pullman. *Washington State College AES Bulletin 333*. July, 1936.

—— "The Growth and Decline of South Dakota Trade Centers, 1901–1933." Brookings. *South Dakota State College AES Bulletin 279*. 1933.

—— "South Dakota Town-Country Trade Relations, 1901–1931." Brookings. *South Dakota State College AES Bulletin 274*. 1932.

Leonard, Olen E., and Loomis, Charles P. "Culture of a Contemporary Rural Community: El Cerrito, New Mexico." Washington, D.C. United States *Department of Agriculture, Rural Life Studies 1*. 1941.

Lindstrom, D. E. "Forces Affecting Participation of Farm People in Rural Organization." Urbana. *University of Illinois AES Bulletin 423*. May, 1936.

Lindstrom, D. E., and Dawson, W. M. "Selectivity of 4-H Club Work: An Analysis of Factors Influencing Membership." Urbana. *University of Illinois AES Bulletin 426*. July, 1936.

Little, Harry A. "Potential Economies in the Reorganization of Local School Attendance Units." New York. *Teachers College, Columbia University, Contributions to Education 628*. 1934.

Lively, C. E. "Growth and Decline of Farm Trade Centers in Minnesota, 1905–1930." St. Paul. *University of Minnesota AES Bulletin 287*. 1932.

Lively, C. E., and Beck, P. G. "The Rural Health Facilities of Ross County, Ohio." Wooster. *Ohio AES Bulletin 412*. October, 1927.

Loomis, Charles P. "The Growth of the Farm Family in Relation to Its Activities." Raleigh. *North Carolina AES Bulletin 298*. June, 1934.

Manny, Theodore B. "Attitudes Towards Rural Government." Washington, D.C. United States Department of Agriculture. 1929. (mimeo.)

Mather, Wm. G., Jr. "The Rural Churches of Allegany County." Ithaca. *Cornell University AES Bulletin 587*. March, 1934.

Mather, Wm. G., Jr.; Townsend, T. H.; and Sanderson, Dwight. "A Study of Rural Community Development in Waterville, New York." Ithaca. *Cornell University AES Bulletin 608*. June, 1934.

McCormick, T. C. "Comparative Study of Rural Relief and Non-Relief Households." Washington, D.C. *Division of Social Research, Works Progress Administration, Research Monograph II*.

Melvin, Bruce L. "Rural Population of New York, 1855 to 1925." Ithaca. *Cornell University AES Memoir 116*. June, 1928.

—— "Rural Youth on Relief." Washington, D.C. *Division of Social Research, Works Progress Administration, Research Monograph XI*. 1937.

—— "Village Service Agencies, New York, 1925." Ithaca. *Cornell University AES Bulletin 493*. 1929.

Morgan, E. L., and Howells, Owen. "Rural Population Groups." Columbia. *University of Missouri Research Bulletin 74*. 1925.

Morgan, E. L., and Sneed, Melvin W. "The Libraries of Missouri: A Survey of Facilities." Columbia. *University of Missouri AES Research Bulletin 236*. April, 1936.

Nelson, Lowry. "A Social Survey of Escalante, Utah." Provo. *Brigham Young University Studies, 1.* 1925.

—— "Some Social and Economic Features of American Fork, Utah." Provo. *Brigham Young University Studies, 4.* 1933.

—— "The Utah Farm Village of Ephraim." Provo. *Brigham Young University Studies, 2.* 1928.

Oyler, Merton. "Community and Neighborhood Groupings in Knott County." Lexington. *University of Kentucky AES Bulletin 366.* October, 1936.

Peattie, Roderick. "The Isolation of the Lower St. Lawrence Valley," *Geographical Review, V,* 1918.

"Report of the Advisory Committee on Education." Washington, D.C. *75th Congress, 3rd Session, House Document 529.* 1938.

"Report of the Country Life Commission." Washington, D.C. *60th Congress, 2nd Session, Senate Document 705.* 1911.

Rice, Stuart A. "Farmers and Workers in American Politics," New York. *Columbia University Studies in History, Economics, and Public Law, CXIII.* 1924.

Richter, H. "Consolidation of Scattered Farm Holdings in Germany," *Foreign Agriculture, II,* 1938.

Sanders, Irwin T., and Ensminger, Douglas. "Alabama Rural Communities: A Study of Chilton County." Montevallo. *Alabama College Bulletin 136.* 1940.

Sanderson, Dwight. "A Survey of Sickness in Rural Areas of Cortland County, New York." Ithaca. *Cornell University AES Memoir 112.* March, 1928.

—— "Locating the Rural Community." Ithaca. *Cornell Country Life Series.* 1920.

—— "Research Memorandum on Rural Life in the Depression." New York. *Social Science Research Council Bulletin 34.* 1937.

Sanderson, Dwight, and Foster, Robert G. "A Sociological Case Study of Farm Families," *The Family, XI,* pp. 107–114, 1930.

Sanderson, Dwight, and Thompson, Warren S. "The Social Areas of Otsego County." Ithaca. *Cornell University AES Bulletin 422.* July, 1923.

Schanck, Richard L. "A Study of a Community and Its Groups and Institutions Conceived As Behaviors of Individuals." Princeton, N.J. *Psychological Reviews Co., Psychological Monograph 195.* 1932.

Schuler, E. A. "Social Status and Farm Tenure—Attitudes and Social Conditions of Corn Belt and Cotton Belt Farmers." Washington, D.C. *United States Department of Agriculture Social Research Report IV.* April, 1938.

—— "Survey of Radio Listeners in Louisiana." Baton Rouge. *The General Extension Division of Louisiana State University.* 1943.

Semple, Ellen Churchill. "The Influence of the Geographic Environment of the Lower St. Lawrence." *Bulletin of the American Geographical Society, XXXVI.* 1904.

Smith, T. Lynn. "Farm Trade Centers in Louisiana, 1901 to 1931." Baton Rouge. *Louisiana State University AES Bulletin 234*. 1933.

────── "The Growth of Population in Louisiana, 1890 to 1930." Baton Rouge. *Louisiana State University AES Bulletin 264*. July, 1935.

Sneed, Melvin W., and Ensminger, Douglas. "The Rural Church in Missouri." Columbia. *University of Missouri AES Research Bulletin 225*. June, 1935.

Taylor, Carl C.; Wheeler, Helen W.; and Kirkpatrick, E. L. "Disadvantaged Classes in American Agriculture." Washington, D.C. *United States Department of Agriculture Social Research Report VIII*. April, 1938.

Taylor, Carl C., and Zimmerman, C. C. "Economic and Social Conditions of North Carolina Farmers." Raleigh. *North Carolina Tenancy Committee, North Carolina State Board of Agriculture*. 1923.

Tetreau, E. D. "The Objectives and Activities of the California Farm Bureau." Berkeley. *California AES Bulletin 563*. 1933.

Thaden, J. F. "Population Trends in Michigan." East Lansing. *Michigan State College AES Special Bulletin 236*. June, 1933.

Thaden, J. F., and Mumford, Eben. "High School Communities in Michigan." East Lansing. *Michigan State College AES Special Bulletin 289*. January, 1938.

Thomas, Dorothy Swaine. "Research Memorandum on Migration Differentials." New York. *Social Science Research Council Bulletin 43*. 1938.

Thompson, Warren S. "Research Memorandum on Internal Migration During the Depression." New York. *Social Science Research Council Bulletin 30*. 1937.

Thurow, Mildred B. "A Study of Selected Factors in Family Life As Described in Autobiographies." Ithaca. *Cornell University AES Memoir 171*. February, 1935.

────── "Interests, Activities and Problems of] Rural Young Folk.— I. Women 15 to 29 Years of Age." Ithaca. *Cornell University AES Bulletin 617*. December, 1934.

Von Tungeln, Geo. H.; Kirkpatrick, E. L.; Hoffer, C. R.; and Thaden, J. F. "The Social Aspects of Rural Life and Farm Tenantry, Cedar County, Iowa." Ames. *Iowa State College AES Bulletin 217*. August, 1923.

Whetten, N. L., and Devereux, E. C. Jr., "Studies of Suburbanization in Connecticut. I. Windsor." Storrs. *Storrs AES Bulletin 212*. 1936.

White, Max R.; Ensminger, Douglas; and Gregory, Cecil L. "Rich Land —Poor People." Indianapolis. *United States Department of Agriculture, Farm Security Administration* (Region 3) *Research Report 1*. January, 1938. (mimeo.)

Williams, B. O. "Occupational Mobility Among Farmers. Part I. Mobility Patterns." Clemson. *South Carolina AES Bulletin 296*. June, 1934.

Willson, E. A.; Hoffsommer, H. C.; and Benton, Alva H. "Rural Changes in Western North Dakota." Fargo. *North Dakota AES Bulletin 214*. January, 1928.

Wilson, Isabella C., and Metzler, William H. "Sickness and Medical

Care in an Ozark Area in Arkansas." Fayetteville. *University of Arkansas AES Bulletin 353.* April, 1938.

Woofter, T. J., Jr. "Landlord and Tenant on the Cotton Plantation." Washington, D.C. *Division of Social Research, Works Progress Administration, Research Monograph V.* 1936.

Zimmerman, C. C. "Farm Trade Centers in Minnesota, 1905–1929." St. Paul. *University of Minnesota AES Bulletin 269.* September, 1930.

## II. *BRITISH ISLES AND EUROPE*

Alpert, Harry. "France's First University Course in Sociology," *American Sociological Review,* Vol. 2, No. 3, June, 1937.

Blaha, Arnost. "Contemporary Sociology in Czechoslovakia," *Social Forces,* Vol. 9, Nos. 1–4, p. 167, October, 1930—May, 1931.

Brandt, Karl. *The Reconstruction of World Agriculture.* New York: W. W. Norton and Co., 1945.

Cépède, Michel. "Agricultural Labor Organization in France," *Rural Sociology,* Vol. 4, No. 1, March, 1939.

Charles, Enid. "Post-War Demographic Problems in Britain," *American Sociological Review,* Vol. 11, No. 5, October, 1946.

Danhoff, Ralph H. "New Zuiderzee Lands: Planned Settlement in the Netherlands," *American Sociological Review,* Vol. 4, No. 4, August, 1939.

Douglas-Irvine, Helen. *The Making of Rural Europe.* London: G. Allen and Unwin, Ltd., 1923.

Goodsell, Willystine. "Housing and the Birth Rate in Sweden," *American Sociological Review,* Vol. 2, No. 6, December, 1937.

Gras, N. S. B. *A History of Agriculture in Europe and America.* Chapter XI, pp. 252–277. New York: F. S. Crofts and Co., 1925.

Hale, Oron James. "The Way of Social Science and History Teaching in Hitler's Germany," *Social Forces,* Vol. 12, Nos. 1–4, p. 187, October, 1933–May, 1934.

Harper, Ernest Bouldin. "Sociology in England," *Social Forces,* Vol. 11, Nos. 1–4, p. 335, October, 1932–May, 1933.

Holt, John B. *German Agricultural Policy, 1918–1934.* Chapel Hill: University of North Carolina Press, 1936.

——— "Recent Changes in German Rural Life," *Rural Sociology,* Vol. 2, No. 3, September, 1937.

Hunter, Neil. *Peasantry and Crisis in France.* Canadian Agent: Ryerson Press. London: Victor Gollancz, 1938.

Hutchinson, E. P. "Internal Migration and Tuberculosis Mortality in Sweden," *American Sociological Review,* Vol. 1, No. 2, April, 1936.

*International Yearbook of Agricultural Statistics, 1940–41,* International Institute of Agriculture, Rome, 1941.

Isbell, Eleanor Collins. "Internal Migration in Sweden and Intervening Opportunities," *American Sociological Review,* Vol. 9, No. 6, December, 1944.

Kirkpatrick, Clifford. "Recent Changes in the Status of Women and the Family in Germany," *American Sociological Review,* Vol. 2, No. 5, October, 1937.

Landheer, Barth. "Dutch Sociology," *Social Forces,* Vol. 12, Nos. 1–4, p. 191, October, 1933—May, 1934.

LaPiere, Richard T. "Race Prejudice: France and England," *Social Forces,* Vol. 7, Nos. 1–4, p. 102, September, 1928—June, 1929.

Laveleye, Emile de. *Primitive Property*. London: Macmillan and Co., Ltd., 1878.

Lindeman, E. C. "New Forces in German Life," *Social Forces*, Vol. 5, Nos. 1–4, p. 456, September, 1926—June, 1927.

Maine, Sir Henry Sumner. *Village Communities in the East and West*. New York: Henry Holt and Co., 1889.

Maitland, F. W. *Domesday Book and Beyond*. Cambridge: University Press, 1897.

Michels, Robert. "The Status of Sociology in Italy," *Social Forces*, Vol. 9. Nos. 1–4, p. 20, October, 1930—May, 1931.

Monachesi, Elio D. "Trends in Criminological Research in Italy," *American Sociological Review*, Vol. 1, No. 3, June, 1936.

Moore, Wilbert E. *Economic Demography of Eastern and Southern Europe*. League of Nations, Geneva, 1945. Printed by Princeton University Press.

Morgan, O. S. (ed.) *Agricultural Systems of Middle Europe: A Symposium*. New York: The Macmillan Company, 1933.

Obrdlík, Antonín. "Social Attitudes of the Czechoslovakian Peasant Towards the Other Occupational Groups," *Rural Sociology*, Vol. 1, No. 3, September, 1936.

Obrdlík, Antonín, and Zwicker, Bruno. "Survey of Recent Sociological Production in Czechoslovakia," *American Sociological Review*, Vol. 2, No. 3, June, 1937.

Opler, Morris Edward. "The Bio-Social Basis of Thought in the Third Reich," *American Sociological Review*, Vol. 10, No. 6, December, 1945.

Peake, Harold. *The English Village*. London: Benn Brothers, Ltd., 1922.

Roucek, Joseph S. "Methods of Meeting Domination: The Czechoslovaks," *American Sociological Review*, Vol. 6, No. 5, October, 1941.

——— "Social Background of Roumanian Politics," *Social Forces*, Vol. 10, Nos. 1–4, p. 419, October, 1931—May, 1932.

——— "Sociology in Roumania," *American Sociological Review*, Vol. 3, No. 1, February, 1938.

——— "The Development of Sociology in Yugoslavia," *American Sociological Review*, Vol. 1, No. 6, December, 1936.

Sanders, Irwin T. "The Social Contacts of a Bulgarian Village," *Rural Sociology*, Vol. 4, No. 3, September, 1939.

Seebohm, Frederic. *The English Village Community*. New York: Longmans, Green and Co., 1926.

Spiegel, H. W. "The Altenteil: German Farmers' Old Age Security," *Rural Sociology*, Vol. 4, No. 2, June, 1939.

Vinogradoff, Paul. *The Growth of the Manor*. New York: The Macmillan Company, 1905.

Warriner, Doreen. *Economics of Peasant Farming*. London: Oxford University Press, 1939.

Znaniecka, Eileen Markley. "Current Sociology in Poland," *American Sociological Review*, Vol. 2, No. 3, June, 1937.

III. *RUSSIA*

Baykov, Alexander. *The Development of the Soviet Economic System*. New York: The Macmillan Company, 1946.

Berman, Nathan. "The Place of the Child in Present-Day Russia," *Social Forces*, Vol. 21, No. 4, May, 1943.

Borders, Karl. "Local Autonomy in Russian Village Life Under the Soviets," *Social Forces*, Vol. 7, Nos. 1–4, p. 409, September, 1928—June, 1929.

Fairchild, Mildred. "The Status of the Family in the Soviet Union Today," *American Sociological Review*, Vol. 2, No. 5, October, 1937.

Maynard, John. *The Russian Peasant and Other Studies*. London: Victor Gollancz, 1943.

Rabinowitch, Dr. Germina. "The Kolkhozes in the Economy of the Union of Socialist Soviet Republics," *Rural Sociology*, Vol. 8, No. 3, September, 1943.

"Recent Social Trends in the Soviet Union," *American Sociological Review*, Vol. 9, No. 3. Entire issue for June, 1944, pp. 217–318.

Timasheff, N. S. "The Population of Soviet Russia," *Rural Sociology*, Vol. 5, No. 3, September, 1940.

—— "Structural Changes in Rural Russia," *Rural Sociology*, Vol. 2, No. 1, March, 1937.

IV. *NEAR AND MIDDLE EAST*

Baber, Ray Erwin. "Marriage and Family Life in Ancient Egypt," *Social Forces*, Vol. 13, Nos. 1–4, p. 409, October, 1934—May, 1935.

Tannous, Afif I. "Agricultural Production and Food Consumption in Iran," *Foreign Agriculture*, 8:2, pp. 27–42, February, 1944.

—— "Missionary Education in Lebanon: A Study in Acculturation," *Social Forces*, Vol. 21, No. 3, March, 1943.

—— "Rural Problems and Village Welfare in the Middle East," *Rural Sociology*, Vol. 8, No. 3, September, 1943.

—— "Social Change in an Arab Village," *American Sociological Review*, Vol. 6, No. 5, October, 1941.

Webster, Donald E. "State Control of Social Change in Republican Turkey," *American Sociological Review*, Vol. 4, No. 2, April, 1939.

V. *INDIA*

Andrus, R. *Rural Reconstruction in Burma*. London: Oxford University Press, 1936.

Bedekar, S. K. "Relationships Between Social and Economic Conditions in Rural India," *Rural Sociology*, Vol. 2, No. 1, March, 1937.

Blunt, Sir Edward. *Social Service in India*. London: His Majesty's Stationery Office, 1938.

Brayne, F. L. *Better Villages*. London: Oxford University Press, 1937.

Chandrasekhar, S. *India's Population: Fact and Policy*, New York: The John Day Co., 1946.

—— "The Emigration and Status of Indians in the British Empire," *Social Forces*, Vol. 24, No. 2, December, 1945.

—— "The Hindu Joint Family," *Social Forces*, Vol. 21, No. 3, March, 1943.

Dutt, R. P. *A Guide to the Problem of Rural India: A Survey of Agrarian Structure, Poverty, and Overpopulation*. London: Victor Gollancz, 1942.

Farley, Miriam. *Speaking of India*. New York: American Council, Institute of Pacific Relations, 1943.

Ghurye, G. S. *Indian Population Problems*. Bombay: Karnatak Publishing House, 1938.

Hatch, S. *Further Upward in Rural India*. London: Oxford University Press, 1938.

Mukherjee, B. B. "Rural Welfare in India," *Social Forces*, Vol. 8, No. 2, pp. 253–254, December, 1929.

Nanavati, Manilal B., and Anjaria, J. J. *The Indian Rural Problem.* Bombay: Indian Society of Agricultural Economics, 1944.

Olcott, Mason. "The Caste System of India," *American Sociological Review,* Vol. 9, No. 6, December, 1944.

Slater, Gilbert. *Some South India Villages.* London: Oxford University Press, 1918.

## VI. *CHINA*

*Agrarian China.* New York: Institute of Pacific Relations, 1938.

Buck, J. L. *Farm Economy in China.* Chicago: University of Chicago Press, 1930.

―――― *Land Utilization in China.* Chicago: University of Chicago Press, 1938. 3 vols.

―――― *Agricultural Survey of Szechwan Province.* New York: International Secretariat, Institute of Pacific Relations, 1943. (mimeo.)

Buck, Pearl. *The Good Earth.* A novel of rural life in China. New York: The John Day Company, 1931.

Burgess, J. S. "Some Observations on Chinese Village Life," *Social Forces,* Vol. 11, No. 3, pp. 402–409, March, 1933.

Buxton, L. H. Dudley. *China, the Land and the People.* New York: Oxford University Press, 1929.

Ch'eng-K'un, Cheng. "Familism the Foundation of Chinese Social Organization," *Social Forces,* Vol. 23, No. 1, October, 1944.

―――― "Regionalism in China's Postwar Reconstruction," *Social Forces,* Vol. 22, No. 1, October, 1943.

*China Handbook, 1937–1943.* Chungking: China Ministry of Information, 1943.

Cressey, George Babcock. *China's Geographic Foundations.* New York: McGraw-Hill Book Co., 1934.

Cressey, Paul Frederick. "Chinese Traits in European Civilization: A Study in Diffusion," *American Sociological Review,* Vol. 10, No. 5, October, 1945.

Dai, Bingham. "Personality Problems in Chinese Culture," *American Sociological Review,* Vol. 6, No. 5, October, 1941.

Fei, Hsiao-Tung. *Peasant Life in China,* New York: E. P. Dutton and Co., 1939; Oxford University Press, 1946.

Kulp, D. H. *Country Life in South China; The Sociology of Familism.* New York: Teachers College Bureau of Publications, 1925.

Lang, Olga. *Chinese Family and Society.* New Haven: Yale University Press, 1946.

Lasker, Bruno. "Shanghai Tomorrow," *Social Forces,* Vol. 19, No. 3, March, 1941.

Price, Harry B. "The Prospects of Rural Industry in China," *Social Forces,* Vol. 14, No. 1, October, 1935.

Price, Maurice T. "Culture Contact in China," *Social Forces,* Vol. 7, No. 2, pp. 270–278, December, 1928.

―――― "The Assumed Isolation of China and Autochthony of her Culture," *American Sociological Review,* Vol. 10, No. 1, February, 1945.

Rossiter, Fred J. "Agriculture in China," *Foreign Agriculture,* Vol. III, No. 10, October, 1939.

Sarvis, Guy Walter. "Western Culture and Social Change in China," *Social Forces,* Vol. 11, No. 1, pp. 86–96, October, 1932.

Tawney, R. H. *Land and Labor in China.* New York: Harcourt, Brace and Co., 1932.

Yang, Hsin-Pao. "Agricultural Planning With the Chinese," *Rural Sociology,* Vol. 10, No. 1, March, 1945.

## VII. *JAPAN, FORMOSA, AND KOREA*

Becker, Howard. "Sociology in Japan," *American Sociological Review.* Vol. 1, No. 3, June, 1936.

Brunner, Edmund deS. *Rural Korea.* New York and London: International Missionary Council, 1928. Also reprinted in *Vol. VI, Proceedings of the International Missionary Council, 1929,* and translated into Japanese by the Governor-General of Chosen.

—— "Rural Problems in Japan," *Social Forces,* Vol. 11, No. 1, pp. 70–75, October, 1932.

Embree, John F. *Suye Mura: A Japanese Village.* Chicago: University of Chicago Press, 1939.

—— *The Japanese Nation: A Social Survey.* New York: Farrar and Rinehart, 1945.

Gillin, John Lewis. "Japan's Prison System," *Social Forces,* Vol. 7, Nos. 1–4, p. 177, September, 1928—June, 1929.

Grajdanzev, Andrew J. *Formosa Today.* New York: Institute of Pacific Relations, 1942.

—— *Modern Korea.* New York: Institute of Pacific Relations, 1944.

*Japanese Population Policy.* Population Index, Vol. 7, No. 4, 1941.

Ladejinsky, W. "Japan's Agriculture Crisis," *Journal of Farm Economics,* Vol. XXI, No. 3, Part 1, August, 1939.

Lee, Hoon K. *Land Utilization and Rural Economy in Korea.* Chicago: University of Chicago Press, 1936.

Masuoka, Jitsuichi. "Changing Food Habits of the Japanese in Hawaii," *American Sociological Review,* Vol. 10, No. 6, December, 1945.

Nasu, S. *Aspects of Japanese Agriculture: A Preliminary Survey.* New York: Institute of Pacific Relations, 1941.

—— *Land Utilization in Japan.* Tokyo: Institute of Pacific Relations, 1929.

Trewartha, Glenn T. *Japan: A Physical, Cultural and Regional Geography.* Especially Chapters IV, V, VII, IX. Madison: University of Wisconsin Press, 1945.

Yoder, Fred R. "The Japanese Rural Community," *Rural Sociology,* Vol. 1, No. 4, December, 1936.

## VIII. *SOUTH AMERICA*

A. GENERAL WORKS

Carlson, Fred A. *Geography of Latin America.* New York: Prentice-Hall, 1942.

Cunha, Euclydes da. *Os Sertoes.* Translated by Samuel Putnam under the title, *Rebellion in the Backlands.* Chicago: University of Chicago Press, 1944.

Davis, Kingsley, and Casis, Ana. "Urbanization in Latin America," *Milbank Memorial Fund Quarterly,* Vol. 24, No. 2, pp. 1–45, April, 1946.

Howard, George P. *Religious Liberty in Latin America.* Philadelphia: Westminster Press, 1944.

Hulbert, Winifred. *Latin American Backgrounds.* New York: The Friendship Press, 1935.

James, Preston E. *Latin America.* New York: The Odyssey Press, 1942.

Mecham, J. Lloyd. *Church and State in Latin America.* Chapel Hill: University of North Carolina Press, 1934.

*Outlook Pamphlets on Latin America.* New York: The Friendship Press.

Platt, Robert S. *Latin America.* New York: McGraw-Hill Book Co., 1943.

Quintanilla, Luiz. *A Latin American Speaks.* New York: The Macmillan Company, 1943.

Schurz, William L. *Latin America.* New York: E. P. Dutton and Co., 1941.

Troncoso, Moises Poblete. "Socio-Agricultural Legislation in the Latin-American Countries," *Rural Sociology,* Vol. 5, pp. 5–16, March, 1940.

―――― "The Social Content of Latin American Constitutions," *Social Forces,* Vol. 21, No. 1, October, 1942.

Whitbeck, R. H., and Williams, F. E. *Economic Geography of South America.* New York: McGraw-Hill Book Co., 1940.

Wythe, George. *Industry in Latin America.* New York: Columbia University Press, 1945.

B. MEXICO

Booth, George C. *Mexico's School-Made Society.* Palo Alto: Stanford University Press, 1941.

Ebaugh, C. D. "Mexico Studies Sex Education," *Social Forces,* Vol. 15, No. 1, October, 1936.

Gruening, Ernest. *Mexico and Its Heritage.* New York: D. Appleton-Century Co., 1931.

Hayner, Norman S. "Criminogenic Zones in Mexico City," *America Sociological Review,* Vol. 11, No. 4, August, 1946.

―――― "Notes on the Changing Mexican Family," *American Sociological Review,* Vol. 7, No. 4, August, 1942.

Humphrey, Norman D. "The Generic Folk Culture of Mexico," *Rural Sociology,* Vol. 8, No. 4, December, 1943.

Lewis, Oscar. "Social and Economic Changes in a Mexican Village: Tepoztlan, 1926–1944." *America Indigena,* Vol. 4, No. 4, pp. 281–314, October, 1944. (Mexico, D. F.)

McBride, George M. *The Land Systems of Mexico.* New York: American Geographical Society, 1923.

Redfield, Robert. *Tepoztlan, A Mexican Village.* Chicago: University of Chicago Publications, 1930.

―――― *"Chan Kom, A Maya Village."* Washington, D.C. *Carnegie Institute of Washington Publication 448.* 1934.

Simpson, E. N. *The Ejido: Mexico's Way Out.* Chapel Hill: University of North Carolina Press, 1937.

Tannenbaum, Frank. *The Mexican Agrarian Revolution.* New York: The Macmillan Company, 1933.

Vasconcellos, José, and Gamio, Manuel. *Aspects of Mexican Civilization.* Chicago: University of Chicago Press, 1926.

C. CENTRAL AMERICA AND THE CARIBBEAN

Biesanz, John and Mavis. *Costa Rican Life.* New York: Columbia University Press, 1944.

Biesanz, John and Mavis. "Mate Selection Standards of Costa Rican Students," *Social Forces*, Vol. 22, No. 2, December, 1943.

Buell, Raymond Leslie. (ed.) *Problems of the New Cuba.* New York: Foreign Policy Association, 1934.

Cahnman, Werner J. "The Mediterranean and Caribbean Regions—A Comparison in Race and Culture Contacts," *Social Forces*, Vol. 22, No. 2, December, 1943.

Chenault, Lawrence R. "The Population Problem of Puerto Rico and Its Forebodings of Malthusianism," *Social Forces*, Vol. 19, No. 3, March, 1941.

Gillin, John. "Parallel Cultures and the Inhibitions to Acculturation in a Guatemalan Community," *Social Forces*, Vol. 24, No. 1, October, 1945.

Hooper, Ofelia. "Rural Panama: Its Needs and Prospects," *Rural Sociology*, Vol. 8, No. 3, September, 1943.

————— "The Plight of Education in Rural Panama," *Rural Sociology*, Vol. 9, No. 1, March, 1944.

Leyburn, James G. *The Haitian People.* New Haven: Yale University Press, 1941.

Linder, Forrest E. "Population and Population Statistics of the Caribbean Area," *Vital Statistics—Special Reports*, Vol. 12, pp. 557–571, 1941.

Macmillan, W. M. *Warning from the West Indies: A Tract for Africa and the Empire.* London: Faber and Faber Ltd., 1936.

*Puerto Rico and Its Problems.* Washington, D.C.: Brookings Institution, 1930.

Rogler, Charles. "Making Personal Contacts in the Study of a Puerto Rican Community," *Social Forces*, Vol. 21, No. 3, March, 1943.

Smith, T. Lynn. "Notes on Population and Rural Social Organization in El Salvador," *Rural Sociology*, Vol. 10, No. 4, December, 1945.

Tugwell, Rexford Guy. *The Stricken Land: The Story of Puerto Rico.* New York: Doubleday and Co., 1947.


D. BRAZIL

Cooke, Morris Llewellyn. *Brazil on the March: A Study in International Cooperation,* New York: McGraw-Hill Book Co., 1944; Whittlesey House, 1945.

Deffontaines, P. "Mountain Settlement in the Central Brazilian Plateau," *Geographical Review*, Vol. 27, 1937.

————— "The Origin and Growth of the Brazilian Network of Towns," *Geographical Review*, Vol. 27, 1938.

Frazier, E. Franklin. "The Negro Family in Bahia Brazil," *American Sociological Review*, Vol. 7, No. 4, August, 1942.

Freyre, Gilberto. *The Masters and the Slaves: A Study in the development of Brazilian Civilization.* Translated from the Portuguese by Samuel Putnam. New York: Alfred A. Knopf, 1946.

Herskovits, Melville J. "The Negro in Bahia, Brazil: A Problem in Method," *American Sociological Review*, Vol. 8, No. 4, August, 1943.

James, P. E. "The Coffee Lands of Southeastern Brazil," *Geographical Review*, Vol. 22, 1932.

————— "The Expanding Settlements of Southern Brazil," *Geographical Review*, Vol. 30, 1940.

James, P. E. "The Changing Patterns of Population in São Paulo State, Brazil," *Geographical Review*, Vol. 27, 1938.

Kelsey, Vera. *Seven Keys to Brazil*. New York: Funk and Wagnalls Co., 1941.

Leão, A. Carneiro. "Problems of Rural Society in Brazil," *Rural Sociology*, Vol. 9, No. 2, June, 1944.

Nash, Roy. *Conquest of Brazil*. New York: Harcourt, Brace and Co., 1926.

Pierson, Donald. *Negroes in Brazil*. Chicago: University of Chicago Press, 1941.

────── "The Negro in Bahia, Brazil," *American Sociological Review*, Vol. 4, No. 4, August, 1939.

Ramos, Arthur. "Contact of Races in Brazil," *Social Forces*, Vol. 19, pp. 533–538, May, 1941.

Ribeiro, Réne. "On the Amaziado Relationship, and Other Aspects of the Family in Recife (Brazil)," *American Sociological Review*, Vol. 10, No. 1, February, 1945.

Schmidt, Carlos B. "Systems of Land Tenure in São Paulo," *Rural Sociology*, Vol. 8, No. 3, September, 1943.

Smith, T. Lynn. *Brazil: People and Institutions*. Baton Rouge: Louisiana State University Press, 1946.

────── "Brazilian Land Surveys, Land Division, and Land Titles," *Rural Sociology*, Vol. 9, No. 3, September, 1944.

────── "The Locality Group Structure of Brazil," *American Sociological Review*, Vol. 8, No. 1, February, 1944.

Von Spix, Johann B., and Von Martius, C. F. Phil. *Travels in Brazil in the Years 1817–1820*. London: Longman, Hurst, Rees, Orme, Browne and Green, 1824.

Will, L. W. "Changes in the Agriculture of South Central Brazil," *Journal of Farm Economics*, Vol. XXV, No. 3, August, 1943.

Willems, Emilio. "Some Aspects of Cultural Conflict and Acculturation in Southern Rural Brazil," *Rural Sociology*, Vol. 7, No. 4. 1942.

Zweig, Stefan. *Brazil: Land of the Future*. Translated by Andrew St. James. New York: The Viking Press, 1941.

E. ARGENTINA

Herring, Hubert. *Good Neighbors, Argentina, Brazil, Chile and Seventeen Other Countries*. New Haven: Yale University Press, 1941.

Jefferson, Mark. *Peopling the Argentina Pampa*. New York: American Geographical Society, 1926.

Marcenaro-Boutell, Roberto. "Farm Housing in Argentina," *Rural Sociology* Vol. 10, No. 2, June, 1945.

Moore, Wilbert E. "Rural-Urban Conflict in Argentine Sociological Theories," *Rural Sociology*, Vol. 6, No. 2, June, 1941.

Taylor, Carl C. "Rural Locality Groups in Argentina," *American Sociological Review*, Vol. 9, No. 2, April, 1944.

────── *Rural Life in Argentina*. Baton Rouge: Louisiana State University Press, 1948.

F. CHILE, BOLIVIA, COLOMBIA, AND OTHERS

McBride, G. M. *Chile: Land and Society*. New York: American Geographical Society, 1936.

McBride, G. M. *The Agrarian Indian Communities of Highland Bolivia.* New York: Oxford University Press, 1921.

Romoli, Kathleen. *Colombia: Gateway to South America.* New York: Doubleday, Doran and Co., 1941.

Schurz, W. L. *Bolivia: A Commercial and Industrial Handbook.* Washington, D.C.: United States Department of Commerce, Bureau of Foreign and Domestic Service, Special Agents Series No. 208, 1921.

Smith, T. Lynn. "The Cultural Setting of Agricultural Extension Work in Colombia," *Rural Sociology*, Vol. 10, No. 3, September, 1945.

Wylie, Kathryn H. "The Agriculture of Colombia." Washington, D.C. *United States Department of Agriculture, Foreign Agricultural Bulletin 1.* October, 1942.

# INDEX OF AUTHORS

(FOR INDEX OF SUBJECTS, SEE PP. 560-568)

# INDEX OF SUBJECTS

## (FOR INDEX OF AUTHORS, SEE PP. 553–559)

Accommodation, 165–170; and accommodative neighborhoods, 81–83; and segregation of Negro, 168; as new *definition of situation*, 167; caste as form of, 166; conflict, competition, and, 149–170; definition of, 165–166; equalitarian form of, 169; of slave and free Negro, 166–168; resulting from rigid stratification, 166–167; role of government in, 169

Acculturation, culture contact, assimilation, and, 187–203; definition of, 187–188

Adams Act of 1906, 414

Adjustment and maladjustment, patterns of, 43–44

Age, composition of population according to, 114–119; differentials in various segments of population, 117; marital, 295–296; migration of youth from farms, 140–141; of sons in transmission of farming as occupation, 232–233; selectivity of migration according to, 140–141; social mobility related to, 229–230

Age-sex pyramid, 115–118

Agencies, health, and health, 491–516; rural welfare and, 471–488; types of welfare, 473–476

Agricultural Adjustment Act of 1933, 458

Agricultural Adjustment Administration, 45, 127, 246–247; influence of, on type-of-farming areas, 37

Agricultural Extension Service, as an educational agency, 414–422; changing emphasis of, 422; community relations of, 420–422; educational differences of participants in, 419; extent of contacts of, 418–420; financial support of, 415–416; historical background of, 414–415; lay leaders in, 417; number of workers in, 416; professional leadership in, 416–417; racial differences of participants in, 419; relation of church to, 421; relation of Farm Bureau to, 421–422; relation of school to, 420–421; tenure differences of participants in, 419; training of personnel of, 417

*Agricultural ladder*, as symbol of vertical mobility, 233; regional differences in, 234–237

Agricultural Marketing Act of 1929, 456

Agriculture, journals dealing with, 430–431; migratory labor in, 137–139; occupation of, 15–19; wide fluctuations of labor needs in, 137

Amalgamation, relation to assimilation, 200–201

Ambivalence, definition of, 172

American Farm Bureau Federation, 209

American Indian, 168–169, 202

American Library Association, 424, 426

American Medical Association, 209

American Society of Equity, 162–163

Anthropology, definition of, 3–4

Applied sociology, definition of, 3

Area, culture, 8

Assimilation, amalgamation as a factor in, 200–201; *Americanization* programs as, 188; as a process, 188; as identification, 189; as influenced by public schools, 194–195; as loss of *social visibility*, 201; as *melting pot*, 202; complete, 201; culture contact and acculturation, 187–203; definition of, 187–188; factors in, 192–201; group versus individual, 203; inevitability of, 201, 202; intermarriage as a measure of, 198–201; language as a barrier to, 194; necessity or desirability of, 202–203; of minority groups, 202–203; reflected in participation, 195–196; religion as a factor in, 196–198; retarded in rural areas, 192–194; rural-urban differences in, 203

Association of American Railroads, 209

Bankhead-Jones Act of 1936, 414

Birth rate, inverse relation of, to education, 112–113; trend of, 106, 279

Bureau of Agricultural Economics, 134, 153

Capital, investment of, in farming, 262

Case study, method, 6

Change, in population, effects on rural life of, 521–522; major forces in rural life leading to, 519–522; rate of, 527; resistance to, 526–527; technology as a factor in, 519–521

Churches, and church membership, 347–352; and social contact, 324; as neighborhood institutions, 331–332; as social institutions, 342–369; auxiliary organizations of, 346–347; clergymen and the, 354–369; congregational type of organization of, 328–329; consolidation of, 335; contributions to, 352–353; definition of undersized, 332–333; denominational distribution of membership of, 350–352; ₁dissenting tradition of American, 325–326; ecological factors affecting rural, 330–332; effect of stratification on membership of, 221–222; expenditures of, 353; financial support of, 352–354; four types

560